CANADIAN SOCIOLOGY

—— A Reader ——

Compiled by DR. GERALD BOOTH

University of Windsor

PEARSON

Custom
Publishing

PEARSON CUSTOM PUBLISHING
75 Arlington Street, Suite 300, Boston, MA 02116
A Pearson Education Company

Contents

Part I
The Sociological Perspective

1. The Promise of Sociology"
   by C. Wright Mills 3
2. The Perspective of Sociology
   by Allan G. Johnson 8
3. Defining Features of Canadian
   Sociology *by Bruce Ravelli* 14

Part II
Sociological Research

4. The Case for Value-Free Sociology
   by Max Weber 23
5. The Importance of Social Research
   by Earl Babbie 25

Part III
Culture

6. Canada and the United States: A
   Comparative View *by Seymour Martin
   Lipset* 31
7. Investigating Canadian and American
   Value Differences Through an Analysis
   of Media Portrayals of Native Issues
   by Bruce Ravelli 41

Part IV
Society

8. Manifesto of the Communist Party
   by Karl Marx and Friedrich Engels 51
9. The Amish: A Small Society
   by John A. Hostetler 59

Part V
Socialization

10. The Self
    by George Herbert Mead 65
11. The Importance of the Family as an
    Agent of Socialization: Developmental
    Pathways and Crime Prevention
    *by Michael C. Boyes, Nancy A. Ogden,
    and Joseph P. Hornick* 73

Part VI
Social Interaction

12. The Presentation of Self
    by Erving Goffman 83
13. Disclaimer Mannerisms of Students:
    How to Avoid Being Labeled as
    Cheaters *by Daniel Albas
    and Cheryl Albas* 89
14. The Body Beautiful: Adolescent Girls
    and Images of Beauty
    by Beverly J. Matthews 98

Part VII
Groups and Organizations

15. The Characteristics of Bureaucracy *by Max Weber*   113
16. McJobs: McDonaldization and the Workplace *by George Ritzer*   117

Part VIII
Deviance

17. The Functions of Crime *by Emile Durkheim*   125
18. Exploring Deviance in Canada *by Linda Deutschman*   128

Part IX
Sexuality

19. Understanding Sexual Orientation *by Alfred C. Kinsey, Wardell B. Pomeroy, and Clyde E. Martin*   141
20. Streets, Strangers, and Solidarity *by Tracy Nielsen*   144

Part X
Social Stratification

21. The Vertical Mosaic: An Analysis of Social Class and Power in Canada *by John Porter*   155
22. Does the Vertical Mosaic Still Exist? Ethnicity and Income in Canada, 1991 *by Jason Z. Lian and David Ralph Matthews*   158

Part XI
Gender

23. Sex and Temperament in Three Primitive Societies *by Margaret Mead*   171
24. Playing by the Rules of the Game: Women's Experiences and Perceptions of Sexual Harassment in Sport *by Vivian Krauchek and Gillian Ranson*   176

Part XII
Race and Ethnicity

25. The Souls of Black Folk *by W. E .B. Du Bois*   187
26. Aboriginal Identity: The Need for Historical and Contextual Perspectives *by Jean-Paul Restoule*   192

Part XIII
Aging and the Elderly

27. The Tragedy of Old Age in America *by Robert N. Butler*   203
28. Aging Families: Have Current Changes and Challenges Been 'Oversold'? *by Carolyn J. Rosenthal*   209

Part XIV
The Economy and Work

29. Alienated Labor *by Karl Marx*   223
30. When Work Disappears *by William Julius Wilson*   227

Part XV
Politics and Government

31. The Power Elite
by C. Wright Mills   239
32. Freedom in the World: A Global
Survey *by Adrian Karatnycky*   245

Part XVI
Family

33. 'His' and 'Her' Marriage
by Jessie Bernard   261
34. Looking Back, Looking Ahead:
Canadian Families in Perspective
by Beverly J. Matthews   267

Part XVII
Religion

35. The Protestant Ethic and the Spirit of
Capitalism *by Max Weber*   285
36. Some Very Good News via Some Very
Bad Myths *by Reginald W. Bibby*   291

Part XVIII
Education

37. Education and Inequality *by Samuel
Bowles and Herbert Gintis*   307
38. The Boundaries of Public Education in
the Knowledge-Based Economy
by Terry Wotherspoon   313

Part XIX
Health and Medicine

39. The Social Structure of Medicine
by Talcott Parsons   327
40. Female Genital Mutilation
by Efua Dorkenoo and Scilla Elworthy
331

Part XX
Population, Urbanization
and the Evironment

41. The Metropolis and Mental Life *by
Georg Simmel*   341
42. Africville: The Life and Death of a
Canadian Black Community
*by Donald H. Clairmont
and Dennis William Magill*   347
43. Rich Planet, Poor Planet: Global
Environment and Poverty in 2001
by Christopher Flavin   359

Part XXI
Collective Behaviour
and Social Movements

44. On the Origins of Social Movements
by Jo Freeman   375

Part XXII
Social Change and Modernity

45. The Disenchantment of Modern Life
by Max Weber   391

46. The Information Age: Aparthied
Cultural Imperialism, or Global
Village? *by R. Alan Hedley*   393

Part I

The Sociological Perspective

1

The Promise of Sociology

C. Wright Mills

Nowadays men often feel that their private lives are a series of traps. They sense that within their everyday worlds, they cannot overcome their troubles, and in this feeling, they are often quite correct: What ordinary men are directly aware of and what they try to do are bounded by the private orbits in which they live; their visions and their powers are limited to the close-up scenes of job, family, neighborhood; in other milieux, they move vicariously and remain spectators. And the more aware they become, however vaguely, of ambitions and of threats which transcend their immediate locales, the more trapped they seem to feel.

Underlying this sense of being trapped are seemingly impersonal changes in the very structure of continent-wide societies. The facts of contemporary history are also facts about the

Source: From *The Sociological Imagination* by C. Wright Mills. Copyright © 1959 by Oxford University Press, Inc. Renewed 1987 by Yaraslava Mills. Used by permission of Oxford University Press, Inc.

success and the failure of individual men and women. When a society is industrialized, a peasant becomes a worker; a feudal lord is liquidated or becomes a businessman. When classes rise or fall, a man is employed or unemployed; when the rate of investment goes up or down, a man takes new heart or goes broke. When wars happen, an insurance salesman becomes a rocket launcher; a store clerk, a radar man; a wife lives alone; a child grows up without a father. Neither the life of an individual nor the history of a society can be understood without understanding both.

Yet men do not usually define the troubles they endure in terms of historical change and institutional contradiction. The well-being they enjoy, they do not usually impute to the big ups and downs of the societies in which they live. Seldom aware of the intricate connection between the patterns of their own lives and the course of world history, ordinary men do not usually know what this connection means for the kinds of men they are becoming and for the kinds of history-making in which they might take part. They do not possess the

3

quality of mind essential to grasp the interplay of man and society, of biography and history, of self and world. They cannot cope with their personal troubles in such ways as to control the structural transformations that usually lie behind them.

Surely it is no wonder. In what period have so many men been so totally exposed at so fast a pace to such earthquakes of change? That Americans have not known such catastrophic changes as have the men and women of other societies is due to historical facts that are now quickly becoming "merely history." The history that now affects every man is world history. Within this scene and this period, in the course of a single generation, one-sixth of mankind is transformed from all that is feudal and backward into all that is modern, advanced, and fearful. Political colonies are freed; new and less visible forms of imperialism installed. Revolutions occur; men feel the intimate grip of new kinds of authority. Totalitarian societies rise, and are smashed to bits—or succeed fabulously. After two centuries of ascendancy, capitalism is shown up as only one way to make society into an industrial apparatus. After two centuries of hope, even formal democracy is restricted to a quite small portion of mankind. Everywhere in the underdeveloped world, ancient ways of life are broken up and vague expectations become urgent demands. Everywhere in the overdeveloped world, the means of authority and of violence become total in scope and bureaucratic in form. Humanity itself now lies before us, the super-nation at either pole concentrating its most coordinated and massive efforts upon the preparation of World War III.

The very shaping of history now outpaces the ability of men to orient themselves in accordance with cherished values. And which values? Even when they do not panic, men often sense that older ways of feeling and thinking have collapsed and that newer beginnings are ambiguous to the point of moral stasis. Is it any wonder that ordinary men feel they cannot cope with the larger worlds with which they are so suddenly confronted? That they cannot understand the meaning of their epoch for their own lives? That—in defense of selfhood—they become morally insensible, trying to remain altogether private men? Is it any wonder that they come to be possessed by a sense of the trap?

It is not only information that they need—in this Age of Fact, information often dominates their attention and overwhelms their capacities to assimilate it. It is not only the skills of reason that they need—although their struggles to acquire these often exhaust their limited moral energy.

What they need, and what they feel they need, is a quality of mind that will help them to use information and to develop reason in order to achieve lucid summations of what is going on in the world and of what may be happening within themselves. It is this quality, I am going to contend, that journalists and scholars, artists and publics, scientists and editors are coming to expect of what may be called the sociological imagination.

The sociological imagination enables its possessor to understand the larger historical scene in terms of its meaning for the inner life and the external career of a variety of individuals. It enables him to take into account how individuals, in the welter of their daily experience, often become falsely conscious of their social positions. Within that welter, the framework of modern society is sought, and within that framework the psychologies of a variety of men and women are formulated. By such means the personal uneasiness of individuals is focused upon explicit troubles and the indifference of publics is transformed into involvement with public issues.

The first fruit of this imagination—and the first lesson of the social science that embodies it—is the idea that the individual can understand his own experience and gauge his own fate only by locating himself within his period, that he can know his own chances in life by becoming aware of those of all individuals in his circumstances. In many ways it is a terrible lesson; in many ways [it is] a magnificent one. We do not know the limits of man's capacities for supreme effort or willing degradation, for agony or glee, for pleasurable brutality or the sweetness of reason. But in our time we have come to know that the limits of "human nature" are frighteningly broad. We have come to know that every individual lives, from one generation to the next, in some society, that he lives out a biography, and that he lives it out within some historical sequence. By the fact of his living he contributes, however minutely, to the shaping of this society and to the course of its history, even as he is made by society and by its historical push and shove.

The sociological imagination enables us to grasp history and biography and the relations between the two within society. That is its task and its promise. To recognize this task and this promise is the mark of the classic social analyst. It is characteristic of Herbert Spencer—turgid, polysyllabic, comprehensive; of E. A. Ross—graceful, muckraking, upright; of Auguste Comte and Emile Durkheim; of the intricate and subtle Karl Mannheim. It is the quality of all that is intellectually excellent in Karl Marx; it is the clue to Thorstein Veblen's brilliant and ironic insight, to Joseph Schumpeter's many-sided constructions of reality; it is the basis of the psychological sweep of W. E. H. Lecky no less than of the profundity and clarity of Max Weber. And it is the signal of what is best in contemporary studies of man and society.

No social study that does not come back to the problems of biography, of history, and of their intersections within a society has completed its intellectual journey. Whatever the specific problems of the classic social analysts, however limited or however broad the features of social reality they have examined, those who have been imaginatively aware of the promise of their work have consistently asked three sorts of questions:

1. What is the structure of this particular society as a whole? What are its essential components, and how are they related to one another? How does it differ from other varieties of social order? Within it, what is the meaning of any particular feature for its continuance and for its change?

2. Where does this society stand in human history? What are the mechanics by which it is changing? What is its place within and its meaning for the development of humanity as a whole? How does any particular feature we are examining affect, and how is it affected by, the historical period in which it moves? And this period—what are its essential features? How does it differ from other periods? What are its characteristic ways of history-making?

3. What varieties of men and women now prevail in this society and in this period? And what varieties are coming to prevail? In what ways are they selected and formed, liberated and repressed, made sensitive and blunted? What kinds of "human nature" are revealed in the conduct and character we observe in this society in this period? And what is the meaning for "human nature" of each and every feature of the society we are examining?

Whether the point of interest is a great power state or a minor literary mood, a family, a prison, a creed—these are the kinds of questions the best social analysts have asked. They are the intellectual pivots of classic studies of man in society—and they are the questions inevitably raised by any mind possessing the sociological imagination. For that imagination is the capacity to shift from one perspective to another—from the political to the psychological; from examination of a single family to comparative assessment of the national budgets of the world; from the theological school to the military establishment; from considerations of an oil industry to studies of contemporary poetry. It is the capacity to range from the most impersonal and remote transformations to the most intimate features of the human self—and to see the relations between the two. [At the b]ack of its use there is always the urge to know the social and historical meaning of the individual in the society and in the period in which he has his quality and his being.

That, in brief, is why it is by means of the sociological imagination that men now hope to grasp what is going on in the world, and to understand what is happening in themselves as minute points of the intersections of biography and history within society. In large part, contemporary man's self-conscious view of himself as at least an outsider, if not a permanent stranger, rests upon an absorbed realization of social relativity and of the transformative power of history. The sociological imagination is the most fruitful form of this self-consciousness. By its use men whose mentalities have swept only a series of limited orbits often come to feel as if [they have] suddenly awakened in a house with which they had only supposed themselves to be familiar. Correctly or incorrectly, they often come to feel that they can now provide themselves with adequate summations, cohesive assessments, comprehensive orientations. Older decisions that once appeared sound now seem to them products of a mind unaccountably dense. Their capacity for astonishment is made lively again. They acquire a new way of thinking, they experience a transvaluation of values: In a word, by their reflection and by their sensibility, they realize the cultural meaning of the social sciences.

Perhaps the most fruitful distinction with which the sociological imagination works is between "the personal troubles of milieu" and "the public issues of social structure." This distinction is an essential tool of the sociological imagination and a feature of all classic work in social science.

Troubles occur within the character of the individual and within the range of his immediate relations with others; they have to do with his self and with those limited areas of social life of which he is directly and personally aware. Accordingly, the statement and the resolution of troubles properly lie within the individual as a biographical entity and within the scope of his immediate milieu—the social setting that is directly open to his personal experience and to some extent his willful activity. A trouble is a

private matter: Values cherished by an individual are felt by him to be threatened.

Issues have to do with matters that transcend these local environments of the individual and the range of his inner life. They have to do with the organization of many such milieux into the institutions of an historical society as a whole, with the ways in which various milieux overlap and interpenetrate to form the larger structure of social and historical life. An issue is a public matter: Some value cherished by publics is felt to be threatened. Often there is a debate about what that value really is and about what it is that really threatens it. This debate is often without focus if only because it is the very nature of an issue, unlike even widespread trouble, that it cannot very well be defined in terms of the immediate and everyday environments of ordinary men. An issue, in fact, often involves a crisis in institutional arrangements, and often too it involves what Marxists call "contradictions" or "antagonisms."

In these terms, consider unemployment. When, in a city of 100,000, only one man is unemployed, that is his personal trouble, and for its relief we properly look to the character of the man, his skills, and his immediate opportunities. But when in a nation of 50 million employees, 15 million men are unemployed, that is an issue, and we may not hope to find its solution within the range of opportunities open to any one individual. The very structure of opportunities has collapsed. Both the correct statement of the problem and the range of possible solutions require us to consider the economic and political institutions of the society and not merely the personal situation and character of a scatter of individuals.

Consider war. The personal problem of war, when it occurs, may be how to survive it or how to die in it with honor; how to make money out of it; how to climb into the higher safety of the military apparatus; or how to contribute to the war's termination. In short, according to one's values, to find a set of milieux and within it to survive the war or make one's death in it meaningful. But the structural issues of war have to do with its causes; with what types of men it throws up into command; with its effects upon economic and political, family and religious institutions, with the unorganized irresponsibility of a world of nation-states.

Consider marriage. Inside a marriage a man and a woman may experience personal troubles, but when the divorce rate during the first four years of marriage is 250 out of every 1,000 attempts, this is an indication of a structural issue having to do with the institutions of marriage and the family and other institutions that bear upon them.

Or consider the metropolis—the horrible, beautiful, ugly, magnificent sprawl of the great city. For many upper-class people, the personal solution to "the problem of the city" is to have an apartment with private garage under it in the heart of the city and, forty miles out, a house by Henry Hill, garden by Garrett Eckbo, on a hundred acres of private land. In these two controlled environments—with a small staff at each end and a private helicopter connection—most people could solve many of the problems of personal milieux caused by the facts of the city. But all this, however splendid, does not solve the public issues that the structural fact of the city poses. What should be done with this wonderful monstrosity? Break it up into scattered units, combining residence and work? Refurbish it as it stands? Or, after evacuation, dynamite it and build new cities according to new plans in new places? What should those plans be? And who is to decide and to accomplish whatever choice is made? These are structural issues; to confront them and to solve them requires us to consider political and economic issues that affect innumerable milieux.

Insofar as an economy is so arranged that slumps occur, the problem of unemployment becomes incapable of personal solution. Insofar as war is inherent in the nation-state system and in the uneven industrialization of the world, the ordinary individual in his restricted milieu will be powerless—with or without psychiatric aid—to solve the troubles this system or lack of system imposes upon him. Insofar as the family as an institution turns women into darling little slaves and men into their chief providers and unweaned dependents, the problem of a satisfactory marriage remains incapable of purely private solution. Insofar as the overdeveloped megalopolis and the overdeveloped automobile are built-in features of the overdeveloped society, the issues of urban living will not be solved by personal ingenuity and private wealth.

What we experience in various and specific milieux, I have noted, is often caused by structural changes. Accordingly, to understand the changes of many personal milieux, we are required to look beyond them. And the number and variety of such structural changes increase as the institutions within which we live become more embracing and more intricately connected with one another. To be aware of the idea of social structure and to use it with sensibility is to be capable of tracing such linkages among a great variety of milieux. To be able to do that is to possess the sociological imagination....

2

The Perspective of Sociology

Allan G. Johnson

I am a practicing sociologist. This book is about what it is that I practice and what it means and why it matters to practice it. This book is about how the practice finds its way into almost every aspect of life, from headlines in the morning paper to the experience of growing older to the ravages of social oppression in the world. It is about things small and things large, things simple and things complex well past what we can imagine.

I practice sociology in many ways. I practice it when I think about how social life works, when I write, when I work with people trying to see what's going on in the world and our lives in it. I practice as a consultant in corporations to help solve the dilemmas of a diverse and difficult world in which race, gender, sexual orientation, and other issues of difference cast dark shadows over people's lives. I practice when I walk down a street, shop in a market, or sit in a sidewalk restaurant, sip a cup of coffee, and watch the world go by and wonder what life *really* is all about, what this stream of interconnected people's lives consists of, what knits it all together and what tears it apart, and what, as my students would say, it's got to do with me.

I practice sociology for many reasons. I practice it because there is so much unnecessary suffering in the world, and to do something about it we need to understand where it comes from. In this sense, practicing sociology has a profoundly moral dimension. I don't mean this in the sense that it's about being good instead of bad. I mean it in a deeper and broader sense of morality that touches on the essence of what we're about as human beings and what our life together consists of. It is impossible to study social life for very long without coming up against the consequences that social life produces, and a lot of these consequences do such damage to people's lives that, unless we find ways to deny or ignore

Source: From "Introduction", by Allan G. Johnson as it appears in *The Forest and the Trees: Sociology as Life, Practice and Promise,* by Allan G. Johnson. Reprinted by permission of Temple University Press. © 1997 by Allan G. Johnson. All Rights Reserved.

the reality of it, we feel compelled to ask "why?" And once we ask that question, we need tools to help make sense of where it leads and to imagine how we might go from there toward something better. We can't help but be part of the problem; practicing sociology is a way to also be part of the solution. This not only helps the world, but makes it easier to live in, especially given how crazy a place it can seem. It helps to be able to see how one thing is connected to another, and, in that, how to find ways to make some small difference. We can't change the world all by ourselves, but we can make informed decisions about how to participate in it, and how that can help turn the world toward something better, even if it's just in our neighborhoods or families or where we work.

I wouldn't do all this if I didn't believe something better was possible, so I have to add faith to my list of reasons for practicing sociology. I believe that the choices we make as individuals matter beyond our lives more than we can imagine, that things don't have to be the way they are, but that they won't get better all by themselves. We need to do something, and what we do needs to be based on more than hunches and personal opinion and prejudice. We need systematic ways to figure things out, and that's what sociological practice offers.

I also practice sociology because it helps to keep me in touch with the essence of my own life in the world, for sociology isn't simply about some larger world "out there." It's also about us in the world and the connection between the two, which means it can take us toward basic truths about who we are and what our lives are about. I practice it because it reminds me that for all that we think we know about things, beneath that is all that we don't know, which is good reason to feel awed from time to time. On some level, for example, I'm amazed that social life works at all, that we're able to live and work together as much as we do, to talk, dream, imagine, fight, and create. There is something miraculous about the simplest conversation, miraculous in the sense that there is a core truth about how it happens that

we can never get to. We can contemplate the miracle of things by taking ourselves toward the limit of what we can know. And we can feel the fringe of core truths and how our lives are part of them. So, while my practice is usually "about" understanding the world, it is also about keeping myself in touch with the essentially unknowable essence of human existence that lies beneath.

Practicing sociology is a way to observe the world and to think about and make sense of it. It is a way to be in the world and *of* the world, to play a meaningful role in the life of our species as it shapes and reshapes itself into the mystery of what's going on and what it's got to do with us....

THE ONE THING

If sociology could teach everyone just one thing with the best chance to lead toward everything else we could know about social life, it would, I believe, be this: *We are always participating in something larger than ourselves, and if we want to understand social life and what happens to people in it, we have to understand what it is that we're participating in and how we participate in it.* In other words, the key to understanding social life isn't just the forest and it isn't just the trees. It's the forest and the trees and how they're related to one another. Sociology is the study of how all this happens.

The "larger" things we participate in are called social systems, and they come in all shapes and sizes. In general, the concept of a system refers to any collection of parts or elements that are connected in ways that cohere into some kind of whole. We can think of the engine in a car as a system, for example, a collection of parts arranged in ways that make the car "go." Or we could think of a language as a system, with words and punctuation and rules for how to combine them into sentences that mean something. We can also think of a family as a system—a collection of elements related to one another in a way that leads us to think of it as a unit. These include things such as the positions of mother, father, wife, husband, parent, child, daughter, son, sister, and brother. Elements also include shared ideas that tie those positions together to make relationships, such as how "good mothers" are supposed to act in relation to children or what a "family" is and what makes family members "related" to one another as kin. If we take the positions and the ideas and other elements, then we can think of what results as a whole and call it a social system.

In similar ways, we can think of corporations or societies as social systems. They differ from one another—and from families—in the kinds of elements they include and how those are arranged in relation to one another. Corporations have positions such as CEOs and stockholders, for example; but the position of "mother" isn't part of the corporate system. People who work in corporations can certainly be mothers in families, but that isn't a position that connects them to a corporation. Such differences are a key to seeing how systems work and produce different kinds of consequences. Corporations are sometimes referred to as "families," for example, but if you look at how families and corporations are actually put together as systems, it's easy to see how unrealistic such notions are. Families don't usually "lay off" their members when times are tough or to boost the bottom line, and they usually don't divide the food on the dinner table according to who's the strongest and best able to grab the lion's share for themselves.[1] But corporations dispense with workers all the time as a way to raise dividends and the value of stock, and top managers routinely take a huge share of each year's profits even while putting other members of the corporate "family" out of work.

What social life comes down to, then, is social systems and how people participate in and relate to them. Note that people *participate* in systems without being *parts* of the systems themselves. In this sense, "father" is a position in my family, and I, Allan, am a person who actually occupies that position. It's a crucial distinction that's easy to

lose sight of. It's easy to lose sight of because we're so used to thinking solely in terms of individuals. It's crucial because it means that people aren't systems, and systems aren't people, and if we forget that, we're likely to focus on the wrong thing in trying to solve our problems.

Thinking of systems as just people is why members of privileged groups often take it personally when someone points out that society is racist or sexist or classist. "The United States is a racist society that privileges whites over other racial groups" is a statement that describes the United States as a social system. It does *not* thereby describe me or anyone else as an individual, for that has more to do with how each of us participates in society. As an individual, I can't avoid participating and can't help but be affected and shaped by that. But how all that plays out in practice depends on many things, including the choices I make about *how* to participate. Born in 1946, I grew up listening to the radio shows of the day, including *Amos and Andy,* which was full of racist stereotypes about blacks (the actors were white). Like any other child, I looked to my environment to define what was "funny." Since this show was clearly defined as "funny" from a white perspective in a white society, and since I was born white, I laughed along with everyone else as we drove down the highway listening to the car radio. I even learned to "do" the voices of "black" characters and regaled my family with renditions of classic lines from the show.

More than forty years later, those racist images are firmly lodged in my memory; once they get in, there's no way to get them out. With the benefit of hindsight, I see the racism in them and how they're connected to massive injustice and suffering in the society I participate in. As an individual, I can't undo the past and I can't undo my childhood. I can, however, choose what to do about race and racism *now.* I can't make my society or the place where I live or work suddenly nonracist, but I can decide how to live as a white person in relation to my privileged *position* as a white person. I can decide whether to laugh or object when I hear racist "humor"; I can decide how to treat people who aren't classified as "white"; I can decide what to do about the consequences that racism produces for people, whether to be part of the solution or merely part of the problem. I don't feel guilty because my country is racist, because that wasn't my doing. But as a white person who *participates* in that society, I feel responsible to consider what to do about it. The only way to get past the potential for guilt and see how I can make a difference is to realize that the system isn't me and I'm not the system.

Nonetheless, systems and people are closely connected to each other, and seeing how that works is a basic part of sociological practice. One way to see this is to compare social systems to a game such as Monopoly. We can think of Monopoly as a social system. It has positions (players, banker); it has a material reality (the board, the pieces, the dice, play money, property deeds, houses and hotels); and it has ideas that connect all of this together in a set of relationships. There are values that define the point of the game—to win—and rules that spell out what's allowed in pursuit of winning, including the idea of cheating. Notice that we can describe the game without saying anything about the personalities, intentions, attitudes, or other characteristics of the people who might play it. The game, in other words, has an existence that we can describe all by itself. "It" exists whether or not anyone is playing it at the moment. The same is true of social systems. We don't have to describe actual basketball players in order to describe "a basketball team" as a kind of system that has characteristics that distinguish it from other systems.

I don't play Monopoly anymore, mostly because I don't like the way I behave when I do. When I used to play Monopoly, I'd try to win, even against my own children, and I couldn't resist feeling good when I did (we're *supposed* to feel good) even if I also felt guilty about it. Why did I act and feel this way? It wasn't because I

have a greedy, mercenary personality, because I know that I don't behave this way when I'm not playing Monopoly. Clearly I am *capable* of behaving this way as an individual, which is part of the explanation. But the rest of it comes down to the simple fact that I behaved that way because winning is what Monopoly is about. When I participate in that system, greedy behavior is presented to me as a path of least resistance. As defined by the game, it's what you're supposed to do; it's the point. And when I play the game, I feel obliged to go by its rules and pursue the values it promotes. I look upon the game as having some kind of authority over the people who play it, which becomes apparent when I consider how rare it is for people to suggest changing the rules ("I'm sorry, honey," I say as I take my kid's last dollar, "but that's just the way the game is played"). If *we* were the game, then we'd feel free to play by any rules we liked. But we tend not to see games—or systems—in that way. We tend to see them as external to us and therefore not ours to shape however we please....

IT'S ABOUT US AND IT'S NOT ABOUT US

If we start from the idea that we're always participating in something larger than ourselves and that social life flows from this relationship, then we have to consider that we're all involved—even if only indirectly—in the social consequences that result, both the good and the bad. By definition, if I participate in a racist society—no matter what my race—then I'm involved in white privilege and racist consequences. As an individual, I may not feel or act in racist ways and in my heart I may even hate racism; but that's beside the core sociological point. I'm *involved* in one way or another by virtue of my participation in society itself.[2] If someone takes what I say more seriously because I'm white, then I've received a benefit of racism whether I'm aware of it or not, and in doing so, I've unwittingly participated in racism. This raises the question of how society works *and* how I participate in it—whether I actively defend white privilege or let people know I'm against racism or just go about my business and pretend there's no problem to begin with.

In diversity training sessions, this simple insight can dramatically alter how people see potentially painful issues and themselves in relation to them. This is especially true for people in privileged groups who otherwise resist looking at the nature and consequences of privilege. Their defensive resistance is probably the biggest single barrier to ending racism, sexism, and other forms of social oppression. Most of the time it happens because, like everyone else, they're stuck in an individualistic model of the world and can't see a way to acknowledge racial privilege as a fact of social life without also feeling personally blamed and guilty for it. And the people who are most likely to feel this way are often the ones who are otherwise most open to doing something to make things better. When they look at a problem like racism sociologically, however, they can see how it's both about them and not about them. It's not about them in the sense that they didn't create the racist society we all live in. As I was growing up white, no one asked me if it was OK with me for white people to use *Amos and Andy* to make fun of black people and keep them in their place beneath white privilege. And if they *had* asked me, I doubt that as a child I'd have known enough to object. In this sense, white people who've grown up in a racist environment have no reason to feel guilty when they hear anger about the existence of white racism and the harm and suffering it causes.

Racism *is* about me personally, however, because whether or not I'm conscious of it, I'm always making choices about how to participate in a society that is organized in racist ways and that makes behavior that perpetuates white privilege a path of least resistance. Regardless of how I behave, as a white person I have privileges that are at the expense of people of other races. Race privilege is built into the system itself, which means I don't have to like it or believe in it or even do anything to receive it. When I go shopping at the mall, sales people and store detectives don't follow me around as if I was going to steal something. They don't swoop down on me and pointedly ask "Can I help you?" as if I was a suspicious character or something other than a serious customer. But black people are mistreated this way all the time, and it usually doesn't matter how well they dress or how much money they have to spend.[3] Most people would agree that everyone should be treated decently, but when some are and some aren't simply because of which group they belong to, then social privilege is at work. And whether I like it or not, as a white person I benefit from that by getting something of value that's denied to them. Once I see this, it's hard to avoid asking about how I participate in the system that produces such racist consequences. What are my responsibilities? What could I do differently that would contribute to different outcomes? How can I be part of the solution to racism rather than merely part of the problem?

In other words, by making me aware that I'm involved in something larger than myself, sociological practice gets me off the hook of personal guilt and blame for a world that I didn't create and that isn't my fault. At the same time, however, it makes me aware of how I choose to participate in that world and how and why that matters. I have no reason to feel guilty simply because I'm white; but I also don't have the luxury of thinking that racism and race privilege have nothing to do with me.[4]...

NOTES

1. There are of course numerous examples of cultures and historical periods where families have behaved in this way, especially in relation to daughters. But in places like the United States where organizations are routinely likened to families, this is not how normal family life is viewed.

2. For more on this way of looking at racism, see David T. Wellman, *Portraits of White Racism,* 2nd ed. (New York: Cambridge University Press, 1993).

3. See, for example, Ellis Cose, *The Rage of a Privileged Class* (New York: HarperCollins, 1993); Joe R. Feagin, "The Continuing Significance of Race: Antiblack Discrimination in Public Places," *American Sociological Review* 56, 1 (1991): 101–16; and Joe R. Feagin and Melvin P. Sikes, *Living with Racism: The Black Middle-Class Experience* (Boston: Beacon Press, 1994).

4. For useful perspectives on how white people can become more aware of how they're connected to a racist society on a personal level, see Paul Kivel, *Uprooting Racism: How White People Can Work for Racial Justice* (Philadelphia: New Society Publishers, 1996).

3

Defining Features of Canadian Sociology

Bruce Ravelli

Canadian sociology often mirrors the nature of Canada itself: a diverse landscape where Canadians struggle to find their unique voice within a chorus dominated by Americans. In fact, some analysts suggest that Canadian sociology is a product of its experiences with, and at times its resistance to, the larger and more dominant American sociological tradition (see Brym & Saint-Pierre, 1997; Hiller, 2001; Hiller & Di Luzio, 2001). The dominance of the American sociological tradition in Canada is largely due to its longer history[1] and its sheer size.[2] However, at least four elements influence the presence of a distinctly Canadian sociology:

1. Canada's physical geography, defined by its vast and often challenging physical environment,

and its regionalism, evidenced in the important role Quebec plays in Canadian sociology's intellectual development

2. Canadian sociology's focus on the political economy

3. The Canadianization movement of the 1960s and 1970s in response to the number of American faculty in our postsecondary institutions

4. The radical nature of Canadian sociology

CANADA'S GEOGRAPHY AND REGIONALISM

Canada, the world's second-largest country—in terms of total area, not population—(Countries of the World, 2002), is blessed with rich natural resources and a beautiful and diverse landscape. As we will see, these environmental factors have influenced Canadian sociology. According to Hiller (2001), Canadian sociology is not simply a culmination of the varieties of sociology practised in Canada; it is instead the product of

Source: Ravelli, Bruce. (2004). Defining Features of Canadian Sociology (Chp. 3). In Macionis, John J., Nijole B. Benokraitis, and Bruce Ravelli (eds.). *Seeing Ourselves: Classic, Contemporary, and Cross-Cultural Readings in Sociology* (Canadian Edition). Toronto: Pearson Education. Reprinted with permission by Pearson Education Canada Inc.

Canadian sociologists' efforts to understand the Canadian experience. For Hiller (2001), one of Canadian sociology's defining pursuits has been the attempt to understand a changing national society. Everett Hughes asserted in 1959 that Canadian sociology should be grounded in its own societal context: as society changes, so too should its sociology (cited in Hiller, 2001). Sociology "should reflect both the unique aspects of the society's character as well as the evolution of that society" (Hiller, 2001: 262).

External and internal forces help to shape and define a Canadian sociology. The particular nature of the relationship between Canada's physical landscape and Canadian sociology is seen clearly in Brym and Saint Pierre (1997). They suggest that one defining characteristic of Canadian sociology is its survivalism (1997: 543) and propose that a core theme of Canadian sociology is the development and maintenance of a community in the face of hostile elements (e.g., geographically, socially) and outside forces (i.e., political and intellectual pressures from the United States and American sociologists). One inside force defining Canadian sociology is the role that regionalism plays in our country's development (e.g., west versus east) and, in particular, Quebec's influence. Quebec has a unique linguistic and cultural influence on Canadian society generally and on Canadian sociology specifically.

The teaching of Canadian francophone sociology began in 1943, when the Faculty of Social Sciences was established at Laval University in Quebec City. Although francophone sociology is comparatively young, it experienced explosive growth from the 1960s to the 1980s, as demonstrated by rising student enrolment and the wealth of research produced by francophone sociologists (Brym & Saint-Pierre, 1997: 544). During the 1960s, a social movement in Quebec called the Quiet Revolution saw the influence of the Catholic Church diminish, replaced by an expanded provincial bureaucracy and, ultimately, a resurgence in nationalistic sentiments (seen in the rising popularity of the separatist movement and the growing influence of the Parti Québécois and its then-leader, René Lévesque).

The Quiet Revolution not only inspired changes in Quebec society and politics, but it also influenced sociologists to focus on issues of social class and social policy (see Brym & Saint-Pierre, 1997; Hiller, 2001). In fact, some Quebec sociologists have played leadership roles in the transformation of francophone society as senior advisors and civil servants for the provincial government (Brym & Saint-Pierre, 1997: 544). This is consistent with Southcott's (1999: 459) position that francophone sociologists are more likely to see themselves as "agents of change" than are their anglophone colleagues. Again, we see that the society in which sociologists work affects their approach to the discipline. One of those approaches involves an interest in the political economy.

CANADIAN FOCUS ON THE POLITICAL ECONOMY

Wallace Clement (2001), a leading figure in Canadian sociology, believes that one of the defining elements of Canadian sociology is its interest in the political economy. The political economy encompasses politics, government, and governing, as well as the social and cultural constitution of markets, institutions, and actors (Clement, 2001: 406). For Clement, this intellectual pursuit is characterized by the attempt to uncover tensions and contradictions within society and use them as the bases for social change.

Arguably, the first Canadian sociologist to investigate Canada's political economy was Harold A. Innis in *The Fur Trade in Canada* (1970/1930) and *The Cod Fisheries* (1954/1940). In these works, Innis develops what has been termed the *staples thesis,* which contends that Canada's development was based on the exploitation of raw materials sent back to

European countries to satisfy their industrial thirsts. Innis suggests that each staple (e.g., commercial: cod, fur, timber; industrial: pulp and paper, minerals) had its own characteristics that imposed a particular logic on its individual development (Clement, 2001: 407). As Canada grew and these economic developments continued, these raw materials were sent abroad, refined into more valuable commodities (e.g., furniture, automobiles), and returned to Canada at vastly inflated prices. Innis suggests that since Canada's economic position was subordinate to Britain and to the United States, Canadians were seen as "hewers of wood, drawers of water"—people who performed menial tasks. Certainly, the historical development of Canada's natural resources suggests that Canadian society has been, at least in part, defined by the realization that Canada is not one of the world's major economic or social forces. This underdog mentality was evident in the attempt by Canadian universities in the 1960s and 1970s to Canadianize our postsecondary education system.

THE CANADIANIZATION MOVEMENT

The development of Canadian anglophone sociology was influenced by American sociology as practised at the University of Chicago (see Brym & Saint-Pierre, 1997; Eichler, 2001; Hiller, 2001; Hiller & Di Luzio, 2001; Langlois, 2000; McKay, 1998).

Founded in 1892 by Albion Small, the department of sociology at the University of Chicago defined the American sociological tradition for much of the early twentieth century. The Chicago School of sociology was dominated by the symbolic-interactionist approach, focusing on social reform and collective social responsibility. The Chicago School's influence was most profound on early francophone sociology in Quebec, particularly at Canada's founding department of sociology, McGill. In fact, many influential sociologists in Canada trained at the University of Chicago (such as C. A. Dawson, Everett Hughes, Harold Innis, A. C. McCrimmon, and Roderick D. McKenzie). The Chicago School was instrumental in defining Canadian sociology, but in the 1950s and 1960s, a movement to increase the number of Canadian faculty teaching at Canadian universities began.

During the late 1960s, Connors and Curtis (1970, cited in Hiller & Di Luzio, 2001: 494) found that more than 60 percent of sociologists in Canada had received their highest degree from a foreign institution. Even in 1971, Hedley and Warburton (1973: 305, cited in Hiller & Di Luzio, 2001: 494) found that in large Canadian sociology departments (those with more than 20 faculty members), more than 50 percent of instructors were American, 20 percent were from other countries, and 30 percent were Canadian. These finding were important as they emphasized the need to hire and train more Canadian sociologists if we ever hoped to investigate and understand Canadian society.

The discipline's Canadianization movement was also prompted by the explosion in the number of university enrolments in Canada beginning in the 1950s. In 1962–63, full-time university enrolment in Canada was 132 681, while only 10 years later (1972–73) it had more than doubled to 284 897. Ten years later (1982–83) the number had reached 640 000 (Hiller & Di Luzio, 2001: 491), and at the end of 1999, the number of full-time Canadian university enrolments hovered around 580 000 (Statistics Canada, 1999). Clearly, the need for Canadian-trained sociologists to teach students about Canadian society was a pressing one. This sentiment was clearly expressed when the Association of Universities and Colleges of Canada appointed a Commission on Canadian Studies in 1972, which resulted in The Symons Report (1975).

The report called on the Canadian academic community to increase its efforts to contribute to the knowledge of their own society. The reaction to this report came in an increase in the number of Canadian society courses taught by sociologists across the country, as well as in an increased focus on publishing sociological materials for Canadian sociology students. The assertion that these measures have worked has some support in the number of part- and full-time students who are undergraduate majors in sociology: the figure rose from 13 638 in 1982–83 to 21 028 in 1996–97 (Hiller & Di Luzio, 2001: 493). These students are making a sociological analysis of their own society, and they are also learning about the comparatively radical nature of Canadian sociology.

THE RADICAL NATURE OF CANADIAN SOCIOLOGY

Brym and Saint-Pierre (1997) suggest that one of the defining features of English-Canadian sociology is its radical nature, seen in its focus on the political economy and feminist ideas and perspectives. The important distinction these authors add, however, is how little of this radicalism is seen by the public (1997: 546). Certainly, Quebec sociologists are more focused on the policy ramifications of their endeavours, but Brym and Saint-Pierre recognize that many leading English-Canadian sociologists (such as Margrit Eichler, Graham Lowe, and Susan McDaniel) are mindful of the impact their ideas have on the larger society (1997: 546). Their investigations into the political economy was instrumental in showing that Canadian sociology was not afraid to uncover the hidden power structures that influence and guide society. Canadian feminist sociologists continue this tradition by looking at how gender acts as a locus of oppression and domination.

Margrit Eichler (2001) suggests that the simultaneous emergence of the Canadianization movement and the feminist movement led to a politics of knowledge that proved helpful to both groups. By expanding university departments by adding Canadian academics during the 1960s and 1970s, the feminist movement found a new voice on university campuses. In Eichler's paper *Women Pioneers in Canadian Sociology: The Effects of a Politics of Gender and a Politics of Knowledge* (2001), she attempts to reverse the politics of erasure that she argues effectively allowed the historical contributions of female sociologists in Canada to be written out of the literature. Eichler undertakes the project by conducting interviews with 10 of the leading female sociologists born before 1930. Through the interviews, Eichler utilizes a life-history approach, allowing the women to tell their own stories about being female sociologists during a period of rapid growth within the university system in general, and sociology departments in particular, as well as in a period when feminist issues first entered the sociological discourse.

One important finding from Eichler's investigation into these women's lives is the fact that they never had problems finding jobs in academe (2001: 393). The expanding university system, as well as the emerging recognition of feminist issues, allowed these women to begin full-time careers with little effort. Although they all faced sexism in some form during their careers, they were able to initiate significant institutional change by their mere presence on campus (e.g., pay equity measures, sexual harassment policies). Their ability to be a critical social presence within the academic community was an important factor in advancing feminist issues on university campuses and in the larger society as the feminist movement gained momentum in Canada.

That impetus led to the establishment of the Royal Commission on the Status of Women in 1967 to "inquire into and report upon the status of women in Canada, and to recommend what steps might be taken by the Federal Government to ensure for women equal opportunities with men in all aspects of Canadian society" (Cross,

2000). The final report was released in 1970 with 167 recommendations and "became the blueprint for mainstream feminist activism" (Womenspace, 2002). The feminist movement inspired women to reflect differently on their social surroundings and reinforced the need to question social convention. The influence on early female sociology pioneers was equally important, as it encouraged them to critique their own intellectual foundations generally and sociology specifically. As Dorothy Smith notes about this time, "Because we were free to take up issues for women, we didn't feel committed to reproducing the discipline,…it had the effect…of really liberating the discipline in general in Canada, so that you now have an orientation where people feel absolutely comfortable in raising current issues, in addressing what's going on in Canada" (cited in Eichler, 2001: 394). The Royal Commission report opened the debate on women's positions in Canadian society and resulted in the formation of the women's caucus at the Canadian Sociology and Anthropology Association, which still exists today. The feminist movement, and sociology's role within it, is just one example of Canadian sociology's critical foundation and how Canada continues to influence the discipline today.

CONCLUSION

Canadian sociology is defined by its geography, focus on the political economy, the Canadianization movement, and its radical approach to social issues. This brief review should give you some appreciation for the flavour of Canadian sociology and how it represents a unique approach to the discipline and to our understanding of what it means to be Canadian.

NOTES

1. The University of Chicago established the first American department of sociology in 1892 and McGill University established the first Canadian one in 1924.

2. The American postsecondary system serves more than 14 800000 students and the Canadian system around 827000 (NCES, 2002; Statistics Canada, 1999). In 1999 more than 2400 departments of sociology existed in the United States (ASA, 2002). Canada had around 45 university departments of sociology—including joint sociology/anthropology departments—(McMaster, 2002) and approximately 150 colleges, the majority of which offered at least introductory sociology (ACCC, 2002).

REFERENCES

ACCC (Association of Canadian Community Colleges). 2002. Membership list. [Online]. Available: **http://www .accc.ca/english/colleges/membership_list.cfm.** Accessed October 27, 2002.

ASA (American Sociological Association). 2002. Departmental listings for 1999. [Online]. Available: **http://www.asanet.org/pubs/dod.html.** Accessed October 27, 2002.

Brym, R., and C. Saint-Pierre. 1997. Canadian sociology. *Contemporary Sociology,* 26(5): 543–46.

Clement, W. 2001. Canadian political economy's legacy for sociology. *Canadian Journal of Sociology,* 26(3): 405–20.

Connor, D. M., and E. Curtis. 1970. *Sociology and anthropology in Canada: Some characteristics of the disciplines and their current university programs.* Montreal: Canadian Sociology and Anthropology Association.

Countries of the World. 2002. Country statistics at a glance. [Online]. Available: **http://www.infoplease.com/ipa/ A0762380.html.** Accessed July 17, 2002.

Cross, P. 2000. Report of the Royal Commission on the Status of Women: Where are we after thirty years? [Online]. Available: **http://www.owjn.org/issues/equality/thirty .htm.** Accessed January 31, 2003.

Eichler, M. 2001. Women pioneers in Canadian sociology: The effects of a politics of gender and a politics of knowledge. *Canadian Journal of Sociology,* 26(3): 375–403.

Hedley, R. A., and R. T. Warburton. 1973. The role of national courses in the teaching and development of sociology: The Canadian case. *Sociological Review,* 21(2): 299–319.

Hiller, H. H. 2001. Legacy for a new millennium: Canadian sociology in the twentieth century as seen through its publications. *Canadian Journal of Sociology,* 26(3): 257–63.

Hiller, H. H., and L. Di Luzio. 2001. Text and context: Another "chapter" in the evolution of sociology in Canada. *Canadian Journal of Sociology,* 26(3): 487–512.

Innis, H. A. 1954. *The cod fisheries: The history of an international economy.* University of Toronto Press (original work published 1940).

———. 1970. *The fur trade in Canada.* Toronto: University of Toronto Press (original work published 1930).

Langlois, S. 2000. A productive decade in the tradition of Canadian sociology. *Canadian Journal of Sociology,* 25(3): 391–97.

McKay, I. 1998. Changing the subject(s) of the "History of Canadian sociology": The case of Colin McKay and Spencerian Marxism, 1890–1940." *Canadian Journal of Sociology,* 23(4): 389–426.

McMaster University. 2002. Sociology institutions—departments. [Online]. Available: **http://www.mcmaster.ca/ socscidocs/w3virtsoclib/cansoc .htm.** Accessed October 27, 2002.

NCES (National Center for Education Statistics). 2002. Digest of education statistics, 2001—Chapter 3: Postsecondary education. [Online]. Available: **http://nces .ed.gov//pubs2002/digest2001/ch3 .asp#1.** Accessed January 31, 2003.

Southcott, C. 1999. The study of regional inequality in Quebec and English Canada: A comparative analysis of perspectives. *Canadian Journal of Sociology,* 24(4): 457–84.

Statistics Canada. 1999. University enrolment, full-time and part-time, by sex. [Online]. Available: **http://www .statcan.ca/english/Pgdb/educ03a.htm.** Accessed October 27, 2002.

Womenspace. 2002. Since the Royal Commission on the Status of Women. [Online]. Available: **http://herstory .womenspace.ca/RCSW.html.** Accessed October 23, 2002.

Part II

Sociological Research

4

The Case for Value-Free Sociology

Max Weber

Let us consider the disciplines close to me: sociology, history, economics, political science, and those types of cultural philosophy that make it their task to interprct the sciences. It is said, and I agree, that politics is out of place in the lecture-room. It does not belong there on the part of the students.... Neither does [it] belong in the lecture-room on the part of the [instructors], and when the [instructor] is scientifically concerned with politics, it belongs there least of all.

To take a practical stand is one thing, and to analyze political structures and party positions is another. When speaking in a political meeting about democracy, one does not hide one's personal standpoint; indeed, to come out clearly and take a stand is one's damned duty. The words one uses in such a meeting are not means of scientific analysis but means of canvassing votes and winning over others. They are not plowshares to loosen the soil of contemplative thought; they are swords against the enemies: Such words are weapons. It

Source: Excerpts from From *Max Weber: Essays in Sociology by Max Weber*, edited by H. H. Gerth and C. Wright Mills. Translation copyright © 1946, 1958 by H. H. Gerth and C. Wright Mills. Used by permission of Oxford University Press, Inc.

would be an outrage, however, to use words in this fashion in a lecture or in the lecture-room. If, for in stance, "democracy" is under discussion, one considers its various forms, analyzes them in the way they function, determines what results for the conditions of life the one form has as compared with the other. Then one confronts the forms of democracy with nondemocratic forms of political order and endeavors to come to a position where the student may find the point from which, in terms of his ultimate ideals, he can take a stand. But the true teacher will beware of imposing from the platform any political position upon the student, whether it is expressed or suggested. "To let the facts speak for themselves" is the most unfair way of putting over a political position to the student.

Why should we abstain from doing this? I state in advance that some highly esteemed colleagues are of the opinion that it is not possible to carry through this self-restraint and that, even if it were possible, it would be a whim to avoid declaring oneself. Now one cannot demonstrate scientifically what the duty of an academic teacher is. One can only demand of the teacher that he have the intellectual integrity to see that it is one thing to state facts, to determine mathematical or logical relations or the internal structure of cultural values, while it is another thing to answer questions of the value of culture and its individual contents and the question of how one should act in the cultural community and in political associations. These are quite heterogeneous problems. If he asks further why he should not deal with both types of problems in the lecture-room, the answer is: because the prophet and the demagogue do not belong on the academic platform.

To the prophet and the demagogue, it is said: "Go your ways out into the streets and speak openly to the world," that is, speak where criticism is possible. In the lecture-room we stand opposite our audience, and it has to remain silent. I deem it irresponsible to exploit the circumstance that for the sake of their career the students have to attend a teacher's course while there is nobody present to oppose him with criticism. The task of the teacher is to serve the students with his knowledge and scientific experience and not to imprint upon them his personal political views. It is certainly possible that the individual teacher will not

entirely succeed in eliminating his personal sympathies. He is then exposed to the sharpest criticism in the forum of his own conscience. And this deficiency does not prove anything; other errors are also possible, for instance, erroneous statements of fact, and yet they prove nothing against the duty of searching for the truth. I also reject this in the very interest of science. I am ready to prove from the works of our historians that whenever the man of science introduces his personal value judgment, a full understanding of the facts ceases....

The primary task of a useful teacher is to teach his students to recognize "inconvenient" facts—I mean facts that are inconvenient for their party opinions. And for every party opinion there are facts that are extremely inconvenient, for my own opinion no less than for others. I believe the teacher accomplishes more than a mere intellectual task if he compels his audience to accustom itself to the existence of such facts. I would be so immodest as even to apply the expression "moral achievement," though perhaps this may sound too grandiose for something that should go without saying.

5

The Importance
of Social Research

Earl Babbie

...We can't solve our social problems until we understand how they come about, persist. Social science research offers a way to examine and understand the operation of human social affairs. It provides points of view and technical procedures that uncover things that would otherwise escape our awareness. Often, as the cliché goes, things are not what they seem; social science research can make that clear. One example illustrates this fact.

Poverty is a persistent problem in the United States, and none of its intended solutions is more controversial than *welfare*. Although the program is intended to give the poor a helping hand while they reestablish their financial viability, many complain that it has the opposite effect.

Part of the public image of welfare in action was crystallized by Susan Sheehan (1976) in her book *A Welfare Mother*, which describes the situation of a three-generation welfare family, suggesting that the welfare system trapped the poor rather than liberate[d] them. Martin Anderson (1978: 56) agreed with Sheehan's assessment and charged that the welfare system had established a caste system in America, "perhaps as much as one-tenth of this nation—a caste of people almost totally dependent on the state, with little hope or prospect of breaking free. Perhaps we should call them the Dependent Americans."

George Gilder (1990) has spoken for many who believe the poor are poor mainly because they refuse to work, saying the welfare system saps their incentive to take care of themselves. Ralph Segalman and David Marsland (1989: 6–7) support the view that welfare has become an intergenerational way of life for the poor in welfare systems around the world. Children raised in welfare families, they assert, will likely live their adult lives on welfare:

This conflict between the intent of welfare as a temporary aid (as so understood by most of the public) and welfare as a permanent right (as understood by the

Source: From *Practice of Social Research (with InfoTrac)*, 8th edition, by E. R. Babbie, copyright © 1998. Reprinted with permission of Wadsworth Publishing, a division of Thomson Learning.

welfare bureaucracy and welfare state planners) has serious implications. The welfare state nations, by and large, have given up on the concept of client rehabilitation for self-sufficiency, an intent originally supported by most welfare state proponents. What was to have been a temporary condition has become a permanent cost on the welfare state. As a result, welfare discourages productivity and self-sufficiency and establishes a new mode of approved behavior in the society—one of acceptance of dependency as the norm.

These negative views of the effects of the welfare system are widely shared by the general public, even among those basically sympathetic to the aims of the program. Greg Duncan (1984: 2–3) at the University of Michigan's Survey Research Center points out that census data would seem to confirm the impression that a hard core of the poor have become trapped in their poverty. Speaking of the percentage of the population living in poverty at any given time, he says,

Year-to-year changes in these fractions are typically less than 1 percent, and the Census survey's other measures show little change in the characteristic of the poor from one year to the next. They have shown repeatedly that the individuals who are poor are more likely to be in families headed by a woman, by someone with low education, and by blacks.

Evidence that one-eighth of the population was poor in two consecutive years, and that those poor shared similar characteristics, is consistent with an inference of absolutely no turnover in the poverty population. Moreover, the evidence seems to fit the stereotype that those families that are poor are likely to remain poor, and that there is a hard-core population of poor families for whom there is little hope of self-improvement.

Duncan continues, however, to warn that such snapshots of the population can conceal changes taking place. Specifically, an unchanging percentage of the population living in poverty does not necessarily mean the *same* families are poor from year to year. Theoretically, it could be a totally different set of families each year.

To determine the real nature of poverty and welfare, the University of Michigan undertook a "Panel Study of Income Dynamics" in which they followed the economic fate of 5,000 families

from 1969 to 1978, or ten years, the period supposedly typified by Sheehan's "welfare mother." At the beginning, the researchers found that in 1978, 8.1 percent of these families were receiving some welfare benefits and 3.5 percent depended on welfare for more than half their income. Moreover, these percentages did not differ drastically over the ten-year period (Duncan 1984: 75).

Looking beyond these surface data, however, the researchers found something you might not have expected. During the ten-year period, about one-fourth of the 5,000 families received welfare benefits at least once. However, only 8.7 percent of the families were ever dependent on welfare for more than half their income. *"Only a little over one-half of the individuals living in poverty in one year are found to be poor in the next, and considerably less than one-half of those who experience poverty remain persistently poor over many years"* (Duncan 1984: 3; emphasis original).

Only 2 percent of the families received welfare each of the ten years, and less than 1 percent were continuously dependent on welfare for the ten years. Table 6.1 summarizes these findings.

These data paint a much different picture of poverty than people commonly assume. In a summary of his findings, Duncan (1984: 4–5) says:

While nearly one-quarter of the population received income from welfare sources at least once in the decade, only about 2 percent of all the population could be characterized as dependent upon this income for extended periods of time. Many families receiving welfare benefits at any given time were in the early stages of recovering from an economic crisis caused by the death, departure, or disability of a husband, a recovery that often lifted them out of welfare when they found full-time employment, or remarried, or both. Furthermore, most of the children raised in welfare families did not themselves receive welfare benefits after they left home and formed their own households.

Many of the things social scientists study— including [the issue of welfare] you've just read about—generate deep emotions and firm convictions in most people. This makes effective

TABLE 5.1 Incidence of Short- and Long-Run Welfare Receipt and Dependence, 1969–1978

	Percent of U.S. Population:	
	Receiving Any Welfare Income	Dependent on Welfare for More than 50% of Family Income
Welfare in 1978	8.1%	3.5%
Welfare in 1 or more years, 1969–78	25.2	8.7
Welfare in 5 or more years, 1969–78	8.3	3.5
Welfare in all 10 years, 1969–78	2.0	0.7
"Persistent welfare" (welfare in 8 or more years), 1969–78	4.4	2.0

Source: Greg J. Duncan, *Years of Poverty, Years of Plenty: The Changing Fortunes of American Workers and Families* (Ann Arbor: University of Michigan, 1984), 75.

inquiry into the facts difficult at best; all too often, researchers manage only to confirm their initial prejudices. The special value of social science research methods is that they offer a way to address such issues with logical and observational rigor. They let us all pierce through our personal viewpoints and take a look at the world that lies beyond our own perspectives. And it is that "world beyond" that holds the solutions to the social problems we face today.

At a time of increased depression and disillusionment, we are continually tempted to turn away from confronting social problems and retreat into the concerns of our own self-interest. Social science research offers an opportunity to take on those problems and discover the experience of making a difference after all. The choice is yours; I invite you to take on the challenge....

REFERENCES

Anderson, M. 1978. *Welfare: The political economy of welfare reform in the United States.* Stanford, Calif.: Hoover Institution Press.

Duncan, G. J., with R. D. Coe, M. E. Corcoran, M. S. Hill, S. D. Hoffman, and J. N. Morgan (eds.). 1984. *Years of poverty, years of plenty: The changing economic fortunes of American workers and families.* Ann Arbor, Mich.: Survey Research Center Institute.

Gilder, G. 1990. The nature of poverty. In *The American polity* reader, eds. A. Serow, W. Shannon, and E. Ladd, 658–63. New York: Norton.

Segalman, R., and D. Marsland. 1989. *Cradle to grave: Comparative perspectives on the state of welfare.* New York: St. Martin's Press.

Sheehan, S. 1976. *A welfare mother.* New York: Mentor.

Part III

Culture

6

Canada and the United States:
A Comparative View

Seymour Martin Lipset

The 23 independent states plus the assorted colonies and autonomous commonwealths of North and South America provide a magnificent laboratory for comparative analysis, of which relatively few social scientists have taken advantage. The obvious advantage for such an analysis of common cultural and linguistic origin among twenty of those societies, the Latin-American republics and Puerto Rico, has not encouraged many systematic efforts to account for their differences. The Caribbean nations offer the diversity of being former colonies of six foreign powers and the similarity of having preponderantly Negro populations of slave descent, providing an interesting and as yet relatively untapped arena for comparative research. English-speaking

Canada and the United States have long presented unused opportunities to analyse the variations in institutional arrangements in highly similar cultural contexts.

As an illustration of the value of such comparative analysis within the Americas, I would like to deal briefly with the two northernmost nations. There is little question that a comprehensive analysis of institutional patterns and groups in the United States and Canada would be enormously fruitful for sociologists. These two nations share a British legacy, frontier areas, immigrants of comparable origin from the same historic epoch, and comparable ecological conditions. Both have attained a high level of economic development and stable democratic political institutions.

Although the United States and English-speaking Canada probably resemble each other as much as any two nations on earth, the fact remains that various observers have noted a consistent pattern of differences between them.

Source: S. M. Lipset. (1964). Canada and the United States: A Comparative View. *The Canadian Review of Sociology and Anthropology*, 1, 173–185. Reprinted by permission of the Canadian Sociology and Anthropology Association.

To analyse the factors which underlie the perpetuation of small differences among nations is one of the more intriguing and difficult tasks in comparative study. What makes the Canadian more law-abiding? Why is there a much lower divorce rate in Canada? Why do fewer Canadians than Americans or Filipinos or Puerto Ricans attend universities? Why is the Canadian "quieter" in many of his behaviour traits than his American neighbour? Many of our assumptions about sources of national differences can be tested in this North American laboratory.

To a considerable extent comparative macroscopic sociology deals with polarity concepts when it seeks to compare core aspects of societies—gemeinschaft-gesellschaft, organic solidarity–mechanical solidarity, inner-directed versus other-directed, diffuseness-specificity, achievement-ascription, traditional-modern, and so forth. As I have attempted to demonstrate elsewhere, one particularly effective set of polarities for systematically classifying the central values of social systems is the pattern variables as originally set forth by Talcott Parsons.[1] Pattern variables are dichotomous categories of interaction in different structures. Those distinctions which seem particularly suitable for the analysis of Canada and the United States are achievement-ascription, universalism-particularism, self-orientation–collectivity-orientation, and equalitarianism-elitism. (The latter is not one of Parsons' distinctions, but one added here.) A society's value system may emphasize that a person in his orientation to others treats them in terms of their abilities and performances or in terms of inherited qualities (achievement-ascription); applies a general standard or responds to some personal attribute or relationship (universalism-particularism); perceives the separate needs of others or subordinates the individual's needs to the defined interests of the larger group (self-orientation–collectivity-orientation); and stresses that all persons must be respected because they are human beings or emphasizes the general superiority of those who hold elite positions (equalitarianism-elitism).[2]

The great mass of literature on these two democracies suggests the United States to be more achievement-oriented, universalistic, equalitarian, and self-oriented than Canada. Because the value differences of Canada and the United States are not great, the test of the utility of the comparative approach to the two North American societies depends upon specifying the special differences that *do* exist and identifying the historic issues and problems which sustain the near differences between them.

Though many factors in the history of these nations account for the variations between them, the following factors may be singled out: varying origins in their political systems and national identities, varying religious traditions, and varying frontier experiences. In general terms, the value orientations of Canada stem from a counter-revolutionary past, a need to differentiate itself from the United States, the influence of monarchical institutions, a dominant Anglican religious tradition, and a less individualistic and more governmentally controlled expansion of the Canadian than of the American frontier.

HOW DIFFERENT, HOW SIMILAR?

Both nations are largely urbanized, heavily industrialized, and politically stabilized. They share many of the same ecological and demographic conditions, approximately the same level of economic development, similar rates of upward and downward social mobility. To a very great extent Canada and the United States share the same values but, as Kaspar Naegele has pointed out, in Canada these values are held much more tentatively.[3] Both are new peoples and new states, but Canada's relationship to Britain has helped perpetuate in a North American nation the elements of a set of values having Old World origins and a conservative character. Thus, while equality and achievement, for example, are values emphasized in both American societies, in Canada the emphasis is somewhat less and therefore the contrast between the nations remains one of degree.

Perhaps no other value emphases are as paramount in American life as the twin values of equalitarianism and achievement. Both have been strongest in the school system where the principles of the "common school," and "equal opportunity for success" remain viable educational ideals. By contrast, in Canada education has held a more elitist and ascriptive import. These value differences are quantitatively indicated by a comparison of college enrolment figures. If we relate the number enrolled in institutions of higher learning to the size of the age cohort 20 to 24, we find that 30.2 per cent in the United States were attending universities in 1960, compared with 9.2 per cent in Canada.[4]

It has been suggested that elitist tendencies among the Canadians account for the education of a limited few at the college level. Some Canadian writers have pointed out that until very recently education in their country was designed to train an ecclesiastical and political *élite* much in the British tradition.[5] Canadian educators, unlike American, have shown resistance to the introduction into higher education of purely vocational training. Technical training has been viewed as corrupting the "aristocracy of intellect," those being educated for political and social leadership.

Status distinctions, which exist in the United States as in all nations, do not have as much legitimacy as in Canada. For example, the greater strength of elitist and ascriptive value emphases in Canada would seem to be reflected comparatively in the paternalistic organization of the family, in the reverence paid to the clergy by the laity, in the diffuse deference granted the old by the young, men by women, teachers by students, and politicians by the electorate.[6] From James Bryce to S. D. Clark, sociological observers have stressed the greater respect in Canada for political leaders than in the United States. The democratic ethos with its stress on populist values derivative from equalitarian emphases in the United States also "leads to certain impatience with legal process and, occasionally, to outright disrespect for the law."[7]

There are several indicators of the differences in Canadian and American respect for public authority. Where diffuse respect for public authority exists, we should expect to find greater reliance on informal social controls based on traditional obligations. One indicator of the relative strength of the informal normative mechanisms of social control as compared with the restrictive emphases of legal sanctions may be the extent to which a nation requires police protection. The data in Table 9.1 indicate that the ratio of police to population is more than one-third greater in the United States than in Canada. In 1961 only one police officer in Canada was killed by criminal action while on duty, compared to 37 police officers killed in the United States. By 1963, the latter figure had risen to 55 police officers in a single year while the former remained at one.[8] (The United States has about ten times the population of Canada.) The proportionately fewer lawyers in private practice in Canada (one for 1,630 people) as compared to the United States (one for 868) suggests the lesser propensity of Canadians to rely on the law even for civil matters.[9]

TABLE 6.1   Number and Rates of Police Protection in Canada and the United States

Country	Number of Police Personnel	Ratio per 100,000 Population
Canada (1961)	26,189	143.2
United States (1962)	360,000	193.8

Source: Canada: Dominion Bureau of Statistics, *Police Administration Statistics*, 1961, 18; United States: United States Department of Commerce, Bureau of the Census, *Statistical Abstracts of the United States*, 1963, 436.

The greater obedience paid to the law by Canadians may be reflected also in the rates of charges for criminal offences in the two countries. Though data on crime rates are far from amenable to accurate cross-national comparisons, both countries offer the same definition and report statistics for several major criminal offences. The data in Table 6.2 indicate that crime rates for particular offences are substantially higher in the United States than in Canada.

The greater respect for the law in Canada, as compared to the United States, may underlie the greater freedom of political dissent, and the lesser corruption.[10] In English-speaking Canada it is not at all unexpected that one writer has remarked that "Canadians are today perhaps more aware of the differences in their attitudes toward the law than anything else distinguishing them from Americans."[11]

The variation in the strength of the achievement and self-orientations in the United States and Canada may account for another political difference, the fact that "free enterprise" ideology, though accepted in Canada, has never been the source of as violent political conflicts there as in the United States. The greater respect for

government and political leaders, derived in part from elitism and in part from the need dictated by special historic circumstances (see below) requiring that the central government intervene repeatedly in economic and local political matters to assure national survival, has inhibited the development of strong economic individualism as a dominant political virtue. Canada has been much more collectivity-oriented than the United States: proposals for medicare, support for large families, government intervention in the economy, and public ownership of major enterprises have encountered much less opposition north of the border than south of it. "The extreme economic individualism expressed by such slogans as 'the best government is the one that governs least' does not have such deep roots in Canada" as it has in the United States.[12] As one English writer notes:

One of the strange contradictions of Canada is that although it has never had anything resembling a Socialist Government in Ottawa, the list of its "nationalized" industries is almost as imposing as Britain's: more than half the railways; the principal airline; most of radio and television; the Atomic Energy Corporation and one of the biggest uranium producers; a big plastics industry; many of the power utilities [and telephone and telegraph]; and the entire liquor retailing business.[13]

TABLE 6.2   Adults Charged on Selected Indictable Offences, by Class of Offence, 1960, for Canada and the United States

	Canada Rate per 100,000		United States* Rate per 100,000	
	Number	Population	Number	Population
Burglary	8,267	46.4	137,800	126.7
Criminal homicide	207	1.16	7,956	7.3
Forgery and counterfeiting	1,158	6.4	25,244	23.2
Fraud and embezzlement	2,414	13.5	42,189	38.8
Theft-larceny	15,545	87.2	237,193	218.1

Source: Canada: Dominion Bureau of Statistics, *Canada Year Book*, 1962, 356; United States: United States Bureau of the Census, *Statistical Abstracts of the United States*, 1962, 152.

*The rate for the United States was computed from a total population base of 108,779,000; for Canada's rates, the population base used was 17,814,000. The weaker authority over local policing of the American federal government as compared to the Canadian makes it more difficult for the former to collect reliable crime statistics; hence the discrepancy in the proportion of the total population for whom data exist.

And as a Canadian points out, "it is interesting to note that at a time when the *laissez-faire* philosophy was prevailing in the rest of the Western World, there was no protest in Canada against government intervention and interference, not even from business circles."[14] Far from turning to McCarthyism or Goldwaterism, Canadian conservatives responded to years of political defeat by renaming their party the *Progressive* Conservatives.

The lower divorce rate in Canada, compared to that in the United States, presented in Table 6.3, may be viewed as another reflection of the strength of collectivity-orientation in the North. The semi-Establishment status of churches in Canada has lent strong support to traditional morality. It is more difficult to obtain a divorce in all the Canadian provinces than in almost all of the American states. S. D. Clark argues that "the institution of the family [in Canada] has found support in much the same set of conservative forces which have upheld the institutions of law and order."[15]

TABLE 6.3   Divorce Rates per 1,000 Marriages for Specified Years in Canada and the United States

Year	Canada	United States
1891	less than 1	60.0
1911	less than 1	93.4
1941	29.3	168.5
1951	41.0	230.4
1956	45.2	233.0
1960	53.5	257.3

Source: Canada: Dominion Bureau of Statistics, *Canada Year Book*, 1962, 209, 211; United States: United States Department of Commerce, Bureau of the Census, *Statistical Abstracts of the United States*, 1962, 52, and United Nations, Demographic Yearbook, 1960 (New York), 607. See also Lincoln Day, "Patterns of Divorce in Australia and the United States," *American Sociological Review*, XXIX, 4, 1964, 509–22, n.b. Table II.

The weakness in Canada of the sort of rugged individualism (self-orientation) and emphasis on achievement so characteristic of its neighbour to the south may be reflected also in the reluctance of Canadians to be over-optimistic, assertive, or experimentally inclined. Alistair Horne points out that Canadian caution manifests itself in several ways: "one is that Canadians take out more insurance per capita than any other race in the world. Another is that they buy considerably less on hire-purchase [installment plan] than the Americans.... The average Canadian is also cautious about his savings, favoring Government bonds and savings banks. Whereas over the years the American big investor has tended to take a risk on the future of Canada and invest heavily in more speculative Canadian enterprises, the wealthy Canadian cautiously puts his money into Standard Oil of New Jersey."[16] It has been more difficult for the Horatio Alger model of success to take hold in Canadian society where there is strong resistance to economic aggressiveness, social informality, and unabashed materialism. A leading Canadian historian, Arthur Lower, has argued that "Henry Ford was a figure who could hardly have been other than American. Canada did not provide a stage for such as he. Yet this was not on account of lack of opportunities here [in Canada] for accumulating wealth, but rather because that process called for more betting on the sure thing than was necessary across the border."[17] The muted effect of the achievement pattern in Canada is also observed by an English commentator: "Canadian 'quietness' extends also to the worlds of both business and politics...the rat race exists, of course; the North American urge to get ahead, to keep up with the Jones's, is all there, but in Canada, it seems to be kept to a healthier mean."[18]

The emphasis on achievement in the United States is strongly linked to universalism. For instance, in the United States there is a proclaimed need to treat everyone according to the same standard. This universalistic objective underlies the concept of the "melting pot" which holds that no one should be disqualified from full participation on the grounds of ethnic origin or other social distinctions. The melting-pot concept is achievement orientation applied to entire ethnic groups.[19] In contradistinction to the melting pot of the United States, Canadians speak of their society as a "mosaic," a concept which embodies in theory the "right to sustained collective individuality."[20] Vincent Massey, a former Governor General, has expressed the Canadian stress on the presentation of particularistic values:

> We have been successful in our manner of adjusting the relations of the varied communities making Canada their home. About one out of three speaks French as his mother tongue. He is no minority assimilated within a common Canadianism, but rather a partner sharing equally in the joint project of Confederation. Then there are the "new Canadians" of whom two million from Great Britain and from Europe have reached our shores since 1945.... We try to fit in the newcomers much as they are, as pieces in the Canadian mosaic.[21]

Canadian particularism has been demonstrated also in the requirement, in existence until recently, that Canadian passports indicated ethnic origin, for example, a Canadian of German origin even though the German origin may go back more than a century. The Canadian Census not only records religious data gathered from each individual, but also reports the national origins of every Canadian, except for Jews. Jews, regardless of country of paternal ancestry, are classified as such under both religion and national origin.

Canada's political party system has witnessed the rise of a number of "particularistic" third parties, various French-Canadian nationalist or separatist movements, plus the Progressives, Social Credit, and the Co-operative Commonwealth Federation (CCF). The latter, a socialist party, has recently joined with the Canadian Labour Congress to form the New Democratic Party which, based on trade unions, is the largest contemporary "third" party. This pattern of Canadian politics—that is, the continued presence of strong particularistic third parties—is consistent with the assumption that Canada is more particularistic (group-attribute conscious) than the seemingly more universalistic United States.

THE ROOTS OF TWO DEMOCRACIES

Many writers seeking to account for value differences between the United States and Canada suggest that they stem in large part from the revolutionary origins of the United States and the counter-revolutionary history of Canada, from two disparate founding ethos. The Loyalist *émigrés* from the American Revolution and Canada's subsequent and repeated fears of encroachment by the United States fostered the institutionalization of a counter-revolutionary or conservative ethos.[22] By contrast the core values of the United States are linked to the idealistic ideology which emerged during the Revolution and were codified in the Declaration of Independence and elaborated in the principles successfully pressed by the Jeffersonian Democrats in the first formative post-Revolutionary decades.

In Canada's counter-revolutionary beginnings we find the clue to the continuance of British ascriptive and elitist value patterns. The Canadian historian, Arthur Lower, has pointed out that "in its new wilderness home and its new aspect of British North Americanism, colonial Toryism made its second attempt to erect on American soil a copy of the English social edifice. From one point of view this is the most significant thing about the Loyalist movement; it withdrew a class concept of life from the south, moved it up north and gave it a second chance."[23] The anti-revolutionary and anti-American character of Canada's political and social development helped strengthen ethnic particularism. The English rulers of French Canada opposed assimilation as a means of resisting Americanization. Falconer indicates that "as late as 1822 Lord Dalhousie favored the French Canadians of the lower province as a make-weight against Americanizing tendencies which he discerned in Upper Canada."[24] Similarly, the unification of the British North American colonies was procured by Empire-oriented Canadian Conservatives who feared expansion by the United States across the border. The decision to provide

Canada with a much stronger central government than that of the United States was based on anti-American feeling.[25]

In distinction to Canada, the United States is a result of a successful Revolution and prolonged War of Independence organized around an ideology which proclaimed the validity of a specific system of equalitarian and universalistic social relations. Populist beliefs were at the root of early demands from the citizenry that the franchise be extended to everyone. Such populist tendencies lead to the "conviction that government should reflect the will of the people.... [It] breeds a suspicion of strong leaders...."[26] The populist demands on American politicians to be competent and deliver rewards to the people were as natural in the Revolutionary era as they are today.

In addition to the norms directly derived from or linked to political concepts, American values have fostered strong positive orientations to hard work and economic development. The emphasis on equality and achievement reinforced the belief that one could and should get ahead by continuous hard work, frugality, self-discipline, and individual initiative. The absence of an aristocratic model in the nation as a whole after the Revolution left the United States free to develop a socially as well as economically dominant class of merchants and manufacturers whose desire for wealth was uninhibited by norms denigrating hard work and the accumulation of capital.

The special character of American religion has been of considerable significance in the development of the related values of equalitarianism and achievement. Much of the United States was heir to a Calvinistic Puritanism, supplanted by Arminian religious beliefs by the early nineteenth century. According to the Arminian doctrines of free will, free grace, and unlimited hope for the conversion of all men, a devout man was an ambitious man and righteousness was to be rewarded both in this life and in the next.[27] It has been argued that this change occurred because "in a period when special privileges of individuals were being called into question or being

destroyed, there would naturally be less favor for that form of theology which was dominated by the doctrine of special election of a part of mankind, a growing favor for forms which seemed more distinctly to be based upon the idea of the natural equality of all men."[28]

The abolition of religious establishment in the United States which followed on the Revolution and the political successes of the Democrats fostered a strong commitment to voluntarism. This commitment, together with the early dominance of the dissenting anti-statist Methodist and Baptist denomination, meant that religion not only contributed to the economic ethos of the country, but reinforced the egalitarian and democratic social ethic as well.

The ecclesiastical character of Canadian religions greatly inhibited the development of achievement and equalitarian values. Religion in Canada, being related to the state, has provided that country with a control hierarchical mechanism rooted in tradition, which is wholly lacking in the history of the United States. Because of the strong tie between church and state in Canada, religious development there, in contrast to religious movements in the United States, has been less prone to fundamentalism and experimentalism.[29]

Some of the flavour of the social distinctions between Canada and the United States which reflect the greater strength of traditionalist and more conservative values in Canada may be traced also to a Canadian frontier fashioned in a spirit of cautious defensiveness against American expansionist tendencies. Rarely did Canada leave its borders unprotected or its frontier communities autonomous. Law and order in the form of the centrally controlled North West Mounted Police moved into frontier settlements before and along with the settlers. Not only did this establish respect for institutions of law and order, but the special constabulary force which followed on the heels of the frontiersman in Canada also meant that the Mounted Police dominated the frontier scene.[30] In addition, the presence of national government controls on the Canadian frontier weakened the development of excessive individualism.

In the United States on the other hand, frontier agricultural, ranching, and mining areas, unrelated for long periods to any central government or policing system, provided uncontrolled opportunities and encouraged settlers to use their own resources as they saw fit. The cowboy, the frontiersman, and even the vigilante, not the uniformed Mountie, are the heroes of western settlement in the United States.

THE PROBLEM OF CANADIAN IDENTITY

It is not unusual for Americans to refer to Canada as if it had no special independent national character; in fact, Americans frequently think of Canada as a northern extension of their own country, a place for fishing in the summer, hunting in the fall, and skiing in the winter. This attitude towards Canada is aptly described by Douglas LePan, a former Canadian diplomat, who once called upon a United States Senator to discuss the building of a bridge across one of the rivers along the border only to find the Senator oblivious to the need for a boundary at all. He reports that he was rather taken aback when the Senator blithely stated: "You know, I have never been able to see why there should be a border between us at all, our two countries so much alike." LePan, remarking on his feelings, reports that "the Senator, for all his generous good nature, seemed quite unaware that if the boundary were obliterated, the result in the case of a country of some 19 million people living alongside a much richer and more powerful country of almost 190 million people would not be some kind of union; it would be simply absorption."[31] The United States views Canada through a myopia of ethnocentrism in which "in a large country...people find it hard to understand that a much smaller country [in terms of population] is just as mature, viable, well-established, and distinct as the larger. Add to this the relatively

small overt differences of culture and language, and one gets a situation in which the larger is inclined to assume that the smaller is an accident which will soon fade away. English Canadians seem to assume that French Canada will go away, that it won't always be French. Americans seem to imply, by many words and deeds, that Canada will not always be Canada."[32]

The existing Canadian national identity is in large part a reaction against a long-term supposed threat to its independence and traditions, against absorption into the American republic.[33] Loyalty to the British Crown has been one effective means of providing sentiment against American intervention and control. The social consequence of Canadian allegiance to a British monarch has been the acceptance of a national purpose based on the principle of "indivisibility of the Commonwealth." As Vincent Massey has put it:

There are some people in Canada with strong nationalist feelings who think that their end could only be achieved through a republican reform of government. There are, happily, very few persons with such views, and they are profoundly misguided in labouring under the delusion that as a republic we could remain an independent nation. We could not. The Crown-in-Parliament is the supreme symbol of our nationhoood and our greatest defense against absorption into a continental state.[34]

There is at present extensive American capital investment in Canada, high consumption of American goods, and a wide audience for American communication media. Many have rebelled against this American penetration into Canadian life.[35] The Canadian nationalist points to such facts as proof of "domination" by the United States.[36]

Nationalism in English-speaking Canada has undergone some curious changes from the time when it represented a left-wing, often pro–United States protest against the Imperial connection, and the closed economic-political-ecclesiastical system sustained by this connection. Today it is often the left-winger who is most anti-American and pro-British. The more traditional form of Canadian nationalism would seem to continue in the French-Canadian protest movements with their anti-English and anti-Establishment overtones directed at those within Canadian borders who represent English cultural, political, and economic domination. As English-speaking Canadians seek to isolate Canada from the United States, French Canadians look for means to assure the safety of their own culture, surrounded as it is by two hundred million English speakers. In a sense both English-speaking and French-speaking Canadians have similar objectives: to protect two minority cultures from being absorbed by more powerful neighbours.[37]

The problem of changing Canadian and American identities is clearly linked to the broad topic of this paper, the nature and sources of the differences in values and institutions of the two North American democracies. In the past decades the image of the United States has changed drastically. Relatively few in the rest of the world still see the United States as it sees itself, the champion of democratic and egalitarian ideals. To the leaders of the underdeveloped nations and the Communist world, and of many others, including Canada, the United States is now the leading defender of conservative traditional social forms, and is governed from within by an oligarchy of power-*élite*. Many Canadians now seek to defend the integrity of Canada against the United States by defining their own country as more humane, more equalitarian, more democratic, and more anti-imperialist than the United States. Many Canadians now view their country as more "leftist" or liberal in its institutions and international objectives than the United States. Whether this shift in the definition of the character of the United States, Canada's chief reference group, will also affect Canadian values remains to be seen. For anyone interested in Canada or in the general problem of how a nation maintains or changes its basic identity, the situation provides a fascinating question for observation and study.

NOTES

1. S. M. Lipset, *The First New Nation* (New York, 1963), n.b. 248–73.

2. Because of the absence of clear indicators and the overlap with the equalitarian-elitist dimension, the specificity-diffuseness pattern variable is not discussed in this paper. For reasons of parsimony, I ignore Parsons' other pattern variables—affectivity, affectivity-neutrality and instrumental-consummatory distinctions. See Talcott Parsons, *The Social System* (Glencoe, Ill., 1951), 58–67. See also Parsons' recent elaboration of the pattern variables in "Pattern Variables Revisited," *American Sociological Review*, xxv, 4, 1960, 467–83.

3. Kaspar D. Naegele, "Canadian Society: Some Reflections," in Bernard Blishen, Frank Jones, Kaspar Naegele, and John Porter, eds., *Canadian Society* (Toronto, 1961), 27. This article is an excellent effort to summarize the general value system of Canada. Naegele argues convincingly that Canada on many matters lies "in the middle between America and England" and that it both accepts and rejects various aspects of the English and American models.

4. The educational data are calculated from materials in UNESCO, *Basic Facts and Figures*, 1960 (Paris, 1963); United Nations *Demographic Yearbook*, 1960 (New York, 1960); 2nd United Nations Compendium of Social Statistics (New York, 1963).

5. Dennis Wrong, *American and Canadian Viewpoints* (Washington, 1955), 20; Wilson Woodside, *The University Question* (Toronto, 1958), 21–2.

6. One of the more subtle signs of certain status distinctions was noted by A. R. M. Lower, *Canadians in the Making* (Toronto, 1958), 446, n. 11, who observed that, to his astonishment, in one midwestern university in the United States known to him, students and faculty actually share the same lavatory. Dennis Wrong points out that "with respect to the position of women, greater conservatism exists in Canada than in the United States...relatively fewer women have achieved prominence as public figures." *American and Canadian Viewpoints*, 11.

7. Wrong, *American and Canadian Viewpoints*, 36–7.

8. Canada: Dominion Bureau of Statistics, *Police Administration Statistics*, 1961, 19; United States: Federal Bureau of Investigation, *Uniform Crime Report—1961*, 20, 110, Table 36, and *Uniform Crime Report—1963*, 33–4. Dennis Wrong notes that "one finds less of the frequent American distrust of lawyers as 'shysters,' or as ambitious politicians, in English-speaking Canada and a greater sense of remoteness and majesty of the law." Wrong argues that the contrast between the popular-culture heroes of American and Canadian frontier expansion indicate the respect among Canadians for the law and the converse for Americans: "...in the United States it is the cowboy, a rugged individualist whose relationship to the forces of law and order was at least ambiguous, who has come to symbolize the frontier, while in Canada the 'mountie,' a policeman who clearly stands for law and order and tradi-

tional institutional authority, is the corresponding symbol of Canadian westward expansion." *Wrong, American and Canadian Viewpoints*, 38.

9. S. M. Lipset, *The First New Nation*, 264–65.

10. For example, S. D. Clark has pointed out that McCarthyism, a populist movement expressing political intolerance, is not likely to emerge in Canada. "In Canada it would be hard to conceive of a state of political freedom great enough to permit the kind of attacks upon responsible leaders of the government which have been carried out in the United States." S. D. Clark, "The Frontier and Democratic Theory," *Transactions of the Royal Society of Canada*, XLVIII, June 1954, 72. Regarding judiciary appointments, see Henry H. Bull, "The Career Prosecutor of Canada," *Journal of Criminal Law, Criminology, and Police Science*, LIII, 1962, 89–96.

11. Wrong, *American and Canadian Viewpoints*, 38.

12. Ibid., 29.

13. Alistair Horne, *Canada and the Canadians* (London, 1961), 248–49. It might be added that hotels are owned by the CNR, and now all provinces except Quebec have hospitalization insurance plans; Canada also has Family Allowances of $6 per month for every child under 10, and $8 for those between 10 and 15 (see Horne, 250).

14. Maurice Lamontagne, "The Role of Government," in G. P. Gilmour, ed., *Canada's Tomorrow* (Toronto, 1954), 125. See also James Byrce's discussion on Canada's resistance to the policy of *laissez-faire: Modern Democracies*, vol. I (London, 1921), 471.

15. S. D. Clark, "The Canadian Community," in G. Brown, ed., *Canada* (Berkeley, California, 1950), 386–87.

16. Horne, *Canada and the Canadians*, 245.

17. Lower, *Canadians in the Making*, 426. In Quebec, also, there has been notable Catholic resistance to aggressive business enterprise, due primarily to the strength of religious and traditionalist views. See Wrong, *American and Canadian Viewpoints*, 29–30.

18. A. Horne, *Canada and the Canadians*, 9.

19. "In the United States the Briton hastened to become a good American; in Canada he has been encouraged to remain a good Briton. Nor has any vigorous effort been made to assimilate continental European peoples in Canada, except through the public school; as with the French Canadians, the break of continental Europeans from their cultural past has tended to expose them to European influences." S. D. Clark, "The Canadian Community," 386–87.

20. Kaspar Naegele, "Canadian Society: Some Reflections," in Blishen et al., *Canadian Society*, 44.

21. Vincent Massey, *Canadians and Their Commonwealth* (Oxford, 1961), 5–6.

22. See J. M. S. Careless, *Canada: A Story of Challenge* (Cambridge, 1963), 111, 112, 113. Even since World War II, as Careless argues, Canada has remained more conservative than the United States: "In comparison with the rich and restless republic [the United States], Canada was a cautious and conservative country: cautious because her path was

harder, more conservative because of her closer bonds with the Old World, and the stronger power of traditions brought from Britain and France" (p. 405).

23. Arthur Lower, *From Colony to Nation* (Toronto, 1946), 114.

24. Sir Robert Falconer, *The United States as a Neighbour* (Cambridge, 1925), 23.

25. W. L. Morton, "The Extension of the Franchise in Canada," *Report of the Canadian Historical Association* (Toronto, 1943), 76.

26. Wrong, *American and Canadian Viewpoints*, 31–2.

27. See Philip Schaff, *America: A Sketch of the Political, Social and Religious Character of the United States of North America* (New York, 1855), 259.

28. Franklin Jameson, *The American Revolution Considered as a Social Movement* (Princeton, 1926), 157.

29. S. D. Clark, *The Developing Canadian Community* (Toronto, 1962), 178. Clark remarks: "Political pressures have forced the community to come to the support of organized religion and such support has placed a definite limitation upon sectarian activity. With the collective weight of the community brought to bear upon them, the sects have been forced either to retreat behind a wall of isolation or build themselves into an integral part of the community, or else to seek denominational supports by aligning themselves with the state and with the traditional institutions of the community."

30. Clark, *The Developing Canadian Community*, 386–87.

31. Douglas V. LePan, "The Outlook for the Relationship," in John Sloan Dickey, ed., *The United States and Canada* (Englewood Cliffs, N.J., 1964), n.b. 155–56.

32. Everett C. Hughes, " A Sociologist's View," in John Sloan Dickey, *The United States and Canada*, 18.

33. "Canadian national life can almost be said to take its rise in the negative will to resist absorption in the American republic. It is largely about the United States as an object that the consciousness of Canadian national unity has grown up..." S. D. Clark, "The Importance of Anti-Americanism in Canadian National Feeling," in H. F. Angus, ed., *Canada and Her Great Neighbor* (Toronto, 1938), 243.

34. Vincent Massey, *Canadians and Their Commonwealth*, 19.

35. The concern of Canadians with the large amount of American investment is not merely based on the historical insecurity of Canada vis-à-vis its more powerful neighbour. It is interesting to note that Americans owned 44 per cent of Canadian manufacturing industry in 1959 and that the United States has more money invested in Canada than in any other area in the world. See Norman L. Nicholson, *Canada in the American* Community (Princeton, N.J., 1963), 119.

36. Harry G. Johnson, "Problems of Canadian Nationalism," *International Journal* (Summer, 1961), 238–49.

37. S. D. Clark, "Canada and Her Great Neighbour," paper presented at the meeting of the *American Sociological Association* (Montreal, Canada), September 3, 1964.

7

Investigating Canadian and American Value Differences Through an Analysis of Media Portrayals of Native Issues

Bruce Ravelli

CULTURE

One of sociology's defining interests is the study of the relationship between the individual and society (Brym with Fox, 1989: 4). A critical component of this investigation is the attempt to understand the role culture plays in defining people's perception of their social environment.

The first section of this article reviews the defining characteristics of culture and many of the concepts that sociologists use to analyze and study it. The second section investigates Canadian and American cultural values, to determine whether they are different. The purpose of this article then is twofold: the first is to acquaint you with the sociological analyses of culture, and the second is to compare and contrast Canadian and American cultures in the hope of helping you appreciate what it means to be Canadian.

DEFINING ELEMENTS OF CANADIAN CULTURE

Before we begin our analysis, it is important to define what sociologists mean when they refer to a society's *culture* and *values*.[1] *Culture* is defined as a broad spectrum of beliefs, values, and material objects that help people define their way of life. For example, Canadians' appreciation of multiculturalism and support for universal health care are two defining attributes of what it means to be Canadian. *Values* are defined in more general terms and involve standards, principles, and broad guidelines as to how people should try to live their lives. For example, a Canadian value might be the belief that it is better to compete fairly and lose than to cheat and win. As we will see, Canadian culture and values are shaped by an intricate and diverse set of physical and social circumstances.

Physically, Canada is the second-largest country in the world (Countries of the World, 2002). Although it boasts a rich and diverse supply of natural resources, it also endures challenging, cold winters. Noted Canadian writer Margaret Atwood believes that Canada's adaptation to its harsh physical environment defines Canadian culture and, to some extent, what it means to be Canadian (Atwood, 1970: 33, cited in Lipset, 1986: 124). Socially, Canadian culture has been defined by the coexistence of, and at times conflict between, the English and the French (Hiller, 1996). The fact that 87 percent of the people living in Quebec identify French as their mother tongue suggests that on this criterion at least, Quebec is certainly *distinct* from the rest of the country (Statistics Canada, 2002). However, Quebec's distinctiveness does not rest solely on language; it also rests on its people's shared history, symbols, ideas, and perceptions of reality (McGuigan, 1997: 52). Clearly, Canada's physical and social environments have influenced its culture, but arguably, they have also influenced its values as well.

Canadian values were of primary interest to a 1991 federal commission called the Citizens' Forum on Canada's Future, or the Spicer Commission (CFCF, 1991: 35–45). In its report, the commission identified seven primary cultural values:

1. *Equality and fairness in a democratic society:* Canadians believe in treating all citizens equally (e.g., people with disabilities).
2. *Consultation and dialogue:* Canadians try to settle differences peacefully through discussion and collective problem solving (e.g., Aboriginal self-government initiatives).
3. *Importance of accommodation and tolerance:* Canadians attempt to accommodate the traditions and customs of various ethnic populations (e.g., Aboriginal peoples and the French in Quebec).
4. *Appreciation for diversity:* Canadians support diversity (e.g., regional, ethnic, linguistic, or cultural differences).
5. *Compassion and generosity:* Canadians value their social safety net as an attempt to provide a fair and accessible society for all (e.g., universal health care, pension plans, economic development programs, openness to refugees, and commitment to reducing regional disparities).
6. *Attachment to Canada's natural beauty:* Canadians believe they have a close connection to the natural environment and feel that governments should do more to protect it from pollution and other forms of industrialization (e.g., environmental protection legislation).
7. *Commitment to freedom, peace, and nonviolent change:* Canadians see themselves as peaceful people who maintain an active role in international peacekeeping (e.g., Canada's support for UN-sponsored peacekeeping initiatives)

(Macionis, Jansson, & Benoit, 2002: 36).

Clearly, Canadian culture and values are a culmination of many physical and social forces, and studying Canadian–American differences fascinates Canadians (Lipset, 1999: 124; 1990: 53; 1986: 123) and Canadian sociologists in particular (Arnold & Tigert, 1974; Brym & Saint-Pierre, 1997; Clark, 1942; Clement, 1975; Hull, 1998: 4; Porter, 1965; Ravelli, 1994; Reitz & Breton, 1994). Seymour Martin Lipset (an American) has based his career on the study of what makes Canadians and Americans different (Tiryakian, 1991: 1040; Waller, 1990: 380). Lipset's book *Continental Divide* (1990) summarizes and consolidates his almost forty-five years of research on Canadian–American differences; in it he justifies his research, arguing that

Knowledge of Canada or the United States is the best way to gain insight into the other North American country. Nations can only be understood in comparative perspective. And the more similar the units being compared, the more possible it should be to isolate the factors responsible for differences between them. Looking intensively at Canada and the United States sheds light on both of them. (1990: xiii)

Canadians, historically at least, defined themselves by what they were not—Americans (Lipset: 1990: 53; 1986: 123). For Lipset, the primordial event that generated the different founding ideologies of Canada and the United States was the American Revolution (Lipset, 1990: 8; 1986: 114; 1985: 160; 1963: 239). The United States emerged from the Revolution as a manifestation of the classic liberal state, rejecting all ties to the throne, ascriptive elitism, noblesse oblige, and communitarianism (1986: 114). English Canada, however, fought to maintain its imperial ties through the explicit rejection of liberal revolutions (Lipset, 1986: 115). Canadian identity was not defined by a successful revolution, but instead a successful counterrevolution (Lipset, 1993: 161; 1990: 42). America, conversely, was defined by a rigid and stable ideology Lipset called Americanism (1950: 181).[2]

Lipset offers evidence that Canadian and American founding ideologies are present in each country's literature (1986: 123). For example, American literature concentrates on themes of winning, opportunism, and confidence, while Canadian writing focuses on defeat, difficult physical circumstances, and abandonment by Britain (Lipset, 1990: 1; 1986: 123). Lipset cites well-known Canadian novelist Margaret Atwood, who suggests that national symbols reveal a great deal about the cultural values a nation embraces. For Atwood, the defining symbol for America was "the frontier," which inspired images of vitality and unrealized potential, while the symbol of "survival" summed up Canada's national character: "Canadians are forever taking the national pulse like doctors at a sickbed; the aim is not to see whether the patient will live well but simply whether he will live at all" (Atwood, 1970: 33, cited in Lipset, 1986: 124). Lipset suggests that the symbols, attitudes, and values of a people do not exist in a vacuum; rather, social and political institutions embody and reinforce them (Lipset, 1990: xiv; 225; 1986: 114, 119; Baer, Grabb, & Johnston, 1990a: 693). For Lipset, values are the basis on which society builds its social and political structures, and different value systems manifest themselves in all social realms, not just literature. (Lipset, 1990: xiv)

Lipset argues that social structures reflect a society's values and beliefs (Baer, Grabb, & Johnston, 1990a: 693; Grabb & Curtis, 1988: 129, 137; Lipset, 1963: 210). To understand the importance of culture in determining a society's social structure, Lipset incorporated Talcott Parsons' (1952) pattern variables typology into his research (Lipset, 1963: 210). Parsons' pattern variables provide researchers with a method for classifying social values that is more sensitive to cultural variation than the older polar concepts of sociology, such as core–periphery, folk–urban, mechanical–organic, and primary–secondary.

Lipset's thesis of cross-national value differences suggests that Canadians are more elitist and ascriptive; appreciate racial and ethnic variation; and are more community-oriented than Americans. Although Lipset is a dominant figure in North American sociology,[3] his Canadian–American research has been the subject of much interest and debate. Various researchers (see Baer, Grabb, & Johnston, 1990a, 1990b, 1990c, 1993; Curtis, Grabb, & Baer, 1992; Grabb & Curtis, 1988) have attempted to test Lipset's thesis but have faced several difficulties, the most challenging being the following:

- Lipset's research is based on subjective data that are difficult, if not impossible, to test systematically.
- Lipset's pattern variables are at times contradictory and often suggest Canadian–American differences that are opposite to what his thesis would predict.
- Lipset fails to recognize how contemporary social change may influence Canadian and American values.
- Lipset's approach ignores regional variations.
- Lipset fails to offer alternative explanations for Canadian and American value differences.

In spite of such pointed criticism, sociologists generally agree that Lipset's fundamental proposition that Canadian and American cultural values are different, is sound (see Brym with Fox, 1989: 16–8; Clark, 1975: 26; Baer, Grabb, & Johnston, 1990a: 708; 1990c: 276; McGuigan, 1990: 127; Ogmundson & Fisher, 1994: 196). One area of investigation that may shed a contemporary light on Canadian–American differences is an analysis of each country's media, looking for evidence of national value differences.[4]

THE MEDIA'S INFLUENCE ON DEFINING CULTURE

In *Inventing Reality* (1993), Michael Parenti argues that although the media may not mould our every opinion, they do mould *opinion visibility* (Parenti, 1993: 23; see also Gamson & Modigliani, 1989: 3). In effect, journalists, reporters, and news anchors set our *perceptual agenda* (a view shared by Adams, 1978: 30; and Smith, 1992: 210). Parenti states, "The media may not always be able to tell us what to think, but they are strikingly successful in telling us what to think about" (1993: 23; see also Smith, 1992: 210). It is not so much that the media construct opinion; it is enough that they give legitimacy to certain views and illegitimacy to others (Parenti, 1993: 24). This ability has important implications for how the media define and reflect our perceptions and guide our interactions with the social world by effectively constructing news that reflects dominant values (Parenti, 1993: 69). Edward Herman and Noam Chomsky explore this issue in *Manufacturing Consent* (1988).

Herman and Chomsky suggest that the media intentionally create a social environment favourable to the dominant classes by *manufacturing consent* through the filtering of stories (Herman & Chomsky, 1988: xi, 2). This filtering takes two forms: (1) deciding not to cover a story and (2) presenting a story in such a way as to diffuse or bias its objective content. This filtering influences how people see and interpret the social world because it defines their reality. Herman and Chomsky suggest that the primary role of mainstream media is to ensure popular support for the economic, social, and political agenda of the privileged classes (1988: 298). Their *propaganda* model reveals many of the techniques media use to manufacture consent.

One way to find evidence for Canadian and American cultural differences would be to study a single social phenomenon common to both countries, such as how the media present a common and familiar issue. This brief review of how the media reflect and define a society's values reinforces the selection of media as one avenue by which to investigate Lipset's thesis of cross-national value differences in more detail. As argued by many, the media are becoming *the* conduit through which much of the world defines and reflects its cultural values (see Adams, 1978: 30; Campbell, 1999; Gamson & Modigliani, 1989: 3; Gitlin, 1980; Herman & Chomsky, 1988: 2; Parenti, 1993: 23; Smith, 1992: 210; Tetzlaff, 1992). My approach uses Native issues as a social phenomenon for study since both Canada and the United States have a long history of Native–White contact (see Berelson & Salter, 1946; Grenier, 1993; Singer, 1982; Skea, 1993).[5]

To test Lipset's thesis, I employed a fifty-year longitudinal study of Canadian and American media and how they presented Native issues. The medium I chose for the comparison was newsmagazines, in particular, *Maclean's* in Canada and *Newsweek* in the United States.[6] These newsmagazines were selected because they are regarded as journalistic leaders (see Roy, 1990: 510; van Driel & Richardson, 1988: 38) and attract national audiences. Thus, they should present national values to the extent that they exist. To test Lipset's theory, I formulated seven hypotheses flowing directly out of his four pattern variables (see Table 7.1).

My sampling frame included all articles referring to Natives in *Maclean's* and *Newsweek* from 1943 to 1993.[7] After locating the articles, I conducted a content analysis to determine whether there were systematic differences between each magazine's coverage of Native issues.

My analysis of *Maclean's* and *Newsweek* incorporated two complementary perspectives, the first a quantitative examination testing whether Lipset's value differences were evident (see Appendix A), and the second a qualitative exploration to detect themes speaking to Lipset's thesis (see Appendix B). The quantitative analysis provides a rudimentary statistical assessment of Lipset's thesis, while the qualitative has greater sensitivity to themes appearing in the articles pertaining to cultural differences. By coding the articles from both quantitative and qualitative perspectives, I hoped to gain a more complete appreciation of their portrayals of Native issues than would be possible by using either approach independently.

Results suggest little quantitative or qualitative support for Lipset's thesis of Canadian–American value differences (see Table 7.2).

TABLE 7.1   Testing Lipset's Thesis

Lipset's Pattern Variable	Hypothesis
Elitism–Egalitarianism	1a: Canadians will view political leaders more positively than Americans. 1b: Canadians will view minority leaders more critically than Americans.
Ascription–Achievement	2a: Canadians will support government-sponsored redistribution programs more than Americans. 2b: Canadians will criticize lawlessness more than Americans.
Particularism–Universalism	3: Canadians will support the mosaic perspective more than Americans.
Diffuseness–Specificity	4a: Canadians will support the collectivist perspective more than Americans. 4b: Canadians will criticize minority challenges to the collective more than Americans.

TABLE 7.2   Qualitative/Quantitative Results Summary

Pattern Variable	Hypothesis	Quantitative Results	Qualitative Results
Elitism versus Egalitarianism	1a: Political Leadership 1b: Native Leadership	Reject Reject	Reject Reject
Ascription versus Achievement	2a: Redistribution Programs 2b: Native Lawlessness	Reject Reject	Support Reject
Particularism versus Universalism	3: Mosaic Perspective	Support	Support
Diffuseness versus Specificity	4a: Collectivist Perspective 4b: Native Challenge to the Collective	Reject Reject	Support Reject

Table 7.2 illustrates that six of the seven quantitative results fail to support Lipset's thesis. Statistical differences existed between *Maclean's* and *Newsweek* and their presentation of Native issues, but the differences were often in the opposite direction of what Lipset's thesis would predict. Qualitative results were similar to the quantitative in that four of the seven hypotheses rejected Lipset's thesis.

1. Elitism versus Egalitarianism is **not supported** as all four tests reject Lipset's hypothesis.
2. Ascription versus Achievement is **not supported** as three of the four tests refute Lipset's hypothesis.
3. Particularism versus Universalism is **supported** as both tests support Lipset's hypothesis.
4. Diffuseness versus Specificity is **not supported** as three of the four tests reject Lipset's hypothesis.

My findings suggest that Canadian and American cultural values do vary, but not in a manner consistent with Lipset's pattern variable thesis. The only pattern variable to be supported was *Particularism versus Universalism*, which suggests that Canadians do recognize and encourage racial and ethnic diversity more than Americans. Although my research found little support for the three remaining pattern variables, it did find evidence to support the common experience that Canadian and American cultures differ (see Reitz & Breton, 1994).

CONCLUSION

After reading almost 400 magazine articles, on at least three separate occasions, I was struck by how often *Maclean's* presented Native issues with emotion and passion and how rarely any empathy was shown for the plight of American Natives in *Newsweek*. For me, this suggests one of the defining differences between Canadians and Americans—the belief in, and support for, multiculturalism. Granted, Canada's record of dealing with Native populations has often been strained and difficult; however, the dialogue between the parties has played a central and defining role in constructing our national value systems. This level of public debate and discussion between American Natives and the larger American society has not yet occurred. Canadians, however, must appreciate that just saying that Canada is a multicultural society is not enough. All people in Canada need to know, and be shown, that for Canadians, multiculturalism is not just an abstract philosophy; it is one of the defining elements of who we are as a people—multiculturalism means nothing if we don't practise what we preach.

APPENDIX A

My quantitative coding tested Lipset's overall thesis of cross-national value differences by comparing how each article portrayed issues that were relevant to Lipset's pattern variables. For example, when an article discussed political leaders (pertinent to hypothesis 1a), I noted every reference to political leaders as positive, negative, or indeterminate in the margins of the article. Positive statements about political leaders were coded as PL+, negative as PL−, and indeterminate as PL? When I completed the coding, I added the number of positive, negative, and indeterminate references and determined an overall coding for that article. That is, if the article had 15 positive statements about the political leader, 3 negative, and 0 indeterminate, I concluded that the article presented a supportive portrayal of political leaders. The statistical analyses were based on these comparisons. An obvious concern at this point is how confident I am that my coding of the articles was reliable.

Research is deemed reliable when the particular research technique, applied repeatedly to the same phenomenon, yields the same results (Babbie, 1995: 124). I am confident that my coding was reliable for two reasons. First, totals for the three possible codings (i.e., PL+, PL−, PL?) were never within 10 percent of each other. This indicates that the article's editorial bias (or lack of one) was readily apparent. Second, even though I was the only person coding the articles, I re-coded a 10 percent random sample of the articles (30 articles from *Maclean's*, 10 from *Newsweek*) six months after I completed my initial coding. The coefficient of reliability between the codings was 72 percent (coefficient of reliability = number of units in identical category/total number of units). Since coefficient values higher than 60 percent are deemed reliable (Jackson, 1995: 72), I am confident that my coding reliably reflects the articles' (and by extension, the newsmagazines') editorial bias.

APPENDIX B

Content analysis is a set of procedures used to study text (Weber, 1990: 9) and is appropriate for most forms of communication (Babbie, 1995: 307). Using content analysis I was able to investigate themes in media content that went beyond those explicitly stated. Robert Weber (1990: 9) suggests that content analysis of media can reveal international differences and uncover the cultural patterns of groups, institutions, or societies. The ability to look beyond the text makes content analysis well suited for a cross-national analysis of culture differences in media (Babbie, 1995: 315).

NOTES

1. The majority of the following analysis is a consolidation of my doctoral dissertation, "Canadian–American Value Differences: Media Portrayals of Native Issues" (1997), unpublished manuscript, Department of Sociology, University of Victoria.
2. An ideology is a system of beliefs, common ideas, perceptions, and values held in common by members of a collective (Parsons, 1952: 349). Ideology can be thought of as the filter through which we interpret our social world.
3. As demonstrated, in part, by his election as president of the American Sociological Association for 1993–94.
4. My working assumption behind this analysis is the belief that media content will reflect national values to secure the widest audience possible and, by extension, the greatest financial benefit for its shareholders.
5. The term "Native" is used to describe the indigenous populations of North America. This terminology was selected over others (e.g., Aboriginal, First Nations, Amerindian, Indian) as it is the standard in contemporary literature (see Francis, 1992: 9).
6. Electronic media are too recent to study and print media lend themselves to better contextual analysis (see Neumann, Just, & Crigler, 1992: 58–9; Vipond, 1992: 27, 78, 128).
7. To locate the articles, I first consulted the Library of Congress subject heading Indians of North America. I then manually searched the *Reader's Guide to Periodical Literature* (Reader's Guide) and the *Canadian Periodical Index* (CPI) for references to the subject title. This strategy located 296 articles in *Maclean's* and 96 in *Newsweek*.

REFERENCES

Adams, W. C. 1978. Network news research in perspective: A bibliographic essay. In *Television network news: Issues in content research*. Washington, DC: George Washington University Press.

Arnold, S. J., and D. J. Tigert. 1974. Canadians and Americans: A comparative analysis. *International Journal of Comparative Sociology*, 15: 68–83.

Atwood, M. 1970. *The journals of Suzanna Moodie: Poems*. Toronto: Oxford University Press.

Babbie, E. 1995. *The practice of social research*, 7th ed. Belmont, Calif.: Wadsworth Publishing Company.

Baer, D., E. Grabb, and W. A. Johnston. 1990a. *The values of Canadians and Americans: A critical analysis and reassessment*. Social Forces, 68(3): 693–713.

———. 1990b. Reassessing differences in Canadian and American values. In *Images of Canada: The sociological tradition*, eds. J. Curtis, and L. Tepperman, 86–97. Scarborough, Ont.: Prentice-Hall Canada.

———. 1990c. The values of Canadians and Americans: A rejoinder. *Social Forces*, 69(1): 273–77.

———. 1993. National character, regional culture, and the values of Canadians and Americans. *Canadian Review of Sociology and Anthropology*, 30(1): 13–36.

Berelson, B., and P. J. Salter. 1946. Majority and minority Americans: An analysis of magazine fiction. *Public Opinion Quarterly*, 10.

Brym, R. J., with B. J. Fox. 1989. *From culture to power: The sociology of English Canada*. Toronto: Oxford University Press.

Brym, R., and C. Saint-Pierre. 1997. Canada: Canadian sociology. *Contemporary Sociology*, 26(5): 543–46.

Campbell, K. 1999. Why we must protect Canadian culture from the U.S. juggernaut. In *Canadian communications: Issues in contemporary media culture*, eds. B. Szuchewycz, and J. Sloniowski, 214–18. Scarborough, Ont.: Prentice Hall/Allyn and Bacon Canada.

CFCF (Citizen's Forum on Canada's Future). 1991. *Report to the People and Government of Canada*. Ottawa: Supply and Services Canada.

Clark, S. D. 1942. *The social development of Canada: An introductory study with select documents*. Toronto: University of Toronto Press.

———. 1975. The post–Second World War Canadian society. *The Canadian Review of Sociology and Anthropology*, 12(1).

Clement, W. 1975. *The Canadian corporate elite: An analysis of economic power*. Toronto: McClelland and Stewart.

Countries of the World. 2002. Country statistics at a glance. [Online]. Available: **http://www.infoplease.com/ipa/A0762380.html**. Accessed July 17, 2002.

Curtis, J. E., E. G. Grabb, and D. E. Baer. 1992. Voluntary association membership in fifteen countries: A comparative analysis." *American Sociological Review*, 57(April): 139–52.

Francis, D. 1992. *The imaginary Indian: The image of the Indian in Canadian culture*. Vancouver: Arsenal Pulp Press.

Gamson, W. A., and A. Modigliani. 1989. Media discourse and public opinion on nuclear power: A constructionist approach." *American Journal of Sociology*, 95(1) : 1–37.

Gitlin, T. 1980. *The whole world is watching*. Berkeley: University of California Press.

Grabb, E. G., and J. E. Curtis. 1988. English Canadian–American differences in orientation toward social control and individual rights. *Sociological Focus*, 21(2): 127–40.

Grenier, M. 1993. Native Indians in the English-Canadian press: The case of the Oka Crisis. *Media, Culture and Society*, 16 (April): 313–36.

Herman, E. S., and N. Chomsky. 1988. *Manufacturing consent: The political economy of the mass media*. New York: Pantheon Books.

Hiller, H. 1996. *Canadian society: A macro analysis*, 3rd ed. Scarborough, Ont.: Prentice Hall Canada.

Hull, J. P. 1998. From many, two: A bibliographic history of Canadian–American relations. *American Studies International*, 36(2): 4–22.

Jackson, W. 1995. *Methods: Doing social research*. Scarborough, Ont.: Prentice Hall Canada.

Lipset, S. M. 1950. *Agrarian socialism: The Cooperative Commonwealth Federation in Saskatchewan*. Berkeley and Los Angeles: University of California Press.

———. 1963. *The first new nation: The United States in historical and comparative perspective*. New York: Basic Books.

———. 1985. Canada and the United States: The cultural dimension. *In Canada and the United States*, eds. C. F. Doran, and J. H. Sigler, 109–160. Englewood Cliffs, N.J.: Prentice Hall.

———. 1986. Historical traditions and national characteristics: A comparative analysis of Canada and the United States. *Canadian Journal of Sociology* 11(2): 113–55.

———. 1990. Continental divide: The values and institutions of the United States and Canada. New York: Routledge.

———. 1993. Revolution and counterrevolution: The United States and Canada. *In A passion for identity: An introduction to Canadian studies*, eds. D. Taras, B. Rasporich, and E. Mandel, 150–61. Scarborough, Ont.: Nelson Canada.

———. 1999. American union density in comparative perspective. *Contemporary Sociology*, 27(2): 123–25.

Macionis, J. J., S. M. Jansson, and C. M. Benoit. 2002. *Society: The basics*, 2nd Cdn ed. Toronto: Pearson Education Canada.

McGuigan, B. 1990. *The comparative sociology of Seymour Martin Lipset: An analysis and critique*. Unpublished master's thesis. University of Calgary.

———. 1997. Issues in Canadian culture. In *Issues in Canadian sociology*, 2nd ed., eds. M. Kanwar, and D. Swenson, 35–60. Dubuque, Iowa: Kendall/Hunt Publishing.

Neumann, R. W., M. R. Just, and A. N. Crigler. 1992. *Common knowledge: News and the construction of political meaning*. Chicago: University of Chicago Press.

Ogmundson, R. L., and L. Fisher. 1994. Beyond Lipset and his critics: An initial reformulation. *Canadian Review of Sociology and Anthropology*, 31(2): 196–99.

Parenti, M. 1993. *Inventing the politics of news media reality*, 2nd ed. New York: St. Martin's Press.

Parsons, T. 1952. *The social system*. London: Tavistock Publications Ltd.

Porter, J. 1965. *The vertical mosaic: An analysis of social class and power in Canada*. Toronto: University of Toronto Press.

Ravelli, B. 1994. Health care in the United States and Canada. In *The Sociological Outlook: A Text with Readings*, 4th ed., ed. R. Luhman, 467–68. San Diego: Collegiate Press.

Reitz, J. G., and R. Breton. 1994. *The illusion of difference: Realities of ethnicity in Canada and the United States*. Toronto: C.D. Howe Institute.

Roy, D. 1990. The U.S. print media and the conventional military balance in Europe. *Armed Forces & Society*, 16(4): 509–28.

Singer, B. D. 1982. Minorities in the media: A content analysis of Native Canadians in the daily press. *Canadian Review of Sociology and Anthropology*, 19(3): 348–59.

Skea, W. H. 1993. The Canadian newspaper industry's portrayal of the Oka Crisis. *Native Studies Review*, 9(1): 15–31.

Smith, R. L. 1992. Media networking: Toward a model for the global management of sociocultural change. In *Mass media effects across cultures*, eds. F. Korzenny et al., 201–28. Newbury Park, Calif.: Sage.

Statistics Canada. 2002. Population by home language, 2001 Census. [Online]. Available: **http://www.statcan.ca/ english/Pgdb/demo29b.htm**. Accessed July 16, 2002.

Tetzlaff, D. 1992. Popular culture and social control in late capitalism. *In Culture and power: A media, culture and society reader*, eds. P. Scannell, P. Schlesinger, and C. Sparks, 48–72. London: Sage.

Tiryakian, E. A. 1991. Book review of *Continental divide: The values and institutions of the United States and Canada* by S. M. Lipset. *American Journal of Sociology*, 96(4): 1040–42.

Van Driel, B., and Richardson, J. T. 1988. *Print media coverage of new religious movements: A longitudinal study*. Journal of Communication, 38(3): 37–61.

Vipond, M. 1992. *The mass media in Canada*. Toronto: James Lorimer & Company.

Waller, H. M. 1990. Book review of *Continental divide: The values and institutions of the United States and Canada* by S. M. Lipset. *Canadian Journal of Political Science*, 23: 380–81.

Weber, R. P. 1990. *Basic content analysis*, 2nd ed. Newbury Park, Calif.: Sage Publications.

Part IV

Society

8

Manifesto of the Communist Party

Karl Marx and Friedrich Engels

BOURGEOIS AND PROLETARIANS[1]

The history of all hitherto existing society[2] is the history of class struggles.

Freeman and slave, patrician and plebeian, lord and serf, guild-master[3] and journeyman, in a word, oppressor and oppressed, stood in constant opposition to one another, carried on an uninterrupted, now hidden, now open fight, a fight that each time ended, either in a revolutionary reconstitution of society at large, or in the common ruin of the contending classes.

In the earlier epochs of history, we find almost everywhere a complicated arrangement of society into various orders, a manifold gradation of social rank. In ancient Rome we have patricians, knights, plebeians, slaves; in the Middle Ages, feudal lords, vassals, guild-masters, journeymen, apprentices, serfs; in almost all of these classes, again, subordinate gradations.

The modern bourgeois society that has sprouted from the ruins of feudal society has not done away with class antagonisms. It has but established new classes, new conditions of oppression, new forms of struggle in place of the old ones.

Our epoch, the epoch of the bourgeoisie, possesses, however, this distinctive feature; it has simplified the class antagonisms. Society as a whole is more and more splitting up into two great hostile camps, into two great classes directly facing each other: Bourgeoisie and Proletariat.

From the serfs of the Middle Ages sprang the chartered burghers of the earliest towns. From these burgesses the first elements of the bourgeoisie were developed.

The discovery of America, the rounding of the Cape, opened up fresh ground for the rising bourgeoisie. The East Indian and Chinese markets, the [colonization] of America, trade with the colonies, the increase in the means of exchange, and in commodities generally, gave to commerce, to navigation, to industry, an impulse never before known, and thereby, to the revolutionary element

Source: From *Manifesto of the Communist Party,* Part I, by Karl Marx and Friedrich Engels.

in the tottering feudal society, a rapid development.

The feudal system of industry, under which industrial production was monopolized by close guilds, now no longer sufficed for the growing wants of the new markets. The manufacturing system took its place. The guild-masters were pushed on one side by the manufacturing middle class; division of labor between the different corporate guilds vanished in the face of division of labor in each single workshop.

Meantime the markets kept ever growing, the demand, ever rising. Even manufacture no longer sufficed. Thereupon, steam and machinery revolutionized industrial production. The place of manufacture was taken by the giant, Modern Industry, the place of the industrial middle class, by industrial millionaires, the leaders of whole industrial armies, the modern bourgeois.

Modern industry has established the world-market, for which the discovery of America paved the way. This market has given an immense development to commerce, to navigation, to communication by land. This development has, in its turn, reacted on the extension of industry; and in proportion as industry, commerce, navigation, railways extended, in the same proportion the bourgeoisie developed, increased its capital, and pushed into the background every class handed down from the Middle Ages.

We see, therefore, how the modern bourgeoisie is itself the product of a long course of development, of a series of revolutions in the modes of production and of exchange.

Each step in the development of the bourgeoisie was accompanied by a corresponding political advance of that class. An oppressed class under the sway of the feudal nobility, an armed and self-governing association in the mediæval commune,[4] here independent urban republic (as in Italy and Germany), there taxable "third estate" of the monarchy (as in France), afterwards, in the period of manufacture proper,

serving either the semi-feudal or the absolute monarchy as a counterpoise against the nobility, and, in fact, cornerstone of the great monarchies in general, the bourgeoisie has at last, since the establishment of modern industry and of the world-market, conquered for itself, in the modern representative State, exclusive political sway. The executive of the modern State is but a committee for managing the common affairs of the whole bourgeoisie.

The bourgeoisie, historically, has played a most revolutionary part.

The bourgeoisie, wherever it has got the upper hand, has put an end to all feudal, patriarchal, idyllic relations. It has pitilessly torn asunder the motley feudal ties that bound man to his "natural superiors," and has left remaining no other nexus between man and man than naked self-interest, than callous "cash payment." It has drowned the most heavenly ecstasies of religious fervour, of chivalrous enthusiasm, of philistine sentimentalism, in the icy water of egotistical calculation. It has resolved personal worth into exchange value, and in place of the numberless indefeasible chartered freedoms, has set up that single, unconscionable freedom—Free Trade. In one word, for exploitation, veiled by religious and political illusions, it has substituted naked, shameless, direct, brutal exploitation.

The bourgeoisie has stripped of its halo every occupation hitherto honoured and looked up to with reverent awe. It has converted the physician, the lawyer, the priest, the poet, the man of science, into its paid [wage-laborers].

The bourgeoisie has torn away from the family its sentimental veil, and has reduced the family relation to a mere money relation.

The bourgeoisie has disclosed how it came to pass that the brutal display of vigour in the Middle Ages, which reactionists so much admire, found its fitting complement in the most slothful indolence. It has been the first to show what man's activity can bring about. It has accomplished wonders far surpassing Egyptian pyramids, Roman aqueducts, and Gothic cathedrals; it has conducted expeditions that put in the shade all former Exoduses of nations and crusades.

The bourgeoisie cannot exist without constantly revolutionizing the instruments of production, and thereby the relations of production, and with them the whole relations of society. Conservation of the old modes of production in unaltered form, was, on the contrary, the first condition of existence for all earlier industrial classes. Constant revolutionizing of production, uninterrupted disturbance of all social conditions, everlasting uncertainty and agitation distinguish the bourgeois epoch from all earlier ones. All fixed, fast-frozen relations, with their train of ancient and venerable prejudices and opinions, are swept away, all new-formed ones become antiquated before they can ossify. All that is solid melts into air, all that is holy is profaned, and man is at last compelled to face with sober senses, his real conditions of life, and his relations with his kind.

The need of a constantly expanding market for its products chases the bourgeoisie over the whole surface of the globe. It must nestle everywhere, settle everywhere, establish [connections] everywhere.

The bourgeoisie has through its exploitation of the world-market given a cosmopolitan character to production and consumption in every country. To the great chagrin of reactionists, it has drawn from under the feet of industry the national ground on which it stood. All old-established national industries have been destroyed or are daily being destroyed. They are dislodged by new industries, whose introduction becomes a life and death question for all civilised nations, by industries that no longer work up indigenous raw material, but raw material drawn from the remotest zones; industries whose products are consumed, not only at home, but in every quarter of the globe. In place of the old wants, satisfied by the productions of the country, we find new wants, requiring for their satisfaction the products of distant lands and climes. In place of the old

local and national seclusion and self-sufficiency, we have intercourse in every direction, universal interdependence of nations. And as in material, so also in intellectual production. The intellectual creations of individual nations become common property. National one-sidedness and narrowmindedness become more and more impossible, and from the numerous national and local literatures there arises a world-literature.

The bourgeoisie, by the rapid improvement of all instruments of production, by the immensely facilitated means of communication, draws all, even the most barbarian, nations into civilization. The cheap prices of its commodities are the heavy artillery with which it batters down all Chinese walls, with which it forces the barbarians' intensely obstinate hatred of foreigners to capitulate. It compels all nations, on pain of extinction, to adopt the bourgeois mode of production; it compels them to introduce what it calls civilization into their midst, i.e., to become bourgeois themselves. In a word, it creates a world after its own image.

The bourgeoisie has subjected the country to the rule of the towns. It has created enormous cities, has greatly increased the urban population as compared with the rural, and has thus rescued a considerable part of the population from the idiocy of rural life. Just as it has made the country dependent on the towns, so it has made barbarian and semi-barbarian countries dependent on the civilised ones, nations of peasants on nations of bourgeois, the East on the West.

The bourgeoisie keeps more and more doing away with the scattered state of the population, of the means of production, and of property. It has agglomerated population, centralized means of production, and has concentrated property in a few hands. The necessary consequence of this was political centralization. Independent, or but loosely connected provinces, with separate interests, laws, governments and systems of taxation, became lumped together in one nation, with one government, one code of laws, one national class-interest, one frontier and one customs-tariff.

The bourgeoisie, during its rule of scarce one hundred years, has created more massive and more colossal productive forces than have all preceding generations together. Subjection of Nature's forces to man, machinery, application of chemistry to industry and agriculture, steam-navigation, railways, electric telegraphs, clearing of whole continents for cultivation, canalization of rivers, whole populations conjured out of the ground—what earlier century had even a present-iment that such productive forces slumbered in the lap of social labor?

We see then: The means of production and of exchange on whose foundation the bourgeoisie built itself up were generated in feudal society. At a certain stage in the development of these means of production and of exchange, the conditions under which feudal society produced and exchanged, the feudal organization of agriculture and manufacturing industry, in one word, the feudal relations of property became no longer compatible with the already developed produc-tive forces; they became so many fetters. They had to burst asunder; they were burst asunder.

Into their places stepped free competition, accompanied by a social and political constitu-tion adapted to it, and by the economical and political sway of the bourgeois class.

A similar movement is going on before our own eyes. Modern bourgeois society with its relations of production, of exchange and of property, a society that has conjured up such gigantic means of production and of exchange is like the sorcerer who is no longer able to control the powers of the nether world whom he has called up by his spells. For many a decade past the history of industry and commerce is but the history of the revolt of modern productive forces against modern conditions of production, against the property relations that are the conditions for the exis-tence of the bourgeoisie and of its rule. It is enough to mention the commercial crises that

by their periodical return put on its trial, each time more threateningly, the existence of the entire bourgeois society. In these crises a great part not only of the existing products, but also of the previously created productive forces, are periodically destroyed. In these crises there breaks out an epidemic that, in all earlier epochs, would have seemed an absurdity—the epidemic of overproduction. Society suddenly finds itself put back into a state of momentary barbarism; it appears as if a famine, a universal war of devastation had cut off the supply of every means of subsistence; industry and commerce seem to be destroyed; and why? Because there is too much civilization, too much means of subsistence, too much industry, too much commerce. The productive forces at the disposal of society no longer tend to further the development of the conditions of bourgeois property; on the contrary, they have become too powerful for these conditions, by which they are fettered, and so [as] soon as they over-come these fetters, they bring disorder into the whole of bourgeois society, endanger the exis-tence of bourgeois property. The conditions of bourgeois society are too narrow to comprise the wealth created by them. And how does the bourgeoisie get over these crises? On the one hand by enforced destruction of a mass of productive forces; on the other, by the conquest of new markets, and by the more thorough exploitation of the old ones. That is to say, by paving the way for more extensive and more destructive crises, and by diminishing the means whereby crises are prevented.

The weapons with which the bourgeoisie felled feudalism to the ground are now turned against the bourgeoisie itself.

But not only has the bourgeoisie forged the weapons that bring death to itself; it has also called into existence the men who are to wield those weapons—the modern working class—the proletarians.

In proportion as the bourgeoisie, i.e., capital, is developed, in the same proportion is the proletariat, the modern working class, developed, a class of laborers, who live only so long as they find work, and who find work only so long as their labor increases capital. These laborers, who must sell themselves piecemeal, are a commodity, like every other article of commerce, and are consequently exposed to all the vicissitudes of competition, to all the fluctuations of the market.

Owing to the extensive use of machinery and to division of labor, the work of the proletarians has lost all individual character, and, consequently, all charm for the workman. He becomes an appendage of the machine, and it is only the most simple, most monotonous and most easily acquired knack that is required of him. Hence, the cost of production of a workman is restricted, almost entirely, to the means of subsistence that he requires for his maintenance, and for the propagation of his race. But the price of a commodity, and also of labor, is equal to its cost of production. In proportion, therefore, as the repulsiveness of the work increases, the wage decreases. Nay more, in proportion as the use of machinery and division of labor increases, in the same proportion the burden of toil also increases, whether by prolongation of the working hours, by increase of the work enacted in a given time, or by increased speed of the machinery, etc.

Modern industry has converted the little workshop of the patriarchal master into the great factory of the industrial capitalist. Masses of laborers, crowded into the factory, are organized like soldiers. As privates of the industrial army they are placed under the command of a perfect hierarchy of officers and sergeants. Not only are they the slaves of the bourgeois class, and of the bourgeois State, they are daily and hourly enslaved by the machine, by the over-looker, and, above all, by the individual bourgeois manufacturer himself. The more openly this despotism proclaims gain to be its end and aim, the more petty, the more hateful and the more embittering it is.

The less the skill and exertion or strength implied in manual labor, in other words, the more modern industry becomes developed, the more is the labor of men superseded by that of women. Differences of age and sex have no longer any distinctive social validity for the working class. All are instruments of labor, more or less expensive to use, according to their age and sex.

No sooner is the exploitation of the laborer by the manufacturer, so far, at an end, that he receives his wages in cash, than he is set upon by the other portions of the bourgeoisie, the landlord, the shopkeeper, the pawnbroker, etc.

The lower strata of the middle class—the small tradespeople, shopkeepers, and retired tradesmen generally, the handicraftsmen and peasants—all these sink gradually into the proletariat, partly because their diminutive capital does not suffice for the scale on which Modern Industry is carried on, and is swamped in the competition with the large capitalists, partly because their specialised skill is rendered worthless by new methods of production. Thus the proletariat is recruited from all classes of the population.

The proletariat goes through various stages of development. With its birth begins its struggle with the bourgeoisie. At first the contest is carried on by individual laborers, then by the workpeople of a factory, then by the operatives of one trade, in one locality, against the individual bourgeois who directly exploits them. They direct their attacks not against the bourgeois conditions of production, but against the instruments of production themselves; they destroy imported wares that compete with their labor, they smash to pieces machinery, they set factories ablaze, they seek to restore by force the vanished status of the workman of the Middle Ages.

At this stage the laborers still form an incoherent mass scattered over the whole country, and broken up by their mutual competition. If anywhere they unite to form more compact bodies, this is not yet the consequence of their own active union, but of the union of the bourgeoisie, which class, in order to attain its own political ends, is compelled to set the whole proletariat in motion, and is moreover yet, for a time, able to do so. At this stage, therefore, the proletarians do not fight their enemies, but the enemies of their enemies, the remnants of absolute monarchy, the landowners, the non-industrial bourgeois, the petty bourgeoisie. Thus the whole historical movement is concentrated in the hands of the bourgeoisie; every victory so obtained is a victory for the bourgeoisie.

But with the development of industry the proletariat not only increases in number, it becomes concentrated in greater masses, its strength grows, and it feels that strength more. The various interests and conditions of life within the ranks of the proletariat are more and more equalized, in proportion as machinery obliterates all distinctions of labor, and nearly everywhere reduces wages to the same low level. The growing competition among the bourgeois, and the resulting commercial crises, make the wages of the workers ever more fluctuating. The unceasing improvement of machinery, ever more rapidly developing, makes their livelihood more and more precarious; the collisions between individual workmen and individual bourgeois take more and more the character of collisions between two classes. Thereupon the workers begin to form combinations (Trades' Unions) against the bourgeois; they club together in order to keep up the rate of wages; they found permanent associations in order to make provision beforehand for these occasional revolts. Here and there the contest breaks out into riots.

Now and then the workers are victorious, but only for a time. The real fruit of their battles lies, not in the immediate result, but in the ever expanding union of the workers. This union is helped on by the improved means of communication that are created by modern industry, and that place the workers of different localities in contact with one another. It was just this contact that was needed to centralize the numerous local struggles, all of the same character, into one national struggle between classes. But every class struggle is a political struggle. And that union, to attain which the burghers of the Middle Ages, with their miserable highways, required centuries, the modern proletarians, thanks to railways, achieve in a few years.

This organization of the proletarians into a class, and consequently into a political party, is continually being upset again by the competition between the workers themselves. But it ever rises up again, stronger, firmer, mightier. It compels legislative recognition of particular interests of the workers, by taking advantage of the divisions among the bourgeoisie itself. Thus the ten-hours'-bill in England was carried.

Altogether collisions between the classes of the old society further, in many ways, the course of development of the proletariat. The bourgeoisie finds itself involved in a constant battle. At first with the aristocracy; later on, with those portions of the bourgeoisie itself, whose interests have become antagonistic to the progress of industry; at all times, with the bourgeoisie of foreign countries. In all these battles it sees itself compelled to appeal to the proletariat, to ask for its help, and thus, to drag it into the political arena. The bourgeoisie itself, therefore, supplies the proletariat with its own elements of political and general education, in other words, it furnishes the proletariat with weapons for fighting the bourgeoisie.

Further, as we have already seen, entire sections of the ruling classes are, by the advance of industry, precipitated into the proletariat, or are at least threatened in their conditions of existence. These also supply the proletariat with fresh elements of enlightenment and progress.

Finally, in times when the class-struggle nears the decisive hour, the process of dissolution going on within the ruling class, in fact within the whole range of old society, assumes such a violent, glaring character, that a small section of the ruling class cuts itself adrift, and joins the revolutionary class, the class that holds the future in its hands. Just as, therefore, at an earlier period, a section of the nobility went over to the bourgeoisie, so now a portion of the bourgeoisie goes over to the proletariat, and in particular, a portion of the bourgeois ideologists, who have raised themselves to the level of comprehending theoretically the historical movements as a whole.

Of all the classes that stand face to face with the bourgeoisie today, the proletariat alone is a really revolutionary class. The other classes decay and finally disappear in the face of modern industry; the proletariat is its special and essential product.

The lower-middle class, the small manufacturer, the shopkeeper, the artisan, the peasant, all these fight against the bourgeoisie, to save from extinction their existence as fractions of the middle class. They are therefore not revolutionary, but conservative. Nay more, they are reactionary, for they try to roll back the wheel of history. If by chance they are revolutionary, they are so, only in view of their impending transfer into the proletariat, they thus defend not their present, but their future interests, they desert their own standpoint to place themselves at that of the proletariat.

The "dangerous class," the social scum, that passively rotting mass thrown off by the lowest layers of old society, may, here and there, be swept into the movement by a proletarian revolution; its conditions of life, however, prepare it far more for the part of a bribed tool of reactionary intrigue.

In the conditions of the proletariat, those of old society at large are already virtually swamped. The proletarian is without property; his relation to his wife and children has no longer anything in common with the bourgeois family-relations; modern industrial labor, modern subjection to capital, the same in England as in France, in America as in Germany, has stripped him of every trace of national character. Law, morality, religion, are to him so many bourgeois prejudices, behind which lurk in ambush just as many bourgeois interests.

All the preceding classes that got the upper hand sought to fortify their already acquired status by subjecting at large to their conditions of appropriation. The proletarians cannot become masters of the productive forces of society, except by abolishing their own previous mode of appropriation, and thereby also every other previous mode of appropriation. They have nothing of their own to secure and to fortify; their mission is to destroy all previous securities for, and insurances of, individual property.

All previous historical movements were movements of minorities, or in the interest of minorities. The proletarian movement is the self-conscious, independent movement of the immense majority, in the interest of the immense majority. The proletariat, the lowest stratum of our present society, cannot stir, cannot raise itself up, without the whole superincumbent strata of official society being sprung into the air.

Though not in substance, yet in form, the struggle of the proletariat with the bourgeoisie is at first a national struggle. The proletariat of each country must, of course, first of all settle matters with its own bourgeoisie.

In depicting the most general phases of the development of the proletariat, we traced the more or less veiled civil war, raging within existing society, up to the point where that war breaks out into open revolution, and where the violent overthrow of the bourgeoisie, lays the foundation for the sway of the proletariat.

Hitherto, every form of society has been based, as we have already seen, on the antagonism of oppressing and oppressed classes. But in order to oppress a class, certain conditions must be assured to it under which it can, at least, continue its slavish existence. The serf, in the period of serfdom, raised himself to membership in the commune, just as the petty bourgeois, under the yoke of feudal absolutism, managed to develop into a bourgeois. The modern laborer, on the contrary, instead of rising with the progress of industry, sinks deeper and deeper below the conditions of existence of his own class. He becomes a pauper, and pauperism develops more rapidly than population and wealth. And here it becomes evident, that the bourgeoisie is unfit any longer to be the ruling class in society, and to impose its conditions of existence upon society as an overriding law. It is unfit to rule, because it is incompetent to assure an existence to its slave within his slavery, because it cannot help letting him sink into such a state, that it has to feed him, instead of being fed by him. Society can no longer live under this bourgeoisie, in other words, its existence is no longer compatible with society.

The essential condition for the existence, and for the sway of the bourgeois class, is the formation and augmentation of capital; the condition for capital is wage-labor. Wage-labor rests exclusively on competition between the laborers. The advance of industry, whose involuntary promoter is the bourgeoisie, replaces the isolation of the laborers, due to competition, by their involuntary combination, due to association. The development of modern industry, therefore, cuts from under its feet the very foundation on which the bourgeoisie produces and appropriates products. What the bourgeoisie therefore produces, above all, are its own grave-diggers. Its fall and the victory of the proletariat are equally inevitable.

CRITICAL THINKING QUESTIONS

1. What are the distinguishing factors of "class conflict"? How does class conflict differ from other kinds of conflict, as between individuals or nations?
2. Why do Marx and Engels argue that understanding society in the present requires investigating the society of the past?
3. On what grounds did Marx and Engels *praise* industrial capitalism? On what grounds did they *condemn* the system?

NOTES

1. By *bourgeoisie* is meant the class of modern capitalists, owners of the means of social production and employers of wage-labor. By *proletariat,* the class of modern wage-laborers who, having no means of production of their own, are reduced to selling their labor-power in order to live.
2. That is, all written history. In 1847, the prehistory of society, the social organization existing previous to recorded history, was all but unknown. Since then, Haxthausen discovered common ownership of land in Russia. Maurer proved it to be the social foundation from which all Teutonic races started in history, and by and by village communities were found to be, or to have been, the primitive form of society everywhere from India to Ireland. The inner organization of this primitive Communistic society was laid bare, in its typical form, by Morgan's crowning discovery of the true nature of the gens and its relation to the tribe. With the dissolution of these primæval communities society begins to be differentiated into separate and finally antagonistic classes. I have attempted to retrace this process of dissolution in "Der Ursprung der Familie, des Privateigenthums und des Staats," 2d ed. Stuttgart 1886.
3. Guild-master, that is, a full member of a guild, a master within, not a head of, a guild.
4. "Commune" was the name taken, in France, by the nascent towns even before they had conquered from their feudal lords and masters, local self-government and political rights as "the Third Estate." Generally speaking, for the economical development of the bourgeoisie, England is here taken as the typical country, [and] for its political development, France.

9

The Amish: A Small Society

John A. Hostetler

Small communities, with their distinctive character—where life is stable and intensely human—are disappearing. Some have vanished from the face of the earth, others are dying slowly, but all have undergone changes as they have come into contact with an expanding machine civilization. The merging of diverse peoples into a common mass has produced tension among members of the minorities and the majority alike.

The Old Order Amish, who arrived on American shores in colonial times, have survived in the modern world in distinctive, viable, small communities. They have resisted the homogenization process more successfully than others. In planting and harvest time one can see their bearded men working the fields with horses and their women hanging out the laundry in neat rows to dry. Many American people have seen Amish families, with the men wearing broad-brimmed black hats and the women in bonnets and long dresses, in railway depots or bus terminals. Although the Amish have lived with industrialized America for over two and a half centuries, they have moderated its influence on their personal lives, their families, communities, and their values.

The Amish are often perceived by other Americans to be relics of the past who live an austere, inflexible life dedicated to inconvenient and archaic customs. They are seen as renouncing both modern conveniences and the American dream of success and progress. But most people have no quarrel with the Amish for doing things the old-fashioned way. Their conscientious objection was tolerated in wartime, for after all, they are meticulous farmers who practice the virtues of work and thrift.

...The Amish are a church, a community, a spiritual union, a conservative branch of Christianity, a religion, a community whose members practice simple and austere living, a familistic entrepreneuring system, and an adaptive human community....

Source: From *Amish Society,* 3rd ed., by John A. Hostetler (Baltimore: The Johns Hopkins University Press, 1980), pp. 3–12. Reprinted with permission.

The Amish are in some ways a little commonwealth, for their members claim to be ruled by the law of love and redemption. The bonds that unite them are many. Their beliefs, however, do not permit them solely to occupy and defend a particular territory. They are highly sensitive in caring for their own. They will move to other lands when circumstances force them to do so.

Commonwealth implies a place, a province, which means any part of a national domain that geographically and socially is sufficiently unified to have a true consciousness of its unity. Its inhabitants feel comfortable with their own ideas and customs, and the "place" possesses a sense of distinction from other parts of the country. Members of a commonwealth are not foot-loose. They have a sense of productivity and accountability in a province where "the general welfare" is accepted as a day-to-day reality. Commonwealth has come to have an archaic meaning in today's world, because when groups and institutions become too large, the sense of commonwealth or the common good is lost. Thus it is little wonder that the most recent dictionaries of the American English language render the meaning of commonwealth as "obsolescent." In reality, the Amish are in part a commonwealth. There is, however, no provision for outcasts.

It may be argued that the Amish have retained elements of wholesome provincialism, a saving power to which the world in the future will need more and more to appeal. Provincialism need not turn to ancient narrowness and ignorance, confines from which many have sought to escape. A sense of province or commonwealth, with its cherished love of people and self-conscious dignity, is a necessary basis for relating to the wider world community. Respect for locality, place, custom, and local idealism can go a long way toward checking the monstrous growth of consolidation in the nation and thus help to save human freedom and individual dignity.

...Anthropologists, who have compared societies all over the world, have tended to call semi-isolated peoples "folk societies," "primitives," or merely "simple societies." These societies constitute an altogether different type in contrast to the industrialized, or so-called civilized, societies.

The "folk society," as conceptualized by Robert Redfield,[1] is a small, isolated, traditional, simple, homogeneous society in which oral communication and conventionalized ways are important factors in integrating the whole life. In such an ideal-type society, shared practical knowledge is more important than science, custom is valued more than critical knowledge, and associations are personal and emotional rather than abstract and categoric.

Folk societies are uncomfortable with the idea of change. Young people do what the old people did when they were young. Members communicate intimately with one another, not only by word of mouth but also through custom and symbols that reflect a strong sense of belonging to one another. A folk society is *Gemeinschaft*-like; there is a strong sense of "we-ness." Leadership is personal rather than institutionalized. There are no gross economic inequalities. Mutual aid is characteristic of the society's members. The goals of life are never stated as matters of doctrine, but neither are they questioned. They are implied by the acts that constitute living in a small society. Custom tends to become sacred. Behavior is strongly patterned, and acts as well as cultural objects are given symbolic meaning that is often pervasively religious. Religion is diffuse and all-pervasive. In the typical folk society, planting and harvesting are as sacred in their own ways as singing and praying.

The folk model lends itself well to understanding the tradition-directed character of Amish society. The heavy weight of tradition can scarcely be explained in any other way. The Amish, for example, have retained many of the customs and small-scale technologies that were common in rural society in the nineteenth century. Through a process of syncretism, Amish religious values have been fused with an earlier period of simple country living when everyone farmed with horses and on a scale where family members could work together. The Amish exist as a folk or "little" community in a rural subculture within the modern state…. The outsider who drives through an Amish settlement cannot help but recognize them by their clothing, farm homes, furnishings, fields, and other material traits of culture. Although they speak perfect English with outsiders, they speak a dialect of German among themselves.

Amish life is distinctive in that religion and custom blend into a way of life. The two are inseparable. The core values of the community are religious beliefs. Not only do the members worship a deity they understand through the revelation of Jesus Christ and the Bible, but their patterned behavior [also] has a religious dimension. A distinctive way of life permeates daily life, agriculture, and the application of energy to economic ends. Their beliefs determine their conceptions of the self, the universe, and man's place in it. The Amish world view recognizes a certain spiritual worth and dignity in the universe in its natural form. Religious considerations determine hours of work and the daily, weekly, seasonal, and yearly rituals associated with life experience. Occupation, the means and destinations of travel, and choice of friends and mate are determined by religious considerations. Religious and work attitudes are not far distant from each other. The universe includes the divine, and Amish society itself is considered divine insofar as the Amish recognize themselves as "a chosen people of God." The Amish do not seek to master nature or to work against the elements, but try to work with them. The affinity between Amish society and nature in the form of land, terrain, and vegetation is expressed in various degrees of intensity.

Religion is highly patterned, so one may properly speak of the Amish as a tradition-directed group. Though allusions to the Bible play an important role in determining their outlook on the world, and on life after death, these beliefs have been fused with several centuries of struggling to survive in community. Out of intense religious experience, societal conflict, and intimate agrarian experience, a mentality has developed that prefers the old rather than the new. While the principle seems to apply especially to religion, it has also become a charter for social behavior. "The old is the best, and the new is of the devil" has become a prevalent mode of thought. By living in closed communities where custom and a strong sense of togetherness prevail, the Amish have formed an integrated way of life and a folklike culture. Continuity of conformity and custom is assured and the needs of the individual from birth to death are met within an integrated and shared system of meanings. Oral tradition, custom, and conventionality play an important part in maintaining the group as a functioning whole. To the participant, religion and custom are inseparable. Commitment and culture are combined to produce a stable human existence.

…A century ago, hardly anyone knew the Amish existed. A half-century ago they were viewed as an obscure sect living by ridiculous customs, as stubborn people who resisted education and exploited the labor of their children. Today the Amish are the unwilling objects of a thriving tourist industry on the eastern seaboard. They are revered as hard-working, thrifty people with enormous agrarian stamina, and by some, as islands of sanity in a culture gripped by commercialism and technology run wild.

NOTE

1. Robert Redfield, "The Folk Society," *American Journal of Sociology,* 52 (Jan. 1947), 293–308. See also his book *The Little Community* (Chicago: University of Chicago Press, 1955).

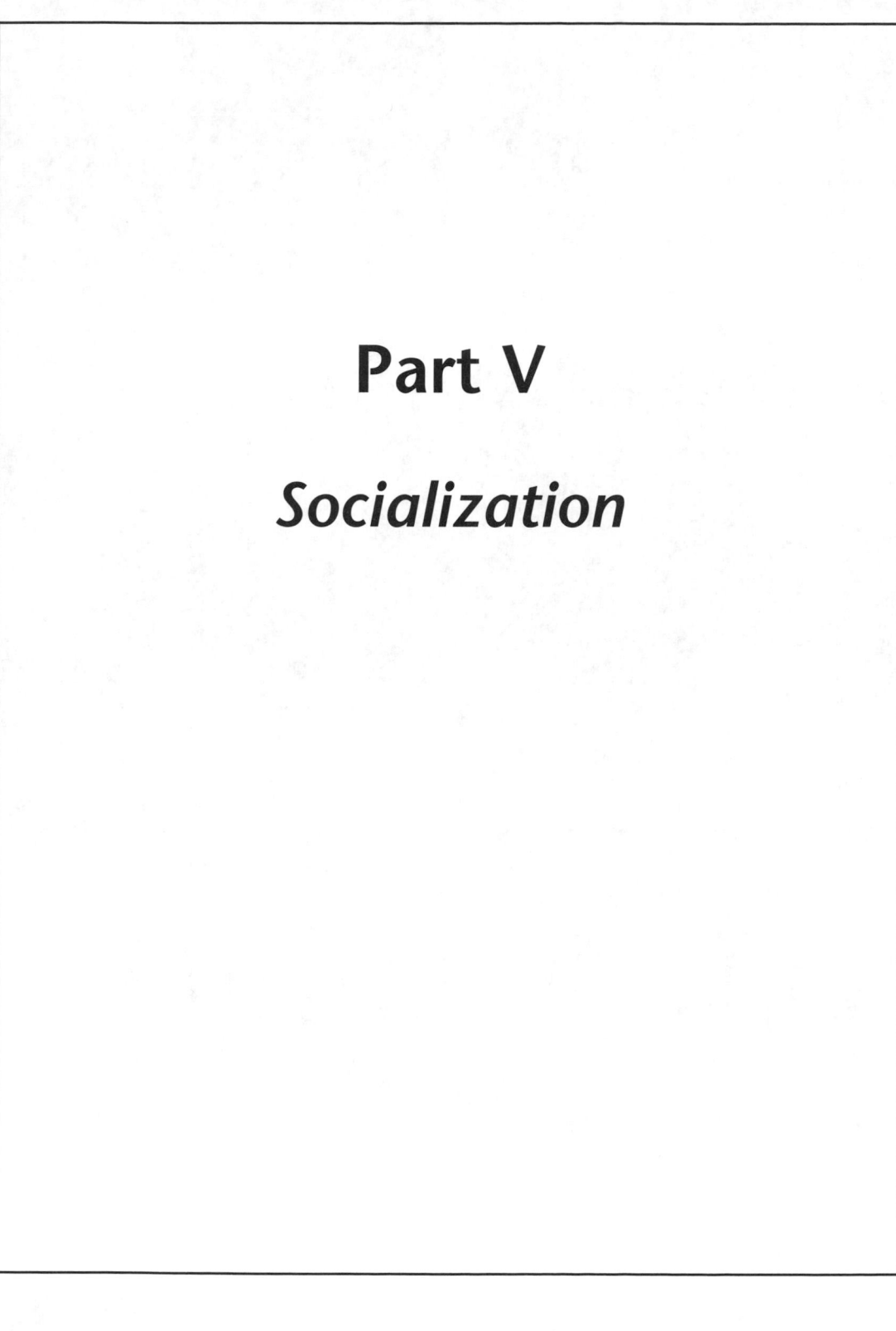

Part V

Socialization

10

The Self

George Herbert Mead

In our statement of the development of intelligence we have already suggested that the language process is essential for the development of the self. The self has a character which is different from that of the physiological organism proper. The self is something which has a development; it is not initially there, at birth, but arises in the process of social experience and activity, that is, develops in the given individual as a result of his relations to that process as a whole and to other individuals within that process....

We can distinguish very definitely between the self and the body. The body can be there and can operate in a very intelligent fashion without there being a self involved in the experience. The self

Source: From *Mind, Self and Society: From the Standpoint of a Social Behaviorist* by George Herbert Mead (Chicago: University of Chicago Press, 1934), pp. 135–42, 144, 149–56, 158, 162–64. Copyright © 1934 by The University of Chicago Press. Reprinted with permission of the University of Chicago Press.

has the characteristic that it is an object to itself, and that characteristic distinguishes it from other objects and from the body. It is perfectly true that the eye can see the foot, but it does not see the body as a whole. We cannot see our backs; we can feel certain portions of them, if we are agile, but we cannot get an experience of our whole body. There are, of course, experiences which are somewhat vague and difficult of location, but the bodily experiences are for us organized about a self. The foot and hand belong to the self. We can see our feet, especially if we look at them from the wrong end of an opera glass, as strange things which we have difficulty in recognizing as our own. The parts of the body are quite distinguishable from the self. We can lose parts of the body without any serious invasion of the self. The mere ability to experience different parts of the body is not different from the experience of a table. The table presents a different feel from what the hand does when one hand feels another, but it is an experience of something with which we come

65

definitely into contact. The body does not experience itself as a whole, in the sense in which the self in some way enters into the experience of the self.

It is the characteristic of the self as an object to itself that I want to bring out. This characteristic is represented in the word "self," which is a reflexive, and indicates that which can be both subject and object. This type of object is essentially different from other objects, and in the past it has been distinguished as conscious, a term which indicates an experience with, an experience of, one's self. It was assumed that consciousness in some way carried this capacity of being an object to itself. In giving a behavioristic statement of consciousness we have to look for some sort of experience in which the physical organism can become an object to itself.[1]

When one is running to get away from someone who is chasing him, he is entirely occupied in this action, and his experience may be swallowed up in the objects about him, so that he has, at the time being, no consciousness of self at all. We must be, of course, very completely occupied to have that take place, but we can, I think, recognize that sort of a possible experience in which the self does not enter. We can, perhaps, get some light on that situation through those experiences in which in very intense action there appear in the experience of the individual, back of this intense action, memories and anticipations. Tolstoi as an officer in the war gives an account of having pictures of his past experience in the midst of his most intense action. There are also the pictures that flash into a person's mind when he is drowning. In such instances there is a contrast between an experience that is absolutely wound up in outside activity in which the self as an object does not enter, and an activity of memory and imagination in which the self is the principal object. The self is then entirely distinguishable from an organism that is surrounded by things and acts with reference to things, including parts of its own body. These latter may be objects like other objects, but they are just objects out there in the field, and they do not involve a self that is an object to the organism. This is, I think, frequently overlooked. It is that fact which makes our anthropomorphic reconstructions of animal life so fallacious. How can an individual get outside himself (experientially) in such a way as to become an object to himself? This is the essential psychological problem of selfhood or of self-consciousness; and its solution is to be found by referring to the process of social conduct or activity in which the given person or individual is implicated. The apparatus of reason would not be complete unless it swept itself into its own analysis of the field of experience; or unless the individual brought himself into the same experiential field as that of the other individual selves in relation to whom he acts in any given social situation. Reason cannot become impersonal unless it takes an objective, noneffective attitude toward itself; otherwise we have just consciousness, not *self*-consciousness. And it is necessary to rational conduct that the individual should thus take an objective, impersonal attitude toward himself, that he should become an object to himself. For the individual organism is obviously an essential and important fact or constituent element of the empirical situation in which it acts; and without taking objective account of itself as such, it cannot act intelligently, or rationally.

The individual experiences himself as such, not directly, but only indirectly, from the particular standpoints of other individual members of the same social group, or from the generalized standpoint of the social group as a whole to which he belongs. For he enters his own experience as a self or individual, not directly or immediately, not by becoming a subject to himself, but only insofar as he first becomes an object to himself just as other individuals are objects to him or in his experience; and he becomes an object to himself only by taking the attitudes of other individuals toward himself within a social environment or context of experience and behavior in which both he and they are involved.

The importance of what we term "communication" lies in the fact that it provides a form of behavior in which the organism or the individual may become an object to himself. It is that sort of communication which we have been discussing— not communication in the sense of the cluck of the hen to the chickens, or the bark of a wolf to the pack, or the lowing of a cow, but communication in the sense of significant symbols, communication which is directed not only to others but also to the individual himself. So far as that type of communication is a part of behavior it at least introduces a self. Of course, one may hear without listening; one may see things that he does not realize; do things that he is not really aware of. But it is where one does respond to that which he addresses to another and where that response of his own becomes a part of his conduct, where he not only hears himself but responds to himself, talks and replies to himself as truly as the other person replies to him, that we have behavior in which the individuals become objects to themselves....

The self, as that which can be an object to itself, is essentially a social structure, and it arises in social experience. After a self has arisen, it in a certain sense provides for itself its social experiences, and so we can conceive of an absolutely solitary self. But it is impossible to conceive of a self arising outside of social experience. When it has arisen we can think of a person in solitary confinement for the rest of his life, but who still has himself as a companion, and is able to think and to converse with himself as he had communicated with others. That process to which I have just referred, of responding to one's self as another responds to it, taking part in one's own conversation with others, being aware of what one is saying and using that awareness of what one is saying to determine what one is going to say thereafter—that is a process with which we are all familiar. We are continually following up our own address to other persons by an understanding of what we are saying, and using that understanding in the direction of our continued speech. We are finding out what we are going to say, what we are going to do, by saying and doing, and in the process we are continually controlling the process itself. In the conversation of gestures what we say calls out a certain response in another and that in turn changes our own action, so that we shift from what we started to do because of the reply the other makes. The conversation of gestures is the beginning of communication. The individual comes to carry on a conversation of gestures with himself. He says something, and that calls out a certain reply in himself which makes him change what he was going to say. One starts to say something, we will presume an unpleasant something, but when he starts to say it he realizes it is cruel. The effect on himself of what he is saying checks him; there is here a conversation of gestures between the individual and himself. We mean by significant speech that the action is one that affects the individual himself, and that the effect upon the individual himself is part of the intelligent carrying-out of the conversation with others. Now we, so to speak, amputate that social phase and dispense with it for the time being, so that one is talking to one's self as one would talk to another person.[2]

This process of abstraction cannot be carried on indefinitely. One inevitably seeks an audience, has to pour himself out to somebody. In reflective intelligence one thinks to act, and to act solely so that this action remains a part of a social process. Thinking becomes preparatory to social action. The very process of thinking is, of course, simply an inner conversation that goes on, but it is a conversation of gestures which in its completion implies the expression of that which one thinks to an audience. One separates the significance of what he is saying to others from the actual speech and gets it ready before saying it. He thinks it out, and perhaps writes it in the form of a book; but it is still a part of social intercourse in which one is addressing other persons and at the same time addressing one's self, and in which one controls the address to other persons by the response made to one's own gesture. That the person should be responding to himself is necessary to the self, and it is this sort of social conduct which provides behavior within which that self appears. I know of no other form of behavior than the linguistic in which the individual is an object to himself, and, so far as I can see, the individual is not a self in the reflexive sense unless he is an object to himself. It is this fact that gives a critical importance to communication, since this is a type of behavior in which the individual does so respond to himself.

We realize in everyday conduct and experience that an individual does not mean a great deal of what he is doing and saying. We frequently say that such an individual is not himself. We come away from an interview with a realization that we have left out important things, that there are parts of the self that did not get into what was said. What determines the amount of the self that gets into communication is the social experience itself. Of course, a good deal of the self does not need to get expression. We carry on a whole series of different relationships to different people. We are one thing to one man and another thing to another. There are parts of the self which exist only for the self in relationship to itself. We divide ourselves up in all sorts of different selves with reference to our acquaintances. We discuss politics with one and religion with another. There are all sorts of different selves answering to all sorts of different social reactions. It is the social process itself that is responsible for the appearance of the self; it is not there as a self apart from this type of experience.

A multiple personality is in a certain sense normal, as I have just pointed out....

The unity and structure of the complete self reflects the unity and structure of the social process as a whole; and each of the elementary selves of which it is composed reflects the unity and structure of one of the various aspects of that process in which the individual is implicated. In other words, the various elementary selves which constitute, or are organized into, a complete self are the various aspects of the structure of that complete self answering to the various aspects of the structure of the social process as a whole; the structure of the complete self is thus a reflection of the complete social process. The organization and unification of a social group is identical with the organization and unification of any one of the

selves arising within the social process in which that group is engaged, or which it is carrying on.[3]

...Another set of background factors in the genesis of the self is represented in the activities of play and the game.... We find in children...imaginary companions which a good many children produce in their own experience. They organize in this way the responses which they call out in other persons and call out also in themselves. Of course, this playing with an imaginary companion is only a peculiarly interesting phase of ordinary play. Play in this sense, especially the stage which precedes the organized games, is a play at something. A child plays at being a mother, at being a teacher, at being a policeman; that is, it is taking different roles, as we say. We have something that suggests this in what we call the play of animals: A cat will play with her kittens, and dogs play with each other. Two dogs playing with each other will attack and defend, in a process which if carried through would amount to an actual fight. There is a combination of responses which checks the depth of the bite. But we do not have in such a situation the dogs taking a definite role in the sense that a child deliberately takes the role of another. This tendency on the part of children is what we are working with in the kindergarten where the roles which the children assume are made the basis for training. When a child does assume a role he has in himself the stimuli which call out that particular response or group of responses. He may, of course, run away when he is chased, as the dog does, or he may turn around and strike back just as the dog does in his play. But that is not the same as playing at something. Children get together to "play Indian." This means that the child has a certain set of stimuli that call out in itself the responses that they would call out in others, and which answer to an Indian. In the play period the child utilizes his own responses to these stimuli which he makes use of in building a self. The response which he has a tendency to make to these stimuli organizes them. He plays that he is, for instance, offering himself something, and he buys it; he gives a letter to himself and takes it away; he addresses himself as a parent, as a teacher; he arrests himself as a policeman. He has a set of stimuli which call out in himself the sort of responses they call out in others. He takes this group of responses and organizes them into a certain whole. Such is the simplest form of being another to one's self. It involves a temporal situation. The child says something in one character and responds in another character, and then his responding in another character is a stimulus to himself in the first character, and so the conversation goes on. A certain organized structure arises in him and in his other which replies to it, and these carry on the conversation of gestures between themselves.

If we contrast play with the situation in an organized game, we note the essential difference that the child who plays in a game must be ready to take the attitude of everyone else involved in that game, and that these different roles must have a definite relationship to each other. Taking a very simple game such as hide-and-seek, everyone with the exception of the one who is hiding is a person who is hunting. A child does not require more than the person who is hunted and the one who is hunting. If a child is playing in the first sense he just goes on playing, but there is no basic organization gained. In that early stage he passes from one to another just as a whim takes him. But in a game where a number of individuals are involved, then the child taking one role must be ready to take the role of everyone else. If he gets in a ball game he must have the responses of each position involved in his own position. He must know what everyone else is going to do in order to carry out his own play. He has to take all of these roles. They do not all have to be present in consciousness at the same time, but at some moments he has to have three or four individuals present in his own attitude, such as the one who is going to throw the ball, the one who is going to catch it, and so on. These responses must be, in some degree, present in his own make-up. In the game, then, there is a set of responses of such others so organized that the attitude of one calls out the appropriate attitudes of the other.

This organization is put in the form of the rules of the game. Children take a great interest in rules. They make rules on the spot in order to help themselves out of difficulties. Part of the enjoyment of the game is to get these rules. Now, the rules are the set of responses which a particular attitude calls out. You can demand a certain response in others if you take a certain attitude. These responses are all in yourself as well. There you get an organized set of such responses as that to which I have referred, which is something more elaborate than the roles found in play. Here there is just a set of responses that follow on each other indefinitely. At such a stage we speak of a child as not yet having a fully developed self. The child responds in a fairly intelligent fashion to the immediate stimuli that come to him, but they are not organized. He does not organize his life as we would like to have him do, namely, as a whole. There is just a set of responses of the type of play. The child reacts to a certain stimulus, and the reaction is in himself that is called out in others, but he is not a whole self. In his game he has to have an organization of these roles; otherwise he cannot play the game. The game represents the passage in the life of the child from taking the role of others in play to the organized part that is essential to self-consciousness in the full sense of the term.

…The fundamental difference between the game and play is that in the former the child must have the attitude of all the others involved in that game. The attitudes of the other players which the participant assumes organize into a sort of unit, and it is that organization which controls the response of the individual. The illustration used was of a person playing baseball. Each one of his own acts is determined by his assumption of the action of the others who are playing the game. What he does is controlled by his being everyone else on that team, at least insofar as those attitudes affect his own particular response. We get then an "other" which is an organization of the attitudes of those involved in the same process.

The organized community or social group which gives to the individual his unity of self may be called "the generalized other." The attitude of the generalized other is the attitude of the whole community.[4] Thus, for example, in the case of such a social group as a ball team, the team is the generalized other insofar as it enters—as an organized process or social activity—into the experience of any one of the individual members of it.

If the given human individual is to develop a self in the fullest sense, it is not sufficient for him merely to take the attitudes of other human individuals toward himself and toward one another within the human social process, and to bring that social process as a whole into his individual experience merely in these terms: He must also, in the same way that he takes the attitudes of other individuals toward himself and toward one another, take their attitudes toward the various phases or aspects of the common social activity or set of social undertakings in which, as members of an organized society or social group, they are all engaged; and he must then, by generalizing these individual attitudes of that organized society or social group itself, as a whole, act toward different social projects which at any given time it is carrying out, or toward the various larger phases of the general social process which constitutes its life and of which these projects are specific manifestations. This getting of the broad activities of any given social whole or organized society as such within the experiential field of any one of the individuals involved or included in that whole is, in other words, the essential basis and prerequisite of the fullest development of that individual's self: Only insofar as he takes the attitudes of the organized social group to which he belongs toward the organized, cooperative social activity or set of such activities in which that group as such is engaged, does he develop a complete self or possess the sort of complete self he has developed. And on the other hand, the complex cooperative processes and activities and institutional functionings of organized human society are also possible only insofar as every individual involved in them or belonging to that society can take the general attitudes of all other such individuals with reference to these processes and activities and institutional functionings, and to the organized social whole of experiential relations and interactions thereby constituted—and can direct his own behavior accordingly.

It is in the form of the generalized other that the social process influences the behavior of the individuals involved in it and carrying it on, i.e., that the community exercises control over the conduct of its individual members; for it is in this form that the social process or community enters as a determining factor into the individual's thinking. In abstract thought the individual takes the attitude of the generalized other[5] toward himself, without reference to its expression in any particular other individuals; and in concrete thought he takes that attitude insofar as it is expressed in the attitudes toward his behavior of those other individuals with whom he is involved in the given social situation or act. But only by taking the attitude of the generalized other toward himself, in one or another of these ways, can he think at all; for only thus can thinking—or the internalized conversation of gestures which constitutes thinking—occur. And only through the taking by individuals of the attitude or attitudes of the generalized other toward themselves is the existence of a universe of discourse, as that system of common or social meanings which thinking presupposes at its context, rendered possible.

...I have pointed out, then, that there are two general stages in the full development of the self. At the first of these stages, the individual's self is considered simply by an organization of the particular attitudes of other individuals toward himself and toward one another in the specific social acts in which he participates with them. But at the second stage in the full development of the individual's self that self is constituted not only by an organization of these particular individual attitudes, but also by an organization of the social attitudes of the generalized other or the social group as a whole to which he belongs.... So the self reaches its full development by organizing these individual attitudes of others into the organized social or group attitudes, and by thus becoming an individual reflection of the general systematic pattern of social or group behavior in which it and the others are all involved—a pattern which enters as a whole into the individual's experience in terms of these organized group attitudes which, through the mechanism of his central nervous system, he takes toward himself, just as he takes the individual attitudes of others.

...A person is a personality because he belongs to a community, because he takes over the institutions of that community into his own conduct. He takes its language as a medium by which he gets his personality, and then through a process of taking the different roles that all the others furnish he comes to get the attitude of the members of the community. Such, in a certain sense, is the structure of a man's personality. There are certain common responses which each individual has toward certain common things, and insofar as those common responses are awakened in the individual when he is affecting other persons he arouses his own self. The structure, then, on which the self is built is this response which is common to all, for one has to be a member of a community to be a self. Such responses are abstract attitudes, but they constitute just what we term a man's character. They give him what we term his principles, the acknowledged attitudes of all members of the community toward what are the values of that community. He is putting himself in the place of the generalized other, which represents the organized responses of all the members of the group. It is that which guides conduct controlled by principles, and a person who has such an organized group of responses is a man who we say has character, in the moral sense.

...I have so far emphasized what I have called the structures upon which the self is constructed, the framework of the self, as it were. Of course we are not only what is common to all: Each one

of the selves is different from everyone else; but there has to be such a common structure as I have sketched in order that we may be members of a community at all. We cannot be ourselves unless we are also members in whom there is a community of attitudes which control the attitudes of all. We cannot have rights unless we have common attitudes. That which we have acquired as self-conscious persons makes us such members of society and gives us selves. Selves can only exist in definite relationships to other selves. No hard-and-fast line can be drawn between our own selves and the selves of others, since our own selves exist and enter as such into our experience only insofar as the selves of others exist and enter as such into our experience also. The individual possesses a self only in relation to the selves of the other members of his social group; and the structure of his self expresses or reflects the general behavior pattern of this social group to which he belongs, just as does the structure of the self of every other individual belonging to this social group.

NOTES

1. Man's behavior is such in his social group that he is able to become an object to himself, a fact which constitutes him a more advanced product of evolutionary development than are the lower animals. Fundamentally it is this social fact—and not his alleged possession of a soul or mind with which he, as an individual, has been mysteriously and supernaturally endowed, and with which the lower animals have not been endowed—that differentiates him from them.

2. It is generally recognized that the specifically social expressions of intelligence, or the exercise of what is often called "social intelligence," depend upon the given individual's ability to take the roles of, or "put himself in the place of," the other individuals implicated with him in given social situations; and upon his consequent sensitivity to their attitudes toward himself and toward one another. These specifically social expressions of intelligence, of course, acquire unique significance in terms of our view that the whole nature of intelligence is social to the very core—that this putting of one's self in the places of others, this taking by one's self of their roles or attitudes, is not merely one of the various aspects or expressions of intelligence or intelligent behavior, but is the very essence of its character. Spearman's "X factor" in intelligence—the unknown factor which, according to him, intelligence contains—is simply (if our social theory of

intelligence is correct) this ability of the intelligent individual to take the attitude of the other, or the attitudes of others, thus realizing the significations or grasping the meanings of the symbols or gestures in terms of which thinking proceeds; and thus being able to carry on with himself the internal conversation with these symbols or gestures which thinking involves.

3. The unity of the mind is not identical with the unity of the self. The unity of the self is constituted by the unity of the entire relational pattern of social behavior and experience in which the individual is implicated, and which is reflected in the structure of the self; but many of the aspects or features of this entire pattern do not enter into consciousness, so that the unity of the mind is in a sense an abstraction from the more inclusive unity of the self.

4. It is possible for inanimate objects, no less than for other human organisms, to form parts of the generalized and organized—the completely socialized—other for any given human individual, insofar as he responds to such objects socially or in a social fashion (by means of the mechanism of thought, the internalized conversation of gestures). Any thing—any object or set of objects, whether animate or inanimate, human or animal, or merely physical—toward which he acts, or to which he responds, socially, is an element in what for him is the generalized other; by taking the attitudes of which toward himself he becomes conscious of himself as an object or individual, and thus develops a self or personality. Thus, for example, the cult, in its primitive form, is merely the social embodiment of the relation between the given social group or community and its physical environment—an organized social means, adopted by the individual members of that group or community, of entering into social relations with that environment, or (in a sense) of carrying on conversations with it; and in this way that environment becomes part of the total generalized other for each of the individual members of the given social group or community.

5. We have said that the internal conversation of the individual with himself in terms of words or significant gestures—the conversation which constitutes the process or activity of thinking—is carried on by the individual from the standpoint of the "generalized other." And the more abstract that conversation is, the more abstract thinking happens to be, the further removed is the generalized other from any connection with particular individuals. It is especially in abstract thinking, that is to say, that the conversation involved is carried on by the individual with the generalized other, rather than with any particular individuals. Thus it is, for example, that abstract concepts are concepts stated in terms of the attitudes of the entire social group or community; they are stated on the basis of the individual's consciousness of the attitudes of the generalized other toward them, as a result of his taking these attitudes of the generalized other and then responding to them. And thus it is also that abstract propositions are stated in a form which anyone—any other intelligent individual—will accept.

11

The Importance of the Family as an Agent of Socialization: Developmental Pathways and Crime Prevention

Michael C. Boyes, Nancy A. Ogden, and Joseph P. Hornick

We will discuss a specific program that operates at the level of the individual family in an attempt to reduce human suffering, both today and in the future, by curtailing the development of criminal activity, particularly violent criminal activity. Considerable evidence supports the existence of a relationship between child maltreatment and subsequent delinquency and criminality. Programs that provide children with healthier beginnings early in life endeavour to prevent such children from choosing the maladaptive pathways that commonly lead to criminality, substance abuse, or both. We'll begin by outlining the basic premises on which such assumptions are based, follow with a discussion about general programs, and conclude with a specific Canadian program and its early findings.

Source: Reprinted by permission of the authors, 2002.

INFLUENCES AT THE BEGINNING OF LIFE

Every human being is a product of their biology as well as their individual and sociocultural experiences. Our genetic blueprint, our heredity, provides us with the basic material for our development but does not absolutely determine our behaviour. Although the self has a strong biological element, most social scientists agree that social influence is critical for creating truly human individuals. In fact, few behaviours are not socially influenced. Sociologists use the term *socialization* to refer to lifelong social experiences through which individuals develop a self-identity and learn culture: the physical, mental, and social skills needed for the survival of both the individual and the society. Human beings create and maintain their own culture and transmit it from one generation to the next through socialization. Socialization serves as the fundamental connection between the individual and society and as such is essential for maintaining the stability of society. Therefore, to support and sustain the existing social structure, individual members of a society must be socialized.

How does society ensure that its newest members receive appropriate socialization? Teaching the infant and young child—and eventually the older child, adolescent, and adult—what they need to know to participate in society is the task of persons, groups, or institutions that are collectively called *agents of socialization*. These agents come in many forms: schools, media, peers, families, and so on. Fitting children into their sociocultural environment is an important responsibility for socialization agents. For most individuals the family is the first and most important agent of socialization and is the centre of the infant and young child's world. Parents are our earliest teachers, transmitting cultural and social values to us. The family provides infants with their first social interactions and is likely to be children's primary contact with the world during the early years. Moreover, the family context places children within society in terms of class, religion, race, and ethnicity. Individuals of various social classes demonstrate different expectations for their children's behaviours. For example, working class parents are more likely to demand obedience and conformity from their children than are middle-class parents.

This socialization process is most effective when individuals adhere to the accepted norms and values of society because they come to recognize the function and importance of those norms and values. Ideally, parents help their children learn to be caring and contributing members of society. "Successfully" socialized children grow into adults who act as their own socialization agents. They choose not to break the rules because to do so would be "wrong." This implies that very early in their lives, children develop a warm and trusting relationship with a parent and *want* to please that parent by doing the things the parent considers "right" or "good." How then does a parent establish such a relationship with a young infant?

The Importance of Early Relationships

The initial love and nurturing children receive from their families, usually their parents, are central to their cognitive, emotional, and physical development. If infants live in such an environment, they learn to trust their caregivers; this makes infants feel secure. Security is vitally important for children's sense of well-being. When infants feel safe, they explore the environment, using the caregiver as a secure base. This pattern is part of the normal development of infants and very young children and is essential for healthy growth and development. Most children are nurtured by their parents and live in secure, loving, trusting environments. But the sad truth is that not all infants and children feel safe. Large numbers of infants and children experience maltreatment at the hands of those whom they depend upon, those whom they cannot leave or reject. These children are insecure. Documented cases of child abuse and neglect indicate that human infants without adequate social interaction with other human beings are unable to fully develop healthy human characteristics.

Child maltreatment includes physical, emotional, and sexual abuse, as well as neglect. Research on the community, family, and individual causes of violence in the lives of children and youth emphasizes the importance of the family as an agent of socialization. Deprivation, poor parenting practices, and dysfunctional family interaction are associated with the development of antisocial and delinquent behaviour (Snyder & Patterson, 1987).

Perhaps you are thinking of someone you know who lived in a dysfunctional environment, yet is not abusing any substances and is not involved in any criminal activity. Perhaps this person is you. Not everyone from an abusive, dysfunctional, or violent home will experience these outcomes. The relationship among family violence, substance abuse, and criminal behaviour is not absolute; these consequences are not inevitable. To determine just who *is* at risk, researchers assess the presence or absence of two types of variables: risk factors and protective factors.

In infants' and children's lives, risk factors in their family, school, and community include variables such as discrimination, family violence and dysfunction, poverty, lack of supervision, violent neighbourhoods, and multiple moves. The presence of any of these risk factors significantly increases children's later risk for negative outcomes such as depression, mental illness, conduct problems, suicide, delinquency and criminality, substance abuse, and aggressive or violent behaviour. The greatest risk factor for the development of nearly all forms of behavioural problems is poverty. The number of children living in poverty continues to increase in most industrialized nations, including Canada (Canadian Council on Social Development, 1997). The National Longitudinal Survey of Children and Youth (in Canadian Council on Social Development, 1997) reports that poverty has a negative impact on family functioning and school performance. Family dysfunction and parental depression are significantly higher in families living below the poverty line.

The presence of four or more risk factors increases the risk of negative outcomes tenfold (Sameroff et al., 1987; Smith et al., 1995). The prevalence of serious delinquency and substance abuse is strongly associated with increased numbers of risk factors. Many risk factors are interrelated. For example, family breakdown is related to high levels of juvenile delinquency, high conflict, lowered income, and parent absence, which are in turn each related to juvenile delinquency (Garbarino, 1999). Thus, the factors involved in criminal offending are complex, cumulative, and can be explained through both individual and social history.

An excellent example of the interrelationship between individual and sociocultural influences is the relatively recent research documenting the destructive consequences of children's exposure to community violence (Bell & Jenkins, 1993; Osofsky et al., 1993; Sheidow et al., 2001). Of course, substantial discrepancy exists in the degree and extent of exposure to violence among children and youth living in inner-city communities. Nevertheless, the Canadian Council on Social Development reports that one in four Canadian children lives in an area that is considered unsafe after dark (Canadian Council on Social Development, 1997). Characteristics of the neighbourhood (such as the percentages of families working or living below the poverty level and the stability of the neighbourhood) and family functioning are important influences on how children function within their local community environments. How important is the family as an agent of socialization in violent communities? Unfortunately, the importance of family functioning is not independent of neighbourhood characteristics; Sheidow et al. (2001) report that in inner-city communities without positive social processes, the risk of exposure to violence cannot be assuaged by family functioning. That is, for many children exposed to violence within their communities, it does not matter how their family is functioning; these children are at risk simply by living within their community. Children in functional families are at risk; children in dysfunctional families are *more* at risk. These observations underscore the importance of understanding the social ecology of development for identifying how risk factors relate to outcomes (Gorman-Smith, Tolan, & Henry, 1999; National Crime Prevention Council, 1995) and serve as an important reminder that the family is not the *only* agent of socialization affecting children.

The impact of violence on children differs with the type of violence, the pattern of violence, the presence of supportive adult caretakers and other support systems, and the age of the child (Perry, 1995). Children at risk at an early age are in greater jeopardy for multiple negative outcomes later in life. This is due in part to the fact that younger children have fewer defensive capabilities (Grizenko & Fisher, 1992; Perry, 1995).

Early Risk and Resilience

Children at risk for later negative outcomes can be identified through particular sets of risk factors. Are researchers equally adept at identifying those factors that will protect children from inferior environments? The answer is, in part, yes. Factors such as high intelligence, secure attachment, average to above average family income, educated parents, and so on, can serve as protection for children in destitute environments, causing them to be more resilient. In fact, most studies of protective factors (see, for example, Losel & Bliesener, 1990) suggest that under adverse circumstances, 80 percent of children will "bounce back" from developmental challenges. This assumption is proving to be overly optimistic (Garbarino, 2001; Perry, 1994). For instance, resilience is drastically diminished under conditions of extreme risk accumulation or if children receive inadequate care in the first two years. Garbarino (2001) suggests that these observations could be interpreted to mean that the children and youth best able to survive functionally are those who have the least to lose morally and psychologically. The data yielded by his conversations with youths incarcerated for murder and other acts of violent crime confirm his theory. He reports that the crimes were unaffected by moral compunction or emotional responsibility for others.

How can this be? The work of Perry and his colleagues (1994, 1995) documents the impact of early neglect and abuse on the development of the brain. This research contends that infant's and children's brains are more plastic (i.e., receptive to inputs from the environment) than more mature brains are: the infant or child is most vulnerable to disadvantaged environments during the first three or four years. These developmental experiences determine how the brain will be organized and therefore how it will function. Early trauma can produce inadequate development of the brain's cortex (the part of the brain that controls higher abilities such as abstract

reasoning and impulse control) by stimulating a stress-related hormone—cortisol—that impedes brain growth.

These findings have implications for research, intervention, and prevention. For example, the earlier an intervention occurs, the more effective and preventative it is likely to be (Blair, Ramey, & Hardin, 1995; Kiser, Heston, & Millsap, 1991; McFarlane, 1987) and thus the more enduring its impact. Furthermore, insightful sociocultural and public policy implications should arise from understanding the critical role that early experience plays in socializing children as they mature and acculturate or identify as traumatized and maladapted, thereby affecting our society for ill or good. Perry forcefully argues that we must stop accepting the myth that children are resilient; evidence contradicts such assertions, and children are irrevocably affected by maltreatment. "Persistence of the pervasive [political acceptance of] maltreatment of children in the face of devastating global and national resources will lead, inevitably, to sociocultural devolution" (Perry, 1994: 12).

In Canada, where children and youth compose 23 percent of the population, nearly one-quarter of police-reported assaults are visited on children and youth (Statistics Canada, 1996). This statistic is disturbing enough; however, of greater concern is the belief of officials that many incidents of maltreatment are not documented because they are either not observed or reported, leading to an underestimate of the extent of the problem. Factors such as the secrecy surrounding the issue, the dependency of the victim on the abuser, and the lack of knowledge about potential sources for help also contribute to underreporting.

We can conclude that the ramifications of the maltreatment of children involve tremendous personal and sociocultural costs. The financial costs are also staggering. In its report *Preventing Crimes by Investing in Families* (1996), the National Crime Prevention Council conservatively estimates that the annual cost of crime in Canada is in the range of 46 *billion* dollars (of which approximately one-quarter may be attributed to youth crime). Family violence escalates social and economic costs to the health care system, affects the civil and criminal justice systems, and creates immeasurable human suffering. The prevention of crime translates into meaningful reductions in human anguish, community victimization, and money spent on services for young offenders and their families. Society must rethink its priorities with respect to dedicating adequate time, energy, and resources to every aspect of prevention. Programs that support families and parents of very young children can significantly reduce child abuse and juvenile crime.

Secure attachments have recently been used to ascertain levels of vulnerability for those at risk of serious criminal behaviour. Many young offenders have been abused or have witnessed abuse in their homes. As already discussed, family violence is a problem that creates lasting physical, psychological, or economic repercussions for children and for society. The impacts of child abuse are experienced throughout the individual's lifetime. For example, 50 percent of those who were abused as children reported also being abused as adults (McCauley et al., 1997).

A DEVELOPMENTAL APPROACH TO CRIME PREVENTION

Over the past few decades, the focus on crime prevention has shifted from treatment and punishment to preventative initiatives targeting the family and parenting skills, using a multi-systemic, developmental approach. It is essential to turn individuals from harmful pathways before maladaptive patterns of behaviour are well established. Thus, early prevention is the most effective strategy. Early intervention approaches involve various aspects of the family and those outside factors that influence family functioning. Willing participation in intensive, high-quality early intervention programs has been shown to be associated with improved developmental outcomes for high-risk children (Ramey & Ramey, 1994). For the first three years of children's lives, home-visiting programs are a successful way to reach high-risk children and their families and to promote resiliency (Luthar & Ziglar, 1991). Farrington (1994) summarizes research evidence attesting to the positive impact that early intervention programs have on deflecting criminal behaviour and other social problems. Interventions at crucial developmental transition points can have a major positive effect on at-risk families and their children, improving quality of life and potentially preventing criminal activity.

The saying "it takes a village to raise a child" does more than simply suggest that raising children requires a lot of work. What it points to is the essential importance of considering *both* the direct contacts that children have as they develop *and* the multiple contexts in which those contacts occur to properly see what facilitates or hampers optimal development. There have been several attempts to capture a broader perspective on development using ecological developmental models. Based on Bronfenbrenner's (1979) pioneering work, ecological models identify the familial and contextual influences that contribute to abuse. However, these influences are transactional; that is, the individual and the immediate and larger social contexts are viewed as actively influencing one another.

From this ecological developmental model perspective, opportunities for risk reduction must be considered in the contexts comprising the child and his or her immediate family, friends, neighbourhood, spiritual community, and school. Other influential contexts include aspects of social and physical geography such as weather, local and national laws, social conventions, and cultural and subcultural values and ideals. How all these contextual forces interact with the child's physical makeup determines the actual developmental course taken by an individual child (Garbarino, 1990).

Interventions for Reducing Risks and Bolstering Protective Factors: The Healthy Families Example

Creating specific programs aimed at reducing stress, enhancing family functioning, and promoting child development was the logical first step in implementing theoretical developmental models. The Healthy Start program in Hawaii was designed to improve family coping skills, as well as family functioning, and promoted positive parenting. The stated purpose of the Hawaii Healthy Start program was to reduce child abuse and neglect. The program identified families at high risk for abuse or neglect by screening newborns and their families in hospital and followed up with home visits from community-based family support services. Families were linked to family physicians or to nursing clinics and connected to a number of community services. Families were followed until the child was five years old. Evaluation of the program revealed that the high-risk families that participated in the program had half the state average for child maltreatment and abuse, whereas the rate of abuse for high-risk families that did not participate in the program was twice the state average.

Since their inception in 1992, Healthy Families America Inc. has modelled their programs on Hawaii's groundbreaking initiative, and has implemented nearly 200 programs throughout the United States. However, escalating health costs in a country without socialized medicine caused the Healthy Families America program interventions to became increasingly focused on helping low income, at-risk families to access state-funded health services. The Health Insurance Association of America (1999) estimates that by the year 2007, 53.5 million people in the United States will be uninsured, and more than one-third of these people will be children. This, coupled with the fact that at both the state and federal levels child and family services (i.e., Child Welfare) are less broadly organized in

the American system, indicated that modifications to the Healthy Families initiative would be necessary if the program were to come to Canada. Canada has a system of socialized medicine that guarantees universal health care and is strongly supported through efficient community public health support. In fact, Canadian children at all income levels make the same average number of visits to doctors, whereas insured American children are eight times more likely to visit a doctor than are uninsured children (Canadian Council on Social Development, 1997). Moreover, Canada boasts more formally organized child and family ministries. These differences enabled Canadian researchers to redefine program objectives and allowed them to focus more intensely and more broadly on the other issues involved in assessing risk.

The Department of Justice Canada, through the National Crime Prevention Centre (NCPC), financed a Healthy Families demonstration project. The main goal of the investment is to establish effective programs for reducing delinquency and crime. Three programs were chosen to pilot the project: "Best Start" in Prince Edward Island, "Healthy Families" in Yukon, and "Success by 6 Healthy Families" in Alberta. Each program and the people they serve were chosen because they represent very different types of communities. The Prince Edward Island program is in a small urban centre with a large rural population, the Yukon program serves an Aboriginal community, and the Edmonton program serves a large urban community. In 1999, the Canadian Research institute for Law and the Family (CRILF), located in Alberta, began a three-year project to complete process and outcome evaluations of these Healthy Families programs.

The Healthy Families program utilized trained paraprofessional visitors to provide home visitation services to families identified by the public health system as requiring assistance. Healthy Families programs administer initial and follow-up screenings and establish schedules for home visits. The model requires that the entire child-raising system be assessed. Evaluators from CRILF used existing measures and developed measures to assess for each child the risk and protective factors that could influence a less than optimal developmental trajectory, potentially influencing the child's vulnerability to delinquent and criminal behaviour.

The overall mandate of all Healthy Families Programs is to optimize the development of young at-risk children and their families and to increase the children's opportunities for later success through early screening, assessment, and intervention. The Canadian focus has been on the transition to parenting, enabling parents to become more effective caregivers. First, the program empowers parents and enables them to access a broad range of community programs and resources (e.g., community kitchens, library reading programs, parenting support groups). Second, the program has an intense focus on the interaction between the parent and the child, with an eye to identifying issues and facilitating positive parent–child interaction and healthy growth and development for both. Program personnel are trained to identify and address maladaptive parenting attitudes and behaviours.

A key issue underlying the Healthy Families project in Canada (and the United States) is whether early experience and intervention make a difference to later occurrence of delinquency or crime. The answer in a recent comprehensive longitudinal review of developmental and early intervention approaches conducted in Australia is unequivocally "yes" (National Crime Prevention, 1999). In Canada, this question will remain unanswered until the young children involved in the Healthy Families project reach adulthood, but initial data from the project are causing researchers to be cautiously optimistic.

Early outcome data from the Canadian project suggest that if at-risk families are involved in a Healthy Families program, they have a reduced likelihood of Child Welfare involve-

ment (both contacts and apprehensions). For example, data from Prince Edward Island indicate Child Welfare involvement in less than 2 percent of the families involved in the program compared with more than 25 percent of families in a matched comparison group. This is of particular note given that the number of children apprehended by Child Welfare agencies across Canada has increased (Canadian Council on Social Development, 1997). Outcomes will not actually be known for another twenty years, but existing data on welfare apprehension and crime suggest that a reduction in apprehensions should lead to better developmental outcomes, which in turn should lower rates of violent crime and incarceration. In the short term, kindergarten teachers will assess every child associated with the Healthy Families program for school readiness, as this is considered a strong indicator of a young child's early developmental experiences, especially whether the child received the enrichment and support that they needed.

To summarize, the foundations for crime are laid early, within the broad social and economic early environment of the child. If society is determined to reduce crime and victimization, it must support families and provide, maintain, and enhance opportunities for children from the beginning of their lives. As Canadians, we need many more proactive strategies of intervention when children are at risk. We should enable child welfare services to be proactively engaged at the moment when children and families need them most. We need to emphasize prevention not punishment, because by the time society intervenes to punish, it is already too late. Programs that work to optimize the socialization of the next generation of Canadians hold the most promise for reducing rates of abuse and crime and brightening Canada's future. The greatest protection society can give itself is to ensure that every individual has access to basic necessities: health care, childcare, housing, education, job training, employment, and recreation.

REFERENCES

Bell, C. C., & E. J. Jenkins. 1993. Community violence and children on Chicago's southside, *Psychiatry,* 56: 46–54.

Blair, C., C. T. Ramey, & J. M. Hardin. 1995. Early intervention for low birthweight, premature infants: Participation and intellectual development. *American Journal on Mental Retardation*, 99: 542–54.

Bronfenbrenner, U. 1979. *The ecology of human development: Experiments by nature and design.* Cambridge, Mass.: Harvard University Press.

Canadian Council on Social Development. 1997. *The progress of Canada's children,* Ottawa: SSCD Publications.

Farrington, D. P. 1994. Early developmental prevention of juvenile delinquency. *Child Behavior and Mental Health*, 4: 209–27.

Garbarino, J. 1990. The human ecology of early risk. In *Handbook of early childhood intervention*, eds. S. J. Meisels, and J. P. Shonkoff. New York: Cambridge University Press.

———. 2001. An ecological perspective on the effects of violence on children. *Journal of Community Psychology,* 29(3): 361–78.

Gorman-Smith, D., P. H. Tolan, & D. B. Henry. 1999. The relation of community and family to risk among urban poor adolescents. In *Where and when: Influence of historical time and place on aspects of psychopathology,* eds. P. Cohen, L. Robins, & C. Slomskoski. Hillsdale, N.J.: Erlbaum.

Grinzenko, N., & Fischer, C. 1992. Review of studies of risk and protective factors for psychopathology in children. *Canadian Journal of Psychiatry*, 37: 711–21.

Health Insurance Association of America. 1999. "Patient protection" bills give short shrift to the uninsured. [Online]. Available: **http://www.hiaa.org/search/content.cfm?ContentID=304**. Accessed July 10, 2002.

Kiser, L., J. Heston, & P. Millsap. 1991. Physical and sexual abuse in childhood: Relationship with post-traumatic stress disorder. *Journal of the American Academy of Child and Adolescent Psychiatry,* 30(2): 776–83.

Losel, F., & T. Bliesener. 1990. Resilience in adolescence: A study on the generalizability of protective factors. In *Health Hazards in Adolescence*, eds. K. Hurrelmann, & F. Losel. New York: Walter de Gruyter.

Luther, S. S., & E. Zigler. January 1991. Vulnerability and competence: A review of research on resilience in childhood. *American Journal of Orthopsychiatry,* 61: 6–22.

McCauley, J., D. Kern, K. Kolodner, L. Dill, A. F. Schroeder, H. K. DeChant, J. Ryden, L. R. Derogatis, and E. B. Bass. 1997. Clinical characteristics of women with a history of child abuse. *Journal of the American Medical Association,* 277(17): 1362–68.

McFarlane, A. C. 1987. Post-traumatic phenomena in a longitudinal study of children following a natural disaster. *Journal of American Academy of Child and Adolescent Psychiatry*, 26: 764–69.

National Crime Prevention Council of Canada (NCPC). 1996. Preventing crime by investing in families: An integrated approach to promote positive outcomes in children. [Online]. Available: **http://www.crime-prevention.org/english/publications/children/family/index.html**. Accessed July 10, 2002.

———. 1995. *Resiliency in young children.* Ottawa: NCPC/CNPC.

———. 1999. *Pathways to prevention: Developmental and early intervention approaches to crime in Australia.* Ottawa: National Crime Prevention, Attorney-General's Department, Canberra.

Ontario Association of Children's Aid Societies. 1998. Child protection: Pay now or pay later, *OACAS Journal,* 42(3): 14–5.

Osofsky, J. D., S. Wewers, D. M. Hann, & A. C. Fick. 1993. Chronic community violence: What is happening to our children? *Psychiatry,* 56: 36–45.

Perry, B. D. 1994. Neurobiological sequelae of childhood trauma: Post-traumatic stress disorders in children. In *Catecholamine function in posttraumatic stress disorder: Emerging concepts,* ed. M. Murburg. Washington: American Psychiatric Press.

———. 1995. Incubated in terror: Neurodevelopmental factors in the "cycle of violence." In *Children, youth, and violence: Searching for solutions*, ed. J. D. Osofsky. New York: Guilford Press.

Ramey, C. T., & S. L. Ramey. 1994. Which children benefit the most from early intervention? *Pediatrics,* 94: 1064–66.

Sameroff, A., R. Seifer, R. Barocas, M. Zax, & S. Greenspan. 1987. Intelligence quotient scores of 4-year-old children: Socio-environmental risk factors. *Pediatrics,* 79: 343–50.

Sheidow, A. J., D. Gorman-Smith, P. H. Tolan, & D. B. Henry. 2001. Family and community characteristics: Risk factors for violence exposure in inner-city youth, *Journal of Community Psychology*, 29(3): 345–60.

Smith, C., A. J. Lizotte, T. P. Thornberry, & M. D. Krohn. 1995. Resilient youth: Identifying factors that prevent high-risk youth from engaging in delinquency and drug use. In *Current perspectives on aging and the life cycle, Volume 4: Delinquency and disrepute in the life course,* eds. Z. S. Blau & J.Hagan, 217–47. London: JAI Press Inc.

Snyder, J., & G. Patterson. 1987. Family interaction and delinquent behaviour. In *Handbook of juvenile delinquency*, ed. H. C. Quay. New York: Wiley Publishing.

Statistics Canada. 1996. *Crime statistics.* [Online]. Available: **http://www.StatCan.ca.Daily.English/970730/d97/0730.htm**. Accessed July 10, 2002.

Part VI

Social Interaction

12

The Presentation of Self

Erving Goffman

When an individual enters the presence of others, they commonly seek to acquire information about him or to bring into play information about him already possessed. They will be interested in his general socioeconomic status, his conception of self, his attitude toward them, his competence, his trustworthiness, etc. Although some of this information seems to be sought almost as an end in itself, there are usually quite practical reasons for acquiring it. Information about the individual helps to define the situation, enabling others to know in advance what he will expect of them and what they may expect of him. Informed in these ways, the others will know how best to act in order to call forth a desired response from him.

For those present, many sources of information become accessible and many carriers (or "sign-vehicles") become available for conveying this information. If unacquainted with the individual, observers can glean clues from his conduct and appearance which allow them to apply their previous experience with individuals roughly similar to the one before them or, more important, to apply untested stereotypes to him. They can also assume from past experience that only individuals of a particular kind are likely to be found in a given social setting. They can rely on what the individual says about himself or on documentary evidence he provides as to who and what he is. If they know, or know of, the individual by virtue of experience prior to the interaction, they can rely on assumptions as to the persistence and generality of psychological traits as a means of predicting his present and future behavior.

However, during the period in which the individual is in the immediate presence of the others, few events may occur which directly provide the others with the conclusive information they will need if they are to direct wisely their own activity. Many crucial facts lie beyond the time and place of interaction or lie concealed within it. For example,

Source: From *The Presentation of Self in Everyday Life* by Erving Goffman, copyright © 1959 by Erving Goffman, Bantam Doubleday Dell Publishing Group, Inc. Reprinted with permission.

the "true" or "real" attitudes, beliefs, and emotions of the individual can be ascertained only indirectly, through his avowals or through what appears to be involuntary expressive behavior. Similarly, if the individual offers the others a product or service, they will often find that during the interaction there will be no time and place immediately available for eating the pudding that the proof can be found in. They will be forced to accept some events as conventional or natural signs of something not directly available to the senses. In Ichheiser's terms,[1] the individual will have to act so that he intentionally or unintentionally *expresses* himself, and the others will in turn have to be *impressed* in some way by him.

The expressiveness of the individual (and therefore his capacity to give impressions) appears to involve two radically different kinds of sign activity: the expression that he *gives,* and the expression that he *gives off.* The first involves verbal symbols or their substitutes which he uses admittedly and solely to convey the information that he and the others are known to attach to these symbols. This is communication in the traditional and narrow sense. The second involves a wide range of action that others can treat as symptomatic of the actor, the expectation being that the action was performed for reasons other than the information conveyed in this way. As we shall have to see, this distinction has an only initial validity. The individual does of course intentionally convey misinformation by means of both of these types of communication, the first involving deceit, the second feigning.

…Let us now turn from the others to the point of view of the individual who presents himself before them. He may wish them to think highly of him, or to think that he thinks highly of them, or to perceive how in fact he feels toward them, or to obtain no clear-cut impression; he may wish to ensure sufficient harmony so that the interaction can be sustained, or to defraud, get rid of, confuse, mislead, antagonize, or insult them. Regardless of the particular objective which the individual has in mind and of his motive for having this

objective, it will be in his interests to control the conduct of the others, especially their responsive treatment of him. This control is achieved largely by influencing the definition of the situation which the others come to formulate, and he can influence this definition by expressing himself in such a way as to give them the kind of impression that will lead them to act voluntarily in accordance with his own plan. Thus, when an individual appears in the presence of others, there will usually be some reason for him to mobilize his activity so that it will convey an impression to others which it is in his interests to convey. Since a girl's dormitory mates will glean evidence of her popularity from the calls she receives on the phone, we can suspect that some girls will arrange for calls to be made, and Willard Waller's finding can be anticipated:

It has been reported by many observers that a girl who is called to the telephone in the dormitories will often allow herself to be called several times, in order to give all the other girls ample opportunity to hear her paged.[2]

Of the two kinds of communication—expressions given and expressions given off—this report will be primarily concerned with the latter, with the more theatrical and contextual kind, the nonverbal, presumably unintentional kind, whether this communication be purposely engineered or not. As an example of what we must try to examine, I would like to cite at length a novelistic incident in which Preedy, a vacationing Englishman, makes his first appearance on the beach of his summer hotel in Spain:

But in any case he took care to avoid catching anyone's eye. First of all, he had to make it clear to those potential companions of his holiday that they were of no concern to him whatsoever. He stared through them, round them, over them—eyes lost in space. The beach might have been empty. If by chance a ball was thrown his way, he looked surprised; then let a smile of amusement lighten his face (Kindly Preedy), looked round dazed to see that there *were* people on the beach, tossed it back with a smile to himself and not a smile *at* the people, and then resumed carelessly his nonchalant survey of space.

But it was time to institute a little parade, the parade of the Ideal Preedy. By devious handlings he gave any who wanted to look a chance to see the title of his book—a Spanish translation of Homer, classic thus, but not daring, cosmopolitan too—and then gathered together his beach-wrap and bag into a neat sand-resistant pile (Methodical and Sensible Preedy), rose slowly to stretch at ease his huge frame (Big-Cat Preedy), and tossed aside his sandals (Carefree Preedy, after all).

The marriage of Preedy and the sea! There were alternative rituals. The first involved the stroll that turns into a run and a dive straight into the water, thereafter smoothing into a strong splashless crawl towards the horizon. But of course not really to the horizon. Quite suddenly he would turn on to his back and thrash great white splashes with his legs, somehow thus showing that he could have swum further had he wanted to, and then would stand up a quarter out of water for all to see who it was.

The alternative course was simpler, it avoided the cold-water shock and it avoided the risk of appearing too high-spirited. The point was to appear to be so used to the sea, the Mediterranean, and this particular beach, that one might as well be in the sea as out of it. It involved a slow stroll down and into the edge of the water—not even noticing his toes were wet, land and water all the same to *him!*—with his eyes up at the sky gravely surveying portents, invisible to others, of the weather (Local Fisherman Preedy).[3]

The novelist means us to see that Preedy is improperly concerned with the extensive impressions he feels his sheer bodily action is giving off to those around him. We can malign Preedy further by assuming that he has acted merely in order to give a particular impression, that this is a false impression, and that the others present receive either no impression at all, or, worse still, the impression that Preedy is affectedly trying to cause them to receive this particular impression. But the important point for us here is that the kind of impression Preedy thinks he is making is in fact the kind of impression that others correctly and incorrectly glean from someone in their midst....

There is one aspect of the others' response that bears special comment here. Knowing that the individual is likely to present himself in a light that is favorable to him, the others may divide what they witness into two parts; a part that is relatively easy for the individual to manipulate at will, being chiefly his verbal assertions, and a part in regard to which he seems to have little concern or control, being chiefly derived from the expressions he gives off. The others may then use what are considered to be the ungovernable aspects of his expressive behavior as a check upon the validity of what is conveyed by the governable aspects. In this a fundamental asymmetry is demonstrated in the communication process, the individual presumably being aware of only one stream of his communication, the witnesses of this stream and one other. For example, in Shetland Isle one crofter's wife, in serving native dishes to a visitor from the mainland of Britain, would listen with a polite smile to his polite claims of liking what he was eating; at the same time she would take note of the rapidity with which the visitor lifted his fork or spoon to his mouth, the eagerness with which he passed food into his mouth, and the gusto expressed in chewing the food, using these signs as a check on the stated feelings of the eater. The same woman, in order to discover what one acquaintance (A) "actually" thought of another acquaintance (B), would wait until B was in the presence of A but engaged in conversation with still another person (C). She would then covertly examine the facial expressions of A as he regarded B in conversation with C. Not being in conversation with B, and not being directly observed by him, A would sometimes relax usual constraints and tactful deceptions, and freely express what he was "actually" feeling about B. This Shetlander, in short, would observe the unobserved observer.

Now given the fact that others are likely to check up on the more controllable aspects of behavior by means of the less controllable, one can expect that sometimes the individual will try to exploit this very possibility, guiding the impression he makes through behavior felt to be reliably informing.[4] For example, in gaining admission to a tight social circle, the participant observer may not only wear an accepting look while listening to an informant, but may also be careful to wear the same look when observing the informant talking to others; observers of the observer will then not as easily discover where he actually stands. A specific illustration may be cited from Shetland Isle. When a neighbor dropped in to have a cup of tea, he would ordinarily wear at least a hint of an expectant warm smile as he passed through the door into the cottage. Since lack of physical obstructions outside the cottage and lack of light within it usually made it possible to observe the visitor unobserved as he approached the house, islanders sometimes took pleasure in watching the visitor drop whatever expression he was manifesting and replace it with a sociable one just before reaching the door. However, some visitors, in appreciating that this examination was occurring, would blindly adopt a social face a long distance from the house, thus ensuring the projection of a constant image.

This kind of control upon the part of the individual reinstates the symmetry of the communication process, and sets the stage for a kind of information game—a potentially infinite cycle of concealment, discovery, false revelation, and rediscovery. It should be added that since the others are likely to be relatively unsuspicious of the presumably unguided aspects of the individual's conduct, he can gain much by controlling it. The others of course may sense that the individual is manipulating the presumably spontaneous aspects of his behavior, and seek in this very act of manipulation some shading of conduct that the individual has not managed to control. This again provides a check upon the individual's behavior, this time his presumably uncalculated behavior, thus re-establishing the asymmetry of the communication process. Here I would like only to add the suggestion that the arts of piercing an individual's effort at calculated unintentionality seem better developed than our capacity to manipulate our own behavior, so that regardless of how many steps have occurred in the information game, the witness is likely to have the advantage over the actor, and the initial asymmetry of the communication process is likely to be retained....

In everyday life, of course, there is a clear understanding that first impressions are important. Thus, the work adjustment of those in service occupations will often hinge upon a capacity to seize and hold the initiative in the service relation, a capacity that will require subtle aggressiveness on the part of the server when he is of lower socioeconomic status than his client. W. F. Whyte suggests the waitress as an example:

The first point that stands out is that the waitress who bears up under pressure does not simply respond to her customers. She acts with some skill to control their behavior. The first question to ask when we look at the customer relationship is, "Does the waitress get the jump on the customer, or does the customer get the jump on the waitress?" The skilled waitress realizes the crucial nature of this question....

The skilled waitress tackles the customer with confidence and without hesitation. For example, she may find that a new customer has seated himself before she could clear off the dirty dishes and change the cloth. He is now leaning on the table studying the menu. She greets him, says, "May I change the cover, please?" and, without waiting for an answer, takes his menu away from him so that he moves back from the table, and she goes about her work. The relationship is handled politely but firmly, and there is never any question as to who is in charge.[5]

When the interaction that is initiated by "first impressions" is itself merely the initial interaction in an extended series of interactions involving the same participants, we speak of "getting off on the right foot" and feel that it is crucial that we do so. Thus, one learns that some teachers take the following view:

You can't ever let them get the upper hand on you or you're through. So I start out tough. The first day I get a new class in, I let them know who's boss.... You've got to start off tough, then you can ease up as you go along. If you start out easy-going, when you try to get tough, they'll just look at you and laugh.[6]

...In stressing the fact that the initial definition of the situation projected by an individual tends to provide a plan for the cooperative activity that follows—in stressing this action point of view—we must not overlook the crucial fact that any projected definition of the situation also has a distinctive moral character. It is this moral character of projections that will chiefly concern us in this report. Society is organized on the principle that any individual who possesses certain social characteristics has a moral right to expect that others will value and treat him in an appropriate way. Connected with this principle is a second, namely that an individual who implicitly or explicitly signifies that he has certain social characteristics ought in fact to be what he claims he is. In consequence, when an individual projects a definition of the situation and thereby makes an implicit or explicit claim to be a person of a particular kind, he automatically exerts a moral demand upon the others, obliging them to value and treat him in the manner that persons of his kind have a right to expect. He also implicitly forgoes all claims to be things he does not appear to be[7] and hence forgoes the treatment that would be appropriate for such individuals. The others find, then, that the individual has informed them as to what is and as to what they *ought* to see as the "is."

One cannot judge the importance of definitional disruptions by the frequency with which they occur, for apparently they would occur more frequently were not constant precautions taken. We find that preventive practices are constantly employed to avoid these embarrassments and that corrective practices are constantly employed to compensate for discrediting occurrences that have not been successfully avoided. When the individual employs these strategies and tactics to protect his own projections, we may refer to them as "defensive practices"; when a participant employs them to save the definition of the situation projected by another, we speak of "protective practices" or "tact." Together, defensive and protective practices [compose] the techniques employed to safeguard the impression fostered by an individual during his presence before others. It should be added that while we may be ready to

see that no fostered impression would survive if defensive practices were not employed, we are less ready perhaps to see that few impressions could survive if those who received the impression did not exert tact in their reception of it.

In addition to the fact that precautions are taken to prevent disruption of projected definitions, we may also note that an intense interest in these disruptions comes to play a significant role in the social life of the group. Practical jokes and social games are played in which embarrassments which are to be taken unseriously are purposely engineered.[8] Fantasies are created in which devastating exposures occur. Anecdotes from the past—real, embroidered, or fictitious—are told and retold, detailing disruptions which occurred, almost occurred, or occurred and were admirably resolved. There seems to be no grouping which does not have a ready supply of these games, reveries, and cautionary tales, to be used as a source of humor, a catharsis for anxieties, and a sanction for inducing individuals to be modest in their claims and reasonable in their projected expectations. The individual may tell himself through dreams of getting into impossible positions. Families tell of the time a guest got his dates mixed and arrived when neither the house nor anyone in it was ready for him. Journalists tell of times when an all-too-meaningful misprint occurred, and the paper's assumption of objectivity or decorum was humorously discredited. Public servants tell of times a client ridiculously misunderstood form instructions, giving answers which implied an unanticipated and bizarre definition of the situation.[9] Seamen, whose home away from home is rigorously he-man, tell stories of coming back home and inadvertently asking mother to "pass the fucking butter."[10] Diplomats tell of the time a near-sighted queen asked a republican ambassador about the health of his king.[11]

To summarize, then, I assume that when an individual appears before others he will have many motives for trying to control the impression they receive of the situation.

NOTES

1. Gustav Ichheiser, "Misunderstandings in Human Relations," supplement to *The American Journal of Sociology* 55 (Sept., 1949), 6–7.

2. Willard Waller, "The Rating and Dating Complex," *American Sociological Review* 2, 730.

3. William Sansom, *A Contest of Ladies* (London: Hogarth, 1956), pp. 230–32.

4. The widely read and rather sound writings of Stephen Potter are concerned in part with signs that can be engineered to give a shrewd observer the apparently incidental cues he needs to discover concealed virtues the gamesman does not in fact possess.

5. W. F. Whyte, "When Workers and Customers Meet," chap. 7, *Industry and Society,* ed. W. F. Whyte (New York: McGraw-Hill, 1946), pp. 132–33.

6. Teacher interview quoted by Howard S. Becker, "Social Class Variations in the Teacher–Pupil Relationship," *Journal of Educational Sociology* 25, 459.

7. This role of the witness in limiting what it is the individual can be has been stressed by Existentialists, who see it as a basic threat to individual freedom. See Jean-Paul Sartre, *Being and Nothingness,* trans. Hazel E. Barnes (New York: Philosophical Library, 1956), pp. 365ff.

8. Goffman, op. cit., pp. 319–27.

9. Peter Blau, "Dynamics of Bureaucracy" (Ph.D. dissertation, Department of Sociology, Columbia University, forthcoming, University of Chicago Press), pp. 127–29.

10. Walter M. Beattie, Jr., "The Merchant Seaman" (unpublished M.A. Report, Department of Sociology, University of Chicago, 1950), p. 35.

11. Sir Frederick Ponsonby, *Recollections of Three Reigns* (New York: Dutton, 1952), p. 46.

13

Disclaimer Mannerisms of Students: How to Avoid Being Labelled as Cheaters

Daniel Albas and Cheryl Albas

Wherever there are rules there will be temptations for people to break them. Consequently, there is always the possibility of people being labelled deviant whether or not they do break the rules. University examinations are rule-riddled events shrouded in a "suspicion awareness context" where suspecting invigilators are on guard against possible cheaters. Students, aware of this, must avoid all taint of suspicion and the dire consequences of being labelled a cheater. These avoidance strategies consist of impression management in the form of disclaimers. It is the purpose of this article to describe the bizarre and seemingly paranoid length students writing exams go to in: the control of their eyes, deployment of books and notes, and choice of space to avoid the stigma of being labelled a cheater. The emphasis is primarily on the innocent noncheaters but there is brief treatment also of the guilty.

INTRODUCTION

Wherever there are rules, there will be temptations to break them, and the possibility of being labelled deviant by those who made the rules or have a vested interest in their observance. The assumption is that these power figures will institute a monitoring regime and sanctions to achieve compliance and control. In such a situation there are four theoretical possibilities (Becker, 1963): A. an actor might break a rule and be labelled; B. an actor might break a rule but escape detection and labelling; C. an actor might break no rule but be wrongfully labelled; D. an actor might break no rule and not be labelled. This article focuses mainly on category "C". There is only brief comment on categories "A" and "B".... Because of the painful results of labelling, which are usually dramatically impressed on all actors, they will make strenuous efforts to avoid being labelled, whether or

Source: Albas, Daniel, and Albas, Cheryl. (1993). Disclaimer mannerisms of students: How to avoid being labelled as cheaters. *Canadian Review of Sociology and Anthropology,* 30(4), 451–67. Reprinted by permission of the Canadian Sociology and Anthropology Association.

not they break the rules. Our focus, then, is on the avoidance that goes on before any labelling occurs as opposed to previous works, particularly by Becker, which focus on the victimized deviants after they have been labelled. Accordingly, the present emphasis as with that of Goffman (1971; 1963a; 1963b; 1959), Lemert (1981), and Matza (1964), is on actors before they are labelled. In addition, we assume actors are aware of the existence of suspicion and are active in its avoidance. We also treat briefly but do not elaborate upon students who actually cheat, are sometimes detected, but continue to try to avoid being labelled. The method of avoidance we shall demonstrate is largely impression management. Such behaviour applies in all suspicion-awareness situations[1] like shop-lifting in department stores and smuggling at customs stations.

In the case with which we are concerned here, students are painfully aware that their identities in the eyes of invigilators are those of potential cheaters. The focus in this paper is on the highly fraught suspicion awareness context of an examination room. The rules of the exam room constitute a "veritable filigree of trip wires" (Goffman, 1971: 106) and the presence of functionaries who, in the eyes of the students, are there principally for catching cheaters and labelling them clearly creates a labelling liable situation. The impression management carried on by the students consists largely of disclaimers. In the usual sense disclaimers are the verbal explanations given by actors before the act of behaviour that might appear to be proscribed and liable to result in labelling. However, in our present study, the disclaimers are largely mannerisms rather than verbalizations (i.e. nonverbal "symbolic gestures" that invite, persuade, and cajole others to respond in one way rather than another). We have chosen this symbolic focus for study here, in part to redress an imbalance in the emphasis on those aspects of the vocabulary of motives (Mills, 1981) which have hitherto stressed the "discursive" (Stone and Farberman, 1981) and largely neglected the nonverbal....

METHOD

This article is part of a larger study of student life and exams conducted over the past 17 years at a large provincial university in Western Canada (Albas and Albas, 1984). The data come from over 300 individuals who comprise four "generations" of university students. The data originate from three principal sources:

1. Examination logs—These are written accounts by students in which they describe in detail how exams influence their daily lives and noted aspects of exam-related events which they perceived as problematic. More specifically, students wrote about what caused them particular difficulty, anxiety, or trouble and how they coped with it....

2. Interviews—These were conducted by us mostly at the examination site where we mingled with students before and after exams, and in classrooms after test papers were returned. We attempted to get from students their spontaneous explanations of behaviour and practices about which we had questions but which had not yet been verified....

3. Comprehensive observations—To complete the triangulation process, information derived from logs and interviews was combined with careful observations of strategies guided by categories that seemed theoretically and semantically apt (e.g., concealment, revelation, or selective revelation)....

DATA

It is possible to categorize the strategies employed by students in seeking to avoid the label of cheating into two major categories of "Actions Avoided" and "Actions Taken". Actions Avoided are in turn mainly counters to imputed signs of cheating and can be further subcategorized as (a) control of eyes, (b) control of books, notes, formulae and any materials that could be considered "cribs," and (c) morality of place. Actions Taken are all exaggerated shows of (a) picayune overconformity with regulations, (b) the expression (or repression) of "creature releases," and (c) shows of innocence by: default, diligence, affability, declarations, pointless questions.

With the schema that follows we propose to describe the activities the students tell us about and we observe that they carry on to give the impression of complete innocence:

Actions Avoided

1. Control of eyes

   The well-understood rule in the examination room is that there should be no looking at other people's papers or exchanging glances with others that might be interpreted as unfair communication. In effect students are expected not to have "roving eyes." On the other hand, it is not humanly possible for students to focus their eyes on their own answer sheet unwaveringly for two or three hours. Accordingly it is necessary to rest and relax from time to time and to remove their eyes from the papers in front of them in order to gather their thoughts. At such times great care is necessary in selecting where to look when they look away from their own papers. A favourite strategy is to keep their eyes fixed on the invigilators. The theory is that if the invigilators see students looking at them, they could not be looking at anybody or anything else. Sometimes this strategy is taken too far and may even backfire so that what is intended as an open, innocent looking into the eyes of another (the invigilator) becomes and is interpreted as a breach of convention—civil inattention (Goffman, 1963a). It may become incriminating if invigilators interpret these long-held glances as an attempt to find an opportunity to cheat when they look away.

   Another strategy is to stare at the ceiling where, as one student says, "There is no earthly possibility of deriving unfair help." (There might be the possibility of fair heavenly help though, if thoughts accompany the eyes!) Other students say they stare at the back of the head of the person immediately in front or a little above. Quite often they state they go off into brief reveries and suddenly wake up to find themselves staring into the eyes of an invigilator. This contingency is coped with differently by different people. One young woman reports that she smiles ingenuously at the invigilator and moves her eyebrows up and down a few times because as she says, "no cheater would be comfortable enough to do a goofy thing like that." One young male student indicates: "I've given the invigilators a sort of 'help me, I'm stuck' look, hoping it would make them

   feel sorry for me and so cancel out any thoughts they may have had that I might be cheating." One interesting case observed was of a female student who, in her reverie, was staring at her hands. She looked up to see the invigilator looking at her. She described her reaction and strategy in this way: Using him as a mirror (reflexive role-taking, Turner, 1955: 321) she intuited that he could interpret her to be reading notes written on her palms. She tried to negate that reading by holding up her hands in front of him, palms forward. She found that the invigilator, who at that time had no suspicious thoughts whatsoever, was hard-pressed to understand her actions and showed his puzzlement. He thought that she perhaps wanted to ask a question. She left her seat, went to the front of the room where the invigilator was standing and proclaimed to him explicitly that she was not cheating by showing him the fronts and palms of her hands!

   In addition to resting the eyes, it is necessary from time to time for students writing an examination to scratch and stretch and turn their heads from side to side "to get the kinks out." This is a time when many say they feel particularly vulnerable to suspicion. In order to avoid suspicion some report that they cover their eyes with their hands as they stretch and affect to rub them. One student reports that he put his face down on his paper and rolled his head from side to side "where I couldn't possibly be seeing anything, not even my own writing."

   Students report that if they drop a pencil or some other object and have to stoop to pick it up they keep their eyes on the invigilator rather than on the object they are trying to pick up in much the same way as touch typists keep their eyes on the copy rather than on the keys.

   Some males come into the examination room wearing baseball caps, in order, they claim to conceal unwashed, greasy or unkempt hair made so by the rigours of study preparation. However, to avoid the possible stigma of reading crib notes from under the peak of the cap, they turn it around so that the peak extends over the back of their necks where any invigilator will know that they do not have eyes. On the other hand, some women who have long bangs which can almost cover their eyes (like horse blinders, especially when their heads are lowered) dramatize the fact that they do not copy from others because they could not possibly see through the blinds.

2. Control of notes, books, etc.

   Examination rules are explicit that students should not have on their persons any "unauthorized books, tables, notes, or other extraneous material"... "Books or tables authorized for use ... must not contain any additional notes, formulae or other extraneous material." Some instructors allow students writing tests to bring such material into the examination room and even to their desks provided that they do not refer to them during the examination. One may wonder why on earth students would want to put themselves unnecessarily in the vulnerable position of being able to be suspected of using these materials. That so many do can only be explained by the fact that having these course materials with them when they write provides such students with a "security blanket" (Albas and Albas, 1988a). Perhaps, even more, there is a magical influence imparted by the closeness of their course materials. One woman reported that she kept hers under her feet as a kind of foot stool and was convinced that inspiration from them came up to her through her legs (Albas and Albas, 1989).

Under such circumstances the management of these materials has to be elaborate and intensive in order to convince invigilators that they are not being used illicitly. One man states that he piles these materials on the floor beside his desk with the ones pertaining to the course and might be of any use at the bottom, then on top go the books for other courses, calculators, and other obviously harmless appurtenances. Many students say that before entering an examination room, they "frisk" themselves to ensure that they have not inadvertently forgotten scraps of paper in their pockets which might have notes or formulae written on them. A student stated that once when he opened his wallet to produce his ID card (a recent regulation to prevent "ghost writing") he was embarrassed by various receipts falling out, which of course were innocent but a possible source of suspicion.

Perhaps the most dramatic action reported by a student to counter the imputation of cheating was when the person beside him passed him a note addressed to him asking for help! He indicates: "I was terrified of being caught because my marks reflected a need to cheat. Furthermore, the other student had addressed me by name and signed his as well." Not wanting to pass the note back and not wishing to keep it on his person he resolved his dilemma as follows: "My solution was to eat the note. Fortunately it was a short note written on a small piece of paper!"

3. Morality of Place

Glassner and Corzine (1978) make the point that physical locations become inured with social iden-

tities and are important to sociological analysis. Lofland (1973) also stresses the importance of physical location "as a shorthand for imputing social identities to individuals" (Glassner and Corzine, 1978: 83). Students writing exams seem implicitly aware of this connection. One reports: "Since trouble makers (cheaters included) tend to cluster at the back of the room, I stay away from there." Accordingly, it is true to say, as a basic generality, that in choosing their seats in the examination room students "try to avoid the limelight." In other words, they endeavour not to be conspicuous. However, there are some exceptions. For example, some students sit directly in front of the invigilator so that they can be ostentatiously innocent. One invigilator complains of being particularly offended by a student in one of these "conspicuous" seats who cheated—the offence experienced was greater than if the student had chosen an inconspicuous seat at the back or somewhere in the middle. In effect, the student cheated not merely by copying or some other such infringement but he also breached the morality of place by violating the mutual expectations of "the game" in that he cheated in a sacrosanct area rather than in a more sporting locale where the invigilator would routinely patrol, and the odds would be even. However, since students are aware that the inconspicuous seats are suspect, many explicitly avoid them. Others say that they avoid seats beside the well-known high achievers because they may be suspected of trying to copy from them. Also avoided are seats next to known cheaters, students say they do this to escape possible guilt by association. A favoured position in the examination room is the aisle seat where it is possible to angle one's body away from the person sitting in the adjoining seat and obviously impossible to see the paper of the person across the aisle. Sitting beside friends is also avoided. If they find themselves so placed they sit with their bodies angled away from each other.

Actions Taken

1. Exaggerated Shows of Picayune Overconformity with Regulations

The cover page of the examination answer booklet lists a number of regulations some of which have been referred to previously. In addition, there are unwritten rules and regulations many of them conveyed dramaturgically in the staging of the examination (Albas and Albas, 1988b). The "trip wires" are numerous—both explicit and implicit. In response students dramatically overconform to these regulations so as to avoid all possible suspicion. The kinds of things they do sometimes approach the bizarre. For example, one male student who had grown a beard since his ID picture was taken says that he strove to recapture on his face the expression he had in the picture so that even with the beard he would be recognizable to the invigilator as the same person. A woman who did not remember her student number which she was required to write at the top of the answer sheet, instead of opening her purse and getting the number from her ID card, waited until she was handing in her paper and with ostentatious innocence got out the ID card and wrote the student number as the invigilator looked on. Her action visibly annoyed him because she slowed down the "traffic" of students handing in their papers and leaving the room. A number of students report that they always hand in their papers before going back to their desk and packing up their effects. This way there can be no possible chance they might sneak a last minute look at notes before the exam paper is turned in. They also say that they pack their equipment while standing up to signal blatantly that they are not doing anything untoward.

These overdrawn precautions by students to escape the suspicion of unfair copying are matched by their efforts to avoid being copied from by exaggerated hunching over their papers, covering them with their hands and, in the case of one person, covering it with a handkerchief. A peculiar example of this ostentatious concealment technique occurs in science laboratory exams in which the room is partially darkened and the questions are flashed on a screen. Because of the darkness and thus increased opportunity for cheating there are usually more invigilators who are also more diligent than in other situations. Accordingly, in order to show that no copying is going on, students turn their answer sheets over as they answer each question. The effect is a periodic, rhythmic "swish" of papers after each question has been answered.

If students have to go into their purses, pencil cases, or bookbags they do so with exaggerated movements designed purposefully to attract attention. They then demonstrate the innocence of the action with the final flourished waving of a [K]leenex like a flag to demonstrate there is no writing on it. One student whose pen ran out of ink shook it violently for a sufficient time to attract the attention of everyone close by and then with two fingers only, delicately extracted a new pen from his jacket pocket.

Students usually attempt to keep a minimum number of irrelevant items like glasses cases, extra pencils, etc. on their desks on the theory that what is not there cannot possibly incriminate them. In contrast to the students mentioned earlier who wear long bangs to "guard their eyes from temptation," others come to the exam with their hair combed tightly back from their faces so that the rectitude of their eyes can be fully observed: "I wear the sides of my hair pulled back so my eyes are more visible."

One student reports that if, after resting her eyes perhaps in the direction of another paper—she becomes aware of being observed by an invigilator, she delays writing anything for a reasonable interval so as to neutralize any possible suspicion that she might be transferring something she saw on the other paper to her own. This happens particularly in tests using IBM sheets which are machine graded.

2. Expression or Repression of Creature Releases

Goffman (1963b) conceptualizes "creature releases" as "fleeting acts that slip through one's self control and momentarily assert one's animal nature," such things as yawning, sneezing, stretching a cramped limb, or relieving the bladder. These acts are either exaggeratedly expressed in order to make clear beyond all doubt that they are genuine and not meant to mask some guilty activity or they are repressed quite frequently to an excruciating extent in order to avoid the possibility of being falsely accused. Examples of exaggerated expressions include spectacular, wide-mouthed yawning, expansive stretching and vigorous rubbing of the eyes....

Some examples of the repression of creature releases are as follows. One woman... knew that since there were no female exam invigilators there would be no one to accompany her to the washroom. Even though she would have been trusted to go alone if she expressed the need desperately enough, she decided not to risk this but rather with great discomfort that brought tears to her eyes, she "held on" to the bitter end. Another student who suffers from asthma and is required from time to time to use an inhaler would not risk taking it from his knapsack during the examination but instead elected to wheeze his way to the end of his examination. Still another student describes how she had a bad cold, a dripping nose and sneezing spasms but was caught without a supply of Kleenex. Even though the student sitting beside her put some Kleenex within her reach, she delayed accepting it "for a long time."

3. Exaggerated Shows of Innocence

Innocence is blatantly declared by a number of techniques:

(i) By default. Many students come to the exam in clothing devoid of pockets or sleeves (at least long ones) and often women do not wear skirts but opt to dress in pants. By so doing there is no possibility of being suspected of concealing notes in any of these styles of dress. Another case of innocence by default is that of a woman who had finished writing her exam, had already packed up her equipment and was ready to leave the room but wished to wait for her friend who was still writing. In order to make it abundantly clear that she was indeed finished and not trying to copy from anyone else she did three things: she turned her paper face down on the desk, put the cap on her pen with a sweeping flourish and an audible "click," and then she fixed her gaze on some distant object beyond the window.

(ii) By diligence. An emergent norm among the collectivity of exam writers is that any pause or lack of activity is damning. Thus, if they are stumped for a time over the answer to some question, while they think about it they put on a show of diligence in which they may move their lips exaggeratedly as they read the question or they underline and circle words on the question paper while others turn to diligent doodling. In general, they assume a posture of great seriousness and frowning industry. One says: "When I take a break from writing, I crease my brow as if in deep thought. This lets the professor know that I'm thinking deeply."

(iii) By affability. Students say that when they have any interaction at all with the invigilator during the exam, for example, when ID cards are being checked, the register is being signed, or even when patrolling is going on, they often affect exaggerated affability. Students say, for example, "I always smile and make a joke." "I try to convey as soft, open and honest impression as I possibly can." "I try to be my most charming." They seem to be saying that no self-respecting, decent invigilator could suspect such open friendliness....

(iv) By verbal declarations. Quite often students realize that they have been caught off guard—quite innocently doing something such as looking at a neighbour's watch or being in the midst of a group of other students who are cheating and particularly if, for some reason, they have been asked by an invigilator to change seats. Such people tell us they make a point, upon leaving the exam room, of letting the invigilator know in no uncertain terms that they were not cheating. Some students say they put this in written notes they leave with the invigilator. They say further that by so doing they neutralize any possible suspicion that they are "sneaking off." Sometimes these declarations are posed as pointless questions. For example, students might invite an invigilator to their seat to explain some obviously clear wording in the question, or to ask whether it would be possible to have the room temperature adjusted, or perhaps, to ask how much time is left. One student says: "It lets the professor know I wasn't cheating. If I were, I would not be able to invite her to come near, look her in the eyes and exchange words with her."

DISCUSSION

It seems clear from the presentation above that the examination room is an area highly fraught with suspicion because of the multitude of rules students must follow and the many temptations which exist to break them and thus the possibilities of being labelled. We noted also that the university's staging of examinations introduces numerous additional guilt threatening situations such as the presence of invigilators and their patrolling activities. We found in these and parallel circumstances elsewhere that in the examination room a great deal of impression management goes on in the form of acted out disclaimers intended to ward off labelling. The descriptions provided might strike the reader as exaggerated or, if not an exaggeration on our part, then an overdramatization on the part of the students in their accounts. Indeed, at first glance, it might seem so. However, if we look more closely at the circumstances surrounding these disclaimer displays, exaggerated as they are, they become sociologically explainable. First there does seem to be some paranoia (a term used by many students to describe their state of mind). But are all students paranoid? If not all [,] which ones and why? We shall now try to answer these questions.

Becker (1963) forcefully established the fact that "deviance" is not merely objectively definable as "breach of the norms" but also involves a subjective component open to numerous interpretations in turn resting upon "social constructions of the act." These social constructions and interpretations of student behaviour by invigilators frequently lead to situations that students perceive as false accusations. Furthermore, whether or not these accusations are actually made overt, students imagine that they are made in the invigilator's minds. Thus it becomes more understandable that students might tend to be paranoid.

However, what is also clear is that the paranoid displays do vary to a certain extent depending on the status of the student, the difficulty and significance of the test in question and the "staging" of the test. What follows is an elaboration of these variables and their relation to the degree of paranoid behaviour expressed by students.

Status of Student

A student's status is a function of a complex combination of circumstances and attributes. First, in relation to the powerful professor invigilators, students are in a low-powered, subordinate position. Students tell us that the tone of voice invigilators use tends to infuse more or less awe. The ones who make official and loud announcements, particularly if these announcements include the dire penalties for cheating (which some invigilators feel constrained to do) sets off the drama on an ominous note. Students say also that invigilators who patrol constantly during the examination disturb them most, particularly when they are nearby. Such patterns are consistent with Lofland's (1976: 54–55) observation that "Acute strategic consciousness seems to be the consciousness of underdogs ... they become highly sensitive to the impression their actions are making on the overdog." Argyle and Williams (1969) consistently found that subordinates in role relationships (i.e. interviewee versus interviewer, adolescent versus older person, etc.) feel more self-conscious and

demonstrate a greater concern with self presentation. Weems and Wolowitz (1969: 191) indicate that "self-perceived power deficit is a demonstrably prominent factor in the dynamics of ... paranoids." Lemert (1981) also makes the same point....

Second, what we are calling the paranoid aspect of disclaimer displays is generally a function of a student's competence and year in program. Very able students evince less paranoia. Their main anxiety is to have a minimum of interruption or interference until they have completed their answers to the questions. They are seemingly largely unaware of being suspected of cheating and in any case would hardly care because they are so secure and conscious of their ability to prove their competence and demonstrate their innocence if necessary. The mediocre and weak students on the other hand are generally aware of deep down temptations in themselves to cheat. They often imagine that invigilators can telepathically determine these urges ... and so they compulsively watch their ps and qs to avoid betraying these temptations. We also found that as students progress within the academic program from first to last year, their exam behaviour seems to become less paranoid. The explanation for this fact might be that in the higher years they feel somewhat closer in status to invigilators, particularly if the latter are graduate students. Another explanation might be that over the years, through practice, they have become so expert in the performance of disclaimers that they are able to be more poised.

A third dimension of status is ethnicity. We found that visible minority students (e.g., First Nations People, Asians) evince more paranoid-seeming displays than do average, white, middle-class students. This is quite in accord with what Glassner and Corzine (1978) lead us to expect by their discussion of "categorical deviance." They imply that people who do labelling (i.e. power figures) group individuals into categories to which they attach different tendencies to deviance. This, of course, puts "minority" students in a pejorative position in the scale of expectations and they know it.

Fourth, students who wear bristling beards, long "pony tails," tattoos, or present a generally scruffy appearance (much as these appearances provide them with self-satisfactions and status within their own peer groups) are at greater "risk" to be labelled (and they know it) in the "straight" (their assessment) environment of the examination room. Once again we have the corroboration of Glassner and Corzine for this assertion.

Difficulty and Significance of Test

Students classify tests and examinations on a continuum from "a piece of cake" to "a real killer." On another scale these tests vary from "class tests" conducted in the rooms in which the courses are taught to "final examinations" conducted in an auditorium or gymnasium. Our findings suggest that the more difficult the test and the more significant it is, the more paranoid-seeming are the displays. These relationships seem explicable as identity protection. The more one's identity is on the line, the higher the identity risk and the more elaborate the display.

Staging

By staging is meant the dramaturgy surrounding the conduct of the examination. It involves rituals such as admission of students to the exam room on the stroke of the hour, the requirement that they sit in designated seats with plyboard dividers between writing areas, and an army of invigilators making announcements, handing out exam papers (face down), patrolling, etc. This type of elaboration occurs for significant final examinations rather than for class tests. However, even for class tests there are certain formalities and restrictions above the everyday level of class conduct that must be observed. We found that the more elaborate the staging the more paranoid seeming the disclaimers.

The exaggerated disclaimer behaviour to avoid labelling we have described for the classroom is common to a wide range of situations in social life. In spite of being so widespread and, for some people, so intense, a large number of such people are completely unaware of its existence. For example, many professors who have themselves been through the exam-writing trauma will have forgotten and are surprised at the seeming paranoia of their students. They find the acted out disclaimers puzzling and even unintelligible. This is what some writers have referred to as the privilege of insensitivity enjoyed by people in power (Thomas et al., 1972; Rose, 1969). Furthermore, many honest people in department stores, who would never think of shoplifting tell us in interviews of the ends to which they go, for example, keeping their hands out of their pockets, not taking shopping bags into stores, avoiding the area of an unattended counter, not leaving the store in too great a hurry, etc. This is clearly paranoid-like behaviour but it is also understandable given the presence of store detectives and television scanners....

In sum, in this paper we have concentrated on category "C" of the typology—people who have broken no rule but strive by impression management to avoid being wrongfully labelled. There are, however, students in both categories "A" and "B" of the typology, namely those who cheat, are caught and labelled and those who cheat but manage to escape detection and labelling. Even students in this latter category who are sometimes detected manage to argue and turn the stigma away from themselves.

NOTES

1. Glazer and Strauss (1981) define awareness context as the total amount of knowledge we have of the identity (friend, enemy, spy, etc.) of the other and/or our own identity in the eyes of the other. They list four possible awareness contexts: 1/Closed awareness context—we are unaware of another's identity and/or of our own identity in the eyes of another; 2/ Suspicion awareness context—we are aware that our identity in the eyes of the other is under suspicion

or the other's identity is suspected by us; 3/ Pretence-awareness context—we are aware of each other's identity, but pretend not to be; 4/ Open awareness context—we are both aware of each other's identity and make it known.

REFERENCES

Albas, C., and D. Albas. 1988a. Emotion work and emotion rules: The case of exams. *Qualitative Sociology,* 11(4): 259–74.

Albas, D., and C. Albas. 1984. *Student life and exams: Stresses and coping strategies.* Dubuque, Ind.: Kendall/Hunt.

———. 1988b. The institutional staging of an examination. *Canadian Journal of Higher Education,* 18(1): 65–73.

———. 1989. Modern magic: The case of exams. *Sociological Quarterly,* 30(4): 603–13.

Argyle, M., and M. Williams. 1969. Observer or observed? A reversible perspective in person perception. *Sociometry,* 32: 396–412.

Becker, H. 1963. *The outsiders.* New York: Free Press of Glencoe.

Glassner, B., and J. Corzine. 1978. Can labeling theory be saved? *Symbolic Interaction,* 1(2): 74–89.

Goffman, E. 1959. *The presentation of self in everyday life.* Garden City, N.J.: Doubleday/Anchor.

———. 1963a. *Behavior in public places.* New York: Free Press of Glencoe.

———. 1963b. *Stigma: Notes on the management of spoiled identity.* Englewood Cliffs, N.J.: Prentice-Hall.

———. 1971. *Relations in public: Microstudies in the public order.* New York: Basic Books.

Lemert, E. 1981. Paranoia and the dynamics of exclusion. In *Social psychology through symbolic interaction,* 2nd ed., eds. G. Stone, and H. Farberman, 415–28. Toronto: John Wiley.

Lofland, J. 1976. *Doing social life.* New York: Wiley–Interscience.

Lofland, L. 1973. *A world of strangers: Order and action in public urban space.* New York: Basic Books.

Matza, D. 1964. *Delinquency and drift.* New York: Wiley.

Mills, C.W. 1981. Situated actions and vocabularies of motive. In *Social psychology through symbolic interaction,* 2nd ed., eds. G. Stone, and H. Farberman, 325–33. Toronto: John Wiley.

Rose, J. 1969. The role of the other in self evaluation. *Sociological Quarterly,* 10: 470–79.

Stone, G., and H. Farberman. 1981. Introduction. In *Social psychology through symbolic interaction,* 2nd ed., eds. G. Stone, and H. Farberman, 1–20. Toronto: John Wiley.

Thomas, D., D. Franks, and J. Calancino. 1972. Role-taking and power in social psychology. *American Sociological Review,* 37(October): 605–15.

Turner, R. 1955. Role-taking, role standpoint and reference group behavior. *American Journal of Sociology,* 61: 316–28.

Weems, L., and H. Wolowitz. 1969. The relevance of power themes among males, negro and white paranoid and non-paranoid schizophrenics. *International Journal of Social Psychiatry,* 15: 189–96.

14

The Body Beautiful: Adolescent Girls and Images of Beauty

Beverly J. Matthews

INTRODUCTION

The tyranny of appearance norms have long been recognized in the lives of women (see Brownmiller, 1984; Greer, 1970; or Freedman, 1986, for example). Both academic literature and the popular media have examined factors which underlie the intense pressure women experience to adhere to a cultural ideal and the price they pay for either attempting to comply or failing to do so (see Chernin, 1981; Shute, 1992; Hesse-Biber, 1996; Bordo, 1993). While we are aware of the problem among older teenagers and adult women, recent studies indicate that even girls in early adolescence are prone to eating problems and a preoccupation with food (Pipher, 1996; Brumberg, 1997). Some of the literature in this area focuses on media images and unhealthy portrayals of beauty and the ways in which women are influ-

Source: Matthews, Beverly J. (2000). The Body Beautiful: Adolescent Girls and Images of Beauty. In Lori G. Beaman (Ed.), *New Perspectives on Deviance: The Construction of Deviance in Everyday Life* (pp. 208–19). Scarborough: Prentice-Hall.

enced by such portrayals (Wolf, 1991). While this has been a fruitful line of inquiry, it is incomplete. It implies that women uncritically, or helplessly, follow a cultural ideal, simply because it is prescribed by society. The findings of this research study into the social world of adolescent girls reveal that straining to conform to the "ideal look" is not always an end in itself, that it is often a purposeful act designed to achieve social goals.

Young women are surrounded by images which define attractiveness as a very particular, thin, "perfect" ideal. While many strive to achieve this goal, they do not all do so out of blind conformity, or simply because they have negative images of themselves. The problem is more complex: many girls use appearance as a means for achieving social status and power; they conform to avoid the costs associated with deviating from the ideal. They experience the gender system in a unique way, because of their stage in life, which compounds the pressures all women experience around appearance; however, these girls are not all misguided individuals passively following a societal definition of beauty. Just like older women, adolescents are working to negotiate and achieve their individual goals within a micro and macro gender structure. They are actively finding their location within the peer arena and their relationships with food and appearance play a key role in this endeavor. In this research, in-depth interviews with adolescent women reveal much about the adolescent world and the importance of appearance norms within it.

EXAMINING THE MULTILEVEL GENDER SYSTEM AND THE SOCIAL WORLD OF ADOLESCENT GIRLS

When studying the social world it is essential to recognize the interplay between the individual and the social context. Although women have the freedom to make their own choices, these choices are constrained by the socially created structures which surround them. Sociologists have long recognized the existence of social structures and have worked to explain their relation to individuals: "social structures create social persons who (re)create social structures who create social persons who (re)create...ad infinitum" (Stryker, 1980: 53). They also recognize that such structures operate on two levels. "[W]e inhabit the *micro-world* of our immediate experience with others in face-to-face relations. Beyond that, with varying degrees of significance and continuity, we inhabit a *macro-world* consisting of much larger structures.... Both worlds are essential to our experience of society" (Berger & Berger, 1975: 8). Sociologists and feminists have studied the creation of the social person and the role that gender plays in that development. They have also examined the gendered dimensions of social structures and their impact upon members of the society (see Risman & Schwartz, 1989; Smith, 1987; Bem, 1993).

Through my research into gender and social behaviour (Matthews & Beaujot, 1997;

Matthews, 1997), it has become clear that the gender system can be more fully understood by acknowledging that it operates on several levels at one time. And that analyses are more complete when three levels are integrated into the explanatory framework. This tri-level model of the gender system includes the individual gender role orientation, a micro structure, and a macro structure. On the most basic level, men and women have individual gender role orientations, which they have developed through socialization and interaction over the course of their lives. These orientations consist of their beliefs about the appropriate roles for women and men and serve as guidelines for choices regarding presentation of self, relationships, and activities, as well as attitudes and values. However, these gender role orientations alone do not determine behaviour. Women's choices about how to behave, and how to present themselves, are also influenced by the micro level gender structure, where they encounter others in daily interaction and negotiate their roles. Conforming to expectations is an integral part of interaction; people play roles in order to facilitate communication and joint action. They are also influenced by the macro level gender structure: the societal context which provides a landscape within which people act out their choices. It is my contention that the combination of the three levels and the way in which they interact, sometimes complementary and sometimes contradictory, can advance our understanding of the gender system and of young women's actions concerning weight and appearance.

For women making decisions about weight, food, and dieting, it is apparent that all three levels of the gender system influence their choices and behaviour. The macro structure, which has evolved over time, emphasizes the importance of appearance for women. While women's accomplishments are many, they continue to be judged by their appearance. It provides media images of "perfect bodies" and advertising which constantly criticizes and undermines women with appearance "flaws" (i.e., extra pounds, "problem" skin, gray hair). On the micro level, appearance is also salient. Because slenderness is the norm, there is some pressure in daily interaction to achieve it. Friends and family often encourage, and occasionally coerce, women into dieting and following the cultural ideal. Choosing not to diet, not following the ideal, seems to imply either slovenliness— "she's really let herself go"—or a personal statement about her unwillingness to conform. It is rarely accepted as a woman choosing to be comfortable with herself as she is. Thus interaction with others is influenced by their interpretation of her appearance. At the individual level, women's understanding of themselves is filtered through the existing social structures. Women know that they may be afforded more attention and respect if they follow the ideal;[1] they may also have internalized the societal standards throughout their lives. Thus, not "measuring up" to the ideal may cause personal anguish.

Women's decisions to diet are bound up with several levels of gender and must be considered in this light. The three levels of gender may be complementary or contradictory. That is, while people all live in a social world that appears to appreciate and promote only one body type, individual micro structures or individual gender role orientations may be in agreement or at odds with this standard. Women may be surrounded by people who disregard the cultural ideal and thus feel less pressure to conform in their interactions. They may have developed a critical stance to the societal ideal and experience no internal misgivings about weight and appearance. Or they may experience pressure on all three levels to follow the ideal. Clearly, in order to understand women's relationships to food and diet it is insufficient to focus on only one level. Women's social contexts and their individual gender role orientations are unique and must be considered as such.

Adolescence compounds the imperatives of the gender system. While all people feel the effects of the gender systems in which they operate, adolescents face unique challenges; adolescence is (1) a time of identity construction and (2) a time to find one's own location in the social world. They must navigate their ways through the layers of gender, making their choices and moderating their behaviours based on the context in which they live. And because individuals in this age group do not necessarily have a strong gender role orientation guiding their choices and actions, they are more vulnerable to the influences of the micro and macro gender structures. Also, because they have moved into a new "adolescent world," they can no longer rely on the "borrowed identity" from their childhood or the social status of their families. They must construct a unique self and establish their own position within the social world. This new self will largely be based on measures of status determined by peer groups and the broader youth culture.

Scholars and clinicians have developed a body of literature which discusses adolescent experience in great detail. We can trace study in this area back to Erikson's theory of stages. He argued that adolescence is a time of identity construction (Erikson, 1956). Until adolescence, identity is acquired through the family; individuals are socialized to see themselves much as the family sees them. In childhood, attitudes, values, and definitions are accepted uncritically. During adolescence, the earlier "borrowed" identity is questioned. Individuals ask themselves whether they agree with what they have been told, what they have learned. While reconstructing themselves, adolescents rely less on families (who played an important role in defining their childhood selves) and, in an effort to become independent and autonomous, turn towards their peers and societal standards. Part of this identity construction is, of course, the gender role orientation. Not just "who am I?" but "who am I as a woman?" "What does this involve?" "How should I act? think?" By the time these girls become adults, most have developed a sense of who they are as women. Therefore, when they are confronted with external stressors—for example, pressure from conflicts among individual, micro, and macro levels of the gender system—they have an internal sense of self that provides direction, which is lacking during early adolescence.

During adolescence, peers play a critical role. They are all experiencing similar changes, though at varying paces. By observing each other, they gain a sense of what is considered desirable and appropriate. While they observe, they are painfully aware that they are also being observed. The "imaginary audience" hypothesis suggests that adolescents are so sensitive to the evaluation/judgement of others that they perceive an audience, and behave accordingly, even when they are not being observed (Elkind & Bowen, 1979). As each adolescent is looking at others she is gathering the "raw resources" to shape her "self." Seltzer calls this the "comparative act" (Seltzer, 1989). Through the evaluation and critique and assessment of peers as well as imitation and experimentation, an adolescent gains the materials necessary to construct her "self." The knowledge that one is both judging and being judged makes adolescents highly conscious of their social desirability. Seltzer describes the adolescent world as the "peer arena," the micro structure where identity is constructed.

A further aspect of adolescence is finding one's location; that is, answering the question "where do I fit in?" This clearly is associated with the "social desirability" mentioned above. Just as the adult society is stratified—around class, race, and gender, for example—and one gains social power through position based on resources, the adolescent world is also hierarchical and also involves social power. The young person must find his or her place in this social structure. The social class from which the adolescent has come is still prevalent, but it is not sufficient to define who has power in the peer arena, because it is based on the parent's resources and not on the adolescent's own characteristics. So the hierarchy among adolescents is based largely on personal resources. Because a significant part of constructing the self at this point is coming to understand gender role orientation and sexuality, the adolescent hierarchy is based in large part on one's presentation of manhood or womanhood. That is to say, the more "manly" men, displaying evidence of the strength, courage, and competence stereotypically expected of males, are considered more desirable than others. And among women, appearance and desirability are key attributes.

The powerful effect of the peer arena determines where any individual will fit in the social world. And in this arena, status is linked to appearance. Do you look the part? Or, as important, are you "playing" the part by dieting and making appearance a key part of your conversations and social world? Drawing messages from the larger macro gender structure, peers set the rules for "fitting in." And the unstable aspect of individual adolescents' own sense of self and their incomplete individual gender role orientation makes withstanding the pressure to conform difficult. By later adolescence, the tendency to conform is reduced (Berndt, 1979); individuals are more sure of themselves, have established their identities and gender role orientations, and may be, therefore, less vulnerable to the pressures of the micro and macro structures.

THIS STUDY

We undertook a qualitative research project in the summer of 1997 in Southern Alberta entitled "Growing Up Female." Through 25 depth interviews and focus groups with 6 girls, we explored adolescents' own perceptions of the challenges they face and how they navigate through the peer arena. The analysis was based on the principles of grounded theory (Glaser & Strauss, 1967; Strauss, 1987). That is, rather than trying to verify a specific hypothesis, we attempted to see their world as adolescents see it and discover how the three levels of the sex/gender system interact in their lives. From listening to the girls, reviewing the tapes, and examining transcripts, patterns emerged. The patterns were then explored more fully in subsequent interviews. The goal was not to quantify, but rather to get a sense of the importance of conforming to appearance norms within the adolescent social hierarchy.

The study began with a "typical" sample of young women chosen to represent different ages, social classes, and family arrangements. We quickly came to recognize that one's location in the hierarchy—insider, outsider, popular, outcast, etc.—was a critical variable and that the sample needed to reflect this diversity as well. (The girls' location in the hierarchy was also seen to influence them in terms of vulnerability to outside pressure and suggestion, but not in the ways one might predict.) The girls interviewed were from junior high, high school (one of whom attended an all girl's high school), post-secondary institutions, and "drop outs" (many of whom had moved to alternative schools).

The importance of qualitative studies is that they can answer the question "why?" While quantitative studies can measure patterns to determine how many suffer from eating disorders and/or depression, and can assess the correlation [among] class, race, family and behaviour numerically, one must look deeper to understand the underlying causal connection between these behaviours and the social factors in the girls' lives. One must try to understand their social world as they define and live it. It is vital for the researchers to avoid directing the discussions so as not to artificially focus on "constraints." Questions about what boys do to them or what society does to them denies the agency of the young women. Instead, this study asked the girls what they did to get along in their world. What are the rules in their world? Where did the rules come from?

Once we had collected information from all of the respondents, we identified patterns and came to understand how fully social hierarchy, and therefore social power, influenced their lives and

how salient appearance is within that hierarchy. The best way to convey these findings is through case studies. In the following section, I will present the cases of women located in each of the various positions in the adolescent hierarchy, allowing each to speak about where they fit and how they came to hold that position. (Obviously, names have been changed but other details are unaltered.)

FINDINGS

Not surprisingly, the study indicates that for adolescent girls, appearance is salient and notions about what is a desirable appearance are influenced by cultural norms: the macro structure provides powerful images and pressures. However, the girls made it clear that they were not all victims blindly following a goal set by the larger society without thought. And not all were dissatisfied with their appearances—not even all of those who spent a considerable amount of time and energy complaining about themselves and dieting. As they explained, appearance equals status. "Life would be easier if you looked like that [like the women on *Melrose Place*] because people give you an easier time if you are pretty. If more guys like you, the girls give you an easier time,…I don't think it should be that way, but I think society puts a lot of importance on your looks and size." And dieting and "fat" talk are also linked to status. The girls say they hate their bodies, or themselves, but when they discuss it more fully they often acknowledge that these statements are a means of fitting in.[2] They see that being part of the group means "obsessing" about their bodies, and group membership leads to success and social power. Those who fit the appearance criteria belong to the elite group, have power, know they have it, and enjoy wielding it. They reinforce their own position by deliberately making others feel inadequate. In fact, the power that they gain from their elite status is the power to exclude others. Their actions enhance their own positions while making appearance more salient for all girls (that is, making the micro structure extremely appearance-based).

The findings indicate that the most difficult time for young women was during junior high school, sooner than most people would like to believe is the case. Why should twelve-year-olds be caught up in issues about body and appearance? Are they trying to attract boys or men? Not really. They perceive other girls as both their audience and their harshest critics. Therefore, their preoccupation with weight and body is not about being desirable to the boys so much as gaining acceptance within the hierarchy. Boys can certainly exacerbate the pressure through name-calling and harassment, but this is only one part of the larger issue: finding your place in the social world is based on playing a role and looking the part. Even girls who attended "all girl schools" were subject to appearance pressures.

By later adolescence, women have already begun to develop a stronger sense of self and [have] grown less vulnerable to the group's definition of who they are. By the end of high school, most girls had worked through much of their confusion and vulnerability. While they continued to talk about dieting and eating, about shape and size, this was much less about really planning to change their physical appearance than about "playing the game." Those who wanted to fit into the social hierarchy recognized that playing by these rules was necessary. However, by this stage, many girls had found their own groups of friends and set their own goals and challenges; they felt freer [to] express their own gender role orientations rather than following the group's definition of "woman."[3]

But in early adolescence, in junior high, most girls are just beginning the process of becoming independent and autonomous. There is a shift from living with the self-image that your parents and family defined for you to finding your "own" self with the assistance of peers. The peers' opin-

ions count for a great deal because they form the social world in which this new self must establish herself. This is for most girls the period of most intense pressure to be autonomous and independent, greatest confusion about self, and therefore greatest vulnerability. And in this setting, young adolescent girls are becoming themselves, adults, and "women."

As indicated, most of the girls had worked through and beyond this understanding that their self worth and status as women was tied to appearance by the time they reached the end of high school. But some girls did not get past this stage as easily as others. They continued to measure themselves by their appearance.

The Elite Group

The first group of those who had trouble moving beyond the adolescent definitions of desirability is made up of girls who were popular in junior high and high school; they were at the top of the social hierarchy. They seemed to be the winners who enjoyed the power that accompanied their status. They basked in the attention of all: other girls, boys, and most teachers. Two of the respondents talked about their experiences at the top of this hierarchy.

Jillian said that she is so good at being part of the group that she has no very clear sense of who she is. While in high school she knew exactly where she belonged. "I was definitely one of the popular ones." She said bluntly, "I consider myself to be pretty, that might have something to do with it [her popularity]. All my friends were popular." In fact, she revelled in the attention she received. She was teased by the boys about her looks ("I have big boobs") but found this flattering rather than intimidating or threatening. Being a part of the elite group was not a problem while in the insulated world of the high school, but she feels completely lost since leaving school. She found that the attributes that had given her power were no longer as valuable and she had no sense of direction. Jillian had allowed herself to be defined by the micro structure of her peer group and did not develop her own identity. She adopted the norms of the group without truly developing her own gender role orientation. Now that she has moved into a new environment, and without the guidance of her own individual gender role orientation, she feels aimless. "Where I stand now I'm not going anywhere. I'm not moving forward, I'm not moving backward, I'm just not going anywhere."

Reva was also very popular in high school, but [she] recognized even at the time that this popularity had no solid foundation. She tried to hang on to status and popularity via appearance but was constantly concerned about it. "I was insecure but I don't know if other people knew it." She was unsure of her "self" and her true desirability. She recognized that popularity in high school was all about "material things, the way things look, everything on the outside." And she knew that she and her friends maintained their position by belittling others: "I think we were back stabbers and snobby, pretty snobby." But at the time this seemed reasonable. Having a boyfriend was an affirmation of Reva's status and her desirability. When she and her boyfriend broke up, she believed that she need only lose weight to regain her social position. "Actually, there were a couple of us that wanted to like, starve ourselves, try to lose weight so we just wouldn't eat." As a result, she developed an eating disorder. Eventually, she went into counselling and slowly has come to recognize the damage that her bulimia caused. But at the time, being thin made sense and gaining even a little bit of weight "really stressed me out."

Being in the elite group is no guarantee of success or well-being. While it worked for some in the short-term because they really did attain power—the power to exclude others—it did not bring long-term contentment. Upon graduation, the micro structure which had given girls power and a valued position was disbanded, leaving them directionless. Even within high school, all

was not well. While this group appeared to dictate what was the appropriate appearance around the school, this was often a reflection of media images. "Popular" respondents mentioned TV shows and magazines that influenced their "style." And maintaining their social position involved a constant effort to keep up with the cultural ideal. For some this seemed easy, but for others like Reva, it was both difficult and undermining.

The "Wannabes"

While this seems like a pejorative term, it's how these girls describe themselves. They believe they will be in the most popular group if they just make a few changes; as a result, they spend their adolescent years struggling to reach the top of the pyramid. Kim is a member of this group. She says she understands the hierarchy and knows how it works: "The pressure increases as you move towards the popular group. You always have to prove yourself—based on how you look." She also knows that she is very close to the top and believes she could get there if she could just play the game right. And despite acknowledging that being popular doesn't always allow you to be a good person—"Popular people are jerks, they don't care about others, are very competitive, and treat people badly"—this doesn't stop her from wanting to be one of them. She works hard to win favour, to accept the rules. She believes that she could be popular if she was just a bit thinner. People in her group tend to diet for real, thinking they are just ten pounds away from having social power. She said the whole group began smoking on the same day when one person found out that it suppressed appetite. "We always talked about weight and how to lose it—drink Slimfast, take Dexatrim." Expending so much energy on reaching the top of the social hierarchy means that Kim spends little time trying to find her own direction or "self." She just knows she isn't happy. She feels "insecure, always beating myself up" and says "trying to fit in is limiting." She does not have a strong sense of self and therefore accepts the peer arena as the ultimate arbiter. The unquestioning acceptance of the peer arena and of the validity of the social hierarchy leaves people in this group, like those in the group "above" them on the popularity scale, vulnerable to a gender system which focuses on appearance. Their gender role orientation reflects this desire to achieve the ideal appearance: being a woman means looking the part.

Life in the Middle

The girls on the next level "down" on the hierarchical scale are the least vulnerable. While girls in this group still cope with pressure in the peer arena, they know they will never be at the top. As a result, they tend to examine it more critically, asking whether increased popularity is worth achieving. The answer is usually no. These girls form their own rules, have outside interests, and define "self" by a standard other than that of the hierarchy. One result of this alternate definition of self is that appearance is less salient than ability.

The individuals in this group often have outside interests—music, sports, religion, or the guiding movement, for example—that seem to help them find a self worth regardless of their status at school. And at school they either are not picked on or don't let it bother them because they know that it isn't real. They construct their "self" based on what they are, not on what someone tells them they should be. Jana is never going to be at the top of the social hierarchy; she knows it and doesn't care. Her parents are of different races and she perceives that being biracial makes her "different." But it isn't a problem for her, she says, she just has to find her own way. When listening to Jana, she convinces you that this makes her stronger. She sees other "kids who try their hardest to be like another person and follow what they do" but distinguishes herself. She says unequivocally, "I am who I am." Racial slurs don't bother her, she makes a joke of it. When her best friend goes on and on about being fat, Jana believes "she

does it just for attention." She isn't affected by media images either: "I'm not saying they're not beautiful but I'm saying that you don't know what's under all that make-up, that's four hours of make-up put on. I could look like that too." In essence, Jana isn't caught up in the gender system because she is not trying to prove herself in the peer arena. She has a strong sense of self and does not accept the salience of appearance. However, she also notes that "I've never gotten fat so it has never been an issue for me." She can be truly comfortable with herself even when others in her world are striving to attain an ideal.

Una is also in this middle group. She is involved in both music and sports and spends much of her time with these activities. She says, "there's no pressure in my group. We don't have to spend time on make-up and hair." They don't want to be skinny partly because "the coach encourages us to stay fit." "I just don't have the time or the money to keep up." But she does acknowledge that it was harder to "be yourself" in junior high: "People were starting to form groups and you were left out if you didn't follow the group." But her close circle of friends didn't value the "popular" behaviours and didn't try to look the part.

Freedom from the tyranny of the gender system—which offers an almost impossible beauty standard—seems much more attainable for these young women. Because they do not have an opportunity to join the elite group, and because they have other qualities which make them strong, they are less vulnerable to its dictates. Not being part of the "in" crowd enables them to critique the hierarchy and its norms. In essence, these girls have developed gender role orientations which conflict with the macro structure and most of them have found a group of peers who also reject the salience of appearance.

On The Fringe

The next group—the "lowest" on the scale I have identified—is that of individuals who define themselves as "outsiders." They believe they are excluded because of their size and shape (though some of them have other characteristics which also contribute to their exclusion). These girls don't have the ability to break out of the outsider role into which they have been cast. For adolescents in this group, not fitting in really hurts; they feel rejected, ridiculed, isolated. Because they are so far from the norm—often very overweight or dealing with severe acne—they feel that they are suffering at the hands of their peers.

Some do come to hate themselves because they are treated so cruelly. Rachel describes one hurtful experience[:] "I was trying to walk through the crowd when one guy said 'R, you don't belong in this crowd.' There was another girl who told me to f— off. I was watching them I guess. I was pretty shy too. But I think *it* made me shy[.]" The "it" she refers to is being excluding for not looking the "right" way. She feels very alone, even though there are several other girls on the "outside." She now "rejects the image thing" because she knows she doesn't fit ("I'm big boned like my dad") but she tried really hard in junior high. She really hated herself, even though she believed she was good on the inside, because of the way she was treated, because her body was devalued. In fact, Rachel feels pressure from her family to try harder to fit in—her mom would like her to change her appearance but she says she "just gave up trying."

Terry was also on the outside because of her weight. She had a couple of close friends "but the rest just left me out." Unlike Rachel, though, she "successfully" lost weight and reaped the rewards of following the group standard. She wanted to be small no matter what and simply stopped eating. At first everyone was pleased. She got more attention at school. People noticed her and talked to her. Initially, Terry liked being popular. "I felt better for a while but then came to realize that my life still sucked. Even when I was skinny I wasn't happy." She came to hate being popular because she could see more clearly than most how artificial the distinction was. Terry believes being skinny actually made her feel worse because the "popular Terry" wasn't the "real Terry." Her peers only saw her outside and still didn't recognize her true worth. Her family and few close friends became worried and did not support her dieting. And "I got tired of measuring every mouthful, having everyone watching and measuring every mouthful, so I started eating again." She gained the weight back and is now more comfortable with herself. "A whole new world opened up when I left school." Both Terry and Rachel understood how the social hierarchy worked. They knew how to gain power by following the mandate of the peer group. But they both chose not to. They lost status within the micro structure but grew more comfortable with themselves.

Karla was in a similar situation and it was terribly damaging. She started out in the popular group but "I found you had to stoop quite low to become popular. You had to be willing to be rude to all the other people." She wanted to be friendly to everyone and eventually the popular crowd turned their backs on her. They began to harass her and single her out; most of the insults were based on her appearance. "After a while, when so many people tell you something, you know you start to believe it's true, like you get it from enough people it starts to seem true, so I got enough people telling me I was ugly enough times, it kind of makes you believe it." Eventually she quit school because it became unbearable. She'd like to go back but "it's hard to get started up again if you live in the same place and you stay in the same place because everyone knows your past.... I can't start over again because the people who knew me, knew me as a geek, a freak." She feels better about herself now but doesn't want to face that kind of pressure again.

Examining the fringe group in terms of the three levels of gender, the "hell" for these girls was the micro gender structure of the peer arena;

however, the values of the microsystem seemed to be reinforced—though not caused—by the larger macro structure. Our society is far more conscious of racism and sexism than of "look-ism," especially as it is manifested in the adolescent world. Rachel and Karla internalized the negative messages directed at them by their peers. And they both came to hate themselves. Fortunately, they also both were able to overcome those feelings and recognize that their value was determined neither by their appearance nor by the critics in the peer arena.

IMPLICATIONS

Why is appearance so salient for adolescent girls? This study reinforces the understanding that at this period in her life, a girl has few measuring sticks and no long list of personal accomplishments. She must seek some means of reassuring herself that she is becoming an adult, a woman, an individual separate from her earlier, family-defined self. The larger macro gender structure of fashion magazines and advertisement sends messages that appearance is an important feature of power and desirability. This notion is adopted by adolescent girls in part because it is a field over which many feel they have some control (however illusory such a perception might be). They think that they can change their bodies, their clothing, their hairstyles. And they recognize that a specific kind of beauty is valued by the society at large. Thus appearance becomes a standard. This means that appearance actually does serve as a means of attaining social acceptability and power within the peer arena. As the study revealed, becoming a woman has less to do with the role one might play and more to do with the body. An interesting—perhaps startling—paradox emerged when we asked the respondents to define "woman." On the one hand, being a woman, they said, does not constrain career choices. They believe women can become

anything they want. As available "sexual" roles grow, women are not defined by filling a specific role—for example, wife or mother. And as they perceive that more and more options are available in the work world, no particular job defines "woman." On the other hand, something distinguishes women from men. And that something is appearance. It is the girl's body that makes her a woman. Therefore, being a woman means one should be preoccupied with one's body and making one's body fit the part. None of the girls we spoke to was trying to diet to avoid growing up into womanhood; indeed, they were dieting to *achieve* womanhood, which they have come to accept is characterized by a very particular physical stature.

Young women are not all passive recipients of society's messages about the body. They perceive that they are not victims, that they are not trying to achieve certain appearances because men or boys want them to. Instead, they see themselves as actively involved in struggles with other women. Their female peers are the harshest critics. Among these critics, appearance brings social power, even if it is only the power to exclude others. They want the right body in order to attain social power and to prove themselves as women. Having a "boyfriend" is important in part because it sends a message to the peer arena that one has successfully achieved the requisite look. This becomes part of the measuring stick.

When the three levels of the gender system—the individual, micro, and macro levels—all agree that appearance is salient, the girl who experiences this will strive to attain the beauty standard. She believes that achieving this look will bring her social acceptance and membership into the elite group. If she fails to measure up to the standard, she faces the painful realization that she will be devalued by those with power in the peer arena. However, if she also learns that the imperatives of the peer arena are not absolute, and she is able to develop her own gender role orientation, then appearance loses its salience, and the elite group loses its power over her. If the three levels do not all agree, if girls have developed gender role orientations which do not incorporate the societal beauty ideal, or they belong to micro structures (as adolescents, perhaps a group of friends, sports team, or social club apart from the school-based peer arena) which value ability rather than appearance, then they are less subject to the appearance standards.

While adolescent girls face an exaggerated version of the gender system, all women are subject to the same forces. We must find our way within a societal landscape that valorizes beauty often above ability. And frequently we must do so in micro structures (in the work place and in our homes) which adopt this standard and devalue our actions. Like these adolescent girls, we remain strong if we develop gender role orientations which do not centre around appearance, and if we foster relationships and micro structures which value women for their strength and skill rather than their outward appearance. The results of this study are suggestive—not yet detailed enough or broad enough to be conclusive—but give us some insight into girls' own perceptions of their world and perhaps into the roots of gender role uncertainty that continues for some women into adulthood.

NOTES

1. Obviously, this is a generalization. An important point of this argument is that individual women—especially adult women—move in microstructures and have developed "selves" that allow them to function effectively in a way inconsistent with the "body beautiful" standards…society.
2. This is not to say that…[none of the] girls…experience[d] genuine pain and self-hatred—their situations will be explored more fully in subsequent sections. It does mean that many girls are not as negative about themselves as it might appear from listening to their conversations among their peers.
3. It is possible that for university women, living in dormitories, food, eating, and weight once again become salient as a new social hierarchy must be established. While this was not investigated in this study, we are currently interviewing women in residences to see if the pattern re-emerges.

REFERENCES

Bem, S. 1993. *The lenses of gender.* New Haven: Yale University Press.

Berger, P., and B. Berger. 1975. *Sociology: A biographical approach.* New York: Basic Books.

Berndt, T. 1979. Developmental changes in conformity to peers and parents. *Developmental Psychology,* 15: 606–16.

Bordo, S. 1993. *Unbearable weight: Feminism, western culture and the body.* Los Angeles: University of California Press.

Brownmiller, S. 1984. *Femininity.* New York: Linden Press.

Brumberg, J. 1997. *The body project: An intimate history of American girls.* New York: Random House.

Chernin, K. 1981. *The obsession: Reflections on the tyranny of slenderness.* New York: Harper and Row.

Elkind, D., and Bowen. 1979. Imaginary audience behaviour in children and adults. *Developmental Psychology,* 15: 33–44.

Erikson, E. 1956. The problem of ego identity. *Journal of the American Psychoanalytic Association,* 4: 56–121.

Freedman, R. 1986. *Beauty bound.* Lexington, Mass.: D.C. Heath and Company.

Glaser, B., and A. Strauss. 1967. *Am I thin enough yet?: The cult of thinness and the commercialization of identity.* New York: Oxford University Press.

Greer, G. 1970. *The female eunuch.* London: MacGibbon & Kee.

Hesse-Biber, S. 1996. *Am I thin enough yet? The cult of thinness and the commercialization of identity.* New York: Oxford University Press.

Matthews, B. 1997. *The gender system and fertility: An examination of the hidden links.* Population Studies Centre: Working Paper.

Matthews, B., and R. Beaujot. 1997. Gender orientations and fertility strategies. *Canadian Review of Sociology and Anthropology,* 34(4): 415–28.

Pipher, M. 1996. *Reviving Ophelia: Saving the selves of adolescent girls.* New York: Ballantine Books.

Risman, B., and P. Schwartz. 1989. *Gender in intimate relationships: A microstructural approach.* Belmont: Wadsworth Publishing Co.

Seltzer, V. 1989. *The psychosocial worlds of the adolescent: Public and private.* New York: John Wiley and Sons.

Shute, J. 1992. *Life size.* New York: Avon Books.

Smith, D. 1987. *The everyday world as problematic: A feminist sociology.* Toronto: University of Toronto Press.

Strauss, A. 1987. *Qualitative analysis for social scientists.* New York: Cambridge University Press.

Stryker, S. 1980. *Symbolic interactionism: A social structural version.* Menlo Park: Benjamin Cummings Publishing.

Wolf, N. 1991. *The beauty myth.* New York: Morrow Books.

Part VII

Groups and Organizations

15

The Characteristics of Bureaucracy

Max Weber

Modern officialdom functions in the following specific manner:

I. There is the principle of fixed and official jurisdictional areas, which are generally ordered by rules, that is, by laws or administrative regulations. (1) The regular activities required for the purposes of the bureaucratically governed structure are distributed in a fixed way as official duties. (2) The authority to give the commands required for the discharge of these duties is distributed in a stable way and is strictly delimited by rules concerning the coercive means, physical, sacerdotal, or otherwise, which may be placed at the disposal of officials. (3) Methodical provision is made for the regular and continuous fulfillment of these duties and for the execution of the corresponding rights; only persons who have the generally regulated qualifications to serve are employed.

Source: From *Max Weber: Essays in Sociology,* by Max Weber, ed. H. H. Gerth and C. Wright Mills. Copyright ©1946 by Max Weber. Used by permission of Oxford University Press, Inc.

In public and lawful government these three elements constitute "bureaucratic authority." In private economic domination, they constitute bureaucratic "management." Bureaucracy, thus understood, is fully developed in political and ecclesiastical communities only in the modern state, and, in the private economy, only in the most advanced institutions of capitalism. Permanent and public office authority, with fixed jurisdiction, is not the historical rule but rather the exception. This is so even in large political structures such as those of the ancient Orient, the Germanic, and Mongolian empires of conquest, or of many feudal structures of state. In all these cases, the ruler executes the most important measures through personal trustees, table-companions, or court-servants. Their commissions and authority are not precisely delimited and are temporarily called into being for each case.

II. The principles of office hierarchy and of levels of graded authority mean a firmly ordered system of super- and subordination in which there is a supervision of the lower offices by the higher ones. Such a system offers the governed the possibility of appealing the decision of a lower office to its higher authority, in a definitely regulated manner. With the full development of the bureaucratic type, the office hierarchy is monocratically organized. The principle of hierarchical office authority is found in all bureaucratic structures: in state and ecclesiastical structures as well as in large party organizations and private enterprises. It does not matter for the character of bureaucracy whether its authority is called "private" or "public."

When the principle of jurisdictional "competency" is fully carried through, hierarchical subordination—at least in public office—does not mean that the "higher" authority is simply authorized to take over the business of the "lower." Indeed, the opposite is the rule. Once established and having fulfilled its task, an office tends to continue in existence and be held by another incumbent.

III. The management of the modern office is based upon written documents ("the files"), which are preserved in their original or draft form. There is, therefore, a staff of subaltern officials and scribes of all sorts. The body of officials actively engaged in a "public" office, along with the respective apparatus of material implements and the files, make up a "bureau." In private enterprise, "the bureau" is often called "the office."

In principle, the modern organization of the civil service separates the bureau from the private domicile of the official, and, in general, bureaucracy segregates official activity as something distinct from the sphere of private life. Public monies and equipment are divorced from the private property of the official.... In principle, the executive office is separated from the household, business from private correspondence, and business assets from private fortunes. The more consistently the modern type of business management has been carried through, the more are these separations the case. The beginnings of this process are to be found as early as the Middle Ages.

It is the peculiarity of the modern entrepreneur that he conducts himself as the "first official" of his enterprise, in the very same way in which the ruler of a specifically modern bureaucratic state spoke of himself as "the first servant" of the state. The idea that the bureau activities of the state are intrinsically different in character from the management of private economic offices is a continental European notion and, by the way of contrast, is totally foreign to the American way.

IV. Office management, at least all specialized office management—and such management is distinctly modern—usually presupposes a thorough and expert training. This increasingly holds for the modern executive and employee of private enterprises, in the same manner as it holds for the state official.

V. When the office is fully developed, official activity demands the full working capacity of the official, irrespective of the fact that his obligatory time in the bureau may be firmly delimited. In the normal case, this is only the product of a long development, in the public as well as in the private office. Formerly, in all cases, the normal state of affairs was reversed: Official business was discharged as a secondary activity.

VI. The management of the office follows general rules, which are more or less stable, more or less exhaustive, and which can be learned. Knowledge of these rules represents a special technical learning which the officials possess. It involves jurisprudence, or administrative or business management.

The reduction of modern office management to rules is deeply embedded in its very nature. The theory of modern public administration, for instance, assumes that the authority to order certain matters by decree—which has been legally granted to public authorities—does not entitle the bureau to regulate the matter by commands given for each case, but only to regulate the matter abstractly. This stands in extreme contrast to the regulation of all relationships through individual privileges and bestowals of favor, which is absolutely domi-nant in patrimonialism, at least insofar as such relationships are not fixed by sacred tradition.

All this results in the following for the internal and external position of the official.

I. Office holding is a "vocation." This is shown, first, in the requirement of a firmly prescribed course of training, which demands the entire capacity for work for a long period of time, and in the generally prescribed and special exam-inations which are prerequisites of employment. Furthermore, the position of the official is in the nature of a duty. This determines the internal structure of his relations, in the following manner: Legally and actually, office holding is not considered a source to be exploited for rents or emoluments, as was normally the case during the Middle Ages and frequently up to the thresh-old of recent times.... Entrances into an office, including one in the private economy, is consid-ered an acceptance of a specific obligation of faithful management in return for a secure exist-ence. It is decisive for the specific nature of modern loyalty to an office that, in the pure type, it does not establish a relationship to a *person,* like the vassal's or disciple's faith in feudal or in patrimonial relations and authority. Modern loyalty is devoted to impersonal and functional purposes....

II. The personal position of the official is patterned in the following way:

(1) Whether he is in a private office or a public bureau, the modern official always strives and usually enjoys a distinct *social esteem* as compared with the governed. His social position is guaranteed by the prescriptive rules of rank order and, for the political official, by special definitions of the criminal code against "insults of officials" and "contempt" of state and church authorities.

The actual social position of the official is normally highest where, as in old civilized countries, the following conditions prevail: a strong demand for administration by trained experts; a strong and stable social differentia-tion, where the official predominantly derives

from socially and economically privileged strata because of the social distribution of power; or where the costliness of the required training and status conventions are binding upon him. The possession of educational certificates—to be discussed elsewhere—are usually linked with qualification for office. Naturally, such certifi-cates or patents enhance the "status element" in the social position of the official....

Usually the social esteem of the officials as such is especially low where the demand for expert administration and the dominance of status conventions are weak. This is especially the case in the United States; it is often the case in new settlements by virtue of their wide fields for profit-taking and the great instability of their social stratification.

(2) The pure type of bureaucratic official is *appointed* by a superior authority. An official elected by the governed is not a purely bureau-cratic figure. Of course, the formal existence of an election does not by itself mean that no appointment hides behind the election—in the state, especially, appointment by party chiefs. Whether or not this is the case does not depend upon legal statutes but upon the way in which the party mechanism functions. Once firmly organ-ized, the parties can turn a formally free election into the mere acclamation of a candidate desig-nated by the party chief. As a rule, however, a formally free election is turned into a fight, conducted according to definite rules, for votes in favor of one of two designated candidates....

(3) Normally, the position of the official is held for life, at least in public bureaucracies; and this is increasingly the case for all similar structures. As a factual rule, *tenure for life* is presupposed, even where the giving of notice or periodic reappoint-ment occurs. In contrast to the worker in a private enterprise, the official normally holds tenure. Legal or actual life-tenure, however, is not recognized as the official's right to the possession of office, as was the case with many structures of authority in the past. Where legal guarantees against arbitrary dismissal of transfer are

developed, they merely serve to guarantee a strictly objective discharge of specific office duties free from all personal considerations....

(4) The official receives the regular *pecuniary* compensation of a normally fixed *salary* and the old age security provided by a pension. The salary is not measured like a wage in terms of work done, but according to "status," that is, according to the kind of function (the "rank") and, in addition, possibly, according to the length of service. The relatively great security of the official's income, as well as the rewards of social esteem, make the office a sought-after position....

(5) The official is set for a *"career"* within the hierarchical order of the public service. He moves from the lower, less important, and lower paid to the higher positions. The average official naturally desires a mechanical fixing of the conditions of promotion: if not of the offices, at least of the salary levels. He wants these conditions fixed in terms of "seniority," or possibly according to grades achieved in a developed system of expert examinations....

16

McJobs: McDonaldization and the Workplace

George Ritzer

In recent years the spread of McDonaldized systems has led to the creation of an enormous number of jobs. Unfortunately, the majority of them can be thought of as McDonaldized jobs, or "McJobs." While we usually associate these types of positions with fast-food restaurants, and in fact there are many such jobs in that setting (over 2.5 million people worked in that industry in the United States in 1992 [Van Giezen, 1994]), McJobs have spread throughout much of the economy with the growing impact of McDonaldization on work settings which had previously experienced relatively little rationalization.

It is worth outlining some of the basic realities of employment in the fast-food industry in the United States since those jobs serve as a model for employment in other McDonaldized settings (Van Giezen, 1994). The large number of people employed in fast-food restaurants accounts for over 40 percent of the approximately 6 million people employed in restaurants of all types. Fast-food restaurants rely heavily on teenage employees—almost 70 percent of their employees are twenty years of age or younger. For many, the fast-food restaurant is likely to be their first employer. It is estimated that the first job for one of every fifteen workers was at McDonald's; one of every eight Americans has worked at McDonald's at some time in his or her life. The vast majority of employees are part-time workers: The average work week in the fast-food industry is 29.5 hours. There is a high turnover rate: Only slightly more than half the employees remain on the job for a year or more. Minorities are over-represented in these jobs—almost two-thirds of employees are women and nearly a quarter are non-white. These are low-paid occupations, with many earning the minimum wage, or slightly more. As a result, these jobs are greatly affected by changes in the minimum wage: An upward

Source: Reprinted by permission of Sage Publications Ltd. from George Ritzer, *The McDonaldization Thesis: Explorations and Extensions*, copyright © 1998 Sage Publications.

revision has an important effect on the income of these workers. However, there is a real danger that many workers would lose their positions as a result of such increases, especially in economically marginal fast-food restaurants.[1]

Although the McDonaldization of society is manifest at all levels and in all realms of the social world, the work world has played a particularly pivotal role in this. On the one hand, it is the main source of many of the precursors of McDonaldization, including bureaucracies, scientific management, assembly lines, and so on. More contemporaneously, the kinds of jobs, work procedures, and organizing principles that have made McDonald's so successful have affected the way in which many businesses now organize much of their work. In fact, it could well be argued that the primary root of the McDonaldization of the larger society is the work world. On the other hand, the McDonaldization of the larger society has, in turn, served to further rationalize the work world. We thus have a self-reinforcing and enriching process that is speeding the growth and spread of McDonaldization.

The process of McDonaldization is leading to the creation of more and more McJobs.[2] The service sector, especially at its lower end, is producing an enormous number of jobs, most of them requiring little or no skill. There is no better example of this than the mountain of jobs being produced by the fast-food industry. However, new occupational creation is not the only source of McJobs: Many extant low-level jobs are being McDonaldized. More strikingly, large numbers of middle-level jobs are also being deskilled and transformed into McJobs.

McJobs are characterized by the five dimensions of McDonaldization. The jobs tend to involve a series of simple tasks in which the emphasis is on performing each as efficiently as possible. Second, the time associated with many of the tasks is carefully calculated and the emphasis on the quantity of time a task should take tends to diminish the quality of the work from the point of view of the worker. That is, tasks are so simplified

and streamlined that they provide little or no meaning to the worker. Third, the work is predictable: employees do and say essentially the same things hour after hour, day after day. Fourth, many nonhuman technologies are employed to control workers and reduce them to robotlike actions. Some technologies are in place, and others are in development, that will lead to the eventual replacement of many of these "human robots" with computerized robots. Finally, the rationalized McJobs lead to a variety of irrationalities, especially the dehumanization of work. The result is the extraordinarily high turnover rate described above and difficulty in maintaining an adequate supply of replacements.[3]

The claim is usually made by spokespeople for McDonaldized systems that they are offering a large number of entry-level positions that help give employees basic skills they will need in order to move up the occupational ladder within such systems (and many of them do). This is likely to be true in the instances in which the middle-level jobs to which they move—for example shift leader, assistant manager, or manager of a fast-food restaurant—are also routinized and scripted. In fact, it turns out that this even holds for the positions held by the routinized and scripted instructors at [McDonald's training program at] Hamburger University who teach the managers, who teach the employees, and so on. However, the skills acquired in McJobs are not likely to prepare one for, help one to acquire, or help one to function well in, the far more desirable postindustrial occupations which are highly complex and require high levels of skill and education. Experience in routinized actions and scripted interactions do not help much when occupations require thought and creativity....

At the cultural level, large numbers of people in the United States, and increasingly throughout much of the rest of the world, have come to value McDonaldization in general, as well as its fundamental characteristics. McDonaldization, as well as its various principles, has become part of our value system. That value system has, in turn, been translated into a series of principles that have been exported to, adopted by, and adapted to, a wide range of social settings....

...For example, the behavior of customers at fast-food restaurants is being affected in much the same way as the behavior of those who work in those restaurants....

The constraints on the behavior of employees and customers in McDonaldized systems are of both a structural and a cultural nature. Employees and customers find themselves in a variety of McDonaldized structures that demand that they behave in accord with the dictates of those structures. For example, the drive-through window associated with the fast-food restaurant (as well as other settings such as banks) structures both what customers in their cars and employees in their booths can and cannot do. They can efficiently exchange money for food, but their positions (in a car and a booth) and the press of other cars in the queue make any kind of personal interaction virtually impossible. Of course, many other kinds of behavior are either made possible, or prohibited, by such structures. In Giddens's (1984) terms, such structures are both enabling and constraining.

At a cultural level, both employees and customers are socialized into, and have internalized, the norms and values of working and living in a McDonaldized society. Employees are trained by managers or owners who are likely, themselves, to have been trained at an institution like McDonald's Hamburger University (Schaaf, 1991). Such institutions are as much concerned with inculcating norms and values as they are with the teaching of basic skills. For their part, customers are not required to attend Hamburger University, but they are "trained" by the employees themselves, by television advertisements, and by their own children who are often diligent students, teachers, and enforcers of the McDonald's way. This "training," like that of those employees who attend Hamburger University, is oriented not only to teaching the "skills" required to be a customer at a fast-food restaurant (e.g. how to queue up in order to order food), but also the norms and values

of such settings as they apply to customers (e.g. customers are expected to dispose of their own debris; they are not expected to linger after eating). As a result of such formal and informal training, both employees and customers can be relied on to do what they are supposed to, and what is expected of them, with little or no personal supervision....

...McJobs are not simply the deskilled jobs of our industrial past in new settings; they are jobs that have a variety of new and distinctive characteristics.... Industrial and McDonaldized jobs both tend to be highly routinized in terms of what people do on the job. However, one of the things that is distinctive about McDonaldized jobs, especially since so many of them involve work that requires interaction and communication, especially with consumers, is that what people *say* on the job is also highly routinized. To put this another way, McDonaldized jobs are tightly scripted: They are characterized by *both* routinized actions (for example, the way McDonald's hamburgers are to be put down on the grill and flipped [Love, 1986: 141–2]) and scripted interactions (examples include, "May I help you?"; "Would you like a dessert to go with your meal?"; "Have a nice day!"). Scripts are crucial because, as Leidner (1993) points out, many of the workers in McDonaldized systems are interactive service workers. This means that they not only produce goods and provide services, but they often do so in interaction with customers.

The scripting of interaction leads to new depths in the deskilling of workers. Not only have employee actions been deskilled; employees' ability to speak and interact with customers is now being limited and controlled. There are not only scripts to handle general situations, but also a range of subscripts to deal with a variety of contingencies. Verbal and interactive skills are being taken away from employees and built into the scripts in much the same way that manual skills were taken and built into various technologies. At one time distrusted in their ability to *do* the right thing, workers now find themselves no longer trusted to *say* the right thing. Once able to create distinctive interactive styles, and to adjust them to different circumstances, employees are now asked to follow scripts as mindlessly as possible....

One very important, but rarely noted, aspect of the labor process in the fast-food restaurant and other McDonaldized systems is the extent to which customers are being led, perhaps even almost required, to perform a number of tasks without pay that were formerly performed by paid employees. For example, in the modern gasoline station the driver now does various things for free (pumps gas, cleans windows, checks oil, even pays through a computerized credit card system built into the pump) that were formerly done by paid attendants. In these and many other settings, McDonaldization has brought the customer *into* the labor process: The customer *is* the laborer! This has several advantages for employers such as lower (even nonexistent) labor costs, the need for fewer employees, and less trouble with personnel problems: Customers are far less likely to complain about a few seconds or minutes of tedious work than employees who devote a full work day to such tasks. Because of its advantages, as well as because customers are growing accustomed to and accepting of it, I think customers are likely to become even more involved in the labor process.

This is the most revolutionary development, at least as far as the labor process is concerned, associated with McDonaldization. As a result of this dramatic change, the analysis of the labor process must be extended to what customers do in McDonaldized systems. The distinction between customer and employee is eroding, or in postmodern terms "imploding," and one can envision more and more work settings in which customers are asked to do an increasing amount of "work." More dramatically, it is also likely that we will see more work settings in which there are no employees at all! In such settings customers, in interaction with nonhuman technologies, will do *all* of the human labor. A widespread example is the ATM in which customers (and the technol-

ogy) do all of the work formerly done by bank tellers. More strikingly, we are beginning to see automated loan machines which dispense loans as high as $10,000 (Singletary, 1996). Again, customers and technologies do the work and, in the process, many loan-officer positions are eliminated. Similarly, the new automated gasoline pumps allow (or force) customers to do all of the required tasks; in some cases and at certain times (late at night) no employees at all are present.

In a sense, a key to the success of McDonaldized systems is that they have been able to supplement the exploitation of employees with the exploitation of customers. Lest we forget, Marx "put at the heart of his sociology—as no other sociology does—the theme of exploitation" (Worsley, 1982: 115). In Marxian theory, the capitalists are seen as simply paying workers less than the value produced by the workers, and as keeping the rest for themselves. This dynamic continues in contemporary society, but capitalists have learned that they can ratchet up the level of exploitation not only by exploiting workers more, but also by exploiting a whole new group of people—consumers. In Marxian terms, customers create value in the tasks they perform for McDonaldized systems. And they are not simply paid less than the value they produce, they are paid *nothing at all*. In this way, customers are exploited to an even greater degree than workers....

While no class within society is immune to McDonaldization, the lower classes are the most affected. They are the ones who are most likely to go to McDonaldized schools, live in inexpensive, mass-produced tract houses, and work in McDonaldized jobs. Those in the upper classes have much more of a chance of sending their children to non-McDonaldized schools, living in custom-built homes, and working in occupations in which they impose McDonaldization on others while avoiding it to a large degree themselves.

Also related to the social class issue...is the fact that the McDonaldization of a significant portion of the labor force does not mean that all, or even most, of the labor force is undergoing this process. In fact, the McDonaldization of some of the labor force is occurring at the same time that another large segment is moving in a postindustrial, that is, more highly skilled, direction (Hage & Powers, 1992). Being created in this sector of society are relatively high-status, well-paid occupations requiring high levels of education and training. In the main, these are far from McJobs and lack most, or all, of the dimensions discussed at the beginning of this [reading]. The growth of such postindustrial occupations parallels the concern in the labor process literature with flexible specialization occurring side by side with the deskilling of many other jobs. This points to a bifurcation in the class system. In spite of appearances, there is no contradiction here; McDonaldization and postindustrialization tend to occur in different sectors of the labor market. However, the spread of McJobs leads us to be dubious of the idea that we have moved into a new postindustrial era and have left behind the kind of deskilled jobs we associate with industrial society.

NOTES

This chapter combines a paper, "McJobs," published in Rich Feller and Garry Walz (eds.), *Career Transitions in Turbulent Times* (Greensboro, N.C.: ERIC/CASS Publications, 1996) and the Invited Plenary Address, International Labour Process Conference, Blackpool, England, April, 1995.

1. Although a study by Katz and Krueger (1992) indicates an employment *increase* accompanying a rise in the minimum wage.
2. As we will see below, other kinds of high-status, high-paying postindustrial occupations are also growing.
3. There are, of course, many other factors involved in turnover.

REFERENCES

Giddens, A. 1984. *The constitution of society: Outline of the theory of structuration*. Berkeley: University of California Press.

Hage, J., and C. H. Powers. 1992. *Post-industrial lives: Roles and relationships in the 21st century*. Newbury Park, Calif.: Sage.

Leidner, R. 1993. *Fast food, fast talk: Service work and the routinization of everyday life*. Berkeley: University of California Press.

Love, J. 1986. *McDonald's: Behind the arches*. Toronto: Bantam Books.

Schaaf, D. 1994. Inside Hamburger University. *Training*, December: 18–24.

Singletary, M. 1996. Borrowing by the touch. *Washington Post*, (30 March): C1, C2.

Van Giezen, R. W. 1994. Occupational wages in the fast-food restaurant industry. *Monthly Labor Review*, August: 24–30.

Worsley, P. 1982. *Marx and Marxism*. Chichester: Ellis Horwood.

Part VIII

Deviance

17

The Functions of Crime

Emile Durkheim

...Crime is present not only in the majority of societies of one particular species but in all societies of all types. There is no society that is not confronted with the problem of criminality. Its form changes; the acts thus characterized are not the same everywhere; but, everywhere and always, there have been men who have behaved in such a way as to draw upon themselves penal repression.... There is, then, no phenomenon that presents more indisputably all the symptoms of normality, since it appears closely connected with the conditions of all collective life. To make of crime a form of social morbidity would be to admit that morbidity is not something accidental, but, on the contrary, that in certain cases it grows

Source: Reprinted with permission of The Free Press, a Division of Simon & Schuster, from *The Rules of Sociological Method* by Emile Durkheim, translated by S. A. Solovay and John H. Mueller. Edited by George E. G. Catlin. Copyright © 1938 by George E. Catlin; copyright renewed 1966 by Sarah A. Solovay, John H. Mueller, and George E. G. Catlin.

out of the fundamental constitution of the living organism; it would result in wiping out all distinction between the physiological and the pathological. No doubt it is possible that crime itself will have abnormal forms, as, for example, when its rate is unusually high. This excess is, indeed, undoubtedly morbid in nature. What is normal, simply, is the existence of criminality....

Here we are, then, in the presence of a conclusion in appearance quite paradoxical. Let us make no mistake. To classify crime among the phenomena of normal sociology is not to say merely that it is an inevitable, although regrettable, phenomenon, due to the incorrigible wickedness of men; it is to affirm that it is a factor in public health, an integral part of all healthy societies. This result is, at first glance, surprising enough to have puzzled even ourselves for a long time. Once this first surprise has been overcome, however, it is not difficult to find reasons explaining this normality and at the same time confirming it.

In the first place crime is normal because a society exempt from it is utterly impossible. Crime, we have shown elsewhere, consists of an act that offends certain very strong collective sentiments. In a society in which criminal acts are no longer committed, the sentiments they offend would have to be found without exception in all individual consciousnesses, and they must be found to exist with the same degree as sentiments contrary to them. Assuming that this condition could actually be realized, crime would not thereby disappear; it would only change its form, for the very cause which would thus dry up the sources of criminality would immediately open up new ones.

Indeed, for the collective sentiments which are protected by the penal law of a people at a specified moment of its history to take possession of the public conscience or for them to acquire a stronger hold where they have an insufficient grip, they must acquire an intensity greater than that which they had hitherto had. The community as a whole must experience them more vividly, for it can acquire from no other source the greater force necessary to control these individuals who formerly were the most refractory. For murderers to disappear, the horror of bloodshed must become greater in those social strata from which murderers are recruited; but, first it must become greater throughout the entire society. Moreover, the very absence of crime would directly contribute to produce this horror; because any sentiment seems much more respectable when it is always and uniformly respected.

One easily overlooks the consideration that these strong states of the common consciousness cannot be thus reinforced without reinforcing at the same time the more feeble states, whose violation previously gave birth to mere infraction of convention—since the weaker ones are only the prolongation, the attenuated form, of the stronger. Thus robbery and simple bad taste injure the same single altruistic sentiment, the respect for that which is another's. However, this same sentiment is less grievously offended by bad taste than by robbery; and since, in addition, the average consciousness has not sufficient intensity to react keenly to the bad taste, it is treated with greater tolerance. That is why the person guilty of bad taste is merely blamed, whereas the thief is punished. But, if this sentiment grows stronger, to the point of silencing in all consciousnesses the inclination which disposes man to steal, he will become more sensitive to the offenses which, until then, touched him but lightly. He will react against them, then, with more energy; they will be the object of greater opprobrium, which will transform certain of them from the simple moral faults that they were and give them the quality of crimes. For example, improper contracts, or contracts improperly executed, which only incur public blame or civil damages, will become offenses in law.

Imagine a society of saints, a perfect cloister of exemplary individuals. Crimes, properly so called, will there be unknown; but faults which appear venial to the layman will create there the same scandal that the ordinary offense does in ordinary consciousnesses. If, then, this society has the power to judge and punish, it will define these acts as criminal and will treat them as such. For the same reason, the perfect and upright man judges his smallest failings with a severity that the majority reserve for acts more truly in the nature of an offense. Formerly, acts of violence against persons were more frequent than they are today, because respect for individual dignity was less strong. As this has increased, these crimes have become more rare; and also, many acts violating this sentiment have been introduced into the penal law which were not included there in primitive times.[1]

...Crime is, then, necessary; it is bound up with the fundamental conditions of all social life, and by that very fact it is useful, because these conditions of which it is a part are themselves indispensable to the normal evolution of morality and law.

Indeed, it is no longer possible today to dispute the fact that law and morality vary from one social type to the next, nor that they change within the same type if the conditions of life are modified. But, in order that these transformations may be possible, the collective sentiments at the basis of morality must not be hostile to change, and consequently must have but moderate energy. If they were too strong, they would no longer be plastic. Every pattern is an obstacle to new patterns, to the extent that the first pattern is inflexible. The better a structure is articulated, the more it offers a healthy resistance to all modification; and this is equally true of functional, as of anatomical, organization. If there were no crimes, this condition could not have been fulfilled; for such a hypothesis presupposes that collective sentiments have arrived at a degree of intensity unexampled in history. Nothing is good indefinitely and to an unlimited extent. The authority which the moral conscience enjoys must not be excessive; otherwise no one would dare criticize it, and it would too easily congeal into an immutable form. To make progress, individual originality must be able to express itself. In order that the originality of the idealist whose dreams transcend his century may find expression, it is necessary that the originality of the criminal, who is below the level of his time, shall also be possible. One does not occur without the other.

Nor is this all. Aside from this indirect utility, it happens that crime itself plays a useful role in this evolution. Crime implies not only that the way remains open to necessary changes but that in certain cases it directly prepares these changes. Where crime exists, collective sentiments are sufficiently flexible to take on a new form, and crime sometimes helps to determine the form they will take. How many times, indeed, it is only an anticipation of future morality—a step toward what will be! According to Athenian law, Socrates was a criminal, and his condemnation was no more than just. However, his crime, namely, the independence of his thought, rendered a service not only to humanity but to his country....

From this point of view the fundamental facts of criminality present themselves to us in an entirely new light. Contrary to current ideas, the criminal no longer seems a totally unsociable being, a sort of parasitic element, a strange and unassimilable body, introduced into the midst of society. On the contrary, he plays a definite role in social life.

NOTE

1. Calumny, insults, slander, fraud, etc.

18

Exploring Deviance in Canada

Linda Deutschmann

DEFINING DEVIANCE

Deviance is not just a whole lot of sex, drugs, and violence; wrongdoing by bad people; or the ramblings of people who have forgotten to take their medication. When we look at deviance in Canada, we find a wide array of behaviours that seem to have little in common with each other.

Those called deviant include nasty individuals such as serial killer Paul Bernardo[1] (Burnside & Cairns, 1995) and sadistic pedophile Karl Toft[2] (Sorenson, 2002). They include people such as John Colapinto ("a boy raised as a girl") who struggle to find a place in a society that has only two mainstream gender categories and little tolerance for anyone just a bit different (Colapinto, 2001; Bloom, 2002; Preves, 2003). They also include temporary and accidental deviants such as the Iranian law

Source: Printed with the author's permission (2003). Linda Deutschmann is also the author of *Deviance and Social Control* (2002).

professor who, on his way to Canada to learn English, told the Air Canada flight attendant to be careful stowing his bag because it might explode (i.e., burst open). His use of English, in the era of post-September 11 sensitivities, resulted in a month in custody and a criminal conviction on mischief charges (MacAfee, 2003). The deviant category includes many other people who find themselves on the outside of social groups because they are seen as unacceptable for some reason. You can argue that each of these people has in some way violated a social norm (or been accused of this) whether they meant to do so or not, and this may be what they all have in common.

Deviance is a violation of a social norm, but not just any violation of a norm. In the course of a regular day, each of us is likely to find situations in which conforming fully to one set of social norms forces us to violate other norms. As we try to balance school and work, family and friends, getting ahead and "having a life," few of us can live up to the expectations of all our social roles all the time. People who violate a few of the rules, and not too often, think of themselves as normal, and usually are thought of by others as normal. What, then, is deviance? What makes a practice or a person or a set of ideas "deviant"?

Whenever we find deviance, whether in Canada or elsewhere, we find that there are *observers,* people who see (or claim to see) some kind of *behaviour or appearance or belief* that violates *normative standards* (norms or rules) regarded as significant (i.e., standards that are worth defending at this time and in this situation). The breaking of rules is not enough, all by itself, to produce consensus that behaviour is deviant. Many rules are used selectively—they are invoked when someone feels such rules are "needed," not every time someone breaks them. If you start looking out for this, you can probably come up with many examples of behaviour that is okay in one situation (e.g., at a rock concert or a hockey rink) but not okay in another (e.g., at a church service), or times when behaviour that has been tolerated for a while will be treated to a "crackdown" and suddenly become the spark for serious regulations.

Notice how this definition places as much emphasis on the *observers* as it does on the behaviour or appearance or belief that is observed. There have been times when the observers have been wrong about, or even lied about, what they have observed. During the witchcraft craze in early Europe, accusers testi-fied about seeing neighbours flying on broom-sticks or calling up hailstorms, and in some villages every woman was burned as a witch because of this testimony (Larner, 1980; Levack, 1992). Even in modern times, it is not uncommon to find that people called deviant are victims of rumours or "bad press" put out by those who do not like them. This definition also places impor-tance on the normative standards that are invoked by the observers. The standards will be those shared by the surrounding culture; otherwise the observers would not be able to get people to agree that deviance has occurred.

Consider the following list:

Deviant Category	Normative Standard
Heretic	Religious belief
Traitor	Loyalty
Homosexual	Traditional male gender role
Obese/Anorexic	Medical weight standards
Delinquent	Laws applicable to youth
Trespasser	Privacy, property rights
Dirty, smelly	Cleanliness

Are some of these standards more defensible (commonly shared) than others? Could an "observer" get people to label someone deviant because the observed person was doing some-thing that violated this normative standard? Are some of these standards changing? In this exer-cise, *you* are acting as the observer.

SEEING DEVIANCE THROUGH THE LENSES OF THEORY

Each of the perspectives of sociology helps us to understand deviance. The definition that we have been using owes a great deal to the *symbolic interaction* perspective, so we will begin with that perspective.

Symbolic Interaction

Making use of this perspective, we can see that even when we notice an important rule has been broken, we may or may not be willing to take action. If we like the person who has committed the perceived offence, we may be reluctant to start the process of stigmatization or labelling that is known as *deviantizing*. We may try to "normalize" what has happened by ignoring, covering up, or excusing the person—for exam-ple, by suggesting that the real problem is stress or overwork. If we do not like the offender, or we are very committed to defending the rule, we may choose to make the most of the offence. It always takes a bit of work (awareness, attention, emotional effort, talk...) to produce the reality of deviance. Some people from the ranks of the observers, or those who listen to the observers, have to care enough to make a big deal about what they see, or what has been reported to them. When they undertake this enterprising work, we call them labellers or *moral entrepreneurs*.[3] The result of their work is a new rule or a newly enforced rule, and often a new deviant or a new class of deviants.

A small-scale moral entrepreneur may be the person in your circle of friends who maintains the group standards by way of enthusiastic telephone gossip. This can lead to the exclusion of nonconforming members, or may just mean that they get a lot of teasing or criticism. A larger-scale moral entrepreneur can be the leader of a group that actively seeks to ban Harry Potter books from a school library,[4] or to keep gay couples from attending the school prom, or to cover up naked public statues. Some large-scale moral entrepreneurs become leaders or spokespersons for social movements that target particular kinds of behaviour and people. Examples of this have been temperance crusaders, who campaigned against alcohol, and eugenics leaders, who argued for such causes as the sterilization of anyone "unfit" to reproduce and the tightening of immigration rules (McLaren, 1990). Canada has had no violent equivalent to Carrie Nation, the hatchet-wielding American anti-alcohol crusader who was arrested more than 30 times for destroying saloons in the early 1900s. Canadian temperance activist Nellie McClung was called "Calamity Nell," but this had to do with her fiery language, and not with violence (Hallett & Davis, 1993).

Moral entrepreneurs often have to work hard to make others agree that certain behaviour is evil and that people who practise such behaviour are morally tainted and deviant. Some moral entrepreneurs have become so wrapped up in their cause that they and their followers have been willing to go to terrible lengths to make it succeed. History is full of the stories of persecutions of so-called deviant populations and the untruths that were told to justify these actions. In the late 1930s and 1940s, the German National Socialists (Nazis) made deviants out of Jewish people by accusing them of undermining the German nation, stigmatizing them by forcing them to wear the Star of David symbol, and eventually entering into a systematic plan for their extermination. Judge Emily Murphy (pen name "Janey Canuck") was a Canadian moral entrepreneur who was an anti-marijuana and anti-Chinese-immigration activist. Her book *The Black Candle* (1922) is full of passages linking marijuana with the destruction of the "white race" in Canada and with allegations that homicide and insanity follow upon even minor use of marijuana[5] (Murphy, 1922). Along with the U.S. materials that this book was largely based on, *The Black Candle* had an effect on Canada's immigration and drug laws (Blackwell & Erickson, 1988).

Sometimes it is useful to distinguish between the moral entrepreneurs (the people who work to bring about moral rules) and the rule enforcers (the police, the school authorities, or the company management). Rule enforcers may sometimes be required to enforce rules that they do not support, or they may act to enforce rules in ways that were not originally intended. Political authorities sometimes make rules for schools that school authorities do not appreciate. When this happens, the rules may be subverted in many ways. Rule enforcers may decide that the enforcement of rules in a particular situation is simply not wise. Thus police at rock concerts rarely wade into the thickest part of the crowd to arrest drug sellers and users. On the other hand, sometimes the conflict between the rule makers and rule enforcers results in a clear resolution. Metropolitan Toronto Police Constable David Packer was forced to resign or be dismissed in the 1980s when he refused to stand guard at the Morgentaler abortion clinic in Toronto (Packer, 1988). Packer apparently had the choice of being deviant within the police organization by refusing to obey its rules, or being deviant within the anti-abortion milieu that he and his wife shared. He resigned from the police force.

Usually those who are labelled deviant face some level of punishment and some degree of social exclusion or banishment. While they may not be taken to an actual courtroom, they are treated to judgment in the eyes of those around them and punished by being stigmatized and possibly shunned. Their presence is treated as contaminating or polluting and "decent" people (the insiders) avoid them. When this happens at school, the deviant may be excluded from desirable friendship groups. The consequences of such exclusion can be cumulative. Youths lacking the protection of respectable friends may be vulnerable to bullying. Their performance in the classroom may suffer. Their response to these ramifications may make the situation even worse. Unless reversed, this *deviance amplification* process may continue until the individual gradually comes to have fewer respectable choices, comes to think of his or her identity as more and more deviant, and becomes more and more committed to deviant lines of action. The final result may be a school dropout, a school shooting, or a suicide.

The daycare scandals of the 1980s and early 1990s also provide a good example of how symbolic interaction theory can help us to understand deviance processes. Beginning in the 1980s, there were many "satanic" daycare scandals. Most of these occurred in the so-called Bible-belt areas of the United States, but some took place in Canada and England (Victor, 1993). They were fuelled by a climate of anxiety over child care and beliefs about children's testimony that have since been shown to be incorrect[6] (Ofshe & Watter, 1994; Butler, Fukurai, et al., 2001). One of these scandals occurred in 1992 in Martensville, Saskatchewan. Nine people, five of them police officers, were accused of sexual and satanic crimes against young children[7] (Harris, 1998). This case started with a mother's concern over her daughter's diaper rash, and escalated through the hyper-awareness of a policewoman who had received training about satanic cults, a

police chief who believed her, and the activities of several overenthusiastic but improperly trained child therapists. The stories of terrible deeds that were elicited by parents and therapists eventually collapsed in the complete absence of relevant physical evidence, but not before many people were accused of Satanist practices and pedophilia, and not before many children were subjected to "therapy" that was traumatic. This case shows how accusations of deviance can snowball in a community, creating conditions whereby people convince themselves that, if so many other people believe that an accusation is true, it must be true. In the process, many lives are ruined.

Not all deviance is falsely attributed, of course, but the process of deviantizing is the same whether the incident has really occurred or is falsely attributed. When deviance takes the form of a serious violation of the Criminal Code—such as bank robbery—the individual may be stigmatized with the label "criminal" and put in prison. He or she will then be excluded from (almost) all forms of civil society for a designated period of time. There will be an awkward point when it comes time to release and reintegrate such an offender, who is still symbolically labelled a criminal but now is about to rejoin free society. When there is a proposal to put in a halfway house so that the offender can gradually rejoin the community in a supervised way, neighbours will often band together in a NIMBY (Not In My Back Yard) movement to keep criminal people "like this" from living in their neighbourhood (Deutschmann, 2002: 345–46). These movements respond to ex-offenders in the same language of fear and rejection as other NIMBY movements respond to dangerous toxic waste (Walsh, Warland, et al., 1993). Symbolic interaction analysis helps us to see the ways in which the social process of criminalization makes offender reintegration a perilous undertaking. Even a falsely accused offender may find it difficult to find a satisfying legitimate career when returning to society from prison, all because the stigma of criminality persists long beyond the sentence of imprisonment and creates a spoiled identity (Goffman, 1959).

People threatened with being labelled as deviant (stigmatization) sometimes fight back. We see this now in the case of homosexuals, marijuana users, and stigmatized minorities. When this happens, interesting *stigma contests* can take place. A stigma contest evolves when those people who denounce and exclude find that the tables have been turned, and that they have become the accused deviants. The prudish book-banners, busybody meddlers, and racist Archie Bunkers can become figures of fun or condemnation. German-born former Canadian resident Ernst Zundel, for example, has become infamous for his writings and speeches on Holocaust denial, and for neo-Nazi and anti-Semitic activities. These have caused him to be deported from the United States, denied Canadian citizenship, and threatened with deportation from Canada to face trial in Germany. This is part of the pattern whereby those who attempt to label and exclude others are sometimes labelled and excluded themselves.

Some of those who have been labelled deviant do not really mind their outsider status: they may enjoy notoriety and not want to fit in with the mainstream dominant groups. They disdain safe, careful, hard-working and sensible "squares" and relish the fear that they can evoke in the hearts of those who follow the rules and abhor violence and extreme adventure. They seek the respect of a different sort of people. While just 1 percent of bikers pride themselves on being outlaws, the other 99 percent are said to be decent, law-abiding people[8] (Harris, 1985; Lavigne, 2000). This disdain for the square and the safe is shared by many elements within youth subcultures, varying from the style rebel punks and goths to the "weekend warriors" to the "street elite" gang youths of the urban downtown scene. Symbolic interaction helps us to understand the identity construction that underlies the symbols that are displayed by all of these groups. They wear the symbols to show that they belong outside the respectable world and to show that they disdain the people who would exclude them. Erving Goffman calls such symbols "identifiers," since they help to tell the observer a great deal about the person wearing them (Goffman, 1959).

Structural Functionalism

The structural functional theoretical perspective in sociology emphasizes a very different aspect of the reality of deviance.

Functionalists argue that deviance can be beneficial for the maintenance of a social system, even if the people in the system do not recognize its beneficial effects. That is, deviance can have *latent functions*. Societies that are under some kind of threat will tend to "find" a lot of deviants, because this aids societal *boundary maintenance*. Moral outrage against deviants dramatizes the rules and reasserts the old boundary or establishes a new one. For example, Kai Erikson has written about how, in the Puritan New England colony of Salem in the 1690s, accusations of witchcraft arose amid uncertainty and disorder related to political problems, relations with the native Indians, changes in the social structure, and illness due to a fungus growing on the crops (Erikson, 1966). There were 19 hangings and one pressing to death by heavy stones before the outbreak came to an end. During the same period, the very stable colonies of New France saw no outbreak of persecution despite the presence of witchcraft beliefs there (Morison, 1955).

Functionalists argue that each successful system has, or finds, just enough deviance to mark and maintain its borders. Deviance can be adjusted up and down simply by adjusting the official level of sensitivity to it (Krauthammer, 1993; Moynihan, 1993). If we have too many deviants, we ignore many of them. If we do not have enough deviants, we can (and do) invent them, as has happened with witches, the "communists" falsely accused in the McCarthy scandals of the 1950s, and other innocent-but-accused scapegoats in the present (Deutschmann, 2002: Chapters 3 and 8).

Functionalists have identified many other latent functions of deviance in addition to boundary maintenance. Deviance is often a way of inducing tension relief in groups under stress, and the punishment of deviants serves a function by demonstrating the value of conformity and by drawing the conformists together in their shared values of conformity. Sometimes the deviant serves as both tension relief and demonstration of the value of conformity, as when the class clown does something really extreme and ends up in the principal's office, and the rest of the class then settles down to work. Deviance is sometimes the way in which new and better ways of doing things are discovered and eventually brought into the mainstream, and sometimes the way in which bureaucratic red tape is subverted for a good cause.

There are also dysfunctions of deviance. Alcoholic airline pilots do not improve airline service. Pedophiles do nothing good for families or for the children they molest. Corrupt politicians do little to improve our desire to participate in politics, and fraudulent corporate behaviour, especially when unpunished, is not good for the economy. These behaviours tend to tear systems apart, and create a society with substantial areas of anomie.

Anomie means, literally, "without law." In Emile Durkheim's writing, anomie refers to a state of normlessness or deregulation, a state of society not having meaningful rules and values (Durkheim, 1951). Anomie is found when society becomes less regulated; it often appears because of rapid social change through modernization and urbanization (Mestrovic, 1985), although it can also develop as an aftermath of war or disaster. Inner-city areas where there is high popula-

tion turnover and little stability of family and work life tend to be characterized by high rates of suicide, mental illness, drug abuse, and delinquency. These forms of deviance can be seen as symptoms of Durkheim's version of anomie.

American sociologist Robert Merton developed the concept of anomie further by adding the idea of social strain (Merton, 1938). He saw anomie as a condition of strain between the things we are socialized to want (cultural goals) and the amount of access we have to them (institutionalized means). While most of us are socialized to want, for example, a home, car, a meaningful job, children, and many consumer goods, not all of us are well placed to get these things in the approved ways. Not all of us are positioned well enough to succeed in the right schools or to get rich by getting the right job or marrying into the right family. Merton argued that people adapt to this kind of anomie in five main ways. First, some people are *conformists*. They are usually well enough placed to achieve the goals with the means they have been given. Other people may accept the goals, but decide that the acceptable means either take too long or are too difficult; they become *innovators*. (Innovation includes what most of us would call cheating.) Innovation is most likely to be used by people who are structurally blocked from being able to achieve the goals that are held out as valid for everyone in the "American Dream." Canadian track star Ben Johnson, who was stripped of his gold medal at the 1988 Olympics in Seoul after a positive drug test and whose running career faltered after he was cut off from steroids, is an example of an innovator (Francis & Coplon, 1990; Issajenko, 1990). A third group adapts to structural strain of anomie by becoming *ritualists*. These people give up on the goals but continue to go through the means in an empty way. This might mean staying in school forever, without having any personal or practical goal in mind, or becoming the kind of bureaucrat who compulsively engages in setting up useless paper-pushing systems. Merton has two categories for people who adapt to anomie by rejecting both the goals and the means. The first of these, and Merton's fourth adaptation to anomie, is the *retreats* category. Retreatists are the social dropouts. The drug-using street people on Vancouver's Lower East Side may be an example of this category. Many of these people have replaced society's goals with the goal of obtaining drugs, and even survival takes second place to this. The second category of rejection, and Merton's fifth adaptation, is the *rebel* category. Rebels reject both the goals and the means, but they continue to engage in society, trying to change the system that does not work for them. Rebels may be seen as deviants by those who are trying to maintain the status quo, but they are often the heroes of the next generation.

Conflict

The conflict perspective is also useful in understanding deviance. Conflict theorists, like functionalists, are interested in the structural level of society. They analyze conflicts by looking at group interests rather than by looking at individual needs, emotions, or personalities. (If this distinction is not kept in mind, you may find it difficult to see that the conflict and symbolic interaction perspectives are very distinct from each other.) Marxist and neo-Marxist theorists analyze class interests, especially economically based class interests, as the most important elements of conflict. Other conflict theorists may look at such interests as those of ethnicity, culture, gender, or age.

Conflict theory looks at how the most powerful groups in society use their power to establish conditions that enhance their own interests and act to keep others from getting into positions that could change these conditions. The kind of power that is important here is the power to make the rules that everyone has to live under. This includes, of course, rules such as the Criminal Code of Canada, but also the rules of companies and schools, and the everyday norms of life that make some cultural groups more comfortable than others. People who are in government and on committees and generally in charge of things get to make the rules; they control how the rules are enforced, and they control how rule breakers are treated. For a very long time, the most comfortable combination of groups in Canada have been the people labelled as White Anglo-Saxon Protestant (WASP) capitalists, and this is shown in the kinds of rules that Canadians, at least those living outside of Quebec, live under. (One aspect of conflict theory is that it tends to point to uncomfortable truths.)

Conflict theorists see it as no accident that Canada's Criminal Code tends to outlaw the things that employers think employees should not do, and things that working-class people are more likely to be caught doing rather than things that rich people are likely to be caught doing. You can attend criminal court in any Canadian city and observe the social class of those caught in the net of the criminal law. You will notice that there are relatively few wealthy defendants before the courts.

In Canada, workplace dangers and shoddy products are much more likely to shorten your life or injure you than are serial killers or street crime, and yet the people responsible are rarely, if ever, identified and called criminal or even deviant (Naylor, 2002). In 1992 the Westray mine explosion killed 26 miners in Nova Scotia. The inquiry that followed revealed that flagrant breaches of health and safety standards had not been attended to or prosecuted. Although the RCMP laid two charges under the Criminal Code, these were dropped. Thus, although 26 human beings died, no one was held criminally responsible (Richard, 1999; Glasbeek, 2002). We fear the criminal in the street. We are oblivious to the much greater threats to our wealth and our health that are hidden from us.[9] While the criminal courts are particularly striking places for conflict analysis, the conflict perspective can help you to understand that there are many other settings—such as schools, clubs, and work-places—in which deviantization takes place.

While Marx himself thought that criminals were part of the "lumpenproletariat" and thus of no use to capitalist society or to the revolution, some of his followers argued that, since the capitalist inequalities and unjust laws make outlaws of the poor and outsiders, criminals were not really bad people. Criminals were simply people who refused to be exploited. In this view, bank robbers are just expressing their opposition to the exploitation of employers and the evils of the banking system, and are really an advance guard of the revolution, perhaps even heroes of a sort. Marxist historian Eric Hobsbawm, for example, sees early bandits as "social bandits" and part of the pre-industrial class structure of early society (Hobsbawm, 2000). This view is now called *left idealism.* Left idealists have been largely displaced by *left realists*, who recognize that criminal deviants such as murderers, robbers, and parents who beat their children "really" do a lot of harm. Thus, while most conflict theorists regard prisons and other repressive institutions as weapons of the dominant classes to control those they dominate, they recognize that some offenders "really" must be controlled at least until something revolutionary can be done to remove the structural inequalities that produce these damaged and dangerous people (Taylor, Walton, et al., 1973; Quinney, 2000).

DEVIANCE AS PART OF SOCIAL CONTROL

Social control includes all those ways, obvious and not so obvious, by which we are encouraged or coerced, tricked, or bribed into particular patterns of behaviour, or, failing that, put away in jails or asylums where decent people do not have to put up with us. All societies that survive have social controls to ensure that their members do the things that are needful for social life to continue, and all societies respond with processes that isolate or banish or execute members who are identified as impossible nonconformists or scapegoats. Deviance occurs everywhere. Thus we can assert that deviance is universal.

Although universal, deviance is not the same in every society. The food, sexual, and burial practices of foreign cultures may be shocking to outsiders. In Japan, many restaurant delicacies are insect-based. In some cultures, burial customs include the eating of body parts (Conklin, 2001). Within a country as large as Canada, there are many cultural groups. What is normal and accepted in one may be deviant in another. For example, the community of Bountiful in British Columbia is settled by the Fundamentalist Church of Jesus Christ of Latter Day Saints (no relation to mainstream Mormons). The leader of Bountiful, Winston Blackmore, has 26 wives and 80 children.[10] What is a normal family in Bountiful is probably not a normal family where you live. One way of expressing this variation is to say that deviance is *relative* to a particular culture and place.

What is very normal and even required in one time and place may be deviant in another. The practices of our own ancestors would shock us if we could return to them today. Women, children, employees, and servants were regularly treated in ways that we would now consider criminal abuse. Until the late 1880s, cannibalism among stranded sailors was "the custom of the sea" and not considered illegal (Hanson, 2000). On the other hand, people who were deviant in their own time may become heroes or saints in a later period. Metis leader Louis Riel was executed as a traitor in 1885, but has since been recognized by some as a father of Confederation[11] (Winsor, 1989). Other examples of people scorned as deviants long ago but now venerated would include Jesus of Nazareth, who was crucified, and Socrates, who was forced to take poison for corrupting the morals of youth by teaching them to argue rationally about conventions of the day (Proietto & Portrer, 1966). As the dominant values change, so do our notions about what, and who, is deviant.

Deviance is relative because deviance depends on the normative standards that the observers are able to invoke when they say that what they observe is deviant, respectable, or even admirable. The same behaviour may be regarded as admirable by some people and deviant by others. Consider the case of great-grandmother Betty Krawczyk, who has been jailed for criminal contempt of court in connection with her role in peaceful protest against logging in old-growth B.C. forest (Krawczyk, 1997). Canadian courts usually use prison sentences to communicate extreme disapproval. But Krawczyk is treated as a heroine in the environmentalist community and is proud of protecting the environment for her great-grandchildren.[12]

There are variations in the level of tolerance for behaviour that might be considered deviant. Summer holidays and major sports events typically allow greater tolerance for differences in clothing styles and public behaviour than do funerals and state functions. Tolerance for social control is also variable. Sometimes we become angry when enforcement of rules is too heavy-handed. In the aftermath of the events of September 11, 2001, Canadians' tolerance for public surveillance and many similar kinds of social control increased dramatically.

NOTES

1. Bernardo and his wife Karla kidnapped and killed schoolgirls in the St. Catharines area of Ontario in the early 1990s.
2. Toft was a guard at Kingsclear Training School in New Brunswick. Some 233 compensation claims have been settled since his plea-bargained conviction on just 34 charges.
3. Actually, you probably call them busybodies or meddlers, but Howard Becker, a symbolic interaction theorist and jazz musician, invented the term moral entrepreneur to describe people who made it their business to enforce morals and who often gained something by it. Moral entrepreneurs sometimes become the heads of organizations devoted to

dealing with the social problem that they have identified. You can find a summary of Becker's ideas at **http://www.criminology.fsu.edu/crimtheory/becker.htm.**
4. J. K. Rowling's Harry Potter novels were the books most subject to censorship attempts in 1999 and 2000. This was because of their focus on wizardry and magic, according to Kranich, 2000.
5. A brief section from this book is scanned at **http://cannabislink.ca/papers/menace.htm.**
6. To summarize a complex literature, children do not make up complex sexual-assault stories on their own, but improperly trained therapists can lead them to do so, and the process can plant false memories that are damaging in the same ways that the memories would be if the assaults had actually occurred.
7. The CBC's Fifth Estate produced a documentary about this called "Hell to Pay," which was broadcast on February 12, 2003. The relevant Web site, which includes documents and resources on the subject, is **http://www.cbc.ca/fifth/martin** (accessed December 31, 2003).
8. The reference to 1 percent traces its origins back to 1947, when an annual biker racing and climbing event at Hollister, California, turned into a drunken rampage. Successive events were also taken over this way. The American Motorcycle Association repeatedly tried to put a distance between itself and the renegade element by stressing that 99 percent of bikers were decent, law-abiding, and civilized. The outlaw biker groups proudly took on the "1%" symbol and wore it on their jackets as part of their so-called identifying patch. Many bikers also wear it as a tattoo (see Lavigne, 1987; Garson, 2003; Veno & Gannon, 2003).
9. Two recent Canadian books can help you to understand the way in which upper-level deviants can make their actions "invisible." See Glasbeek, 2002; Naylor, 2002.
10. More information was available on the CBC Fifth Estate Web site, as updated February 2003 at **http://www.cbc.ca/fifth/polygamy.** The government of British Columbia provides a school to this community despite public criticism that the community is immoral.
11. The Louis Riel Institute, created by an act of the Manitoba Legislature in 1995, is responsible for promoting awareness of the history, culture, and values of the Metis people in Manitoba.
12. Information on the environmentalist side of this issue may be found at **http://media.wildernesscommittee.org/.**

REFERENCES

Blackwell, J. C., and P. G. Erickson. 1988. *Illicit drugs in Canada: A risky business.* Toronto: Nelson Canada.

Bloom, A. 2002. *Normal: Transsexual CEOs, crossdressing cops, and hermaphrodites with attitude.* New York: Random House.

Burnside, S., and A. Cairns. 1995. *Deadly innocence: The true story of Paul Bernardo, Karla Homolka and the schoolgirl murders.* New York: Time Warner.

Butler, E. W., H. Fukurai, et al. 2001. *Anatomy of the McMartin child molestation case.* Lanham, Md.: University Press of America.

Colapinto, J. 2001. *As nature made him: The boy who was raised as a girl.* Toronto: Perennial (HarperCollins).

Conklin, B. A. 2001. *Consuming grief: Compassionate cannibalism in Amazonian society.* Austin, Tex.: University of Texas Press.

Deutschmann, L. 2002. *Deviance and social control.* Scarborough, Ont.: Nelson Thompson Learning.

Durkheim, E. 1951. *Suicide.* New York: Free Press (original work published 1897).

Erikson, K. T. 1966. *Wayward puritans: A study in the sociology of deviance.* New York: John Wiley.

Francis, C., and J. Coplon. 1990. *Speed trap.* Toronto: Lester and Orpen Dennys.

Garson, P. 2003. *Born to be wild: A history of the American biker and bikes 1947–2002.* New York: Simon and Schuster.

Glasbeek, H. 2002. *Wealth by stealth: Corporate crime, corporate law, and the perversion of democracy.* Toronto: Between the Lines.

Goffman, E. 1959. *The presentation of self in everyday life.* Garden City, N.Y.: Doubleday.

Hallett, M., and M. Davis. 1993. *Firing the heather.* Saskatoon: Fifth House.

Hanson, N. 2000. *The custom of the sea.* New York: John Wiley.

Harris, F. 1998. *Martensville: Truth or justice?* Toronto: Dundurn Press.

Harris, M. 1985. *Bikers: Birth of a modern day outlaw.* London: Faber and Faber.

Hobsbawm, E. 2000. *Bandits.* New York: New Press.

Issajenko, A., as told to M. O'Malley and K. O'Reilly. 1990. *Running risks.* Toronto: Macmillan.

Kranich, N. 2000. Develop yourself: Expose your mind to a banned book. Speech available online through American Library Association. http://www.ala.org. Accessed in 2003.

Krauthammer, C. 1993. *Defining deviance up. New Republic* (November): 20–25.

Krawczyk, B. S. 1997. *Clayoquot: The sound of my heart.* Victoria: Orca Book Publishers.

Larner, C. 1980. *Crimen exceptum? The crime of witchcraft in Europe.* In *Crime and the law: The social history of crime in Western Europe since 1500,* eds. V. A. C. Gatrell, B. Lenman, and G. Parker. London: Europa, 49–75.

Lavigne, Y. 1987. *Hell's Angels: Taking care of business.* Toronto: Ballantine Books.

———. 2000. *Hells Angels at war: The alarming story behind the headlines.* Toronto: HarperCollins.

Levack, B. P., ed. 1992. *Witchcraft, women and society,* vol. 10 of Articles on witchcraft, magic and demonology. New York: Garland.

MacAfee, M. 2003. Iranian law professor convicted of mischief in Air Canada case. Man told attendant his briefcase might explode if pushed under the seat. *Halifax Herald* (January 23).

McLaren, A. 1990. *Our own master race: Eugenics in Canada, 1885–1945.* Toronto: McClelland and Stewart.

Merton, R. K. 1938. Social structure and anomie. *American Sociological Review* 3: 672–82.

Mestrovic, S. G. 1985. Durkheim's concept of anomie as dérèglement. *Social Problems* 33(2): 81–99.

Morison, S. E. 1955. *The Parkman reader: From the works of Francis Parkman.* Boston: Little, Brown.

Moynihan, D. P. 1993. Defining deviancy down. *American Scholar* 62(1): 17–20.

Murphy, E. F. 1922. *The black candle.* Toronto: Thomas Allen.

Naylor, R. T. 2002. *Wages of crime: Black markets, illegal finance, and the underworld economy.* Montreal: McGill-Queen's University Press.

Ofshe, R., and E. Watter, 1994. *Making monsters: False memories, psychotherapy, and sexual hysteria.* New York: Scribner's.

Packer, A. 1988. *A matter of conscience.* Nazareth Homestead, Constable, N.Y.: Our Lady's Book Service.

Preves, S. E. 2003. *Intersex and identity: The contested self.* Rutgers, N.J.: Rutgers University Press.

Proietto, R., and J. N. Portrer. 1966. Socrates: A sociological understanding of the production of an outcast. *Economy and Society* 25(1): 1–35.

Quinney, R. 2000. *Bearing witness to crime and social justice.* Albany, N.Y.: State University of New York Press.

Richard, Justice K. Peter. 1999. *The Westray mine explosion—aftermath.* In Papers from the 1999 Congress on Medical-Legal Aspects of Work Injuries.

Sorenson, K. 2002. View from parliament. http://www.crowfoot.ca/mpcolumns.htm. Accessed September 2003.

Taylor, I., P. Walton, et al. 1973. *The new criminology: For a social theory of deviance.* London: Routledge/Keegan Paul.

Veno, A., and E. Gannon. 2003. *The brotherhoods: Inside the outlaw motorcycle clubs.* Sydney: Allen and Unwin.

Victor, J. S. 1993. *Satanic panic: The creation of a contemporary legend.* Chicago: Open Court.

Walsh, E. J., R. Warland, et al. 1993. Backyards, NIMBYs and incinerator sitings: Implications for social movement theory. *Social Problems* 40(1): 25–38.

Winsor, H. 1989. Tories urged to recognize Riel as a father of Confederation. *Globe and Mail* (August 18).

Part IX

Sexuality

19

Understanding Sexual Orientation

*Alfred C. Kinsey, Wardell B. Pomeroy,
and Clyde E. Martin*

THE HETEROSEXUAL-HOMOSEXUAL BALANCE

Concerning patterns of sexual behavior, a great deal of the thinking done by scientists and laymen alike stems from the assumption that there are persons who are "heterosexual" and persons who are "homosexual," that these two types represent antitheses in the sexual world, and that there is only an insignificant class of "bisexuals" who occupy an intermediate position between the other groups. It is implied that every individual is innately—inherently—either hetero-

Source: From *Sexual Behavior in the Human Male,* by Alfred C. Kinsey, Wardell B. Pomeroy, and Clyde E. Martin. Indiana University Press, 1948, pp. 636–39.

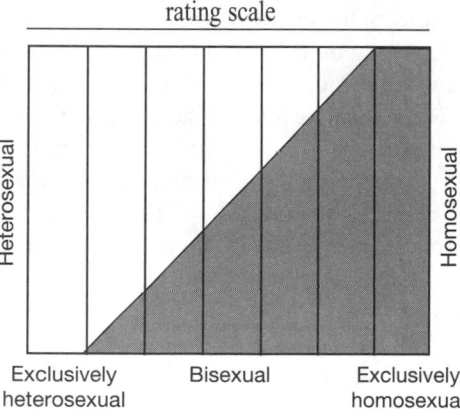

Figure 19.1   Heterosexual-homosexual rating scale

Exclusively heterosexual — Bisexual — Exclusively homosexual

sexual or homosexual. It is further implied that from the time of birth one is fated to be one thing or the other, and that there is little chance for one to change his pattern in the course of a lifetime.

It is quite generally believed that one's preference for a sexual partner of one or the other sex is correlated with various physical and mental qualities, and with the total personality which makes a homosexual male or female physically, psychically, and perhaps spiritually distinct from a heterosexual individual. It is generally thought that these qualities make a homosexual person obvious and recognizable to anyone who has a sufficient understanding of such matters. Even psychiatrists discuss "the homosexual personality" and many of them believe that preferences for sexual partners of a particular sex are merely secondary manifestations of something that lies much deeper in the totality of that intangible which they call the personality.

It is commonly believed, for instance, that homosexual males are rarely robust physically, are uncoordinated or delicate in their movements, or perhaps graceful enough but not strong and vigorous in their physical expression. Fine skins, high-pitched voices, obvious hand movements, a feminine carriage of the hips, and peculiarities of walking gaits are supposed accompaniments of a preference for a male as a sexual partner. It is commonly believed that the homosexual male is artistically sensitive, emotionally unbalanced, temperamental to the point of being unpredictable, difficult to get along with, and undependable in meeting specific obligations. In physical characters there have been attempts to show that the homosexual male has a considerable crop of hair and less often becomes bald, has teeth which are more like those of the female, a broader pelvis, larger genitalia, and a tendency toward being fat, and that he lacks a linea alba. The homosexual male is supposed to be less interested in athletics, more often interested in music and the arts, more often engaged in such occupations as bookkeeping, dress design, window display, hairdressing, acting, radio work, nursing, religious service, and social work. The converse to all of these is supposed to represent the typical heterosexual male. Many a clinician attaches considerable weight to these things in diagnosing the basic heterosexuality or homosexuality of his patients. The characterizations are so distinct that they seem to leave little room for doubt that homosexual and heterosexual represent two very distinct types of males....

It should be pointed out that scientific judgments on this point have been based on little more than the same sorts of impressions which the general public has had concerning homosexual persons. But before any sufficient study can be made of such possible correlations between patterns of sexual behavior and other qualities in the individual, it is necessary to understand the incidences and frequencies of the homosexual in the population as a whole, and the relation of the homosexual activity to the rest of the sexual pattern in each individual's history.

The histories which have been available in the present study make it apparent that the heterosexuality or homosexuality of many individuals is not an all-or-none proposition. It is true that there are persons in the population whose histories are exclusively heterosexual, both in regard to their overt experience and in regard to their psychic reactions. And there are individuals in the population whose histories are exclusively homosexual, both in experience and in psychic reactions. But the record also shows that there is a considerable portion of the population whose members have combined, within their individual histories, both homosexual and heterosexual experience and/or psychic responses. There are some whose heterosexual experiences predominate, there are some whose homosexual experiences predominate, there are some who have had quite equal amounts of both types of experience [see Figure 19.1].

Some of the males who are involved in one type of relation at one period in their lives may have only the other type of relation at some later period. There may be considerable fluctuation of patterns from time to time. Some males may be involved in both heterosexual and homosexual activities within the same period of time. For instance, there are some who engage in both heterosexual and homosexual activities in the same year, or in the same month or week, or even in the same day. There are not a few individuals who engage in group activities in which they may make simultaneous contact with partners of both sexes.

Males do not represent two discrete populations, heterosexual and homosexual. The world is not to be divided into sheep and goats. Not all things are black nor all things white. It is a fundamental of taxonomy that nature rarely deals with discrete categories. Only the human mind invents categories and tries to force facts into separated pigeon-holes. The living world is a continuum in each and every one of its aspects. The sooner we learn this concerning human sexual behavior the sooner we shall reach a sound understanding of the realities of sex.

20

Streets, Strangers, and Solidarity

Tracy Nielsen

In New York City, my girlfriend and I were walking, holding hands, down a busy East Village sidewalk. We passed a couple of lesbians. All four of us exchanged quick (knowing) glances and subtle nods. The more femme looking one held my gaze for a prolonged moment and smiled. I remarked, jokingly, to my partner that she must have liked me. A few seconds after we passed each other, we all turned our heads to look back at each other. Being caught in the act of obvious recognition was both exhilarating and a bit embarrassing. My partner called out, "Hey, she's mine." We all laughed and then kept on our way. This passing exchange, so seemingly inconsequential that most people on the street did not notice it, created a surge of validation for four lesbians on a New York City sidewalk. In a world surrounded by heterosexual norms, complete strangers shared a moment of "queer pride."

(Fieldnotes)

Source: Reprinted by permission of the author, 2002.

As unexceptional as this incident may appear, the interactions within it are sociologically significant. The essential role of strangers in building social solidarity in cities has been greatly underestimated. Urban public places have traditionally been viewed as populated by anti-social types who care little about the fellow human beings with whom they share space.

Such an anti-urban attitude is based on a profound misunderstanding of the way urbanites operate. Studious observation of interaction between strangers reveals that, far from being interactional wastelands, public places are sites of rich and dynamic social life (Lofland, 1990). It is difficult to grasp the meaning of fleeting engagements between strangers, such as the one described above, not only because they are short lived, but also because they are so routine that they are often engaged in unconsciously. Marginalized people are necessarily more conscious of their actions than members of dominant groups. I have drawn on this heightened consciousness to illustrate the ways lesbians build nonintimate solidarity, thereby stressing the significance of stranger interaction in the urban public realm.

As an insider in the lesbian subculture, I was able to use a unique empirical method to study the interactional patterns of this group. I actively engaged in participant observation of lesbians in public places in a number of North American cities. After detecting other lesbians on the streets and sharing acknowledgment rituals with them, I stopped them to talk about what had occurred between us and asked them to take part in a survey that I had designed to encourage lesbians to think about their public realm experiences. The empirical materials for this article came from my fieldnotes on these unusual encounters, informal interviews, and completed questionnaires from 38 participants.[1]

SEXUAL IDENTITY AND URBAN SPACES

For gay people, the urban public realm is both challenging and rewarding (Gardner, 1994). In heterosexually dominated urban spaces, gay people often experience the magnified vulnerability and sense of isolation that accompany a stigmatized identity. However, like members of other minorities, when gay people connect, they are more likely to experience moments of heightened civility than people whose identities are in sync with the dominant reality.

Lesbians often possess an enhanced awareness of the presence of other gay people in public places. Interactionally, it is possible to turn this awareness to their advantage. However, lesbians must always be vigilant about the risks that accompany being "out" in a homophobic society.[2] These risks range from breaches in civility, such as staring and harassment, to more serious attacks, such as physical assault. Interesting subcultural rituals have developed over time, as lesbians negotiate the dual processes of building solidarity by recognizing and responding to each other, while dealing

with issues of trust and risk. Strategies used by lesbians revolve around the interrelated concepts of *recognition*, *acknowledgment*, and *encounters*. Signals of recognition (gaydar) and acknowledgment (lesbian interaction rituals) that pass between lesbians often lead to prolonged and more spontaneous engagement (encounters). These interactional episodes, often strategically subtle, have profound effects on the lesbian subculture.

READING STRANGERS' IDENTITIES

The public realm is the world of strangers. City life would not be possible if strangers did not categorize each other so as to define situations and to know how to act toward each other. Habitually drawing on stereotypes or typifications to categorize strangers is a ubiquitous urban phenomenon.[3] Because much of this "ordering of the urban populace" (Lofland, 1973) is automatic and relatively unproblematic, many people are unaware of the influence that these everyday categorization processes have on subsequent social actions and interactions.

Lesbians, however, can take little for granted with respect to their sexual identities. Because a lesbian identity is largely indiscernible, most strangers will assume the "default sexuality" (heterosexuality) unless a lesbian identity is clearly presented to the public world. Although most urbanites tend to have a sophisticated grasp of the diverse identities of the strangers they encounter, based, for example, on age, race, class, and occupation, many are unaware of the signals and cues that represent a lesbian identity.

It would be a mistake to assume that public realm invisibility is an objective for lesbians. The ability to "pass" as straight can be desirable for lesbians who are not out or who feel vulnerable about their sexual orientation. However, it is also common for lesbians to claim that they are troubled by the omnipresent assumption of heterosexuality and therefore to challenge it by designing their presentation of self (Goffman, 1959) towards lesbian visibility. As indicated by this Vancouver lesbian's struggle to explain her presentation of self, impression management is never simple.

I always prefer that people identify me as lesbian—to experience interaction in any other way makes me feel that I am being "accepted" based on an incorrect assumption of heterosexuality. For years I presented myself as a stereotypical dyke, accentuating every possible visual and spatial cue to ensure that I would be recognized by all members of the public. Interestingly, though, I now identify as a more femme lesbian and it rarely occurs to me that I may appear straight. Although I wear make up and have grown my hair to a considerable length, I generally take up a great deal of energy or space in many public settings. I have an open stance, very strong (I hesitate to say masculine) gait and sit most frequently with my legs apart. I also perceive my shoes to be a give-away. I always wear "comfortable" (read: masculine or male-identified) shoes.

The desire to be visible to other lesbians has resulted in an elaborate impression management system in the lesbian subculture. The signalling and receiving behaviour that takes place between gay people in the public realm has been playfully named "gaydar" by the gay/lesbian subculture. Many heterosexuals express disbelief when gay people say they can, in the words of one survey participant, "*spot the queers a mile away*."[4] Those who do think they can detect lesbians often rely on superficial stereotypes. However, lesbians are aware that reading a lesbian identity requires a more finely tuned grasp of coding signals than the presence of masculine traits on a female body. Lesbians are a diverse subculture. If lesbians relied on simplistic readings to detect other lesbians, they would overlook the majority of lesbians in public places. A survey participant discusses the complexity of the New York City subculture.

In New York, there are so many types of lesbians that gaydar is quite complicated. There are the women who wear baggy pants and oversized shirts. Then you have the ones who dress alternatively and have many piercings and tattoos. Then I also see the business/professional types. Then you have the athletic types.... Come to think of it, lesbians are just as diverse as heterosexuals.

Although gaydar is unique to the gay subculture, this concept illustrates the tentative and contingent nature of stranger interaction in general. In attempting to make sense of situations, urbanites continually test their conceptions of strangers.[5] Through expressions given and given off (Goffman, 1959), lesbians signify their identities to an audience (i.e., lesbian strangers). The presence of "surface signs" may make a lesbian take a second look at a stranger for more "subtle signs" to confirm a gaydar reading. Surface signs are those more obvious cues signifying a lesbian identity that even some outsiders can discern (e.g., very short hair, a butch appearance or public displays of affection between women). Subtle signs include those cues whose meanings are clear mainly to insiders (e.g., strong stance, lesbian insignia, or prolonged eye contact).

Strangers assess each other's roles and identities using cues based on appearance (e.g., clothing, hairstyles, and jewellery), behaviour (e.g., actions, facial expressions, and body language) and space (e.g., where they are located in the city).[6] A lesbian from New York City made the following humorous observation about appearential cues.

Sometimes I need a set of cues for my gaydar to go off. Short hair, of course, makes me think twice, especially if it is spiky, slicked back, anything butch. In NYC it can get tricky because straight women have co-opted many dyke looks. If a woman has long hair but has piercings in places other than her ears or tattoos I might think she's a dyke. The other things that make me think "hmmm" are clunky black shoes or boots, those damn rainbows, shirts that say "dyke" are pretty easy, baggy jeans hanging off someone's hips, thick black leather belts, torn clothing that looks like it was found under a rock and anything that is considered, by the outside world, as belonging to men.

Although strangers often gain first impressions from appearance cues, appearances can be deceiving. Thus, deeper cues must often be used. A Winnipeg lesbian stressed the importance of assessing behavioural cues.

I think there is more than just clothes and hair—it is a combination that includes body language. A straight woman can wear masculine attire but I have my doubts that she is gay because the *cues are broader*. For example, I have a co-worker who I am sure is a lesbian (it turns out she has a female "roommate" and they seem more involved than sharing house bills). This woman will wear stereotypical feminine clothing but her "sporty" gait makes me think she'd be more comfortable in a ball field. She seems a bit more masculine in voice, manner and body movement. To me this is a common giveaway. Straight women rarely express their body language in that way (and when they do I usually think they are bisexual or closeted).

Like all urbanites, lesbians also assess spatial cues in making lesbian identity placements. As gay/lesbian spaces become more popular as hangouts, these cues can be misleading. As a New Yorker points out:

I am more likely to assume that someone is queer if she is in a lesbian space (i.e., bar, bookstore, pride march) but in the East Village of Manhattan, I do recognize that there are many queer-friendly exceptions even within those spaces.

With the exception of very clear cues such public displays of affection (PDAs) between women, most signals of a lesbian identity are ambiguous. Perhaps for this reason, many lesbians find themselves looking beyond appearential, behavioural, and spatial cues for an attitudinal variable. A lesbian from Toronto put it this way:

I believe there are a thousand hidden cues that we give to one another that we then interpret as a feeling. But there is a feeling I get when I discover another lesbian. I am having a hard time narrowing it down.... It's a look, a feeling, a vibe that they send you that says, I see you, I recognize you. Now I don't believe in ESP so I think it must be a form of nonverbal communication, but it's hard to put my finger on exactly what it is.

All urbanites interpret signals from strangers that are so subtle that describing them is very difficult. These cues are often picked up subconsciously. Because lesbians are motivated to recognize other lesbians, they find it easier to verbalize the nature of these intangible cues. Lesbians often say that their radar picks up a "dyke energy" or "lesbian vibe." A Winnipeg lesbian expressed it

this way: "I identify women as lesbian (I admit it) based on hair, clothes, and mannerisms but also their 'essence.' Lesbians have an indescribable trait that just screams 'I'm a lesbian!'"

A critical reader might ask why lesbians are so concerned about recognizing other lesbians in public places. Although it might be tempting to dismiss gaydar as a frivolous notion, the emotional responses elicited by sighting other lesbians captures the significance of gaydar for the lesbian community. Consider these comments from survey respondents from Minneapolis, Toronto, and New York, respectively.

I feel affirmed, energized and empowered and proud of myself and the lesbians I encounter. It makes me feel that I'm not alone in the world and that I am okay.

I look for lesbians everywhere. Especially at straight functions. It's kind of a game and it makes the experience less lonely. I get thrilled to see lesbians and will work to connect with them in some manner. There is definitely a feeling I get when I discover another lesbian. It's so damn exciting!

Seeing a queer person in a crowd of strangers is like seeing a friend, even if we don't connect, I feel comforted and less alone.

If lesbians engage their "dyke spotting" abilities and invest these sightings with a heightened importance, can we conclude that the process of gaydar ends with recognition and the fleeting "warm and fuzzy" feelings that accompany spotting a "friend" in a crowd of hostile strangers?

ACKNOWLEDGING STRANGERS

The assessment of strangers' identities is, in fact, simply one step in a dynamic interactional process. Symbolic interactionists suggest that all social action stems from these initial categorizations. However, a strong urban norm dictates that strangers appear to pay little heed to each other. Goffman's (1963) concept of "civil inattention" describes the urban interaction ritual in which trust and mutual respect are routinely secured in instances of co-presence between strangers. In a quick scanning of a stranger's eyes, we assess the other's identity and in an equally quick "dimming of the lights" (looking away) we convey respect for the sacredness of the other's self.

Using gaydar can lead to situations of heightened civility where gay strangers momentarily eschew the norms of civil inattention that structure the urban world as they become more attentive to each other based on shared marginalized sexual identity. This "reciprocal responsiveness" (Couch, 1989) takes varied forms. The smallest exchanges between lesbian strangers involve ritualistic mutual acknowledgement. I refer to these actions as "acknowledgement rituals" to capture their habitual nature.

Returning to the scenario described at the beginning of the article, we find that once the four lesbians had read each other's identities, a number of actions followed. These rituals would not likely have been shared among heterosexual strangers. Six lesbian interaction rituals took place on the New York City sidewalk: prolonged eye contact, nodding, smiling, subtle checking out, brief words, and low-level flirting. These rituals have developed historically in lesbian subcultures as ways to show that recognition has occurred and to take that recognition further by displaying solidarity. A Winnipeg lesbian described a number of these rituals.

It is all in the eyes! Initially eye contact and then a subtle smile. If possible, then a longer look to figure out why I think she is or isn't. If I am with another queer person, then we play the "Is She or Isn't She?" game. If it is at all appropriate in the setting, I will engage in low-level flirting. Some lesbians of course carefully avoid any acknowledgment but those who have at least some comfort with who they are make eye contact, smile knowingly, nod hello.

Rituals of acknowledgement in public places are not unique to lesbians. Strangers often find occasion to nod or smile at each other and even to exchange brief greetings. It is the motivation behind the increased interactional civility between lesbians that is unique. In a world where lesbian identity can be problematic, strangers send signals of identity validation to each other

through mutual acknowledgment in the form of small gestures filled with amplified meaning. Certain characteristics of these rituals make them specific to the subculture as in the "Is She or Isn't She?" game described above. The persistent use of folk terms such as "the knowing smile," "the butch nod," or "the subtle check out" to describe the ways lesbians respond to each other suggests their ubiquity in the lesbian subculture.

The interactions described in the opening scenario could not have taken place without the most basic of rituals: eye contact. Mutual eye contact is "perhaps the most direct and purest reciprocity which exists anywhere" (Simmel, 1970: 301). In the simplest gestures the most profound messages are sent. It is for this reason that the eye is said to be the window to the soul.

Civil inattention is often altered when lesbians are co-present. Lesbians repeatedly state that they can detect another lesbian by the intensity of the eye contact she makes. Despite the apparent simplicity and brevity of this ritual, its message is profound and its effects in guiding social action enormous. Folk terms for this slightly longer eye contact include "the knowing look," "the prolonged glance," or "the lingering gaze." In a very short time, lasting only a second or two, lesbians convey in "the look" that a secret knowledge is shared. As a Toronto resident put it, "If you catch a woman looking at you (twice or in a cautious but lingering way—apart from the 'through you' stares of public transit) then it is a signal that you are being checked out and read as queer or whatever."

Due to its secretive nature, lesbians often describe intense or prolonged eye contact as exciting. A Winnipeg lesbian observes, "Making eye contact with dykes conjures up feeling of pleasure, delight, a sense of power that we know something about each other that maybe other people on the street don't recognize—or if they recognize it they are not part of it."

Eye contact is both a behavioural cue of recognition and an action of acknowledgment. One way that lesbians determine the accuracy of a gaydar reading is by assessing the quality and length of eye contact they receive from a stranger. In the scenario below, described by a Toronto lesbian, eye contact is the only cue available. It is such a powerful cue, however, that it is enough to solidify a gaydar reading.

My first experience recognizing a lesbian came about when I was 16 years old. A new teacher had come to our school. She dressed femmy, had a good figure and long blond hair. I was in the empty hall going through my locker when she came out of her classroom. It was just she and me in the hallway. I looked up at her and our eyes locked. And I knew, and I knew that she knew. I was almost knocked over with the surprise of it all. I started to laugh and she started to laugh and we just stood there in the hallway smiling and laughing and seeing each other. The bell rang and the hallway filled with students. So what was it? It wasn't her look or anything she wore. It wasn't situational, the high-school hallway. It was the way she looked at me. Like she knew who I was. Like we shared something. It was also wild to know this thing that I was sure no one else in the school knew. That she was willing to let herself be recognized by recognizing me. That was my first real experience with recognizing a lesbian stranger: it was strange and joyful. Later when I told my gay friends about the experience, I couldn't really explain how I knew, but I was and still am 100% certain. I knew because she told me [in the way she looked at me].

Few lesbians, I suspect, would read this story without emotion. This moment, described so lucidly, captures the essence of what gaydar means to many lesbians. Neither of the lesbians in the scenario was "out," in the full meaning of the term, and yet they shared a brief moment of solidarity that placed them outside the heterosexual norm.

Prolonged or intense eye contact seals an identity placement made through assessment of cues. Further rituals (e.g., smiling, nodding, or exchanging greetings) follow eye contact. If the situation is conducive, more spontaneous actions, such as low-level flirting, may take place.[7] These rituals of recognition and acknowledgement temporarily imbue public places with lesbian meaning. Hence, they can ease the difficulties that lesbians experience in negotiating a heterosexist society. Are engagements between lesbian strangers always so subtle and ritualistic?

ENCOUNTERS

Anti-urbanites view the idea of stranger interaction as an oxymoron (Lofland, 1990). The following quote sums up an attitude toward the public realm that continues to influence both the sociological imagination (Mills, 1959) and common-sense beliefs about urbanite interaction:

On the street, in the subway, on the bus [the city dweller] comes in contact with hundreds of people. But these brief incidental associations are based neither on sharing of common values nor on a co-operation for a common purpose. They are formal in the most complete sense of the term in that they are empty of content. (Spykman, 1926: 58)

Is this pessimistic conjecture a reality? Not so, according to urban ethnographers.[8] On the contrary, a moral order underlies the apparent chaos and impersonality of city streets. This "interaction order" (Goffman, 1983) is sustained differently from the morality found in primary groups. Strangers on city streets do not display the kinds of close interaction found in smaller settings; that would be impossible. Yet civil intentions can be detected between strangers, affirming the existence of a collective urban civility.

Being openly gay in public places carries a degree of risk. Despite this fact, or perhaps because of it, gay people may find more opportunities than heterosexuals to engage in encounters. Heightened civility between lesbian strangers, then, moves beyond politeness and a collective effort to sustain an orderly society. Such actions also send messages of solidarity. Once the transitory actions of mutual acknowledgement take place, openings in the norms of silence between strangers may be created where lesbians make contacts that are spontaneous and enduring in nature. These encounters range from small gestures of helping behaviour to more sustained interactions, such as making friends or romantic connections.

Lesbians often state that they are more willing to help a stranger if they perceive her to be gay. They may look for reasons to assist a woman they have tagged as lesbian in order to connect. Two lesbians, from Minneapolis and Vancouver, respectively, illustrate this point.

I always try to be extra nice to the dykes who checkout at my register (give them free stuff, talk more, flirt, etc.). There is a lot of negativity and homophobia out there, so I smile and make eye contact a lot. Sometimes I try to start conversation if it is reasonable.

I decided in my mind which of the staff at a bookstore I shopped at in Vancouver were lesbians based on which ones were more overtly friendly to me when I was buying or browsing through lesbian-themed books. When I worked in retail and lesbians (or women I assumed or suspected were lesbians) came into the store, I was much more friendly to them than to general customers.

Always aware of safety issues, lesbians are often subtle in their interactions with lesbian strangers. Although the events described below by a New Yorker do not typify normal subway riding behaviour, the incident is unexceptional. Though no words are exchanged, the meaning of the nonverbal communication is clear.

My girlfriend and I were riding the subway home, and it was fairly late. A very interesting couple sat across from us holding hands. The younger of the two was an androgynous, butchy dyke, and her girlfriend was much older and clearly femme. My girlfriend was holding my hand and we all very subtly, casually glanced at each other. They were getting off the subway at the same stop as us, and when the subway doors opened, the butchy dyke stood at the opening *holding the door* until her girlfriend, *my* girlfriend and *myself* had safely exited. The funny thing is, we would have made it through the door just fine on our own, I mean we'd definitely done it many times before...*but*, it was simply the *beauty*, and *respect* and *recognition* and *pride* of the gesture that really struck me. The subway is definitely one of the scariest places to be out, because you are surrounded by some of the scariest people in New York ya know? It was just so beautiful how this woman *without* words made such as huge statement to me and my girl, by showing concern and recognizing us.

The exchange among the four subway riders can be interpreted as a silent honouring of the boldness of being "out" in one of the cities "scariest places." In a marginalized subculture, signals of solidarity are political in nature, even when not intended as political statements. Through displays of solidarity, the subculture is strengthened and heterosexual hegemony is challenged.

Political and safety issues aside, strangers connect for the pure pleasure of engaging with fellow human beings (Lofland, 1990). Nonintimate social interaction, although qualitatively different from intimate social interaction, can be deeply satisfying. In fact, these encounters have certain advantages, not the least of which are that differences are not immediately threatening and group dynamics do not come into play. Jane Jacobs has referred to "sidewalk terms" to capture the nature of these types of social engagements. In public places, it is possible to connect with people "without unwelcome entanglements, without boredom, necessity for excuses, explanations, fears of giving offence, embarrassments respecting impositions or commitments and all such paraphernalia of obligations which accompany less limited relationships. It is possible to be on excellent sidewalk terms with people who are very different from oneself" (Jacobs, 1961: 62).

Sidewalk connections are made easily among lesbians because they share a symbolic culture that facilitates the breaking down of boundaries. A New Yorker recalls an encounter with a stranger that transformed her bus riding experience. Take notice of the way the interaction unfolded. The mutual reading of identity cues (assisted by subtle actions) was followed by acknowledgement, which led to an encounter.

I was on a city bus. It was extremely crowded with people pushing and shoving their way home. A woman sat down next to me and, although we did not initially acknowledge one another, I read her as a dyke right away. She was middle-aged, with a short haircut and style that I read as 70s feminist lesbian. I realize that I did something I often do when I see others I perceive as queer. I picked up my backpack so that the rainbow beads on the zipper were visible. Whether or not any conversation takes place, I feel a sense of connection with others when I know they've recognized a common sign. I got out my book and began reading. I noticed the woman next to me peering over at the page. Normally I'd be irritated by this, but I was interested to connect with this woman I perceived to be "family" in this straight crowd. I acknowledged her glance by looking back in a friendly way. She mentioned her surprise to see the book and said she [had known] the author long ago. We spoke about the book and about where one might buy the book and she mentioned that she hosts a poetry night at Bluestockings [a lesbian bookstore collective] once a month. We got off the bus at the same stop and went our separate ways...but, speaking with her even just briefly created a sense of connection to the community in me that stayed with me the whole day.

The fact that this episode took place in an ordinary public place is important. The creation of "free territories" in the city is a resistance tactic of marginalized people (Lyman & Scott, 1970). Lesbian territories are spaces where lesbians can interact, free from heterosexual constraints. In more restrictive times, lesbians and gays forged urban spaces in underground places such as bars (Nestle, 1997). With the advent of the gay rights movement, many lesbian spaces, such as coffee shops, bookstores, and urban neighbourhoods with large numbers of lesbians living in them, have become available (Valentine, 1995). Recently, however, the gay community, refusing to be ghettoized, has emphasized the right to be "out" in heterosexually dominated public places.

Considering the historical restriction of lesbian interaction to specified spaces, it is no surprise that interacting as lesbians in nongay public places is exciting. This strategy of being visible in public has become progressively, politically significant.

Such visibility reacts against the confined space of the "closet," which has been perhaps the most compelling metaphor for visibility and identity within gay and lesbian narratives. The closet symbolizes the space of denial, darkness, confinement. To come out depends on emerging from the spatial structures of the closet and into the public, onto the street. Therefore, the process of attaining an authentic gay identity relies on the movement from one space to another—from the closet to the street (Polchin, 1997: 386).

As lesbians struggle to express themselves freely in public places, the connection between lesbian visibility and street level solidarity continues to grow in importance. Each time lesbians engage with each other in public places, they strengthen the subculture and challenge the right of heterosexuals to dominate those spaces. These interactions infuse a lesbian reality into a society that would otherwise render lesbians invisible. The significance of gaydar and the interactions that follow, then, cannot be underestimated nor dismissed as the trivial imaginings of an elitist subculture. They are parts of the dynamic identity and community building processes that occur on city streets. As Giddens (1984) has argued, it is through the collective actions of individual social actors that structures of society are created and recreated. Indeed Goffman (1967: 91) expressed it best when he observed: "The gestures which we sometimes call empty are perhaps in fact the fullest things of all."

NOTES

1. This article is drawn from my Ph.D. dissertation. For details of the methodology, theoretical outcomes, and in-depth quotations from participants see Nielsen (2002), "Streets Strangers and Solidarity: A Study of Lesbian Interaction in the Public Realm." Unpublished dissertation. The University of Manitoba.

2. The word "out" is used by gays and lesbians to refer to being open (i.e., "out of the closet") about their sexual identity.

3. Outright condemnation of stereotyped thinking is unrealistic. Although it is tempting to relegate stereotyping to the rigid attitudes of prejudiced people, in reality all people must employ stereotypes to organize the kaleidoscopic flow of events around them. A more realistic approach is to confront the dual reality of these "enabling conventions" (Goffman, 1971) as both distorters of reality and doorways to social engagement.

4. Note that as part of the "gay pride" movement, gays and lesbians have re-appropriated pejorative labels such as queer, dyke, fag, and homo. By adopting these labels for their own use, the subculture has reduced their power to stigmatize.

5. Turner's (1990) concept of "role making" describes the way that social actors impose meanings on situations through the process of testing the inferences they make about others in social situations.

6. For a detailed analysis of the ways that strangers use these different types of cues (appearential, behavioural, and spatial) in making sense of the chaotic "world of strangers" see Lofland (1973).

7. For an explanation of why low-level flirting takes on ritualistic qualities in the lesbian subculture as both a gaydar cue and a recognition strategy, see Nielsen (2002). The dissertation outlines the details of these rituals and the situational variables that affect whether they take place (i.e., safety, spatial concerns, racial variables, and outness levels).

8. Urban ethnographers have steadily chipped away at the pervasive belief in the emptiness of urban interaction. See Lofland (1998) for an overview of these ethnographic studies.

REFERENCES

Couch, C. 1989. *Social processes and relationships*. New York: General Hall.

Giddens, A. 1984. *The constitution of society: Outline of the theory of structuration*. Cambridge: Polity Press.

Gardner, C. B. 1994. A family among strangers: Kinship claims among gay men in public places. In *The community of the streets*, eds. L. Lofland, and S. Cahill, 95–120. London: JAI Press Inc.

Goffman, E. 1959. *The presentation of self in everyday life*. New York: Anchor.

———. 1963. *Behavior in public places*. New York: Free Press of Glencoe.

———. 1967. *Interaction ritual*. New York: Pantheon Books.

———. 1971. *Relations in public*. New York: Basic Books.

———. 1983. The interaction order. *American Sociological Review,* 48: 1–17.

Jacobs, J. 1961. *The death and life of great American cities*. New York: Vintage Books.

Lofland, L. 1973. *A world of strangers: Order and action in urban public space*. New York: Basic Books.

———. 1990. Social interaction: Continuities and complexities in the study of nonintimate sociality. In *Sociological perspectives on social psychology*, eds. K. Cook, G. Fine, and J. House, 176–201. Boston: Allyn and Bacon.

———. 1998. *The public realm: Exploring the city's quintessential social territory*. New York: Basic Books.

Lyman, S., and M. Scott.1970. Territoriality: A neglected sociological dimension. In *Social psychology through symbolic interactionism*, eds. G. Stone, and H. Faberman, 214–26. Massachusetts: Xerox College Publishing.

Mills, C. W. 1959. *The sociological imagination*. London: Oxford University Press.

Nestle, J. 1997. Restriction and reclamation: Lesbian bars and beaches in the 1950s. In *Queers in space: Communities, public places, resistance*, eds. G. Ingram, A. Bouthilette, and Y. Retter, 61–8. Seattle: Bay Press.

Nielsen, T. 2002. Streets, strangers and solidarity: A study of lesbian interaction in the public realm. Unpublished dissertation. Winnipeg: University of Manitoba.

Polchin, J. 1997. Having something to wear: The landscape of identity on Christopher Street. In *Queers in space: Communities, public places, resistance*, eds. G. Ingram, A. Bouthilette, and Y. Retter, 381–90. Seattle: Bay Press.

Simmel, G. 1970. On visual interaction. In *Social psychology through symbolic interactionism*, eds. G. Stone, and H. Farberman, 300–02. Massachusetts: Xerox College Publishing.

Spykman, N. 1926. A social philosophy of the city. In *The urban community: Selected papers from the proceedings of the American Sociological Society*, ed. E. Burgess. Chicago: University of Chicago Press.

Turner, R. 1990. Role-taking: Process versus conformity. In *Life as theatre: A dramaturgical sourcebook*, eds. D. Brissett, and C. Edgley, 85–100. New York: Aldine de Gruyter.

Valentine, G. 1995. Out and about: Geographies of lesbian landscapes. *International Journal of Urban and Regional Research*, 19: 96–112.

Part X

Social Stratification

21

The Vertical Mosaic:
An Analysis of Social Class
and Power in Canada

John Porter

THE CANADIAN MIDDLE CLASS IMAGE

One of the most persistent images that Canadians have of their society is that it has no classes. This image becomes translated into the assertion that Canadians are all relatively equal in their possessions, in the amount of money they earn, and in the opportunities which they and their children have to get on in the world. An important element in this image of classlessness is that, with the absence of formal aristocracy and aristocratic institutions, Canada is a society in which equalitarian values have asserted themselves over authoritarian values. Canada, it is thought, shares not only a continent with the United States, but also a democratic ideology which rejects the historical class and power structures of Europe.

Source: From *The Vertical Mosaic* by John Porter. Toronto: University of Toronto Press, 1965, pp. 3–6. Reprinted with the permission of the publisher.

Social images are one thing and social realities another. Yet the two are not completely separate. Social images are not entirely fictional characters with only a coincidental likeness to a real society, living or dead. Often the images can be traced to an earlier historical period of the society, its golden age perhaps, which, thanks to the historians, is held up, long after it has been transformed into something else, as a model way of life. As well as their historical sources, images can be traced to their contemporary creators, particularly in the world of the mass media and popular culture. When a society's writers, journalists, editors, and other image-creators are a relatively small and closely linked group, and have more or less the same social background, the images they produce can, because they are consistent, appear to be much more true to life than if their group were larger, less cohesive, and more heterogeneous in composition.

The historical source of the image of a classless Canada is the equality among pioneers in the frontier environment of the last century. In the early part of the [twentieth] century there was a similar equality of status among those who were settlers in the west, although, as we shall see, these settlers were by no means treated equally. A rural, agricultural, primary producing society is a much less differentiated society than one which has highly concentrated industries in large cities. Equality in the rural society may be much more apparent than real, but the rural environment has been for Canada an important source of the image of equality. Later we shall examine more closely how the historical image has become out of date with the transformation of Canadian society from the rural to the urban type.

Although the historical image of rural equality lingers, it has gradually given way in the urban industrial setting to an image of a middle level classlessness in which there is a general uniformity of possessions. For families these possessions include a separate dwelling with an array of electrical equipment, a car, and perhaps a summer cottage. Family members, together or as individuals, engage in a certain amount of ritualistic behaviour in churches and service clubs. Modern advertising has done much to standardize the image of middle class consumption levels and middle class behaviour. Consumers' magazines are devoted to the task of constructing the ideal way of life through articles on child-rearing, homemaking, sexual behaviour, health, sports, and hobbies. Often, too, corporations which do not produce family commodities directly will have large advertisements to demonstrate how general social well-being at this middle level is an outcome of their own operations.

That there is neither very rich nor very poor in Canada is an important part of the image. There are no barriers to opportunity. Education is free. Therefore, making use of it is largely a question of personal ambition. Even university education is available to all, except that it may require for some a little more summer work and thrift. There

is a view widely held by many university graduates that they, and most other graduates, have worked their way through college. Consequently it is felt anyone else can do the same.

In some superficial respects the image of middle class uniformity may appear plausible. The main values of the society are concerned with the consumption of commodities, and in the so-called affluence that has followed World War II there seem to have been commodities for everybody, except, perhaps, a small group of the permanently poor at the bottom. Credit facilities are available for large numbers of low-income families, enabling them, too, to be consumers of commodities over and above the basic necessities of life. The vast array of credit facilities, some of them extraordinarily ingenious, have inequalities built into them, in that the cost of borrowing money varies with the amount already possessed. There are vast differences in the quality of goods bought by the middle income levels and the lower income levels. One commodity, for instance, which low-income families can rarely purchase is privacy, particularly the privacy of a house to themselves. It is perhaps the value of privacy and the capacity to afford it which has become the dividing line between the real and the apparent middle class.

If low-income families achieve high consumption levels it is usually through having more than one income earner in the household. Often this is the wife and mother, but it may be an older child who has left school, and who is expected to contribute to the family budget. Alternatively, high consumption levels may be achieved at a cost in leisure. Many low-income family heads have two jobs, a possibility which has arisen with the shorter working day and the five-day week. This "moonlighting," as it is called in labour circles, tends to offset the progress which has been made in raising the level of wages and reducing the hours of work. There is no way of knowing how extensive "moonlighting" is, except that we know that trade unions denounce it as a practice which tends to take away the gains which have been obtained for workers. For large segments of the population, therefore, a high level of consumption is obtained by means which are alien to a true middle class standard. [When]…we…examine closely the distribution of income, we …see what a small proportion of Canadian families were able to live a middle class style of life in the middle 1950s, the high tide of post-war affluence.

At the high end of the social class spectrum, also in contrast to the middle level image, are the families of great wealth and influence. They are not perhaps as ostentatious as the very wealthy of other societies, and Canada has no "celebrity world" with which these families must compete for prestige in the way Mills has suggested is important for the very rich in American society.[1]

Almost every large Canadian city has its wealthy and prominent families of several generations. They have their own social life, their children go to private schools, they have their clubs and associations, and they take on the charitable and philanthropic roles which have so long been the "duty" of those of high status. Although this upper class is always being joined by the new rich, it still contributes, as we shall see later, far more than its proportionate share to the elite of big business.

The concentration of wealth in the upper classes is indicated by the fact that in Canada in 1955 the top one per cent of income recipients received about 40 per cent of all income from dividends.

Images which conflict with the one of middle class equality rarely find expression, partly because the literate middle class is both the producer and the consumer of the image. Even at times in what purports to be serious social analy-sis, middle class intellectuals project the image of their own class onto the social classes above and below them. There is scarcely any critical analysis of Canadian social life upon which a conflicting image could be based. The idea of class differences has scarcely entered into the stream of Canadian academic writing despite the fact that class differences stand in the way of implementing one of the most important values of western society, that is equality.[2] The fact, which we shall see later, that Canada draws its intellectuals either from abroad or from its own middle class, means that there is almost no one producing a view of the world which reflects the experience of the poor or the underprivileged. It was as though they did not exist. It is the nature of these class differences and their consequences for Canadian society that [we]…seek to explore.

Closely related to differences in class levels are differences in the exercising of power and decision-making in the society: Often it is thought that once a society becomes an electoral democracy based on universal suffrage, power becomes diffused throughout the general population so that everyone participates somehow in the selection of social goals. There is, however, a whole range of institutional resistances to the transfer of power to a democratic political system.…

NOTES

1. C. W. Mills, *The Power Elite* (New York, 1956), chap. 4.
2. Nor does class appear as a theme in Canadian literature. See R. L. McDougall, "The Dodo and the Cruising Auk," *Canadian Literature*, no. 18 (Autumn 1963).
3. For a comparative study of social mobility see S. M. Lipset and R. Bendix, *Social Mobility in Industrial Society* (Berkeley, 1959).

22

Does the Vertical Mosaic Still Exist? Ethnicity and Income in Canada, 1991*

Jason Z. Lian and David Ralph Matthews

This paper updates our knowledge about the relationship between ethnicity and social class in Canada using *The Public Use Microdata File for Individuals* drawn from the 1991 Census of Canada. We provide three levels of analysis. First, we examine the relationship between ethnicity and education by ethnic group. Second, we examine the "return to education" in terms of income for those of various ethnic groups. Third, we use log-linear regression to examine the relationship between ethnicity, education, and income while controlling for the effects of a variety of other social variables. We find that, at

*This is a revised version of a paper presented at the Canadian Ethnic Studies Association, Biennial Meeting, Gimli, Manitoba, October 1995. We thank Margaret Denton, John Fox, and Wulong Gu for helpful suggestions and comments. The manuscript of this article was submitted in February 1997 and accepted in July 1997.

Source: Jason Z. Lian and David Matthews. 1998. Does the Vertical Mosaic Still Exist? Ethnicity and Income in Canada, 1991. *The Canadian Review of Sociology and Anthropology*, 35(4), 461–81. Reprinted by permission of the Canadian Sociology and Anthropology Association.

most educational levels, Canadians of French ethnicity now earn significantly more than those of British ethnicity when other variables are controlled. With this exception, for those of European ethnic backgrounds there are now virtually no significant differences in income within educational levels when other social variables are controlled. However, those who belong to visible minorities have significantly lower incomes than other Canadians at all educational levels. Race is now the fundamental basis of income inequality in Canada.

In 1965, John Porter described Canadian society as a "vertical mosaic" stratified along ethnic lines (1965: 60–103). Porter argued that the British and French, as the first ethnic groups to come into Canada, became the "charter groups" and to a considerable extent dictated the circumstances under which other ethnic groups were subsequently permitted to enter. He argued that "entrance status" was generally granted to those of other ethnic groups who were willing to accept lower level occupational roles (63–73) and that, as a result, "immigration and ethnic affilia-tion...have been important factors in the forma-tion of social classes in Canada" (73). Porter used census data from the 1931 to 1961 period to demonstrate that the British dominated the French in all of the most prestigious occupational categories, and that other ethnic groups were generally distributed in a hierarchy below them.

Since then, considerable effort has been expended by researchers to support or refute Porter's thesis and to examine the extent to which ethnic social class mobility has occurred as previ-ous immigrants overcame their "entrance status" and moved up the social class hierarchy. Proponents of the vertical mosaic thesis have argued that differences in occupational status among Canadian ethnic groups remain substantial. Over the past thirty years, they have demonstrated that, for the two charter groups, the occupational status of the British has remained significantly higher than that of the French (Royal Commission, 1969: 34–45; Breton & Roseborough, 1971; Boyd et al., 1981). They have argued that among other groups, Jews and those from the north and west of Europe are generally in favourable positions, South Europeans and visible minorities are gener-ally in disadvantaged positions, and Aboriginal Peoples are at the bottom of the Canadian occupa-tional hierarchy (Reitz, 1980; Porter, 1985; Jabbra & Cosper, 1988; Li, 1988; Lautard & Guppy, 1990). Thus, in 1984, Lautard and Loree could still claim that "occupational inequality is still substan-tial enough to justify the use of the concept 'verti-cal mosaic' to characterize this aspect of ethnic relations in Canada" (343).

In contrast, a number of other researchers have argued that the influence of ethnicity in the process of social mobility was and/or is minimal in Canada, and that ethnic affiliation did not operate as a significant block to social mobility as Porter had suggested. Most such works have examined the relationship between ethnicity and occupation, while controlling for a range of other variables. Using such methods, they have argued that the association between ethnicity and

occupational status was minimal and declining (Pineo, 1976; Darroch, 1979; Ornstein, 1981) and that the contention of the vertical mosaic thesis that the status of immigrants groups has been rigidly preserved is "patently false" (Tepperman, 1975: 156). Other researchers have suggested that a convergence process in occupa-tional status among ethnic groups in Canada has become more apparent since Porter's original analysis (Reitz, 1980: 150–53), the relationship between ethnic origin and class position has been in flux (Nakhaie, 1951), and that gains by non-charter groups have been significantly greater than those of the charter groups (Boyd et al., 1981; Pineo & Porter, 1985: 382–83). Porter, himself, has argued that the situation he described in 1965 may have been in existence only for a relatively short period in Canadian history (Pineo & Porter, 1985: 390). It is also argued that, to the extent that any ethnic status hierarchy remains, Porter's status hierarchy of ethnic groups has changed dramatically with the British dropping from the top to the middle and the Asians moving to the top with the Jews (Herberg, 1990). As a result, it has been stated recently that ethnicity is no longer a drawback for social mobility in Canada (Isajiw, Sev'er & Driedger, 1993).

In many such works, the relation of educa-tion and ethnicity has come under considerable scrutiny. Thus, proponents of the ethnic inequality thesis have argued that the Canadian education system has been a mechanism to reproduce social inequality (Shamai, 1992: 44–5) and that educational opportunity was not equally accessible to all groups (Li, 1988: 77–96). Alternatively, those who have been crit-ical of the ethnic inequality thesis have argued that there is little evidence of ethnic inequality in education in Canada and that a *"contest-achieved"* system of status attainment is oper-ating (Herberg, 1990). Indeed, Porter was himself involved in work which argued that non-charter groups have gained significantly in educational achievement compared to the

British (Pineo & Porter, 1985: 384) and that the educational system has worked to help minority Canadians overcome the disadvantages of their background (391).

The general conclusion of this body of work would seem to be that there is a collapsing of the vertical mosaic. However, there is growing evidence (see Li, 1988; Reitz, 1980; Agocs & Boyd, 1993) that Canada has retained what Geschwender and Guppy have called a "colour-coded vertical mosaic" (1995: 2). Such works suggest that, whereas ethnic stratification has lessened among white European groups, differences between racial groups have persisted and that, in effect, Canada's mosaic has been reduced to a division based principally on skin colour (1995: 2).

This paper will examine the evidence for and against ethnic inequality in Canada with respect to income distribution, using *The Public Use Microdata Files for Individuals* (PUMFI) provided by Statistics Canada, which constitutes a 3% sample of the 1991 Census. Such files have been made available since 1971, but the 1991 PUMFI provides both a more extensive list of ethnic groups and a more detailed categorization of other variables that may be employed as controls than were available in previous issues. Thus, the present paper is able to provide more current information on the relationship between ethnicity and income than most previous studies, and also is able to identify ethnicity more precisely and use more stringent control variables in the analysis.

To carry out the analysis we have used those respondents in the PUMFI who were in the "working population," and from this group have eliminated those respondents for whom data were not available or who had zero or negative earnings.[1] These latter reductions reduce the number of respondents in the working population sample by 4.78%, nearly half of whom had zero or negative earnings in 1990. As a result of these adjustments, the average earnings of the sample increased by approximately 4%, but the ethnic composition

changed very little.... Thus, for purposes of the present study which focuses on ethnicity, our sample was not affected significantly.

ETHNICITY AND EDUCATION

In any study of ethnic stratification and mobility, education is seen as a critically important intervening variable between ethnicity and income. A fundamental question in such studies is whether educational achievement is distributed equally among ethnic groups. Earlier we noted the diverging positions on this subject in Canada—some argued that the educational system has functioned to reproduce the existing socio-economic hierarchy in favour of the dominant groups (Li, 1988: 73–7; Shamai, 1992: 53–5), and others argued that the educational system has functioned as a source of upward mobility for Canadian minority groups since the early decades of this century (Herberg, 1990).

It is not possible to test this issue fully using data from a single time period. However, data from the 1991 PUMFI show a considerable variation in education among ethnic groups when compared with the Canadian average and this variation remains even when one separates out the Canadian born from the foreign born. This indicates that, among native-born Canadians, educational achievement is unevenly distributed by ethnicity....

In 1991, approximately 30% of the employed labour force in Canada had less than secondary education, just over 54% had secondary or non-university post-secondary education, and almost 17% had post-secondary education. About two-thirds of the European groups and half of the visible minority groups were close to this Canadian average. However, several Southern European groups (Italians, Greeks, Portuguese), Vietnamese, and Aboriginal Peoples had proportionally more persons with this lower educational level while Arabs, West Asians, Jews and Filipinos were under-represented in the lower educational groups.

At the other extreme, in terms of post-secondary (university) education most European groups were around the national average, Poles were moderately above and Jews were nearly three times likely to have a university degree than were those of European origin *per se*. With the exception of the Black/Caribbean and Aboriginal groups who ranked substantially below the national level, the remaining visible minority groups had high rates of university education. This was particularly the case for those of Arab, West Asian, South Asian, Chinese, Filipino and Other East and Southeast Asian ethnic backgrounds.

To some considerable degree this latter finding is a reflection of Canadian immigration policy since the 1970s, which has favoured those with high levels of education and training. Thus, Arab, West Asian, South Asian, Filipino, and Vietnamese foreign born were generally better educated than their Canadian-born counterparts. This relationship held for most other groups with the notable exception of the Greek, Italian, and Balkan ethnic groups among whom the native born were generally better educated than recent immigrants.

EDUCATION AND INCOME DIFFERENCES AMONG ETHNIC GROUPS

While differences in education by ethnic group, particularly among the Canadian-born, are an indication of possible ethnic discrimination, the more significant indication is whether the "returns for education" are also unequal among ethnic groups. That is, does similar education (at whatever level) generate significantly different incomes among the ethnic groups?...

At the national level, those with secondary education earned about 50% more than those without secondary education and those with university education earned about 150% more than those without secondary education.... However, there are extreme ethnic differences at all three educational levels.

The following analyses are all based on comparisons with the national average for each of the educational categories. Looking first at the two "charter groups," workers of British origin with non-secondary education earned 3% more than the national average for this educational level, those with secondary education earned 7% more, while those with university education earned 8% more. In comparison, workers of French ethnicity with non-secondary education earned 12% more than the national average, those with secondary education earned 1% less and those with university education earned 4% more. Thus, in contrast to Porter's finding that the French were rewarded significantly less than the British for their educational achievement, at the lower educational level they now have a significant edge over the British, and are above the national average in income at the higher educational levels.

Those of Western European ethnic background earned considerably higher incomes than the Canadian average in each of the education categories, the exception being university educated persons of Dutch and German ethnic backgrounds who earned only marginally more. Eastern Europeans also tended to earn more than the Canadian average, with Hungarians and Ukrainians earning substantially more at all levels. Persons of Polish ethnicity with lower as well as middle levels of education earned more than average, but better educated persons of Polish ethnicity earned less.

For those whose Jewish ethnic background was recorded, those with the lowest level of education earned 9% more than the Canadian average income for that level, while those with university education earned 19% more than the Canadian university educated average income. However, those with secondary education earned 4% less than the average Canadians at their educational level.

The pattern for Southern Europeans is mixed. At the lowest educational level, most of these ethnic groups earned above the Canadian average income with those of Italian, Portuguese, Greek, and Balkan origin earning considerably higher than that average. However, at higher educational levels Southern Europeans were generally disadvantaged.

However, it is when we consider visible minorities that the largest discrepancies between education and income are apparent. At the lower education levels all 10 visible minority groups earned less than an average Canadian with similar education, ranging from 5% less for those of Arab ethnicity to 33% less for those of Filipino ethnic background and 42% less for Aboriginal Peoples. Likewise, among those with secondary education, all 10 visible minority groups earned substantially less than the comparable Canadian average. Similarly, amongst those with post-secondary education, while those of Black and Chinese ethnicity earned only somewhat less than the Canadian average, those in the other eight visible minority groups received earning[s] substantially below that level.

The overall conclusion to be drawn from these two tables is that persons of European background generally receive above average income for their educational level with the exception of persons with higher education from some Eastern and Southern European ethnic groups. Indeed, persons from many such ethnic backgrounds now receive incomes relative to education that are higher than for either of the two "charter groups." *However, for visible minorities a very different picture emerges. For all visible ethnic groups and at all educational levels, the rewards for education are substantially below the Canadian average.*

ETHNICITY AND INCOME DIFFERENCES WITHIN EDUCATIONAL CATEGORIES, TAKING INTO ACCOUNT OTHER VARIABLES

Although the preceding analysis has provided strong indications that the rewards for education vary by ethnic group and particularly that workers of visible minorities receive comparatively less than other workers with similar education, it is possible that these results are not due to ethnicity *per se* but to a range of other factors such as the age composition, marital status, or period of immigration of workers from various ethnic groups. Thus, if one wants to measure directly the effect of ethnicity on earnings within educational categories, it is necessary to take into account the effect of these other earnings-related variables.

To do this, we developed a semi-logarithmic regression model of earnings determination with interaction terms constructed of ethnicity and education, controlling for gender; age and age squared; marital status; province of residence; metropolitan versus non-metropolitan area of residence; geographic mobility in the past five years; period of immigration; knowledge of official languages; occupational level; industrial sector; weeks worked and weeks worked squared; and full versus part-time weeks worked. Controlling for these factors in a semi-logarithmic regression yields an adjusted R square of 0.58007, indicating that 58% of the variations in log earnings have been accounted for by the variables included in the model.

Because of the dominant position of the British in Canadian society both numerically and socio-economically, we have used them as the base line category in the regression for an estimation of the net log earnings of the other ethnic groups at each educational level. While persons of British ethnicity with "no degree, certificate, or diploma" were used as the reference category for all other interactive categories of ethnicity and education in the regression, for easy interpretation, we have converted the partial coefficients for the other ethnic groups as deviations from those of their category of "no degree, certificate, or diploma" for the British. The coefficients derived in this manner have been converted into percentages and displayed in Table 22.1

As an example of how to interpret the table, we would note that the 3.1% in the cell for French with "no degree, certificate, or diploma" indicates that workers of French ethnic origin earned 3.1% more than their British counterparts with comparable education when all the dimensions in our model have been taken into account. Similarly,

TABLE 22.1 Adjusted Earnings[1] of Persons of Different Ethnic Origins[2] as Percentage Differences from Those of Persons of British Origin by Educational Level, Canada, 1990

Ethnic Origin	No Degree, Certificate, or Diploma	High School Graduation Certificate	Trades Certificate	Other Non-University Certificate	University Certificate below Bachelor Level	Bachelor's Degree(s)	University Certificate above Bachelor Level	Masters Degree(s)	Earned Doctorate	Degree in Medicine[3]
British[4]		13.2**	16.8***	21.3***	27.3***	39.6***	47.4***	58.3***	76.6***	141.7***
French	3.1**	1.7**	3.0**	5.3*	8.1**	2.3*	2.8	1.2	5.4	4.2
Dutch	0.5	2.8	1.6	-2.0	-18.4**	-3.9	-3.9	-12.4*	1.9	-40.6**
German	3.7**	-0.5	-2.1	0.7	3.7	-2.6	-3.4	-7.0	-3.4	-14.7
Other W European	14.0**	5.2	1.0	14.3**	16.2	0.9	-7.4	2.4	6.1	-24.4
Hungarian	-2.4	-2.1	-1.3	-11.3**	-18.7	-2.0	4.4	11.4	-17.0	8.3
Polish	-3.6	-1.1	1.8	1.1	-19.2*	0.6	-3.0	-14.4**	-6.1	-12.5
Ukrainian	2.7	3.1	2.7	4.0**	-14.4**	5.6*	-2.2	-3.4	-13.8	6.3
Balkan	2.4	-3.6	-2.0	5.3	4.6	-2.1	-5.6	-5.8	-8.6	-3.4
Greek	-6.3**	-6.6**	0.4	-1.7	-32.5**	-9.3	-15.7	-2.4	-25.9	-50.1**
Italian	-0.6	2.7*	-0.0	7.1**	8.3	-1.1	-2.1	3.6	-1.8	-26.4*
Portuguese	11.0**	3.1	4.8	2.8	-22.5*	-4.9	5.3	0.6	–	41.7
Spanish	4.1	-14.4**	0.7	-6.0	-13.1	-14.7	0.5	-20.2	48.5	14.6
Jewish	21.9**	8.0**	3.3	3.1	3.2	4.4	6.7	0.7	6.7	-2.2
Arab	1.4	-6.2*	-12.6**	1.6	-22.7**	-17.8**	-22.3**	-18.1**	1.6	-27.7**
West Asian	-5.4	-10.4**	-5.3	-0.6	-10.2	-7.5	-15.6	-18.2**	-25.7	-30.5*
South Asian	2.9	-3.9*	-8.6**	-4.1	-0.7	-17.7**	-12.8*	-18.9**	-6.8	-15.9*
Chinese	-4.4**	5.3**	-3.3	-5.6**	-6.6	-7.3**	-14.1**	-10.3**	-26.3**	-15.2*
Filipino	-6.4	-2.1	-12.5**	-8.2*	-7.5	-12.4**	-12.5	-20.9*	–	13.0
Vietnamese	0.8	-11.9**	-19.7**	3.2	-19.3*	-12.7*	-39.2**	-6.9	-7.0	-42.7**
Other E & SE Asian	-4.2	-10.2**	-3.7	-6.8	20.2*	-14.6**	-10.1	-12.1	-27.5	-35.1**
Latin American	3.7	-11.7**	-2.3	-29.8**	-7.8	-24.4**	-31.1**	-18.7	-30.4	-40.6
Black	-8.1**	-3.1	-3.3	-10.4**	-3.7	-10.0**	10.6	-12.4	-10.3	-10.2
Aboriginal	-18.8**	-16.0**	-20.0**	-24.7**	-1.9	-8.0	-24.2	-20.2	-49.4	-76.7*
Others	-2.7**	-0.3	-1.7*	-0.9	0.3	-3.7**	-2.5	-6.7**	-2.6	-7.2

Source: Public Use Microdata File for Individuals, 1991 Census of Canada.

1. Controlling for gender, age, marital status, province of residence, metropolitan/non-metropolitan area, geographic mobility, period of immigration, knowledge of official languages, occupation, industrial sector, weeks worked, and part-time/full-time weeks worked.
2. The earnings of workers of various ethnic origins are expressed as percentage differences from the earnings of workers of British origin in the same educational category.…
3. Including degrees in medicine, dentistry, veterinary medicine, and optometry.
4. The category of "no degree, certificate, or diploma" for the British is the base category for other categories for the British.…

*Significant at 0.10
**Significant at 0.05

persons of British origin with "no degree, certificate, or diploma" are used as the base category for their British counterparts at other levels of education. Thus, for example, workers of British origin with "high school graduate certificates" earned 13.2% more than their counterparts of British origin, who had "no degree, certificate, or diploma," when all the other factors in our [regression] were taken into account. As also noted, this difference is significant at the 0.05 level.

Looking first at the two "charter groups," it is obvious that the net economic returns to education for workers of British origin is significant, with each advancing educational category providing progressively higher returns. It is clear that the economic value of education for persons of British origin in the Canadian labour market is beyond doubt.

However, of more significance is the somewhat surprising finding that, after the other factors are controlled, persons of French origin at *all* educational levels had earnings above that for persons of British origin. Moreover, at the Bachelor's degree level and below, these differences of income between the French and the British are statistically significant. Hence, whatever may have been the situation in the past, it is clear that any suggestion that today the French are discriminated against in terms of the returns they receive for their education, is clearly not the case. Indeed, especially at lower levels, the French are significantly favoured over the British in terms of this relationship.

Among Europeans, whether from the north, east, or south of Europe, most ethnic groups had approximately the same income levels as their British counterparts with similar education. Notable exceptions were the Dutch and Poles who, in several of the upper educational levels earned significantly less, and those of Jewish ethnicity in the lowest educational categories who earned significantly more. The most significant discrepancies occurred, not in relation to any ethnicity, but in terms of certain educational categories. Thus, where respondents held either a "university certificate below the bachelor's level" or a "degree in medicine," persons from continental Europe were quite likely to have incomes significantly below that of the British when other factors were taken into account. The frequency of such discrepancies in these two categories suggests that this may have to do with the evaluation of educational qualification at these levels rather than just ethnicity.

In sharp contrast to the situation for Europeans, adjusted earnings of visible minorities were much lower than for the British at most educational levels. Compared to their British counterparts, out of the 10 educational categories, most visible minority groups earned less than their British counterparts in the majority of categories. Moreover, in many of the educational categories, visible minorities earned *significantly* less than their British counterparts.

Given this obvious evidence of discrimination against all visible minority groups, it is difficult to single out any one or two groups as being more hard done by than others. Perhaps persons of Chinese background might fit this category as they earned less than those of British ethnicity in all 10 educational categories and significantly less than the British in 8 of the 10 educational categories. However, Aboriginal Peoples and West Asians also earned less in 10 categories, and most other visible minority groups earned less in nine of them. While the Arabs might seem better off amongst visible minorities in that they earned lower in only 7 categories, they were significantly less in all 7, a level of earnings discrimination surpassed only by those of Chinese ethnicity.

Whereas one might have thought that increased level of education would lead to lower levels of discrimination, there is little in Table 32.1 to support such a position. From high school to doctorate there is clear evidence of lower earnings amongst visible minorities compared to their British counterparts at the same educational level. Thus, all visible minorities earned less than the British at the high school graduate level, at the level of bachelors degree holder, master's degree holder and, with the exception of Arabs, at the level of doctorate degree holder. Likewise, all visible minorities who held degrees in medicine earned less than their British counterparts, as did all but the Blacks among those who held a university certificate above bachelor's but below master's level. Moreover, in the majority of cases *these differences were either significant or highly significant. In sum, it is clear from these findings that educational achievement at any level fails to protect persons of visible minority background from being disadvantaged in terms of the income they receive.*

SUMMARY AND DISCUSSION

We began this paper with the question, "Does the 'vertical mosaic' still exist?" It has been our assumption that the most appropriate place to look for evidence to either support or refute the vision of Canadian society as a "vertical mosaic" is through an examination of the relationship between ethnicity and income, first controlling for educational level, and then controlling for other key social variables so that this relationship can be measured more directly and precisely.

Our conclusion is that, by 1991, for the majority of ethnic groups in Canada there is no evidence that the traditionally accepted image of a vertical mosaic still remains. Among the two charter groups, the French now earn more for comparable education than their British counterparts when other factors are controlled. Likewise, many ethnic groups from all parts of Europe who had entered Canada with generally little education and hence occupied lower income positions, have now moved up the educational and income hierarchies and there is very little evidence of discrimination against any such ethnic groups.

On the other hand, there is also clear evidence that visible minorities have not fared well. When education and a range of other social variables are controlled, Aboriginal Peoples still remain mired at the bottom of Canadian society. Almost all Asian groups and most of those of Latin American and Middle Eastern ethnicity were also similarly disadvantaged.

In sum, the evidence indicates that similar educational qualifications carried different economic values in the Canadian labour market for individuals of different "racial" origins. All visible minority groups had below-average earnings in each of the categories, while most of those of European ethnicity had above-average earnings.

It is possible that there are some other variables than "race" which systematically operate to discriminate against people of colour in Canadian society. However, the 1991 *Public Use Microdata File for Individuals* permits more "controls" for other possible variables than has ever previously been possible in such a large data set based on Canadian society. Thus, we have controlled for most of the other competing factors and their interaction effects which might conceivably affect the fundamental relationship between education and income that lies at the centre of our analysis. If there are other factors which might affect this relationship, we cannot easily discern what these might be. More importantly, the large literature on the relationship between education, income, and ethnicity in Canada which we have reviewed provides no clue of any other factor or factors which might have such a significant influence.

Consequently, whereas we began this paper with the question, "Does the vertical mosaic still exist?," we must end it with an even more serious question, namely, "Is Canada a racist society?" Canadians have long prided themselves on their policy of ethnic pluralism in contrast to the "melting pot" of the United States. We have also generally seen ourselves as a more racially tolerant society than the American one. However, our data suggest that there are limits to our tolerance of cultural and racial divisions. While we are apparently willing to accept cultural differences (particularly from a wide range of European cultures) in terms of the income received relative to level of education, we show no such tolerance for those who are racially "visible" from the white majority in Canadian society. All our evidence suggests that, while our traditional "vertical mosaic" of ethnic differences may be disappearing, it has been replaced by a strong "coloured mosaic" of racial differences in terms of income rewards and income benefits. While this does not necessarily mean that we have racial discrimination when it comes to other social benefits such as location of residence, access to public facilities, and the extreme forms of discrimination that have characterized some other societies, our evidence leads us to conclude that there *is* some considerable level of racial discrimination in Canada in terms of financial rewards for educational achievement. In this respect at least, yes, we are a racist society.

NOTES

1. The analysis is based on 425,107 cases. The 1991 PUMFI contains 809,654 cases. Respondents who did not work in 1990 (nearly half of whom were under age 15) have been excluded, thereby dropping the sample to 446,478 cases representing the working population of Canada in 1990. A small number of persons were on employment authorizations or Minister's permits or were refugee claimants. As the income of such persons could have been significantly affected by factors atypical of the Canadian labour market, they have been excluded, thereby reducing the sample to 443,161 cases. Also eliminated were a small number of cases with missing information on education, age, marital status, geographic mobility, and period of immigration (i.e., the factors of earning determination used in this study), thereby reducing the sample to 439,959 cases. Finally, to estimate the net effect of ethnicity on earnings with educational categories, we employed linear least-squares regression with logarithms of earnings as the dependent variable…, and this meant persons with zero or negative earnings had to be eliminated. This further reduced the sample to 425,107 persons.

REFERENCES

Agocs, C., and M. Boyd. 1993. The Canadian ethnic mosaic recast for the 1990s. In *Social inequality in Canada: Patterns, problems, policies,* eds. J. Curtis, E. Grabb, and N. Guppy, 330–60. Scarborough, Ont.: Prentice-Hall Canada Inc..

Barringer, H., and G. Kassebaum. 1989. Asian Indians as a minority in the United States: The effects of education, occupations, and gender on income. *Sociological Perspectives,* 32(4): 501–20.

Beggs, J. J. 1995. The institutional environment: Implications for race and gender inequality in the U.S. labour market. *American Sociological Review,* 60 (August): 612–33.

Boyd, M., J. Goyder, F. E. Jones, H. A. McRoberts, P. C. Pineo, and J. Porter. 1981. Status attainment in Canada: Findings of the Canadian mobility study. *Canadian Review of Sociology and Anthropology,* 18(5): 657–73.

Breton, R., and H. Roseborough. 1971. Ethnic differences in status. In *Canadian society: Sociological perspectives,* eds. B. R. Blishen, F. E. Jones, K. D. Naegele, and J. Porter, 450–68. Toronto: Macmillan of Canada Ltd.

Darroch, A. G. 1979. Another look at ethnicity, stratification and social mobility in Canada. *Canadian Journal of Sociology,* 4(1): 1–24.

Featherman, D. L., and R. M. Hauser. 1978. *Opportunity and change.* New York: Academic Press.

Fox, B. J. and J. Fox. 1986. Women in the labour market, 1931–81: Exclusion and competition. *The Canadian Review of Sociology and Anthropology,* 23(1): 1–21.

Geschwender, J. A., and N. Guppy. 1995. Ethnicity, educational attainment and earned income among Canadian-born men and women. *Canadian Ethnic Studies,* 27(1): 67–84.

Halvorsen, R., and R. Palmquist. 1980. The interpretation of dummy variables in semilogarithmic equations. *American Economic Review,* 70(3): 474–75.

Herberg, E. N. 1990. The ethno-racial socioeconomic hierarchy in Canada: Theory and analysis of the new vertical mosaic. *International Journal of Comparative Sociology,* 31(3–4): 206–20.

Isajiw, W. W., A. Sev'er, and L. Dreidger. 1993. Ethnic identity and social mobility: A test of the "drawback model." *Canadian Journal of Sociology,* 18(2): 177–96.

Jabbra, N. W., and R. L. Cosper. 1988. Ethnicity in Atlantic Canada: A survey. *Canadian Ethnic Studies,* 20(3): 6–27.

Lautard, E. H., and N. Guppy. 1990. The vertical mosaic revisited: Occupational differentials among Canadian ethnic groups. In *Race and ethnic relations in Canada,* ed. P. S. Li, 189–208. Toronto: Oxford University Press.

Lautard, E. H., and D. J. Loree. 1984. Ethnic stratification in Canada, 1931–1971. *Canadian Journal of Sociology,* 9: 333–43.

Li, P. S. 1988. *Ethnic inequality in a class society.* Toronto: Thompson Educational Publishing Inc.

Nakhaie, M. R. 1995. Ownership and management position of Canadian ethnic groups in 1973 and 1989. *Canadian Journal of Sociology,* 20(2): 167–92.

Ornstein, M. D. 1981. The occupational mobility of men in Ontario. *The Canadian Review of Sociology and Anthropology,* 18(2): 181–215.

Pineo, P. C. 1976. Social mobility in Canada: The current picture. *Sociological Focus,* 9(2): 109–23.

Pineo, P. C., and J. Porter. 1985. Ethnic origin and occupational attainment. In *Ascription and achievement: Studies in mobility and status attainment in Canada,* eds. M. Boyd, J. Goyder, F. E. Jones, H. A. McRoberts, P. C. Pineo, and J. Porter, 357–92. Ottawa: Carleton University Press.

Porter, J. 1965. *The vertical mosaic.* Toronto: University of Toronto Press.

Reitz, J. G. 1980. *The survival of ethnic groups.* Toronto: McGraw-Hill Ryerson, Ltd.

Royal Commission on Bilingualism and Biculturalism, Canada. 1969. *Report of the Royal Commission on Bilingualism and Biculturalism,* Vol. 3A. Ottawa: Queen's Printer.

Sandefur, G. D., and W. J. Scott. 1983. Minority group status and the wages of Indian and Black males. *Social Science Research,* 12(1): 44–68.

Shamai, S. 1992. Ethnicity and educational achievement in Canada: 1941–1981. *Canadian Ethnic Studies,* 24(1): 41–57.

Statistics Canada. 1993. *Standard occupational classification, 1991.* Ottawa: Ministry of Industry, Science and Technology.

———. 1994. *User documentation for public use microdata file for individuals, 1991 Census.* Catalogue No.: 48-030E. Ottawa: Statistics Canada.

Tepperman, L. 1975. *Social mobility in Canada.* Toronto: McGraw-Hill Ryerson.

Winn, C. 1988. The socio-economic attainment of visible minorities: Facts and policy implications. In *Social inequality in Canada: Patterns, problems, policies,* eds. J. Curtis, E. Grabb, N. Guppy, and S. Gilbert, 195–213. Scarborough, Ont.: Prentice-Hall Canada.

Part XI

Gender

23

Sex and Temperament in Three Primitive Societies

Margaret Mead

We have…considered in detail the approved personalities of each sex among three primitive peoples. We found the Arapesh—both men and women—displaying a personality that, out of our historically limited preoccupations, we would call maternal in its parental aspects, and feminine in its sexual aspects. We found men, as well as women, trained to be cooperative, unaggressive, responsive to the needs and demands of others. We found no idea that sex was a powerful driving force either for men or for women. In marked contrast to these attitudes, we found among the Mundugumor that both men and women developed as ruthless, aggressive, positively sexed individuals, with the maternal cherishing aspects of personality at a minimum. Both men and women approximated to a personality type that we in our culture would find only in an undisciplined and very violent male. Neither the Arapesh nor the Mundugumor profit by a contrast between the sexes; the Arapesh ideal is the mild, responsive man married to the mild, responsive woman; the Mundugumor ideal is the violent aggressive man married to the violent aggressive woman. In the third tribe, the Tchambuli, we found a genuine reversal of the sex attitudes of our own culture, with the woman the dominant, impersonal, managing partner, the man the less responsible and the emotionally dependent person. These three situations suggest, then, a very definite conclusion. If those temperamental attitudes which we have traditionally regarded as feminine—such as passivity, responsiveness, and a willingness to cherish children—can so easily be set up as the masculine pattern in one tribe, and in another be outlawed for the majority of women as well as for the majority of men, we no longer have any basis for regarding such aspects of behaviour as sex-linked. And this conclusion becomes even stronger when we consider the actual reversal in Tchambuli of the position of dominance of the two sexes, in spite of the existence of formal patrilineal institutions.

Source: From *Sex and Temperament in Three Primitive Societies*, pp. 279–88, by Margaret Mead, copyright © 1935, 1950, 1963, by Margaret Mead. Reprinted by permission of HarperCollins Publishers, Inc./William Morrow.

The material suggests that we may say that many, if not all, of the personality traits which we have called masculine or feminine are as lightly linked to sex as are the clothing, the manners, and the form of head-dress that a society at a given period assigns to either sex. When we consider the behaviour of the typical Arapesh man or woman as contrasted with the behaviour of the typical Mundugumor man or woman, the evidence is overwhelmingly in favour of the strength of social conditioning. In no other way can we account for the almost complete uniformity with which Arapesh children develop into contented, passive, secure persons, while Mundugumor children develop as characteristically into violent, aggressive, insecure persons. Only to the impact of the whole of the integrated culture upon the growing child can we lay the formation of the contrasting types. There is no other explanation of race, or diet, or selection that can be adduced to explain them. We are forced to conclude that human nature is almost unbelievably malleable, responding accurately and contrastingly to contrasting cultural conditions. The differences between individuals who are members of different cultures, like the differences between individuals within a culture, are almost entirely to be laid to differences in conditioning, especially during early childhood, and the form of this conditioning is culturally determined. Standardized personality differences between the sexes are of this order, cultural creations to which each generation, male and female, is trained to conform. There remains, however, the problem of the origin of these socially standardized differences.

While the basic importance of social conditioning is still imperfectly recognized—not only in lay thought, but even by the scientist specifically concerned with such matters—to go beyond it and consider the possible influence of variations in hereditary equipment is a hazardous matter. The following pages will read very differently to one who has made a part of his thinking a recognition of the whole amazing mechanism of cultural conditioning—who has really accepted the fact that the same infant could be developed into a full participant in any one of these three cultures—than they will read to one who still believes that the minutiae of cultural behaviour are carried in the individual germ-plasm. If it is said, therefore, that when we have grasped the full significance of the malleability of the human organism and the preponderant importance of cultural conditioning, there are still further problems to solve, it must be remembered that these problems come *after* such a comprehension of the force of conditioning; they cannot precede it. The forces that make children born among the Arapesh grow up into typical Arapesh personalities are entirely social, and any discussion of the variations which do occur must be looked at against this social background.

With this warning firmly in mind, we can ask a further question. Granting the malleability of human nature, whence arise the differences between the standardized personalities that different cultures decree for all of their members, or which one culture decrees for the members of one sex as contrasted with the members of the opposite sex? If such differences are culturally created, as this material would most strongly suggest that they are, if the new-born child can be shaped with equal ease into an unaggressive Arapesh or an aggressive Mundugumor, why do these striking contrasts occur at all? If the clues to the different personalities decreed for men and women in Tchambuli do not lie in the physical constitution of the two sexes—an assumption that we must reject both for the Tchambuli and for our own society—where can we find the clues upon which the Tchambuli, the Arapesh, the Mundugumor, have built? Cultures are manmade, they are built of human materials; they are diverse but comparable structures within which human beings can attain full human stature. Upon what have they built their diversities?

We recognize that a homogeneous culture committed in all of its gravest institutions and slightest usages to a cooperative, unaggressive course can bend every child to that emphasis, some to a perfect accord with it, the majority to an easy acceptance, while only a few deviants fail to receive the cultural imprint. To consider such traits as aggressiveness or passivity to be sex-linked is not possible in the light of the facts. Have such traits, then, as aggressiveness or passivity, pride or humility, objectivity or a preoccupation with personal relationships, an easy response to the needs of the young and the weak or a hostility to the young and the weak, a tendency to initiate sex-relations or merely to respond to the dictates of a situation or another person's advances—have these traits any basis in temperament at all? Are they potentialities of all human temperaments that can be developed by different kinds of social conditioning and which will not appear if the necessary conditioning is absent?

When we ask this question we shift our emphasis. If we ask why an Arapesh man or an Arapesh woman shows the kind of personality that we have considered in the first section of this book, the answer is: Because of the Arapesh culture, because of the intricate, elaborate, and unfailing fashion in which a culture is able to shape each new-born child to the cultural image. And if we ask the same question about a Mundugumor man or woman, or about a Tchambuli man as compared with a Tchambuli woman, the answer is of the same kind. They display the personalities that are peculiar to the cultures in which they were born and educated. Our attention has been on the differences between Arapesh men and women as a group and Mundugumor men and women as a group. It is as if we had represented the Arapesh personality by a soft yellow, the Mundugumor by a deep red, while the Tchambuli female personality was deep orange, and that of the Tchambuli male, pale green. But if we now ask whence came the original direction in each culture, so that one now shows yellow, another red, the third orange and green by sex, then we must peer more closely. And leaning closer to the picture, it is as if behind the bright consistent yellow of the Arapesh, and

the deep equally consistent red of the Mundugumor, behind the orange and green that are Tchambuli, we found in each case the delicate, just discernible outlines of the whole spectrum, differently overlaid in each case by the monotone which covers it. This spectrum is the range of individual differences which lie back of the so much more conspicuous cultural emphases, and it is to this that we must turn to find the explanation of cultural inspiration, of the source from which each culture has drawn.

There appears to be about the same range of basic temperamental variation among the Arapesh and among the Mundugumor, although the violent man is a misfit in the first society and a leader in the second. If human nature were completely homogeneous raw material, lacking specific drives and characterized by no important constitutional differences between individuals, then individuals who display personality traits so antithetical to the social pressure should not reappear in societies of such differing emphases. If the variations between individuals were to be set down to accidents in the genetic process, the same accidents should not be repeated with similar frequency in strikingly different cultures, with strongly contrasting methods of education.

But because this same relative distribution of individual differences does appear in culture after culture, in spite of the divergence between the cultures, it seems pertinent to offer a hypothesis to explain upon what basis the personalities of men and women have been differently standardized so often in the history of the human race. This hypothesis is an extension of that advanced by Ruth Benedict in her *Patterns of Culture.* Let us assume that there are definite temperamental differences between human beings which if not entirely hereditary at least are established on a hereditary base very soon after birth. (Further than this we cannot at present narrow the matter.) These differences finally embodied in the character structure of adults, then, are the clues from which culture works, selecting one temperament, or a combination of related and congruent types, as desirable, and embodying this choice in every thread of the social fabric—in the care of the young child, the games the children play, the songs the people sing, the structure of political organization, the religious observance, the art and the philosophy.

Some primitive societies have had the time and the robustness to revamp all of their institutions to fit one extreme type, and to develop educational techniques which will ensure that the majority of each generation will show a personality congruent with this extreme emphasis. Other societies have pursued a less definitive course, selecting their models not from the most extreme, most highly differentiated individuals, but from the less marked types. In such societies the approved personality is less pronounced, and the culture often contains the types of inconsistencies that many human beings display also; one institution may be adjusted to the uses of pride, another to a casual humility that is congruent neither with pride nor with inverted pride. Such societies, which have taken the more usual and less sharply defined types as models, often show also a less definitely patterned social structure. The culture of such societies may be likened to a house the decoration of which has been informed by no definite and precise taste, no exclusive emphasis upon dignity or comfort or pretentiousness or beauty, but in which a little of each effect has been included.

Alternatively, a culture may take its clues not from one temperament, but from several temperaments. But instead of mixing together into an inconsistent hotchpotch the choices and emphases of different temperaments, or blending them together into a smooth but not particularly distinguished whole, it may isolate each type by making it the basis for the approved social personality for an age-group, a sex-group, a caste-group, or an occupational group. In this way society becomes not a monotone with a few discrepant patches of an intrusive colour, but a mosaic, with different groups displaying different personality traits. Such specializations as these may be based upon any facet of human endow-

ment—different intellectual abilities, different artistic abilities, different emotional traits. So the Samoans decree that all young people must show the personality trait of unaggressiveness and punish with opprobrium the aggressive child who displays traits regarded as appropriate only in titled middle-aged men. In societies based upon elaborate ideas of rank, members of the aristocracy will be permitted, even compelled, to display a pride, a sensitivity to insult, that would be deprecated as inappropriate in members of the plebeian class. So also in professional groups or in religious sects some temperamental traits are selected and institutionalized, and taught to each new member who enters the profession or sect. Thus the physician learns the bedside manner, which is the natural behaviour of some temperaments and the standard behaviour of the general practitioner in the medical profession; the Quaker learns at least the outward behaviour and the rudiments of meditation, the capacity for which is not necessarily an innate characteristic of many of the members of the Society of Friends.

So it is with the social personalities of the two sexes. The traits that occur in some members of each sex are specially assigned to one sex, and disallowed in the other. The history of the social definition of sex-differences is filled with such arbitrary arrangements in the intellectual and artistic field, but because of the assumed congruence between physiological sex and emotional endowment we have been less able to recognize that a similar arbitrary selection is being made among emotional traits also. We have assumed that because it is convenient for a mother to wish to care for her child, this is a trait with which women have been more generously endowed by a carefully teleological process of evolution. We have assumed that because men have hunted, an activity requiring enterprise, bravery, and initiative, they have been endowed with these useful attitudes as part of their sex-temperament.

Societies have made these assumptions both overtly and implicitly. If a society insists that warfare is the major occupation for the male sex, it is therefore insisting that all male children display bravery and pugnacity. Even if the insistence upon the differential bravery of men and women is not made articulate, the difference in occupation makes this point implicitly. When, however, a society goes further and defines men as brave and women as timorous, when men are forbidden to show fear and women are indulged in the most flagrant display of fear, a more explicit element enters in. Bravery, hatred of any weakness, of flinching before pain or danger— this attitude which is so strong a component of *some human* temperaments has been selected as the key to masculine behaviour. The easy unashamed display of fear or suffering that is congenial to a different temperament has been made the key to feminine behaviour.

Originally two variations of human temperament, a hatred of fear or willingness to display fear, they have been socially translated into inalienable aspects of the personalities of the two sexes. And to that defined sex-personality every child will be educated, if a boy, to suppress fear, if a girl, to show it. If there has been no social selection in regard to this trait, the proud temperament that is repelled by any betrayal of feeling will display itself, regardless of sex, by keeping a stiff upper lip. Without an express prohibition of such behaviour the expressive unashamed man or woman will weep, or comment upon fear or suffering. Such attitudes, strongly marked in certain temperaments, may by social selection be standardized for everyone, or outlawed for everyone, or ignored by society, or made the exclusive and approved behaviour of one sex only.

Neither the Arapesh nor the Mundugumor have made any attitude specific for one sex. All of the energies of the culture have gone towards the creation of a single human type, regardless of class, age, or sex. There is no division into age-classes for which different motives or different moral attitudes are regarded as suitable. There is no class of seers or mediums who stand apart drawing inspiration from psychological sources not available to the majority of the people. The Mundugumor have, it is true, made

one arbitrary selection, in that they recognize artistic ability only among individuals born with the cord about their necks, and firmly deny the happy exercise of artistic ability to those less unusually born. The Arapesh boy with a tinea infection has been socially selected to be a disgruntled, antisocial individual, and the society forces upon sunny cooperative children cursed with this affliction a final approximation to the behaviour appropriate to a pariah. With these two exceptions no emotional role is forced upon an individual because of birth or accident. As there is no idea of rank which declares that some are of high estate and some of low, so there is no idea of sex-difference which declares that one sex must feel differently from the other. One possible imaginative social construct, the attribution of different personalities to different members of the community classified into sex-, age-, or caste-groups, is lacking.

When we turn however to the Tchambuli, we find a situation that while bizarre in one respect, seems nevertheless more intelligible in another. The Tchambuli have at least made the point of sex-difference; they have used the obvious fact of sex as an organizing point for the formation of social personality, even though they seem to us to have reversed the normal picture. While there is reason to believe that not every Tchambuli woman is born with a dominating, organizing, administrative temperament, actively sexed and willing to initiate sex-relations, possessive, definite, robust, practical and impersonal in outlook, still most Tchambuli girls grow up to display these traits. And while there is definite evidence to show that all Tchambuli men are not, by native endowment, the delicate responsive actors of a play staged for the women's benefit, still most Tchambuli boys manifest this coquettish play-acting personality most of the time. Because the Tchambuli formulation of sex-attitudes contradicts our usual premises, we can see clearly that Tchambuli culture has arbitrarily permitted certain human traits to women, and allotted others, equally arbitrarily, to men.

24

Playing by the Rules of the Game: Women's Experiences and Perceptions of Sexual Harassment in Sport

Vivian Krauchek and Gillian Ranson*

This paper explores the experiences and perceptions of sexual harassment among women athletes coached by men in the male-dominated world of elite sport. Drawing on interviews with 32 female athletes, we focus on the women's own interpretations of the behaviours they encounter, and locate their experiences of sexual harassment within the broader context of gender harassment and discrimination which shapes much of their experience in sport. We consider the possibility of challenging sexual harassment in sport by changing the terms of women's participation.

*The authors would like to thank Barbara Crow, Leslie Miller, Aysan Sev'er and the CRSA reviewers for helpful comments on an earlier draft of this paper. The manuscript of this article was submitted in June 1999 and accepted in August 1999.

Source: Vivian Krauchek and Gillian Ranson. 1999. Playing by the Rules of the Game: Women's Experiences and Perceptions of Sexual Harassment in Sport. *The Canadian Review of Sociology and Anthropology,* 36(4), 585–600. Reprinted by permission of the Canadian Sociology and Anthropology Association.

Sexual harassment has now been established as not merely a personal trouble for individual women but a social problem "rooted in power dynamics" (Sev'er, 1996: 188). However, in spite of the wide variety of sites in which sexual harassment is experienced, much of the scholarly work on the subject has focussed on workplaces and educational institutions.

In this paper, our interest is in the experience of sexual harassment in an environment that has received much less attention. We report here on a study of female athletes coached by men in the male-dominated world of elite sport. Our study is strategic because of the ways coach–athlete relationships, and the sporting context in which they occur, *differ* in important ways from more conventional workplace or educational relationships and settings. First, the authority exerted by the men as coaches is, self-evidently, over women's bodies and the physical performances of those bodies. Second, while the athletes' performances take place in public, much of the "work" to achieve them is not so public. While coaches may share some accountability for their athletes' performances—the "ends" of the relationship—they are generally not accountable for what happens off the field. Brackenridge (1997) describes several features of the coach–athlete relationship that may make female athletes particularly vulnerable to sexual harassment from male coaches: the dependence of the athlete on the coach's expertise—and the heavy pressure *not* to leave the sport or drop out that is placed on highly talented athletes; the construction of coach and team members as "family" and the special intimacy of the coach–athlete relationship; the apolitical, laissez-faire attitude to inequality that makes sport "a particularly active site of social exploitation" (Brackenridge, 1997: 115). On the latter point, Canadian scholars (e.g., Hall et al., 1989; Lenskyj, 1992; Kirby, 1995; Hall, 1995, 1996) point to the general unwillingness of national sports organizations in Canada to view sexual harassment as an institutional, rather than an individual, problem.

Our particular focus on female athletes is not meant to discount the sexual harassment known to have been perpetrated by male coaches against male athletes. It is rather that, as Tomlinson and Yorganci (1997) point out, the relations of power and control that characterize all coach–athlete interactions are particularly acute when the coach is a man and the athlete—competing in male-dominated terrain—is a woman.

SEXUAL HARASSMENT IN SPORT

...Among the earliest scholarly studies of sexual harassment in sport are Lackey's (1990) survey of 264 Nebraska women college and university athletes, and Yorganci's (1993) survey of 149 female athletes in the U.K. Lackey found that at least 20% of the female athletes he surveyed identified harassment as occurring in each of three categories: profanity, intrusive physical contacts (for example, "slapping on the butt"), and demeaning language, in other words language that is "embarrassing,

derogatory, containing sexual innuendoes that male athletes are superior to females" (Lackey, 1990: 23). However, he found his respondents accepted much of the behaviour as "part of the game"; only 17% acknowledged sexual harassment as a problem. In Yorganci's study, 54% of respondents had experienced or knew of someone who had experienced demeaning language, verbal intrusion, physical contact, fondling or pressure to have sexual intercourse from their male coaches. Of these, 43% felt that the behaviour was not sexual harassment. Similar patterns have been reported by Lenskyj (1992), Kirby and Greaves (cited in Smith, 1996), Tomlinson and Yorganci (1997), and Volkwein et al. (1997).

These studies suggest that women in sport, like those studied in other contexts, are not only unwilling to take formal action against their harassers (Fitzgerald et al., 1988; Cairns, 1997; Thomas & Kitzinger, 1997); they are also unwilling to label as sexual harassment many of the behaviours that would certainly be recognized as such both in law and by researchers studying the issue. The various explanations cited for this anomalous situation centre on a recognition of the sporting world as emphatically masculine, and women's participation in it as contingent on their willingness to accept the (masculine) rules of the game.

Male dominance in sport has been demonstrated in the literature on several fronts. Barriers to women's participation in sports, historically on the grounds that it endangered their feminine physiology, have been only slowly and grudgingly removed (Messner, 1992; Hargreaves, 1994). Feminist critics point to the role of the media in sexualizing and trivializing women's athleticism (Lenskyj, 1987; Messner et al., 1993; Hargreaves, 1994; Burton-Nelson, 1994). Other studies note the absence of women in the hierarchies of authority and administration in sport (White & Brackenridge, 1985; Lenskyj, 1992; Hargreaves, 1994; Hall et al., 1989; Hall, 1995, 1996)....

ISSUES IN THE STUDY OF SEXUAL HARASSMENT

...A major problem for researchers is to decide which behaviours should be included in the definition of sexual harassment. Attempts to specify such behaviours (e.g., Fitgerald et al., 1988) have generally proposed a continuum of severity, ranging from the verbal level of sexist and offensive comments, to the more serious level of actual or attempted intercourse. But more recent work by Fitzgerald and her colleagues (Fitzgerald & Hesson-McInnis, 1989; Fitzgerald & Shullman, 1993) suggests that the continuum model oversimplifies what is a multi-dimensional construct. In particular, they draw attention to *gender* harassment as conceptually distinct from the more commonly identified forms of sexual harassment. Gender harassment is exemplified in sexist behaviour or remarks, or gender favouritism (as in the male professor clearly favouring the male students in a co-ed class). There is some dispute about whether the conceptual distinctiveness of gender harassment actually disqualifies it from inclusion in a study of sexual harassment; Gruber (1992), for example, describing his own category of sexual remarks/comments, considers that sexist comments, while contributing to a hostile environment, are not *technically* instances of sexual harassment. However, Fitzgerald and her colleagues clearly locate sexist behaviour, as well as sexually offensive behaviour, within the general category of sexual harassment behaviours known as "conditions of work" or "environment."[1] They argue that until questions about how to study sexual harassment as a *process* are resolved, "[r]esearchers should inquire about the full range of potentially sexually harassing behaviors, from gender harassment to sexual assault" (Fitzgerald & Shullman, 1993: 9).

Exactly how to conduct such inquiry raises the second methodological (and epistemological) question. Critics of much of the survey research on sexual harassment (e.g., Gruber, 1990, 1992; Arvey & Cavanaugh, 1995; Welsh & Nierobisz, 1997) suggest ways to improve surveys. But while useful in helping us to understand the incidence of particular behaviours among large populations, surveys are not always sensitive to the context in which those behaviours occur. More importantly, they are less appropriate tools for exploring individuals' own interpretations of behaviours and contexts.

We draw from the work of Fitzgerald and her colleagues, described above, the need to take account of a wide range of behaviours and contexts. We argue that, in our particular case, local "contexts" of coach–athlete interaction are part of the institutional context of masculine hegemony in sports in which sexual harassment is almost normative. This commits us to a study of sexual harassment which does not bracket off certain specific behaviours for particular attention, but which attempts to explore behaviours and perceptions of behaviours in *both* the local *and* the broader institutional context. In other words, we need to pay close attention to environment, not merely as a category of sexual harassment, but as the place in which it may be cultivated.

We also take seriously the issues related to women's recognition and acknowledgement of sexually harassing behaviours. These issues are critical if social harassment as a problem is to be effectively addressed. A stable finding in the literature, as noted above, is that women generally do *not* see sexual harassment for what it is. To ask, "Why not?" as we wish to do, clearly commits us to a study which also pays close attention to how women *do* see such behaviour, and how they themselves interpret the details and the context of their relationships.

RESEARCH DESIGN AND METHODOLOGY

Our study design is significantly shaped by the two imperatives noted above: the need to pay attention to context, and the need to hear women's own interpretations of it. Our approach was to use a semi-structured interview in which all questions were open-ended. Details of the interview guide are discussed elsewhere (Krauchek, 1999). Briefly, however, we included questions that addressed issues of power and control in the coach–athlete relationship, as well as questions relating to gender and sexuality. While not explicitly asking about sexual harassment, we provided ample opportunity for a discussion of sexually harassing behaviours to emerge. For example, we asked about the coach's coaching style, what he was like outside of sport, whether the athlete's athletic career (or her life) would have looked different had she not worked with the coach, the athlete's image of an ideal coach (and how well the coach in question measured up), whether she had ever thought of quitting (and why), how she would feel about a daughter (or a son) playing with the coach in question.

Interviews were conducted by the first author, herself an athlete who had competed at provincial, national and international levels in her sport, and whose entire sporting career had involved relationships with male coaches. Clearly this experience also informed the interview guide, and shaped "the discourse between interviewer and respondent as they try to make continuing sense of what they are saying to each other" (Mishler, 1986: 53–4). Interviews took place between March and September 1997. All were taped and transcribed verbatim....

EXPERIENCES OF SEXUAL HARASSMENT

In the context of a discussion of sexual harassment by male coaches, it is important to record that of at least some male coaches, only good things were said. Indeed, about a quarter of the women believed that in at least one of their coaches, they had gained a friend and an important figure in their lives. They spoke of some of these coaches as "father figures" whom "everybody really loved," as men to whom they would entrust their children for coaching.

But what also emerged, for about two-thirds of the women, were experiences along the range of sexually harassing behaviours from gender harassment to what Gruber (1992) would call "sexual imposition." A now-retired athlete reported the most serious incident of the study, as follows:

> We were coming back on the plane, it was my second year with him, and I was sitting next to him on the plane. I was awakened by him fondling me, I kid you not, and I just kept my eyes closed and was thinking, "This cannot be happening—he cannot be doing this." His hands were all over, he was rubbing my legs and my stomach. I thought, "This can't be happening to me." So I just got up really quickly and went to the bathroom and then sat down in another seat. I guess I just never thought he would take advantage of me while I was sleeping. I trusted him.... I never thought he'd do that. That blew anything that ever happened between us and anything he ever said to me after that. I can't believe he stepped over this boundary.... I was shattered.

At the time, she took no action. More than a year later, she changed coaches. But the incident clearly sensitized her to the prevalence of sexual harassment in sport. As a coach herself now, she actively counsels the teenage girls she encounters in her sport about who to avoid on the coaching circuit, because "many coaches are male predators."

Five of the women talked about what they described as "womanizing" behaviour on the part of a coach, summed up by one of them as follows:

> [A]t the banquets when he's got a bit of liquor in him he is incredibly opposite from what he always is. He's flirty and he's always touchy-feely when he's dancing with you. I don't like to dance with him..., he'll take your hand and pull you in anyways.

Though "womanizing" behaviour was described similarly by all five women, their reactions to it varied. One said, albeit with a laugh, "I would charge him." One commented that the behaviour showed a side of the coach that she was "a little sceptical or hesitant about"; it was behaviour that made her "shiver a little bit." One commented that "if someone from the outside was looking in, it might not seem appropriate. She added, however, that as long as the offending coach treated her respectfully as coach to athlete, "I don't have a problem with him." The fourth commented that her coach was "actually pretty fun to be around" even though he could sometimes "cross the line" with behaviour that's "not anything big, just a little peck on the cheek," but "somewhat inappropriate or uncharacteristic for a coach, I think." The fifth remarked that she was really "turned off" by the way a former coach "always went after the athletes on the other teams," and this was one reason why she changed coaches. Yet, asked if she would allow him to coach her daughter, she said, "Oh, yes, I think he's fine."

While all these experiences concerned behaviour that was explicitly sexual, and caused some level of discomfort for all the women concerned, none of them *spoke* of "sexual harassment" even though these were the experiences that ought to have been most likely to warrant the label. And there were some startling differences of interpretation, not only between the individual women, but also in the way individual perceptions could be clearly distinguished from how "someone from the outside" might see things. Knowing that someone else might view certain behaviours as constituting sexual harassment does not necessarily change the insider's view.

The "womanizing behaviour" examples also indicate another dimension of sexual harassment, namely that while individual women may seem to be its overt targets, observation of the behaviour by other women greatly extends its effects. This is one of the ways in which environments become "toxic" (Welsh & Nierobisz, 1997). What is further suggested here is the difficulty of separating "environment" harassment from the more serious forms of sexual intrusion or coercion which target individuals.

Much more common in the interviews, however, were experiences in the category labelled by Fitzgerald and Shullman (1993) as gender harassment, and defined as including sexist remarks and behaviour, and gender favouritism. Some of these comments related to women's bodies, and so could be seen as verging on more sexualized terrain. For example, Ann[2] reported comments about body weight being directed at women rather than men. "When the guys get bulky you don't hear a whole lot about it, but when a girl starts putting on weight…a lot is said and it's embarrassing for women because I think they beat themselves up enough about it." Nadine agreed:

Just the girls would have to go running after workout because in his words, "they were all fat." …He made little comments, "You're being lazy. You're getting fat." It was never like that for the guys, which drove me insane because there were some fat guys compared to the girls—they didn't have to run.

Traci commented:

He's always, always making little comments, like if you see somebody walk by…he'll say, "Oh, look at that," just really negative toward women in general. And then you wonder what he says about you behind your back.

Other comments and reported behaviours included a wide variety of other forms of gender harassment. For example, Ann reported being upset by her coach when, informed of her education plans, he said, "Oh, you don't want to be a doctor. You'll just be a nurse." Clare heard her coach say that "women aren't as tough as men." Sue elaborated the same basic story:

He would say, "I know women, I know athletic women, when you coach them they're going to cry, they're going to sulk, they're wimps, you have to deal with their emotional side."

Gail spoke of an incident with a swim coach before a competition:

He was doing something on the board and a bunch of us were sitting around the board looking at it and we had lots of time for warm-up, but he chose to yell in our direction, but he only said the female names, "Get in the water!" And he said it really nasty. Meanwhile there were three guys standing with us and he never said a word to them. And he was talking to us as if we were kids.

These are only a few of the very many similar stories that emerged during the interviews.

We see them as illuminating the environment in which the more serious and explicitly sexual episodes of harassment occur. Sexual harassment as a *process*, as Fitzgerald and Shullman (1993) point out, is difficult to assess. But attention to environment and context makes it much easier to understand. The woman whose coach makes her feel embarrassed because of her weight has had a different experience from the woman who watches her coach come on to other team members at a banquet. But both experiences grow out of an environment where women are degraded. And it is the behaviour labelled as gender harassment that produces that degradation on a daily basis.

THE BROADER CONTEXT: PLAYING BY MEN'S RULES

This perspective returns us to the broader context of women's participation in sports. Sexual harassment, according to the theoretical analyses outlined earlier, is a means of upholding the masculine hegemony of sport in the face of increasing participation and challenge by women. Yet even the women who do encroach on this male turf do not participate on the same terms. For heuristic purposes, we can specify three possible ideological positions for the women in the male-dominated elite sporting world of our study. They can adopt the male model of sporting participation by becoming "one of the boys"; they can, in the terms of Disch and Kane (1996), adopt the "apologetic" code of conduct that continues to affirm male supremacy by allowing themselves and other women to be "second-class citizens"; or they can challenge the rules of the game.

These positions have serious implications in terms of how women as athletes might respond, both personally and generally, to the sexual harassment of women in sport. We argue that women who resist the masculine rules of the game, and who want to compete in sport on their own terms, are most likely to challenge and confront sexual harassment in all its forms. This is the transformative potential described earlier by Birrell and Theberge (1994). On the other hand, we see women who are "one of the boys," or who consent to second-class status, as accepting the rules of the game, and by extension unlikely to challenge sexual harassment. It is beyond the scope of our data and this paper to test these propositions, but we see them as theoretically plausible. And as a first attempt at mapping the terrain of women's resistance to, and accommodation of, sexual harassment in sport, we can certainly offer examples from the interviews of the three positions outlined above.

We begin with the "resisters"—those who challenge the rules of the game. Several comments illustrated women's resistance both to men's rules, and to men's perceptions of women as athletes. Ellen's resistance was to her coach's ideas about body weight:

> I know he doesn't think I'm lean enough. But I told him, "I don't care what you think about that"—it's bad for you to be less. He wants us to be 12% body weight.... That's where you start screwing things up. So I always say, "No, I'm never going to be that low."

...Comments representative of the position of "one of the boys," or of women as second-class athletes, were much more common in the interviews. The extent to which women become "one of the boys" is most clearly demonstrated in their talk about pain and injury. The tenet "no pain, no gain" is widely recognized to be a central ideological component of masculinist sport (Connell, 1990; Kidd, 1990; Sabo, 1994; Young et al., 1994). But our interviews suggest the extent to which elite women athletes are also prepared to "suck it up." In most cases of dealing with injury, they "worked through it," "got used to it," "learned to play with it," and "expected it." As Maureen commented, "you have to sacrifice your body" in order to compete. The interviews yielded a long list of descriptions of injuries, including shoulder strains, groin injuries, chronic back injuries, pulled hamstrings, sprained ankles among many others. Pain and injury were thoroughly normalized. According to Traci, "you take eight ibuprofen and anti-inflammatories and you run." Sue recalled staying on the field to play after pulling a hamstring: "I could hardly walk and I didn't leave. I still thought I could make a difference."

...Nowhere, however, was the articulation of women's lower status in the sporting world made more clear than in the strongly stated preferences of several women for men, rather than women, as coaches. While it must be noted that information about gender preferences was volunteered and not deliberately sought, only three of the nine women who raised the issue could see advantages to having a woman as a coach. Much more typical was Traci's comment:

> I think it's awful to say it but you sort of respect male coaches more...boys especially look up to male coaches. And it's horrible but I think women do too. And that makes it a lot harder for women to be coaches, to get the same recognition and respect as a male coach does. And that's horrible. But I think a lot of people would agree with me.

Others commented that they had only experienced male coaches, and had no basis of comparison. But this only supported the view of another athlete that "it's almost ingrained in a person that the male is the coach."

Having given examples from our study of the discourse representative of the three ideological positions available to female athletes, we note that our concern is to map the ideological terrain rather than assess the relative strength of each position. In any case, individual women at different times during the interview moved across the ideological space from one position to another. That said, the fact that we heard much more accommodation than resistance has implications for the way the serious problems of sexual harassment in sport might be addressed.

IMPLICATIONS FOR CHANGE

This discussion of the broader institutional context in which our athletes and their coaches interact brings us back to the first theoretical proposition informing the study—the radical feminist claim that sexual harassment constitutes a defence of male turf against intrusion by women, and that women's entry into the male-dominated world of elite sport is conditional and on male terms. Our interviews have suggested that the athletes' experiences, which have included sexual harassment in its most inclusive sense, have occurred in a context in which they generally accept the "rules of the game." Our interviews did not produce any evidence of the specific, sexually coercive behaviour known as quid pro quo harassment. But we suggest that women's tolerance of ongoing gender and "environment" harassment as a condition of their participation in sport and because "it's just something that happens" (Thomas & Kitzinger, 1994) is a quid pro quo of a different kind.

What then of the second theoretical proposition, that women's entry into the sporting world represents resistance that brings with it the potential for transformation of the existing structures of power and control? As we have noted, not all women who do enter the world of elite sport participate on the same terms. Women who construct themselves as "one of the boys," or who acquiesce to second-class status, are unlikely to transform power relations unless the prevailing model of masculine behaviour changes also.

Recognition by men in the sports world that the model needs to change would be helpful, and educational efforts in this direction (such as the mandatory workshops now being offered by Calgary's National Sports Centre for all its athletes) are to be commended. So are initiatives like the Coaching Code of Ethics developed by the Canadian Professional Coaches Association. But while continuing to encourage these efforts, we need to acknowledge that those who are well served by the status quo, as we suggest is the case for men in sports, have little motivation to change. We should not pin all our hopes for ending sexual harassment on work with men.

Drawing on some of the findings of our study, we want to suggest that transformation of the power relations which enable sexual harassment in the sporting world could *also* be effected by changing women—but in a way that we hope might be exciting and emancipatory. We have argued earlier that the female athletes most likely to resist sexual harassment, and the model of behaviour which enables it, are those who are not willing to play by men's rules. We gave examples of women—the resisters—who seemed to want to claim their place in sport on their own terms. These were the women who spoke passionately about their love for their sport; who talked in positive terms about their strong, athletic bodies, their size and speed; who relished the hard work and the competition but who most highly valued the friendships they made on the field.

There is much to work with here—at least partly because elements of this discourse of resistance are available to women who in some situations may self-identify more readily as "one of the boys," or continue to think that female athletes "always kind of suck." Clearly what is needed here is perceptual reframing on a fairly large scale, and on (at least) two levels. The more women are able to celebrate their own sporting achievements, and win them on their own terms, the less likely they are to see themselves as inferior. And the more confidently they claim their place in this way, the less willing they will be to tolerate behaviour like sexual harassment that denigrates or impedes their performance.

NOTES

1. This category is generally contrasted with quid pro quo harassment, defined as sexual cooperation that is coerced by promises of rewards or fear of punishment (Fitzgerald & Hesson-McInnis, 1989: 510).
2. Names have been changed, and other identifying details withheld, to maintain confidentiality.

REFERENCES

Arvey, R., and M. Cavanaugh. 1995. Using surveys to assess the prevalence of sexual harassment: Some methodological problems. *Journal of Social Issues,* 51(1): 39–52.

Birrell, S., and N. Theberge. 1994. Feminist resistance and transformation in sport. In *Women and sport: Interdisciplinary perspectives,* eds. D. Costa, and S. Guthrie, 361–76. Champaign, Ill.: Human Kinetics.

Brackenridge, C. 1997. 'He owned me basically...' Women's experience of sexual abuse in sport. *International Review for the Sociology of Sport,* 32(2): 115–30.

Burton-Nelson, M. 1994. *The stronger women get, the more men love football.* New York: Harcourt Brace & Co.

Cairns, K. 1997. 'Femininity' and women's silence in response to sexual harassment and coercion. In *Sexual harassment: Contemporary feminist perspectives,* eds. A. Thomas, and C. Kitzinger, 91–111. Buckingham: Open University Press.

Connell, R. W. 1990. An iron man: The body and some contradictions of hegemonic masculinity. In *Sport, men and the gender order,* eds. M. Messner and D. Sabo, 83–95. Champaign, Ill.: Human Kinetics Books.

Disch, I., and M. Kane. 1996. When a looker is really a bitch: Lis Olson, sport, and the heterosexual matrix. *Signs,* 21(2): 278–308.

Fitzgerald, L., S. Shullrnan, N. Bailey, M. Richards, J. Swecker, Y. Gold, M. Ormerod, and L. Weitzman. 1988. The incidence and dimensions of sexual harassment in academia and the workplace. *Journal of Vocational Behavior,* 32: 152–75.

Fitzgerald, L., and M. Hesson-McInnis. 1989. The dimensions of sexual harassment: A structural analysis. *Journal of Vocational Behavior,* 35: 308–26.

Fitzgerald, L., and S. Shullman. 1993. Sexual harassment: A research analysis and agenda for the 1990s. *Journal of Vocational Behavior,* 42: 5–27.

Gruber, J. 1990. Methodological problems and policy implications in sexual harassment/research. *Population Research and Policy Review,* 9: 235–54.

———. 1992. A typology of personal and environmental sexual harassment: Research and policy implications for the 1990s. *Sex Roles,* 26(11–12): 447–63.

Hall, M. A. 1995. Women and sport: From liberal activism to radical cultural struggle. In *Changing methods,* eds. S. Burr, and L. Code, 265–99. Peterborough, Ont.: Broadview.

———. 1996. *Feminism and sporting bodies: Essays on theory and practice.* Champaign, Ill.: Human Kinetics.

Hall, M. A., D. Cullen, and T. Slack. 1989. Organizational elites recreating themselves: The gender structure of national sports organizations. *Quest,* 41: 28–45.

Hargreaves, J. 1994. *Sporting females: Critical issues in the history and sociology of women's sport.* London: Routledge.

Kidd, B. 1990. The men's cultural centre: Sports and the dynamic of women's oppression/men's repression. In *Sport, Men and the gender order,* eds. M. Messnet and D. Sabo, 31–43. Champaign, Ill.: Human Kinetics.

Kirby, S. 1995. Not in my backyard: Sexual harassment and abuse in sport. *Canadian Woman Studies,* 15(4): 58–62.

Krauchek, V. 1999. In the hands of the coach? Women's interpretations of athleticism and their relationships with men as coaches. Unpublished Master's thesis, Department of Sociology, University of Calgary.

Lackey, D. 1990. Sexual harassment in sports. *Physical Educator,* 47(2): 22–6.

Lenskyj, H. 1987. Canadian women and physical activity. In *From fair sex to feminism: Sport and the socialization of women in the industrial and post-industrial eras,* eds. J. Mangan and R. Park, 208–31. London: Frank Cass and Co. Ltd.

———. 1990. Power and play: Gender and sexuality issues in sport and physical activity. *International Review for the Sociology of Sport,* 25(3): 235–43.

———. 1992. Sexual harassment: Female athletes' experiences and coaches' responsibilities. *Sports,* 12(6): 1–5.

Messner, M. 1992. *Power at play: Sports and the problem of masculinity.* Boston: Beacon Press.

Messner, M., M. Duncan, and K. Jensen. 1993. Separating the men from the girls: The gendered language of televised sport. *Gender & Society,* 7(1): 121–37.

Mishler, E. 1986. *Research interviewing: Context and narrative.* Cambridge: Harvard University Press.

Sabo, D. 1994. Pigskin, patriarchy and pain. In *Sex, violence and power in sports,* eds. M. Messner, and D. Sabo, 82–8. Freedom, Calif.: The Crossing Press.

Sev'er, A. 1996. Mainstream neglect of sexual harassment as a social problem. *Canadian Journal of Sociology,* 21(2): 185–202.

Smith. B. 1996. Abuse prevalent in elite sport, survey indicates. *The Globe and Mail,* (July 17): A1.

Theberge, N. 1994. Toward a feminist alternative to sport as a male preserve. In *Women, sport and culture*, eds. S. Birrell, and C. Cole, 181–92. Champaign, Ill.: Human Kinetics.

Thomas, A., and C. Kitzinger. 1994. "It's just something that happens": The invisibility of sexual harassment in the workplace. *Gender, Work and Organization,* 1(3): 151–61.

———. 1997. Sexual harassment: Reviewing the field. In *Sexual harassment: Contemporary feminist perspectives,* eds. A. Thomas, and C. Kitzinger, 1–18. Buckingham: Open University Press.

Tomlinson, A., and I. Yorganci. 1997. Male coach/female athlete relations: Gender and power relations in competitive sport. *Journal of Sport and Social Issues,* 21(2): 134–55.

Volkwein, K., F. Schnell, D. Sherwood, and A. Livezey. 1997. Sexual harassment in sport: Perceptions and experiences of American female student-athletes. *International Review for the Sociology of Sport,* 32(3): 283–95.

Welsh, S., and A. Nierobisz. 1997. How prevalent is sexual harassment? A research note on measuring sexual harassment in Canada. *Canadian Journal of Sociology,* 22(4): 505–22.

White, A., and C. Brackenridge. 1985. Who rules sport? Gender divisions in the power structure of British sports organizations from 1960. *International Review for the Sociology of Sport,* 20: 1–11.

Yorganci, I. 1993. Preliminary findings from a survey of gender relationships and sexual harassment in sport. In *Body matters: Leisure images and lifestyles,* ed. C. Brackenridge, 197–203. Brighton: Leisure Studies Association.

Young, K., P. White, and B. McTeer. 1994. Body talk: Male athletes reflect on sport, injury, and pain. *Sociology of Sport Journal,* 11: 175–94.

Part XII

Race and Ethnicity

25

The Souls of Black Folk

W. E. B. Du Bois

Between me and the other world there is ever an unasked question: unasked by some through feelings of delicacy; by others through the difficulty of rightly framing it. All, nevertheless, flutter round it. They approach me in a half-hesitant sort of way, eye me curiously or compassionately, and then, instead of saying directly, How does it feel to be a problem? they say, I know an excellent colored man in my town; or, I fought at Mechanicsville; or, Do not these Southern outrages make your blood boil? At these I smile, or am interested, or reduce the boiling to a simmer, as the occasion may require. To the real question, How does it feel to be a problem? I answer seldom a word.

And yet, being a problem is a strange experience—peculiar even for one who has never been anything else, save perhaps in babyhood and in

Source: From *The Souls of Black Folk* by W. E. B. Du Bois (New York: Penguin, 1982; orig. 1903), pp. 43–53.

Europe. It is in the early days of rollicking boyhood that the revelation first bursts upon one, all in a day, as it were. I remember well when the shadow swept across me. I was a little thing, away up in the hills of New England, where the dark Housatonic winds between Hoosac and Taghkanic to the sea. In a wee wooden schoolhouse, something put it into the boys' and girls' heads to buy gorgeous visiting-cards—ten cents a package—and exchange. The exchange was merry, till one girl, a tall newcomer, refused my card—refused it peremptorily, with a glance. Then it dawned upon me with a certain suddenness that I was different from the others; or like, mayhap, in heart and life and longing, but shut out from their world by a vast veil. I had thereafter no desire to tear down that veil, to creep through; I held all beyond it in common contempt, and lived above it in a region of blue sky and great wandering shadows. That sky was bluest when I could beat my mates at examination-time, or beat them at a foot-race, or even beat their stringy heads. Alas, with the years all this fine contempt began to fade; for the words I longed for, and all their dazzling opportunities, were theirs, not mine. But they should not keep these prizes, I said; some, all, I would wrest from them. Just how I would do it I could never decide: by reading law, by healing the sick, by telling the wonderful tales that swam in my head—some way. With other black boys the strife was not so fiercely sunny: Their youth shrunk into tasteless sycophancy, or into silent hatred of the pale world about them and mocking distrust of everything white; or wasted itself in a bitter cry, Why did God make me an outcast and a stranger in mine own house? The shades of the prison-house closed round about us all: walls strait and stubborn to the whitest, but relentlessly narrow, tall, and unscalable to sons of night who must plod darkly on in resignation, or beat unavailing palms against the stone, or steadily, half hopelessly, watch the streak of blue above.

After the Egyptian and Indian, the Greek and Roman, the Teuton and Mongolian, the Negro is a sort of seventh son, born with a veil, and gifted with second-sight in this American world—a world which yields him no true self-consciousness, but only lets him see himself through the revelation of the other world. It is a peculiar sensation, this double-consciousness, this sense of always looking at one's self through the eyes of others, of measuring one's soul by the tape of a world that looks on in amused contempt and pity. One ever feels his twoness—an American, a Negro; two souls, two thoughts, two unreconciled strivings; two warring ideals in one dark body, whose dogged strength alone keeps it from being torn asunder.

The history of the American Negro is the history of this strife, this longing to attain self-conscious manhood, to merge his double self into a better and truer self. In this merging he wishes neither of the older selves to be lost. He would not Africanize America, for America has too much to teach the world and Africa. He would not bleach his Negro soul in a flood of white

Americanism, for he knows that Negro blood has a message for the world. He simply wishes to make it possible for a man to be both a Negro and an American, without being cursed and spit upon by his fellows, without having the doors of Opportunity closed roughly in his face.

This, then, is the end of his striving: to be a coworker in the kingdom of culture, to escape both death and isolation, to husband and use his best powers and his latent genius. These powers of body and mind have in the past been strangely wasted, dispersed, or forgotten. The shadow of a mighty Negro past flits through the tale of Ethiopia the Shadowy and of Egypt the Sphinx. Through history, the powers of single black men flash here and there like falling stars, and die sometimes before the world has rightly gauged their brightness. Here in America, in the few days since Emancipation, the black man's turning hither and thither in hesitant and doubtful striving has often made his very strength to lose effectiveness, to seem like absence of power, like weakness. And yet it is not weakness—it is the contradiction of double aims. The double-aimed struggle of the black artisan on the one hand to escape white contempt for a nation of mere hewers of wood and drawers of water, and on the other hand to plough and nail and dig for a poverty-stricken horde—could only result in making him a poor craftsman, for he had but half a heart in either cause. By the poverty and ignorance of his people, the Negro minister or doctor was tempted toward quackery and demagogy; and by the criticism of the other world, toward ideals that made him ashamed of his lowly tasks. The would-be black *savant* was confronted by the paradox that the knowledge his people needed was a twice-told tale to his white neighbors, while the knowledge which would teach the white world was Greek to his own flesh and blood. The innate love of harmony and beauty that set the ruder souls of his people a-dancing and a-singing raised but confusion and doubt in the soul of the black artist; for the beauty revealed to him was the soul-beauty of a race which his larger audience despised, and he could not articulate the message of another people. This waste of double aims, this seeking to satisfy two unreconciled ideals, has wrought sad havoc with the courage and faith and deeds of ten thousand thousand people, has sent them often wooing false gods and invoking false means of salvation, and at times has even seemed about to make them ashamed of themselves.

Away back in the days of bondage they thought to see in one divine event the end of all doubt and disappointment; few men ever worshipped Freedom with half such unquestioning faith as did the American Negro for two centuries. To him, so far as he thought and dreamed, slavery was indeed the sum of all villainies, the cause of all sorrow, the root of all prejudice; Emancipation was the key to a promised land of sweeter beauty than ever stretched before the eyes of wearied Israelites. In song and exhortation swelled one refrain Liberty; in his tears and curses the God he implored had Freedom in his right hand. At last it came, suddenly, fearfully, like a dream. With one wild carnival of blood and passion came the message in his own plaintive cadences:

Shout, O children!
Shout, you're free!
For God has bought your liberty!

Years have passed away since then,—ten, twenty, forty; forty years of national life, forty years of renewal and development, and yet the swarthy spectre sits in its accustomed seat at the Nation's feast. In vain do we cry to this our vastest social problem:

Take any shape but that, and my firm nerves
Shall never tremble!

The Nation has not yet found peace from its sins; the freedman has not yet found in freedom his promised land. Whatever of good may have come in these years of change, the shadow of a deep disappointment rests upon the Negro people—a disappointment all the more bitter because the unattained ideal was unbounded save by the simple ignorance of a lowly people.

The first decade was merely a prolongation of the vain search for freedom, the boon that seemed ever barely to elude their grasp, like a tantalizing will-o'-the-wisp, maddening and misleading the headless host. The holocaust of war, the terrors of the Ku-Klux Klan, the lies of carpet-baggers, the disorganization of industry, and the contradictory advice of friends and foes, left the bewildered serf with no new watchword beyond the old cry for freedom. As the time flew, however, he began to grasp a new idea. The ideal of liberty demanded for its attainment powerful means, and these the Fifteenth Amendment gave him. The ballot, which before he had looked upon as a visible sign of freedom, he now regarded as the chief means of gaining and perfecting the liberty with which war had partially endowed him. And why not? Had not votes made war and emancipated millions? Had not votes enfranchised the freedmen? Was anything impossible to a power that had done all this? A million black men started with renewed zeal to vote themselves into the kingdom. So the decade flew away, the revolution of 1876 came, and left the half-free serf weary, wondering, but still inspired. Slowly but steadily, in the following years, a new vision began gradually to replace the dream of political power—a powerful movement, the rise of another ideal to guide the unguided, another pillar of fire by night after a clouded day. It was the ideal of "book-learning"; the curiosity, born of compulsory ignorance, to know and test the power of the cabalistic letters of the white man, the longing to know. Here at last seemed to have been discovered the mountain path to Canaan; longer than the highway of Emancipation and law, steep and rugged, but straight, leading to heights high enough to overlook life.

Up the new path the advance guard toiled, slowly, heavily, doggedly; only those who have watched and guided the faltering feet, the misty minds, the dull understandings, of the dark pupils of these schools know how faithfully, how piteously, this people strove to learn. It was weary work. The cold statistician wrote down the inches of progress here and there, noted also where here and there a foot had slipped or some one had fallen. To the tired climbers, the horizon was ever dark, the mists were often cold, the Canaan was always dim and far away. If, however, the vistas disclosed as yet no goal, no resting-place, little but flattery and criticism, the journey at least gave leisure for reflection and self-examination; it changed the child of Emancipation to the youth with dawning self-consciousness, self-realization, self-respect. In those sombre forests of his striving his own soul rose before him, and he saw himself, darkly as through a veil; and yet he saw in himself some faint revelation of his power, of his mission. He began to have a dim feeling that, to attain his place in the world, he must be himself, and not another. For the first time he sought to analyze the burden he bore upon his back, that dead-weight of social degradation partially masked behind a half-named Negro problem. He felt his poverty; without a cent, without a home, without land, tools, or savings, he had entered into competition with rich, landed, skilled neighbors. To be a man is hard, but to be a poor race in a land of dollars is the very bottom of hardships. He felt the weight of his ignorance, not simply of letters, but of life, of business, of the humanities; the accumulated sloth and shirking and awkwardness of decades and centuries shackled his hands and feet. Nor was his burden all poverty and ignorance. The red stain of bastardy, which two centuries of systematic legal defilement of Negro women had stamped upon his race, meant not only the loss of ancient African chastity, but also the hereditary weight of a mass of corruption from white adulterers, threatening almost the obliteration of the Negro home.

A people thus handicapped ought not to be asked to race with the world, but rather allowed to give all its time and thought to its own social problems. But alas! while sociologists gleefully count his bastards and his prostitutes, the very soul of the toiling, sweating black man is darkened by the shadow of a vast despair. Men call the shadow prejudice, and learnedly explain it as the natural defence of culture against barbarism, learning against ignorance, purity against crime, the "higher" against the "lower" races. To which the Negro cries Amen! and swears that to so much of this strange prejudice as is founded on just homage to civilization, culture, righteousness, and progress, he humbly bows and meekly does obeisance. But before that nameless prejudice that leaps beyond all this he stands helpless, dismayed, and well-nigh speechless; before that personal disrespect and mockery, the ridicule and systematic humiliation, the distortion of fact and wanton license of fancy, the cynical ignoring of the better and the boisterous welcoming of the worse, the all-pervading desire to inculcate disdain for everything black, from Toussaint to the devil—before this there rises a sickening despair that would disarm and discourage any nation save that black host to whom "discouragement" is an unwritten word.

But the facing of so vast a prejudice could not but bring the inevitable self-questioning, self-disparagement, and lowering of ideals which ever accompany repression and breed in an atmosphere of contempt and hate. Whisperings and portents came borne upon the four winds: Lo! we are diseased and dying, cried the dark hosts; we cannot write, our voting is vain; what need of education, since we must always cook and serve? And the Nation echoed and enforced this self-criticism saying: Be content to be servants, and nothing more; what need of higher culture for half-men? Away with the black man's ballot, by force or fraud—and behold the suicide of a race! Nevertheless, out of the evil came something of good—the more careful adjustment of education to real life, the clearer perception of the Negroes' social responsibilities, and the sobering realization of the meaning of progress.

So dawned the time of *Sturm und Drang:* Storm and stress today rocks our little boat on the mad waters of the world-sea; there is within and without the sound of conflict, the burning of body and rending of soul; inspiration strives with doubt, and faith with vain questionings. The bright ideals of the past—physical freedom, political power, the training of brains and the training of hands—all these in turn have waxed and waned, until even the last grows dim and overcast. Are they all wrong, all false? No, not that, but each alone was over-simple and incomplete—the dreams of a credulous race-childhood, or the fond imaginings of the other world which does not know and does not want to know our power. To be really true, all these ideals must be melted and welded into one. The training of the schools we need today more than ever—the training of deft hands, quick eyes and ears, and above all the broader, deeper, higher culture of gifted minds and pure hearts. The power of the ballot we need in sheer self-defence—else what shall save us from a second slavery? Freedom, too, the long-sought, we still seek, the freedom of life and limb, the freedom to work and think, the freedom to love and aspire. Work, culture, liberty—all these we need, not singly but together, not successively but together, each growing and aiding each, and all striving toward that vaster ideal that swims before the Negro people, the ideal of human brotherhood, gained through the unifying ideal of Race; the ideal of fostering and developing the traits and talents of the Negro, not in opposition to or contempt for other races, but rather in large conformity to the greater ideals of the American Republic, in order that some day on American soil two world-races may give each to each those characteristics both so sadly lack. We the darker ones come even now not altogether empty-handed: There are today no truer exponents of the pure human spirit of the Declaration of Independence than the American Negroes; there is no true American music but the wild sweet melodies of the Negro slave, the American fairy tales and folklore are Indian and African; and, all in all, we black men seem the sole oasis of simple faith and reverence in a dusty desert of dollars and smartness. Will America be poorer if she replace[s] her brutal dyspeptic blundering with light-hearted but determined Negro humility? or her coarse and cruel wit with loving jovial good-humor? or her vulgar music with the soul of the Sorrow Songs?

Merely a concrete test of the underlying principles of the great republic is the Negro Problem, and the spiritual striving of the freedmen's sons is in the travail of souls whose burden is almost beyond the measure of their strength, but who bear it in the name of an historic race, in the name of this the land of their fathers' fathers, and in the name of human opportunity.

26

Aboriginal Identity: The Need for Historical and Contextual Perspectives

Jean-Paul Restoule

Employing a perspective that distinguishes between "identity" and "identifying" demonstrates the limitations inherent in typical conceptions of cultural identity. Identifying is situational and historical, shaped by the time and place in which it occurs, whereas identity is thought to transcend history and social situations. Identity is represented in the Indian Act and its definition of "Indian." Métis efforts for recognition as an Aboriginal people in their own right is seen as identifying. The potential harm of identity is demonstrated by the Crown's arguments in the case for Gitksan-Wet'suwet'en Aboriginal title.

I recently attended a conference where a number of us were discussing issues concerning Aboriginal identity. We talked about how our parents had tried to hide any semblance of their Aboriginal identity and how in our experience

today it was not only acceptable, but indeed desirable to be Aboriginal. In our experience dreamcatchers were everywhere and Aboriginal plays and events in the city were sold out. "What happened?" we asked each other. Then someone pointed out that where she came from there was not the luxury to talk about identifying as Aboriginal as if it were a choice. Shame about being Aboriginal continued to exist in her community. Most of the people from her community would hide their Aboriginality if possible. For many of them it was not even an option. They were "known" as Aboriginal people. Also, in her experience the issue of drug abuse, AIDS, diabetes, unemployment, spousal abuse, and others were seen as more pressing concerns than identity.

Her words had quite an impact on me. How can some of us talk about the struggle for identity when on a daily basis so many of us struggle just to survive? Is writing about these matters really helping to change anything? I keep coming back to this idea that some of the people in her community would hide their Aboriginality if they

Source: Jean-Paul Restoule. 2000. Aboriginal Identity: The Need for Historical and Contextual Perspectives. *Canadian Journal of Native Education*, 24(2), 102–12. Abridged with the permission of the Canadian Journal of Native Education, University of Alberta and University of British Columbia.

could. Understanding what influences our pride or shame in identifying as Aboriginal people is important. How we feel about ourselves contributes to and arises from the issues my colleague felt were more urgent to discuss than identity. I have seen examples where pride in Aboriginal identity is the basis for fighting addiction and where shame in identity is a factor in developing a habit of substance abuse (Restoule, 1999). It is important to explore what identifying as Aboriginal means and what is gained and lost in attempting to erase that identity, as well as what it means to change the referents of what is meant by Aboriginal identity.

IDENTITY AND IDENTIFYING

The term *identity* expressed popularly, as well as in academic circles, implies a fixed nature over a given time period. In psychology, identity is often qualified as, for example, sex-role identity or racial identity (Sutherland, 1989). These qualities are assumed to have some continuity over time for the individual. In Piaget's work, identity refers to a state of awareness that something holds its value despite surface appearances to the contrary (Sutherland, 1989). In logic, identity refers to two words, properties, or statements that are so similar that they can substitute one for the other in an equation without altering the meaning (Sutherland). In sum, identity has been conceived to mean sameness. For social scientists discussing cultural identity, the sameness inherent in the definition of identity refers to the shared norms, traits, and habits of members of a cultural group at one historical moment. Unfortunately, there are educators, lawyers, and policymakers who make the error of assuming Aboriginal identity must hold over several generations.

To talk about Aboriginal identity assumes a sameness and continuity that belies the fluidity and change that Aboriginal people experience and demonstrate. When this assumed permanence of character is run through institutions like the education and court systems "Aboriginal

identity" can be constrictive and colonizing. I return to this idea below with a discussion of the case for Gitksan-Wet'suwet'en Aboriginal title. If we change the focus from *identity* to *identifying*, we move from noun to verb and set off a potentially liberating way of conceiving and talking about self-definition. *Identity* implies fixedness; that the "things" that make one Indian remain the same and should be the same as those things associated with Indianness by the Europeans at the time of historical "first" contact. Identity places power in the observer who observes Aboriginal people from the outside and defines them, giving them an identity. *Identifying* shifts control to the self, and motivations come to the fore. This perspective favors a set of referents that are put into action at the historical time one identifies as an Aboriginal person and in the contextual place where one identifies. Identifying is a process of being and becoming what one is in the moment. The power is placed in the self, for the Aboriginal person who emphasizes his or her Indigenous roots at a particular place and time. This allows for the salient components of an Aboriginal identity to be expressed as the actor feels is expedient, allowing for cultural change and adaptation. Identifying is situational and historical, whereas identity is thought to transcend history and social situations.

In this article I use a number of examples to make clearer the distinction between identity and identifying. Dunn's (2001) research on the Métis of the Red River region shows that the tension between identity and identifying existed even in the 1800s. I provide a brief overview of Canadian legislation defining "Indians" as an example of identity as I characterize it above. As a point of contrast, Métis participation in the Constitutional Conferences of the 1980s and the Royal Commission on Aboriginal Peoples (RCAP, 1996) demonstrate identifying.

Employing a perspective that distinguishes between identity and identifying might help us problematize typical conceptions of cultural identity limited in their ability to reflect the situational and contextual identifying that exists in contemporary Aboriginal life. To demonstrate the limitations of an identity perspective, I look at Fitzgerald's (1977) notion of cultural identity as an interplay between color, culture, and class. This conception of cultural identity, I feel, is fairly typical. I refer to work by Valentine (1995) and Pinneault and Patterson (1997) to demonstrate that identity/identifying is indeed contextual and is shaped by the time and place in which it occurs....

LIMITATIONS OF IDENTITY IN ABORIGINAL NORTH AMERICA

Identity is a complicated concept. Cultural identity is often conceived as an interplay between biology, socioeconomic status, and cultural knowledge. Fitzgerald (1977), in his study of Maori students, refers to these three components as color, culture, and class. To Fitzgerald color represents a biological connection to the original peoples. In other words, it is the blood connection, the lineage that can be traced to Aboriginal communities and families. By culture Fitzgerald means knowledge of the traditions, language, and ceremonies or the "markers" of the race. Class stands for socioeconomic position in the greater society. Society is perceived as the greater economic and political entity where many cultures coexist. Each culture participates in the larger society where it is located, although the cultural norms of the group may be distinct from the rest of the society.

Race is often conflated with class, so that a racial group or cultural group is likely to be thought of as occupying a particular class position in relation to the greater society. Power is maintained by barriers that keep racial groups from advancing socioeconomically. Although certain individuals may succeed in being upwardly mobile, much of the group continues to experience difficulty. As Fitzgerald (1993) observed, "The central tensions between groups do not seem to be essentially cultural but originate in inequalities over power and participation in society. More and more, groups are trying to invent cultures through identity assertions" (p. 221). Identity tends to be more persistent and stable over time, whereas cultures are in a constant state of reinvention. This is because identity often has to do with how the out-group culture views the in-group. Fitzgerald (1977) found that some Maoris he studied validated their right of acceptance in the Maori group by overemphasizing their biological connections and/or class position, especially if they knew little about the culture. I suspect this to be the case among Aboriginal people in Canada. Those who know little about the Aboriginal culture to which they claim a connection probably will emphasize their blood ties to an Aboriginal culture. Claiming to be born "Ojibwe" or "Blackfoot" does not necessarily entail a familiarity with the music, ceremonies, or language. This is a reality of living in a dispersed culture where there have been generations of increased pressure not to exhibit these cultural knowledges.

The interplay of biology, culture, and class cannot maintain its integrity when applied to Aboriginal cultures in North America. Perhaps in the mid-nineteenth century most Aboriginal people could be slotted by class, culture, and biology such that the categories remained relatively stable. Aboriginal persons for the most part were not only able to demonstrate who they were related to (biology), but also could make their way in their culture and were probably lower-class citizens in relation to the class structure of British North America. Today these factors are not necessarily applicable to each Aboriginal person, and it is impossible to predict with any certainty one's placement in each of these categories. For example, today many Aboriginal people may be slotted into lower socioeconomic categories in relation to Canadian class structure, but individual Aboriginal people are not necessarily reducible to a particular class. Also, many people with Aboriginal cultural knowledge have no ties to their home communities or to an officially recognized community. Conversely, many Aboriginal people with blood ties to Aboriginal communities have little or no Aboriginal cultural knowledge. The instability of these categories is evident when one looks at contemporary Aboriginal people on Turtle Island today.

IDENTIFYING AS SITUATIONAL AND CONTEXTUAL

Fitzgerald's (1977) observation that "cultural identity has relevance only in a situation of cultural homogeneity" (p. 59) appears to be supported by the research of both Valentine (1995) and Pinneault and Patterson (1997). Valentine lived and worked among the Anishinabe of Lynx Lake, Ontario where the community is composed almost entirely of Aboriginal families. As Valentine explains,

> In southern Ojibwe communities, where forced contact with the White matrix society has been long standing, Native people tend to define themselves vis-à-vis the "other." Thus, if something is "White" then it is necessarily "not-Indian" and vice versa.... In the north, where there has been relatively little and generally recent contact with Whites, the Native people define themselves internally. In a situation such as that in Lynx Lake, it is moot to ask if one element or another is "White" or even "borrowed." If the people are using it, the item is being used "Natively." The question asked by the people of Lynx Lake is "Will X be useful to us?" not "Will the use of X compromise our Nativeness?" (p. 164)

Here the question of what is Aboriginal is raised only in comparison with cultures outside the community.

Contrast the Lynx Lake community with Pinneault and Patterson's (1997) work in urban schools in the Niagara region of Ontario. Here Pinneault and Patterson counsel youth who struggle with debunking myths and labels or with trying to find where they fit in. Pinneault and Patterson describe the situation thus.

> Attempt to put yourself in the following story. You are living in a land which is the first and only foundation of your philosophy, spiritual beliefs, historical patterns, cultural distinction, and ancestral connections. At the same time, you never see a reflection of yourself within the philosophy of others, the educational system, popular culture, or day-to-day events within the community. Stereotyping remains entrenched in most societal situations and you are constantly in a position of needing to defend your rights and position. When you are able to visualize yourself, it is through the interpretation of others who have little understanding of who you are. You are constantly being defined and redefined from an outside system. (p. 27)

Many students in the south are struggling with the creation of safe places to increase self-esteem and build understanding and acceptance of some of the Aboriginal cultural traditions. Obviously identity issues come to the fore when there is sustained contact between culturally different groups, and especially when they are valued differently on the social scale.

Another way to understand the differences between the disparate groups in Niagara and Lynx Lake is to discuss identifying rather than identity. Identifying in Niagara has different meanings and consequences than it does in Lynx Lake. Aboriginal people in Lynx Lake do not identify as "Native" in Lynx Lake because the homogeneous nature of the population makes it redundant to do so. The identity of the people in the distant communities is not different necessarily. Rather the factors that influence an Aboriginal person's choice to identify change from one region to another are different....

LEGISLATIVE DEFINITIONS AS IDENTITY

The Indian Act has been the source of many problems in the history of Aboriginal survival. It has been the legal support for violence enacted against Aboriginal peoples in the form of regulations imposed on personal mobility, language use, and participation in cultural activities. Relevant to this discussion is its peculiar claim of distinction as a rare piece of legislation that sets out in law a definition of a people. This definition has had a profound impact not only in how we are understood by non-Aboriginal people, but also in how we have come to understand ourselves....

In early legislation designed to contain potential violence between Aboriginal people and newcomers, a broad definition of *Indian* was set into law. For example, the 1850 Indian Protection Act defined Indians broadly:

> The following classes of persons are and shall be considered as Indians belonging to the Tribe or body of Indians interested in such lands: First—All persons of Indian blood, reputed to belong to the particular Body or Tribe of Indians interested in such lands, and their descendants. Secondly—All persons intermarried with any such Indians and residing amongst them, and the descendants of all such persons. Thirdly—All persons residing among such Indians, whose parents on either side were or are Indians of such Body or Tribe, or entitled to be considered as such: And Fourthly—All persons adopted in infancy by any such Indians, and residing in the Village or upon the lands of such Tribe or Body of Indians, and their descendants.

The only important distinction was between European and Indian. Interestingly enough, early definitions of Indian like this one allowed for men and women of European descent who lived with an Aboriginal community to be considered Indian before the law. What mattered more than blood (although this too was important) was the evidence that one lived as an Indian. One would have to assume this distinction was relatively simple to make in the nineteenth century. Otherwise the definition would have been drafted differently.

As laws governing Indian lands were consolidated, the definition of an Indian in law was redrafted to exclude more Aboriginal people and to encourage the assimilation of registered Indians into the Canadian body politic (RCAP, 1996). Assimilation is genocide according to the United Nations Genocide Convention, signed by Canada in 1949 and unanimously adopted in Parliament in 1952. Chrisjohn and Young with Maraun (1997) have argued that Canada could be tried in violation of the geno-

cide convention for the operation of residential schools. The Canadian Civil Liberties Union, in debates held before Canada enabled legislation in 1952, recognized the potential for Canada's transfer of Indian children to residential schools to be seen as genocide (Churchill, 1997). Enfranchisement was also a key tool of assimilation or genocide.

Enfranchisement, along with definitions privileging patrilineal descent, reduced the number of Indians eligible for the Register. The children of interracial marriages were counted as Indians only when the father was Indian. Native women who married non-Native men were removed from the Register and often distanced from their communities. Over the years there were many ways Indians could lose their status. Some examples include earning a university degree, requesting the right to vote in a federal election, or requesting removal from the Indian Register for a share of the monies that would have gone to the band on their behalf. Most significantly, Indian women who married non-Indian men were enfranchised involuntarily, and the children of these marriages were ineligible for status. Clearly the goal of the Gradual Enfranchisement Act, and its subsequent absorption into the Indian Act, was assimilation (RCAP, 1996).

The Métis, as an Aboriginal people, found themselves caught in the middle of the changing legal definitions. The numbers of Métis who would have been entitled to receive the benefits of Indian status in 1850 were gradually reduced by arbitrary legislation. Great pains were taken to extinguish Métis claims to Aboriginal title, and they were not accorded any benefits in exchange for the land. This does not mean that only "full-blooded" Indians were entitled to be registered. What mattered was whether it was one's father or mother who was officially recognized as Indian. Often these non-status Indians would align themselves politically with the cultural Métis, who had for the most part been denied any rights as

Aboriginal people. This denial occurred despite Métis treaties with Canada in the Manitoba Act and the Dominion Lands Act(s).

BEING AND BECOMING MÉTIS AS AN EXAMPLE OF IDENTIFYING

The Métis provide an interesting example of how colonial definitions are played out and affect self-definitions. Most people believe that Métis means simply "mixed" denoting the mixing of the blood of European and Indian parents in their child. The word has been used to designate various groups with a tie to Aboriginal peoples present on the continent before European settlement. How were the new populations that were a result of the new inter-relationships between Indian and non-Indian characterized or written about in the earliest times? How did Métis, which originally meant simply mixed, come to mean specific kinds of mixes and in specific times and locations?

Dunn (2001), a descendant of the Red River Métis and consultant to the RCAP, has an excellent Web site (www.otherMétis.net) that catalogues the many terms and names that have been used to describe the intermixing of European and Aboriginal peoples. It is important to note that there is little evidence of what these groups of people under discussion preferred to be called in the nineteenth century, and few records of what they called themselves exist. Most of these terms were used by colonial bureaucrats and traders who thought it important enough and necessary to write about this growing and influential population in their particular region.... The diversity of names used indicates at least two important points. First, the groups now known as Métis were seen as a distinct social fact by most of the social groups sharing the same region. Second, the names accorded these groups of "mixed-race" people are ways for people external to the group to make an identity for them. Obviously

some terms are meant to be disparaging. Dunn's ancestors were called Half-breed by the government officials of the day. At the same time, Dunn's great-great-grandfather used the term *Natives of the country* when referring to his group. In any case, as Dunn points out, "the external application of terminology does not guarantee that the term accurately communicates the expression of an internal identity" (para. 22). Identity is a process of being and becoming, and nouns cannot adequately be used to describe identity; rather they merely serve to label and fix a group of persons (Peterson & Brown, 1985). The attributes of the group that make it identifiable as distinct from others are constantly changing, and the words that are used to fix the group also change their referents. The use of the word Métis was taken up by these groups of "mixed blood" or "ancestry" and applied in different ways and for different ends.

At the constitutional conferences in the mid-1980s the leader of the Métis National Council (1986) stated:

> Surely it is more than racial characteristics that makes a people. What about a common history, culture, political consciousness? Our origins, like that of any people when traced back far enough, are mixed, but once we evolved into a distinct aboriginal people, the amount of this much or that much ancestry mattered less than being Métis.

Note that he stressed the acceptance of the community and identification with the community.

This distinction was promoted by the 1996 *Report of the Royal Commission on Aboriginal Peoples*, although it made some concessions for the Congress of Aboriginal Peoples definition of Métis, which is based solely on Aboriginal ancestry (blood). The RCAP (1996) recommendation is as follows:

> The Commission recommends that Métis Identity 4.5.2 Every person who (a) identifies himself or herself as Métis and (b) is accepted as such by the nation of Métis people with which that person wishes

to be associated, on the basis of criteria and procedures determined by that nation be recognized as a member of that nation for purposes of nation-to-nation negotiations and as Métis for that purpose. (vol. 4: 203)

This definition, although leaving the choice of political affiliation to the individual claimant, is broad enough to include both Métis National Council and Native Council of Canada/Congress of Aboriginal Peoples members.

It should be noted that the Commission's recommendation above is made in respect to the sphere of political rights. The Commission (1996) recognizes that the identification of Aboriginal communities for legal purposes has taken a different approach. Essentially, after some analysis, the Commission laid out three elements that seemed to be acceptable to courts in determining membership in an Aboriginal community:

• some ancestral family connection (not necessarily genetic) with the particular Aboriginal people;
• self-identification of the individual with the particular Aboriginal people; and
• community acceptance of the individual by the particular Aboriginal people. (vol. 4: 297–98)

A fourth element was mentioned as also being of relevance in some cases: "a rational connection, consisting of sufficient objectively determinable points of contact between the individual and the particular Aboriginal people" (vol. 4: 298). Acceptable criteria include residence, family connections, cultural ties, language, and religion (vol. 4: 298).

In many ways it seems as if we have come full circle. Early attempts to legislate who is an Indian were broad and inclusive and allowed for anyone living in an Aboriginal community to qualify as Indian under the law. Definitions became increasingly exclusive, causing inequities and suffering and dissension among Aboriginal peoples. The RCAP (1996) recommended that all Aboriginal peoples be entitled to rights as members of an Aboriginal community. But history has seen individuals with Aboriginal "blood" migrate to urban areas where they may not live in Aboriginal communities that are located in a tight geographical configuration. As sound and fair as it may appear for legal reasoning to recognize only Aboriginal communities and members of those communities, in practice it may again turn out to be a politically expedient way of reducing the numbers of Aboriginal people whom the government must recognize. In the end it really may be up to the individuals in communities of interest to decide what factors of their personality and culture make them distinctly Aboriginal and continue a process of being and becoming that cannot be legislated.

THE IMPACT OF IDENTITY

Once when I was talking to a friend and tenant at a native housing co-op where I worked, I told her that my lack of knowledge on a particular issue was because I was not a politically active person. She replied, "For an Indian, being born is political." I realize now that she meant that from the time we are born, as Indians we are in a particular relationship with the Canadian state by virtue of the treaties, the Indian Register, and the Indian Act. She also meant that because the state had been seeking our disappearance for centuries, each time one more of us is born we are directly in opposition to the goals of the state. Each of us through our birth proved we would not disappear. When we are born, we are defined by the state as a particular kind of Indian. Either we are eligible for the Indian Register and designated a Status Indian, or we are denied the rights that this heritage should lend itself to. There were times when not being registered was an advantage because the strict enforcement of the Indian Act imposed many measures on recognized Indians. The drawback, of course, was that many identifiable Indians were disallowed connections with their extended families and some of the treaty rights their ancestors had negotiated.

Using strictly the legal view of Indianness, in my family's experience, my father was born an

Indian, later "earned the right not to be an Indian" through enfranchisement, and many years later was seen as a Status Indian once again. I was not born an Indian and was given Indian Status only after passage of the amended Indian Act of 1985. Receiving that card in the mail made me question a lot of things, and it caused me to look at my family in a new way. I was confused about how we had an identity decided for us. Why was it not a given that we could define for ourselves who we were?

The issue of Aboriginal identity is most often played out in Canadian law. Aboriginal "difference" from others is used to maintain inequities in power when it is convenient for those with power (Macklem, 1993). However, when our difference results in what is seen as privilege, arguments are made that treating Aboriginal people differently is "un-Canadian" because it is in opposition to the stated goal of equality among individuals before the law. There is a constructed image of what Indians are supposed to be that has to be played into or against in order to make advances in Canadian institutions, especially courts of law (Crosby, 1992; Razack, 1998). If we do not appear Indian enough or do not exhibit enough of the traits that are somewhat expected of Indians, then we will be judged to be no longer different enough from the Euro-Canadian assumption of the mainstream, and thus no longer Aboriginal. We will, in fact, be assumed to have assimilated into the assumed mainstream Canadian norm.

This line of logic has been argued by lawyers for the Crown in the case for Gitksan-Wet'suwet'en Aboriginal title (Crosby, 1992). The Crown argued that because the contemporary Gitksan eat pizza from microwaves and drive cars, they have essentially given up their Aboriginality. Indian rights flow only to those who meet the criteria for authenticity established by the Eurocentric courts (Crosby, 1992). Sustained colonization has caused many Aboriginal people to move away from a subsistence economy to a market economy, often without their choice. Many of the traditional ways of

life seen from the Eurocentric position as "authentic Indian ways" have been altered by the imposition of colonial policies and laws, and then these very charges are used against us as arguments that we are no longer Aboriginal people.

The criteria accepted in the legal system, however, are often limited to material "stuff." What makes one Aboriginal is not the clothes one wears or the food one eats, but the values one holds. There is more to Aboriginal cultures than "fluff and feathers" (Doxtator, 1992). Johnston (1995), an Ojibwe ethnologist, recalls the time a young student in an elementary school, having spent five weeks learning about tipis, buskskin, canoes, and so much other stuff, asked him, "Is that all there is?" Johnston wanted people to know that there was more to Anishinabe culture than mere stuff, and this led him to write books like *Ojibway Heritage* (1976), *Ojibway Ceremonies* (1982), and *The Manitous* (1995). Unfortunately, in museums, movies, and courts of law it is the stuff that is exhibited. We are not Indian unless we prove that we still cling to the stuff that defined us in the eyes of others over 100 years ago. This conception will continue as long as we talk about identity and not identifying.

An interesting exercise is to turn these arguments around and apply them to the Eurocentric arguments for our assimilation. Does the lawyer who said the Gitksan-Wet'suwet'en drive cars realize that Europeans did not drive cars at the point of contact either? Was this lawyer wearing the same clothes his forefathers wore in 1763? Does this lawyer use the number zero? I think the use of zero may be been a case of cultural adoption, not unlike the Aboriginal people who adopt the use of snowmobiles. The culture that made the law is privileged to adapt and change over time, whereas the Aboriginal cultures are denied this same privilege. Although it may not be the stated objective of the law, the result is often the maintenance of inequitable relations of power. Keeping Indians in the place they had at confederation is a goal of the consolidated Indian Act of 1876.

CONCLUSION

The Indian Act had as its goal nothing less than the assimilation of Aboriginal people in Canada (RCAP, 1996). A key strategy in achieving this goal was increasingly to limit who is an Indian by law and to change the status of those who were already on the list through enfranchisement. In this law "Indians" are identical to one another, but "different" from the Canadian power majority. The writers of legislation did not consider our cultures and histories important. Our identity as Indians was invented. Although at times we have used this identity to our own interests, forming coalitions across cultures to seek political gains (such as inclusion in the Constitution Act, 1982), we have also used these invented identities against one another, allowing these government categories to intrude on our social and cultural affairs (Coates, 1999). In our lives, in our work, in our efforts to educate others, let us identify as Aboriginal people from our inside place, from ourselves, our communities, our traditions. Let us not allow others to decide our identity for us.

ACKNOWLEDGMENTS

I would like to thank the anonymous reviewers of an earlier draft for their comments.

REFERENCES

Chrisjohn, R., & Young, S., with Maraun, M. 1997. *The circle game: Shadows and substance in the Indian residential school experience in Canada.* Penticton, B.C.: Theytus.

Churchill, W. 1997. *A little matter of genocide: Holocaust and denial in the Americas 1492 to the present.* San Francisco, CA: City Lights Books.

Coates, K. 1999. Being Aboriginal. In *Futures and identities: Aboriginal peoples in Canada,* ed. M. Behiels, 23–41. Montreal: Association for Canadian Studies.

Crosby, M. 1992. Construction of the imaginary Indian. In *Vancouver anthology: The institutional politics of art,* ed. S. Douglas, 267–91. Burnaby, B.C.: Talonbooks.

Doxtator, D. 1992. *Fluff and feathers: An exhibit of the symbols of Indianness.* Brantford, Ont.: Woodland Cultural Centre.

Dunn, M. 2001, January. Métis identity—A source of rights? Paper presented at Trent University. [Online]. Available: **http://www.otherMétis.net/index.html/Papers/trent/ trent1.html#Terminology**. Retrieved January 4, 2001,

Fitzgerald, T. K. 1977. *Education and identity: A study of the New Zealand Maori graduate.* Wellington: New Zealand Council for Educational Research.

Johnston, B. 1976. *Ojibway heritage.* Toronto: McClelland and Stewart.

———. 1982. *Ojibway ceremonies.* Toronto: McClelland and Stewart.

———. 1995. *The Manitous: The spiritual world of the Ojibway.* Toronto: Key Porter Books.

Macklem, P. 1993. Ethnonationalism, Aboriginal identities, and the law. In *Ethnicity and Aboriginality: Case studies in ethnonationalism,* ed. M. D. Levin, 9–28. Toronto: University of Toronto Press.

Peterson, J., & J. S. H. Brown (eds.). 1985. *The new peoples: Being and becoming Métis in North America.* Winnipeg: University of Manitoba Press.

Pinneault, A., & Patterson, C. 1997. Native support circles in urban schools. *Orbit,* 28(1): 27–9.

Razack, S. 1998. *Looking white people in the eye: Gender, race and culture in courtrooms and classrooms.* Toronto: University of Toronto Press.

Restoule, J. P. 1999. Making movies, changing lives. Aboriginal film and identity. In *Futures and identities: Aboriginal peoples in Canada,* ed. M. Behiels, 180–89. Montreal: Association for Canadian Studies.

Royal Commission on Aboriginal Peoples. 1996. *Report of the Royal Commission on Aboriginal Peoples.* Ottawa: Ministry of Supply and Services.

Sutherland, N. S. 1989. *The international dictionary of psychology.* New York: Continuum.

The Métis Nation. 1986. 2(1): Winter.

Valentine, L. P. 1995. *Making it their own: Severn Ojibwe communicative practices.* Toronto: University of Toronto Press.

Part XIII

Aging and the Elderly

27

The Tragedy of Old Age in America

Robert N. Butler

What is it like to be old in the United States? What will our own lives be like when we are old? Americans find it difficult to think about old age until they are propelled into the midst of it by their own aging and that of relatives and friends. Aging is the neglected stepchild of the human life cycle. Though we have begun to examine the socially taboo subjects of dying and death, we have leaped over that long period of time preceding death known as old age. In truth, it is easier to manage the problem of death than the problem of living as an old person. Death is a dramatic, one-time crisis while old age is a day-by-day and year-by-year confrontation with powerful external and internal forces, a bittersweet coming to terms with one's own personality and one's life.

Those of us who are not old barricade ourselves from discussions of old age by declar-

Source: From *Why Survive? Being Old in America* by Robert N. Butler, M.D., pp. 1–2, 6–12, 15–16, copyright © 1975 by Robert N. Butler, M.D., HarperCollins Publishers, Inc. Reprinted with permission of HarperCollins Publishers, Inc.

ing the subject morbid, boring, or in poor taste. Optimism and euphemism are other common devices. People will speak of looking forward to their "retirement years." The elderly are described respectfully as "senior citizens," "golden agers," "our elders," and one hears of old people who are considered inspirations and examples of how to "age well" or "gracefully." There is the popularly accepted opinion that Social Security and pensions provide a comfortable and reliable flow of funds so the elderly have few financial worries. Medicare has lulled the population into reassuring itself that the once terrible financial burdens of late-life illnesses are now eradicated. Advertisements and travel folders show relaxed, happy, well-dressed older people enjoying recreation, travel, and their grandchildren. If they are no longer living in the old family home, they are pictured as delighted residents of retirement communities with names like Leisure World and Sun City, with lots of grass, clean air, and fun. This is the American ideal of the "golden years" toward which millions of citizens are expectantly toiling through their workdays.

But this is not the full story. A second theme runs through the popular view of old age. Our colloquialisms reveal a great deal: Once you are old you are "fading fast," "over the hill," "out to pasture," "down the drain," "finished," "out of date," an "old crock," "fogy," "geezer," or "biddy." One hears children saying they are afraid to get old, middle-aged people declaring they want to die after they have passed their prime, and numbers of old people wishing they were dead.

What can we possibly conclude from these discrepant points of view? Our popular attitudes could be summed up as a combination of wishful thinking and stark terror. We base our feelings on primitive fears, prejudice, and stereotypes rather than on knowledge and insight. In reality, the way one experiences old age is contingent upon physical health, personality, earlier-life experiences, the actual circumstances of late-life events (in what order they occur, how they occur, when they occur), and the social supports one receives: adequate finances, shelter, medical care, social roles, religious support, recreation. All of these are crucial and interconnected elements which together determine the quality of late life....

MYTHS AND STEREOTYPES ABOUT THE OLD

In addition to dealing with the difficulties of physical and economic survival, older people are affected by the multitude of myths and stereotypes surrounding old age:

An older person thinks and moves slowly. He does not think as he used to or as creatively. He is bound to himself and to his past and can no longer change or grow. He can learn neither well nor swiftly and, even if he could, he would not wish to. Tied to his personal traditions and growing conservatism, he dislikes innovations and is not disposed to new ideas. Not only can he not move forward, he often moves backward. He enters a second childhood caught up in increasing egocentricity and demanding more from his environment than he is willing to give to it. Sometimes he becomes an intensification of himself, a caricature of a lifelong personality. He becomes

irritable and cantankerous, yet shallow and enfeebled. He lives in his past; he is behind the times. He is aimless and wandering of mind, reminiscing and garrulous. Indeed, he is a study in decline, the picture of mental and physical failure. He has lost and cannot replace friends, spouse, job, status, power, influence, income. He is often stricken by diseases which, in turn, restrict his movement, his enjoyment of food, the pleasures of well-being. He has lost his desire and capacity for sex. His body shrinks, and so too does the flow of blood to his brain. His mind does not utilize oxygen and sugar at the same rate as formerly. Feeble, uninteresting, he awaits his death, a burden to society, to his family and to himself.

In its essentials, this view I have sketched approximates the picture of old age held by many Americans. As in all clichés, stereotypes, and myths there are bits of truth. But many of the current views of old age represent confusions, misunderstandings, or simply a lack of knowledge about old age. Others may be completely inaccurate or biased, reflecting prejudice or outright hostility. Certain prevalent myths need closer examination.

The Myth of "Aging"

The idea of chronological aging (measuring one's age by the number of years one has lived) is a kind of myth. It is clear that there are great differences in the rates of physiological, chronological, psychological, and social aging within the person and from person to person. In fact, physiological indicators show a greater range from the mean in old age than in any other age group, and this is true of personality as well. Older people actually become more diverse rather than more similar with advancing years. There are extraordinarily "young" eighty-year-olds as well as "old" eighty-year-olds. Chronological age, therefore, is a convenient but imprecise indicator of physical, mental, and emotional status. For the purposes of this book old age may be considered to commence at the conventionally accepted point of sixty-five.

We do know that organic brain damage can create such extensive intellectual impairment that people of all types and personalities may become dull-eyed, blank-faced, and unresponsive. Massive destruction of the brain and body has a "leveling" effect which can produce increasing homogeneity among the elderly. But most older people do not suffer impairment of this magnitude during the greater part of their later life.

The Myth of Unproductivity

Many believe the old to be unproductive. But in the absence of diseases and social adversities, old people tend to remain productive and actively involved in life. There are dazzling examples like octogenarians Georgia O'Keeffe continuing to paint and Pope John XXIII revitalizing his church, and septuagenarians Duke Ellington composing and working his hectic concert schedule and Golda Meir acting as her country's vigorous Prime Minister. Substantial numbers of people become unusually creative for the first time in old age, when exceptional and inborn talents may be discovered and expressed. What is most pertinent to our discussion here, however, is the fact that many old people continue to contribute usefully to their families and community in a variety of ways, including active employment. The 1971 Bureau of Labor Statistics figures show 1,780,000 people over sixty-five working full time and 1,257,000 part time. Since society and business practice do not encourage the continued employment of the elderly, it is obvious that many more would work if jobs were available.

When productive incapacity develops, it can be traced more directly to a variety of losses, diseases, or circumstances than to that mysterious process called aging. Even then, in spite of the presence of severe handicaps, activity and involvement are often maintained.

The Myth of Disengagement

This is related to the previous myth and holds that older people prefer to disengage from life, to withdraw into themselves, choosing to live alone or perhaps only with their peers. Ironically, some gerontologists themselves hold these views. One study, *Growing Old: The Process of Disengagement*, presents the theory that mutual separation of the aged person from his society is a natural part of the aging experience. There is no evidence to support this generalization. Disengagement is only one of many patterns of reaction to old age.

The Myth of Inflexibility

The ability to change and adapt has little to do with one's age and more to do with one's lifelong character. But even this statement has to be qualified. One is not necessarily destined to maintain one's character in earlier life permanently. True, the endurance, the strength, and the stability in human character structure are remarkable and protective. But most, if not all, people change and remain open to change throughout the course of life, right up to its termination. The old notion, whether ascribed to Pope Alexander VI or Sigmund Freud, that character is laid down in final form by the fifth year of life can be confidently refuted. Change is the hallmark of living. The notion that older people become less responsive to innovation and change because of age is not supported by scientific studies of healthy older people living in the community or by everyday observations and clinical psychiatric experience.

A related cliché is that political conservatism increases with age. If one's options are constricted by job discrimination, reduced or fixed income, and runaway inflation, as older people's are, one may become conservative out of economic necessity rather than out of qualities innate in the psyche. Thus an older person may vote against the creation of better schools or an expansion of social services for tax reasons. His property—his home—may be his only equity, and his income is likely to be too low to weather increased taxes. A perfectly sensible self-interest rather than "conservatism" is at work here.

Naturally, conservatives do exist among the elderly, but so do liberals, radicals, and moderates. Once again diversity rather than homogeneity is the norm.

The Myth of "Senility"

The notion that old people are senile, showing forgetfulness, confusional episodes, and reduced attention, is widely accepted. "Senility" is a popularized layman's term used by doctors and the public alike to categorize the behavior of the old. Some of what is called senile is the result of brain damage. But anxiety and depression are also frequently lumped within the same category of senility, even though they are treatable and often reversible. Old people, like young people, experience a full range of emotions, including anxiety, grief, depression, and paranoid states. It is all too easy to blame age and brain damage when accounting for the mental problems and emotional concerns of later life.

Drug tranquilization is another frequent, misdiagnosed, and potentially reversible cause of so-called senility. Malnutrition and unrecognized physical illnesses, such as congestive heart failure, may produce "senile behavior" by reducing the supply of blood, oxygen, and food to the brain. Alcoholism, often associated with bereavement, is another cause. Because it has been so convenient to dismiss all these manifestations by lumping them together under an improper and inaccurate diagnostic label, the elderly often do not receive the benefits of decent diagnosis and treatment.

Actual irreversible brain damage,[1] of course, is not a myth, and two major conditions create mental disorders. One is cerebral arteriosclerosis (hardening of the arteries of the brain); the other, unfortunately referred to as senile brain disease, is due to a mysterious dissolution of brain cells. Such conditions account for some 50 percent of the cases of major mental disorders in old age, and the symptoms connected with these conditions are the ones that form the basis for what has come to be known as senility. But, as I wish to emphasize again, similar symptoms can be found in a number of other conditions which *are* reversible through proper treatment.

The Myth of Serenity

In contrast to the previous myths, which view the elderly in a negative light, the myth of serenity portrays old age as a kind of adult fairyland Now at last comes a time of relative peace and serenity when people can relax and enjoy the fruits of their labors after the storms of active life are over. Advertising slogans, television, and romantic fiction foster the myth. Visions of carefree, cookie-baking grandmothers and rocking-chair grandfathers are cherished by younger generations. But, in fact, older persons experience more stresses than any other age group, and these stresses are often devastating. The strength of the aged to endure crisis is remarkable, and tranquility is an unlikely as well as inappropriate response under these circumstances. Depression, anxiety, psychosomatic illnesses, paranoia, garrulousness, and irritability are some of the internal reactions to external stresses.

Depressive reactions are particularly widespread in late life. To the more blatant psychotic depressions and the depressions associated with organic brain diseases must be added the everyday depressions that stem from long physical illness or chronic discomfort, from grief, despair, and loneliness, and from an inevitably lowered self-esteem that comes from diminished social and personal status.

Grief is a frequent companion of old age—grief for one's own losses and for the ultimate loss of one's self. Apathy and emptiness are a common sequel to the initial shock and sadness that come with the deaths of close friends and relatives. Physical disease and social isolation can follow bereavement.

Anxiety is another common feature. There is much to be anxious about; poverty, loneliness, and illness head the list. Anxiety may manifest itself in many forms: rigid patterns of thinking and behaving, helplessness, manipulative behavior, restlessness and suspiciousness, sometimes to the point of paranoid states.[2]

Anger and even rage may be seen:

Mary Mack, 73, left her doctor's office irritable, depressed, and untreated. She was angry at the doctor's inattention. She charged that he simply regarded her as a complainer and did not take the necessary time to examine her carefully. She had received the same response from other doctors. Meanwhile her doctor entered the diagnosis in his file: hypochondriasis with chronic depression. No treatment was given. The prognosis was evidently considered hopeless.

John Barber, an elderly black man, spent all his life working hard at low wages for his employers. When he was retired he literally went on strike. He refused to do anything. He would sit all day on his front porch, using his family as the substitute victim of his years of pent-up anger. He had always been seen as mild mannered. Now he could afford to let himself go into rages and describe in vicious detail what he was going to do to people. A social worker viewing his behavior declared to his family that he was "psychotic." But Mr. Barber was not insane; he was angry.

AGEISM—THE PREJUDICE AGAINST THE ELDERLY

The stereotyping and myths surrounding old age can be explained in part by lack of knowledge and by insufficient contact with a wide variety of older people. But there is another powerful factor operating—a deep and profound prejudice against the elderly which is found to some degree in all of us. In thinking about how to describe this, I coined the word "ageism" in 1968:

Ageism can be seen as a process of systematic stereotyping of and discrimination against people because they are old, just as racism and sexism accomplish this with skin color and gender. Old people are categorized as senile, rigid in thought and manner, old-fashioned in morality and skills.... Ageism allows the younger generations to see older people as different from themselves; thus they subtly cease to identify with their elders as human beings.

Ageism makes it easier to ignore the frequently poor social and economic plight of older people.

We can avoid dealing with the reality that our productivity-minded society has little use for nonproducers—in this case those who have reached an arbitrarily defined retirement age. We can also avoid, for a time at least, reminders of the personal reality of our own aging and death.

Ageism is manifested in a wide range of phenomena, both on individual and institutional levels—stereotypes and myths, outright disdain and dislike, or simply subtle avoidance of contact; discriminatory practices in housing, employment, and services of all kinds; epithets, cartoons, and jokes. At times ageism becomes an expedient method by which society promotes viewpoints about the aged in order to relieve itself of responsibility toward them. At other times ageism serves a highly personal objective, protecting younger (usually middle-aged) individuals—often at high emotional cost—from thinking about things they fear (aging, illness, death)....

Older people are not always victims, passive and fated by their environment. They, too, initiate direct actions and stimulate responses. They may exploit their age and its accompanying challenges to gain something they want or need, perhaps to their own detriment (for example, by demanding services from others and thus allowing their own skills to atrophy). Exploitation can backfire; excessive requests to others by an older person may be met at first, but as requests increase they are felt as demands—and may indeed be demands. Younger people who attempt to deal with a demanding older person may find themselves going through successive cycles of rage, guilt, and overprotectiveness without realizing they are being manipulated. In addition to his "age," the older person may exploit his diseases and his impairments, capitalizing upon his alleged helplessness. Invalids of all ages do this, but older people can more easily take on the appearance of frailty when others would not be allowed this behavior. Manipulation by older people is best recognized for what it is—a valuable clue that there is energy available which should be redirected toward greater benefit for themselves and others.

It must also be remembered that the old can have many prejudices against the young. These may be a result of their attractiveness, vigor, and sexual prowess. Older people may be troubled by the extraordinary changes that they see in the world around them and blame the younger generation. They may be angry at the brevity of life and begrudge someone the fresh chance of living out a life span which they have already completed.

Angry and ambivalent feelings flow, too, between the old and the middle-aged, who are caught up in the problems unique to their age and position within the life cycle. The middle-aged bear the heaviest personal and social responsibilities since they are called upon to help support— individually and collectively—both ends of the life cycle: the nurture and education of their young and the financial, emotional, and physical care of the old. Many have not been prepared for their heavy responsibilities and are surprised and overwhelmed by them. Frequently these responsibilities trap them in their careers or life styles until the children grow up or their parents die. A common reaction is anger at both the young and the old. The effects of financial pressures are seen primarily in the middle and lower economic classes. But the middle-aged of all classes are inclined to be ambivalent toward the young and old since both age groups remind them of their own waning youth. In addition—with reason— they fear technological or professional obsolescence as they see what has happened to their elders and feel the pressure of youth pushing its way toward their position in society. Furthermore, their responsibilities are likely to increase in the future as more and more of their parents and grandparents live longer life spans.

NOTES

1. Human beings react in varying ways to brain disease just as they do to other serious threats to their persons. They may become anxious, rigid, depressed, and hypochondriacal. (Hypochondriasis comprises bodily symptoms or fear of diseases that are not due to physical changes but to emotional concerns. They are no less real simply because they do not have a physical origin.) These reactions can be ameliorated by sensitive, humane concern, talk, and understanding even though the underlying physical process cannot be reversed. Therefore, even the irreversible brain syndromes require proper diagnosis and treatment of their emotional consequences.

2. No less a thinker than Aristotle failed to distinguish between the intrinsic features of aging and the reaction of the elderly to their lives. He considered cowardice, resentment, vindictiveness, and what he called "senile avarice" to be intrinsic to late life. Cicero took a warmer and more positive view of old age. He understood, for example, "If old men are morose, troubled, fretful, and hard to please...these are faults of character and not of age." So he explained in his essay *"De Senectute."*

28

Aging Families: Have Current Changes and Challenges Been "Oversold"?

Carolyn J. Rosenthal

INTRODUCTION

Apocalyptic demography is typically invoked in relation to state-supported pension and health-care programs. Is there also an apocalyptic demography of the family, or what one might call apocalyptic thinking about the family? How is population aging reflected at the level of the family? What aspects of these demographic and associated changes have been "oversold"? Once we have identified how families are changing, we may then ask whether these changes are indeed apocalyptic and, further, what the real challenges are.

Source: Excerpted from "Aging Families: Have Current Changes and Challenges Been 'Oversold'?" by Carolyn J. Rosenthal in *The Overselling of Population Aging: Apocalyptic Demography, Intergenerational Challenges, and Social Policy* edited by Ellen M. Gee and Gloria M. Gutman. Copyright © Oxford University Press Canada 2000. Reprinted by permission of Oxford University Press Canada.

Most, though not all, of the major changes in contemporary families, as compared to families in the past, are related to demographic changes. Over the course of this century, there have been significant changes in family structure, patterns of marriage and divorce, the occurrence and timing of various family life-course events, and women's paid labour force participation. Increases in life expectancy have resulted in families typically including elderly members. The dynamic aspect of this is a much increased overlap of lives between familial generations. During the past century, widowhood became a typical experience for women—a normative life event. Divorce began to increase when Canadian laws were liberalized in the late 1960s. Female employment began to rise sharply in the early 1970s, with a resultant trend to dual-earner families replacing the traditional male breadwinner/female homemaker family as the normative pattern in husband-wife families.

Apocalyptic thinking about these changes in families has focused mainly on caregiving—either the increased likelihood that middle-aged adults will be faced with an older parent who requires care or the increased likelihood that older people who need care will not have family to whom to turn. In various places in this chapter I will argue that empirical research fails to support such apocalyptic thinking and its related claims. At the same time, I will frequently offer the reminder—and plea—that there is more to family life than caregiving and that we very much need research that goes beyond caregiving in studying what these changes mean to families and family life.

THE CHANGING STRUCTURE OF FAMILIES

How has the structure of families changed? What are the challenges associated with these changes? Have these challenges been overstated? Identifying changes in family structure is not simply a matter of academic interest. Policy-makers and the general public are very interested in the implications of these changes. Anne Martin-Matthews and I (1993) have used the term "structural potential" to denote how family structure creates the potential for experiencing various types of family role demands. This is distinguished from actually facing demands and providing help or care, an issue to which I will turn later in this chapter.

The Increasing Likelihood of Having an Older Parent Alive

Almost all young adult Canadians have living parents (Table 28.1). A majority have a living parent until ages 55–9, when about 4 in 10 are still in the adult child role. At ages 60–4, only 2 in 10 still occupy this role. It is also important to note that from age 45 onward, a majority of men and women who do have a parent alive have only one parent, a situation that potentially increases

responsibility on adult children. If one is ultimately interested in the potential burden placed on adult children by having older parents, it is important to consider the structural feature of having a living parent in the context of that parent's age. Table 28.1 shows that among those in their late thirties and early forties, the average age of parents is relatively young. If we take age 75 and older as the time when health downturns typically occur (Marshall et al., 1983), then we may expect Canadian men and women in their thirties and early forties to have healthy parents who do not require help. Even in their late forties, children are unlikely to have mothers whose age suggests the need for help. Fathers are in a vulnerable age group by this time in their children's lives, but, typically, these fathers will still have their wives to provide such help as is needed. Adult children in their early fifties have parents nearing age 80 and very substantial minorities have only one parent. By age 55 and over, a majority have only one parent alive and that parent is typically over age 80. In other words, by age 50 and more clearly by age 55, we might speculate that the structural potential for needing to help parents may well translate into actual help provision.

The Increasing "Generational Overlap" of Lives

To this point I have presented cross-sectional data on the likelihood of having a parent alive at different ages, a likelihood that has increased over the course of this century. This is clearly seen when we examine the increase in the likelihood of a middle-aged adult having a surviving parent. Gee (1990) compares the proportion of three Canadian birth cohorts having a surviving parent at age 50 and age 60. Among Canadians born in 1910, only 33 per cent of individuals at age 50 had a surviving parent. This rose to 49 per cent of those born in 1930 and is expected to rise to 60 per cent of those born in 1960. The likelihood of having a surviving parent at age 60 has

TABLE 28.1: Percentage of Canadians with Parent/s Alive, by Age and Gender

Age	35–9		40–4		45–9		50–4		55–9		60–4	
Number of parents	Women	Men	Women	Men	Women	Men	Women	Men	Women	Men	Women	Men
0	8.9	7.5	14.7	14.6	20.7	26.4	46.6	41.0	60.6	62.3	79.4	82.0
1	35.8	36.1	46.2	41.4	52.2	46.7	39.3	46.2	34.6	33.4	17.6	16.8
2	55.3	56.4	39.1	44.0	27.1	26.8	14.1	12.8	4.8	4.3	2.7	1.2
Age of mother (x)	64.2	65.1	69.8	69.3	74.4	73.3	77.5	78.2	82.0	82.8	85.8	86.4
Age of father (x)	66.8	67.7	72.4	72.0	75.6	76.8	79.0	79.3	82.5	84.1	85.9	86.0

Source: General Social Survey of Canada, 1990.

increased from 8 per cent of those born in 1910 to 16 per cent for those born in 1930 and is predicted to rise to 23 per cent for those born in 1960. It has thus become the majority pattern to have a surviving parent at age 50 and it is becoming more common to have one even at age 60. A related phenomenon is the growing likelihood that young adults still have a grandparent alive. These are, in my view, very positive changes.... The longer duration of grandparents' presence in a family ought to create benefits in terms of family cohesion and continuity. It certainly creates the opportunity to be an adult grandchild and for grandparents to have relationships with their grandchildren that extend into the latter's adulthood. Yet research on adult grandchildren is extremely limited. What are the challenges of having older family members? The one challenge that has received extensive research attention is caregiving—the burden on middle generations imposed by older family members with chronic illness or disability who require care. This is an important issue, but surely caregiving is only one aspect of a broad spectrum of family relations.

Changing Patterns of Marriage, Widowhood, and Divorce

Table 28.2 presents data on marital status at different ages for three cohorts of women in order to provide an indication of changing patterns. Among today's elderly women, widowhood is an expectable life event (Martin-Matthews, 1987), while the normative marital status among older men is married (Table 28.2). Divorce was almost unknown among older women who were aged 65–74 in 1991. Similar patterns are seen in the following cohort (women aged 55–64 in 1991), although members of this cohort are somewhat less likely to be widowed as they enter old age, largely due to the declines in mortality rates of males in mid-life. Among those outside of marriage, however, women in this cohort are somewhat less likely to be widowed and more likely to be divorced compared to the previous cohort (Rosenthal et al., forthcoming).

Since the liberalization of Canadian divorce laws in the late 1960s, divorce rates have increased markedly. Divorce has an impact on older families in two ways—directly (i.e., the individual has experienced divorce) and indirectly (i.e., one's children have experienced divorce). Divorce in the adult child generation may increase needs for support from older parents, particularly for the parents of the custodial child (Gladstone, 1988). Conversely, for others, maintaining contact with grandchildren may become problematic. Some grandparents face serious barriers to maintaining relationships with grandchildren following middle-generation divorce, and indeed we read quite a bit about this situation in articles about the grandparent rights movement. We also read (especially in the U.S. press and literature) about grandparents who

TABLE 28.2 Marital Status Trends, Women, 1961–1991: Percentage Distributions by Cohort and Marital Status

Marital Status	1971	1981	1991	Cohort
Married:				
Age in 1991				
65–74	48.9	51.1	53.9	Born 1917–26
55–64	69.9	72.8	71.8	Born 1927–36
45–54	83.8	83.1	77.2	Born 1937–46
Widowed:				
Age in 1991				
65–74	39.6	37.8	34.8	Born 1917–26
55–64	18.6	17.1	14.6	Born 1927–36
45–54	6.9	5.9	4.7	Born 1937–46
Divorced:				
Age in 1991				
65–74	0.9	2.1	4.0	Born 1917–26
55–64	1.6	3.5	7.1	Born 1927–36
45–54	1.9	5.1	9.2	Born 1937–46

Source: Statistics Canada, *The Nation* (1993), Catalogue No. 93-310, p. 33.

become surrogate parents, for example, when the adult child is a drug addict. Between these two extremes, however, is what I speculate is the majority of grandparents, who join in the struggle that is part of the aftermath of divorce—trying to help adult children through the difficult divorce transition, trying to provide continuity and stability for grandchildren, trying to maintain relationships in non-custodial situations, in short, trying to muddle through.

Divorce may also be experienced directly, not simply as a parent or grandparent. Having the marital status of "divorced" is rare among today's elderly but will be somewhat more common in the cohort about to enter old age. It is difficult to predict precisely the proportion of women in the future who will enter old age as divorced persons because some of today's divorced women will remarry.

What impact will these changes have on older people? Divorce legally severs some kin relationships; for example, daughters-in-law

become ex-daughters-in-law. Remarriage, on the other hand, creates new relatives; for example, the remarriage of a daughter brings not only a new son-in-law but perhaps stepgrandchildren. One's own remarriage may bring not only a new spouse but stepchildren. We do not know very much, though, about the extent to which such relationships become attenuated following the dissolution of marriage through death or divorce. Nor do we know much about the extent to which kin acquired later in the life course, that is in mid-life or later life, are supportive and/or remain so following the death of the "linking" person. (For example, if a woman remarries in her fifties and is married for 15 years before her "new" spouse dies, what relationship would be maintained between her and her stepchildren after she is widowed?) Riley and Riley (1993) refer to a "latent matrix of kin relationships," created by increasing longevity and increasing prevalence of divorce and remarriage. Matilda Riley (1983: 451) argues that the "kinship structure has become more extensive and complex, the temporal and spatial boundaries of the family have been altered, and the opportunities for close family relationships have proliferated." Riley's concept of a latent matrix is similar to the concept of "structural potential" that I referred to earlier (Martin-Matthews & Rosenthal, 1993). Uhlenberg (1993), however, argues that although divorce may lead to a larger web of relationships, research suggests that divorce weakens many types of family relationships. Therefore, although there may be notable exceptions, in the general case the expansion of relationships in reconstituted families does not translate into increased support for older people. Having said this, however, I think we need a lot more research on what happens to kin relationships following divorce or death of the "linking" individual. For example, we need research beyond that which simply tells us that this type of relative provides less support than another type of relative (e.g., blood kin).

The "Shrinking" Supply of Children

We hear regularly that the birth rate has fallen and that the average family size (i.e., number of children) has decreased. But what does this mean with respect to actual families, who are not "averages," and to potential support for older people? Uhlenberg (1993: 225) points out that while it is true that over the long term the demographic transition means a reduced average number of children for the elderly, "assertions about the future supply of children for the elderly can be misleading unless two important questions are addressed: What changes in family size make a significant difference? What is the timing of changes in the family size of the elderly?" Uhlenberg argues that:

Although total support received from children is positively related to number of children, the marginal benefits from each additional child beyond the second or third is small. The most critical distinction regarding family size is between having none versus having some, and the second-most important distinction is between having one compared with having two or more. Thus, interest in changing family size should pay less attention to changes in mean number and more attention to proportion with zero or only one child. (Ibid)

...Gee (1995) argues that, in old age, it is the number of surviving children, not the number of children ever born, that is critical. The 1990 Canadian General Social Survey showed that 21 per cent of all men and 24 per cent of all women aged 75 and over have no surviving children (remarkably similar to the U.S. figure for childlessness among women aged 85 and over...). The trends described here indicate that upcoming cohorts of old and middle-aged adults, particularly the parents of the baby boom, will be more likely than their predecessors to be able to draw upon support from children. The challenges engendered by changes in fertility rates need to be viewed in historical perspective (many are not new) and linked to cohort analysis. It is fair to say that alarm calls about the shrinking supply of children are an overstatement—if not a distortion of reality.

The Changing Structure of Multi-generational Families

All of the changes discussed so far combine to produce changes in the generational structure of families. For at least 20 years, social scientists have described the generational structure of families as becoming "long and thin." Bengston et al. (1990) use the term "beanpole" family to describe a family form that contains several generations—four or even five—but relatively few people in each generation. This structure implies a heavy burden on middle generations to care for younger and older generation members, with the prospect of someone in old age caring for someone in very old age. This structure is said to have become increasingly common and, indeed, to be the prototypical family form....

What about the beanpole family type? Uhlenberg asks "how accurate is the often repeated assertion that four- and five-generation families are becoming increasingly common as a result of increased longevity?" He points out that no estimates for the population based on representative samples exist to back up this claim. Rossi and Rossi (1990), based on their study of 1400 adults in Boston, contend that popular beliefs about the prevalence of multi-generational families are exaggerated. Data from the National Survey of Families and Households in the United States (Winsborough et al., 1991) suggest that about one-third of adults aged 45–64 are members of four-generation families. All indications are that very few individuals are or ever will be part of a five-generation family. Moreover, Uhlenberg concludes that the four-generation family will not be the dominant lineage type. Therefore, while the beanpole family, in the sense of generational depth, is probably more common than in the past, we need to be cautious about making sweeping statements about its prevalence....

The Scattering of the Family

Another component of apocalyptic thinking at the level of family change is that, should older people require care, their children will be too far away to provide it. This view encompasses assumptions about both living arrangements and wider geographic dispersion.

Considering living arrangements first. [S]ince about 1960 there has been a trend for older Canadians to live either as a married couple or alone. This trend in living alone is especially pronounced among women (Connidis, 1989; Wister, 1985). Between 1961 and 1991, the proportion of women aged 65 and over living alone more than doubled, from 16 per cent to 34 per cent. Among widowed women, the proportion living alone is close to 80 per cent (Martin-Matthews, 1991: 79). In my view, this is a positive rather than a negative change, one that reflects not only changing norms but, more fundamentally, the opening up of options to women in that Old Age Security and subsidized housing make independent living possible. "One woman, one kitchen" seem to be a strong cultural preference in North America. We have enough evidence that older people like to see their children regularly but do not want to share the same household that we can put to rest arguments promoting shared living between older parents and adult children as an optimal arrangement for most older people....

The fact that most older people do not live in the same household as their children, however, does not necessarily mean that they do not live near their children. Assumptions and statements about the decreasing proximity of older parents and adult children because of increased rates of geographic mobility have perhaps been more common in the U.S. than in Canada, but these statements are not rare in Canada. Proximity is an important issue because it is strongly related to contact and the exchange of help (although much less related to emotional closeness and support). Uhlenberg (1993) shows that mobility rates in the United States were considerably lower in the 1970s and 1980s than they were in the 1950s and 1960s. The data, therefore, do not show a trend that would produce greater dispersion of kin over time. Moreover, the 1987–8 National Survey of

Families and Households found that about three-quarters of older people who have an adult child have a child living within 25 miles. This is almost identical to the percentage of older parents with a child living nearby that was reported by Ethel Shanas in 1968 and—to add some Canadian data—very similar to the percentages Victor Marshall, Jane Synge, and I found in our Hamilton study in 1980 (Rosenthal, 1987). We found that, among people aged 70 and over who had children, about two-thirds lived either in the same household or the same city as a child, and just about 90 per cent lived within an hour and one-half travel time of a child.

This is not to say that older people do not have a child who lives at some distance from them. Most studies only examine the proximity of the nearest child; this obscures the reality that, when people have more than one child, they may have some children close by and others more distant.... In other words, total family dispersion is very unusual, no dispersion beyond one and one-half hours' travel time is characteristics of a large minority of older families, and—importantly—partial dispersion is the most common pattern. We also need to be aware that proximity is something we typically measure at one point in time. In real life, however, proximity is fluid. Adult children may move to another city, only to move back to their city of origin later on. Older parents may make a retirement move to another city. Or, they may move at retirement or later on to be closer to a child. In sum, the geographic dispersion issue seems to have been oversold. My intention here is not to underrate the experience of geographically distant children and parents, particularly when the parents need care; it is simply to emphasize that this is far from the typical experience and it is not on a sharp rise.

Increased Participation of Women in the Paid Labour Force

A well-known trend that must be considered when discussing changing families is the trend towards increased female labour force participation. Consider, for example, women's labour force participation at ages 45–54. Among women who were aged 45–54 in 1991, 72 per cent were in the paid labour force, up from 56 per cent among women of those ages in 1981 and 44 per cent in 1971. Especially noteworthy are the increases in paid employment among married women and women with children at home. These trends mean that combining work and family roles has become much more common than in the past. By 1994, dual-earner families made up 60 per cent of all husband-wife families, compared with 33 per cent in 1967 (Statistics Canada, 1996)....

One major change that has not been overstated with regard to its occurrence is the increased likelihood that adult Canadians will have a parent alive and the related increased generational overlap of lives. These changes create the structural potential for experiencing care-related needs from older parents, but to what degree does this structural potential translate into actually experiencing such demands? Has the extent to which this potential translates into actual demands been oversold? I address this question in the next section.

THE OVERSELLING OF THE DEPENDENCY BURDEN ON FAMILIES

We saw earlier that the structural potential to have aging parents who require help exists for a large percentage of Canadian women. Much media attention is currently given to the potential burden of old family members on those in middle generations. A particularly difficult version of this is the burden and conflict experienced by middle-generation adults who have care responsibilities for family members in both older and younger generations.

While the care-related needs of older parents may present a daunting challenge for families, empirical research suggests that issues of prevalence and burden have been overstated. While the chances are we will all experience the death of our parents, there is great variability in the need for and extent of involvement of adult children, and in the duration of care. We will not all become primary caregivers, many of us will provide only a little or no care to our parents, some of us will have intense involvement for a very short period of time and still others will have intermittent periods of involvement as parents move in and out of health crises.

The Extent of Provision of Help to Parents

There has been an enormous amount of research on caregiving over the past two decades, but it is important to note that much of this research uses non-representative samples and focuses only on primary caregivers, and only on elders who need substantial amounts of care. This does not give us much of a perspective on how much help adult children typically provide to older parents. Data from the 1990 Canadian General Social Survey (Rosenthal et al., 1996) show that only small proportions of adult Canadian sons and daughters actually help parents once a month or more. Respondents were asked about five kinds of help: housework, transportation, personal care, financial support, and outside work/household maintenance. Across five-year age categories from age 35 to age 64, from 11 to 22 per cent of daughters and 7 to 12 per cent of sons provided at least one of these types of help monthly or more often. Based on these data, we may say that only small minorities of adult children can be considered to be "active" helpers.

Personal care is arguably the most important type of help to examine, both because it may signify that the parent is highly dependent and because it is the most demanding and intensive type of care. Very small percentages of daughters provided personal care monthly or more often, although the percentages increased with age; at ages 35–49, between 1.2 and 2.0 per cent of daughters provided personal care. This rose to 5.6 per cent at ages 50–4 and 7 per cent at ages 55–9, then dropped to 0 per cent at ages 60–4. Among sons, a high of 1 per cent provided personal care at least monthly.

When we talk about dependency and need for help in the family context, we are usually referring to informal care. An additional type of dependency, however, is the need for financial assistance.... Data from the General Social Survey indicate that very small percentages of Canadian daughters or sons provide financial assistance to parents: the highest proportion in any age group to provide financial support monthly or more was 2 per cent of daughters and 3 per cent of sons. The percentages who had provided financial support in the past year were not much higher—4 per cent of daughters and 5 per cent of sons. Whatever increases we might see in the future, this type of help is very uncommon at present, and speculation about the future must be placed in this context. For example, even if the percentages giving this type of help doubled, small proportions of adult children would be involved.

The "Sandwich Generation"

The particular manifestation of the need to help older parents that has caught the public imagination is the woman facing care demands from parents and children—popularly termed the "sandwich generation." David Foot (1996), in his best-selling book, *Boom, Bust, and Echo*, devotes a chapter to how demographics can affect family life, but the only issue specifically related to older family members is the sandwich generation—the increased likelihood that one will have an aged parent in declining health and in need of assistance, occurring in the context of being "sandwiched" or pulled between the needs of one's parents and children. When people read Foot's book—and many Canadians have read it—the message about aging families they receive is that more and more women are being sandwiched. However, Foot makes the leap from the demographic fact that women have the family

structure that makes multiple and conflicting demands potentially possible to the assumption that they actually experience such demands.

It is ironic that Foot highlights the sandwich generation issue as emblematic of the impact of demographic change on older families, since it is becoming well established that this is one aspect of demographic change that has been overstated (Rosenthal et al., 1996; Spitze & Logan, 1990; Uhlenberg, 1993).... In our analysis of 1990 General Social Survey data, Anne Martin-Matthews, Sarah Matthews, and I (Rosenthal et al., 1996) found that the proportion of women with the structural potential to be sandwiched between the roles of adult child and parent of a dependent child (defined as a child in the household) dropped from 71 per cent among women aged 35–9 to 51 per cent among women aged 45–9 and to 24 per cent among women aged 50–4. The most difficult combination of roles is paid worker, adult child, and parent of a dependent child. This role configuration holds the greatest structural potential for competing demands, should an older parent need care. This combination dropped from 42 per cent in the 40–4 age group to 35 per cent for women in their later forties and to very small proportions after that.

Among women with the structural potential to be sandwiched, what proportion actually provides tangible help to parents? Among daughters who had a parent alive and a child at home, the highest percentage in any age group who helped a parent at least monthly was 13 per cent. In the potentially most problematic group, those who had a living parent, a child at home, and a paid job, the highest percentage in any age group who helped a parent at least monthly was 7 per cent....

The fact that few adult children seem to be providing assistance at any one point in time does not mean the family is a great untapped resource that can provide much more free labour so that society can save money on the formal health-care system. Creating this impression is one of the dangers of presenting this kind of data (although, clearly, I have had other purposes in mind)....

Women's Labour Force Participation and the "Caregiving Crunch"

The trend to female employment has led to the concern that women will no longer be available to fulfil their traditional roles of family caregivers to older parents, based on the seemingly logical speculation that employment reduces availability of women to provide family care. Myles (1991) uses the term "caregiving crunch" to refer to the crisis stemming from the decreased supply of informal caregivers as a result of women's increased employment outside the home. Myles refers to a crisis in caregiving, the result of the "dramatic decline in the amount of unpaid working time available to the women who have traditionally performed these tasks." Myles sees this caregiving crunch as the next crisis of the welfare state, one that we are already experiencing. A caregiving crunch is very familiar to women who combine employment with family responsibilities, whether those are for older or younger family members. Research has documented the strains on such women, including the impact of care responsibilities on employment careers (Martin-Matthews & Rosenthal, 1993). It is important to recognize, however, that most employed women whose parents require care continue in paid employment. Further, they appear to provide as much help to parents as their non-employed peers. In other words, the "crunch" does not seem to result in a decreased amount of care to older people. In an analysis of 1996 General Social Survey data (Rosenthal et al., 1999), there were minimal differences between employed and non-employed women in the type of help provided to parents and in the amount of time spent helping parents. This issue needs more examination, and I am not implying that everything is fine because employed women seem to provide care despite their job responsibilities. The point is that the so-called "caregiving crunch," to the extent that it exists, is not yet a crisis for the state; it may well be a crisis, however, for those women faced with these multiple demands. The question becomes one of appropriate policy directions. While policies that provide workplace flexibility and support for employed caregivers are important, it is equally or more important to provide policies that create options to family-provided care.

CONCLUSION

While family structure is changing, some aspects of these changes have been oversold—namely, the shrinking supply of children, the beanpole family, and geographic dispersion. On the other hand, families are more likely to have senior-generation members alive. We have tended to accept speculations about the implications of these changes—implications about the growing dependency burden on families—without testing them against empirical data. In examining three of these assumptions—that most adult children are swamped by the need to help parents, that the sandwich generation is a common predicament, and that women's employment is having a profound impact on care provision—we can see they have been oversold. Demographic change in families is not leading us into the apocalypse. It is important to maintain this perspective, in part because it means government programs to assist people who are in these situations are not likely to face massive hordes of caregivers but rather a comparatively small but highly needy segment of the population at any one point in time.

How do we counteract the tendency towards thinking apocalyptically about changes in older families? First of all, we need to identify carefully what is really happening and to pay attention to cohorts and trends over time. Second, we need to investigate the implications of these trends, rather than simply speculate about what they might be. Third, we need to look beyond averages, a point that is well demonstrated by examining the data on number of children ever born to different cohorts of women. To the extent that we have been able to address these issues, the apocalyptic position appears greatly overstated and indeed unsupportable. This is not to say that families are not changing, for they are changing significantly. The point is rather that they are not changing in ways that set kin relations adrift....

It is important to uncover the realities of social organization and social life, and for this reason we need to understand how the family is changing and what the implications of those changes are. However, there is a real danger that findings may be wrongly interpreted and/or used in support of policies that would not be good for families. I recognize that in much of my own work, for example, work that asks what the changes in family structure mean for support to older people, the implicit or explicit dependent variable is family support. This is a perfectly legitimate and important question. However, it is vital that our questions do not stop there. Whether families are or will be capable of providing needed support to older relatives must take second place to the question of who should be responsible for the care of older people. My position, one that is growing stronger over the years as I continue to learn more about older families, is that the care of the elderly is a public, not a private, issue and that responsibility lies with the state. Within that framework, we may then examine the role families might play if they are able and willing.

REFERENCES

Bengston, V. L., C. J. Rosenthal, and L. Burton. 1990. Families and aging: Diversity and heterogeneity. In *Handbook of aging and the social sciences,* eds. R. H. Binstock, and L. K. George, 263–87. New York: Academic Press.

Connidis, I. 1989. *Family ties and aging.* Toronto: Butterworths.

Foot, D. K., with Daniel Stoffman. 1996. *Boom, bust, and echo: How to profit from the coming demographic shift.* Toronto: Macfarlane Walter and Ross.

Gee, E. M. 1990. Demographic change and intergenerational relations in Canadian families: Findings and social policy implications. *Canadian Public Policy,* 16(2): 191–99.

———. 1995. Families in later life. In *Family over the life course: Current demographic analysis,* eds. Roderic Beaujot, Gee, Fernando, Rajulton, and Zenaida Ravanera, 7–113. Ottawa: Statistics Canada Demography Division.

Gladstone, J. 1988. Perceived changes in grandmother-grandchild relations following a child's separation or divorce, *Gerontologist,* 28(1): 66–72.

Marshall, V. W., C. J. Rosenthal, and J. Synge. 1983. Concerns about parental health. In *Older women,* ed. Elizabeth W. Markson, 253–73. Lexington, Mass.: Lexington Books.

Martin-Matthews, A. 1987. Widowhood as an expectable life event. In *Aging in Canada: Social Perspectives,* 2nd ed., ed. V. W. Marshall, 343–66. Markham, Ont.: Fitzhenry and Whiteside.

———. 1991. *Widowhood in later life.* Toronto: Butterworths.

Martin-Matthews, A., and C. J. Rosenthal. 1993. Balancing work and family in an aging society: The Canadian experience. In *Annual review of gerontology and geriatrics,* vol. 13, eds. G. Maddox, and M. P. Lawton, 96–119. New York: Springer.

Myles, J. 1991. Women, the welfare state and caregiving. *Canadian Journal on Aging,* 10(2): 82–5.

Riley, M. W. 1983. The family in an aging society: A matrix of latent relationships. *Journal of Family Issues,* 4: 439–54.

Riley, M. W., and J. W. Riley. 1993. Connections: Kin and cohorts. In *The changing contract across generations,* eds. V. L. Bengston, and W. A. Achenbaum. New York: Aldine de Gruyter.

Rosenthal, C. J. 1987. Aging and intergenerational relations in Canada. In *Aging in Canada: Social perspectives,* 2nd ed., ed. V. W. Marshall, 311–42. Markham, Ont.: Fitzhenry and Whiteside.

Rosenthal, C. J., A. Martin-Matthews, and S. Matthews. 1996. Caught in the middle? Occupancy in multiple roles and help to parents in a national probability sample of Canadian adults. *Journal of Gerontology: Social Sciences,* 51B(6): S274–83.

Rosenthal, C. J., A. Martin-Matthews, L. Hayward, and M. Denton. 1999. Women's multiple roles: How constraining is employment on the provision of parent care? Paper presented at the 52nd Annual Scientific Meeting of the Gerontological Society of America, San Francisco.

Rosenthal, C. J., M. Denton, A. Martin-Matthews, and S. French. Forthcoming. Changes in work and family over the life course: Implications for economic security of today's and tomorrow's older women. In *Independence and economic security in old age,* eds. F. Denton, D. Fretz, and B. Spencer. Vancouver: University of British Columbia Press.

Rossi, A. S., and P. H. Rossi. 1990. *Of human bonding: Parent-child relations across the life course.* New York: Aldine de Gruyter.

Spitze, G., and J. R. Logan. 1990. More evidence on women (and men) in the middle. *Research on Aging,* 12: 182–98.

Statistics Canada. 1996. *Characteristics of dual-earner families 1994*. Ottawa: Minister of Industry, Catalogue No. 13-215-XPB.

Uhlenberg, P. 1993. Demographic change and kin relationships in later life. In *Annual Review of Gerontology and Geriatrics*, vol. 13, eds. G. Maddox, and M. P. Lawton, 219–38. New York: Springer.

Winsborough, H., L. Bumpass, and W. Aguilino. 1991. *The death of parents and the transitions to old age*. National Survey of Families and Households Working Paper No. 39. Madison: University of Wisconsin.

Wister, A. 1985. Living arrangement choices among the elderly. *Canadian Journal on Aging,* 4(3): 127–44.

Part XIV

The Economy and Work

29

Alienated Labor

Karl Marx

...[We] have shown that the worker sinks to the level of a commodity, and to a most miserable commodity; that the misery of the worker increases with the power and volume of his production; that the necessary result of competition is the accumulation of capital in a few hands, and thus a restoration of monopoly in a more terrible form; and finally that the distinction between capitalist and landlord, and between agricultural laborer and industrial worker, must disappear, and the whole of society divide into the two classes of property *owners* and *propertyless* workers....

Thus we have now to grasp the real connexion between this whole system of alienation—private property, acquisitiveness, the separation of labor, capital and land, exchange and competition, value and the devaluation of man, monopoly and competition—and the system of *money*....

Source: "Alienated Labor," by Karl Marx from *Karl Marx: Early Writings,* trans. and ed. by T. B. Bottomore. Copyright © 1963, McGraw-Hill Companies. Reprinted by permission of The McGraw-Hill Companies.

We shall begin from a *contemporary* economic fact. The worker becomes poorer the more wealth he produces and the more his production increases in power and extent. The worker becomes an ever cheaper commodity the more goods he creates. The *devaluation* of the human world increases in direct relation with the *increase in value* of the world of things. Labor does not only create goods; it also produces itself and the worker as a *commodity,* and indeed in the same proportion as it produces goods.

This fact simply implies that the object produced by labor, its product, now stands opposed to it as an *alien being,* as a *power independent* of the producer. The product of labor is labor which has been embodied in an object and turned into a physical thing; this product is an *objectification* of labor. The performance of work is at the same time its objectification. The performance of work appears in the sphere of political economy as a *vitiation*[1] of the worker, objectification as a *loss* and as *servitude to the object,* and appropriation as *alienation.*

223

So much does the performance of work appear as vitiation that the worker is vitiated to the point of starvation. So much does objectification appear as loss of the object that the worker is deprived of the most essential things not only of life but also of work. Labor itself becomes an object which he can acquire only by the greatest effort and with unpredictable interruptions. So much does the appropriation of the object appear as alienation that the more objects the worker produces the fewer he can possess and the more he falls under the domination of his product, of capital.

All these consequences follow from the fact that the worker is related to the *product of his labor* as to an *alien* object. For it is clear on this presupposition that the more the worker expends himself in work the more powerful becomes the world of objects which he creates in face of himself, the poorer he becomes in his inner life, and the less he belongs to himself. It is just the same as in religion. The more of himself man attributes to God the less he has left in himself. The worker puts his life into the object, and his life then belongs no longer to himself but to the object. The greater his activity, therefore, the less he possesses. What is embodied in the product of his labor is no longer his own. The greater this product is, therefore, the more he is diminished. The *alienation* of the worker in his product means not only that his labor becomes an object, assumes an *external* existence, but that it exists independently, *outside himself,* and alien to him, and that it stands opposed to him as an autonomous power. The life which he has given to the object sets itself against him as an alien and hostile force.

Let us now examine more closely the phenomenon of *objectification;* the worker's production and the *alienation* and *loss* of the object it produces, which is involved in it. The worker can create nothing without *nature,* without the *sensuous external world.* The latter is the material in which his labor is realized, in which it is active, out of which and through which it produces things.

But just as nature affords the *means of existence* of labor, in the sense that labor cannot *live* without objects upon which it can be exercised, so also it provides the *means of existence* in a narrower sense; namely the means of physical existence for the *worker* himself. Thus, the more the worker *appropriates* the external world of sensuous nature by his labor the more he deprives himself of *means of existence,* in two respects: First, that the sensuous external world becomes progressively less an object belonging to his labor or a means of existence of his labor, and secondly, that it becomes progressively less a means of existence in the direct sense, a means for the physical subsistence of the worker.

In both respects, therefore, the worker becomes a slave of the object; first, in that he receives an *object of work,* i.e., receives *work,* and secondly, in that he receives *means of subsistence.* Thus the object enables him to exist, first as a *worker* and secondly, as a *physical subject.* The culmination of this enslavement is that he can only maintain himself as a *physical subject* so far as he is a *worker,* and that it is only as a *physical subject* that he is a worker.

(The alienation of the worker in his object is expressed as follows in the laws of political economy: The more the worker produces the less he has to consume; the more value he creates the more worthless he becomes; the more refined his product the more crude and misshapen the worker; the more civilized the product the more barbarous the worker; the more powerful the work the more feeble the worker; the more the work manifests intelligence the more the worker declines in intelligence and becomes a slave of nature.)

Political economy conceals the alienation in the nature of labor insofar as it does not examine the direct relationship between the worker (work) *and production.* Labor certainly produces marvels for the rich but it produces privation for the worker. It produces palaces, but hovels for the worker. It produces beauty, but deformity for the worker. It replaces labor by machinery, but it casts some of the workers back into a barbarous kind of work and turns the others into machines. It produces intelligence, but also stupidity and cretinism for the workers.

The direct relationship of labor to its products is the relationship of the worker to the objects of his production. The relationship of property owners to the objects of production and to production itself is merely a *consequence* of this first relationship and confirms it. We shall consider this second aspect later.

Thus, when we ask what is the important relationship of labor, we are concerned with the relationship of the *worker* to production.

So far we have considered the alienation of the worker only from one aspect; namely, *his relationship with the products of his labor.* However, alienation appears not merely in the result but also in the *process of production,* within *productive activity* itself. How could the worker stand in an alien relationship to the product of his activity if he did not alienate himself in the act of production itself? The product is indeed only the *résumé* of activity, of production. Consequently, if the product of labor is alienation, production itself must be active alienation—the alienation of activity and the activity of alienation. The alienation of the object of labor merely summarizes the alienation in the work activity itself.

What constitutes the alienation of labor? First, that the work is *external* to the worker, that it is not part of his nature; and that, consequently, he does not fulfill himself in his work but denies himself, has a feeling of misery rather than well-being, does not develop freely his mental and physical energies but is physically exhausted and mentally debased. The worker, therefore, feels himself at home only during his leisure time, whereas at work he feels homeless. His work is not voluntary but imposed, *forced labor.* It is not the satisfaction of a need, but only a *means* for satisfying other needs. Its alien character is clearly shown by the fact that as soon as there is no physical or other compulsion it is avoided like the plague. External labor, labor in which man alienates himself, is a labor of self-sacrifice, of mortification. Finally, the external character of work for the worker is shown by the fact that it is not his own work but work for someone else, that in work he does not belong to himself but to another person....

We arrive at the result that man (the worker) feels himself to be freely active only in his animal functions—eating, drinking and procreating, or at most also in his dwelling and in personal adornment—while in his human functions he is reduced to an animal. The animal becomes human and the human becomes animal.

Eating, drinking, and procreating are of course also genuine human functions. But abstractly considered, apart from the environment of human activities, and turned into final and sole ends, they are animal functions.

We have now considered the act of alienation of practical human activity, labor, from two aspects: (1) the relationship of the worker to the *product of labor* as an alien object which dominates him. This relationship is at the same time the relationship to the sensuous external world, to natural objects, as an alien and hostile world; (2) the relationship of labor to the *act of production* within *labor.* This is the relationship of the worker to his own activity as something alien and not belonging to him, activity as suffering (passivity), strength as powerlessness, creation as emasculation, the *personal* physical and mental energy of the worker, his personal life (for what is life but activity?), as an activity which is directed against himself, independent of him and not belonging to him. This is *self-alienation* as against the [afore]mentioned alienation of the *thing.*

We have now to infer a third characteristic of *alienated labor* from the two we have considered. Man is a species-being not only in the sense that he makes the community (his own as well as those of other things) his object both practically and theoretically, but also (and this is simply another expression for the same thing) in the sense that he treats himself as the present, living species, as a *universal* and consequently free being.

Species-life, for man as for animals, has its physical basis in the fact that man (like animals) lives from inorganic nature, and since man is more universal than an animal so the range of inorganic nature from which he lives is more universal. Plants, animals, minerals, air, light, etc. constitute, from the theoretical aspect, a part of human consciousness as objects of natural science and art; they are man's spiritual inorganic nature, his intellectual means of life, which he must first prepare for enjoyment and perpetuation. So also, from the practical aspect, they form a part of human life and activity. In practice man lives only from these natural products, whether in the form of food, heating, clothing, housing, etc. The universality of man appears in practice in the universality which makes the whole of nature into his inorganic body: (1) as a direct means of life; and equally (2) as the material object and instrument of his life activity. Nature is the inorganic body of man; that is to say nature, excluding the human body itself. To say that man *lives* from nature means that nature is his *body* with which he must remain in a continuous interchange in order not to die. The statement that the physical and mental life of man, and nature, are interdependent means simply that nature is interdependent with itself, for man is a part of nature.

Since alienated labor (1) alienates nature from man; and (2) alienates man from himself, from his own active function, his life activity; so it alienates him from the species. It makes *species-life* into a means of individual life. In the first place it alienates species-life and individual life, and secondly, it turns the latter, as an abstraction, into the purpose of the former, also in its abstract and alienated form.

For labor, *life activity, productive life,* now appear to man only as *means* for the satisfaction of a need, the need to maintain his physical existence. Productive life is, however, species-life. It is life creating life. In the type of life activity resides the whole character of a species, its species-character; and free, conscious activity is the species-character of human beings. Life itself appears only as a *means of life.*

The animal is one with its life activity. It does not distinguish the activity from itself. It is *its activity.* But man makes his life activity itself an object of his will and consciousness. He has a conscious life activity. It is not a determination with which he is completely identified. Conscious life activity distinguishes man from the life activity of animals. Only for this reason is he a species-being. Or rather, he is only a self-conscious being, i.e., his own life is an object for him, because he is a species-being. Only for this reason is his activity free activity. Alienated labor reverses the relationship, in that man because he is a self-conscious being makes his life activity, his *being,* only a means for his *existence.*

NOTE

1. Debasement.

30

When Work Disappears

William Julius Wilson

The disappearance of work in the ghetto cannot be ignored, isolated or played down. Employment in America is up. The economy has churned out tens of millions of new jobs in the last two decades. In that same period, joblessness among inner-city blacks has reached catastrophic proportions. Yet in this Presidential election year, the disappearance of work in the ghetto is not on either the Democratic or the Republican agenda. There is harsh talk about work instead of welfare but no talk of where to find it.

The current employment woes in the inner city continue to be narrowly defined in terms of race or lack of individual initiative. It is argued that jobs are widely available, that the extent of inner-city poverty is exaggerated. Optimistic policy analysts—and many African Americans—would prefer that more attention be devoted to the successes and struggles of the black working class and the expanding black middle class. This is understandable. These two groups, many of whom have recently escaped from the ghetto, represent a majority of the African American population. But ghetto joblessness still afflicts a substantial—and increasing—minority: It's a problem that won't go away on its own. If it is not addressed, it will have lasting and harmful consequences for the quality of life in the cities and, eventually, for the lives of all Americans. Solutions will have to be found— and those solutions are at hand.

For the first time in the twentieth century, a significant majority of adults in many inner-city neighborhoods are not working in a typical week. Inner cities have always featured high

Source: From *When Work Disappears* by William Julius Wilson. Copyright © 1996 by William Julius Wilson, Alfred A. Knopf, Inc. Reprinted by permission of Alfred A. Knopf, Inc.

levels of poverty, but the current levels of joblessness in some neighborhoods are unprecedented. For example, in the famous black-belt neighborhood of Washington Park on Chicago's South Side, a majority of adults had jobs in 1950; by 1990, only one in three worked in a typical week. High neighborhood joblessness has a far more devastating effect than high neighborhood poverty. A neighborhood in which people are poor but employed is different from a neighborhood in which people are poor and jobless. Many of today's problems in the inner-city neighborhoods—crime, family dissolution, welfare—are fundamentally a consequence of the disappearance of work.

What causes the disappearance of work? There are several factors, including changes in the distribution and location of jobs, and in the level of training and education required to obtain employment. Nor should we overlook the legacy of historic racial segregation. However, the public debate around this question is not productive because it seeks to assign blame rather than recognizing and dealing with the complex realities that have led to economic distress for many Americans. Explanations and proposed solutions to the problem are often ideologically driven.

Conservatives tend to stress the importance of values, attitudes, habits, and styles. In this view, group differences are reflected in the culture. The truth is, cultural factors do play a role; but other, more important variables also have to be taken into account. Although race is clearly a significant variable in the social outcomes of inner-city blacks, it's not the *only* factor. The emphasis on racial differences has obscured the fact that African Americans, whites, and other ethnic groups have many common values, aspirations, and hopes.

An elderly woman who has lived in one inner-city neighborhood on the South Side of Chicago for more than forty years reflects: "I've been here since March 11, 1953. When I moved in, the neighborhood was intact. It was intact with homes, beautiful homes, minimansions, with stores, Laundromats, with Chinese clean-ers. We had drugstores. We had hotels. We had doctors over on 39th street. We had doctors' offices in the neighborhood. We had the middle class and upper middle class. It has gone from affluent to where it is today. And I would like to see it come back, that we can have some of the things we had. Since I came in young, and I'm a senior citizen now, I would like to see some of the things come back so I can enjoy them like we did when we first came in."

In the neighborhood of Woodlawn, on the South Side of Chicago, there were more than 800 commercial and industrial establishments in 1950. Today, it is estimated that only about 100 are left. In the words of Loïc Wacquant, a member of one of the research teams that worked with me over the last eight years: "The once-lively streets—residents remember a time, not so long ago, when crowds were so dense at rush hour that one had to elbow one's way to the train station—now have the appearance of an empty, bombed-out war zone. The commercial strip has been reduced to a long tunnel of charred stores, vacant lots littered with broken glass and garbage, and dilapidated buildings left to rot in the shadow of the elevated train line. At the corner of 63d Street and Cottage Grove Avenue, the handful of remaining establishments that struggle to survive are huddled behind wrought-iron bars.... The only enterprises that seem to be thriving are liquor stores and currency exchanges, those 'banks of the poor' where one can cash checks, pay bills and buy money orders for a fee."

The state of the inner-city public schools was another major concern expressed by our urban-poverty study respondents. The complaints ranged from overcrowded conditions to unqualified and uncaring teachers. Sharply voicing her views on these subjects, a twenty-five-year-old married mother of two children from a South Side census tract that just recently became poor stated: "My daughter ain't going to school here. She was going to a nursery school where I paid and of course they took the time and spent it with her, because they was getting the money.

But the public schools, no! They are over-crowded and the teachers don't care."

A resident of Woodlawn who had left the neighborhood as a child described how she felt upon her return about the changes that had occurred: "I was really appalled. When I walked down 63d Street when I was younger, everything you wanted was there. But now, coming back as an adult with my child, those resources are just gone, completely.... And housing, everybody has moved, there are vacant lots everywhere."

Neighborhoods plagued by high levels of joblessness are more likely to experience low levels of social organization: The two go hand in hand. High rates of joblessness trigger other neighborhood problems that undermine social organization, ranging from crime, gang violence, and drug trafficking to family breakups. And as these controls weaken, the social processes that regulate behavior change.

Industrial restructuring has further accelerated the deterioration of many inner-city neighborhoods. Consider the fate of the West Side black community of North Lawndale in Chicago: Since 1960, nearly half of its housing stock has disappeared; the remaining units are mostly run-down or dilapidated. Two large factories anchored the economy of this neighborhood in its good days—the Hawthorne plant of Western Electric, which employed more than 43,000 workers, and an International Harvester plant with 14,000 workers. But conditions rapidly changed. Harvester closed its doors in the late 1960s. Sears moved most of its offices to the Loop in downtown Chicago in 1973. The Hawthorne plant gradually phased out its operations and finally shut down in 1984.

"Jobs were plentiful in the past," attested a twenty-nine-year-old unemployed black man who lives in one of the poorest neighborhoods on the South Side. "You could walk out of the house and get a job. Maybe not what you want, but you could get a job. Now, you can't find anything. A lot of people in this neighborhood, they want to work but they can't get work. A few, but a very few, they just don't want to work."

The more rapid the neighborhood deterioration, the greater the institutional disinvestment. In the 1960s and 1970s, neighborhoods plagued by heavy abandonment were frequently redlined (identified as areas that should not receive or be recommended for mortgage loans or insurance); this paralyzed the housing market, lowered property values and encouraged landlord abandonment.

As the neighborhood disintegrates, those who are able to leave depart in increasing numbers; among these are many working- and middle-class families. The lower population density in turn creates additional problems. Abandoned buildings increase and often serve as havens for crack use and other illegal enterprises that give criminals—mostly young blacks who are unemployed—footholds in the community. Precipitous declines in density also make it even more difficult to sustain or develop a sense of community. The feeling of safety in numbers is completely lacking in such neighborhoods.

Problems in the new poverty or high-jobless neighborhoods have also created racial antagonism among some of the high-income groups in the city. The high joblessness in ghetto neighborhoods has sapped the vitality of local businesses and other institutions and has led to fewer and shabbier movie theaters, bowling alleys, restaurants, public parks and playgrounds, and other recreational facilities. When residents of inner-city neighborhoods venture out to other areas of the city in search of entertainment, they come into brief contact with citizens of markedly different racial or class backgrounds. Sharp differences in cultural style often lead to clashes.

Some behavior on the part of residents from socially isolated ghetto neighborhoods—for instance, the tendency to enjoy a movie in a communal spirit by carrying on a running conversation with friends and relatives or reacting in an unrestrained manner to what they see on the screen—is considered offensive by other groups, particularly black and white members of the middle class. Expressions of disapproval, either overt or with subtle hostile glances, tend to trigger belligerent responses from the ghetto residents, who then purposely intensify the behavior that is the source of irritation. The white and even the black middle-class moviegoers then exercise their option and exit, expressing resentment and experiencing intensified feelings of racial or class antagonism as they depart.

The areas surrendered in such a manner become the domain of the inner-city residents. Upscale businesses are replaced by fast-food chains and other local businesses that cater to the new clientele. White and black middle-class citizens complain bitterly about how certain areas of the central city have changed—and thus become "off-limits"—following the influx of ghetto residents.

The negative consequences are clear: Where jobs are scarce, many people eventually lose their feeling of connectedness to work in the formal economy; they no longer expect work to be a regular, and regulating, force in their lives. In the case of young people, they may grow up in an environment that lacks the idea of work as a central experience of adult life—they have little or no labor-force attachment. These circumstances also increase the likelihood that the residents will rely on illegitimate sources of income, thereby further weakening their attachment to the legitimate labor market.

A twenty-five-year-old West Side father of two who works two jobs to make ends meet condemned the attitude toward work of some inner-city black males:

They try to find easier routes and had been conditioned over a period of time to just be lazy, so to speak. Motivation nonexistent, you know, and the society that they're affiliated with really don't advocate hard work and struggle to meet your goals such as education and stuff like that. And they see who's around them and they follow that same pattern, you know.... They don't see nobody getting up early in the morning, going to work or going to school all the time. The guys they be with don't do that...because that's the crowd that you choose—well, that's been presented to you by your neighborhood.

Work is not simply a way to make a living and support one's family. It also constitutes a frame-work for daily behavior because it imposes discipline. Regular employment determines where you are going to be and when you are going to be there. In the absence of regular employment, life, including family life, becomes less coherent. Persistent unemployment and irregular employment hinder rational planning in daily life, the necessary condition of adaptation to an industrial economy.

It's a myth that people who don't work don't want to work. One mother in a new poverty neighborhood on the South Side explained her decision to remain on welfare even though she would like to get a job:

I was working and then I had two kids. And I'm struggling. I was making, like, close to $7 an hour.... I had to pay a baby-sitter. Then I had to deal with my kids when I got home. And I couldn't even afford medical insurance.... I was so scared, when my kids were sick or something, because I have been turned away from a hospital because I did not have a medical card. I don't like being on public aid and stuff right now. But what do I do with my kids when the kids get sick?

Working mothers with comparable incomes face, in many cases, even greater difficulty. Why? Simply because many low-wage jobs do not provide health-care benefits, and most working mothers have to pay for transportation and spend more for child care. Working mothers also have to spend more for housing because it is more difficult for them to qualify for housing subsidies. It is not surprising, therefore, that many welfare-reliant mothers choose not to enter the formal labor market. It would not be in their best economic interest to do so. Given the economic realities, it is also not surprising that many who are working in these low-wage jobs decide to rely on or return to welfare, even though it's not a desirable alternative for many of the black single mothers. As one twenty-seven-year-old welfare mother of three children from an impoverished West Side neighborhood put it: "I want to work. I do not work but I want to work. I don't want to just be on public aid."

As the disappearance of work has become a characteristic feature of the inner-city ghetto, so too has the disappearance of the traditional married-couple family. Only one-quarter of the black families whose children live with them in inner-city neighborhoods in Chicago are husband-wife families today, compared with three-quarters of the inner-city Mexican families, more than one-half of the white families and nearly one-half of the Puerto Rican families. And in census tracts with poverty rates of at least 40 percent, only 16.5 percent of the black families with children in the household are husband-wife families.

There are many factors involved in the precipitous decline in marriage rates and the sharp rise in single-parent families. The explanation most often heard in the public debate associates the increase of out-of-wedlock births and single-parent families with welfare. Indeed, it is widely assumed among the general public and reflected in the recent welfare reform that a direct connection exists between the level of welfare benefits and the likelihood that a young woman will bear a child outside marriage.

However, there is little evidence to support the claim that Aid to Families With Dependent Children plays a significant role in promoting out-of-wedlock births. Research examining the association between the generosity of welfare benefits and out-of-wedlock childbearing and teen-age pregnancy indicates that benefit levels have no significant effect on the likelihood that African American girls and women will have children outside marriage. Likewise, welfare rates have either no significant effect or only a small effect on the odds that whites will have children outside marriage. The rate of out-of-wedlock teen-age childbearing has nearly doubled since 1975—during years when the value of A.F.D.C., food stamps, and Medicaid fell, after adjusting for inflation. And the smallest increases in the number of out-of-wedlock births have not occurred in states that have had the largest declines in the inflation-adjusted value of A.F.D.C. benefits. Indeed, while the real value of cash welfare benefits has plummeted over the past twenty years, out-of-wedlock childbearing has increased, and postpartum marriages (marriages following the birth of a couple's child) have decreased as well.

It's instructive to consider the social differences between inner-city blacks and other groups, especially Mexicans. Mexicans come to the United States with a clear conception of a traditional family unit that features men as breadwinners. Although extramarital affairs by men are tolerated, unmarried pregnant women are "a source of opprobrium, anguish or great concern," as Richard P. Taub, a member of one of our research teams, put it. Pressure is applied by the kin of both parents to enter into marriage.

The family norms and behavior in inner-city black neighborhoods stand in sharp contrast. The relationships between inner-city black men and women, whether in a marital or nonmarital situation, are often fractious and antagonistic. Inner-city black women routinely say that black men are hopeless as either husbands or fathers and that more of their time is spent on the streets than at home.

The men in the inner city generally feel that it is much better for all parties to remain in a nonmarital relationship until the relationship dissolves rather than to get married and then have to get a divorce. A twenty-five-year-old unmarried West Side resident, the father of one child, expressed this view:

> Well, most black men feel now, why get married when you got six to seven women to one guy, really. You know, because there's more women out here mostly than men. Because most dudes around here are killing each other like fools over drugs or all this other stuff.

The fact that blacks reside in neighborhoods and are engaged in social networks and households that are less conducive to employment than those of other ethnic and racial groups in the inner city clearly has a negative effect on their search for work. In the eyes of employers in metropolitan Chicago, these differences render inner-city blacks less desirable as workers, and therefore are reluctant to hire them. The white chairman of a car transport company, when asked if there were differences in the work ethic of whites, blacks, and Hispanics, responded with great certainty:

Definitely! I don't think, I know: I've seen it over a period of thirty years. Basically, the Oriental is much more aggressive and intelligent and studious than the Hispanic. The Hispanics, except Cubans of course, they have the work ethnic [*sic*]. The Hispanics are *mañana, mañana, mañana*—tomorrow, tomorrow, tomorrow.

As for native-born blacks, they were deemed "the laziest of the bunch."

If some employers view the work ethic of inner-city poor blacks as problematic, many also express concerns about their honesty, cultural attitudes and dependability—traits that are frequently associated with the neighborhoods in which they live. A white suburban retail drugstore manager expressed his reluctance to hire someone from a poor inner-city neighborhood. "You'd be afraid they're going to steal from you," he stated. "They grow up that way. They grow up dishonest and I guess you'd feel like, geez, how are they going to be honest here?"

In addition to qualms about the work ethic, character, family influences, cultural predispositions and the neighborhood milieu of ghetto residents, the employers frequently mentioned concerns about applicants' language skills and educational training. They "just don't have the language skills," stated a suburban employer. The president of an inner-city advertising agency highlighted the problem of spelling:

I needed a temporary a couple months ago, and they sent me a black man. And I dictated a letter to him. He took shorthand, which was good. Something like "Dear Mr. So-and-So, I am writing to ask about how your business is doing." And then he typed the letter, and I read the letter, and it's "I am writing to ax about your business." Now you hear them speaking a different language and all that, and they say "ax" for "ask." Well, I don't care about that, but I didn't say "ax," I said "ask."

Many inner-city residents have a strong sense of the negative attitudes that employers tend to have toward them. A thirty-three-year-old employed janitor from a poor South Side neighborhood had this observation: "I went to a couple jobs where a couple of the receptionists told me in confidence: 'You know what they do with these applications from blacks as soon as the day is over?' They say, 'We rip them and throw them in the garbage.'" In addition to concerns about being rejected because of race, the fears that some inner-city residents have of being denied employment simply because of their inner-city address or neighborhood are not unfounded. A welfare mother who lives in a large public housing project put it this way:

Honestly, I believe they look at the address and the—your attitudes, your address, your surround—you know, your environment has a lot to do with your employment status. The people with the best addresses have the best chances. I feel so, I feel so.

It is instructive to study the fate of the disadvantaged in Europe. There, too, poverty and joblessness are on the increase; but individual deficiencies and behavior are not put forward as the culprits. Furthermore, welfare programs that benefit wide segments of the population like child care, children's allowances (an annual benefit per child), housing subsidies, education, medical care and unemployment insurance have been firmly institutionalized in many Western European democracies. Efforts to cut back on these programs in the face of growing joblessness have met firm resistance from working- and middle-class citizens.

My own belief is that the growing assault on welfare mothers is part of a larger reaction to the mounting problems in our nation's inner cities. When many people think of welfare they think of young, unmarried black mothers having babies. This image persists even though roughly equal numbers of black and white families received A.F.D.C. in 1994, and there were also a good many Hispanics on the welfare rolls. Nevertheless, the rise of black A.F.D.C. recipients was said to be symptomatic of such larger problems as the decline in family values and the dissolution of the family. In an article published in *Esquire*, Pete Hamill wrote:

The heart of the matter is the continued existence and expansion of what has come to be called the Underclass...trapped in cycles of welfare dependency, drugs, alcohol, crime, illiteracy and disease, living in anarchic and murderous isolation in some of the richest cities on the earth. As a reporter, I've covered their miseries for more than a quarter of a century.... And in the last decade, I've watched this group of American citizens harden and condense, moving even further away from the basic requirements of a human life: work, family, safety, the law.

One has the urge to shout, "Enough is enough!"

What can be done? I believe that steps must be taken to galvanize Americans from all walks of life who are concerned about human suffering and the public policy direction in which we are now moving. We need to generate a public-private partnership to fight social inequality. The following policy frameworks provide a basis for further discussion and debate. Given the current political climate, these proposals might be dismissed as unrealistic. Nor am I suggesting that we can or should simply import the social policies of the Japanese, the Germans, or other Western Europeans. The question is how we Americans can address the problems of social inequality, including record levels of joblessness in the inner city, that threaten the very fabric of our society.

CREATE STANDARDS FOR SCHOOLS

Ray Marshall, former [U.S.] Secretary of Labor, points out that Japan and Germany have developed policies designed to increase the number of workers with "higher-order thinking skills." These policies require young people to meet high performance standards before they can graduate from secondary schools, and they hold each school responsible for meeting these standards.

Students who meet high standards are not only prepared for work but they are also ready for technical training and other kinds of postsec-

ondary education. Currently, there are no mandatory academic standards for secondary schools in the United States. Accordingly, students who are not in college-preparatory courses have severely limited options with respect to pursuing work after high school. A commitment to a system of performance standards for every public school in the United States would be an important first step in addressing the huge gap in educational performance between the schools in advantaged and disadvantaged neighborhoods.

A system of at least local performance standards should include the kind of support that would enable schools in disadvantaged neighborhoods to meet the standards that are set. State governments, with federal support, not only would have to create equity in local school financing (through loans and scholarships to attract more high-quality teachers, increased support for teacher training and reforms in teacher certification) but would also have to insure that highly qualified teachers are more equitably distributed in local school districts.

Targeting education would be part of a national effort to raise the performance standards of all public schools in the United States to a desirable level, including schools in the inner city. The support of the private sector should be enlisted in this national effort. Corporations, local businesses, civic clubs, community centers and churches should be encouraged to work with the schools to improve computer-competency training.

IMPROVE CHILD CARE

The French system of child welfare stands in sharp contrast to the American system. In France, children are supported by three interrelated government programs, as noted by Barbara R. Bergmann, a professor of economics at American University: child care, income support, and medical care. The child-care program includes establishments for infant care, high-quality nursery schools (*écoles maternelles*), and paid leave for parents of newborns. The income-support program includes child-support enforcement (so that the absent parent continues to contribute financially to his or her child's welfare), children's allowances, and welfare payments for low-income single mothers. Finally, medical care is provided through a universal system of national health care financed by social security, a preventive-care system for children, and a group of public-health nurses who specialize in child welfare.

ESTABLISH CITY-SUBURBAN PARTNERSHIPS

If the other industrial democracies offer lessons for a long-term solution to the jobs problem involving relationships between employment, education, and family-support systems, they also offer another lesson: the importance of city-suburban integration and cooperation. None of the other industrialized democracies have allowed their city centers to deteriorate as has the United States.

It will be difficult to address growing racial tensions in American cities unless we tackle the problems of shrinking revenue and inadequate social services and the gradual disappearance of work in certain neighborhoods. The city has become a less desirable place in which to live, and the economic and social gap between the cities and suburbs is growing. The groups left behind compete, often along racial lines, for declining resources, including the remaining decent schools, housing, and neighborhoods. The rise of the new urban poverty neighborhoods has worsened these problems. Their high rates of joblessness and social disorganization have created problems that often spill over into other parts of the city. All of these factors aggravate race relations and elevate racial tensions.

Ideally, we would restore the federal contribution to city revenues that existed in 1980 and sharply increase the employment base. Regardless of changes in federal urban policy, however, the fiscal crises in the cities would be significantly eased if the employment base could be substantially increased. Indeed, the social

dislocations caused by the steady disappearance of work have led to a wide range of urban social problems, including racial tensions. Increased employment would help stabilize the new poverty neighborhoods, halt the precipitous decline in density, and ultimately enhance the quality of race relations in urban areas.

Reforms put forward to achieve the objective of city-suburban cooperation range from proposals to create metropolitan governments to proposals for metropolitan tax-base sharing (currently in effect in Minneapolis-St. Paul), collaborative metropolitan planning, and the creation of regional authorities to develop solutions to common problems if communities fail to reach agreement. Among the problems shared by many metropolises is a weak public transit system. A commitment to address this problem through a form of city-suburban collaboration would benefit residents of both the city and the suburbs.

The mismatch between residence and the location of jobs is a problem for some workers in America because, unlike the system in Europe, public transportation is weak and expensive. It's a particular problem for inner-city blacks because they have less access to private automobiles and, unlike Mexicans, do not have a network system that supports organized car pools. Accordingly, they depend heavily on public transportation and therefore have difficulty getting to the suburbs, where jobs are more plentiful. Until public transit systems are improved in metropolitan areas, the creation of privately subsidized car-pool and van-pool networks to carry inner-city residents to the areas of employment, especially suburban areas, would be a relatively inexpensive way to increase work opportunities.

The creation of for-profit information and placement centers in various parts of the inner city not only could significantly improve awareness of the availability of employment in the metropolitan area but could also serve to refer workers to employers. These centers would recruit or accept inner-city workers and try to place them in jobs. One of their main purposes would be to make persons who have been persistently unemployed or out of the labor force "job ready."

REINTRODUCE THE W.P.A.

The final proposal under consideration here was advanced by the perceptive journalist Mickey Kaus of *The New Republic,* who has long been concerned about the growth in the number of welfare recipients. Kaus's proposal is modeled on the Works Progress Administration (W.P.A.), the large public-works program initiated in 1935 by President Franklin D. Roosevelt. The public-works jobs that Roosevelt had in mind included highway construction, slum clearance, housing construction, and rural electrification. As Kaus points out:

In its eight-year existence, according to official records, the W.P.A. built or improved 651,000 miles of roads, 953 airports, 124,000 bridges and viaducts, 1,178,000 culverts, 8,000 parks, 18,000 playgrounds and athletic fields, and 2,000 swimming pools. It constructed 40,000 buildings (including 8,000 schools) and repaired 85,000 more. Much of New York City—including La Guardia Airport, F.D.R. Drive, plus hundreds of parks and libraries—was built by the W.P.A.

A neo-W.P.A. program of employment, for every American citizen over eighteen who wants it, would provide useful public jobs at wages slightly below the minimum wage. Like the work relief under Roosevelt's W.P.A., it would not carry the stigma of a cash dole. People would be earning their money. Although some workers in the W.P.A.-style jobs "could be promoted to higher-paying public service positions," says Kaus, most of them would advance occupationally by moving to the private sector. "If you have to work anyway," he says, "why do it for $4 an hour?"

Under Kaus's proposal, after a certain date, able-bodied recipients on welfare would no longer receive cash payments. However, unlike the welfare-reform bill that Clinton has agreed to sign, Kaus's plan would make public jobs available to those who move off welfare. Also, Kaus argues that to allow poor mothers to work, government-financed day care must be provided for their children if needed. But this service has to be integrated into the larger system of child care for other families in the United States to avoid creating a "day-care ghetto" for low-income children.

A W.P.A.-style jobs program will not be cheap. In the short run, it is considerably cheaper to give people cash welfare than it is to create public jobs. Including the costs of supervisors and materials, each subminimum-wage W.P.A.-style job would cost an estimated $12,000, more than the public cost of staying on welfare. That would represent $12 billion for every 1 million jobs created.

The solutions I have outlined were developed with the idea of providing a policy framework that could be easily adopted by a reform coalition. A broad range of groups would support the long-term solutions—the development of a system of national performance standards in public schools, family policies to reinforce the learning system in the schools, a national system of school-to-work transition, and the promotion of city-suburban integration and cooperation. The short-term solutions, which range from job information and placement centers to the creation of W.P.A.-style jobs, are more relevant to low-income people, but they are the kinds of opportunity-enhancing programs that Americans of all racial and class backgrounds tend to support.

Although my policy framework is designed to appeal to broad segments of the population, I firmly believe that if adopted, it would alleviate a good deal of the economic and social distress currently plaguing the inner cities. The immediate problem of the disappearance of work in many inner-city neighborhoods would be confronted. The employment base in these neighborhoods would be increased immediately by the newly created jobs, and income levels would rise because of the expansion of the earned-income tax credit. Programs like universal health care and day care would increase the attractiveness of low-wage jobs and "make work pay."

Increasing the employment base would have an enormous positive impact on the social organization of ghetto neighborhoods. As more people become employed, crime and drug use would subside; families would be strengthened and welfare receipt would decline significantly; ghetto-related culture and behavior, no longer sustained and nourished by persistent joblessness, would gradually fade. As more people became employed and gained work experience, they would have a better chance of finding jobs in the private sector when they became available. The attitudes of employers toward inner-city workers would change, partly because the employers would be dealing with job applicants who had steady work experience and would furnish references from their previous supervisors.

This is not to suggest that all the jobless individuals from the inner-city ghetto would take advantage of these employment opportunities. Some have responded to persistent joblessness by abusing alcohol and drugs, and these handicaps will affect their overall job performance, including showing up for work on time or on a consistent basis. But such people represent only a small proportion of inner-city workers.

Most of them are ready, willing, able and anxious to hold a steady job.

The long-term solutions that I have advanced would reduce the likelihood that a new generation of jobless workers will be produced from the youngsters now in school and preschool. We must break the cycle of joblessness and improve the youngsters' preparation for the new labor market in the global economy.

My framework for long-term and immediate solutions is based on the notion that the problems of jobless ghettos cannot be separated from those of the rest of the nation. Although these solutions have wide-ranging application and would alleviate the economic distress of many Americans, their impact on jobless ghettos would be profound. Their most important contribution would be their effect on the children of the ghetto, who would be able to anticipate a future of economic mobility and harbor the hopes and aspirations that for so many of their fellow citizens help define the American way of life.

Part XV

Politics and Government

31

The Power Elite

C. Wright Mills

The powers of ordinary men are circumscribed by the everyday worlds in which they live, yet even in these rounds of job, family, and neighborhood they often seem driven by forces they can neither understand nor govern. "Great changes" are beyond their control, but affect their conduct and outlook nonetheless. The very framework of modern society confines them to projects not their own, but from every side, such changes now press upon the men and women of the mass society, who accordingly feel that they are without purpose in an epoch in which they are without power.

But not all men are in this sense ordinary. As the means of information and of power are centralized, some men come to occupy positions in American society from which they can look down upon, so to speak, and by their decisions mightily affect, the everyday worlds of ordinary men and women. They are not made by their jobs; they set

up and break down jobs for thousands of others; they are not confined by simple family responsibilities; they can escape. They may live in many hotels and houses, but they are bound by no one community. They need not merely "meet the demands of the day and hour"; in some part, they create these demands, and cause others to meet them. Whether or not they profess their power, their technical and political experience of it far transcends that of the underlying population. What Jacob Burckhardt said of "great men," most Americans might well say of their elite: "They are all that we are not."

The power elite is composed of men whose positions enable them to transcend the ordinary environments of ordinary men and women; they are in positions to make decisions having major consequences. Whether they do or do not make such decisions is less important than the fact that they do occupy such pivotal positions: Their failure to act, their failure to make decisions, is itself an act that is often of greater consequence than the decisions they do make. For they are in command of the major hierarchies and organizations of modern society. They rule the big corporations. They run the machinery of the state and claim its prerogatives. They direct the military establishment. They occupy the strategic command posts of the social structure, in which are now centered the effective means of the power and the wealth and the celebrity which they enjoy.

The power elite are not solitary rulers. Advisers and consultants, spokesmen and opinion-makers are often the captains of their higher thought and decision. Immediately below the elite are the professional politicians of the middle levels of power, in the Congress and in the pressure groups, as well as among the new and old upper classes of town and city and region. Mingling with them, in curious ways which we shall explore, are those professional celebrities who live by being continually displayed but are never, so long as they remain celebrities, displayed enough. If such celebrities are not at the head of any dominating hierarchy, they do often have the power to distract the attention of the public or afford sensations to the masses, or, more directly, to gain the ear of those who do occupy positions of direct power. More or less unattached, as critics of morality and technicians of power, as spokesmen of God and creators of mass sensibility, such celebrities and consultants are part of the immediate scene in which the drama of the elite is enacted. But that drama itself is centered in the command posts of the major institutional hierarchies.

The truth about the nature and the power of the elite is not some secret which men of affairs know but will not tell. Such men hold quite various theories about their own roles in the sequence of event and decision. Often they are uncertain about their roles, and even more often they allow their fears and their hopes to affect their assessment of their own power. No matter how great their actual power, they tend to be less acutely aware of it than of the resistances of others to its use. Moreover, most American men of affairs have learned well the rhetoric of public

relations, in some cases even to the point of using it when they are alone, and thus coming to believe it. The personal awareness of the actors is only one of the several sources one must examine in order to understand the higher circles. Yet many who believe that there is no elite, or at any rate none of any consequence, rest their argument upon what men of affairs believe about themselves, or at least assert in public.

There is, however, another view: Those who feel, even if vaguely, that a compact and powerful elite of great importance does now prevail in America often base that feeling upon the historical trend of our time. They have felt, for example, the domination of the military event, and from this they infer that generals and admirals, as well as other men of decision influenced by them, must be enormously powerful. They hear that the Congress has again abdicated to a handful of men decisions clearly related to the issue of war or peace. They know that the bomb was dropped over Japan in the name of the United States of America, although they were at no time consulted about the matter. They feel that they live in a time of big decisions; they know that they are not making any. Accordingly, as they consider the present as history, they infer that at its center, making decisions or failing to make them, there must be an elite of power.

On the one hand, those who share this feeling about big historical events assume that there is an elite and that its power is great. On the other hand, those who listen carefully to the reports of men apparently involved in the great decisions often do not believe that there is an elite whose powers are of decisive consequence.

Both views must be taken into account, but neither is adequate. The way to understand the power of the American elite lies neither solely in recognizing the historic scale of events nor in accepting the personal awareness reported by men of apparent decision. Behind such men and behind the events of history, linking the two, are the major institutions of modern society. These hierarchies of state and corporation and army constitute the means of power; as such they are now of a consequence not before equaled in human history— and at their summits, there are now those command posts of modern society which offer us the sociological key to an understanding of the role of the higher circles in America.

Within American society, major national power now resides in the economic, the political, and the military domains. Other institutions seem off to the side of modern history, and, on occasion, duly subordinated to these. No family is as directly powerful in national affairs as any major corporation; no church is as directly powerful in the external biographies of young men in America today as the military establishment; no college is as powerful in the shaping of momentous events as the National Security Council. Religious, educational, and family institutions are not autonomous centers of national power; on the contrary, these decentralized areas are increasingly shaped by the big three, in which developments of decisive and immediate consequence now occur.

Families and churches and schools adapt to modern life; governments and armies and corporations shape it; and, as they do so, they turn these lesser institutions into means for their ends. Religious institutions provide chaplains to the armed forces where they are used as a means of increasing the effectiveness of its morale to kill. Schools select and train men for their jobs in corporations and their specialized tasks in the armed forces. The extended family has, of course, long been broken up by the industrial revolution, and now the son and the father are removed from the family, by compulsion if need be, whenever the army of the state sends out the call. And the symbols of all these lesser institutions are used to legitimate the power and the decisions of the big three.

The life-fate of the modern individual depends not only upon the family into which he was born or which he enters by marriage, but increasingly upon the corporation in which he spends the most alert hours of his best years; not only upon the

school where he is educated as a child and adolescent, but also upon the state which touches him throughout his life; not only upon the church in which on occasion he hears the word of God, but also upon the army in which he is disciplined.

If the centralized state could not rely upon the inculcation of nationalist loyalties in public and private schools, its leaders would promptly seek to modify the decentralized educational system. If the bankruptcy rate among the top 500 corporations were as high as the general divorce rate among the 37 million married couples, there would be economic catastrophe on an international scale. If members of armies gave to them no more of their lives than do believers to the churches to which they belong, there would be a military crisis.

Within each of the big three, the typical institutional unit has become enlarged, has become administrative, and, in the power of its decisions, has become centralized. Behind these developments there is a fabulous technology, for as institutions, they have incorporated this technology and guide it, even as it shapes and paces their developments.

The economy—once a great scatter of small productive units in autonomous balance—has become dominated by two or three hundred giant corporations, administratively and politically interrelated, which together hold the keys to economic decisions.

The political order, once a decentralized set of several dozen states with a weak spinal cord, has become a centralized, executive establishment which has taken up into itself many powers previously scattered, and now enters into each and every cranny of the social structure.

The military order, once a slim establishment in a context of distrust fed by state militia, has become the largest and most expensive feature of government, and, although well-versed in smiling public relations, now has all the grim and clumsy efficiency of a sprawling bureaucratic domain.

In each of these institutional areas, the means of power at the disposal of decision makers have

242 Politics and Governmemt

increased enormously; their central executive powers have been enhanced; within each of them modern administrative routines have been elaborated and tightened up.

As each of these domains becomes enlarged and centralized, the consequences of its activities become greater, and its traffic with the others increases. The decisions of a handful of corporations bear upon military and political as well as upon economic developments around the world. The decisions of the military establishment rest upon and grievously affect political life as well as the very level of economic activity. The decisions made within the political domain determine economic activities and military programs. There is no longer, on the one hand, an economy, and, on the other hand, a political order containing a military establishment unimportant to politics and to money-making. There is a political economy linked, in a thousand ways, with military institutions and decisions. On each side of the world-split running through central Europe and around the Asiatic rimlands, there is an ever-increasing interlocking of economic, military, and political structures. If there is government intervention in the corporate economy, so is there corporate intervention in the governmental process. In the structural sense, this triangle of power is the source of the interlocking directorate that is most important for the historical structure of the present.

The fact of the interlocking is clearly revealed at each of the points of crisis of modern capitalist society—slump, war, and boom. In each, men of decision are led to an awareness of the interdependence of the major institutional orders. In the nineteenth century, when the scale of all institutions was smaller, their liberal integration was achieved in the automatic economy, by an autonomous play of market forces, and in the automatic political domain, by the bargain and the vote. It was then assumed that out of the imbalance and friction that followed the limited decisions then possible a new equilibrium would in due course emerge. That can no longer be

assumed, and it is not assumed by the men at the top of each of the three dominant hierarchies.

For given the scope of their consequences, decisions—and indecisions—in any one of these ramify into the others, and hence top decisions tend either to become coordinated or to lead to a commanding indecision. It has not always been like this. When numerous small entrepreneurs made up the economy, for example, many of them could fail and the consequences still remain local; political and military authorities did not intervene. But now, given political expectations and military commitments, can they afford to allow key units of the private corporate economy to break down in slump? Increasingly, they do intervene in economic affairs, and as they do so, the controlling decisions in each order are inspected by agents of the other two, and economic, military, and political structures are interlocked.

At the pinnacle of each of the three enlarged and centralized domains, there have arisen those higher circles which make up the economic, the political, and the military elites. At the top of the economy, among the corporate rich, there are the chief executives; at the top of the political order, the members of the political directorate; at the top of the military establishment, the elite of soldier-statesmen clustered in and around the Joint Chiefs of Staff and the upper echelon. As each of these domains has coincided with the others, as decisions tend to become total in their consequence, the leading men in each of the three domains of power—the warlords, the corporation chieftains, the political directorate—tend to come together, to form the power elite of America.

The higher circles in and around these command posts are often thought of in terms of what their members possess: They have a greater share than other people of the things and experiences that are most highly valued. From this point of view, the elite are simply those who have the most of what there is to have, which is generally held to include money, power, and prestige—as well as all the ways of life to which these lead. But the elite are not simply those who have the most, for they could not "have the most" were it not for their positions in the great institutions. For such institutions are the necessary bases of power, of wealth, and of prestige, and at the same time, the chief means of exercising power, of acquiring and retaining wealth, and of cashing in the higher claims for prestige.

By the powerful we mean, of course, those who are able to realize their will, even if others resist it. No one, accordingly, can be truly powerful unless he has access to the command of major institutions, for it is over these institutional means of power that the truly powerful are, in the first instance, powerful. Higher politicians and key officials of government command such institutional power; so do admirals and generals, and so do the major owners and executives of the larger corporations. Not all power, it is true, is anchored in and exercised by means of such institutions, but only within and through them can power be more or less continuous and important.

Wealth also is acquired and held in and through institutions. The pyramid of wealth cannot be understood merely in terms of the very rich; for the great inheriting families, as we shall see, are now supplemented by the corporate institutions of modern society: Every one of the very rich families has been and is closely connected—always legally and frequently managerially as well—with one of the multimillion-dollar corporations.

The modern corporation is the prime source of wealth, but, in latter-day capitalism, the political apparatus also opens and closes many avenues to wealth. The amount as well as the source of income, the power over consumer's goods as well as over productive capital, are determined by position within the political economy. If our interest in the very rich goes beyond their lavish or their miserly consumption, we must examine their relations to modern forms of corporate property as well as to the state; for such relations now determine the chances of men to secure big property and to receive high income.

Great prestige increasingly follows the major institutional units of the social structure. It is obvious that prestige depends, often quite decisively, upon access to the publicity machines that are now a central and normal feature of all the big institutions of modern America. Moreover, one feature of these hierarchies of corporation, state, and military establishment is that their top positions are increasingly interchangeable. One result of this is the accumulative nature of prestige. Claims for prestige, for example, may be initially based on military roles, then expressed in and augmented by an educational institution run by corporate executives, and cashed in, finally, in the political order, where, for General Eisenhower and those he represents, power and prestige finally meet at the very peak. Like wealth and power, prestige tends to be cumulative: The more of it you have, the more you can get. These values also tend to be translatable into one another: The wealthy find it easier than the poor to gain power; those with status find it easier than those without it to control opportunities for wealth.

If we took the 100 most powerful men in America, the 100 wealthiest, and the 100 most celebrated away from the institutional positions they now occupy, away from their resources of men and women and money, away from the media of mass communication that are now focused upon them—then they would be powerless and poor and uncelebrated. For power is not of a man. Wealth does not center in the person of the wealthy. Celebrity is not inherent in any personality. To be celebrated, to be wealthy, to have power requires access to major institutions, for the institutional positions men occupy determine in large part their chances to have and to hold these valued experiences.

The people of the higher circles may also be conceived as members of a top social stratum, as a set of groups whose members know one another, see one another socially and at business, and so, in making decisions, take one another into account. The elite, according to this conception, feel themselves to be, and are felt by others to be, the inner circle of "the upper social classes." They form a more or less compact social and psychological entity; they have become self-conscious members of a social class. People are either accepted into this class or they are not, and there is a qualitative split, rather than merely a numerical scale, separating them from those who are not elite. They are more or less aware of themselves as a social class and they behave toward one another differently from the way they do toward members of other classes. They accept one another, understand one another, marry one another, tend to work and to think if not together at least alike.

Now, we do not want by our definition to prejudge whether the elite of the command posts are conscious members of such a socially recognized class, or whether considerable proportions of the elite derive from such a clear and distinct class. These are matters to be investigated. Yet in order to be able to recognize what we intend to investigate, we must note something that all biographies and memoirs of the wealthy and the powerful and the eminent make clear: No matter what else they may be, the people of these higher circles are involved in a set of overlapping "crowds" and intricately connected "cliques." There is a kind of mutual attraction among those who "sit on the same terrace"—although this often becomes clear to them, as well as to others, only at the point at which they feel the need to draw the line; only when, in their common defense, they come to understand what they have in common, and so close their ranks against outsiders.

The idea of such ruling stratum implies that most of its members have similar social origins, that throughout their lives they maintain a network of informal connections, and that to some degree there is an interchangeability of position between the various hierarchies of money and power and celebrity. We must, of course, note at once that if such an elite stratum does exist, its social visibility and its form, for very solid historical reasons, are quite different from those of the noble cousinhoods that once ruled various European nations.

That American society has never passed through a feudal epoch is of decisive importance to the nature of the American elite, as well as to American society as a historic whole. For it means that no nobility or aristocracy, established before the capitalist era, has stood in tense opposition to the higher bourgeoisie. It means that this bourgeoisie has monopolized not only wealth but prestige and power as well. It means that no set of noble families has commanded the top positions and monopolized the values that are generally held in high esteem; and certainly that no set has done so explicitly by inherited right. It means that no high church dignitaries or court nobilities, no entrenched landlords with honorific accouterments, no monopolists of high army posts have opposed the enriched bourgeoisie and in the name of birth and prerogative successfully resisted its self-making.

But this does *not* mean that there are no upper strata in the United States. That they emerged from a "middle class" that had no recognized aristocratic superiors does not mean they remained middle class when enormous increases in wealth made their own superiority possible. Their origins and their newness may have made the upper strata less visible in America than elsewhere. But in America today there are in fact tiers and ranges of wealth and power of which people in the middle and lower ranks know very little and may not even dream. There are families who, in their well-being, are quite insulated from the economic jolts and lurches felt by the merely prosperous and those farther down the scale. There are also men of power who in quite small groups make decisions of enormous consequence for the underlying population....

32

Freedom in the World: A Global Survey

Adrian Karatnycky

MORE FREE COUNTRIES THAN EVER

Despite a year that saw violent civil war in the Republic of the Congo, attempts at ethnic cleansing in Kosovo, ethnic and political violence in Indonesia, and severe economic turbulence in many of the world's emerging markets, freedom made significant strides in 1998. As the year drew to a close, 88 of the world's 191 countries (46 percent) were rated as Free, meaning that they maintain a high degree of political and economic freedom and respect basic civil liberties. This was the largest number of Free countries on record, and represented a net gain of seven from last year—the second-largest increase in the twenty-six-year history of the *Survey*. Another 53 countries (28 percent of the world total) were rated as Partly Free, enjoying more

limited political rights and civil liberties, often in a context of corruption, weak rule of law, ethnic strife, or civil war. This represented a drop of four from the previous year. Finally, 50 countries (26 percent of the world total) that deny their citizens basic rights and civil liberties were rated as Not Free. This represented a drop of three from the previous year.

There were seven new entrants into the ranks of Free countries in 1998, including India, which had been rated as Partly Free since 1991, a year that saw the killing of former prime minister Rajiv Gandhi, intense labor strife, and an escalation of intercommunal violence resulting in thousands of deaths. India's return to the ranks of Free countries was the consequence of greater internal stability, fewer instances of intercommunal violence, and the peaceful democratic transfer of power to an opposition-led government. Other entrants into the ranks of Free countries were the Dominican Republic, where a democratically elected government has made efforts to strengthen the administration of justice; Ecuador, which

Source: From *Freedom in the World: The Annual Survey of Political Rights and Civil Liberties, 1998–1999*, ed. Adrian Karatnycky (New York: Freedom House, 1999). Reprinted by permission of Freedom House.

Table 32.1:   Freedom in the World, 1998–1999

The population of the world this year is estimated at 5,908.7 billion persons, who reside in 191 sovereign states and 61 related and disputed territories—a total of 252 entities. The level of political rights and civil liberties as shown comparatively by the Freedom House Survey is:

Free: 2,354.0 billion (39.84 percent of the world's population) live in 88 of the states and in 44 of the related and/or disputed territories.
Partly Free: 1,570.6 billion (26.59 percent of the world's population) live in 53 of the states and 4 of the related and/or disputed territories.
Not Free: 1,984.1 billion (33.58 percent of the world's population) live in 50 of the states and 13 of the related and/or disputed territories.

A Record of the Survey
(population in billions)

Survey Date	Free		Partly Free		Not Free		World Population
January '81	1,613.0	(35.90%)	970.9	(21.60%)	1,911.9	(42.5%)	4,495.8
January '83	1,665.4	(36.32%)	918.8	(20.04%)	2,000.2	(43.64%)	4,584.1
January '85	1,671.4	(34.85%)	1,117.4	(23.30%)	2,007.0	(41.85%)	4,795.8
January '87	1,842.5	(37.10%)	1,171.5	(23.60%)	1,949.9	(39.3%)	4,963.9
January '89	1,992.8	(38.86%)	1,027.9	(20.05%)	2,107.3	(41.09%)	5,128.0
January '90	2,034.4	(38.87%)	1,143.7	(21.85%)	2,055.9	(39.28%)	5,234.0
January '91	2,088.2	(39.23%)	1,485.7	(27.91%)	1,748.7	(32.86%)	5,322.6
January '92 (a)	1,359.3	(25.29%)	2,306.6	(42.92%)	1,708.2	(31.79%)	5,374.2
January '93	1,352.2	(24.83%)	2,403.3	(44.11%)	1,690.4	(31.06%)	5,446.0
January '94	1,046.2	(19.00%)	2,224.4	(40.41%)	2,234.6	(40.59%)	5,505.2
January '95	1,119.7	(19.97%)	2,243.4	(40.01%)	2,243.9	(40.02%)	5,607.0
January '96	1,114.5	(19.55%)	2,365.8	(41.49%)	2,221.2	(38.96%)	5,701.5
January '97	1,250.3	(21.67%)	2,260.1	(39.16%)	2,260.6	(39.17%)	5,771.0
January '98	1,266.0	(21.71%)	2,281.9	(39.12%)	2,284.6	(39.17%)	5,832.5
January '99 (b)	2,354.0	(39.84%)	1,570.6	(26.59%)	1,984.1	(33.58%)	5,908.7

(a) The large shift in the population figure between 1991 and 1992 is due to India's change from Free to Partly Free.
(b) The large shift in the population figure between 1998 and 1999 is due to India's change from Partly Free to Free.

recently concluded free and fair elections; Nicaragua, where improved relations between civilian authorities and a military formerly dominated by the Sandinistas contributed to the strengthening of democratic stability and where greater attention was paid to the problems of indigenous peoples on the country's Atlantic coast; Papua New Guinea, which saw a January 1998 peace agreement put an end to a destabilizing nine-year secessionist rebellion on Bougainville Island; Slovakia, where free and fair elections brought to power a government dominated by reformers; and Thailand, where the government of Prime Minister Chuan Leekpai has fostered increasing political accountability.

In addition, three countries formerly ranked as Not Free—Indonesia, Nigeria, and Sierra Leone—made tangible progress and are now rated as Partly Free. In Indonesia, the downfall of Suharto has led to the reemergence of political parties and civic groups and the promise of free elections. Although the country's economic crisis has sparked ethnic violence targeting the Chinese minority (and some violence has occurred during student demonstrations), some political controls have loosened, political parties and movements have begun to gain strength, and the media have become more outspoken. In Nigeria, the death of military dictator Sani Abacha has led to a political opening that holds out the promise of multiparty elections and already has seen the reemergence of public debate, a resurgence of political parties, the return of exiled leaders, relatively free and fair local elections, and the rise of an increasingly vibrant press. In Sierra Leone, the defeat of a military coup has put an end to chaos and violence and restored power to the country's democratically elected civilian authorities.

MORE FREE PEOPLE THAN EVER

As a result of the gains in freedom in 1998—especially in India, the world's most populous democracy—2.354 billion people (40 percent of the world's population) now live in Free societies, 1.570 billion (26.5 percent) live in countries that are Partly Free, and 1.984 billion (33.5 percent) live in Not Free countries. The proportion of the world's population living in freedom is the highest in the history of the *Survey*.

In addition to these shifts from one category to another, the 1998 survey recorded more modest improvements in freedom in twenty-one countries. Not all trends for the year were positive. The survey registered more modest declines in freedom in ten countries. These changes are reflected by upward or downward arrows, signifying improvements or declines in a country's score on the freedom scale. One country which registered worrying trends was Argentina, which suffered from the destabilizing effects of political sex scandals and efforts to blackmail political leaders.

Thirteen countries were judged to be the world's most repressive and have received Freedom House's lowest rating: scores of 7 for political rights and 7 for civil liberties. In these states, basic political rights and civil liberties are nonexistent, there is no free press, and independent civic life is suppressed. The most repressive countries, the "world's worst" in terms of freedom, include Iraq, North Korea, Cuba, and Sudan. The others are Afghanistan, Burma, Equatorial Guinea, Libya, Saudi Arabia, Somalia, Syria, Turkmenistan, and Vietnam. It is notable that of

Table 32.2: The Global Trend

	Free	Partly Free	Not Free
1988–1989	61	39	68
1993–1994	72	63	55
1998–1999	88	53	50

Tracking Democracy

	Number of Democracies
1988–1989	68
1993–1994	108
1998–1999	117

the thirteen least free states, three are one-party Marxist-Leninist states and eight are predominantly Islamic. The number of countries that received Freedom House's lowest rating (7,7) has declined from twenty-one at the close of 1994.

The *Survey of Freedom* also found that at the end of 1998 there were 117 electoral democracies, representing over 61 percent of the world's countries and nearly 55 percent of its population. The Freedom House roster of electoral democracies is based on a stringent standard requiring that all elected national authority must be the product of free and fair electoral processes. Thus, in the estimation of the *Survey*, neither Mexico (whose 1997 national legislative elections were judged free and fair, but whose last national presidential elections failed to meet that standard) nor Malaysia (whose governing United Malays National Organization enjoys huge and unfair advantages in national elections) qualifies as an electoral democracy. After a period in which electoral democracies increased dramatically from 69 in 1987, their number has remained stagnant at 117 since 1995.

The survey team identified five events that represented important gains for freedom in 1988 and five which signaled setbacks for freedom.

The 13 Worst Rated Countries

Afghanistan
Burma
Cuba
Equatorial Guinea
Iraq
Korea, North
Libya
Saudi Arabia
Somalia
Sudan
Syria
Turkmenistan
Vietnam

The Worst Rated Related Territory

Kosovo (Yugoslavia)

The Worst Rated Disputed Territory

Tibet (China)

TOP FIVE GAINS FOR FREEDOM IN 1998

1. *Nigeria:* Developments have moved in a promising direction since the death of the tyrannical General Abacha, with many civil liberties restored, political parties legalized, and national elections pledged for 1999. A good omen was the holding of local elections which were deemed free and fair.

2. *Indonesia:* President Suharto's resignation has been accompanied by indications of changes towards electoral democracy and enhanced civil liberties. On the negative side has been mounting violence against the Chinese minority and bloody clashes between students and the army.

3. *Corruption alert:* The governments of the United States and other leading democracies, along with the World Bank, are focusing increased attention on the role of corruption in undermining political and economic reform in transitional societies. A positive sign: Demands for improvements in the rule of law are increasingly being incorporated into decisions on foreign assistance.

4. *Freedom on the Net:* Several years ago China and other authoritarian regimes announced plans to control the Internet's political content. Those efforts have failed. In the future, the Internet will play a growing role in linking democratic forces within repressive societies and in building a global network of freedom activists.

5. *Dictators beware:* Both current and former dictators had reason for concern. Though controversial, the effort to bring General Pinochet to justice sent a chilling message to tyrants around the world. Yugoslavia's Milosevic was under increased pressure, Indonesia's Suharto resigned, and Congo's Kabila traveled abroad only after securing assurance that he would not be arrested.

TOP FIVE SETBACKS FOR FREEDOM IN 1998

1. *Russia:* The assassination of democracy advocate Galina Staravoitova was the most tragic development in a bad year for Russian reformers. With President Yeltsin enfeebled, a coalition of neo-Communists and hardline nationalists gained increased influence, and succeeded in bringing down a reformist government. A new government, dominated by former Communists, made little progress in stemming corruption or reviving the economy.

2. *Malaysia:* President Mahathir Mohamad responded to his country's economic decline in all the wrong ways: repressing political critics, tightening political control, and placing restrictions on the economy. Here is a prime example of everything that is wrong with "Asian values."

3. *Congo:* Events moved from bad to worse in the Democratic Republic of Congo. President Kabila showed no sign of relaxing his repressive policies. Much of the country remained contested territory, with forces from a half dozen African nations pillaging the countryside and terrorizing the populace.

4. *Religious persecution:* The persecution of religious minorities, especially Christians, remained a serious problem in a number of countries. Among the worst violators: Pakistan, Egypt, China, and Iran. Persecution was most serious in Sudan, where Christians and animists in the southern regions were killed, starved, and forced into exile by forces of the Moslem North.

5. *Nuclear proliferation:* The detonation of nuclear devices by India and Pakistan was a jolting reminder of the menace still posed by weapons of mass destruction. Other reasons to worry included Iraq's determination to rebuild its nuclear, chemical, and biological arsenal, North Korea's nuclear saber-rattling, and the role of Russian scientists in the development of weapons for Iran and other states.

ELECTORAL DEMOCRACY AND FREEDOM

Despite the emergence of electoral democracy as the world's predominant form of government, major violations of human rights and civil liberties remain the norm in a majority of countries containing some three-fifths of the world's population. This disjunction arises from the fact that many electoral democracies fall short of being Free. In an influential 1997 article in *Foreign Affairs*, Fareed Zakaria drew on Freedom House data underlining this fact to suggest that the world had entered an era characterized by "The Rise of Illiberal Democracy." Yet there are signs that electoral democracy eventually does have a positive effect on freedom. Particularly notable in the 1998 *Survey* was the growing respect for civil liberties in a number of electoral democracies. In fact, it appears that the trend to which political scientists were pointing had peaked in the first half of the 1990s—a period of rapid democratic expansion in the wake of the collapse of Marxist-Leninist regimes.

Freedom House's most current data suggest that, as the 1990s draw toward a close, we are observing a decline in the number of "illiberal democracies" and an increase in the number and proportion of the world's electoral democracies that are also liberal (i.e., Free) democracies. In 1995, for example, the *Survey* found there were 117 electoral democracies, of which 76 were rated Free (64.9 percent), 40 were judged to be Partly Free (over 34 percent), and one—war-ravaged Bosnia-Herzegovina—was Not Free. Today, out of 117 electoral democracies, 88 (over 75 percent) are Free, while the remaining 29 are Partly Free.

Since 1995, the electoral democracies that have seen a deepening climate of respect for political rights and civil liberties and thus have entered the ranks of Free countries include the Dominican Republic, El Salvador, Honduras, India, Mali, Nicaragua, Papua New Guinea, the Philippines, Romania, Taiwan, and Thailand. These gains have been partly offset by setbacks in some formerly Free electoral democracies, for a net gain of ten Free countries. Ecuador, Slovakia, and Venezuela have oscillated between the Free and Partly Free categories since 1995.

While electoral democracy allows space to emerge for competing political interests and holds out the promise of greater freedom and respect for human rights, the record of some electoral democracies remains marred by political restrictions and violations of civil liberties. Not all these Partly Free democracies suffer from an identical set of problems: Some have weak governments incapable of guaranteeing basic civil liberties in the face of violent political movements (Colombia and Georgia); others must contend with powerful and politically influential militaries (Turkey and Paraguay), or: internal security forces that can act with impunity (Brazil). Some are plagued by powerful oligarchic forces and/or the weak rule of law (Russia and Ukraine); in other cases, democratically elected leaders seek to centralize their power or to exercise power arbitrarily. Yet these phenomena should not obscure the overall global record: Most democratically elected leaders function within the context of effective checks and balances on their power, and most are able to marshal democratic legitimacy in their efforts to govern effectively and responsibly.

At the close of 1998, the Partly Free democracies were twenty-nine in number. The record of the *Survey* in recent years shows that precisely these flawed, Partly Free electoral democracies hold the greatest potential for the expansion of freedom. For where there is free electoral competition among political parties, there is also the possibility for open criticism of government policies and the airing of alternative viewpoints. Many new democracies are just beginning the arduous process of institutionalizing the rule of law; creating a vibrant civil society; instituting procedures that protect minority rights; fostering a sense of moderation and tolerance among competing political forces; developing economically and politically independent broadcast media; and ensuring effective civilian control over the police and the military. All this takes time. It should therefore come as no surprise that most new democracies make more rapid progress in the areas of political processes and political rights than in the area of civil liberties. Nonetheless, though complete freedom may be long in coming, citizens of Partly Free electoral democracies can at least engage in serious debate over public policy—a right rarely, if ever, enjoyed in nondemocratic regimes. Some critics have suggested that electoral democracy leads to bad governance, increases instability, places ethnic minorities at peril, and legitimizes efforts to suppress political opponents. But the record suggests otherwise. There are eighty-eight electoral democracies that successfully protect a broad range of political and civil rights. Moreover, even the twenty-nine electoral democracies that Freedom House rates as only Partly Free are not states that brutally suppress basic freedoms. Rather, they are generally countries in which civic institutions are weak, poverty is rampant, and intergroup tensions are acute. This is not surprising, as many such fragile democracies are emerging from protracted periods of intense civil strife, and some are building new states.

The *Survey* shows evidence of improvements in civil liberties in countries that had previously established democratic electoral practices. This sequence makes sense because free and fair elections take less time to implement than the more complex processes that produce the rule of law and a strong civil society. As the Freedom House data suggest, illiberal democracy tends toward liberal democracy so long as there is internal or external pressure for further reform. Moreover, the regular transfer of power between competing political elites, or even the prospect of such a transfer, appears to improve the chances for the deepening of civil liberties.

Clearly, some Partly Free (or illiberal) democracies lack respect for the rule of law, checks and balances among the branches of government, and protections for the rights of minorities. It is also true that in some circumstances (especially in multiethnic settings) open electoral processes can be occasions for the emergence of political demagogy directed against ethnic minorities. Indeed, almost three in ten electoral democracies fail adequately to safeguard basic freedoms for these sorts of reasons. At the same time, the *Survey of Freedom* suggests that, over the last twenty years, the emergence of electoral democracies has been the best indicator of subsequent progress in the areas of civil liberties and human rights.

ETHNICITY AND NATIONALISM

The Freedom House data also suggest that countries without a predominant ethnic majority are less successful in establishing open and democratic societies than ethnically homogeneous countries. For the purposes of making this comparison, we define countries in which over two-thirds of the population belong to a single ethnic group as mono-ethnic, and those without such a two-thirds majority as multiethnic.

According to this definition, 66 of the 88 Free countries (75 percent) are mono-ethnic, while 22 (25 percent) are multiethnic. Of the 114 countries in the world that possess a dominant ethnic group, 66 (58 percent) are Free, 22 (19 percent) are Partly Free, and 26 (23 percent) are Not Free. By contrast, among multiethnic countries only 22 of 77 (29 percent) are Free, 31 (40 percent) are Partly Free, and 24 (31 percent) are Not Free. A mono-ethnic country, therefore, is twice as likely to be Free as a multiethnic one.

A similar pattern can be found among the 117 electoral democracies, which include 77 mono-ethnic and 40 multiethnic countries. Of the 77 mono-ethnic democracies, 66 (86 percent) are

Free, and 11 (14 percent) are Partly Free. Among multiethnic democracies, 22 (55 percent) are Free and 18 are Partly Free (45 percent). Thus multiethnic democracies are nearly two-and-a-half times more likely to be only Partly Free than are mono-ethnic ones.

In the face of ethnic conflicts in Africa, the former Yugoslavia, and elsewhere, many analysts have recently focused on the destructive power of contemporary nationalism. Yet the fact that nation-states appear to provide the most durable basis for political freedom and respect for civil liberties deserves greater attention. At the same time, while the survey suggests that democracies are more likely to be Free if they do not face significant ethnic cleavages, there also is compelling evidence that multiethnic societies can preserve a broad array of political and civil freedoms. Successful multiethnic societies include established democracies like Canada, Belgium, and Switzerland, as well as such new democracies as Estonia, Latvia, Mali, Namibia, and South Africa. India's return to the ranks of Free countries is an indication that, even in an ethnically charged environment, it is possible for multiethnic societies to establish a climate and framework of significant respect for personal freedoms, the rule of law, and the rights of religious and ethnic minorities.

The set of forty multiethnic electoral democracies merits closer investigation. Are there common characteristics among the Free multiethnic democracies? Is there a significant correlation between certain patterns of population distribution in multiethnic societies and greater freedom? Are homogeneous concentrations of particular ethnic groups more or less conducive to stability and freedom? Is the dispersion of ethnic minorities throughout a country more compatible with democratic stability and the expansion of freedom? Do different forms of state organization contribute to a higher degree of freedom? Are federal arrangements more or less conducive to the development of freedom? When are federal arrangements successful and when do they provoke ethnic conflict or separatism? Under

what circumstances do federal arrangements break down? What is the effect of external diasporas and the forces of irredentism on the political development of multiethnic states?

It is clear that in some settings political appeals based on ethnicity make it impossible for democratic systems that feature a regular transfer of power to function. Yet the example of numerous free and democratic multiethnic societies shows that it is possible to transcend ethnic appeals in politics, to avert the permanent disenfranchisement of ethnic minorities, and to establish durable democracies.

In the aftermath of the Cold War, nationalism has come to be identified with violence and intolerance. The *Survey* makes clear, however, that nation-states—many of which are the products of nationalist ideas of state organization—tend to be more compatible with stable democratic rule and political freedom. Indeed, in the 1980s and 1990s, most successful ethnic struggles for national self-determination and even nationhood have been peaceful, involving mass protests, independent civic organization, strikes, and other forms of opposition activity. In the former Soviet bloc, such activism contributed to the downfall of oppressive regimes and the creation of a number of free and democratic states. Where nationalism has led to violence and bloody warfare, another factor has often been present—that of irredentism.

In several instances, ethnic and national aspirations to autonomy or independence have received military support from neighboring nation-states ruled by the very ethnic group that is seeking sovereignty or separation. In such cases (for example, Bosnia's Serb Republic; ethnically Armenian Nagorno-Karabakh in Azerbaijan; the Transdniester Republic in Moldova; to a lesser but considerable degree, the Kosovo Liberation Army; and the Rwandan-aided rebellions in the Republic of the Congo), what is at work may be support provided by an existing state seeking to extend its borders rather than the aspiration to create a new nation-state.

REGIONAL VARIATIONS

Democracy and freedom have been on the upswing since the mid-1970s. Clearly, this trend has been visible across all continents and in most cultures, underscoring that human liberty and democracy are not Western constructs, but universal aspirations. Yet while the expansion of democracy and freedom has been global, it has not everywhere proceeded at the same pace. There have been important geographical and cultural variations that deserve attention and deeper understanding.

At the close of 1998, democracy and freedom are the dominant trends in Western and East-Central Europe, in the Americas, and increasingly in the Asian-Pacific region. In the former Soviet Union the picture is decidedly more mixed, with the growth of freedom stalled and a number of countries evolving into dictatorships. In Africa, too, Free societies and electoral democracies remain a distinct minority. Moreover, there are no democracies or Free societies within the Arab world, and few in other predominantly Muslim societies.

Of the 53 countries in Africa, 9 are Free (17 percent), 21 are Partly Free (40 percent) and 23 are Not Free (43 percent). Only 17 African countries (less than one-third) are electoral democracies. As of the end of 1998, Lesotho's democracy fell, while at the same time, the *Survey* noted positive trends in Nigeria and Sierra Leone.

In Asia, 19 of the region's 38 countries are Free (50 percent), 9 are Partly Free (24 percent), and 10 are Not Free (26 percent). Despite the looming presence of Communist China and the rhetoric of "Asian values," 24 (63 percent) of the region's polities are electoral democracies.

In East-Central Europe and the former USSR, there are growing signs of a deepening chasm. In Central Europe and parts of Eastern Europe, including the Baltic states, democracy and freedom prevail; in the former USSR, however, progress toward the emergence of open societies has stalled or failed. Overall, 19 of the 27 post-Communist countries of East-Central Europe and the former USSR are electoral democracies. Ten of the region's states are Free, 11 are Partly Free, and 6 are Not Free. Of the 12 non-Baltic former Soviet republics, 7 countries are Partly Free, 5 are Not Free, and none are Free.

Among the 35 countries in the Americas, 31 are electoral democracies. Twenty-five states are rated as Free, 9 are Partly Free, and 1—Cuba—is Not Free.

In the Middle East (excluding North Africa), the roots of democracy and freedom are weakest. In this region there is only one Free country, Israel; there are three Partly Free states, Jordan, Kuwait, and Turkey; and there are ten countries that are Not Free. Israel and Turkey are the region's only two electoral democracies.

Western Europe is the preserve of Free countries and democracies, with all twenty-four states both free and democratic.

In addition to these regional breakdowns, Freedom House has examined the state of freedom and democracy in the Arab world. Among the sixteen states with an Arab majority, there are no Free countries, Three predominantly Arab states—Jordan, Kuwait, and Morocco—are Partly Free. There are no electoral democracies in the Arab world.

The *Survey* also reveals some interesting patterns in the relationship between cultures and political development. While there are broad differences within civilizations, and while democracy and human rights find expression in a wide array of cultures and beliefs, the *Survey* shows some important variations in the relationship between religious belief or tradition and political freedom.

Of the eighty-eight countries that are rated Free, seventy-nine are majority Christian by tradition or belief. Of the nine Free countries that are not majority Christian, one is Israel, often considered part of a Judeo-Christian tradition, and two others, Mauritius and South Korea, have significant Christian communities representing at least a third of their population. Of the six remaining Free countries, Mali is predominantly Muslim; nearly half of Taiwan's population is Buddhist; Mongolia and Thailand are chiefly Buddhist; Japan has a majority that observes both Buddhist and Shinto traditions; and India is predominantly Hindu.

While seventy-nine of the eighty-eight Free countries are predominantly Christian, just eleven of the sixty-seven countries with the poorest record in terms of political rights and civil liberties are predominantly Christian. By this indicator, a predominantly Christian country is nearly five-and-a-half times as likely to be Free and democratic as it is to be repressive and nondemocratic. There is also a strong correlation between electoral democracy and Hinduism (India, Mauritius, and Nepal), and there are a significant number of Free countries among traditionally Buddhist societies and societies in which Buddhism is the most widespread faith (Japan, Mongolia, Taiwan, and Thailand).

At the close of the twentieth century, the Islamic world remains most resistant to the spread of democracy and civil liberties, especially the Arab countries. Only one country with a Muslim majority—Mali—is Free, fourteen are Partly Free, and twenty-eight are Not Free. Six countries with a predominantly Muslim population are electoral democracies: Albania, Bangladesh, Kyrgyzstan, Mali, Pakistan, and Turkey. Yet the year's trends also showed that the Islamic world is not completely resistant to the expansion of freedom. There was limited progress in Indonesia, the world's most populous Islamic county, and in Nigeria, where half the population is Muslim, there was momentum toward a democratic political opening.

Although we tend to think of civilizations and cultures as fixed and stable entities, it should be kept in mind that political transformations within civilizations can spread rapidly. For example, before the Third Wave of democratization was launched in the 1970s, the majority of predominantly Catholic countries were tyrannies; they included Latin America's oligarchies and military dictatorships, East-Central Europe's Marxist-Leninist states, Iberia's authoritarian-corporalist

systems, and the Philippine dictatorship of Ferdinand Marcos. Social scientists speculated about the influence that Catholicism's hierarchical system of church authority might have on Catholic attitudes toward politics. Today, of course, most Catholic countries have become Free and democratic, and some would argue that it was precisely the internal discipline of the Catholic church which made possible the rapid spread of pro-democratic values following Vatican II and under the papacy of John Paul II.

THE GLOBAL EXPANSION OF FREEDOM

The last quarter century has seen a rapid expansion of democratic governance along with a more gradual expansion of civil society and civil liberties. There is little question that the *Survey's* findings reflect significant gains for human freedom at the dawn of a new millennium. Still, many of the new electoral democracies and newly Free countries remain fragile, and political reversals cannot be excluded. Moreover, there appears to be little forward momentum for democratic change and freedom in many of the Not Free countries. In particular, there is little evidence of progress toward democracy in the Arab world and in the world's remaining Marxist-Leninist states.

The global expansion of political and civic freedoms has coincided with the expansion of market-based economies. Indeed, on the basis of the Freedom House *Survey* and parallel efforts to monitor and assess global economic change, there is growing empirical evidence of the links between economic freedom and political freedom.[1]

Not only does economic freedom help establish the conditions for political freedom by promoting the growth of prosperous middle and working classes, but successful market economies appear to require political freedom as a barrier against economic cronyism, rent seeking, and other anticompetitive and inefficient practices. Open and democratically accountable societies and economies have also shown themselves capable of weathering economic setbacks—a likely consequence of their political legitimacy (rooted in democratic accountability) and economic legitimacy (rooted in property rights). Moreover, while open societies are not immune to corruption scandals, they have strong instruments for combating graft and bribery, including a free press, the separation of powers, alternations in power between various political elites, and independent judicial systems.

While the *Survey* can be used to examine broad trends, it is important that such trends not be equated with iron laws of history or be interpreted one-dimensionally. For example, while the *Survey* findings show that liberal economic change at times leads to liberal political reform, there are also numerous other cases where political openings lead the way to economic liberalization. The more careful conclusion from an examination of the twenty-six-year record of the *Survey* is that both trends manifest themselves in close proximity to one another. Opposition to the dominance of the state in economic life is usually accompanied by opposition to the dominance of the state in personal life and in the life of civil society. Certainly, there appears to be growing awareness of this relationship, as indicated by the growing emphasis on democracy promotion in the foreign assistance policies of the advanced industrial democracies, and by the stress on issues of good governance and effective anti-corruption regimes by multilateral donors like the World Bank.

POLICY IMPLICATIONS

What challenges issue from the *Survey's* findings? What are the policy implications?

The Freedom House findings make it clear that the world is becoming more free. This trend is mainly the consequence of the strengthening of the rule of law, of improvements in civilian control over militaries and police, the successful management of divisive group conflicts, and the growing effectiveness of civil society.

Most of this progress toward respect for political rights and civil liberties is unfolding in countries which have already undergone more limited democratic openings. The *Survey* finds that such societies over time grow receptive to a further deepening of freedom. This suggests that U.S. and international efforts to promote democratic transitions and to give some priority to material and technical assistance to democratic regimes are having a positive effect. But it also means that most progress is occurring in already Partly Free countries. This year, only a small number of Not Free countries registered meaningful progress. Moreover, after a decade of the rapid expansion of electoral democracies, the number of democracies in 1998, 117, is the same as the figure for 1994.

Yet while there is an extremely active and intelligently conceived U.S. policy to promote democratic transitions once limited political openings have occurred, far fewer resources are being directed at promoting democratic openings in the most repressive societies. For example, USAID efforts in closed societies focus mainly on limited technical assistance in support of modest economic reforms, rather than on support for democratic forces in these closed societies. Moreover, USAID does not devote significant resources to promoting political openings in closed societies. Such efforts are primarily undertaken by the independent, Congressionally funded National Endowment for Democracy.

While the United States has something approaching a consistent policy with regard to several rogue and pariah states that also violate basic human rights on a massive scale—Burma, Cuba, Iran, Iraq, Libya, and North Korea specifically—that policy mainly seeks to isolate these countries, and few resources are devoted to efforts that might actively promote change within them.

In the cases of some of the world's most important countries in which basic freedoms are broadly suppressed, U.S. policy consists of occasional—and at times muted—criticism of human rights violations and general expectations that the forces of economic change and trade will somehow inevitably lead to improvements in political and civil liberties. Among the countries in which there is little effort to promote democratic change are China, Vietnam, and—with the exception of the Palestinian National Authority—the Arab world.

Admittedly, some of the world's most closed societies (for example, North Korea) may be impervious to U.S. and other efforts to promote democratic ideas and foster the emergence of democratic movements. But the example of the collapse of communism in Central and Eastern Europe shows that totalitarian societies cannot forever withstand the pressures of an increasingly open and interdependent world.

Moreover, new technologies and the force of modest market-oriented change in some of the most repressive countries suggest that the capacity of the state to exert day-to-day control over information and private life is lessening, even if repression of political dissent is not.

OPENING UP CLOSED SOCIETIES

A comprehensive strategy to open up closed societies should be developed in cooperation with the nongovernmental sector. The mission of USAID should be expanded to allow it to be more active in fostering the development of the nongovernmental sector in closed countries. Aid and assistance for radio broadcasting, book publishing, contact with independent civic forces, and the transfer of information through the Internet should be expanded.

PROTECTING AGAINST REVERSALS

While 1998 saw the expansion of freedom in many parts of the world, forward momentum appears to have stalled in the twelve non-Baltic former republics of the Soviet Union, including Russia and Ukraine. Setbacks for reform and the weakening of reformist voices is likely a temporary phenomenon. It should not be seen as a signal to scale back drastically U.S. engagement. Rather, it requires a more efficient and precise

deployment of resources oriented around assisting reformers in their efforts to win the political battle of ideas.

Reversals of democratic progress should meet with active diplomatic and nongovernmental initiatives. In a period of some economic turmoil and social difficulties in transitional societies, the preservation of gains for civil liberties and political rights must be an urgent priority for U.S. policymakers and the international democratic community.

ECONOMIC FREEDOM AND POLITICAL LIBERTY

The economic crisis that rocked emerging markets in 1998 has not resulted in a reversal of progress toward greater political and economic freedom. Indeed, economic difficulties have not led to a worldwide resurgence of statism. On the contrary, economic failures have rightly been identified with a lack of transparency, cronyism, and corruption. In short, the case for a link between more open and democratically accountable government and economic success is gaining greater credence. The acknowledgment of such a relationship appears to have played a key role in the political openings in Indonesia and Nigeria. The ability of democratic states like the Philippines, Thailand, South Korea, and Brazil to implement policies to address the looming economic crisis have also done much to convince the international financial community that democratic accountability and legitimacy of rule is an important instrument for political reform.

But international donors and financial institutions need to take more resolute policy steps to act on these trends. The changing attitude of some international financial and aid organizations is a positive sign. The World Bank, in particular, has been innovative in its efforts to introduce issues of governance, corruption, and transparency into its programming and to begin to reach out to civil society and nongovernmental groups.

There is growing understanding among some policymakers of the link between the functioning of an effective rule of law system—a system that requires the checks and balances of a free society, a free press, and democratic accountability—and effective economic performance.

INTERNATIONAL STRUCTURES

In 1998, the fiftieth anniversary of the Universal Declaration of Human Rights was celebrated and efforts were made to intensify international action against basic rights violations. There were welcome efforts to arrest and prosecute those guilty of genocide and war crimes, including those guilty of atrocities in Rwanda and in Bosnia.

Many countries—though not the United States, which, for convincing reasons, was opposed—voted to adopt a charter for a far-reaching International Criminal Court. Yet while international action to eradicate rights abuses can be helpful, it must be limited in scope. Above all, international structures should not jeopardize or weaken the ability of democratic states to act to preserve or to protect freedom. Regrettably, many of the provisions in the proposed Criminal Court would have just such an effect.

As the Freedom House findings suggest, freedom is making important gains around the world. Nevertheless, the majority of mankind still lives in societies in which many or all basic freedoms are violated, and in a majority of countries the rule of law is absent or weak. Any body that emerges from an international consensus that includes undemocratic and unfree states is likely to be problematic in its composition. Adequate safeguards must exist to prevent such a court from acting capriciously. The United States is right to object to the current form of the proposed international Criminal Court. A far better policy would be the promotion of new structures made up of the growing community of free and democratic countries that could coordinate cooperation on behalf of human rights and against genocide and war crimes.

CONCLUSIONS

The remarkable expansion of human freedom recorded in the twenty-six years of the *Survey of Freedom* has not proceeded in a straight line. It has featured reversals as well as gains. Therefore, nothing in the findings should suggest that the expansion of democracy and freedom is inevitable. Indeed, much of the progress the *Survey* has recorded is the byproduct of a growing and systematic collaboration between established and new democracies, between democracies and countries in transition, and between established civic groups operating in the context of freedom and their pro-democratic counterparts seeking to promote change in closed societies. The findings of the *Survey* in future years will depend in no small measure on the success of such collaboration and on the elaboration of effective U.S. government policies to extend freedom to parts of the world where it is largely absent.

NOTE

1. Recent comparisons of the relationship between political freedom and economic liberty conducted by Freedom House (Adrian Karatnycky, Alexander Motyl, and Charles Graybow, eds., *Nations in Transit 1998*, New Brunswick, N.J.: Transaction Books, 1998) and the Heritage Foundation (Bryan T. Johnson, "Comparing Economic Freedom and Political Freedom," in Bryan T. Johnson, Kim R. Homes, and Melanie Kirkpatrick. eds., *1999 Index of Economic Freedom*, Washington, D.C.: The Heritage Foundation and Dow Jones Company, Inc., 1999, 29–34), respectively, have found a high correlation between the two variables. According to the authors of *Nations in Transit 1998*, post-Communist countries that are consolidated democracies also tend to have consolidated their market economies. When these countries' performance with respect to political and economic freedom is related to economic growth, the study found that consolidated democracies and market economies averaged a growth rate of 4.7 percent in 1997, transitional polities and economies registered an average growth rate of 1.4 percent, and consolidated autocracies and statist economies in the region averaged close to a 3 percent drop in GDP. The study similarly found high correlations between more open political systems and lower levels of corruption. Moreover, societies with lower levels of corruption were significantly more successful in generating economic growth. The region's least corrupt countries, for example, grew at an average rate of 4.7 percent in 1997,

while states registering high levels of corruption averaged a decline of nearly 1 percent. Researchers at the Heritage Foundation found a high degree of correlation between political rights and civil liberties (as measured by Freedom House) and economic freedom (as measured by the Heritage Foundation's surveys).

Part XVI

Family

33

"His" and "Her" Marriage

Jessie Bernard

...[T]here is by now a very considerable body of well-authenticated research to show that there really are two marriages in every marital union, and that they do not always coincide.

"HIS" AND "HER" MARRIAGES

...[T]he differences in the marriages of husbands and wives have come under the careful scrutiny of a score of researchers. They have found that when they ask husbands and wives identical questions about the union, they often get quite different replies. There is usually agreement on the number of children they have and a few other such verifiable items, although not, for example, on length of premarital acquaintance and of engagement, on age at marriage, and interval between marriage and birth of first child. Indeed, with respect to even such basic components of the marriage as

Source: From *The Future of Marriage* by Jessie Bernard. Copyright © 1972. Reprinted with permission.

frequency of sexual relations, social interaction, household tasks, and decision making, they seem to be reporting on different marriages. As, I think, they are.

In the area of sexual relations, for example, Kinsey and his associates found different responses in from one- to two-thirds of the couples they studied. Kinsey interpreted these differences in terms of selective perception. In the generation he was studying, husbands wanted sexual relations oftener than the wives did, thus "the females may be overestimating the actual frequencies" and "the husbands...are probably underestimating the frequencies." The differences might also have been vestiges of the probable situation earlier in the marriage when the desired frequency of sexual relations was about six to seven times greater among husbands than among wives. This difference may have become so impressed on the spouses that it remained in their minds even after the difference itself had disappeared or even been reversed. In a sample of happily married, middle-class couples a generation later, Harold Feldman found that both spouses attributed to their mates more influence in the area of sex than they did to themselves.

Companionship, as reflected in talking together, he found, was another area where differences showed up. Replies differed on three-fourths of all the items studied, including the topics talked about, the amount of time spent talking with each other, and which partner initiated conversation. Both partners claimed that whereas they talked more about topics of interest to their mates, their mates initiated conversations about topics primarily of interest to themselves. Harold Feldman concluded that projection in terms of needs was distorting even simple, everyday events, and lack of communication was permitting the distortions to continue. It seemed to him that "if these sex differences can occur so often among these generally well-satisfied couples, it would not be surprising to find even less consensus and more distortion in other less satisfied couples."

Although, by and large, husbands and wives tend to become more alike with age, in this study of middle-class couples, differences increased with length of marriage rather than decreased, as one might logically have expected. More couples in the later than in the earlier years, for example, had differing pictures in their heads about how often they laughed together, discussed together, exchanged ideas, or worked together on projects, and about how well things were going between them.

The special nature of sex and the amorphousness of social interaction help to explain why differences in response might occur. But household tasks? They are fairly objective and clear-cut and not all that emotion-laden. Yet even here there are his-and-her versions. Since the division of labor in the household is becoming increasingly an issue in marriage, the uncovering of differing replies in this area is especially relevant. Hard as it is to believe, Granbois and Willett tell us that more than half of the partners in one sample disagreed on who kept track of money and bills. On the question, who mows the lawn?

more than a fourth disagreed. Even family income was not universally agreed on.

These differences about sexual relations, companionship, and domestic duties tell us a great deal about the two marriages. But power or decision making can cover all aspects of a relationship. The question of who makes decisions or who exercises power has therefore attracted a great deal of research attention. If we were interested in who really had the power or who really made the decisions, the research would be hopeless. Would it be possible to draw any conclusion from a situation in which both partners agree that the husband ordered the wife to make all the decisions? Still, an enormous literature documents the quest of researchers for answers to the question of marital power. The major contribution it has made has been to reveal the existence of differences in replies between husbands and wives.

The presence of such inconsistent replies did not at first cause much concern. The researchers apologized for them but interpreted them as due to methodological inadequacies; if only they could find a better way to approach the problem, the differences would disappear. Alternatively, the use of only the wife's responses, which were more easily available, was justified on the grounds that differences in one direction between the partners in one marriage compensated for differences in another direction between the partners in another marriage and thus canceled them out. As, indeed, they did. For when Granbois and Willett, two market researchers, analyzed the replies of husbands and wives separately, the overall picture was in fact the same for both wives and husbands. Such canceling out of differences in the total sample, however, concealed almost as much as it revealed about the individual couples who composed it. Granbois and Willett concluded, as Kinsey had earlier, that the "discrepancies…reflect differing perceptions on the part of responding partners." And this was the heart of the matter.

Differing reactions to common situations, it should be noted, are not at all uncommon. They are recognized in the folk wisdom embedded in the story of the blind men all giving different replies to questions on the nature of the elephant. One of the oldest experiments in juridical psychology demonstrates how different the statements of witnesses of the same act can be. Even in laboratory studies, it takes intensive training of raters to make it possible for them to arrive at agreement on the behavior they observe.

It has long been known that people with different backgrounds see things differently. We know, for example, that poor children perceive coins as larger than do children from more affluent homes. Boys and girls perceive differently. A good deal of the foundation for projective tests rests on the different ways in which individuals see identical stimuli. And this perception—or, as the sociologists put it, definition of the situation—is reality for them. In this sense, the realities of the husband's marriage are different from those of the wife's.

Finally, one of the most perceptive of the researchers, Constantina Safilios-Rothschild, asked the crucial question: Was what they were getting, even with the best research techniques, family sociology or wives' family sociology? She answered her own question: What the researchers who relied on wives' replies exclusively were reporting on was the wife's marriage. The husband's was not necessarily the same. There were, in fact, two marriages present:

> One explanation of discrepancies between the responses of husbands and wives may be the possibility of two "realities," the husband's subjective reality and the wife's subjective reality—two perspectives which do not always coincide. Each spouse perceives "facts" and situations differently according to his own needs, values, attitudes, and beliefs. An "objective" reality could possibly exist only in the trained observer's evaluation, if it docs exist at all.

Interpreting the different replies of husbands and wives in terms of selective perception, projection of needs, values, attitudes, and beliefs, or different definitions of the situation, by no means renders them trivial or incidental or justifies dismissing or ignoring them. They are, rather, fundamental for an understanding of the

two marriages, his and hers, and we ignore them at the peril of serious misunderstanding of marriage, present as well as future.

IS THERE AN OBJECTIVE REALITY IN MARRIAGE?

Whether or not husbands and wives perceive differently or define situations differently, still sexual relations are taking place, companionship is or is not occurring, tasks about the house are being performed, and decisions are being made every day by someone. In this sense, some sort of "reality" does exist. David Olson went to the laboratory to see if he could uncover it.

He first asked young couples expecting babies such questions as these: Which one of them would decide whether to buy insurance for the newborn child? Which one would decide the husband's part in diaper changing? Which one would decide whether the new mother would return to work or to school? When there were differences in the answers each gave individually on the questionnaire, he set up a situation in which together they had to arrive at a decision in his laboratory. He could then compare the results of the questionnaire with the results in the simulated situation. He found neither spouse's questionnaire response any more accurate than the other's; that is, neither conformed better to the behavioral "reality" of the laboratory than the other did.

The most interesting thing, however, was that husbands, as shown on their questionnaire response, perceived themselves as having more power than they actually did have in the laboratory "reality," and wives perceived that they had less. Thus, whereas three-fourths (73 percent) of the husbands overestimated their power in decision making, 70 percent of the wives underestimated theirs. Turk and Bell found similar results in Canada. Both spouses tend to attribute decision-making power to the one who has the "right" to make the decision. Their replies, that is, conform to the model of marriage that has characterized civilized mankind for millennia. It is this model rather than their own actual behavior that husbands and wives tend to perceive.

We are now zeroing in on the basic reality. We can remove the quotation marks. For there is, in fact, an objective reality in marriage. It is a reality that resides in the cultural—legal, moral, and conventional—prescriptions and proscriptions and, hence, expectations that constitute marriage. It is the reality that is reflected in the minds of the spouses themselves. The differences between the marriages of husbands and of wives are structural realities, and it is these structural differences that constitute the basis for the different psychological realities.

THE AUTHORITY STRUCTURE OF MARRIAGE

Authority is an institutional phenomenon; it is strongly bound up with faith. It must be believed in; it cannot be enforced unless it also has power. Authority resides not in the person on whom it is conferred by the group or society, but in the recognition and acceptance it elicits in others. Power, on the other hand, may dispense with the prop of authority. It may take the form of the ability to coerce or to veto; it is often personal, charismatic, not institutional. This kind of personal power is self-enforcing. It does not require shoring up by access to force. In fact, it may even operate subversively. A woman with this kind of power may or may not know that she possesses it. If she does know she has it, she will probably disguise her exercise of it.

In the West, the institutional structure of marriage has invested the husband with authority and backed it by the power of church and state. The marriages of wives have thus been officially dominated by the husband. Hebrew, Christian, and Islamic versions of deity were in complete accord on this matter. The laws, written or unwritten, religious or civil, which have defined the marital union have been based on male conceptions, and they have undergirded male authority.

Adam came first. Eve was created to supply him with companionship, not vice versa. And God himself had told her that Adam would rule over her; her wishes had to conform to his. The New Testament authors agreed. Women were created for men, not men for women; women were therefore commanded to be obedient. If they wanted to learn anything, let them ask their husbands in private, for it was shameful for them to talk in the church. They should submit themselves to their husbands, because husbands were superior to wives; and wives should be as subject to their husbands as the church was to Christ. Timothy wrapped it all up: "Let the woman learn in silence with all subjection. But I suffer not a woman to teach, nor to usurp authority over the man, but to be in silence." Male Jews continued for millennia to thank God three times a day that they were not women. And the Koran teaches women that men are naturally their superiors because God made them that way; naturally, their own status is one of subordination.

The state as well as the church had the same conception of marriage, assigning to the husband and father control over his dependents, including his wife. Sometimes this power was well-nigh absolute, as in the case of the Roman *patria potestas*—or the English common law, which flatly said, "The husband and wife are as one and that one is the husband." There are rules still lingering today with the same, though less extreme, slant. Diane B. Schulder has summarized the legal framework of the wife's marriage as laid down in the common law:

> The legal responsibilities of a wife are to live in the home established by her husband; to perform the domestic chores (cleaning, cooking, washing, etc.) necessary to help maintain that home; to care for her husband and children.... A husband may force his wife to have sexual relations as long as his demands are reasonable and her health is not endangered.... The law allows a wife to take a job if she wishes. However, she must see that her domestic chores are completed, and, if there are children, that they receive proper care during her absence.

A wife is not entitled to payment for household work; and some jurisdictions in the United States expressly deny payment for it. In some states, the wife's earnings are under the control of her husband, and in four, special court approval and in some cases husband's consent are required if a wife wishes to start a business of her own.

The male counterpart to these obligations includes that of supporting his wife. He may not disinherit her. She has a third interest in property owned by him, even if it is held in his name only. Her name is required when he sells property.

Not only divine and civil law but also rules of etiquette have defined authority as a husband's prerogative. One of the first books published in England was a *Boke of Good Manners,* translated from the French of Jacques Le Grand in 1487, which included a chapter on "How Wymmen Ought to Be Gouerned." The thirty-third rule of Plutarch's *Rules for Husbands and Wives* was that women should obey their husbands; if they "try to rule over their husbands they make a worse mistake than the husbands do who let themselves be ruled." The husband's rule should not, of course, be brutal; he should not rule his wife "as a master does his chattel, but as the soul governs the body, by feeling with her and being linked to her by affection." Wives, according to Richard Baxter, a seventeenth-century English divine, had to obey even a wicked husband, the only exception being that a wife need not obey a husband if he ordered her to change her religion. But, again, like Plutarch, Baxter warned that the husband should love his wife; his authority should not be so coercive or so harsh as to destroy love. Among his twelve rules for carrying out the duties of conjugal love, however, was one to the effect that love must not be so imprudent as to destroy authority.

As late as the nineteenth century, Tocqueville noted that in the United States the ideals of democracy did not apply between husbands and wives:

Nor have the Americans ever supposed that one consequence of democratic principles is the subversion of marital power, or the confusion of the natural authorities in families. They hold that every association must have a head in order to accomplish its objective, and that the natural head of the conjugal association is man. They do not therefore deny him the right of directing his partner; and they maintain, that in the smaller association of husband and wife, as well as in the great social community, the object of democracy is to regulate and legalize the powers which are necessary, not to subvert all power.

This opinion is not peculiar to men and contested by women; I never observed that the women of America consider conjugal authority as an unfortunate usurpation [by men] of their rights, nor that they thought themselves degraded by submitting to it. It appears to me, on the contrary, that they attach a sort of pride to the voluntary surrender of their own will, and make it their boast to bend themselves to the yoke, not to shake it off.

The point here is not to document once more the specific ways (religious, legal, moral, traditional) in which male authority has been built into the marital union—that has been done a great many times—but merely to illustrate how different (structurally or "objectively" as well as perceptually or "subjectively") the wife's marriage has actually been from the husband's throughout history.

THE SUBVERSIVENESS OF NATURE

The rationale for male authority rested not only on biblical grounds but also on nature or natural law, on the generally accepted natural superiority of men. For nothing could be more self-evident than that the patriarchal conception of marriage, in which the husband was unequivocally the boss, was natural, resting as it did on the unchallenged superiority of males.

Actually, nature, if not deity, is subversive. Power, or the ability to coerce or to veto, is widely distributed in both sexes, among women as well as among men. And whatever the theoretical or conceptual picture may have been, the actual, day-by-day relationships between husbands and wives have been determined by the men and women themselves. All that the institutional machinery could do was to confer authority; it could not create personal power, for such power cannot be conferred, and women can generate it as well as men.... Thus, keeping women in their place has been a universal problem, in spite of the fact that almost without exception institutional patterns give men positions of superiority over them.

If the sexes were, in fact, categorically distinct, with no overlapping, so that no man was inferior to any woman or any woman superior to any man, or vice versa, marriage would have been a great deal simpler. But there is no such sharp cleavage between the sexes except with respect to the presence or absence of certain organs. With all the other characteristics of each sex, there is greater or less overlapping, some men being more "feminine" than the average woman and some women more "masculine" than the average man. The structure of families and societies reflects the positions assigned to men and women. The bottom stratum includes children, slaves, servants, and outcasts of all kinds, males as well as females. As one ascends the structural hierarchy, the proportion of males increases, so that at the apex there are only males.

When societies fall back on the lazy expedient—as all societies everywhere have done—of allocating the rewards and punishments of life on the basis of sex, they are bound to create a host of anomalies, square pegs in round holes, societal misfits. Roles have been allocated on the basis of sex which did not fit a sizable number of both sexes—women, for example, who chafed at subordinate status and men who could not master superordinate status. The history of the relations of the sexes is replete with examples of such misfits. Unless a modus vivendi is arrived at, unhappy marriages are the result.

There is, though, a difference between the exercise of power by husbands and by wives. When women exert power, they are not rewarded; they may even be punished. They are "deviant." Turk and Bell note that "wives who…have the greater influence in decision making may experience guilt over this fact." They must therefore dissemble to maintain the illusion, even to themselves, that they are subservient. They tend to feel less powerful than they are because they *ought* to be.

When men exert power, on the other hand, they are rewarded; it is the natural expression of authority. They feel no guilt about it. The prestige of authority goes to the husband whether or not he is actually the one who exercises it. It is not often even noticed when the wife does so. She sees to it that it is not.

There are two marriages, then, in every marital union, his and hers. And his…is better than hers. The questions, therefore, are these: In what direction will they change in the future? Will one change more than the other? Will they tend to converge or to diverge? Will the future continue to favor the husband's marriage? And if the wife's marriage is improved, will it cost the husband's anything, or will his benefit along with hers?

34

Looking Back, Looking Ahead: Canadian Families in Perspective

Beverly J. Matthews

Who do you live with? A roommate? Your parents? Your children? A lover? Your cat? Whatever your answer, there is a good chance that it is not the same answer that your grandparents or great-grandparents would have given when they were your age. North American family patterns and household arrangements have changed dramatically since the early 20th century. For example, in 1901, 69 percent of Canadian families consisted of married couples and their children (Vanier, 2000). By 2001, only 44 percent of family households contained two parents and their children (Statistics Canada, 2002f). In 1921 there were only 6.4 divorces for every 100,000 Canadians (Statistics Canada, 2002d), but in the year 2000 there were 231 divorces for every 100,000, or 71,144 divorces (Statistics Canada, 2002c).

These patterns suggest that family life has undergone a profound shift. Many people are concerned that these trends are indicators of seri-ous problems in Canadian families. In fact, a 1994 Angus Reid poll published in *Maclean's* magazine found that 63 percent of Canadians believed that the Canadian family was in a state of crisis (Nemeth, 1994). Family sociologists and demographers measure these trends and analyze their causes and consequences. And, of course, they are of great interest to us, as they influence the family arrangements we experience and the choices available to us. If we look back at trends in Canadian family life and explore some of their underlying causes, we will be better equipped to look ahead and consider the future of families in Canada.

DEFINITIONS

To begin, we must consider what we mean by "family." This seems like a simple undertaking. After all, if you ask people you meet on the street "Who is in your family?" they will all have an answer. However, what you may not realize is that our societal understanding of what constitutes a

Source: Printed with permission of the author (2003).

family has changed over time. If you asked a senior social scientist in your department to find his or her oldest text on families and read out the definition, you would probably hear something like this: Family is

a social group characterized by common residence, economic cooperation, and reproduction. It includes adults of both sexes, at least two of whom maintain a socially approved sexual relationship and one or more children, own or adopted, of the sexually cohabiting adults. (Murdock, 1949: 1)

or

a social arrangement based on marriage and the marriage contract, including the rights and duties of parenthood, common residence for husband, wife and children, and reciprocal economic obligations between husband and wife. (Stephens, 1963: 5)

Do these definitions still hold true today? Are you a member of a family according to Murdock and Stephens? If you live alone, with a roommate (or with your cat), you are not; if you aren't married but live with an intimate partner, you are not. Even if you are married but because of career requirements your spouse and children live in another city, you do not qualify as a family according to Murdock and Stephens. Their definitions are quite narrow and consequently exclude large portions of the population. More recently, our understanding of what constitutes family has expanded substantially: Family is

Any combination of two or more persons who are bound together over time by ties of mutual consent, birth and/or adoption or placement who, together, assume responsibilities for variant combinations of some of the following:

• physical maintenance and care of group members

• addition of new members through procreation or adoption

• socialization of children

• social control of members

• production, consumption, distribution of goods and services

• affective nurturance—love

(Vanier, 2000: v)

This definition is broad enough to encompass all manner of familial arrangements. Virtually everyone reading this chapter will recognize that their family fits this definition. Today, social scientists tend to define family by the relationships between the members, rather than by the identified statuses (e.g., husband, wife) of its members.

For the purposes of this chapter, we are going to rely on Statistics Canada data to examine changes in family patterns, so we will utilize their definition: a family household

refers to a married couple (with or without children of either or both spouses), a couple living common-law (with or without children of either or both partners) or a lone parent of any marital status, with at least one child living in the same dwelling. A couple living common-law may be of opposite or same sex. "Children" in a census family include grandchildren living with their grandparent(s) but with no parents present. (Statistics Canada, 2002a: 1)

You will probably have noticed that this definition does not consider a person living alone to be a member of a family household. Statistics Canada provides many definitions of types of families (e.g., census families, economic families, family households), but the dictionary does not contain an all-encompassing definition of "family" (Statistics Canada, 2002a). Statistics Canada does not specifically preclude people in single-person households from being members of families, but for the purposes of counting and identifying household types, single-person households are considered non-family units. Statistics Canada has a long history of collecting information on family patterns, which enables us to study the evolving patterns of family life.[1]

LOOKING BACK: THE TRENDS

The following graphs, tables, and charts show various trends in family patterns. Unless otherwise stated, the information comes from Statistics Canada census data.

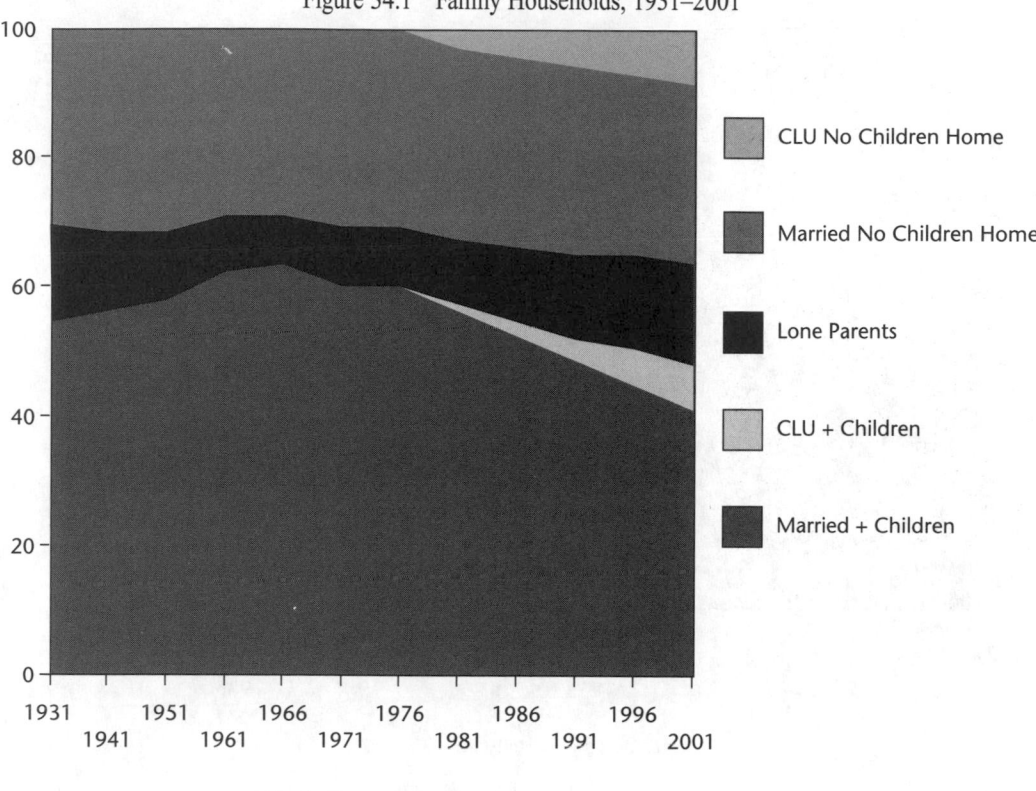

Figure 34.1   Family Households, 1931–2001

Year by Household Type

Source: Data compiled from **http://www12.statcan.ca/english/census01/products/analytic/companion/fam/timeline.cfm.**
Accessed July 15, 2003.

A. Family Households

The membership of family households has changed over time. As you can see in Figure 34.1, the proportion of family households with two married parents and their children is declining. Even when children living with parents in a common-law union (CLU) are included, the decline is evident. The proportion of married couples with no children has remained fairly steady at approximately 30 percent of all family households (ranging between 28.1 percent and 32.5 percent over 70 years). However, if you combine all couples (married and CLU) with no

children at home, there has been an increase (36.6 percent in 2001, up from 30.8 percent in 1981). The major shift, though, has been the increase in lone-parent families.

B. Family Size

Family size changed substantially over the 20th century. The entire Western world experienced a long-term decline in fertility, part of the demographic transition, throughout the 19th century and into the 20th. Canadian fertility rates similarly declined, from 6.8 children per woman in 1851 to 3.53 children in 1921.[2] Figure 34.2

Figure 34.2   Total Fertility Rate, 1921–97

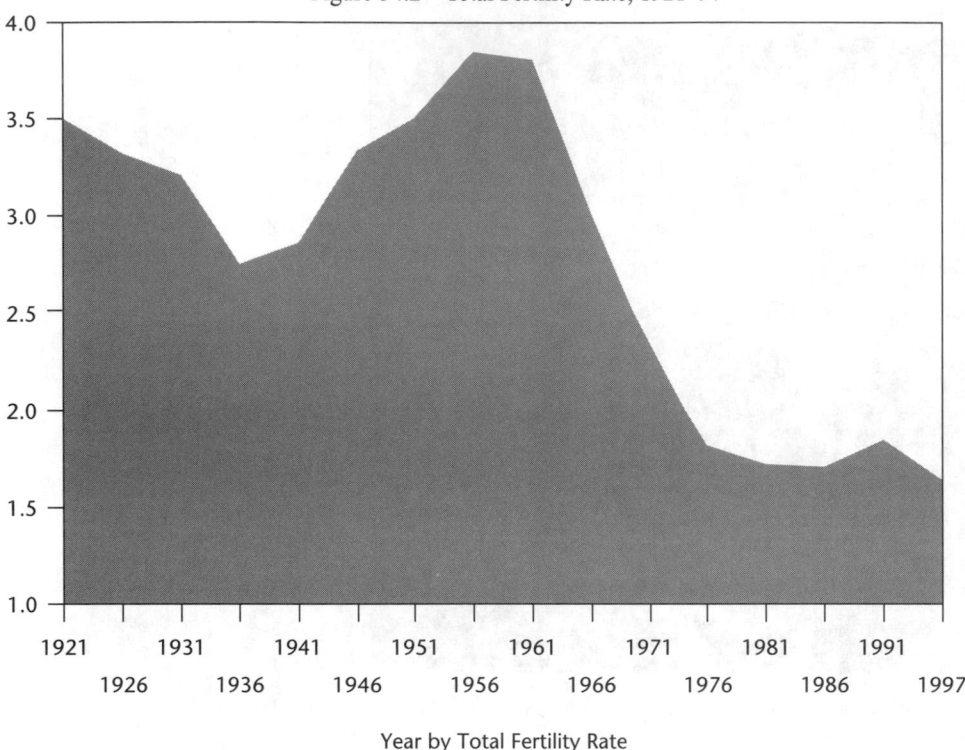

Year by Total Fertility Rate

Source: Adapted from the Statistics Canada publications, "Vital statistics compendium", 1996, Catalogue 84-214, November 1999, page 23, from "Health reports", Supplement 14, 1992, Catalogue 82-003, Vol. 4, No. 1, Table 16, and from "Births and deaths", 1997, Catalogue 84-210, September 1999, Table 1.4.

shows that this rate has changed significantly since then.

The sharp peak indicates the baby boom years, when couples who had delayed childbearing during the Depression and the Second World War began their families, as did younger couples who reached marriageable age during the 1950s. The abrupt decline beginning in the 1960s has been described as the "baby bust" (Romaniuc, 1984). During this time, fewer people were marrying and the number of common-law unions and divorces was increasing, as was the number of single-person households.

In recent years, an increasing proportion of young adults have either returned to or remained in their parents' household [Table 34.1]. This coincides with an increase in levels of education, a tendency to delay marriage, and an increase in partnership dissolution.

Table 34.1   Percentage of Young Adults in the Parental Home, 1961–2001

Age	1981	1991	2001
Age 20–24	42.1%	51.2%	58.0%
Age 25–29	11.8%	17.8%	23.7%

Source: Data from **http://142.206.72.67/02/02d/02d_graph/ 02d_graph_002_1e.htm.** Accessed 7/15/2003.

C. Single-Person and Two-Person Households

The number of Canadians living alone has been steadily increasing. By 2001, more than a quarter of all households contained only one resident. Just under 10 percent of all Canadians live by themselves. Living in single-person households are adults from across the age spectrum: some young, some elderly, and some whose unions have ended (either marriages or common-law relationships). Two-person households have also become more common [Table 34.2].

Table 34.2   Percentage of Single- and Two-Person Households, 1981–2001

Year	1981	2001
Single-Person	20%	25%
Two-Person	29%	33%

Source: Data compiled from **http://www12.statcan.ca/english/census01/products/analytic/companion/fam/canada.cfm.** Accessed July 15, 2003.

D. Cohabitation

As Figure 34.3 shows, when common-law unions were first counted in the 1981 census, they accounted for less than 6 percent of all family households. In only 20 years, they have grown to account for almost 14 percent of Canadian families. We can also see that the number of CLU families with children has tripled from less than 2 percent to 6.3 percent of families in that time span.

The link between age and the probability of a person's first union being a CLU is also telling: Figure 34.4 shows an increasing likelihood of this occurring with each generation. People in their 20s right now are more likely to have a first union that is NOT a marriage.

E. Same-Sex Couples

In 2001, the Canadian Census measured same-sex households for the first time (similar questions are asked in the United States and New Zealand). While this new question tells us the current number of such households, it is not

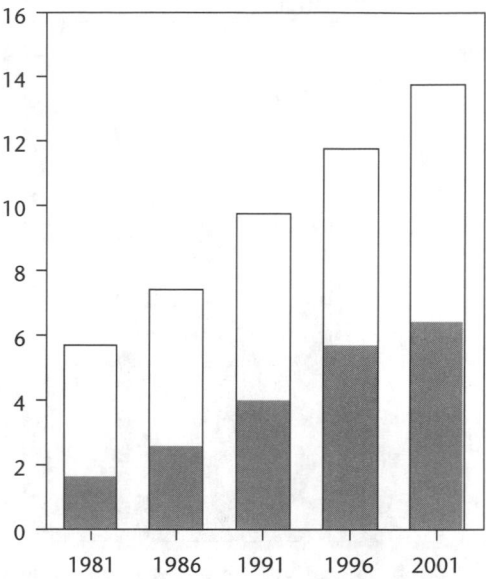

Figure 34.3   Common-Law Unions, 1981–2001

Year by Percentage of Common-Law Families

☐ CLU without Children

■ CLU with Children

Source: Data compiled from **http://www12.statcan.ca/english/census01/products/analytic/companion/fam/timeline.cfm.** Accessed July 15, 2003.

possible to effectively assess whether this is a growing trend using census data. It is important to realize that the question was not designed to measure sexual orientation. So the findings do not tell us the number of gay and lesbian Canadians, only how many people self-identified as living in a same-sex union. Of these 34,200 same-sex couples, 19,000 were males and 15,200 were female. Table 34.3 shows the breakdown of types of two-adult-family households.

Table 34.3   Type of Union, 2001

Married	CLU: 2 sexes	CLU: same sex
83.5%	15.9%	0.5%

Source: Data compiled from **http://www.statcan.ca/Daily/English/ 021022/d021022a.htm.** Accessed July 15, 2003.

Figure 34.4 Probability of First Union Being CLU or Marriage, 2001

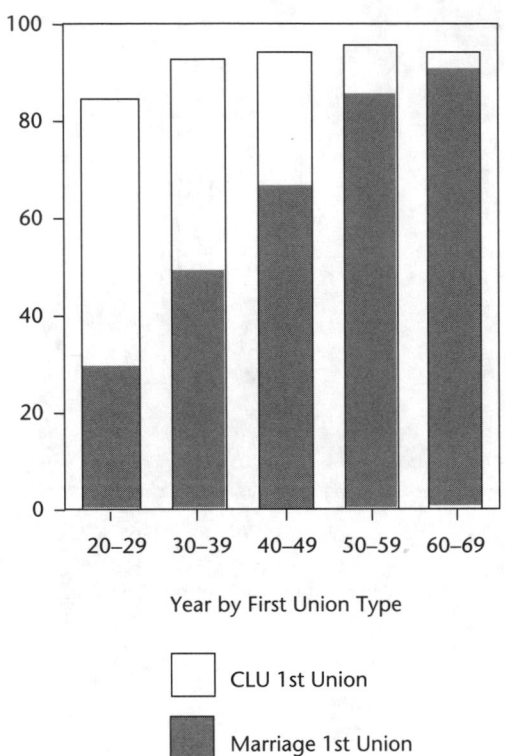

Year by First Union Type

☐ CLU 1st Union

■ Marriage 1st Union

Source: Data compiled from **http://142.206.72.67/02/02d/ 02d_001b_e.htm.** Accessed June 17, 2003.

F. Divorce

The trends in divorce were not uniform over the 20th century. Figure 34.5 [page 176] shows periods when divorce rates increased substantially and then returned to a lower level. Figure 34.6 [page 177] provides a more detailed graph of the 15-year span between 1985 and 1999. These dramatic fluctuations are linked to changes in the divorce laws and the availability of legal aid (Statistics Canada, 2002c).

G. Lone-Parent Families

As previously noted, the number of lone-parent families is increasing [Figure 34.1]. However, this trend has not been uniform. Early in the 20th century, approximately 13.6 percent of family households contained a single parent. This percentage dropped to a low of 8.2 percent in 1966 and has now risen to 15.7 percent [Figure 34.7, page 273].

It is important to note that even though there is not a much larger proportion of lone-parent families now than in the 1930s, the causes of lone parenthood have changed. Earlier in the 20th century, one-parent households were usually the result of the death of one spouse (recall that the divorce rates were very low and life expectancy was shorter than today). Now, children living in lone-parent households typically have a non-residential parent, still alive and living elsewhere. "In the 1950s and 1960s, more than 60 percent of lone parents were widowed. This proportion fell to 20 percent in the 1990s, as a result of the growing incidence of divorce, separation and birth outside marriage" (Statistics Canada, 2003). Table 34.4 shows us the pattern of current family arrangements.

Table 34.4 Percentage of Families by Parental Status, 2001

Parental Status	Percent
Married	70%
CLU	14%
Lone Mothers	13%
Lone Fathers	3%

Source: Data compiled from **http://www.statcan.ca/english/ Pgdb/famil54a.htm.** Accessed July 15, 2003.

H. Step/Blended Families

Just as there were lone-parent families in the past, there were also "stepfamilies." Life expectancy was shorter then, so there was an increased likelihood of parents dying before their children had left home. The remaining parent would often remarry, creating a stepfamily.[3] Stepfamilies today are much more likely to have been created by divorce rather than death. In 2001 there were 503,100 stepfamilies, 12 percent of all families

Figure 34.5   Divorce Trend, 1921–2000

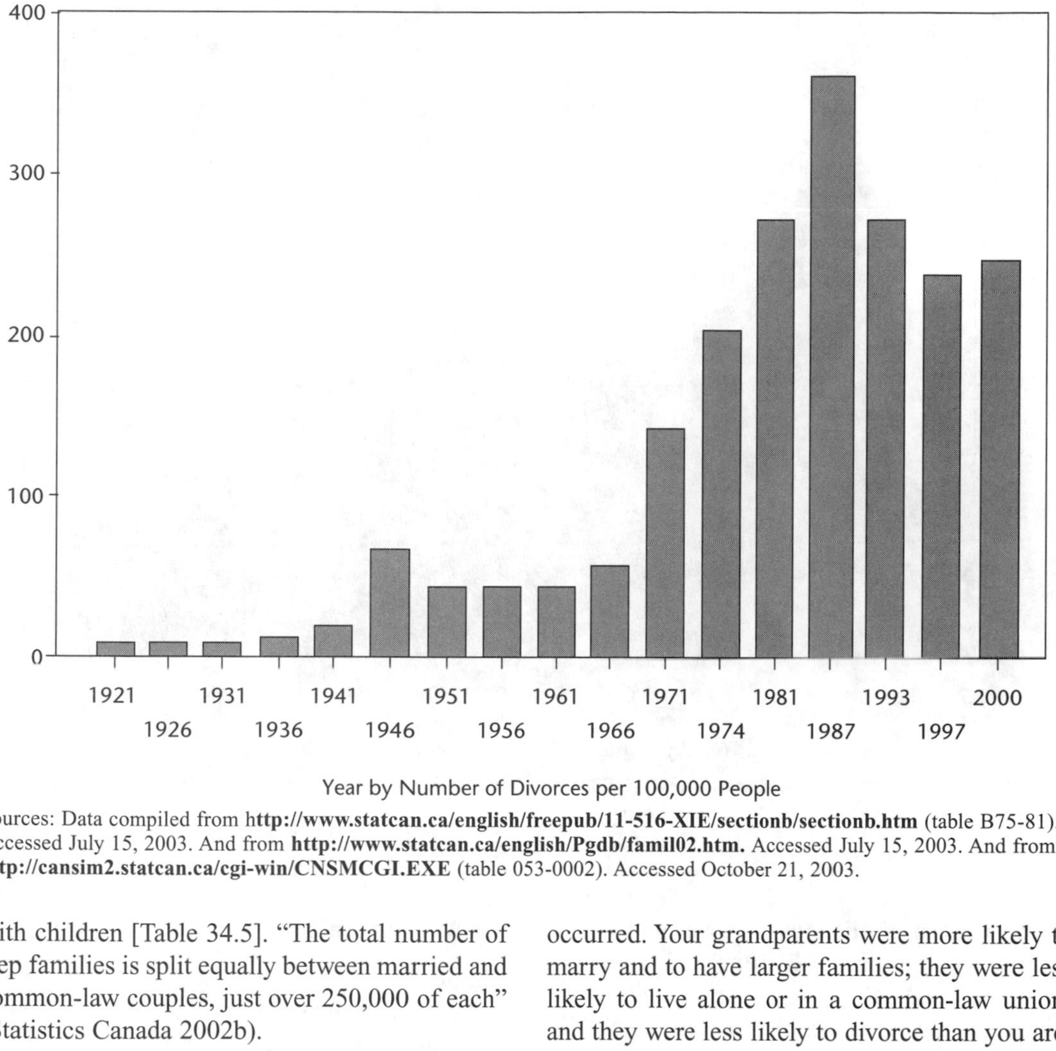

Year by Number of Divorces per 100,000 People

Sources: Data compiled from **http://www.statcan.ca/english/freepub/11-516-XIE/sectionb/sectionb.htm** (table B75-81). Accessed July 15, 2003. And from **http://www.statcan.ca/english/Pgdb/famil02.htm.** Accessed July 15, 2003. And from **http://cansim2.statcan.ca/cgi-win/CNSMCGI.EXE** (table 053-0002). Accessed October 21, 2003.

with children [Table 34.5]. "The total number of step families is split equally between married and common-law couples, just over 250,000 of each" (Statistics Canada 2002b).

Table 34.5   Step/Blended Families, 2001

Type of Stepfamily	Percent
His Children	10%
Her Children	50%
Blended Family (children in common)	32%
Blended Family (no children in common)	8%

Source: Data from **http://www.statcan.ca/Daily/English/ 020711/ d020711a.htm.** Accessed July 15, 2003.

After examining all of these patterns and figures, we can see that profound changes have occurred. Your grandparents were more likely to marry and to have larger families; they were less likely to live alone or in a common-law union; and they were less likely to divorce than you are.

EXPLANATIONS

When you ask people on the street why family patterns have changed so dramatically, they provide a wide range of answers. Explanations I have been given include the following: "People don't try as hard to keep marriages together as they used to"; "The laws around marriage and divorce are too complex, so people prefer just to

Figure 34.6   Divorce Trend, 1985–99

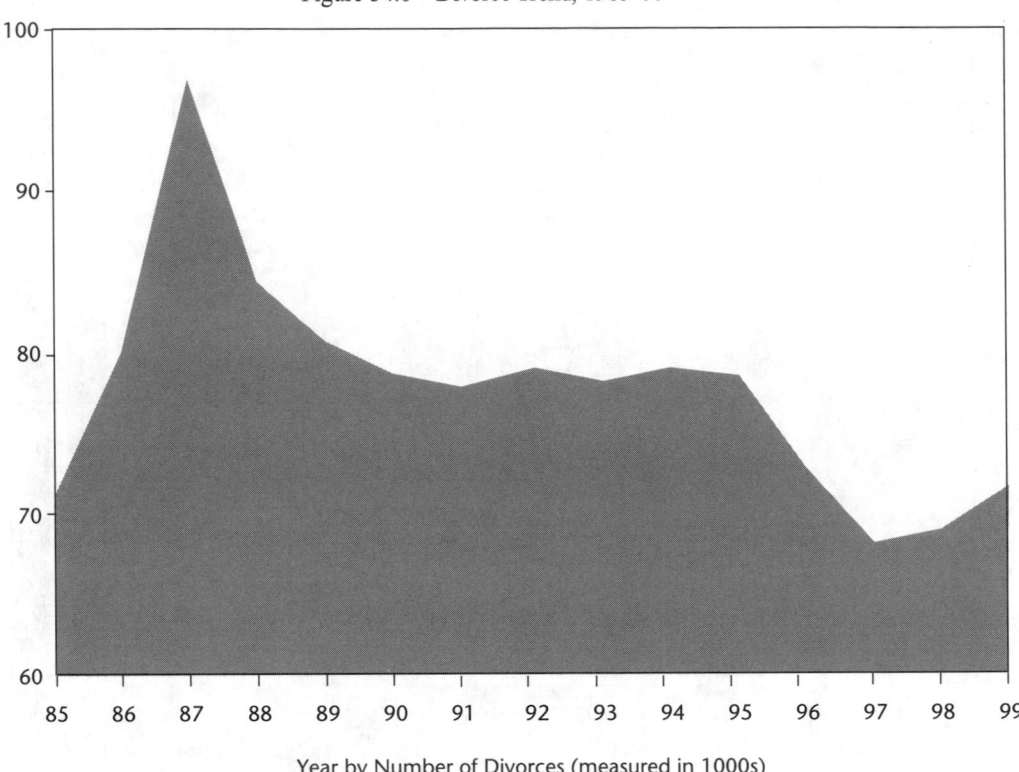

Year by Number of Divorces (measured in 1000s)

Source: Data from **http://cansim2.statcan.ca/cgi-win/CNSMCGI.EXE** (table 053-0002). Accessed October 21, 2003.

live together"; "Feminists have undermined family relationships"; "Conflicting job demands pull people apart"; "The stresses associated with the economy mean people have fewer children and marriages are less stable"; and "Society's values have changed so much that people can live any way they want—it's OK to be gay."

In fact, there are elements of truth in many of these responses. But in order to understand the changing patterns more fully, we must consider multiple causes. Keep in mind that entire books have been written to explain these trends,[4] but we will focus on three key factors: economic, technological, and social.

A. Economic Factors

At the beginning of the 20th century, the majority of Canadians lived in rural areas, working on the land. The population in 1901 was approximately 5,400,000, and only 35 percent of these people lived in towns and cities (Beaujot & McQuillan, 1982). It wasn't until 1941 that the number of urban dwellers surpassed the rural population in Canada. In one century, the economy shifted from an emphasis on the resource sector (agriculture, forestry, mining, etc.) to manufacturing, and then later to the service and information sectors. These economic changes influenced family patterns in several ways.

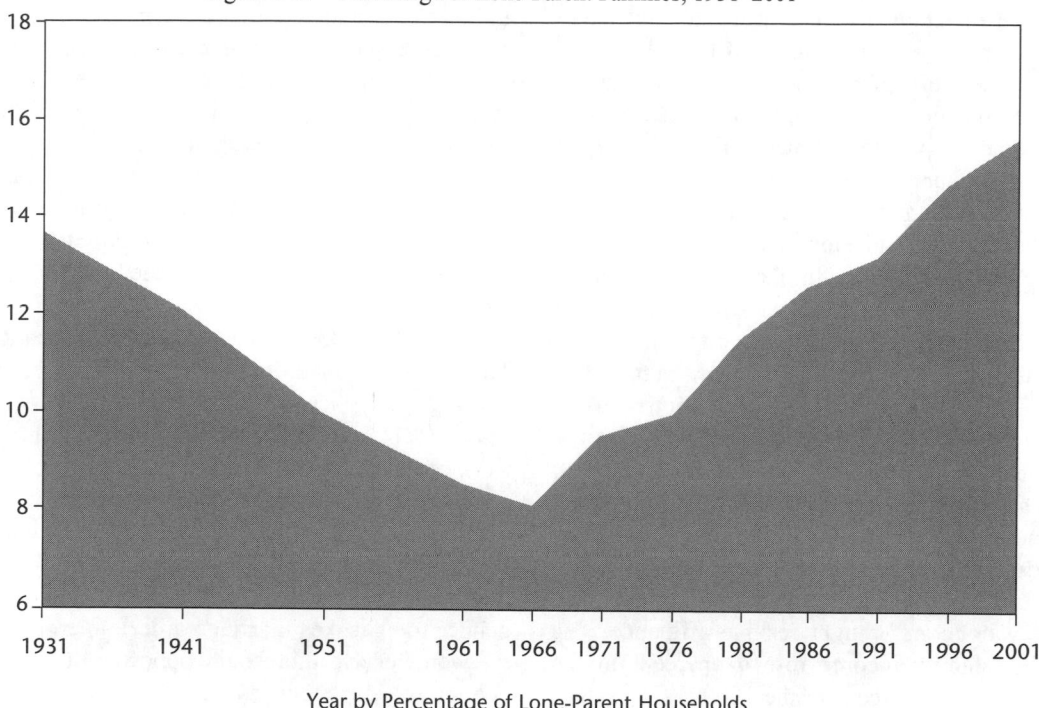

Figure 34.7   Percentage of Lone-Parent Families, 1931–2001

Year by Percentage of Lone-Parent Households

Source: Data compiled from **http://www12.statcan.ca/english/census01/products/analytic/companion/fam/timeline.cfm**. Accessed July 15, 2003.

First, when the majority of families were engaged in farming activities there was an obvious need for large families to undertake the necessary work. The labour of men, women, and children was vital to the success of the family farm. Caldwell (1982) developed the idea of "wealth flows." He argues that, as societies grow away from an agricultural base and become more urban, the contribution of children changes:

children begin to cost parents more (including the cost of educating them as demanded by a modernizing society), and the amount of support that parents get from children begins to decline (starting with the income lost because children are in school rather than working). As the wealth flow reverses and parents begin to spend their income on children, rather than deriving income from them, the economic value of children declines. (Weeks, 1999: 99)

Caldwell's theory was developed to explain the decline in family size in Europe, but it provides insight into the Canadian situation also. In Canada, agriculture and manufacturing developed side by side with the opening up of new territory and the influx of immigrants. The country grew increasingly urban during the 20th century (Beaujot & McQuillan). Urban couples sought to limit family size in part because of the downward flow of wealth that Caldwell described. He notes that if childbearing decisions were based entirely on economic factors, couples would most likely forgo having any children at all (Caldwell, 1982). But, of course, our family formation and childbearing patterns are not solely based on rational, economic decisions: cultural factors also play a profound role (Matthews, 1994).

Second, family patterns changed when the division of labour between husbands and wives was altered by the separation of household and workplace. This reflects the pattern known as the "traditional family," where men worked outside the home for pay and women mainly engaged in unpaid labour in the household. Many people mistakenly believe that the "traditional family" existed throughout history until its predominance waned in the 1960s. In fact, this two-sphere arrangement was relatively short-lived, occurring with urbanization and the transition from agriculture to industrially based economies (Nett, 1988). Its decline began before the Depression years of the 1930s, but it reappeared briefly during the baby boom years of the 1950s (Beaujot, 1991). After the Second World War, the North American economy grew rapidly. "In the mid 1940s one-third of U.S. homes did not have running water and half did not have electric refrigerators, the post war boom brought relative affluence. The median family income rose 42 percent in the 1950s and 38 percent in the 1960s" (Hackstaff, 1999: 32, citing Cherlin, 1992: 35). Prosperity, combined with post-war and post-Depression optimism, influenced family patterns: birth rates rose and divorce rates fell as we saw in Figures 34.2 and 34.5. It was not only the economy that influenced family patterns in the 1950s; the culture and social changes associated with the end of the war also played a significant role (Weiss, 2000).

Third, as the service and information sectors gained economic primacy, the nature of work changed again. Physical strength and endurance became less important than interpersonal communication, computer, and critical thinking skills. Women's perceived physical disadvantage became less salient in this emerging work world, enhancing their career opportunities. The move to the information age further eroded the gender division of labour that identified housework as women's work and paid work as men's work—changing the dynamic within both the household and in the workplace (Hochschild, 1989). Often a higher level of formal education for both women and men is required for career-type jobs, meaning people spend more time in post-secondary education. Marriage and childbearing are delayed (and common-law union is seen as a viable option) or, in some cases, forgone completely (e.g., average age at marriage for first-time brides in 1996 was 27 and first-time grooms was 29 (Statistics Canada, 2002e). The opportunities for women to be financially independent may reduce the necessity of marrying or remaining in a marriage that they perceive to be unworkable. Thus, job opportunities potentially decrease marriage and increase separation and divorce. This widely accepted argument is based on the work of Parsons (1949) and Becker (1981).

Parsons believed that stable marriages must involve a gender-specific division of labour. Becker advanced this premise with the notion that mutual dependence of spouses based on gender roles makes marriage a desirable option. As women have more paid opportunities, their economic dependence in marriage—which Parsons and Becker described—becomes unnecessary. It must be noted that women's so-called economic independence, in and of itself, is not a sufficient explanation for the lowered marriage rates and increased divorce rates. Oppenheimer (1997), in a comprehensive study of this issue, finds little support for this assertion. While it is true that cross-sectional, aggregate analyses show a correlation between women's increasing labour force activity and increasing divorce rates, quite a different pattern emerges when we use time series data and family history data.

Micro-level event history analyses that follow cohorts through their young adulthood generally show that women's educational attainment, employment, and earnings have little or no effect on marriage formation, or, where they do have an effect, find it to be positive. (Oppenheimer, 1997: 449)

Thus it seems that enhanced economic opportunities for women work in concert with other factors to influence family and household patterns.

Finally, the economic prosperity that emerged in North America after the Second World War raised our standard of living substantially. This prosperity has enabled more people to live alone. Many single-person households contain either post-divorce individuals or seniors. "In 2001, 35% of women aged 65 and over lived alone and 16% of men in this age group did so.... For women aged 85 and over, the proportion of seniors living alone grew from 25% in 1981 to 38% in 2001" (Statistics Canada, 2002f: 6). The ability to earn sufficient income to save for retirement is possible in part because of the rise in income in the second half of the 20th century (improved pensions also play an important role; Lindsay, 1999). Even with long-term growth in the economy, though, we have also experienced economic downswings that influence family patterns. One result is the return of adult offspring to the family household or a delay in leaving the parental home when job opportunities are limited. A total of "64% of men aged 20–24 lived with their parents in 2001, while this was the case for 52% of women in the same age group.... According to the 2001 General Social Survey, about 33% of men and 27% of women aged 20–29 returned home at least once after an initial departure" (Statistics Canada, 2002f). Table 34.1 gives an indication of how many young adults live in their parents' homes.

Clearly economic phenomena are linked to family patterns. When we look to the future, then, we should acknowledge that economic realities, like the continued widening of the gap between the rich and poor and short-term economic fluctuations, will influence the choices we make.

B. Technological Factors

Anyone who lived through the decades of the late 20th century knows how much technology has advanced. Computer-based technology has revolutionized production, transportation, communication, health care services, and countless other elements of our social world. Not surprisingly, then, technology has had an impact on family life. Several of these changes are connected to the changing economy. Obviously, it was technological change, in part, that led to a decreasing emphasis on the manufacturing sector and the primacy of service and information-based jobs (as discussed in the previous section).

But technology has also contributed to changes in health care and, thus, in demographic patterns. We live longer now than our ancestors did in large part because of technology. Early declines in mortality rates were linked to the improved standard of living that accompanied modernization and the availability of relatively safe and secure food and water supplies (Davis, 1986). More recently, technology has allowed us to eradicate many infectious diseases through vaccines and to treat other health concerns with antibiotics and medical therapies. It has led to treatments for cancer and diabetes that may not be "cures" but that extend life nevertheless. The average life expectancy for women in Canada is over 80 years and it is almost 76 years for men (Statistics Canada, 2002f). Another major impact of technology on demographic patterns is through contraception. Of course, various means of contraception have existed throughout history (McLaren & McLaren, 1997) but it wasn't until the 20th century that safe, effective, and relatively unobtrusive contraceptives became available.

The combination of much longer lives and fewer children has revolutionized family arrangements (Davis, 1986). Where our grandparents, early in the 20th century, would have spent the vast majority of their adult lives childrearing, and most would die before their last child was grown (average life expectancy in 1921 was 60.6 years for women and 58.8 years for men [Chappell et al., 2003]), Canadians now expect to live the majority of their adult lives in activities other than childrearing. Think of it: if you live to be 80, even if you spend 25 years raising your children, you could still have 35 or more adult years in a child-free household.

The chances of living alone after the death of a spouse increased for women over the 20th century as the gap between life expectancies of the two sexes expanded. This difference in life expectancy is often exaggerated by the common practice of women marrying men slightly older than themselves. Although this gap has narrowed slightly since 1980, there is still a preponderance of elderly women. In 2001, there were 2,315 women and 740 men over 99 years old (three times more women than men; Statistics Canada, 2002g).

Some have even argued that the risk of divorce increases as life expectancy is extended: "improved longevity increases the number of years that marriages can survive; however the number of years that marriages are exposed to the risk of divorce correspondingly increases. This change has undoubtedly influenced the recent escalation in divorce and separation rates" (McVey & Kalbach, 1995: 205). But, of course, increased life expectancy alone is not sufficient to explain these changes.

Looking ahead, we have good reason to believe that technological advances will continue to have a marked impact on family life. Medical researchers are developing ever more powerful reproductive technologies either to avert pregnancies or to create them. Cloning and genetic engineering open the door to the creation of human life without conception as we currently understand it. Similarly, improved technologies that promote health and reduce the impact of disease and injury will likely result in even greater numbers of Canadians reaching their 9th and 10th decades of life.

C. Cultural Factors

Looking back over the past century, we have clearly seen that economic patterns and technological advances have had a profound influence on family arrangements. However, the importance of cultural changes in norms and values, as well as the programs and laws, must not be underestimated. There have been many changes in North American culture in the past 100 years and it is well beyond the scope of this chapter to consider them all. However, we will focus on three major changes in values that have influenced our normative expectations about family life, on the one hand, and the laws and programs that support (or undermine) it, on the other hand. These three changes are secularization, individualism, and egalitarianism. In combination, they have a tremendous impact on all our family decisions.

Secularization refers to a long-term decline in people's participation in organized religions, and the reduced significance of religious institutions in their daily lives (Abercrombie, et al., 1988). This pattern varies by country, culture, and region, but it has been noted in most Western societies. Contrary to the expectation of some early sociologists (e.g., Max Weber), religion has not been entirely replaced by science and rationalism, but it certainly has declined. According to the World Values Survey, only 27 percent of Canadians attend weekly church services, and only 51 percent of Canadians responded that God was important in their lives (Nevitte, 1996). Secularization is linked to family patterns because organized religions tend to support certain family arrangements: they frequently sanction marriage and censure divorce (Hackstaff, 1999), encourage childbearing and oppose abortion, support male dominance, and oppose same-sex families. If religion is salient in our lives, we will follow its doctrines, and our family arrangements will reflect its tenets: fewer divorces, fewer common-law and same-sex unions, more children, and fewer blended families.[5] Hackstaff associates religion with a "marriage culture." She argues that the kind of "family values" many religions support have diminished as our society has experienced secularization (1999). Along with secularization, the value shift toward individualism also influences family patterns. Individualism is a belief that one's own needs and goals should take precedence over the needs of others and the larger community. The movement toward individualism has been linked with an increased desire for personal autonomy, privacy, and independence. Hackstaff (1999) argues that we are moving away from the "marriage culture" toward a pattern of greater individualism.

Marriage culture should be understood as a cluster of beliefs, symbols and practices, framed by material conditions that reinforce marriage and deter divorce. It is constituted by three beliefs that reflect a stance toward marriage *and* divorce: marrying is a given, marriage is forever, and divorce is a last resort. (Hackstaff, 1999: 1)

Over time, our ideas have changed and people are less willing to initiate or continue in relationships that they perceive would irrevocably harm their individual needs and goals. This is illustrated in opinion polls and in behaviour (Thornton, 1989; Matthews, 1994). Hackstaff argues that now people are more inclined to believe "marrying is an option; marriage is contingent; and divorce is a gateway" (1999: 2). People are willing to live alone, in CLUs and in same-sex unions, if these arrangements fulfill their needs. They are also willing to end CLUs or marriages, should they find the union unfulfilling. Like Hackstaff, Inglehart (1977, 1990) also discusses value change in Western society. He argues that it's not simply secularization that has led to these patterns, but that increased affluence and security leads people to adopt post-materialist values. These post-materialist values reflect the importance of individual freedom of choice. Lesthaeghe (1983) connects this value shift directly to demographic change, showing the link between increasing individualism and fertility decline.

The final cultural change we will consider is egalitarianism, specifically the move toward gender equality. Throughout the 20th century in North America, we have seen tremendous changes in the experiences of women. Remember, women were not allowed to vote and were considered to be legal "minors" in 1899. Now women's full equality is entrenched in the Canadian Charter of Rights and Freedoms. In Canada it is not legal to exclude women from educational and employment opportunities. Of course, laws and practices aren't entirely compatible—the protection of equal rights doesn't guarantee that women have equal opportunity. But we have certainly seen an improvement over time. The increasing equality of opportunity for women is reflected in the changing division of labour we discussed in the section on economic factors. This equality challenges the status quo that existed under the "marriage culture" (Hackstaff, 1999) and has been linked to changing roles within families (Hochschild, 1989), to the higher divorce rates (Goldscheider & Waite, 1991), and to lower fertility (Davis, 1984). This does not mean that all feminists are avoiding family arrangements. In fact, there is evidence that existing sex role attitudes don't predict the occurrence of divorce in the future (Thornton et al., 1983) and some evidence shows that improved opportunities for individual women have "a positive effect on marriage formation" (Oppenheimer, 1997: 449). What it does mean is that the gender revolution has an impact on the opportunities and choices of women and men. When this is combined with other elements of our society (such as secularization, individualism, economic, and technological change), we can see a noticeable change in the family patterns of Canadians.

As our values and behaviours change, so to do the laws, policies, and programs that have an impact on family arrangements. I will offer two examples to illustrate. First, divorce laws and policies are changing. As we saw in Figures 34.5 and 34.6, divorce rates have peaked and dropped dramatically in particular years. In 1968 Canada revolutionized its divorce laws to reduce the adversarial nature of divorce proceedings. It was no longer necessary to prove that one spouse was guilty of a marital offence; instead, divorces were granted if the individuals had lived separately for three years (in the United States, this is known as "no-fault divorce"). Divorce rates climbed immediately after this change, showing that many marriages had already ended in all but the legal sense. The law was changed again in 1985 to reduce the three-year waiting period to only one year; again the divorce rates rose. Divorce rates declined slightly in 1996–97, leading many to hope that marriages were becoming more stable and that the high divorce rate would fall. However, on further study it became apparent that the rates were a reflection of a new policy in Ontario that cut the number of divorces legal aid funded by almost 6,000. Thus, many poor people could no longer get financial assistance to pay for a divorce and the rate dropped (Statistics Canada, 1998). This is just one example of how changing laws and policies influence family arrangements. A second example is the much-improved pension system for Canadian seniors. Pension reform that provided a new benefit, called the Guaranteed Income Supplement, for the poorest people had a profound impact on their standard of living. For instance, between 1971 and 1986 "the income of unattached women aged 65 and over increased by 61 percent and went up 36 percent for men in this age group"(Lindsay & Donald, as quoted in Novak & Campbell, 2001: 158). Instituting a pension structure that raises seniors' incomes increases the likelihood of their living independently—a third of the people living in single-person households are over the age of 65 (Ram, 1990).

It is not possible to look ahead and accurately predict how our values and policies will change. But we can easily see that values, policies, and family patterns are intricately connected and that change is inevitable. A case in point is the discussion that erupted in 2003, in the media and among politicians and citizens, about the right to have legally recognized same-sex marriages. The Charter of Rights and Freedoms is a reflection of Canadian values, and yet its protection of non-heterosexual families became a divisive issue. Some Canadians argued that marriage is sacred and should be reserved for heterosexual couples. Others accepted the premise that in an egalitarian society it is discriminatory to privilege heterosexual unions. (The issue remained unresolved as this chapter went to press).

LOOKING AHEAD

Family patterns have changed dramatically over the past century, as our exploration of the Canadian census data has shown us. Despite changes in the membership and activities of families, though, the "ties of mutual consent" (Vanier, 2000: v) at the heart of all families are likely to endure. We have explored some of the many causes for these trends and now we look to the future. Given what you know, who do you think your grandchildren will live with? Their parents? Their children? Their lovers? Their cats? Or, maybe you won't have any grandchildren at all. Obviously, no one can perfectly predict the future, but you can use the insights you have gained to consider possibilities. How do you think future economic fluctuations and the widening gap between the rich and poor will influence you? What about genetic engineering and increased longevity? Finally, how might the growing emphasis on egalitarianism, individualism, and secularization affect your choices? Your answers to these questions are the key to the future. The decisions you and your generation make about marriage, divorce, cohabitation, and childrearing will determine the trends for the coming century.

NOTES

1. Statistics Canada collects census data on all Canadians, every five years. In addition, numerous national surveys are undertaken to assess Canadians' activities and behaviours on a regular basis (e.g., the General Social Survey and the Labour Force Survey). It is required by law that someone from every household responds to a questionnaire, detailing the membership of that household (age, sex, marital status—including common-law and same-sex unions). One in five households must complete a longer questionnaire that asks about a wider range of information

(e.g., ethnicity, religion, language, and birthplace; Statistics Canada, 2002e).

2. The expected number of children per woman is calculated using a measure called the Total Fertility Rate. It indicates how many children each woman would have if she followed the same childbearing pattern, throughout her lifetime, that all Canadian women experienced in that particular year.

3. "Stepfamily" refers to a family in which at least one of the children in the household is from a previous relationship of one of the parents. In a "simple" stepfamily, the child(ren) of one of the spouses lives in the household. A "blended" family contains children from both spouses from one or more previous unions or one or more children from the current union and one or more children from previous unions. (Statistics Canada, 2002a)

4. See, for example, Ram, 1990; Goldsheider & Waite, 1991; Beaujot, 1991; Hackstaff, 1999; Beaujot, 2000; Weiss, 2000; Wu, 2000.

5. To illustrate: the doctrines of Roman Catholicism oppose most forms of contraception. At one time, demographers could readily discern distinct trends in the childbearing patterns of Catholic and Protestant families. As the salience of church doctrine diminished, the gap in fertility rates disappeared (Westoff & Ryder, 1977).

REFERENCES

Abercrombie, et al. 1988. *Dictionary of sociology*, 2nd ed. London: Penguin Books.

Beaujot, R. 1991. *Population change in Canada*. Toronto: McClelland and Stewart.

———. 2000. *Earning and caring in Canadian Families*. Peterborough, Ont.: Broadview Press.

Beaujot, R., and K. McQuillan. 1982. *Growth and dualism*. Toronto: Gage Publishing.

Becker, G. 1981. *A treatise on the family*. Cambridge: Harvard University Press.

Caldwell, J. 1982. *Theory of fertility decline*. New York: Academic Press.

Chappell N., et al. 2003. *Aging in contemporary Canada*. Toronto: Prentice Hall.

Cherlin, A. 1992. *Marriage, divorce and remarriage,* revised and enlarged ed. Cambridge: Harvard University Press.

Davis, K. 1984. Wives and work: The sex role revolution and its consequences. *Population and Development Review,* 10(3): 397–417.

———. 1986. Low fertility in evolutionary perspective. In "Below replacement fertility in industrial societies," supplement to *Population and Development Review,* 12: 48–65.

Goldscheider, F., and L. Waite. 1991. *New families, no families?* Berkeley: University of California Press.

Hackstaff, K. 1999. *Marriage in a culture of divorce*. Philadelphia: Temple University Press.

Hochschild, A., with A. Machung. 1989. *The second shift*. New York: Viking.

Inglehart R. 1977. *The silent revolution: Changing values and political styles among western publics*. Princeton: Princeton University Press.

———. 1990. *Culture shift in advanced industrial society*. Princeton: Princeton University Press.

Lesthaeghe, R. 1983. A century of demographic and cultural change in Western Europe: An exploration of the underlying dimensions. In *Population and Development Review,* 9(3): 411–35.

Lindsay, C. 1999. *A portrait of Canadian seniors*, 2nd ed. Ottawa: Statistics Canada.

Lindsay, C., and S. Donald. 1988. Income of Canadian seniors. *Canadian Social Trends* (Autumn): 20–25.

Matthews, B. 1994. The relationship between gender and fertility strategies. Ph.D. dissertation. Sociology Department, University of Western Ontario.

McLaren, A., and A. Tigar McLaren.1997. *Bedroom and the state : The changing practices and politics of contraception and abortion in Canada*, Toronto: Oxford University Press.

McVey, W., and W. Kalbach. 1995. *Canadian population*. Toronto: Nelson Canada.

Murdock, G. 1949. *Social structure*. New York: Macmillan.

Nemeth, M. 1994. The family. *Maclean's* (June14): 30–38.

Nett, E. 1988. *Canadian families: Past and present*. Toronto: Butterworth's.

Nevitte, N. 1996. *The decline of deference*. Peterborough, Ont.: Broadview Press.

Novak M., and L. Campbell. 2001. *Aging and society: A Canadian perspective*, 4th ed. Toronto: Nelson.

Oppenheimer, V. 1997. Women's employment and the gain to marriage: The specialization and trading model. *Annual Review of Sociology*, 23: 431–53.

Parsons, T. 1949. The social structure of family. In *The family: Its function and destiny,* ed. R. Anshem, 173–201. New York: Harper and Brothers.

Ram, B. 1990. *New trends in the family*. Ottawa: Statistics Canada.

Romaniuc, A. 1984. *Fertility in Canada: From baby boom to baby bust*. Ottawa: Statistics Canada.

Statistics Canada, 1998. Marriages and divorces, 1996. *The Daily* (January 29).

———. 2002a. *Census dictionary.* 2001 Census reference material.

———. 2002b. Changing conjugal life in Canada. *The Daily* (July 11).

———. 2002c. Divorces. *The Daily* (December 2).

———. 2002d. *Divorces: Historical statistics of Canada.* Catalogue no. 82-573 GIE.

———. 2002e. *History of the census of Canada.* 2001 Census general information.

———. 2002f. *Profile of Canadian families and households: Diversification continues.* 2001 Census analysis series.

———. 2002g. *Profiles of the Canadian population by age and sex: Canada ages.* 2001 Census analysis series.

———.2003. *The people: Household and family life.* Canada e-book.

Stephens, W. 1963. *The family in cross cultural perspective.* New York: Holt Rinehart and Winston.

Thornton, A. 1989. Changing attitudes towards family issues in the United States. *Journal of Marriage and Family,* 51(4): 873–93.

Thornton, A., et al. 1983. Causes and consequences of sex role attitudes and attitude change. *American Sociological Review,* 48: 211–27.

Vanier Institute for the Family. 2000. *Profiling Canada's families II.*

Weeks, J. 1999. *Population: An introduction to concepts and issues,* 7th ed. Belmont: Wadsworh Publishing.

Weiss, J. 2000. *To have and to hold: Marriage, the baby boom and social change.* Chicago: University of Chicago Press.

Westoff, C., and N. Ryder. 1977. *The contraceptive revolution.* Princeton: Princeton University Press.

Wu, Z. 2000. *Cohabitation: An alternative form of family living.* Don Mills, Ont.: Oxford University Press.

Part XVII

Religion

35

The Protestant Ethic
and the Spirit of Capitalism

Max Weber

A product of modern European civilization, study-ing any problem of universal history, is bound to ask himself to what combination of circumstances the fact should be attributed that in Western civi-lization, and in Western civilization only, cultural phenomena have appeared which (as we like to think) lie in a line of development having *universal* significance and value.... All over the world there have been merchants, wholesale and retail, local and engaged in foreign trade....

But in modern times the Occident has devel-oped, in addition to this, a very different form of capitalism which has appeared nowhere else: the rational capitalistic organization of (formally) free labour. Only suggestions of it are found elsewhere. Even the organization of unfree labour reached a considerable degree of rationality only on planta-tions and to a very limited extent in the *Ergasteria* of antiquity. In the manors, manorial workshops,

Source: From *The Protestant Ethic and the Spirit of Capitalism* by Max Weber, copyright © 1988, Prentice-Hall, Inc. Reprinted by permission.

and domestic industries on estates with serf labour it was probably somewhat less developed. Even real domestic industries with free labour have definitely been proved to have existed in only a few isolated cases outside the Occident....

Rational industrial organization, attuned to a regular market, and neither to political nor irra-tionally speculative opportunities for profit, is not, however, the only peculiarity of Western capi-talism. The modern rational organization of the capitalistic enterprise would not have been possi-ble without two other important factors in its development: the separation of business from the household, which completely dominates modern economic life, and closely connected with it, rational book-keeping....

Hence in a universal history of culture the central problem for us is not, in the last analysis, even from a purely economic view-point, the development of capitalistic activity as such, differing in different cultures only in form: the adventurer type, or capitalism in trade, war, poli-tics, or administration as sources of gain. It is rather the origin of this sober bourgeois capitalism with its rational organization of free labour. Or in terms of cultural history, the problem is that of the origin of the Western bourgeois class and of its peculiarities, a problem which is certainly closely connected with that of the origin of the capitalistic organization of labour, but is not quite the same thing. For the bourgeois as a class existed prior to the development of the peculiar modern form of capitalism, though, it is true, only in the Western hemisphere.

Now the peculiar modern Western form of capitalism has been, at first sight, strongly influenced by the development of technical possibilities. Its rationality is today essentially dependent on the calculability of the most important technical factors. But this means fundamentally that it is dependent on the peculiarities of modern science, especially the natural sciences based on mathematics and exact and rational experiment. On the other hand, the development of these sciences and of the technique resting upon them now receives important stimulation from these capitalistic interests in its practical economic application. It is true that the origin of Western science cannot be attributed to such interests. Calculation, even with decimals, and algebra have been carried on in India, where the decimal system was invented. But it was only made use of by developing capitalism in the West, while in India it led to no modern arithmetic or book-keeping. Neither was the origin of mathematics and mechanics determined by capitalistic interests. But the *technical* utilization of scientific knowledge, so important for the living conditions of the mass of people, was certainly encouraged by economic considerations, which were extremely favourable to it in the Occident. But this encouragement was derived from the peculiarities of the social structure of the Occident. We must hence ask, from *what* parts of that structure was it derived, since not all of them have been of equal importance?

Among those of undoubted importance are the rational structures of law and of administration.

For modern rational capitalism has need, not only of the technical means of production, but of a calculable legal system and of administration in terms of formal rules. Without it adventurous and speculative trading capitalism and all sorts of politically determined capitalisms are possible, but no rational enterprise under individual initiative, with fixed capital and certainty of calculations. Such a legal system and such administration have been available for economic activity in a comparative state of legal and formalistic perfection only in the Occident. We must hence inquire where that law came from. Among other circumstances, capitalistic interests have in turn undoubtedly also helped, but by no means alone nor even principally, to prepare the way for the predominance in law and administration of a class of jurists specially trained in rational law. But these interests did not themselves create that law. Quite different forces were at work in this development. And why did not the capitalistic interests do the same in China or India? Why did not the scientific, the artistic, the political, or the economic development there enter upon that path of rationalization which is peculiar to the Occident?

For in all the above cases it is a question of the specific and peculiar rationalism of Western culture.... It is hence our first concern to work out and to explain genetically the special peculiarity of Occidental rationalism, and within this field that of the modern Occidental form. Every such attempt at explanation must, recognizing the fundamental importance of the economic factor, above all take account of the economic conditions. But at the same time the opposite correlation must not be left out of consideration. For though the development of economic rationalism is partly dependent on rational technique and law, it is at the same time determined by the ability and disposition of men to adopt certain types of practical rational conduct. When these types have been obstructed by spiritual obstacles, the development of rational economic conduct has also met serious inner resistance. The magical and religious forces, and the ethical ideas of duty based upon them, have in the past always been among the most important formative influences on conduct. In the studies collected here we shall be concerned with these forces.

Two older essays have been placed at the beginning which attempt, at one important point, to approach the side of the problem which is generally most difficult to grasp: the influence of certain religious ideas on the development of an economic spirit, or the *ethos* of an economic system. In this case we are dealing with the connection of the spirit of modern economic life with the rational ethics of ascetic Protestantism. Thus we treat here only one side of the causal chain....

...[T]hat side of English Puritanism which was derived from Calvinism gives the most consistent religious basis for the idea of the calling.... For the saints' everlasting rest is in the next world; on earth man must, to be certain of his state of grace, "do the works of him who sent him, as long as it is yet day." Not leisure and enjoyment, but only activity serves to increase the glory of God according to the definite manifestations of His will.

Waste of time is thus the first and in principle the deadliest of sins. The span of human life is infinitely short and precious to make sure of one's own election. Loss of time through sociability, idle talk, luxury, even more sleep than is necessary for health, six to at most eight hours, is worthy of absolute moral condemnation. It does not yet hold, with Franklin, that time is money, but the proposition is true in a certain spiritual sense. It is infinitely valuable because every hour lost is lost to labour for the glory of God. Thus inactive contemplation is also valueless, or even directly reprehensible if it is at the expense of one's daily work....

[T]he same prescription is given for all sexual temptation as is used against religious doubts and a sense of moral unworthiness: "Work hard in your calling." But the most important thing was that even beyond that labour came to be considered in itself the end of life, ordained as such by God. St. Paul's "He who will not work shall not eat" holds

unconditionally for everyone. Unwillingness to work is symptomatic of the lack of grace.

Here the difference from the mediæval viewpoint becomes quite evident. Thomas Aquinas also gave an interpretation of that statement of St. Paul. But for him labour is only necessary *naturali ratione* for the maintenance of individual and community. Where this end is achieved, the precept ceases to have any meaning. Moreover, it holds only for the race, not for every individual. It does not apply to anyone who can live without labour on his possessions, and of course contemplation, as a spiritual form of action in the Kingdom of God, takes precedence over the commandment in its literal sense. Moreover, for the popular theology of the time, the highest form of monastic productivity lay in the increase of the *Thesaurus eccleslicæ* through prayer and chant.

...For everyone without exception God's Providence has prepared a calling, which he should profess and in which he should labour. And this calling is not, as it was for the Lutheran, a fate to which he must submit and which he must make the best of, but God's commandment to the individual to work for the divine glory. This seemingly subtle difference had far-reaching psychological consequences, and became connected with a further development of the providential interpretation of the economic order which had begun in scholasticism.

It is true that the usefulness of a calling, and thus its favour in the sight of God, is measured primarily in moral terms, and thus in terms of the importance of the goods produced in it for the community. But a further, and, above all, in practice the most important, criterion is found in private profitableness. For if that God, whose hand the Puritan sees in all the occurrences of life, shows one of His elect a chance of profit, he must do it with a purpose. Hence the faithful Christian must follow the call by taking advantage of the opportunity. "If God show you a way in which you may lawfully get more than in another way (without wrong to your soul or to any other), if you refuse this, and choose the less gainful way, you cross one of the ends of your calling, and you refuse to be God's steward, and to accept His gifts and use them for Him when He requireth it: you may labour to be rich for God, though not for the flesh and sin."…

The superior indulgence of the *seigneur* and the parvenu ostentation of the *nouveau riche* are equally detestable to asceticism. But, on the other hand, it has the highest ethical appreciation of the sober, middle-class, self-made man. "God blesseth His trade" is a stock remark about those good men who had successfully followed the divine hints. The whole power of the God of the Old Testament, who rewards His people for their obedience in this life, necessarily exercised a similar influence on the Puritan who…compared his own state of grace with that of the heroes of the Bible.…

Although we cannot here enter upon a discussion of the influence of Puritanism in all…directions, we should call attention to the fact that the toleration of pleasure in cultural goods, which contributed to purely aesthetic or athletic enjoyment, certainly always ran up against one characteristic limitation: They must not cost anything. Man is only a trustee of the goods which have come to him through God's grace. He must, like the servant in the parable, give an account of every penny entrusted to him, and it is at least hazardous to spend any of it for a purpose which does not serve the glory of God but only one's own enjoyment. What person, who keeps his eyes open, has not met representatives of this viewpoint even in the present? The idea of a man's duty to his possessions, to which he subordinates himself as an obedient steward, or even as an acquisitive machine, bears with chilling weight on his life. The greater the possessions the heavier, if the ascetic attitude toward life stands the test, the feeling of responsibility for them, for holding them undiminished for the glory of God and increasing them by restless effort. The origin of this type of life also extends in certain roots, like so many aspects of the spirit of capitalism,

back into the Middle Ages. But it was in the ethic of ascetic Protestantism that it first found a consistent ethical foundation. Its significance for the development of capitalism is obvious.

This worldly Protestant asceticism, as we may recapitulate up to this point, acted powerfully against the spontaneous enjoyment of possessions; it restricted consumption, especially of luxuries. On the other hand, it had the psychological effect of freeing the acquisition of goods from the inhibitions of traditionalistic ethics. It broke the bonds of the impulse of acquisition in that it not only legalized it, but (in the sense discussed) looked upon it as directly willed by God.…

As far as the influence of the Puritan outlook extended, under all circumstances—and this is, of course, much more important than the mere encouragement of capital accumulation—it favoured the development of a rational bourgeois economic life; it was the most important, and above all the only consistent influence in the development of that life. It stood at the cradle of the modern economic man.

To be sure, these Puritanical ideals tended to give way under excessive pressure from the temptations of wealth, as the Puritans themselves knew very well. With great regularity we find the most genuine adherents of Puritanism among the classes which were rising from a lowly status, the small bourgeois and farmers while the *beati possidentes,* even among Quakers, are often found tending to repudiate the old ideals. It was the same fate which again and again befell the predecessor of this worldly asceticism, the monastic asceticism of the Middle Ages. In the latter case, when rational economic activity had worked out its full effects by strict regulation of conduct and limitation of consumption, the wealth accumulated either succumbed directly to the nobility, as in the time before the Reformation, or monastic discipline threatened to break down, and one of the numerous reformations became necessary.

In fact the whole history of monasticism is in a certain sense the history of a continual struggle with the problem of the secularizing influence of wealth. The same is true on a grand scale of the worldly asceticism of Puritanism. The great revival of Methodism, which preceded the expansion of English industry toward the end of the eighteenth century, may well be compared with such a monastic reform. We may hence quote here a passage from John Wesley himself which might well serve as a motto for everything which has been said above. For it shows that the leaders of these ascetic movements understood the seemingly paradoxical relationships which we have here analysed perfectly well, and in the same sense that we have given them. He wrote:

I fear, wherever riches have increased, the essence of religion has decreased in the same proportion. Therefore I do not see how it is possible, in the nature of things, for any revival of true religion to continue long. For religion must necessarily produce both industry and frugality, and these cannot but produce riches. But as riches increase, so will pride, anger, and love of the world in all its branches. How then is it possible that Methodism, that is, a religion of the heart, though it flourishes now as a green bay tree, should continue in this state? For the Methodists in every place grow diligent and frugal; consequently they increase in goods. Hence they proportionately increase in pride, in anger, in the desire of the flesh, the desire of the eyes, and the pride of life. So, although the form of religion remains, the spirit is swiftly vanishing away. Is there no way to prevent this—this continual decay of pure religion? We ought not to prevent people from being diligent and frugal; *we must exhort all Christians to gain all they can, and to save all they can; that is, in effect, to grow rich.*

As Wesley here says, the full economic effect of those great religious movements, whose significance for economic development lay above all in their ascetic educative influence, generally came only after the peak of the purely religious enthusiasm was past. Then the intensity of the search for the Kingdom of God commenced gradually to pass over into sober economic virtue; the religious roots died out slowly, giving way to utilitarian worldliness. Then, as Dowden puts it, as in *Robinson Crusoe,* the isolated economic man who

carries on missionary activities on the side takes the place of the lonely spiritual search for the Kingdom of Heaven of Bunyan's pilgrim, hurrying through the market-place of Vanity....

A specifically bourgeois economic ethic had grown up. With the consciousness of standing in the fullness of God's grace and being visibly blessed by Him, the bourgeois business man, as long as he remained within the bounds of formal correctness, as long as his moral conduct was spotless and the use to which he put his wealth was not objectionable, could follow his pecuniary interests as he would and feel that he was fulfilling a duty in doing so. The power of religious asceticism provided him in addition with sober, conscientious, and unusually industrious workmen, who clung to their work as to a life purpose willed by God.

Finally, it gave him the comforting assurance that the unequal distribution of the goods of this world was a special dispensation of Divine Providence, which in these differences, as in particular grace, pursued secret ends unknown to men....

One of the fundamental elements of the spirit of modern capitalism, and not only of that but of all modern culture: Rational conduct on the basis of the idea of the calling, was born—that is what this discussion has sought to demonstrate—from the spirit of Christian asceticism. One has only to re-read the passage from Franklin, quoted at the beginning of this essay, in order to see that the essential elements of the attitude which was there called the spirit of capitalism are the same as what we have just shown to be the content of the Puritan worldly asceticism, only without the religious basis, which by Franklin's time had died away....

Since asceticism undertook to remodel the world and to work out its ideals in the world, material goods have gained an increasing and finally an inexorable power over the lives of men as at no previous period in history. Today the spirit of religious asceticism—whether finally, who knows?—has escaped from the cage. But victorious capitalism, since it rests on mechanical foundations, needs its support no longer. The rosy blush of its laughing heir, the Enlightenment, seems also to be irretrievably fading, and the idea of duty in one's calling prowls about in our lives like the ghost of dead religious beliefs. Where the fulfilment of the calling cannot directly be related to the highest spiritual and cultural values, or when, on the other hand, it need not be felt simply as economic compulsion, the individual generally abandons the attempt to justify it at all. In the field of its highest development, in the United States, the pursuit of wealth, stripped of its religious and ethical meaning, tends to become associated with purely mundane passions, which often actually give it the character of sport.

No one knows who will live in this cage in the future, or whether at the end of this tremendous development entirely new prophets will arise, or there will be a great rebirth of old ideas and ideals, or, if neither, mechanized petrification, embellished with a sort of convulsive self-importance. For of the last stage of this cultural development, it might well be truly said: "Specialists without spirit, sensualists without heart; this nullity imagines that it has attained a level of civilization never before achieved."

But this brings us to the world of judgments of value and of faith, with which this purely historical discussion need not be burdened....

Here we have only attempted to trace the fact and the direction of its influence to their motives in one, though a very important point. But it would also further be necessary to investigate how Protestant Asceticism was in turn influenced in its development and its character by the totality of social conditions, especially economic. The modern man is in general, even with the best will, unable to give religious ideas a significance for culture and national character which they deserve. But it is, of course, not my aim to substitute for a one-sided materialistic an equally one-sided spiritualistic causal interpretation of culture and of history. Each is equally possible, but each, if it does not serve as the preparation, but as the conclusion of an investigation, accomplishes equally little in the interest of historical truth.

36

Some Very Good News via Some Very Bad Myths

Reginald Bibby

I grew up as a Baptist. Funny thing when you're a Baptist: you don't think of yourself as particularly strange. In fact, you look out at people in other Protestant denominations—friends and neighbours who are United, Anglican, Lutheran, Presbyterian—and see *them* as the ones who are different. And, to be honest, to a ten-year-old Baptist, groups like Catholics, not to mention Mormons or Buddhists, seem *especially* different. Their services are not ones into which Baptists readily wander.

It therefore comes as something of a surprise to Baptists when I tell them about my study of the Toronto Anglican Diocese in the mid-80s—where an Anglican woman who was concerned about changes in liturgy, commented, "We need to be careful, or one day we will end up like the Baptists"! What the Anglican woman probably

Source: Bibby, Reginald W. (2002). Some Very Good News via Some Very Bad Myths. In Reginald W. Bibby, *Restless Gods:The Renaissance of Religion in Canada* (Chp. 2, pp.33–54). Toronto: Stoddart Publishing Co. Ltd. Reprinted with permission of the author (2003).

didn't realize, of course, is that a Baptist in *her* worship service would also feel like the proverbial duck badly in need of some water.

To have conversations with people who are part of other religious groups is to receive a mini-revelation: *everyone thinks that their traditions are the norm*—their beliefs, their kind of worship, their music, their type of ministry. Consequently, to grow up anything is to feel a measure of comfort with one's own group and a measure of discomfort with other "different" groups. What's true of Baptists and Anglicans can just as readily be seen when a Catholic and a Pentecostal who are dating attempt to alternate pews, or when two United and Jewish friends agree to attend their respective services together on a back-to-back Saturday and Sunday. Sometimes the ecclesiastical trip may be short, such as Anglican to Catholic or Baptist to Alliance; the occasion may also be brief—a wedding, a funeral, or a Christmas service. Regardless, confusion and uneasiness are common. People don't know what they are supposed to do when the music and prayers and rituals and gestures are foreign. What's happening somehow doesn't resonate with the kinds of things that may have moved one in the past, or moves one in the present.

All of this is to say that faith, however personal, invariably has a pronounced social and cultural dimension. To be raised Baptist or United or Catholic or Mormon is to acquire a religious identity, which is accompanied by ideas and ways of expressing faith that one sees as normative. As basic as such a reality is, it is not one that Canadian religious leaders readily grasped, to the detriment of both their groups and millions of inactive religious people across the country.

A common impression about the attendance drop-off in the post-1960s is that it was associated with millions of Canadians jettisoning their respective religious groups. To borrow some sports jargon, to the extent that people were not involved in the groups of their childhoods, they were seen as having become religious free agents who were shopping their services to new teams. Or, to use the language of the market model, those who wanted to have their religious and spiritual needs met were said to be spending time browsing in an array of "meaning malls" and "spiritual marketplaces." Allegedly, their consumer choices were determined primarily by their personal tastes and whims. In such an environment, people were seen as having little or no regard for the religions of their parents and grandparents. Those, after all, were the "old-time religions." This was a new day—a day of individualism, freedom, and post-denominationalism. Bring on the competition, New Movements, New Age, and all.

It was a poorly informed and extremely naive reading of the times. If all we had been looking at was religion as a set of ideas, then people could have said goodbye to religious groups just as readily as they had reluctantly said goodbye to beliefs about Santa and the Easter Bunny and tooth fairies. If the churches had been no more than religious department stores that had become outdated and no longer competitive, people could have said goodbye to them just as readily as they waved goodbye to Eaton's and headed for Wal-Mart.

But religious groups carry with them cultures and poignant memories. Some two in three Canadians say they attended Sunday schools and services when they were growing up, frequently accompanied by parents, and sometimes by relatives. These were the places where millions of people heard stories, sang choruses, participated in youth groups, were introduced to faith, and made commitments. These were settings in which many of their grandparents and parents, brothers and sisters, aunts and uncles, and closest friends were involved. These places bring back memories of poignant, moving times when they and people they loved were baptized and married, and when they said final farewells to cherished family members and friends.

As we will see, for those who look at the world through theistic eyes, there are signs that the gods are shaking up Canadians from coast to coast, leading them to ask vital questions about life and death, communicating with them directly, and giving them hints of transcendence. In the midst of it all, large numbers of Canadians seem to continue to think that at least some of the answers to what they are experiencing lie in the religious traditions of their parents and grandparents. Most are reluctant to wander very far from their religious homes and many are open to greater involvement—if they can be shown that it is worth their while.

These realities have not been well understood by the country's churches. It's time to clear up the confusion once and for all.

A MONOPOLY VERSUS A MOSAIC

A key to understanding the nature of organized religion in Canada is recognizing that the country's long-established religious groups have had and continue to have a considerable advantage over newer and smaller counterparts in ministering to Canadians. Their longevity has meant that they have sizeable pools of people who have been socialized in their traditions. Their numerical strength has meant, in turn, that they typically gain far more people than they lose through religious intermarriage. This is not to disparage the presence and expansion efforts of newer and smaller religious organizations; it's simply to recognize the competitive facts of Canadian religious life....

There were three key reasons why Canada's religious market broke down. First, contrary to what [Rodney] Stark and many religious leaders had assumed, the country's well-established churches continued to have a considerable competitive advantage because of the latent loyalty of the people who identified with them—those I refer to as "affiliates." People were very reluctant to switch. The market was not as open as everyone had thought. Second, there was a widespread assumption that affiliates who attended sporadically or not at all had dropped out of their groups and had become part of a growing pool of "unchurched" people. Their affiliate religious bodies essentially gave up on them, a fact graphically illustrated by the strange delight many congregations took in cleaning the alleged "deadwood" off their rolls. Because religious groups, and just about everyone else for that matter, were working from these two false assumptions about switching and dropping out, large numbers of people failed to be touched by their churches' ministries and huge amounts of potential resources went untapped. Third, it was widely believed that people who had ceased to be active were not receptive to greater involvement. And if they weren't, neither were their offspring. A prevalent stereotype was that people no longer involved were typically hostile—"poisoned" by bad experiences. Better to turn elsewhere in pursuing recruitment leads.

Ironically, few congregations appear to have carried out systematic studies of their marginal and inactive affiliates. If they had, they would

Table 36.1 Canada's Religious Families, 2002

	Approximate % of the Canadian Population*
Roman Catholics outside Quebec	23
Roman Catholics in Quebec	19
Mainline Protestants *United (9), Anglican (6), Lutheran (2), Presbyterian (2)*	19
Conservative Protestants *including Baptists, Pentecostals, Mennonites, Alliance, Nazarenes*	8
Other Faith Groups *including Jews, Muslims, Buddhists, Hindus, Sikhs*	6
Religious Nones	20

*A residual 5% or so, mostly Protestants, identify with varied groups that neither fall into any of these six categories nor collectively represent a family with compatible characteristics.

Source: Projection based on *Project Canada* and Statistics Canada data.

have found that (a) many were, in fact, receptive to greater involvement and (b) especially in urban areas, many were among the Canadians who had moved once in the past five years and simply had not reconnected with churches after having been involved somewhere else.[1] They needed to be contacted; often no one called. It all added up to a bad misreading of what was happening.

Religious organizations should have known better. For some time they and academics who make a living from studying them had known well how they grow: the primary source of new additions is biological, in the form of family members. An example is a 52-year-old evangelical from Fredericton who playfully told us recently, "I started attending church nine months before I was born, have been carried to church, pushed to church, towed to church, and shoved to church. Now going to church is one of my favourite things."[2] The research is definitive: religious groups grow by growing their own. On national and international scales, growth also takes place through the recruitment of geographically mobile members, whether they arrive from Ontario or Saskatchewan, England or Asia. To the extent that groups recruit people outside their boundaries, the key factors are friendship and marriage—people on the inside befriend them or marry them. Frankly, for all the talk about outreach and evangelism, the research shows that "people from the outside" represent a very limited, bonus source of growth.[3]

This apparent "bad news" about the difficulty Canadian groups have experienced in recruiting outsiders had and continues to have a "good news" flip side with enormously important implications: well-established religious organizations do not lose many people to their competitors. Maybe the Canadian situation is unique, and maybe it's not. But the proverbial bottom line here is that, on the "demand side," Canadians are reluctant to try just any supplier. Most tenaciously stick with the choices of their parents and grandparents' traditions. In the last part of the 20th century, no new or old religious "company" made significant headway in moving in and recruiting Catholics and Protestants who, ostensibly, were no longer involved in their respective groups.[4] What's more, there is little indication that such a preference for the groups of their parents and grandparents is about to change.

Consequently, for well-established religious organizations that want to grow, the starting point should be obvious: they need to relate to those uninvolved Canadians with whom they have the greatest affinity—those millions of people who identify with their traditions, people who "think" they are Roman Catholic, United, Baptist, Lutheran, Jewish, and so on.

As obvious as such a point should have been, it was almost obliterated in recent decades by the debilitating myths of switching, drop-out, and non-receptivity. If these were merely issued to be debated at professional meetings by academics, it wouldn't matter. Unfortunately, however, these have been "very bad myths" because of the practical implications they have had for how leaders have carried out ministry—who, for example, they have targeted and what they have brought to them. To the extent that leaders have accepted the

three myths, explicit strategies for finding affiliates and ministering to them have seldom been formulated and put into place. In the process, they have blown their competitive advantage. The myths that have led to this debacle are so distracting and unproductive that it's worth looking at them more closely.[5]

MYTH NO. 1: PEOPLE ARE SWITCHING

In recent years, some congregational experts and academics in North America—notably, Lyle Schaller and Robert Wuthnow—have led the way in propagating the idea that there has been a sharp decline in the importance being given to religious group loyalties. People are said to be abandoning allegiances to individual Protestant denominations and even to broader religious families such as Protestantism and Catholicism.[6] Congregational gurus tell us that North Americans who continue to want to participate in religious groups are commonly gravitating toward churches that are in touch with their needs, and they are showing little concern for denominational and religious family labels.[7] Such an alleged decline in religious group loyalties is seen as consistent with a more general decline in loyalty to institutions of all types over the last half of this century.[8] Themes such as freedom, inclusiveness, and the dismantling of boundaries are widespread. The saints are said to be circulating freely....

Consistent with what I have been saying, basic learning in sociology suggests there is little reason to expect that large amounts of prounounced religious switching will take place. In view of the pervasive tendency of children to identify with the religion of their parents, switching almost amounts to a form of deviant behaviour.... We all know that the prospect of ... intermarital "defection" is frequently greeted with a wide range of social controls, ranging from stigma to ostracism, particularly when the potential partner is a fair distance removed from one's religious "home."

The inclination to switch is also limited to the reality of cultural commonality. Most people attended services with some regularity when they were growing up. The majority turn to their identification groups when they require rites of passage, want to attend a seasonal service, or feel the need to expose their children to religious activities. That's why people see the religious cultures of their groups as normative. That's why they feel comfortable or uncomfortable in certain worship settings... prefer hymns and pipe organ to songs and a band, appreciate or feel disdain for a written prayer, feel reverence as they look at candles versus laser lights, kneel rather than stand, bow their heads versus raise their arms, pray silently or pray loudly. Culturally, it's a substantial stretch to move from a Jewish to a Pentecostal world—or even from a United to a Baptist world—and vice versa.

Our current emphases on inclusiveness and acceptance of religious diversity should not blind us to another ongoing reality: there are some people who are not interested in turning elsewhere for the simple reason that they favour their groups' versions of truth. So it is that an 82-year-old Catholic from rural Nova Scotia—who, incidentally, has participated in all of our *Project Canada* surveys dating back to 1975 when he was in his late 50s—told us that he was not comfortable going to a Protestant church, not because of bigotry but because "I cannot in good conscience take part in a non-Catholic service. I can go to a funeral of a friend, but I cannot participate in the service." His age notwithstanding, this candid individual is not alone.

As a result of such social and personal factors, there is little reason to believe that Canadians are open to being recruited by other groups, especially those with whom they have few common theological and cultural ties. To the extent that switching occurs at all, it would be expected both to be limited and to follow fairly predictable lines of affinity. People would be expected to circulate primarily among "the religious families" of their parents.

But don't take my word for it. Let's listen to what Canadians have been saying.

Intergroup Switching

For all the rhetoric about evangelism, outreach, and seeker-sensitive ministries, Canadians who are not actively involved in churches (a) are seldom recruited by such aggressive "outside" groups and (b) if they do become involved, tend to become involved with groups with which they already identify.[9]

Our *Project Canada* surveys show that in the course of acquiring a religious identification, most people continue to more or less "inherit" the religion of their parents, with relatively few switching to other religious families.

- Approximately nine in ten *Catholics in Quebec* and eight in ten *Catholics in the rest of the country* identify with the religion of their parents. To the extent that they don't, the tendency is to say they have no religion.

- The same pattern characterizes some 80% of people from *Mainline Protestant* homes, as well as roughly 70% of Canadians whose parents identified with *Conservative Protestant* or *Other Faith* groups.

- To the extent that people with *Conservative Protestant* backgrounds switch, they tend to move into *Mainline Protestant* denominations.

- The *Religious None* category is characterized by a very high level of switching in and switching out. This category is more like a hotel than a home for many people.

This is not to say that religious switching never takes place. Obviously, some people cross family lines. But proportionately speaking, switching is the exception rather than the norm, particularly among the largest religious families, Catholics and Mainliners....

In the 2000 *Project Canada* survey, we bluntly asked Canadians two questions pertaining to religious identification: *"How important is your religious tradition to you (that is, being Catholic, United, Buddhist, etc.)?"* and *"Are you open to*

Table 36.2   Extent and Nature of Intergenerational Switching, 2000

Respondent's Religion	RC	MLPROT	CPROT	OTHER	NONE
Mother's Religion					
RCs outside Quebec	80%	4%	1%	3%	12%
RCs in Quebec	89	<1	<1	1	9
Mainline Protestants	6	78	4	3	9
Conservative Protestants	<1	18	71	<1	11
Other Faiths	7	4	<1	71	18
No Religion	11	11	5	<1	73
Father's Religion					
RCs outside Quebec	80	7	<1	2	10
RCs in Quebec	91	<1	<1	<1	8
Mainline Protestants	4	82	4	2	8
Conservative Protestants	<1	14	76	<1	10
Other Faiths	8	4	<1	80	8
No Religion	20	13	4	5	58

Source: Bibby, Project Canada 2000.

the possibility of switching to a different tradition?"

- Some six in ten Canadians who identify with a religious group say that their religious tradition is "very important" or "somewhat important" to them, including 92% of *weekly attenders* and 50% of those who attend less often. Variations between religious families tend to be fairly small.

- More than eight in ten people say they are not open to the possibility of switching to a different tradition, led by 97% of *Quebec Catholics*. But here, differences by attendance are small: infrequent attenders are only moderately less likely to be closed to the idea of switching traditions—and in Quebec, there is no difference by attendance! As Ron Graham has observed about the legacy of Catholicism in Quebec, "Three centuries of mysticism do not evaporate in three decades of materialism."[10]

- Although the *Other Faith* sample is small, the preliminary evidence is that this is the category most vulnerable to "defections." Still, even here, resistance to switching characterizes the majority of people.

A Footnote for the Critics

Invariably, some people will say they know of exceptions to the rule. Of course, exceptions exist. I'm not saying that switching never occurs—only that it is relatively rare. And switching typically involves fairly short theologi-

Table 36.3   Intergenerational Identification by Religious Families: Panel, 1975 and 1995

1975 IDENTIFICATION	NUMBER	STAYED	SWITCHED TO:				
			MLPROT	CPROT	RC	OTHER	NONE
Mainline Protestant	196	88%		4	3	2	3
Conservative Protestant	31	83	11		<1	6	0
Roman Catholic	102	90	3	4		2	1
Other Faith	15	63	5	22	5		5
No Religion	19	39	33	<1	28	<1	
Totals*	363	85	4	4	3	2	2

*Identification data for 1975 or 1995 missing for 37 respondents.

Source: Bibby, 1999: 157.

Table 36.4   Importance of Tradition and Openness to Switching Traditions

	NAT	RCOQ	RCQ	MLPROT	CPROT	OF
Tradition Important						
"Very" or "Somewhat"	61%	70%	62%	54%	72%	53%
Weekly attenders	92	96	96	93	85	*
Others attending less often	50	57	52	46	55	*
Open to Switching						
"No"	83	87	97	75	81	61
Weekly attenders	92	93	98	86	87	*
Others attending less often	80	83	97	72	72	*

*Numbers insufficient to permit stable percentaging.

Source: Bibby, Project Canada 2000.

cal and cultural trips. As American sociologists Dean Hoge, Ben Johnson, and Don Luidens have pointed out, the size of our *tolerance zones* for acceptable religious traditions appears to exceed

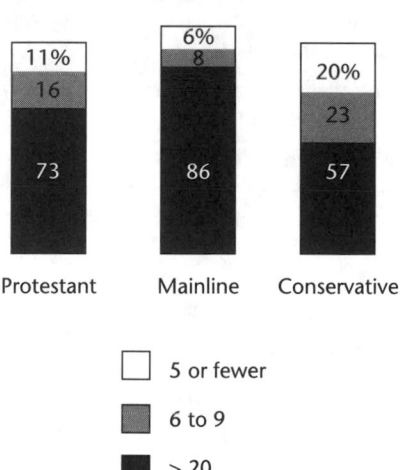

Figure 36.1 Years of Denominational Involvement

Monthly-Plus Attenders

Protestant   Mainline   Conservative

☐ 5 or fewer

▨ 6 to 9

■ > 20

Nearly 75% of Protestants, led by Mainliners, have been with their current denominations for more than 20 years. Taking age into account, Mainline Protestants on average have been involved with their current denominations for 80% of their lives, Conservatives for only 57%. Much of the Conservative switching between denominations, however, is within "the family," where choices outnumber those available to Mainliners.

Source: Bibby, Project Canada 2000.

our personal *comfort zones* with those traditions. They noted in the case of Presbyterian Baby Boomers, for example, that tolerance zones have expanded over the years, whereas personal comfort zones "are surprisingly narrow and traditional." "For the great majority," they wrote, "the comfort zone extends no farther than Mainline Protestantism, and quite a few draw the line at the Episcopal [Anglican] Church.[11] Sociologists Kirk Hadaway and Penny Marler have concluded that "when Americans do switch, they often remain within the same broad denominational family."[12] It's not that North Americans never switch groups: at least 40% of people in both Canada and the United States have switched denominations at one time or another.[13] However, as Hadaway and Marler have put it, "Americans switch more today than they did in the early 1970s, but when they switch they are more likely to remain in the same larger denominational family."[14]...

The same patterns of limited switching and switching within religious families appear to hold for Canada. The decline in active participation has not been associated with a widespread tendency for Canadians to move to other religious families, or to the No Religion category. In marketing language, the religious economy of Canada continues to be characterized by a very tight market, where the expansion of market shares through the recruitment of people from rival groups is extremely difficult. To the extent that switching does take place, it follows fairly predictable lines of affinity, frequently associated with the breaking down of family-related "social controls." But overall, the market is not particularly open; intergroup movement is very limited.

MYTH NO. 2: PEOPLE ARE DROPPING OUT

Closely related to the loyalty myth is the belief that if people are not attending on a regular basis, they have dropped out. Here it is assumed that identification without involvement simply doesn't count. If, for example, someone says that she or he is an "Anglican" or "Roman Catholic" or "Pentecostal" but seldom attends a service, such a self-designation is typically assumed to mean very little. In part, this is a theological assumption: if people are not involved, they have abandoned the faith. Policy-wise, such individuals are typically viewed by leaders as "unchurched" and, as such, are seen as "up for grabs" in the competitive religious marketplace. Officially, they are the prime targets of groups whose ministries are aimed at evangelism and service.

On the surface, the assumption that people have dropped out seems to be reasonable. If they aren't coming, they must have left. The assumption has led to common dichotomous classifications along the lines of "churched–unchurched," "active–inactive," and "practising–lapsed"—not to mention more pejorative dualities such as "saved–unsaved" and "saint–sinner." Even though this dropping-out myth is older, it has been reinforced by the more recent myth about loyalty

decline. People are assumed to be dropping out in part because they have little group loyalty, and it is thought that where they attend next will not, in turn, be guided by group loyalty, but by a consumer-like response to the group that comes up with the most attractive and engaging offer.

Religious Identification

In contrast to radically declining attendance figures, religious identification in Canada stood at 88% in 1991 and at about 85% in 2000. But individuals who indicate that they have "no religion" tend to be disproportionately young. Research shows that such a situation is short-lived for many, who frequently re-adopt the religious group identification of their parents in the course of requesting and receiving religious rites of passage.[15] Their links to their parents' religious groups appear to be sustained not so much by religious content as by family history and these rites of passage.

What is perhaps rather remarkable is not that large numbers of North Americans *identify but are not involved*, but rather that they continue to *identify even though they are not involved*. They can be chastised, ignored, and removed from congregational lists—and they frequently are. But still, they don't really leave. Psychologically, emotionally, and culturally, they continue to identify with the traditions of their childhood.

The Meaning of Religious Identification

The *Project Canada* surveys have also asked respondents directly about their inclination to stay versus switching or dropping out, while

Table 36.5 Accuracy of the Religious Identification Statement: Canadians Identifying and Attending Less Than Monthly, 1985 and 2000

	NAT	RCOQ	RCQ	MLPROT	CPROT	OF
1985	87	84	94	88	86	74
2000	85	89	88	82	86	70

Source: Bibby, Project Can85 and Project Canada 2000.

probing the meaning of their ongoing involvement. Beginning with the 1985 national survey, respondents "not attending religious services regularly" were asked "how well" the following observation describes them:

Some observers maintain that few people are actually abandoning their religious traditions. Rather, they draw selective beliefs and practices, even if they do not attend services frequently. They are not about to be recruited by other religious groups. Their identification with their religious tradition is fairly solidly fixed, and it is to these groups that they will turn when confronted with marriage, death, and, frequently, birth.

Through 2000, about 85% of Canadians who *identify but attend less than monthly* have said that the statement describes them either "very accurately" or "somewhat accurately." Nationally, there has been little change since the mid-80s in the tendency of inactive attenders to acknowledge the accuracy of the description.

It adds up to a situation where, beyond the 20% or so Canadians who attend services almost every week or more, there are another 60%-plus who continue to identify with the country's dominant traditions. Most people in this latter category attend occasionally, believe and practise selectively, are not about to be recruited by alternatives, and are looking to their identification groups for rites of passage. They most definitely have not "dropped out."

As I mentioned at the outset of this chapter, the confusion over switchers and drop-outs involves far more than academic wrangling. It has critically important implications for how religious groups relate to Canadians. If groups see the religious market as essentially wide open, Americans and Canadians will be viewed as religious free agents who can be recruited through effective ministry and evangelism. The problem with such a viewpoint is that it will result in congregations wasting much of their recruitment resources. More seriously, Canadians who might benefit from good ministry will not be identified and pursued.

In contrast, if religious groups would concentrate less on the switcher and drop-out exceptions and more on "the on-going identification rule," they would be in a position to target the very people to whom they have the best chance of ministering—the women and men who already identify with them. Identification represents a measure of affinity; as such, it is the logical place to begin in connecting with people.

Figure 36.2   "Thinking Concentrically" about Religion Identification

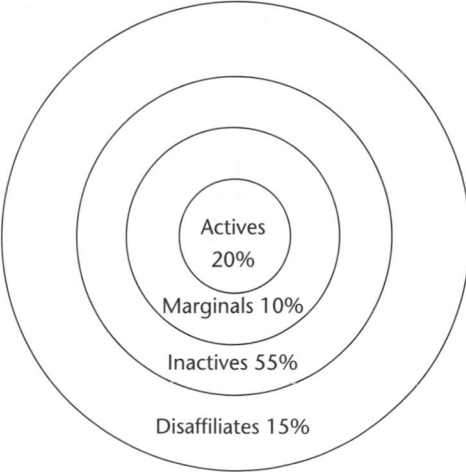

Source: Bibby, 1995: 49.

Table 36.6   Receptivity to Greater Involvement: People Attending Less Than Monthly, 2000

	Adults	Teens
NATIONALLY	55%	39%
Roman Catholics	56	46
Quebec	55	41
Outside Quebec	56	51
Protestants	64	47
Mainline	63	44
Conservative	73*	55
Other Faiths	67*	4
No Religion	34	21

*Numbers only 16 and 33, respectively; percentages unstable. Included here for heuristic purposes.

Sources: Bibby, Project Canada 2000 and Project Teen Canada 2000.

Given the pervasiveness of ongoing religious identification, congregations would be wise to follow Kirk Hadaway's lead in seeing their members and others who identify with their denomination as a series of concentric rings, ranging from active members at the centre through less active individuals to an outer ring of reactive people.[16] Working with such a model, congregations need to develop creative strategies for finding people, exploring their interests and needs, and responding—doing tangible things that I discuss in detail in my 1995 book *There's Got to Be More!*

MYTH NO. 3: PEOPLE ARE NOT RECEPTIVE

One of the most common observations I have heard over the years from religious leaders and from the media is that people "just aren't interested in organized religion anymore." Such a statement is a gross overgeneralization.

As mentioned briefly earlier in the context of Catholicism in Quebec, the latest *Project Canada* national surveys of adults and teenagers have uncovered a finding that speaks volumes about the opportunity that is staring the country's religious groups in the face. In the adult survey, Canadians who attend services less than once a month were asked, *"Would you consider the possibility of being more involved in a religious group if you found it to be worthwhile for yourself or your family?"* The teen survey posed much the same question, asking young people to respond to the statement, *"I'd be open to more involvement with religious groups if I found it to be worthwhile."*[17] Keeping in mind that only 21% of adults and 22% of teens are currently weekly attenders, it's highly significant that 55% of adults and 39% of teens answered yes.

- Across adult religious families, the receptivity levels are about 55%, even among Quebec Catholics. What's more, one in three Canadians who say they have no religious affiliation maintain that they would be receptive to greater involvement in a religious group "if..."
- Among 15-to-19-year-olds, the receptivity levels are some 40% or more across groups, with about one in five teens with no religious affiliation saying they are open to more involvement.

Rather than acting either hostile or indifferent to their identification groups, significant numbers of people are obviously receptive to greater participation. The 55% figure for adults represents almost three times the number who indicate they are currently highly involved; the teen figure is almost double the proportion of young people who presently attend weekly.

- Those 55% of adults who say they would consider being more involved in the country's religious

Table 36.7   Receptivity to Greater Involvement by Select Variables, 2000

	NAT (764)	RCOQ (133)	RCQ (143)	PROT (270)	NONE (160)
TOTALS	57%	56%	55%	64%	34%
Yearly	64	64	57	72	48
Never	36	42	33	42	27
18–34	59	58	61	79	42
35–54	57	64	56	66	27
55+	49	*	52	55	23
Female	56	62	53	71	30
Male	56	57	61	58	39

*Numbers insufficient to permit stable percentaging.

Source: Bibby, Project Canada 2000.

groups include some two in three of the people who attend several times a year to yearly; and one in three who say they never attend.

- They are most frequently found in the 18-to-34 and 35-to-44 age cohorts, with receptivity particularly common among younger Protestant adults.

- Males and females are equally likely to indicate that they are open to greater involvement, although there are some variations between groups....

These findings suggest that noteworthy numbers of Canadians are receptive to greater involvement in the country's religious groups. However, the findings also point to a critical qualifier: people have to find that such involvement is worthwhile for themselves and their families. The observation of a mother of three from Saskatchewan illustrates the hurdles that need to be overcome: "We don't attend often and when we do, it leaves much to be desired." The obvious, burning question is, "What do such people see as worthwhile?" A 66-year-old disenchanted Anglican from Vancouver provides us with a key clue: "Their role should be to minister to people who need them."...

One additional piece of information that has emerged from the national adult and youth surveys speaks not only to receptivity but also to accessibility. Canadians young and old are continuing to look to religious groups for rites of passage.

- Almost nine in ten teenagers indicate they anticipate turning to religious groups for future ceremonies relating to marriage and funerals, and seven in ten say the same in the case of births—a response very similar to levels in the mid-1980s.

- In the case of adults, the levels of anticipated weddings, birth-related ceremonies, and funerals are all up, compared to the mid-80s.

As I have emphasized over the years, these Canadians' choices will not be random. The latent religious identification we have been documenting in this chapter will come to the surface during those times when couples are reflecting on what kind of wedding they want, what should "be done" now that the baby has arrived, or what kind of arrangements should be made for a relative's funeral. And it's not necessarily a case of just bowing to family pressures. Ministers frequently encounter people who, frankly, have little understanding of theology, yet have a sometimes vaguely articulated sense that "God needs to be brought in on the event."[18] With respect to accessibility, think what the desire for rites of passage means: religious groups will not have to go out and find these people; they will be taking the initiative in contacting groups. To put it mildly, such a position would be envied by any number of businesses in the corporate sector.

To sum up, the findings so far show that the "supply side" of religion, the country's churches,

Table 36.8   Desire for Rites of Passage in the Future

"In the future, do you anticipate having any of the following carried out for you by a minister, priest, rabbi, or some other religious figure?"

% Responding "Yes"	Wedding Ceremony	Birth-Related Ceremony	Funeral
Teenagers			
1980s*	87	76	87
2000	89	70	86
Adults			
1980s	19	14	44
2000	24	20	57

*1980s teen data computed from Project Teen Canada 87. "Don't know"s have been included with "no"s; otherwise the respective figures increase to 93%, 85%, and 93%.
Sources: Bibby, Project Teen Canada 2000, Project Can 85, and Project Canada 2000.

have not read the "demand side" very well. At least three major myths have functioned as serious obstacles to effective ministry. The fact that affiliates have refused to switch and haven't dropped out has been bewildering and frustrating to would-be religious competitors who have misread their market opportunity. But more seriously, because misinformed established groups have failed to understand their market advantage, significant numbers of affiliates who need ministry have not been reached by Canada's dominant religious groups....

NOTES

1. Bibby, 1997.
2. *Project Canada* Quota Sample, Winter, 2001–02.
3. For documentation, see Bibby, 1993: 29ff.
4. For a discussion of this failure, see Beyer, 1997: 284ff.
5. Much of the following material dealing with Myths No. 1 and No. 2 is based on Bibby, 1999.
6. See, for example, Schaller, 1987; Wuthnow, 1988; Mead, 1991; Posterski & Barker, 1993; Hoge, Johnson, & Luidens, 1994.
7. See, for example, Barna, 1991; Anderson, 1992; Easum, 1993; Schaller, 1995; Woods, 1996; Bandy, 1997.
8. Americans such as Robert Bellah (1985) and his associates have written that accelerated individualism has been severely threatening group life at all levels, while Allan Bloom (1987) similarly claimed that the individualistic and relativistic legacies of the 1960s have been devastating for relationships and disastrous for institutions. In Canada, Peter C. Newman (1995) maintains that nothing short of a revolution took place between the mid-1980s and 90s, characterized by Canadians moving from a mood of "deference to defiance" in virtually every area of life. I myself (1990) have similarly noted that individualism and relativism have functioned to severely fragment Canadian society, creating unity problems well beyond the threat of Quebec separation.
9. Bibby, 1993: 32, 36–37. According to observers such as Demerath and Yang (1997:5), the situation is similar in the United States as well.
10. Graham, 1990: 123.
11. Hoge, Johnson, & Luidens, 1994: 120.
12. Hadaway & Marler, 1993: 97.
13. Roof & McKinney, 1987: 167; Posterski & Barker, 1993: 51.
14. Hadaway & Marler, 1993: 102.
15. For details, see Bibby, 1993: 157–59.
16. Hadaway, 1990: 46.

17. The adult survey response options were "Yes," "Perhaps," and "No"; receptivity levels combine "Yes" and "Perhaps." In the youth survey, the options were "Strongly Agree," "Agree," "Disagree," and "Strongly Disagree," with receptivity levels being a combination of "Strongly Agree" and "Agree."
18. Bibby, 2001: 118, 197.

REFERENCES

Anderson, L. 1992. *A church for the 21st century.* Minneapolis: Bethany House.

Bandy, T. G. 1997. *Kicking habits: Welcome relief for addicted churches.* Nashville: Abingdon.

Barna, G. 1991. *User friendly churches.* Ventura, Calif.: Regal Books.

Bellah, R., R. Madsen, W. Sullivan, A. Swidler, and S. Tipton. 1985. *Habits of the heart.* New York: Harper and Row.

Beyer, P. 1997. Religious vitality in Canada. *Journal for the Scientific Study of Religion,* 36: 272–88.

Bibby, R. W. 1990. *Mosaic madness: Pluralism without a cause.* Toronto: Stoddart.

———. 1993. *Unknown gods: The ongoing story of religion in Canada.* Toronto: Stoddart.

———. 1997. Going, going, gone: The impact of geographical mobility on religious involvement. *Review of Religious Research,* 38: 289–307.

———. 1999. On boundaries, gates, and circulating saints: A longitudinal look at loyalty and loss. *Review of Religious Research,* 40: 149–64.

———. 2001. *Canada's teens: Today, yesterday, and tomorrow.* Toronto: Stoddart.

Bloom, A. 1987. *The closing of the American mind.* New York: Simon and Schuster.

Demerath, N. J. III, and Y. Yang. 1997. A religious change and changing religions: Who's switching where and why? Paper presented at the annual meeting of the SSSR, San Diego (November).

Easum, B. 1993. *Dancing with dinosaurs.* Nashville: Abingdon.

Graham, R. 1990. *God's dominion: A sceptic's quest.* Toronto: McClelland and Stewart.

Hadaway, C. K. 1990. *What can we do about church dropouts?* Nashville: Abingdon.

Hadaway, C. K., and P. L. Marler. 1993. All in the family: Religious mobility in America. *Review of Religious Research,* 35: 97–116.

Hoge, D. R., B. Johnson, and D. A. Luidens. 1994. *Vanishing Boundaries*. Louisville, Ky.: Westminster/John Knox Press.

Mead, L. B. 1991. *The once and future church*. Washington, D.C.: The Alban Institute.

Newman, P. C. 1995. *The Canadian revolution: From deference to defiance*. Toronto: Viking.

Posterski, D. C., and I. Barker. 1993. *Where's a good church?* Winfield, B.C.: Wood Lake Books.

Roof, W. C., and W. McKinney. 1987. *American mainline religion*. New Brunswick, N.J.: Rutgers University Press.

Schaller, L. E. 1987. *It's a different world: The challenge of today's pastor*. Nashville: Abingdon.

———. 1995. *The new reformation: Tomorrow arrived yesterday*. Nashville: Abingdon.

Woods, C. J. 1996. *Congregational megatrends*. Betheseda, Md.: The Alban Institute.

Wuthnow, R. 1988. *The restructuring of American religion*. Princeton, N.J.: Princeton University Press.

Part XVIII

Education

37

Education and Inequality

Samuel Bowles and Herbert Gintis

Universal education is the power, which is destined to overthrow every species of hierarchy. It is destined to remove all artificial inequality and leave the natural inequalities to find their true level. With the artificial inequalities of caste, rank, title, blood, birth, race, color, sex, etc., will fall nearly all the oppression, abuse, prejudice, enmity, and injustice, that humanity is now subject to.
—*Lester Frank Ward,* Education, 1872

A review of educational history hardly supports the optimistic pronouncements of liberal educational theory. The politics of education are better understood in terms of the need for social control in an unequal and rapidly changing economic order. The founders of the modern U.S. school system understood that the capitalist economy produces great extremes of wealth and poverty, of social elevation

Source: From *Schooling in Capitalist America: Educational Reform and the Contradictions of Economic Life* by Samuel Bowles and Herbert Gintis. Copyright © 1976 by Basic Books, Inc. Reprinted with permission of Basic Books, Inc., a division of HarperCollins Publishers, Inc.

and degradation. Horace Mann and other school reformers of the antebellum period knew well the seamy side of the burgeoning industrial and urban centers. "Here," wrote Henry Barnard, the first state superintendent of education in both Connecticut and Rhode Island, and later to become the first U.S. Commissioner of Education, "the wealth, enterprise and professional talent of the state are concentrated...but here also are poverty, ignorance, profligacy and irreligion, and a classification of society as broad and deep as ever divided the plebeian and patrician of ancient Rome."[1] They lived in a world in which, to use de Tocqueville's words, "...small aristocratic societies...are formed by some manufacturers in the midst of the immense democracy of our age [in which]...some men are opulent and a multitude...are wretchedly poor."[2] The rapid rise of the factory system, particularly in New England, was celebrated by the early school reformers; yet, the alarming transition from a relatively simple rural society to a highly stratified industrial economy could not be ignored. They shared the fears that de Tocqueville had expressed following his visit to the United States in 1831:

When a workman is unceasingly and exclusively engaged in the fabrication of one thing, he ultimately does his work with singular dexterity; but at the same time he loses the general faculty of applying his mind to the direction of the work.... [While] the science of manufacture lowers the class of workmen, it raises the class of masters.... [If] ever a permanent inequality of conditions...again penetrates into the world, it may be predicted that this is the gate by which they will enter.[3]

While deeply committed to the emerging industrial order, the farsighted school reformers of the mid-nineteenth century understood the explosive potential of the glaring inequalities of factory life. Deploring the widening of social divisions and fearing increasing unrest, Mann, Barnard, and others proposed educational expansion and reform. In his Fifth Report as Secretary of the Massachusetts Board of Education, Horace Mann wrote:

Education, then beyond all other devices of human origin, is the great equalizer of the conditions of men—the balance wheel of the social machinery.... It does better than to disarm the poor of their hostility toward the rich; it prevents being poor.[4]

Mann and his followers appeared to be at least as interested in disarming the poor as in preventing poverty. They saw in the spread of universal and free education a means of alleviating social distress without redistributing wealth and power or altering the broad outlines of the economic system. Education, it seems, had almost magical powers:

The main idea set forth in the creeds of some political reformers, or revolutionizers, is, that some people are poor because others are rich. This idea supposed a fixed amount of property in the community...and the problem presented for solution is, how to transfer a portion of this property from those who are supposed to have too much to those who feel and know that they have too little. At this point, both their theory and their expectation of reform stop. But the beneficent power of education would not be exhausted, even though it should peaceably abolish all the miseries that spring from the coexistence, side by side, of enormous wealth and squalid want. It has a higher function. Beyond the power of diffusing old wealth, it has the prerogative of creating new.[5]

The early educators viewed the poor as the foreign element that they were. Mill hands were recruited throughout New England, often disrupting the small towns in which textile and other rapidly growing industries had located. Following the Irish potato famine of the 1840s, thousands of Irish workers settled in the cities and towns of the northeastern United States. Schooling was seen as a means of integrating this "uncouth and dangerous" element into the social fabric of American life. The inferiority of the foreigner was taken for granted. The editors of the influential *Massachusetts Teacher,* a leader in the educational reform movement, writing in 1851, saw "...the increasing influx of foreigners..." as a moral and social problem:

Will it, like the muddy Missouri, as it pours its waters into the clear Mississippi and contaminates the whole united mass, spread ignorance and vice, crime and disease, through our native population?

If...we can by any means purify this foreign people, enlighten their ignorance and bring them up to our level, we shall perform a work of true and perfect charity, blessing the giver and receiver in equal measure....

With the old not much can be done; but with their children, the great remedy is *education.* The rising generation must be taught as our own children are taught. We say *must be* because in many cases this can only be accomplished by coercion.[6]

Since the mid-nineteenth century the dual objectives of educational reformers—equality of opportunity and social control—have been intermingled, the merger of these two threads sometimes so nearly complete that it becomes impossible to distinguish between the two. Schooling has been at once something done for the poor and to the poor.

The basic assumptions which underlay this commingling help explain the educational reform movement's social legacy. First, educational reformers did not question the fundamental economic institutions of capitalism: Capitalist ownership and control of the means of production and dependent wage labor were taken for granted. In fact, education was to help preserve and extend the capitalist order. The function of the school system was to accommodate workers to its most rapid possible development. Second, it was assumed that people (often classes of people or "races") are differentially equipped by nature or social origins to occupy the varied economic and social levels in the class structure. By providing equal opportunity, the school system was to elevate the masses, guiding them sensibly and fairly to the manifold political, social, and economic roles of adult life.

Jefferson's educational thought strikingly illustrates this perspective. In 1779, he proposed a two-track educational system which would prepare individuals for adulthood in one of the two classes of society: the "laboring and the learned."[7] Even children of the laboring class would qualify for leadership. Scholarships would allow "...those persons whom nature hath endowed with genius and virtue..." to "...be rendered by liberal education worthy to receive and able to guard the sacred deposit of the rights and liberties of their fellow citizens."[8] Such a system, Jefferson asserted, would succeed in "...raking a few geniuses from the rubbish."[9] Jefferson's two-tiered educational plan presents in stark relief the outlines and motivation for the stratified structure of U.S. education which has endured up to the present. At the top, there is the highly selective aristocratic tradition, the elite university training future leaders. At the base is mass education for all, dedicated to uplift and control. The two traditions have always coexisted although their meeting point has drifted upward over the years, as mass education has spread upward from elementary school through high school, and now up to the post-high-school level.

Though schooling was consciously molded to reflect the class structure, education was seen as a means of enhancing wealth and morality, which would work to the advantage of all. Horace Mann, in his 1842 report to the State Board of Education, reproduced this comment by a Massachusetts industrialist:

The great majority always have been and probably always will be comparatively poor, while a few will possess the greatest share of this world's goods. And it is a wise provision of Providence which connects so intimately, and as I think so indissolubly, the greatest good of the many with the highest interests in the few.[10]

Much of the content of education over the past century and a half can only be construed as an unvarnished attempt to persuade the "many" to make the best of the inevitable.

The unequal contest between social control and social justice is evident in the total functioning of U.S. education. The system as it stands today provides eloquent testimony to the ability of the well-to-do to perpetuate in the name of equality of opportunity an arrangement which consistently yields to themselves disproportional advantages, while thwarting the aspirations and needs of the working people of the United States. However grating this judgment may sound to the ears of the undaunted optimist, it is by no means excessive in light of the massive statistical data on inequality in the United States. Let us look at the contemporary evidence.

We may begin with the basic issue of inequalities in the years of schooling. As can be seen in [Figure 37.1], the number of years of schooling attained by an individual is strongly associated with parental socioeconomic status. This figure presents the estimated distribution of years of schooling attained by individuals of varying socioeconomic backgrounds. If we define socioeconomic background by a weighted sum of income, occupation, and educational level of the parents, a child from the ninetieth percentile may expect, on the average, five more years of schooling than a child in the tenth percentile.[11]

...We have chosen a sample of white males because the most complete statistics are available for this group. Moreover, if inequality for white males can be documented, the proposition is merely strengthened when sexual and racial differences are taken into account.

FIGURE 37.1   Educational Attainments Are Strongly Dependent on Social Background
Even for People of Similar Childhood IQs

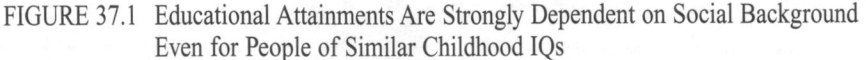

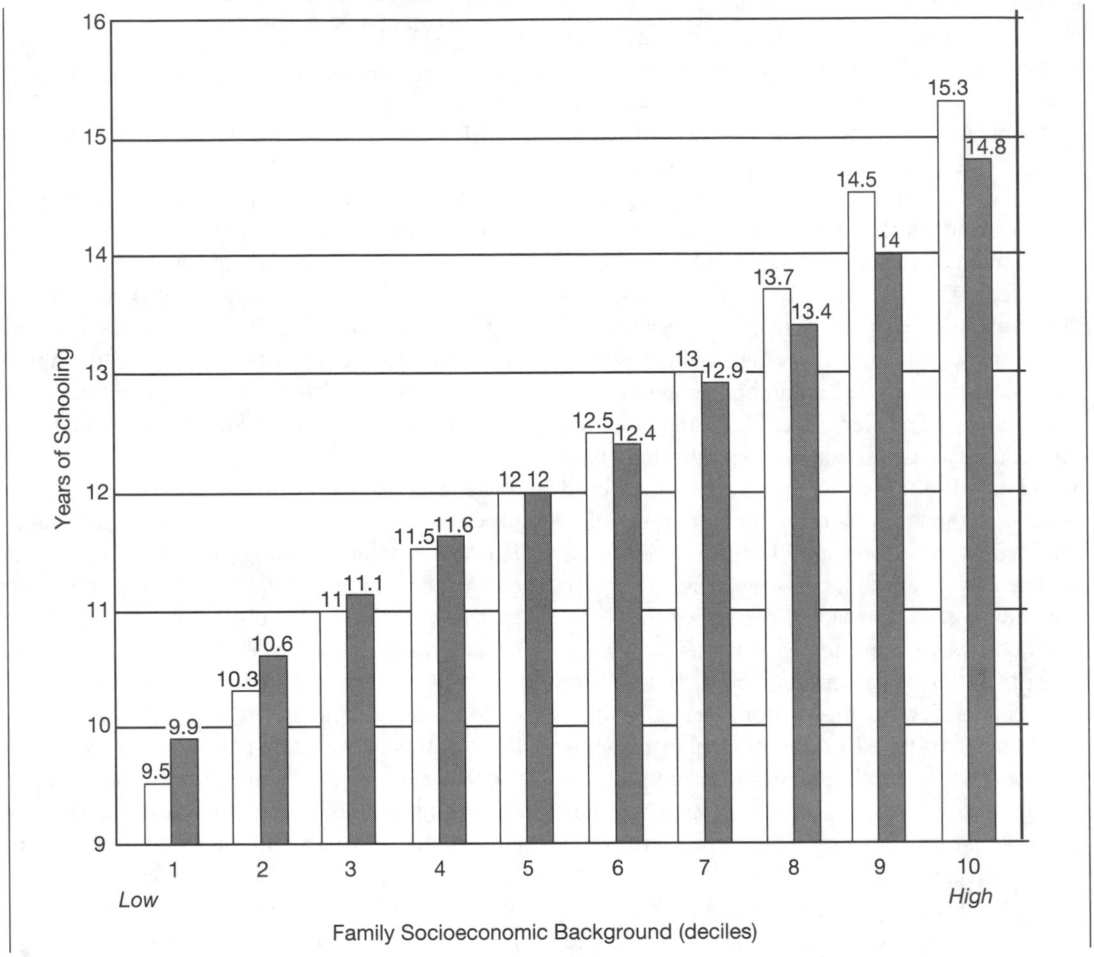

Notes: For each socioeconomic group, the left-hand bar indicates the estimated average number of years of schooling attained by all men from that group. The right-hand bar indicates the estimated average number of years of schooling attained by men with IQ scores equal to the average for the entire sample. The sample refers to "non-Negro" men of "nonfarm" backgrounds, aged 35–44 years in 1962.

Source: Samuel Bowles and Valerie Nelson, "The 'Inheritance of IQ' and the Intergenerational Transmission of Economic Inequality," *The Review of Economics and Statistics,* vol. LVI, no. 1 (Feb. 1974).

Additional census data dramatize one aspect of educational inequalities: the relationship between family income and college attendance. Even among those who had graduated from high school in the early 1960s, children of families earning less than $3,000 per year were over six times as likely *not* to attend college as were the children of families earning over $15,000.[12] Moreover, children from less well-off families are *both* less likely to have graduated from high school and more likely to attend inexpensive, two-year community colleges rather than a four-year B.A. program if they do make it to college.[13]

Not surprisingly, the results of schooling differ greatly for children of different social backgrounds. Most easily measured, but of limited importance, are differences in scholastic achievement. If we measure the output of schooling by scores on nationally standardized achievement tests, children whose parents were themselves highly educated outperform the children of parents with less education by a wide margin. Data collected for the U.S. Office of Education Survey of Educational Opportunity reveal, for example, that among white high-school seniors, those whose parents were in the top education decile were, on the average, well over three grade levels in measured scholastic achievement ahead of those whose parents were in the bottom decile.[14]

Given these differences in scholastic achievement, inequalities in years of schooling among individuals of different social backgrounds are to be expected. Thus one might be tempted to argue that the close dependence of years of schooling attained on background displayed in the left-hand bars of [Figure 55.1] is simply a reflection of unequal intellectual abilities, or that inequalities in college attendance are the consequences of differing levels of scholastic achievement in high school and do not reflect any additional social class inequalities peculiar to the process of college admission.

This view, so comforting to the admissions personnel in our elite universities, is unsupported by the data, some of which is presented in [the figure]. The right-hand bars of [the figure] indicate that even among children with identical IQ test scores at ages six and eight, those with rich, well-educated, high-status parents could expect a much higher level of schooling than those with less-favored origins. Indeed, the closeness of the left-hand and right-hand bars in [the figure] shows that only a small portion of the observed social class differences in educational attainment is related to IQ differences across social classes.[15] The dependence of education attained on back-

ground is almost as strong for individuals with the same IQ as for all individuals. Thus, while [the figure] indicates that an individual in the ninetieth percentile in social class background is likely to receive five more years of education than an individual in the tenth percentile, it also indicates that he is likely to receive 4.25 more years schooling than an individual from the tenth percentile with the same IQ. Similar results are obtained when we look specifically at access to college education for students with the same measured IQ. Project Talent data indicates that for "high ability" students (top 25 percent as measured by a composite of tests of "general aptitude"), those of high socioeconomic background (top 25 percent as measured by a composite of family income, parents' education, and occupation) are nearly twice as likely to attend college than students of low socioeconomic background (bottom 25 percent). For "low ability" students (bottom 25 percent), those of high-social background are more than four times as likely to attend college as are their low-social background counterparts.[16]

Inequality in years of schooling is, of course, only symptomatic of broader inequalities in the educational system. Not only do less well-off children go to school for fewer years, they are treated with less attention (or more precisely, less benevolent attention) when they are there. These broader inequalities are not easily measured. Some show up in statistics on the different levels of expenditure for the education of children of different socioeconomic backgrounds. Taking account of the inequality in financial resources for each year in school and the inequality in years of schooling obtained, Jencks estimated that a child whose parents were in the top fifth of the income distribution receives roughly twice the educational resources in dollar terms as does a child whose parents are in the bottom fifth.[17]

The social class inequalities in our school system, then, are too evident to be denied. Defenders of the educational system are forced back on the assertion that things are getting better; the inequalities of the past were far worse. And, indeed, there can be no doubt that some of the inequalities of the past have been mitigated. Yet new inequalities have apparently developed to take their place, for the available historical evidence lends little support to the idea that our schools are on the road to equality of educational opportunity. For example, data from a recent U.S. Census survey reported in Spady indicate that graduation from college has become no less dependent on one's social background. This is true despite the fact that high-school graduation is becoming increasingly equal across social classes.[18] Additional data confirm this impression. The statistical association (coefficient of correlation) between parents' social status and years of education attained by individuals who completed their schooling three or four decades ago is virtually identical to the same correlation for individuals who terminated their schooling in recent years.[19] On balance, the available data suggest that the number of years of school attained by a child depends upon family background as much in the recent period as it did fifty years ago.

Thus, we have empirical reasons for doubting the egalitarian impact of schooling.... We conclude that U.S. education is highly unequal, the chances of attaining much or little schooling being substantially dependent on one's race and parents' economic level. Moreover, where there is a discernible trend toward a more equal educational system—as in the narrowing of the black education deficit, for example—the impact on the structure of economic opportunity is minimal at best.

NOTES

1. H. Barnard, *Papers for the Teacher: 2nd Series* (New York: F. C. Brownell, 1866), pp. 293–310.
2. A. de Tocqueville, as quoted in Jeremy Brecher, *Strike!* (San Francisco: Straight Arrow Books, 1972), pp. xi, xii.
3. Ibid., p. 172.
4. Horace Mann as quoted in Michael Katz, ed., *School Reform Past and Present* (Boston: Little, Brown, 1971), p. 141.
5. Ibid., p. 145.
6. *The Massachusetts Teacher* (Oct., 1851), quoted in Katz, pp. 169–70.
7. D. Tyack, *Turning Points in American Educational History* (Waltham, Mass.: Blaisdell, 1967), p. 89.
8. Ibid., p. 10.
9. Ibid., p. 89.
10. Mann, quoted in Katz, p. 147.
11. This calculation is based on data reported in full in Samuel Bowles and Valerie Nelson, "The 'Inheritance of IQ' and the Intergenerational Transmission of Economic Inequality," *The Review of Economics and Statistics,* 56, 1 (Feb., 1974). It refers to non-Negro males from nonfarm backgrounds, aged 35–44 years. The zero-order correlation coefficient between socioeconomic background and years of schooling was estimated at 0.646. The estimated standard deviation of years of schooling was 3.02. The results for other age groups are similar.
12. These figures refer to individuals who were high-school seniors in October 1965, and who subsequently graduated from high school. College attendance refers to both two- and four-year institutions. Family income is for the twelve months preceding October 1965. Data is drawn from U.S. Bureau of the Census, *Current Population Reports,* Series P-60, No. 183 (May, 1969).
13. For further evidence, see ibid.; and Jerome Karabel, "Community Colleges and Social Stratification," *Harvard Educational Review,* 424, 42 (Nov., 1972).
14. Calculation based on data in James S. Coleman et al., *Equality of Educational Opportunity* (Washington, D.C.: U.S. Government Printing Office, 1966), and the authors.
15. The data relating to IQ are from a 1966 survey of veterans by the National Opinion Research Center; and from N. Bayley and E. S. Schaefer, "Correlations of Maternal and Child Behaviors with the Development of Mental Ability: Data from the Berkeley Growth Study," *Monographs of Social Research in Child Development,* 29, 6 (1964).
16. Based on a large sample of U.S. high-school students as reported in John C. Flannagan and William W. Cooley, *Project Talent, One Year Follow-up Study,* Cooperative Research Project, No. 2333 (Pittsburgh: University of Pittsburgh, School of Education, 1966).
17. C. Jencks et al., *Inequality: A Reassessment of the Effects of Family and Schooling in America* (New York: Basic Books, 1972), p. 48.
18. W. L. Spady, "Educational Mobility and Access: Growth and Paradoxes," in *American Journal of Sociology,* 73, 3 (Nov. 1967); and Peter Blau and Otis D. Duncan, *The American Occupational Structure* (New York: John Wiley, 1967). More recent data support the evidence of no trend toward equality. See U.S. Bureau of Census, op. cit.
19. Ibid., Blau and Duncan.

38

The Boundaries of Public Education in the Knowledge-Based Economy

Terry Wotherspoon

INTRODUCTION

Education, long regarded as a fundamental institutional feature of highly developed societies, has gained a place of higher prominence in contemporary societies. We now have various interrelated terms—including the *new economy,* the *knowledge economy,* the *learning society,* and the *information society*—to characterize the social and economic relationships that are emerging in an environment associated with intense global market competition driven by revolutionary developments in both production and information and communications technologies (ICT). These trends, as the terminology reveals, signify a newfound importance for education. When it is understood within the broader framework of lifelong learning, education is valued for its contributions to human capital formation, which lies at the heart of any strategy to promote economic growth and development. In the

Source: Printed with permission of the author (2003).

process, education and training are being transformed as they come to be guided increasingly by particular kinds of economic imperatives.

The altered educational landscape holds the possibility of expanding opportunities for segments of the population that previously faced limited chances for social participation and economic advancement, but it also carries the danger that educational requirements and practices could become marginalizing rather than enabling for many segments of the population. Educational processes, when they are extended and modified within and beyond formal schooling, enter a realm in which personal and social relationships are reconstituted as market economic relationships that produce serious personal and family risks for those in positions of competitive disadvantage. This chapter assesses the mixed implications that the knowledge-based economy holds for Canadian education systems and for diverse groups of participants within those systems.

VARIED DIMENSIONS OF EDUCATION SYSTEMS

Sociologists and policy analysts in other fields have long recognized the importance of the connection between schooling and work, although the relationships are understood in diverse ways. Liberal theorists emphasize the social or individual utility of education for economic advancement, while critical theorists highlight the importance of power relations that privilege dominant groups over others, but the two camps agree generally that formal education assumes increasing importance in industrial and post-industrial societies as a way of selecting and orienting people to gain the knowledge, skills, and predispositions that are essential for the performing of socially necessary tasks. Most commentators acknowledge that education, since it provides a crucial opportunity for social and personal development, cannot be reduced to its economic functions. Such diverse groups as youth, parents, governments, business, community organizations, and educators agree strongly on the need for more highly integrated transitions between schooling and work, and education systems are taking several measures to address this issue and to ensure that persons in the labour force have continuous opportunities to upgrade their skills in appropriate forms. Nevertheless, there continues to be considerable debate over the extent to which education is—and should be—aligned with economic priorities (Council of Ministers of Education Canada, 1998: 19; Wotherspoon, 2004).

These debates reflect, to a large extent, the importance of education as an area around which various social groups and interests engage in struggles for strategic positioning. Education offers access to desired knowledge, credentials, and capacities relevant to labour market entry and job performance, but it also has more general social, cultural, and ideological significance as a means by which we come to develop particular understandings about the world and our places within it, along with habits, expectations, and practical capabilities that have other social applications. In the same way that some groups may use educational credentials as a way of controlling access to particular jobs or positions and securing their own competitive advantage relative to others (Collins, 1979), different groups can also attempt to use education, variously, as a vehicle to convert social or cultural resources into economic ones, or to block this conversion process (Bourdieu & Passeron, 1990).

One way in which to make sense of the competing and often contradictory forces that shape education in contemporary societies is through the tension between what Carnoy and Levin (1985) call the capitalist imperative and the democratic imperative. The former refers to the processes by which schooling contributes to the changing labour force requirements to maintain profitable production within capitalist economies. Whereas the capitalist imperative is driven by corporate interests that perpetuate inequality and hierarchy, the democratic imperative is guided by popular demands for participation, expansion of social and economic opportunity, and social justice for all social groups. Carnoy and Levin (1985: 247) argue that, while the balance between these two forces shifts periodically, schools remain a focus for public controversy and conflict "because they have the dual role of preparing workers and citizens."

The historical development of education in Canada reveals these dynamics at work, in part, through changing "boundaries" and mechanisms of inclusion and exclusion (Wotherspoon, 2002). Public education is hypothetically open to all citizens, providing opportunities for social participation that contribute to differing credentials and levels of success that, in turn, become translated into job opportunities and other socio-economic prospects. In practice, however, various processes of exclusion, discrimination, and marginalization have made it more difficult for some groups, relative to others, to advance in and through education. The current emphasis on the changing requirements of education for the knowledge society or new economy provides an opportunity to analyze the educational significance of economic transformations that are grounded in appeals to the apparent compatibility between both social and economic roles and responsibilities.

EDUCATION AND THE KNOWLEDGE ECONOMY

Concepts related to the new economy or knowledge society have appeared with increasing frequency over the past four decades in policy discussions and analysis of changing economic environments. The term *new economy* generally refers to the process that has resulted in the industrial production and distribution of material goods being increasingly altered and replaced by a rapid expansion in productivity made possible by revolutionary advances in information and communications technologies, which have brought with them unprecedented capacities to produce, store, and manipulate data. Knowledge is an essential resource because it enables firms and organizations to develop and implement technological innovations, thereby contributing to enhanced productivity both directly and as a result of adjustments made from monitoring existing procedures. Human capital, in turn, in the form of a highly educated, skilled, innovative, and adaptable workforce (understood as both existing and potential workers), is posed as the motor that drives the production and application of knowledge. In previous incarnations, human capital was conceptualized as an individual attribute that had benefits for society more generally; now it is seen more as an attribute to be harnessed within social and technical relationships that advance the interests of specific firms or organizations.

Globalization is a central characteristic of new economies, both through intensified competition among firms and nations on a global basis and in the accelerated movement of people, goods and services, and data across national boundaries. These trends are accompanied by a central contradiction: the quest for innovation and flexibility is accompanied by demands that there be open markets for goods, services, expertise, technologies, and workers, and conditions that make it difficult for governments to regulate what happens within specific boundaries, yet there is a parallel search for measures to coordinate the development and flow of data, resources, and people.

There is also a political and social dimension to these relationships in the sense that economic and labour market transformations contribute to considerable uncertainty and displacement in people's lives. As jobs, enterprises, or industries are restructured, some of the consequences include periodic job loss; shifts between education and employment for training or retraining; economic insecurity; migration from one locale or nation to another; and the modification of family life to accompany new working arrangements. Governments and community agencies are confronted with pressures to intervene, not only to ensure that labour market demands for the new economy can be fulfilled, but also to devise policy solutions to social displacement. One common response in highly industrialized nations is renewed emphasis on strategies for social cohesion, social integration, and social capital built around notions that social inclusion and participation in economic arrangements, combined with relations of trust and cooperation, are the best safeguard against social unrest and division.

Recent employment trends illustrate the impact these changes are having on the structure of work. The Organisation for Economic Cooperation and Development (2001: 55–56), for instance, reports that between 1992 and 1999, employment in the United States and European Union nations grew by 3.3 percent for knowledge workers (defined as scientists, engineers, and information and communications technology specialists and technical workers who produced new knowledge), compared to 2.2 percent for service workers, 1.6 percent for management workers, and 0.9 percent for data workers, while employment declined by 0.2 percent among workers in goods-producing industries. Canadian data reveal similar trends, with nearly half of the job growth between 1991 and 2001 in highly skilled occupations that normally require a university education; employment in service-producing sectors, which reached parity with goods-producing industries in the late 1950s, had grown to three-quarters of the labour market by the end of the 1990s (Crompton & Vickers, 2000: 7–8; Statistics Canada, 2003a: 7).

Governments, businesses, policy consortia, and other agencies have produced a steady stream of documents and agendas that attempt to guide and monitor the transition to a knowledge-based economy. The prevailing message in these statements is the notion that global competition through knowledge-based economic development is inevitable and generally beneficial, producing a set of conditions to which individuals, firms, and nations must adjust in order to remain competitive and offset any limitations that arise along the way. They also represent a consensus-building exercise, through language that signals an understanding that all individuals and parties stand to gain from these developments, accompanied by exhortations for all participants to take responsibility and act to ensure that the proper adjustments and conditions can be fulfilled.

Statements and recommendations contained within two recent publications—one from the Organisation for Economic Co-operation and Development (OECD, 2001) and the other from the Government of Canada (2002)—are typical of many such documents. The OECD (2001: 97) highlights the importance of information and communications technologies, in conjunction with a broad range of other economic and social policy developments, in capturing the ability to exploit new economic conditions:

Governments today are faced with a new economic environment. ICT has emerged as a key technology with the potential to transform economic and social activity and has led to more rapid growth in countries where the conditions for macroeconomic stability are in place. While it is too early to say how important ICT's transformations will be compared with those of previous innovations, like electricity, government should nonetheless take action to manage adjustment and keep the social costs low. All governments can do more to exploit this new technology further, by accelerating its diffusion, providing the right skills and building confidence. But ICT is not the only factor explaining growth disparities and policies to bolster these technologies will not on their own steer countries on to a higher growth path. Indeed, growth is not the result of a single policy or institutional arrangement, but a comprehensive and co-ordinated set of actions to create the right conditions for future change and innovation.

The OECD report outlines a series of policy recommendations (echoed in similar reports by various business and government agencies or consortia) directed to enhance economic productivity and growth, including several oriented to education and other dimensions of "human capital enhancement":

- Investment in high-quality early education and child care;
- Raising completion of basic and vocational education and improving the quality of the system;
- Improving school-to-work transitions;
- Strengthening the links between higher education and the labour market in a cost-effective way;
- Providing wider training opportunities; and
- Reducing obstacles to workplace changes and giving workers a greater voice. (OECD, 2001: 70)

Statements and recommendations in the report reveal economic logic (evident in the notion that education and child care are "investments" and strategies to enhance and employ labour market developments for economic productivity), mixed with relatively progressive social visions offering participation and opportunity for all social groups (enhancing child care, improving educational participation and attainment, and facilitating employee input) that appear beneficial, reasonable, and politically neutral.

Similar analyses, recommendations, and calls for action are outlined in the federal document *Knowledge Matters*, which was presented as one of the two core papers outlining the Canadian government's innovation strategy. The paper stresses that "further action is required by all" in order "for Canadians to have the skills they need to participate fully in society, and to secure Canada's position as a leader in the world economy" (Canada, 2002: 12). It continues by calling for a unified vision in which "all Canadians work together to develop a common understanding of the challenges we face, articulate a shared vision of where we want to go, and create a plan of action to get us there," including measures to strengthen four main areas of skill and learning development:

- Building a foundation for lifelong learning for children and youth;
- Strengthening accessibility and excellence in post-secondary education;
- Building a world class workforce; and
- Helping immigrants achieve their full potential. (Canada, 2002: 12)

Hale (2002: 23) emphasizes that the innovation agenda to position Canada for successful global competition is accompanied by an inclusion agenda that is oriented toward securing widespread economic participation and managing political and social tensions brought about in the course of economic restructuring:

The government's evolving innovation strategy is linked to a broader economic paradigm in which government has a distinct, facilitative role in fostering business competitiveness in a dynamic, open economy, organizing both economic and social infrastructure, and facilitating widespread access to and participation in the benefits of the emerging knowledge-based economy. Government policies intended to enhance access to education and to improve incentives for employ-

ment-related training are critical to increasing the number of potential "winners" and to reduce the potential "casualties" of continuing economic and technological change.

Hale's account highlights, as well, a recurrent theme that even the most ardent promoters of the benefits of the new economy acknowledge—risks and disparities are likely to be part of the new landscape, so it is better to play to competitive advantage than be left behind. The sections that follow examine how these challenges affect education systems and participants.

CONTEMPORARY EDUCATIONAL REFORMS

Prescriptions for economic innovation come hand in hand with a broader public sentiment that education systems, while contributing significantly to advances in knowledge and skill levels among the population as a whole, must be transformed in order to ensure a better fit and relevance for new economic requirements. The main thrust in the demands for educational reform, signalled in documents such as those cited in the previous section, includes the upgrading of general levels of education, skill, and training across the board; improved participation in higher education; and a better fit among education, labour market requirements, and job placement.

Measures to reposition education for competitive performance in new economic environments are occurring together with broader transformations in education systems. Common patterns of educational reform are evident in Canada and other post-industrial societies, although the nature and scope of these changes are somewhat unique in each context. In addition to the growing emphasis on lifelong learning, blurring of the boundaries between academic and vocational education, and substantial growth in educational programming and participation beyond high school levels, education systems over the past two decades have experienced funding constraint and restructuring; devolution of decision-making from central to more local levels; and neo-conservative reforms promoting individualism and choice that attempt to align education with markets through which goods and services are produced and exchanged (Brown, Halsey, Lauder, & Wells, 1997: 19–21). The impetus for educational reform is grounded in claims that education must be made more accountable and responsible to the public, and that it must better reflect contemporary economic and labour market conditions. But, while there is general consensus among most social groups that coordinated educational planning and reforms are essential, strong discrepancies are evident in proposed changes and their outcomes. Job-related education means different things to different observers, so that employer demands oriented to training specific types of workers may be at odds with students' interests in gaining professional credentials. At the same time, initiatives to involve parent groups and local organizations more fully in the educational decision-making process are likely to be ineffective when they are offset by government measures to tighten central control over the terms and limits of educational finance and other important matters.

Regardless of the images portrayed in various debates, Canada is positioned well, relative to most other nations, to embrace the challenge to become a highly educated, electronically integrated society. Canada is at or near the top in most international comparisons of general educational achievement and educational attainment rates in post-secondary education (OECD, 2002). Educational attainment continues to expand in both depth and scope as more and more people achieve increasingly higher levels of education and training. About one out of five Canadians in all age cohorts are engaged in full-time educational studies; in addition, between 1 and 2 percent of Canadian adults are engaged in post-secondary studies on a part-time basis, while

about one in four are involved in other formal adult education and training programs (calculated from Statistics Canada, 2002b: 48–49). Whereas in 1951 only 1.9 percent of the Canadian adult population had completed a university degree, by 2001 that figure had risen to 15.4 percent, while about half of the adult population overall had completed at least some post-secondary education (Statistics Canada, 2003b: 26). The median levels of education among Canadians aged 25 to 44 increased from 8.2 years in 1951 to 13.5 in 1996 (Schweitzer, Crocker, & Gilliss, 1995: 23; Statistics Canada, 2001: 199). Canadians are also highly engaged in the development, application, and use of information and communications technologies. Canada ranks at or near the top in the world on many indicators associated with computer access and availability and use of the Internet at home, work, and school (Statistics Canada, 2002a).

Within these general trends lie a number of sources of concern for educators, policy-makers and policy analysts. Educational participation rates in Canada are relatively low in comparison with other highly developed nations, standing at or below the mean participation rates among OECD countries for nearly all age cohorts (OECD, 2002, Table C1.2). Amid mounting rhetoric and initiatives oriented to keep youth in school, the number of high school dropouts remains high: in 1999, about 12 percent of 20-year-olds had left before completing high school, although the comparable proportion was 18 percent in 1991, and many early leavers eventually complete their high school later (Bowlby & McMullen, 2002: 26–27). Substantial proportions of the Canadian adult population have low literacy skills, especially in comparison with many European nations, and considerable inequalities in literacy skills are evident across regions, provinces, socio-economic groups, and age cohorts (Willms 1997). One-quarter or more of Canadian children experience learning and behavioural problems, while the fastest-growing segments of the child and youth population include many groups—such as Aboriginal children and youth, immigrants who speak neither English nor French, and children from low-income families—that are often associated with difficulties with education and integration into labour markets of temporary or longer-term duration (Willms, 2002; Wotherspoon & Schissel, 2001).

Increasing attention is also being directed to the extensive levels of education, skills, and capacity that people have attained in forms that are not officially acknowledged within formal and continuing education. Employers, policy-makers, and some educational institutions are beginning to acknowledge two major dimensions of this phenomenon: non-recognition of foreign credentials, in response to which some agencies are taking steps to address a common problem for immigrants who are not granted full-equivalent credit within Canadian institutions for degrees, certificates, and training attained in other countries, and Prior Learning Assessment Recognition, which refers to procedures established by educational institutions, employers, and other agencies to determine credit equivalency for specific types of non-formal learning and work experiences. There is substantial additional evidence that our understanding of lifelong learning needs to be broadened extensively to take into account not only the need for more learning, but also to acknowledge the diverse knowledges and skills that emerge through people's social and community experiences. Individuals and groups throughout the population enrich their lives and capacities through regular engagement in informal learning as they engage in deliberate (as opposed to incidental) efforts to learn new knowledge, skills, or understandings related to work, community, home, personal interests, and other social spheres (Livingstone, 1999: 11, 35). Aboriginal people, among other communities, also maintain and disseminate distinct forms of indigenous knowledge expressed through long-

standing social, environmental, and spiritual relations. While detractors emphasize its irrelevance to contemporary economic circumstances, indigenous knowledge has numerous applications that are coming to be acknowledged for their bio-medical, ecological, socio-legal, and economic as well as cultural significance. Many persons, both on their own and through interaction with others, also develop highly sophisticated understandings and skills related to their performance of specific tasks or response to practical problems they encounter in their daily lives and work, while others turn to private tutors, Web-based research, or mentors to acquire information and skills they wish to apply in various settings.

The multiple dimensions of intense learning engagement, collectively, suggest that people are simultaneously taking seriously widespread demands to pursue lifelong learning and better job-related training while they encounter a problem that is more fundamental than the issue of knowledge deficit. The concern that many people have limited opportunities to apply and gain recognition for their diverse skills and capacities, however, has not received the same high profile that is accorded questions of educational upgrading and reform. Livingstone (1999: 6), pointing to the uncritical management perspective that dominates much of the analysis of the knowledge economy, highlights the consequence: "*A vicious circle of more learning for fewer jobs is now well established.* More education may generally be personally enriching and learning for its own sake should never be discouraged. But more schooling and training have not created more jobs in any direct sense, nor is much formal education even actually required to perform many current and prospective jobs." The significance accorded knowledge and learning in the knowledge-based economy appears to be oriented more toward specific kinds and applications of knowledge than learning in general.

INEQUALITIES IN EDUCATION AND LEARNING

The benefits of the new economy are widely promoted through attention to high-profile jobs related to the creation and application of sophisticated information technologies and management of information and systems related to those technologies. Clearly, many people are well positioned to benefit from the advantages associated with the knowledge-based economy, especially among those able to translate a combination of education, ingenuity, and organizational or entrepreneurial status into recognized forms of innovation. However, many of the jobs that are being created, especially in the rapidly expanding service sector, do not require advanced levels of formal training or involve job tasks that can be learned relatively quickly. Among the fastest-growing occupations in Canada are customer service and information clerks (notably through employment in telephone call centres) and food counter attendants and kitchen assistants; the top-10 lists also include, for men, grocery clerks and store shelf-stockers, truck drivers, and materials handlers, and, for women, general office clerks, visiting homemakers and housekeepers, and teaching assistants (Statistics Canada, 2003a: 26). In other instances, workers whose jobs are more directly related to their higher-level skills and credentials often have limited scope to exercise discretion and employ the capacities they have. The advent of high-powered computers, wireless technology, sophisticated applications, and Web-based links, for instance, has enhanced the work and productivity of many workers, but these technological innovations along with other types of organizational restructuring have also meant that professional and highly qualified workers can spend much of their time meeting administrative requirements and completing clerical tasks that lie outside their main areas of competence and focus. Information technology can fragment work as well as enhance it, often involving mundane tasks or operations that bypass complex worker skills. Both technology and knowledge enter into economic arrangements more fully for their ability to increase productivity and profit margins than their human benefits. Within the setting of the knowledge-based economy, Lowe (2000: 81) observes labour markets' limited capacity to meet most workers' rising expectations that they will attain meaningful jobs to match their increasing levels of qualifications, and he emphasizes the increasing polarization that occurs "between high- and low-paid jobs, while the rise of a contingent workforce of part-time, contract, temporary, and solo self-employed individuals suggests a further deterioration in the overall quality of work—a trend that is exacerbated by the growing divide between large employers and the small businesses and solo self-employment where most new job creation is taking place."

Nonetheless, the analyses by Livingstone, Lowe, and other observers highlight how these trends are intensified by a compelling logic that, for individuals, drives competition and increases pressure to attain even higher-level credentials and expanding repertoires of skills and training. In the pursuit of these objectives, individual learners and their parents are often inclined to take steps that position them for competitive advantage both in the types of education they engage in and the strategies they adopt to ensure their education and other resources yield desirable employment or entrepreneurial outcomes. Thus, increasing numbers of children are enrolled in early child-care programs and a broad range of extracurricular activities; provided with stimuli to enrich their learning; given access to resources such as tutoring services to ensure their successful progress through schooling; pressured to enter programs and institutions deemed to be high in status and quality; and encouraged to take other actions that will give them an educational advantage.

This competitive logic also intensifies the pressures on schooling, both from below (through rising expectations from parents and students about educational quality and relevance) and above (through the various reforms promoted by governments, businesses, and educational managers). Education is regarded increasingly as a business in which each institution or program is considered a service provider that enters the marketplace offering particular kinds of products to attract and maintain consumer loyalty. The capitalist imperative, apparent not only within specific dimensions of educational funding, organization, and programming, comes to be embedded more deeply in the entire conception and structure of contemporary education systems as lean, flexible agencies producing knowledge and workers for the new economy (Sears, 2003).

The transformations now underway in education systems contain numerous contradictions for learners from diverse backgrounds. Significant boundaries around and within education are widening, so that increasing numbers of people face expanded options related to specific needs and interests that have arisen from emerging issues as well as those that previously have been ignored by education systems. Students can select courses from different institutions or even within the same institution that emphasize, for instance, Aboriginal cultural programming and nanotechnology studies. Education, understood as part of a continuum of lifelong transitions rather than an isolated institution, has tended to broaden its focus from an orientation on program delivery to ensure that programs are supported by services and resources that recognize the diverse needs and life circumstances of students. Many of these programs and institutions are more inclusive in various ways, enabling greater participation through more open admission criteria; greater diversity in the ways that courses are delivered; enhanced support services for students with special needs; programming initiatives that respond to student interests; and stronger linkages among education institutions, communities, and work settings.

However, the reorganization of education also means that substantial segments of the population face restricted educational options and horizons.

Funding cutbacks and institutional restructuring have contributed to the deletion of core courses and services in many educational programs; shifted institutional and research priorities from educational enhancement to revenue generation; left institutions unable to meet student demand for specific programs; and burdened students with additional costs as tuitions and other expenditures related to education have risen. As governments have reduced educational funding or shifted the basis on which it is allocated, corporate sponsorships and other private sources have come to play an increasing part both directly and indirectly in classrooms and educational organizations, influencing everything from the brands of consumer products used or marketed in educational institutions to the types of programs, curricula, resources, and teaching methods available for students, educators and researchers. In many educational institutions, the teachers, professors and other educational workers are monitored and subject to work roles and performance measures based typically on industrial standards rather than on the whole range of characteristics that are essential for effective teaching-learning and scholarly relationships. Educational offerings have become increasingly fragmented and stratified as schools, postsecondary institutions, and other agencies cater to particular clientele, especially when they are no longer regarded as universal services open to all members of a particular neighborhood, community, or region. An ethos of competitiveness has reduced some educational relationships to utilitarian quests for grades, spaces in desirable programs, and credentials, leaving many students to opt or be forced out of desired educational pathways as they become marginalized, overwhelmed, or unable to balance educational requirements and other demands.

Changing educational boundaries and practices have not heralded the disappearance of significant exclusionary dimensions of education despite efforts to address problems for students with initial disadvantage or those confronted with serious life-transition difficulties. Female students have moved into many non-traditional areas, and have increased their educational participation, attainment, and success to such an extent that media and policy attention has come to focus on questions about whether the education system is failing males. However, these trends often overshadow more serious issues related to how and why gender-based differentiation processes continue to channel males and females into education and career paths that are often highly segregated and unequal. Similarly, several encouraging developments suggest the closing of persistent "gaps" in education and employment for Aboriginal people compared to Canadians as a whole, even as critical inequalities in life conditions and prospects persist and even expand between and within these population groups. Aboriginal people and persons in visible minority groups also experience overt and covert forms of racism and—in common with many other groups, including people with physical and emotional disabilities and those with alternative lifestyles—various forms of discrimination that pose barriers to their educational and occupational success. Educational opportunities, resources, and outcomes also vary by region, with persons living in remote or rural areas, or inner cities, the most likely to experience educational difficulties. All of these factors are influenced by or interact with social class inequalities and related circumstances, such as poverty, that have a significant impact on educational pathways and attainment levels (Guppy & Davies, 1998; Wotherspoon, 2002, 2004). The knowledge-based economy is likely to provide new opportunities for members of some of these groups, but corresponding labour market, educational and policy changes also contribute to an environment that perpetuates and even increases significant socio-economic inequalities.

CONCLUSION

The advent of a knowledge-based society carries mixed implications for education and the people who participate as learners and workers in educational institutions. Many people have unprecedented chances to benefit from significant increases in educational attainment and participation in formal and informal educational learning activities as education and training gain enhanced profiles within new economic arrangements. However, this promise is limited insofar as economic structures that rely on fundamental inequalities are intensified more than they are transformed. In the process, educational relationships that in the broadest sense are about the expansion of human capacities and social interaction become redefined to emphasize productivity, economic growth, and commodity markets.

It is essential to recognize that what has been identified as the capitalist imperative, accompanied by initiatives to transform education into a business or marketplace, are powerful tendencies but they are not all-pervasive, irreversible forces. Education, and the social environments that educational improvement can enhance, are also guided by elements of a democratic imperative that thrives when there are meaningful opportunities for the expression of voices and action representing the full range of diversity among social participants, including children and youth. Education is not merely a business and economic tool, but a social process that at its best contains prospects to foster human growth and social transformation.

Despite widespread demands for educational reform and assurances that schooling will be relevant to emerging job futures, there are diverse visions, linked by general notions of human improvement, about what education systems should become. Debate and dialogue about education are not new, representing instead a fundamental characteristic of cultural, social, and intellectual diversity in a democratic society. A more significant challenge for education and those concerned with its future lies in the need to sustain democratic diversity while simultaneously ensuring that such diversity means more than enduring inequalities, technical problems managed by efficiency experts, or marketplace choices for consumers.

REFERENCES

Bourdieu, P., and J.-C. Passeron. 1990. *Reproduction in education, society, and culture*. Newbury Park, Calif.: Sage.

Bowlby, J. W., and K. McMullen. 2002. *At a crossroads: First results for the 18 to 20-year-old cohort of the youth in transition survey*. Catalogue no. 81-591. Ottawa: Human Resources Development Canada and Statistics Canada.

Brown, P., A. H. Halsey, H. Lauder, and A. Stuart Wells. 1997. The transformation of education and society: An introduction. In *Education: Culture, economy, society*, eds. A. H. Halsey, H. Lauder, P. Brown, and A. Stuart Wells, 1–44. Oxford: Oxford University Press.

Canada. 2002. *Knowledge matters: Skills and learning for Canadians. Canada's innovation strategy*. Ottawa: Human Resources Development Canada.

Carnoy, M., and H. M. Levin. 1985. *Schooling and work in the democratic state*. Stanford, Calif.: Stanford University Press.

Collins, R. 1979. *The credential society: An historical sociology of education and stratification*. New York: Academic Press.

Council of Ministers of Education Canada. 1998. *The transition from initial education to working life: A Canadian report for an OECD thematic review*. Toronto: Council of Ministers of Education Canada.

Crompton, S., and M. Vickers. 2000. One hundred years of labour force. *Canadian Social Trends* (Summer): 1–13.

Guppy, N., and S. Davies. 1998. *Education in Canada: Recent trends and future challenges*. Ottawa: Minster of Industry.

Hale, G. E. 2002. Innovation and inclusion: Budgetary policy, the skills agenda, and the politics of the new economy. In *How Ottawa spends 2002–03: The security aftermath and national priorities*, ed. G. B. Doern, 20–47. Don Mills, Ont.: Oxford University Press.

Livingstone, D. W. 1999. *The education-jobs gap: Underemployment or economic democracy*. Toronto: Garamond Press.

Lowe, G. S. 2000. *The quality of work: A people-centred agenda*. Don Mills, Ont.: Oxford University Press.

Organisation for Economic Co-operation and Development (OECD). 2001. *The new economy: Beyond the hype. The OECD growth project*. Paris: OECD.

———. 2002. *Education at a glance 2002*. Paris: OECD.

Schweitzer, T. T., R. K. Crocker, and G. Gilliss. 1995. *The state of education in Canada*. Montreal: Institute for Research on Public Policy.

Sears, A. 2003. *Retooling the mind factory: Education in a lean state*. Aurora, Ont.: Garamond Press.

Statistics Canada. 2001. *Education in Canada 2000*. Catalogue no. 810-229. Ottawa: Minister of Industry.

———. 2002a. Computer access at school and at home. *The Daily* (October 29).

———. 2002b. Education at a glance. *Education Quarterly Review*, 8(3): 48–53. Catalogue no. 81-003.

———. 2003a. *The changing profile of Canada's labour force. 2001 Census: Analysis series*. Statistics Canada catalogue no. 96F0030XIE2001009. Ottawa: Minister of Industry.

———. 2003b. *Education in Canada: Raising the standard. 2001 Census: Analysis series*. Statistics Canada catalogue no. 96F0030XIE2002012. Ottawa: Minister of Industry.

Willms, J. D. 1997. *Literacy skills of Canadian youth: International adult literacy survey*. Statistics Canada catalogue no. 89-552. Ottawa: Minister of Industry.

———. 2002. The prevalence of vulnerability. In *Vulnerable children: Findings from Canada's national longitudinal survey of children and youth*, ed. J. Douglas Willms, 45–69. Edmonton: University of Alberta Press and Human Resources Development Canada.

Wotherspoon, T. 2002. *The dynamics of social inclusion: Public education and Aboriginal people in Canada*. Toronto: The Laidlaw Foundation, Perspectives on Social Inclusion Working Paper Series (December).

———. 2004. *The sociology of education in Canada: Critical perspectives*, 2nd ed. Toronto: Oxford University Press.

Wotherspoon, T., and B. Schissel. 2001. The business of placing Canadian children and youth "at-risk." *Canadian Journal of Education*, 26(3): 321–39.

Part XIX

Health and Medicine

39

The Social Structure
of Medicine

Talcott Parsons

A little reflection will show immediately that the problem of health is intimately involved in the functional prerequisites of the social system.... Certainly by almost any definition health is included in the functional needs of the individual member of the society so that from the point of view of functioning of the social system, too low a general level of health, too high an incidence of illness, is dysfunctional. This is in the first instance because illness incapacitates for the effective performance of social roles. It could of course be that this incidence was completely uncontrollable by social action, an independently given condition of social life. But insofar as it is controllable, through rational action or otherwise, it is clear that there is a functional interest of the society in its control, broadly in the minimization of illness. As one special aspect of this, attention

Source: From *The Social System* by Talcott Parsons. Copyright © 1951, copyright renewed 1979 by Talcott Parsons. Reprinted with the permission of The Free Press, a Division of Simon & Schuster.

may be called to premature death. From a variety of points of view, the birth and rearing of a child constitute a "cost" to the society, through pregnancy, child care, socialization, formal training, and many other channels. Premature death, before the individual has had the opportunity to play out his full quota of social roles, means that only a partial "return" for this cost has been received.

All this would be true were illness purely a "natural phenomenon" in the sense that, like the vagaries of the weather, it was not, to our knowledge, reciprocally involved in the motivated interactions of human beings. In this case illness would be something which merely "happened to" people, which involved consequences which had to be dealt with and conditions which might or might not be controllable but was in no way an expression of motivated behavior.

This is in fact the case for a very important part of illness, but it has become increasingly clear, by no means for all. In a variety of ways motivational factors accessible to analysis in action terms are involved in the etiology of many illnesses, and conversely, though without exact correspondence, many conditions are open to therapeutic influence through motivational channels. To take the simplest kind of case, differential exposure, to injuries or to infection, is certainly motivated, and the role of unconscious wishes to be injured or to fall ill in such cases has been clearly demonstrated. Then there is the whole range of "psychosomatic" illness about which knowledge has been rapidly accumulating in recent years. Finally, there is the field of "mental disease," the symptoms of which occur mainly on the behavioral level....

Summing up, we may say that illness is a state of disturbance in the "normal" functioning of the total human individual, including both the state of the organism as a biological system and of his personal and social adjustments. It is thus partly biologically and partly socially defined....

Medical practice...is a "mechanism" in the social system for coping with the illnesses of its members. It involves a set of institutionalized roles.... The immediately relevant social structures consist in the patterning of the role of the medical practitioner himself and, though to common sense it may seem superfluous to analyze it, that of the "sick person" himself....

The role of the medical practitioner belongs to the general class of "professional" roles, a subclass of the larger group of occupational roles. Caring for the sick is thus not an incidental activity of other roles though, for example, mothers do a good deal of it—but has become functionally specialized as a full-time "job." This, of course, is by no means true of all societies. As an occupational role it is institutionalized about the technical content of the function which is given a high degree of primacy relative to other status-determinants. It is thus inevitable both that incumbency of the role should be achieved and that performance criteria by standards of technical competence should be prominent. Selection for it and the context of its performance are to a high degree segregated from other bases of social status and solidarities....

Unlike the role of the businessman, however, it is collectivity-oriented not self-oriented.

The importance of this patterning is, in one context, strongly emphasized by its relation to the cultural tradition. One basis for the division of labor is the specialization of technical competence. The role of physician is far along the continuum of increasingly high levels of technical competence required for performance. Because of the complexity and subtlety of the knowledge and skill required and the consequent length and intensity of training, it is difficult to see how the functions could, under modern conditions, be ascribed to people occupying a prior status as one of their activities in that status, following the pattern by which, to a degree, responsibility for the health of her children is ascribed to the mother-status. There is an intrinsic connection between achieved statuses and the requirements of high technical competence....

High technical competence also implies specificity of function. Such intensive devotion to expertness in matters of health and disease precludes comparable expertness in other fields. The physician is not, by virtue of his modern role, a generalized "wise man" or sage—though there is considerable folklore to that effect—but a specialist whose superiority to his fellows is confined to the specific sphere of his technical training and experience. For example one does not expect the physician as such to have better judgment about foreign policy or tax legislation than any other comparably intelligent and well-educated citizen. There are of course elaborate subdivisions of specialization within the profession.... The physician is [also] expected to treat an objective problem in objective, scientifically justifiable terms. For example, whether he likes or dislikes the particular patient as a person is supposed to be irrelevant, as indeed it is to most purely objective problems of how to handle a particular disease.

...The "ideology" of the profession lays great emphasis on the obligation of the physician to put the "welfare of the patient" above his personal interests, and regards "commercialism" as the most serious and insidious evil with which it has to contend. The line, therefore, is drawn primarily vis-à-vis "business." The "profit motive" is supposed to be drastically excluded from the medical world. This attitude is, of course, shared with the other professions, but it is perhaps more pronounced in the medical case than in any single one except perhaps the clergy....

An increasing proportion of medical practice is now taking place in the context of organization. To a large extent this is necessitated by the technological development of medicine itself, above all the need for technical facilities beyond the reach of the individual practitioner, and the fact that treating the same case often involves the complex co-operation of several different kinds of physicians as well as of auxiliary personnel. This greatly alters the relation of the physician to the rest of the instrumental complex. He tends to be relieved of much responsibility and hence necessarily of freedom, in relation to his patients other than in his technical role. Even if a hospital executive is a physician himself he is not in the usual sense engaged in the "practice of medicine" in performing his functions any more than the president of the Miners' Union is engaged in mining coal.

As was noted, for common sense there may be some question of whether "being sick" constitutes a social role at all—isn't it simply a state of fact, a "condition"? Things are not quite so simple as this. The test is the existence of a set of institutionalized expectations and the corresponding sentiments and sanctions.

There seem to be four aspects of the institutionalized expectation system relative to the sick role. First is the exemption from normal social role responsibilities, which of course is relative to the nature and severity of the illness. This exemption requires legitimation by and to the various actors involved and the physician often serves as a court of appeal as well as a direct legitimatizing agent. It is noteworthy that like all institutionalized patterns the legitimation of being sick enough to avoid obligations can not only be a right of the sick person but an obligation upon him. People are often resistant to admitting they are sick and it is not uncommon for others to tell them that they *ought* to stay in bed. The word generally has a moral connotation. It goes almost without saying that this legitimation has the social function of protection against "malingering."

The second closely related aspect is the institutionalized definition that the sick person cannot be expected by "pulling himself together" to get well by an act of decision or will. In this sense also he is exempted from responsibility—he is in a condition that must "be taken care of." His "condition" must be changed, not merely his "attitude." Of course the process of recovery may be spontaneous but while the illness lasts he can't "help it." This element in the definition of the state of illness is obviously crucial as a bridge to the acceptance of "help."

The third element is the definition of the state of being ill as itself undesirable with its obligation to want to "get well." The first two elements of legitimation of the sick role thus are conditional in a highly important sense. It is a relative legitimation so long as he is in this unfortunate state which both he and alter hope he can get out of as expeditiously as possible.

Finally, the fourth closely related element is the obligation—in proportion to the severity of the condition, of course—to seek *technically competent* help, namely, in the most usual case, that of a physician and to *cooperate* with him in the process of trying to get well. It is here, of course, that the role of the sick person as patient becomes articulated with that of the physician in a complementary role structure.

It is evident from the above that the role of motivational factors in illness immensely broadens the scope and increases the importance of the institutionalized role aspect of being sick. For then the problem of social control becomes much more than one of ascertaining facts and drawing lines. The privileges and exemptions of the sick role may become objects of a "secondary gain" which the patient is positively motivated, usually unconsciously, to secure or to retain. The problem, therefore, of the balance of motivations to recover becomes of first importance. In general motivational balances of great functional significance to the social system are institutionally controlled, and it should, therefore, not be surprising that this is no exception.

A few further points may be made about the specific patterning of the sick role and its relation to social structure. It is, in the first place, a "contingent" role into which anyone, regardless of his status in other respects, may come. It is, furthermore, in the type case temporary. One may say that it is in a certain sense a "negatively achieved" role, through failure to "keep well," though, of course, positive motivations also operate, which by that very token must be motivations to deviance....

The orientation of the sick role vis-à-vis the physician is also defined as collectively-oriented. It is true that the patient has a very obvious self-interest in getting well in most cases, though this point may not always be so simple. But once he has called in a physician the attitude is clearly marked, that he has assumed the obligation to cooperate with that physician in what is regarded as a common task. The obverse of the physician's obligation to be guided by the welfare of the patient is the latter's obligation to "do his part" to the best of his ability. This point is clearly brought out, for example, in the attitudes of the profession toward what is called "shopping around." By that is meant the practice of a patient "checking" the advice of one physician against that of another without telling physician A that he intends to consult physician B, or if he comes back to A that he has done so or who B is. The medical view is that if the patient is not satisfied with the advice his physician gives him he may properly do one of two things, first he may request a consultation, even naming the physician he wishes called in, but in that case it is physician A not the patient who must call B in, the patient may not see B independently, and above all not without A's knowledge. The other proper recourse is to terminate the relation with A and become "B's patient." The notable fact here is that a pattern of behavior on the part not only of the physician but also of the patient, is expected which is in sharp contrast to perfectly legitimate behavior in a commercial relationship. If he is buying a car there is no objection to the customer going to a number of dealers before making up his mind, and there is no obligation for him to inform any one dealer what others he is consulting, to say nothing of approaching the Chevrolet dealer only through the Ford dealer.

The doctor-patient relationship is thus focused on these pattern elements. The patient has a need for technical services because he doesn't—nor do his lay associates, family members, etc.— "know" what is the matter or what to do about it, nor does he control the necessary facilities. The physician is a technical expert who by special training and experience, and by an institutionally validated status, is qualified to "help" the patient in a situation institutionally defined as legitimate in a relative sense but as needing help....

40

Female Genital Mutilation

Efua Dorkenoo and Scilla Elworthy

THE FACTS

…[F]emale genital mutilation covers four types of operation:

1. *Circumcision,* or cutting of the prepuce or hood of the clitoris, known in Muslim countries as Sunna (tradition). This, the mildest type, affects only a small proportion of the millions of women concerned. It is the only type of mutilation that can correctly be called circumcision, though there has been a tendency to group all kinds of mutilations under the misleading term "female circumcision."

2. *Excision,* meaning the cutting of the clitoris and of all or part of the labia minora.

3. *Infibulation,* the cutting of the clitoris, labia minora and at least part of the labia majora. The two sides of the vulva are then pinned together by silk or catgut sutures, or with thorns, thus obliterating the vaginal introitus except for a very small opening, preserved by the insertion of a tiny piece of wood or a reed for the passage of urine or menstrual blood. These operations are done with special knives, with razor blades or pieces of glass. The girl's legs are then bound together from hip to ankle and she is kept immobile for up to forty days to permit the formation of scar tissue.

4. *Intermediate,* meaning the removal of the clitoris and some parts of the labia minora or the whole of it. Various degrees are done according to the demands of the girl's relatives.…

Most frequently these operations are performed by an old woman of the village or by a traditional birth attendant and only rarely by qualified nurses or doctors. The age at which the mutilations are carried out varies from area to area, and according to whether legislation against the practice is foreseen or not. It varies from a few days old (for example, the Jewish Falashas in Ethiopia, and the nomads of the Sudan) to about seven years (as in Egypt and many countries of Central Africa) or—more rarely—adolescence, as among the Ibo of Nigeria. Most experts are agreed that the age of mutilation is becoming younger, and has less and less to do with initiation into adulthood.[1]

Source: From "Female Genital Mutilation," by Efua Dorkenoo and Scilla Elworthy, in *Female Genital Mutilation: Proposals for Change,* an MRG Report, 92/3. Reprinted with permission.

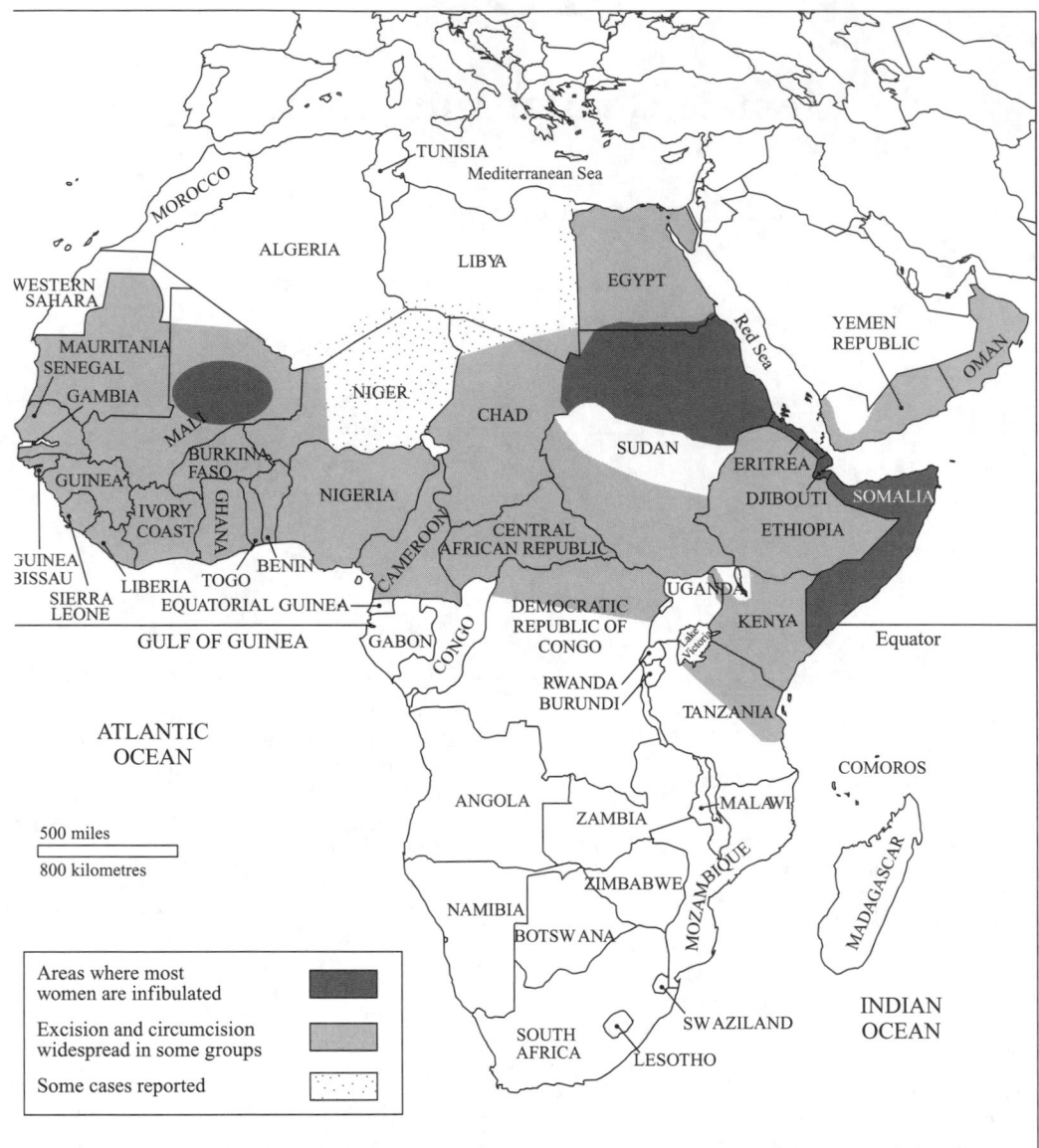

FIGURE 40.1 Female genital mutilation in Africa

Physical Consequences

Health risks and complications depend on the gravity of the mutilation, hygienic conditions, the skill and eyesight of the operator, and the struggles of the child. Whether immediate or long term, they are grave.[2] Death from bleeding is not uncommon, while long-term complications include chronic infections of the uterus and vagina, painful menstruation, severe pain during intercourse, sterility and complications during childbirth. Though evidence has yet to be collected, it is also likely that bleeding or open wounds increase the likelihood of HIV transmission and AIDS.

There is great difficulty in obtaining accurate research on the sexual experiences of mutilated women, because the majority are reluctant to speak on the subject and are generally ambivalent on questions of sexual enjoyment.[3] However, in all types of mutilation, even the "mildest" clitoridectomy, a part of a woman's body containing nerves of vital importance to sexual pleasure is amputated.

Psychological Consequences

Even less research has been done to date on the psychological consequences of these traditions. However, many personal accounts and research findings contain repeated references to anxiety prior to the operation, terror at the moment of being seized by an aunt or village matron, unbearable pain, and the subsequent sense of humiliation and of being betrayed by parents, especially the mother. On the other hand, there are references to special clothes and good food associated with the event, to the pride felt in being like everyone else, in being "made clean," in having suffered without screaming.

To be different clearly produces anxiety and mental conflict. An unexcised, non-infibulated girl is despised and made the target of ridicule, and no one in her community will marry her. Thus what is clearly understood to be her life's work, namely marriage and child-bearing, is denied her. So, in tight-knit village societies where mutilation is the rule, it will be the exceptional girl who will suffer psychologically, unless she has another very strong identity which she has lost.[4]

There is no doubt that genital mutilation would have overwhelming psychological effects on an unmotivated girl, unsupported by her family, village, peers and community. To those from other cultures unfamiliar with the force of this particular community identity, the very concept of amputation of the genitals carries a shock value which does not exist for most women in the areas concerned. For them, not to amputate would be shocking.

These observations concern social-psychological factors rather than the central question, namely, what effects do these traumatic operations have on little girls at the moment of operation and as they grow up? The fact is that we simply don't know. We do not know what it means to a girl or woman when her central organ of sensory pleasure is cut off, when her life-giving canal is stitched up amid blood and fear and secrecy, while she is forcibly held down and told that if she screams she will cause the death of her mother or bring shame on the family.

THE PRACTICE

The Area Covered

The countries where one or more forms of female genital mutilation are practised number more than twenty in Africa, from the Atlantic to the Red Sea, the Indian Ocean and the eastern Mediterranean. Outside Africa, excision is also practised in Oman, South Yemen and in the United Arab Emirates (UAE). Circumcision is practised by the Muslim populations of Indonesia and Malaysia and by Bohra Muslims in India, Pakistan and East Africa.[5]

On the map of Africa, an uninterrupted belt is formed across the centre of the continent, which then expands up the length of the Nile. This belt, with the exception of the Egyptian buckle, corresponds strikingly with the pattern of countries that have the highest child mortality rates (more than 30 percent for children from one to four years of age).[6] These levels reflect deficiencies of medical care, of clean drinking water, of sanitary infrastructure and of adequate nutrition in most of the countries.

The gravity of the mutilations varies from country to country. Infibulation is reported to affect nearly all the female population of Somalia, Djibouti and the Sudan (except the non-Muslim population of southern Sudan), southern Egypt, the Red Sea coast of Ethiopia, northern Kenya, northern Nigeria and some parts of Mali. The most recent estimate of women mutilated is 74 million.[7]

Ethnic groups closely situated geographically are by no means affected in the same way: For example, in Kenya, the Kikuyu practise excision and the Luo do not; in Nigeria, the Yoruba, the Ibo and the Hausa do, but not the Nupes or the Fulanis; in Senegal, the Woloff have no practice of mutilation. There are many other examples.

As the subject of female genital mutilation began to be eligible at least for discussion, reports of genital operations on non-consenting females have appeared from many unexpected parts of the world. During the 1980s, women in Sweden were shocked by accounts of mutilations performed in Swedish hospitals on daughters of immigrants. In France, women from Mali and Senegal have been reported to bring an *exciseuse* to France once a year to operate on their daughters in their apartments.[8] In July 1982 a Malian infant died of an excision performed by a professional circumciser, who then fled to Mali. In the same year, reports appeared in the British press that excision for non-medical reasons had been performed in a London private clinic.

Legislation

In Africa. Formal legislation forbidding genital mutilation, or more precisely infibulation, exists in the Sudan. A law first enacted in 1946 allows for a term of imprisonment up to five years and/or a fine. However, it is not an offence (under Article 284 of the Sudan Penal Code for 1974) "merely to remove the free and projecting part of the clitoris."

Many references have been made to legislation in Egypt, but after researching the available materials, all that has been traced is a resolution signed by the Minister of Health in 1959, recommending only partial clitoridectomy for those who want an operation, to be performed only by doctors.[9]

In late 1978, largely due to the efforts of the Somali Women's Democratic Organization (SWDO), Somalia set up a commission to abolish infibulation. In 1988 at a seminar held in Mogadishu, it was recommended that SWDO should propose a bill to the competent authorities to eradicate all forms of female genital mutilation.

In September 1982, President Arap Moi took steps to ban the practices in Kenya, following reports of the deaths of fourteen children after excision. A traditional practitioner found to be carrying out this operation can be arrested under the Chiefs Act and brought before the law.

Official declarations against female genital mutilation were made by the late Captain Thomas Sankara and Abdou Diouf, the heads of state in Burkina Faso and Senegal respectively.

In Western Countries. A law prohibiting female excision, whether consent has been given or not, came into force in Sweden in July 1982, carrying a two-year sentence. In Norway, in 1985, all hospitals were alerted to the practice. Belgium has incorporated a ban on the practice. Several states in the U.S.A. have incorporated female genital mutilation into their criminal code.

In the U.K., specific legislation prohibiting female circumcision came into force at the end of 1985. A person found guilty of an offence is liable to up to five years' imprisonment or to a fine. Female genital mutilation has been incorporated into child protection procedures at local authority levels. As yet no person has been committed in the English courts for female circumcision but since 1989 there have been at least seven local authority legal interventions which prevented parents from sexually mutilating their daughters or wards.

France does not have specific legislation on female sexual mutilation but under Article 312–3 of the French Penal Code, female genital mutilation can be considered as a criminal offence. Under this code, anybody who exercises violence or seriously assaults a child less than fifteen years old can be punished with imprisonment from ten to twenty years, if the act of violence results in a mutilation, amputation of a limb, the loss of an eye or other parts of the body or has unintentionally caused the death of the child.

In 1989, a mother who had paid a traditional woman exciser to excise her week-old daughter, in 1984, was convicted and given a three-year suspended jail sentence. In 1991 a traditional exciser was jailed for five years in France.

Contemporary Practices

Opinions are very divided as to whether the practice is disappearing because of legislation or social and economic changes. Esther Ogunmodede, for instance, believes that in Nigeria, Africa's most populous country, the tradition is disappearing but extremely slowly, with millions of excisions still taking place. She reports that in areas where the operations are done on girls of marriageable age, they are "running away from home to avoid the razor." This confirms Fran Hosken's assertion that operations are being done at earlier and earlier ages, in order that the children should be "too young to resist." Fran Hosken does not think that the custom is dying out, and she indisputably has the best published range of information concerning all the countries where the practice is known.

An interesting development took place in Ethiopia during the years of civil warfare which only ended in 1991. When the Eritrean People's Liberation Front (EPLF) occupied large areas from January 1977 to December 1978, among many other reforms they categorically and successfully forbade genital mutilation and forced marriage. In fact, the reason given for the large numbers of young women in the EPLF army was that they were running away from home in other parts of Ethiopia to avoid forced marriage and the knife.[10] Although it appears the practice continues in remote areas, because the consciousness of Eritrean women has changed dramatically during the war years, it is easier to persuade men and women to let go of this practice.

Since 1983, the number of educational programmes initiated to raise public awareness of the health risk associated with female genital mutilation at local, national and international levels have increased. The media have played a major role in bringing this issue from the domestic to the public domain. As a result of these efforts it can be said that the taboo surrounding even public mention of the practice has at last been broken. There is an increase in public awareness of the harmful effects of female genital mutilation.

It has been noted that female genital mutilation is becoming unpopular amongst the urban elite in some African countries. In Sierra Leone, for example, Koso-Thomas claims that urban men are willing to marry uncircumcised women, in particular when the marriage is not pre-arranged.[11]

In general, among urban educated women, reasons often cited against female genital mutilation include the pointlessness of mutilation, health risks and reduction of sexual sensitivity. The last reason points to a changing attitude towards women's fundamental human rights amongst urban Africans.

In the main, the practice continues to be widespread among large sectors and groups within Africa. Those in favour of the practice are noted in the 1986 UN study to be a passive majority who refer back to traditional society, without necessarily sharing that society's values.[12] In some cases, the practice appears to be spreading to population groups who traditionally never practised female genital mutilation, as observed with city women in Wau, Sudan, who regard it as fashionable, and among converted Muslim women in southern Sudan who marry northern Sudanese men.[13] Furthermore, even in areas where some groups are turning against the practice, the absolute numbers affected may be increasing. Rapid population growth in Africa means greater numbers of female children are born, who in turn are exposed to the risk of mutilation.

THE ISSUES

Female genital mutilation is a complex issue, for it involves deep-seated cultural practices which affect millions of people. However, it can be divided into (at least) four distinct issues.

Rights of Women

Female genital mutilation is an extreme example of the general subjugation of women, sufficiently extreme and horrifying to make women and men question the basis of what is done to women, what women have accepted and why, in the name of society and tradition.

The burning of Indian widows and the binding of the feet of Chinese girl children are other striking examples, sharp enough and strange enough to throw a spotlight on other less obvious ways in which women the world over submit to oppression. It is important to remember that all these practices are, or were, preserved under centuries of tradition, and that foot-binding was only definitively stopped by a massive social and political revolution (replacing the many traditions which it swept away by offering an entirely new social system, revolutionary in many aspects: land ownership, class system, education, sex equality, etc.) which had been preceded by years of patient work by reformers.

Thus, to be successful, campaigns on female genital mutilation should consider carefully not only eliminating but also replacing the custom. (The example of Eritrea, previously quoted, is illuminating here.) Furthermore, such success may be predicated on long-term changes in attitudes and ideologies by both men and women.

A major international expression of the goal of equal rights for women was taken in December 1979, when the U.N. General Assembly adopted the Convention on the Elimination of All Forms of Discrimination Against Women. This came into force in September 1981. The comprehensive convention calls for equal rights for women, regardless of their marital status, in all fields: political, economic, social, cultural and civil. Article 5(a) obliges states' parties to take:

All appropriate measures to modify the social and cultural patterns of conduct of men and women, with a view to achieving the elimination of prejudices and customary and all other practices which are based on the idea of the inferiority or superiority of either of the sexes or on stereotyped roles for men and women.

To succeed in abolishing such practices will demand fundamental attitudinal shifts in the way that society perceives the human rights of women. The starting point for change should be educational programmes that assist women to recognize their fundamental human rights. This is where UNESCO, the U.N. Centre for Human Rights and international agencies could help by supporting awareness-building programmes.

Rights of Children

An adult is free to submit her or himself to a ritual or tradition, but a child, having no formed judgement, does not consent but simply undergoes the operation (which in this case is irrevocable) while she is totally vulnerable. The descriptions available of the reactions of children—panic and shock from extreme pain, biting through the tongue, convulsions, necessity for six adults to hold down an eight-year-old, and death—indicate a practice comparable to torture.

Many countries signatory to Article 5 of the Universal Declaration of Human Rights (which provides that no one shall be subjected to torture, or to cruel, inhuman or degrading treatment) violate that clause. Those violations are discussed and sometimes condemned by various U.N. commissions. Female genital mutilation, however, is a question of torture inflicted not on adults but on girl children, and the reasons given are not concerned with either political conviction or military necessity but are solely in the name of tradition.

The Declaration of the Rights of Children, adopted in 1959 by the General Assembly, asserts that children should have the possibility to develop physically in a healthy and normal way in conditions of liberty and dignity. They should have adequate medical attention, and be protected from all forms of cruelty.

It is the opinion of Renée Bridel, of the Fédération Internationale des Femmes de Carrières Juridiques, that "One cannot but consider Member

States which tolerate these practices as infringing their obligations as assumed under the terms of the Charter [of the U.N.].[14]

In September 1990, the United Nations Convention on the Rights of the Child went into force. It became part of international human rights law. Under Article 24(3) it states that: "States Parties shall take all effective and appropriate measures with a view to abolishing traditional practices prejudicial to the health of children." This crucial article should not merely remain a paper provision, to be given lip service by those entrusted to implement it. Members of the U.N. should work at translating its provisions into specific implementation programmes at grassroots level. Much could be learned (by African states in particular) from countries with established child protection systems.

The Right to Good Health

No reputable medical practitioner insists that mutilation is good for the physical or mental health of girls and women, and a growing number offer research indicating its grave permanent damage to health and underlining the risks of death. Medical facts, carefully explained, may be the way to discourage the practice, since these facts are almost always the contrary of what is believed, and can be shown and demonstrated.

Those U.N. agencies and government departments specifically entrusted with the health needs of women and children must realize that it is their responsibility to support positive and specific preventative programmes against female genital mutilation, for while the practice continues the quality of life and health will inevitably suffer. However, this approach, if presented out of context, ignores the force of societal pressures which drive women to perform these operations, regardless of risk, in order to guarantee marriage for their daughters, and to conform to severe codes of female behaviour laid down by male-dominated societies.

The Right to Development

The practice of female genital mutilation must be seen in the context of underdevelopment,[15] and the realities of life for the most vulnerable and exploited sectors—women and children. International political and economic forces have frequently prevented development programmes from meeting the basic needs of rural populations. With no access to education or resources, and with no effective power base, the rural and urban poor cling to traditions as a survival mechanism in time of socio-economic change.

In societies where marriage for a woman is her only means of survival, and where some form of excision is a prerequisite for marriage, persuading her to relinquish the practice for herself or for her children is an extraordinarily difficult task. Female (and some male) African analysts of development strategies are today constantly urging that the overall deteriorating conditions in which poor women live be made a major focus for change, for unless development affects their lives for the better, traditional practices are unlikely to change.

DIRECTIONS FOR THE FUTURE

The mutilation of female genitals has been practised in many areas for centuries. The greatest determination, combined with sensitivity and understanding of local conditions, will be needed if it is to be abolished. In every country and region where operations are carried out, the situation is different, as is the political will, whether at local or national levels. In Western countries the way forward is relatively clear. In Africa the problem is more profound and the economic and political conditions vastly more difficult, while international agencies have hardly begun to explore their potential role.

What all three have in common is that, to date, nearly all programmes have been individual or *ad hoc* efforts, with little integration into other structures, with minimal evaluation or monitoring, and lacking in long-term goals and strategies. To achieve real change will require more resources, more detailed planning, and more real, sustained commitment from governments and international organizations.

NOTES

1. Fran Hosken, *The Hosken Report—Genital and Sexual Mutilation of Females* (third enlarged/revised edition, Autumn, 1982, published by Women's International Network News, 187 Grant St, Lexington, Mass. 02173, USA). This is the most detailed and comprehensive collection of information available.

2. The consequences of sexual mutilations on the health of women have been studied by Dr. Ahmed Abu-el-Futuh Shandall, Lecturer in the Department of Obstetrics and Gynaecology at the University of Khartoum, in a paper entitled, "Circumcision and Infibulation of Females" (*Sudanese Medical Journal,* Vol. 5, No. 4, 1967); and by Dr. J.A. Verzin, in an article entitled "The Sequelae of Female Circumcision," (*Tropical Doctor,* October, 1975). A bibliography on the subject has been prepared by Dr. R. Cook for the World Health Organization.

3. Readers interested to read more about research on the sexual experience of circumcised women may want to read Hanny Lightfoot-Klein, *Prisoners of Ritual: An Odyssey into Female Genital Mutilation in Africa* (New York, The Haworth Press, 1989).

4. These feelings of rejection are clearly articulated by Kenyan girls in "The Silence over Female Circumcision in Kenya," in *Viva,* August, 1978.

5. Q.R. Ghadially, "Ali for 'Izzat': The Practice of Female Circumcision among Bohra Muslims," *Manushi,* No. 66, New Delhi, India, 1991.

6. See map of Childhood Mortality in the World, 1977 (Health Sector Policy Paper, World Bank, Washington, D.C., 1980).

7. See Hosken for details and estimates of ethnic groups involved.

8. *F Magazine,* No. 4, March, 1979 and No. 31, October, 1980.

9. Marie Assaad, *Female Circumcision in Egypt—Current Research and Social Implications* (American University in Cairo, 1979), p. 12.

10. "Social Transformation of Eritrean Society," paper presented to the People's Tribunal, Milan, 24–26 May 1980, by Mary Dines of Rights and Justice.

11. Koso-Thomas, *The Circumcision of Women: A Strategy for Elimination* (London, Zed Books, 1987).

12. UN Commission on Human Rights, Report of the Working Group on Traditional Practices Affecting Women and Children, 1986.

13. Ellen Ismail et al., *Women of the Sudan* (Bendestorf, Germany, EIS, 1990).

14. *L'enfant mutilé* by Renée Bridel, delegate of the FIFCJ to the UN, Geneva, 1978. See also Raqiya Haji Dualeh Abdalla, *Sisters in Affliction* (London, Zed Press, 1982) and Asma El Dareer, *Woman Why Do You Weep?* (London, Zed Press, 1982).

15. Belkis Woldes Giorgis, *Female Circumcision in Africa,* ST/ECA/ATRCW 81/02.

Part XX

Population, Urbanization and the Environment

41

The Metropolis and Mental Life

Georg Simmel

The deepest problems of modern life derive from the claim of the individual to preserve the autonomy and individuality of his existence in the face of overwhelming social forces, of historical heritage, of external culture, and of the technique of life. The fight with nature which primitive man has to wage for his *bodily* existence attains in this modern form its latest transformation. The eighteenth century called upon man to free himself of all the historical bonds in the state and in religion, in morals and in economics. Man's nature, originally good and common to all, should develop unhampered. In addition to more liberty, the nineteenth century demanded the functional specialization of man and

his work; this specialization makes one individual incomparable to another, and each of them indispensable to the highest possible extent. However, this specialization makes each man the more directly dependent upon the supplementary activities of all others. Nietzsche sees the full development of the individual conditioned by the most ruthless struggle of individuals; socialism believes in the suppression of all competition for the same reason. Be that as it may, in all these positions the same basic motive is at work: The person resists to being leveled down and worn out by a social-technological mechanism. An inquiry into the inner meaning of specifically modern life and its products, into the soul of the cultural body, so to speak, must seek to solve the equation which structures like the metropolis set up between the individual and the superindividual contents of life. Such an inquiry must answer the question of how the personality accommodates itself in the adjustments to external forces. This will be my task today.

Source: Reprinted and abridged with the permission of The Free Press, a Division of Simon & Schuster from *The Sociology of Georg Simmel*, translated and edited by Kurt H. Wolff. Copyright © 1950, copyright renewed 1978 by The Free Press.

The psychological basis of the metropolitan type of individuality consists in the *intensification of nervous stimulation* which results from the swift and uninterrupted change of outer and inner stimuli. Man is a differentiating creature. His mind is stimulated by the difference between a momentary impression and the one which preceded it. Lasting impressions, impressions which differ only slightly from one another, impressions which take a regular and habitual course and show regular and habitual contrasts—all these use up, so to speak, less consciousness than does the rapid crowding of changing images, the sharp discontinuity in the grasp of a single glance, and the unexpectedness of onrushing impressions. These are the psychological conditions which the metropolis creates. With each crossing of the street, with the tempo and multiplicity of economic, occupational and social life, the city sets up a deep contrast with small town and rural life with reference to the sensory foundations of psychic life. The metropolis exacts from man as a discriminating creature a different amount of consciousness than does rural life. Here the rhythm of life and sensory mental imagery flows more slowly, more habitually, and more evenly. Precisely in this connection the sophisticated character of metropolitan psychic life becomes understandable—as over against small town life, which rests more upon deeply felt and emotional relationships. These latter are rooted in the more unconscious layers of the psyche and grow most readily in the steady rhythm of uninterrupted habituations. The intellect, however, has its locus in the transparent, conscious, higher layers of the psyche; it is the most adaptable of our inner forces. In order to accommodate to change and to the contrast of phenomena, the intellect does not require any shocks and inner upheavals; it is only through such upheavals that the more conservative mind could accommodate to the metropolitan rhythm of events. Thus the metropolitan type of man—which, of course, exists in a thousand individual variants—develops an organ protecting him against the threatening currents and discrepancies of his external environment which would uproot him. He reacts with his head instead of his heart. In this an increased awareness assumes the psychic prerogative. Metropolitan life, thus, underlies a heightened awareness and a predominance of intelligence in metropolitan man. The reaction to metropolitan phenomena is shifted to that organ which is least sensitive and quite remote from the depth of the personality. Intellectuality is thus seen to preserve subjective life against the overwhelming power of metropolitan life, and intellectuality branches out in many directions and is integrated with numerous discrete phenomena.

The metropolis has always been the seat of the money economy. Here the multiplicity and concentration of economic exchange gives an importance to the means of exchange which the scantiness of rural commerce would not have allowed. Money economy and the dominance of the intellect are intrinsically connected. They share a matter-of-fact attitude in dealing with men and with things; and, in this attitude, a formal justice is often coupled with an inconsiderate hardness. The intellectually sophisticated person is indifferent to all genuine individuality, because relationships and reactions result from it which cannot be exhausted with logical operations. In the same manner, the individuality of phenomena is not commensurate with the pecuniary principle. Money is concerned only with what is common to all: It asks for the exchange value, it reduces all quality and individuality to the question: How much? All intimate emotional relations between persons are founded in their individuality, whereas in rational relations man is reckoned with like a number, like an element which is in itself indifferent. Only the objective measurable achievement is of interest. Thus metropolitan man reckons with his merchants and customers, his domestic servants and often even with persons with whom he is obliged to have social intercourse. These features of intellectuality contrast with the nature of the small circle in which the inevitable knowledge of individuality as inevitably produces a warmer tone of behavior, a behavior which is beyond a mere objective balancing of service and return. In the sphere of the economic psychology of the small group it is of importance that under primitive conditions production serves the customer who orders the goods, so that the producer and the consumer are acquainted. The modern metropolis, however, is supplied almost entirely by production for the market, that is, for entirely unknown purchasers who never personally enter the producer's actual field of vision. Through this anonymity the interests of each party acquire an unmerciful matter-of-factness; and the intellectually calculating economic egoisms of both parties need not fear any deflection because of the imponderables of personal relationships. The money economy dominates the metropolis; it has displaced the last survivals of domestic production and the direct barter of goods; it minimizes, from day to day, the amount of work ordered by customers. The matter-of-fact attitude is obviously so intimately interrelated with the money economy, which is dominant in the metropolis, that nobody can say whether the intellectualistic mentality first promoted the money economy or whether the latter determined the former. The metropolitan way of life is certainly the most fertile soil for this reciprocity, a point which I shall document merely by citing the dictum of the most eminent English constitutional historian: Throughout the whole course of English history, London has never acted as England's heart but often as England's intellect and always as her moneybag!

In certain seemingly insignificant traits, which lie upon the surface of life, the same psychic currents characteristically unite. Modern mind has become more and more calculating. The calculative exactness of practical life which the money economy has brought about corresponds to the ideal of natural science: to transform the world into an arithmetic problem, to fix every part of the world by mathematical formulas. Only money

economy has filled the days of so many people with weighing, calculating, with numerical determinations, with a reduction of qualitative values to quantitative ones. Through the calculative nature of money a new precision, a certainty in the definition of identities and differences, an unambiguousness in agreements and arrangements has been brought about in the relations of life-elements—just as externally this precision has been effected by the universal diffusion of pocket watches. However, the conditions of metropolitan life are at once cause and effect of this trait. The relationships and affairs of the typical metropolitan usually are so varied and complex that without the strictest punctuality in promises and services the whole structure would break down into an inextricable chaos. Above all, this necessity is brought about by the aggregation of so many people with such differentiated interests, who must integrate their relations and activities into a highly complex organism. If all clocks and watches in Berlin would suddenly go wrong in different ways, even if only by one hour, all economic life and communication of the city would be disrupted for a long time. In addition an apparently mere external factor, long distances, would make all waiting and broken appointments result in an ill-afforded waste of time. Thus, the technique of metropolitan life is unimaginable without the most punctual integration of all activities and mutual relations into a stable and impersonal time schedule. Here again the general conclusions of this entire task of reflection become obvious, namely, that from each point on the surface of existence—however closely attached to the surface alone—one may drop a sounding into the depth of the psyche so that all the most banal externalities of life finally are connected with the ultimate decisions concerning the meaning and style of life. Punctuality, calculability, exactness are forced upon life by the complexity and extension of metropolitan existence and are not only most intimately connected with its money economy and intellectualistic character. These traits must also color the contents of life and favor the exclusion of those irrational, instinctive, sovereign traits and impulses which aim at determining the mode of life from within, instead of receiving the general and precisely schematized form of life from without....

The same factors which have thus coalesced into the exactness and minute precision of the form of life have coalesced into a structure of the highest impersonality; on the other hand, they have promoted a highly personal subjectivity. There is perhaps no psychic phenomenon which has been so unconditionally reserved to the metropolis as has the blasé attitude. The blasé attitude results first from the rapidly changing and closely compressed contrasting stimulations of the nerves. From this, the enhancement of metropolitan intellectuality, also, seems originally to stem. Therefore, stupid people who are not intellectually alive in the first place usually are not exactly blasé. A life in boundless pursuit of pleasure makes one blasé because it agitates the nerves to their strongest reactivity for such a long time that they finally cease to react at all. In the same way, through the rapidity and contradictoriness of their changes, more harmless impressions force such violent responses, tearing the nerves so brutally hither and thither that their last reserves of strength are spent; and if one remains in the same milieu they have no time to gather new strength. An incapacity thus emerges to react to new sensations with the appropriate energy. This constitutes that blasé attitude which, in fact, every metropolitan child shows when compared with children of quieter and less changeable milieus.

This physiological source of the metropolitan blasé attitude is joined by another source which flows from the money economy. The essence of the blasé attitude consists in the blunting of discrimination. This does not mean that the objects are not perceived, as is the case with the half-wit, but rather that the meaning and differing values of things, and thereby the things themselves, are experienced as insubstantial. They appear to the blasé person in an evenly flat and gray tone; no one object deserves preference over any other. This mood is the faithful subjective reflection of the completely internalized money economy. By being the equivalent to all the manifold things in one and the same way, money becomes the most frightful leveler. For money expresses all qualitative differences of things in terms of "how much?" Money, with all its colorlessness and indifference, becomes the common denominator of all values; irreparably it hollows out the core of things, their individuality, their specific value, and their incomparability. All things float with equal specific gravity in the constantly moving stream of money. All things lie on the same level and differ from one another only in the size of the area which they cover. In the individual case this coloration, or rather discoloration, of things through their money equivalence may be unnoticeably minute. However, through the relations of the rich to the objects to be had for money, perhaps even through the total character which the mentality of the contemporary public everywhere imparts to these objects, the exclusively pecuniary evaluation of objects has become quite considerable. The large cities, the main seats of the money exchange, bring the purchasability of things to the fore much more impressively than do smaller localities. That is why cities are also the genuine locale of the blasé attitude. In the blasé attitude the concentration of men and things stimulate the nervous system of the individual to its highest achievement so that it attains its peak. Through the mere quantitative intensification of the same conditioning factors this achievement is transformed into its opposite and appears in the peculiar adjustment of the blasé attitude. In this phenomenon the nerves find in the refusal to react to their stimulation the last possibility of accommodating to the contents and forms of metropolitan life. The self-preservation of certain personalities is brought at the price of devaluating the whole objective world, a devaluation which in the end unavoidably drags one's own personality down into a feeling of the same worthlessness.

Whereas the subject of this form of existence has to come to terms with it entirely for himself, his self-preservation in the face of the large city demands from him a no less negative behavior of a social nature. This mental attitude of metropolitans toward one another we may designate, from a formal point of view, as reserve. If so many inner reactions were responses to the continuous external contacts with innumerable people as are those in the small town, where one knows almost everybody one meets and where one has a positive relation to almost everyone, one would be completely atomized internally and come to an unimaginable psychic state. Partly this psychological fact, partly the right to distrust which men have in the face of the touch-and-go elements of metropolitan life, necessitates our reserve. As a result of this reserve we frequently do not even know by sight those who have been our neighbors for years. And it is this reserve which in the eyes of the small-town people makes us appear to be cold and heartless. Indeed, if I do not deceive myself, the inner aspect of this outer reserve is not only indifference but, more often than we are aware, it is a slight aversion, a mutual strangeness and repulsion, which will break into hatred and fight at the moment of a closer contact, however caused. The whole inner organization of such an extensive communicative life rests upon an extremely varied hierarchy of sympathies, indifferences, and aversions of the briefest as well as of the most permanent nature. The sphere of indifference in this hierarchy is not as large as might appear on the surface. Our psychic activity still responds to almost every impression of somebody else with a somewhat distinct feeling. The unconscious, fluid, and changing character of this impression seems to result in a state of indifference. Actually this indifference would be just as unnatural as the diffusion of indiscriminate mutual suggestion would be unbearable. From both these typical dangers of the metropolis, indifference and indiscriminate suggestibility, antipathy protects us. A latent antipathy and the preparatory stage of practical antagonism affect the distances and aversions without which this mode of life could not at all be led. The extent and the mixture of this style of life, the rhythm of its emergence and disappearance, the forms in which it is satisfied—all these, with the unifying motives in the narrower sense, form the inseparable whole of the metropolitan style of life. What appears in the metropolitan style of life directly as dissociation is in reality only one of its elemental forms of socialization.

This reserve with its overtone of hidden aversion appears in turn as the form or the cloak of a more general mental phenomenon of the metropolis: It grants to the individual a kind and an amount of personal freedom which has no analogy whatsoever under other conditions. The metropolis goes back to one of the large developmental tendencies of social life as such, to one of the few tendencies for which an approximately universal formula can be discovered. The earliest phase of social formations found in historical as well as in contemporary social structures is this: a relatively small circle firmly closed against neighboring, strange, or in some way antagonistic circles. However, this circle is closely coherent and allows its individual members only a narrow field for the development of unique qualities and free, self-responsible movements. Political and kinship groups, parties and religious associations begin in this way. The self-preservation of very young associations requires the establishment of strict boundaries and a centripetal unity. Therefore they cannot allow the individual freedom and unique inner and outer development. From this stage social development proceeds at once in two different, yet corresponding, directions. To the extent to which the group grows—numerically, spatially, in significance and in content of life—to the same degree the group's direct, inner unity loosens, and the rigidity of the original demarcation against others is softened through mutual relations and connections. At the same time, the individual gains freedom of movement, far beyond the first jealous delimitation. The individual also gains a specific individuality to which the division of labor in the enlarged group gives both occasion and necessity....

It is not only the immediate size of the area and the number of persons which, because of the universal historical correlation between the enlargement of the circle and the personal inner and outer freedom, has made the metropolis the locale of freedom. It is rather in transcending this visible expanse that any given city becomes the seat of cosmopolitanism. The horizon of the city expands in a manner comparable to the way in which wealth develops; a certain amount of property increases in a quasi-automatical way in ever more rapid progression. As soon as a certain limit has been passed, the economic, personal, and intellectual relations of the citizenry, the sphere of intellectual predominance of the city over its hinterland, grow as in geometrical progression. Every gain in dynamic extension becomes a step, not for an equal, but for a new and larger extension. From every thread spinning out of the city, ever new threads grow as if by themselves, just as within the city the unearned increment of ground rent, through the mere increase in communication, brings the owner automatically increasing profits. At this point, the quantitative aspect of life is transformed directly into qualitative traits of character. The sphere of life of the small town is, in the main, self-contained and autarchic. For it is the decisive nature of the metropolis that its inner life overflows by waves into a far-flung national or international area....

The most profound reason, however, why the metropolis conduces to the urge for the most individual personal existence—no matter whether justified and successful—appears to me to be the following: The development of modern culture is characterized by the preponderance of what one may call the "objective spirit" over the "subjective spirit." This is to say, in language as well as in law, in the technique of production as well as in art, in science as well as in the objects of the domestic environment, there is embodied a sum of spirit. The individual in his intellectual development follows the growth of this spirit very imperfectly and at an ever increasing distance. If, for instance, we view the immense culture which for the last hundred years has been embodied in things and in knowledge, in institutions and in comforts, and if we compare all this with the cultural progress of the individual during the same period—at least in high status groups—a frightful disproportion in growth between the two becomes evident. Indeed, at some points we notice a retrogression in the culture of the individual with reference to spirituality, delicacy, and idealism. This discrepancy results essentially from the growing division of labor. For the division of labor demands from the individual an ever more one-sided accomplishment, and the greatest advance in a one-sided pursuit only too frequently means dearth to the personality of the individual. In any case, he can cope less and less with the overgrowth of objective culture. The individual is reduced to a negligible quantity, perhaps less in his consciousness than in his practice and in the totality of his obscure emotional states that are derived from this practice. The individual has become a mere cog in an enormous organization of things and powers which tear from his hands all progress, spirituality, and value in order to transform them from their subjective form into the form of a purely objective life. It needs merely to be pointed out that the metropolis is the genuine arena of this culture which outgrows all personal life. Here in buildings and educational institutions, in the wonders and comforts of space-conquering technology, in the formations of community life, and in the visible institutions of the state, is offered such an overwhelming fullness of crystallized and impersonalized spirit that the personality, so to speak, cannot maintain itself under its impact. On the one hand, life is made infinitely easy for the personality in that stimulations, interests, uses of time, and consciousness are offered to it from all sides. They carry the person as if in a stream, and one needs hardly to swim for oneself. On the other hand, however, life is composed more and more of these impersonal contents and offerings which tend to displace the genuine personal colorations and incomparabilities. This results in the individual's summoning the utmost in uniqueness and particularization, in order to preserve his most personal core. He has to exaggerate this personal element in order to remain audible even to himself....

42

Africville: The Life and Death of a Canadian Black Community

Donald H. Clairmont
and Dennis William Magill

To seek social change, without due recognition of the manifest and latent functions performed by the social organization undergoing change, is to indulge in social ritual rather than social engineering.[1]

— *Robert K. Merton*

Halifax, the foundation city of English-speaking Canada, experienced much change during its first two hundred years of existence. Yet the facelift and redevelopment it has undergone since the late 1950s have effected a change as dramatic as the 1917 explosion that levelled much of the city. Stimulated by the Stephenson Report of 1957,[2] urban renewal and redevelopment have resulted in the relocation of thousands of people, the demolition of hundreds of buildings, and the

construction of impressive business and governmental complexes. The Africville relocation was part of the larger redevelopment pattern; Africville residents constituted some eight to ten percent of the people affected by approved urban renewal schemes in the city of Halifax during the relocation years.

Africville was a black community within the city of Halifax, inhabited by approximately four hundred people, comprising eighty families, many of whom were descended from settlers who had moved there over a century ago. Tucked away in a corner of the city, relatively invisible, and thought of as a "shack town," Africville was a depressed community both in physical and in socioeconomic terms. Its dwellings were located beside the city dump, and railroad tracks cut across the one dirt road leading into the area. Sewerage, lighting, and other public services were conspicuously absent. The people had little education, very low incomes, and many were underemployed. Property claims were in chaos. Only a handful of families could establish legal title;

Source: From Donald H. Clairmont and Dennis W. Magill. 1999. *Africville: The Life and Death of a Canadian Black Community*, Third Edition (pp. 1–19). Toronto: Canadian Scholars' Press. Reprinted by permission of Canadian Scholars' Press Inc.

others claimed squatter rights; and still others rented. Africville, long a black mark against society, had been designated for future industrial and harbour development. Many observers reported that despite these liabilities there was a strong sense of community and that some residents expressed satisfaction with living in Africville.

In 1964 the small black ghetto of Africville began to be phased out of existence. By that time most residents of Halifax, black and white, had come to think of Africville as "the slum by the dump." Most Haligonians, including some Africville residents, did not regard the community as viable and recognized a need for planned social change. The relocation plan announced by the city of Halifax, which purported to be more than simply a real estate operation, appeared to be a response to this need. The plan emphasized humanitarian concern, included employment and education programs, and referred to the creation of new opportunities for the people of Africville. To the general public, the proposed relocation was a progressive step.

In addition to official pronouncements, there were other indications that the Africville program would be more humane and progressive than the typical North American urban relocation. Halifax city council had adopted recommendations contained in a report submitted by a noted Canadian welfare specialist experienced in urban renewal. There was much preliminary discussion of the relocation by city officials among themselves, with Africville residents, and with a "caretaker" group of black and white professionals associated with the Halifax Human Rights Advisory Committee. Relocation plans were not *ad hoc* and haphazard. City officials were required to articulate their policies well and in detail; many implications and alternatives were considered.

There were also indications in the relocation decision-making structure that the Africville program might realize its official rhetoric. A social worker was appointed by the city to take front-line responsibility for the varied aspects of the relocation and to act as liaison between the

city administration and the relocatees. The social worker, who was on loan from the Nova Scotia Department of Public Welfare, had a measure of autonomy vis-à-vis the city and an independent contingency fund to meet day-to-day emergencies and opportunities with a minimum of bureaucratic delay. In negotiating the real estate aspects of relocation, the social worker brought proposed agreements before a special advisory committee consisting of aldermen and several members of the Halifax Human Rights Advisory Committee.

In terms of its rationale, public rhetoric, and organizational structure, the Africville relocation seemed worthy of study. The plan was *liberal-oriented* (that is, aimed at ending segregation and providing improved opportunities for the disadvantaged), *welfare-oriented* (that is, it hoped to coordinate employment, educational, and rehabilitative programs with the rehousing of people), and run by experts (that is, the planning, execution, and advise were provided by professionals). An examination of the Africville relocation could be expected to yield greater fundamental insight into planned social change than would a study of typical relocation programs that were accomplished by administrative fiat and stressed primarily the physical removal of persons. It seemed important to study and evaluate the Africville relocation both in its particularity and against the background of general relocation issues.

There were additional reasons for studying the Africville relocation. First, Africville was part of a trend in the 1960s for governmental initiative in relocation programs, and there was reason to expect that other tentative relocations in Nova Scotia and elsewhere would be patterned after the Africville experience. Second, Africville had attracted national and even international notice, and there was broad public interest in the relocation. Third, accounts of pre-relocation social conditions and attitudes were available. Two surveys had been conducted[3] and other material was available in city records. Finally, in 1968 the Africville relocation had already been acclaimed locally as a success. One city alderman noted:

The social significance of the Africville program is already beginning to show positive results as far as individual families are concerned. The children are performing more satisfactorily in school and they seem to take more of an interest in their new surroundings. This report is not intended to indicate that the program has been 100 percent successful; however I believe it can be said that it has been at least 75 percent, judging by the comments of the relocated families.[4]

Private communication with city officials and relocation officials in the United States and Canada brought forth praise for the organization and rhetoric of the Africville relocation.

Was the Africville relocation a success? If so, from whose perspective? To what extent? What accounted for the success or lack of it? It is hoped that answers to these and related questions will contribute to an appreciation of the Africville relocation and of relocation generally.

THE RELOCATION PHENOMENON

Relocation must be seen in the context of a general North American mobility pattern, and certain distinctive features should be noted. The most important distinction is that relocation is part of planned social change carried out, or at least approved, by public agency. The initiation of relocation, as seen by the relocatees, is usually involuntary and an immediate function of the political process. Our present concern is with relocation as it pertains to private residences, involves neighbourhoods or communities, and is a function of comprehensive programs of social change. This kind of relocation accounts for but a small measure of the mobility noted in Canada and the United States, but it was significant because it was distinctive. It was noted earlier that the Africville relocation was itself part of a much larger redevelopment project in the city of Halifax. In terms of the sweep of lifestyle change, even such large urban projects have been dwarfed by post–Second World War Canadian relocation projects in the Arctic and in Newfoundland. In 1953, Newfoundland, with 6000 miles of coastline and

approximately 1150 settlements, undertook a program to move people from the small outposts to larger viable communities which could be serviced efficiently. Between 1965 and 1970 over 3250 households were moved.[5]

As many low-income Americans and Canadians can testify, urban renewal is a prime example of forced relocation. Urban renewal legislation began in the 1940s in both countries. By 1968 approximately forty-five Canadian urban redevelopments had been initiated at a cost of 270 million dollars for 1500 cleared acres.[6] While the scope of urban renewal in Canada was quite small in the light of American experience, the Canadian program was significant enough that one can complain that there were too few Canadian studies looking into the politics, issues, and human consequences of renewal programs. To overcome this lack of knowledge and to place the Africville relocation in perspective, more comprehensive themes will be discussed in this [selection].

From a political-administrative perspective there are four relocation models: the traditional, development, liberal-welfare, and political. The Africville project is the best Canadian example of the liberal-welfare type of relocation.... [T]hese models vary along six dimensions: (1) ideological premises; (2) formulation of policy; (3) implementation of policy; (4) intended beneficiaries; (5) central actors and organizational units; and (6) key problems. These models are ideal types to which actual relocation programs correspond to a greater or lesser degree.

THE DEVELOPMENT MODEL

The development model was the most prevalent political-administrative approach to relocation in North America. This type of relocation was usually justified in terms of supposed benefits for the system as a whole, whether the system is society, the city, etc. It was usually initiated by order of political authorities and administered by bureaucrats; it was not anticipated that relocatees would benefit other than indirectly. The underlying ideology of the development model was system-oriented and neo-capitalist; an accurate statement of its premise in urban renewal has been offered by Wallace: "[it considers] renewal, as a public activity, to be intervention in a market and competitive system and to be justified by the need to make up for imperfections in the market mechanism that impede the adjustment process, to eliminate conditions which are economic or social liabilities."[7] In the context of contemporary urban renewal, the development model incorporated the usual city-design approach, focusing on questions of beautification, zoning, and structure,[8] and was usually intended to increase the city tax base and achieve civic pride or attract industry.

The development model can be illustrated by past urban renewal programs in Toronto. Ignoring relocatees as viable interest groups the programs operated implicitly on the basis of certain ideological premises: to correct imperfections in the social system (removal of so-called slums) and overall system development (economic growth), or both. As is the case in many Canadian cities, Toronto's past development policy was closely linked to the businesses and commercial-property industry which provided homes, apartment buildings, shopping centres, and industrial complexes. Thus the elimination of "blight areas" and construction of highrise apartment and office buildings generated an important source of urban revenue. Referring to this policy of "dollar planning," Fraser observed:

As long as Toronto, [in 1972] like all other municipalities in Canada has to depend upon property taxes as its sole source of income, the overwhelming power of development interests in determining the direction and quality of Toronto's growth will remain unchallenged.

…[T]he key to a municipality's prosperity remains its rate of growth; Toronto planners have been consistently ignored by city councils that have been over the years almost exclusively uninterested in any discussions about the quality of that development.[9]

A non-urban example of the development model of relocation has been described by John Matthiasson, in his study of the forced relocation of a band of Cree Indians in Northern Manitoba. The Cree were relocated to make way for a gigantic power project; they were not involved in the project planning and despite their displeasure "they accepted in a fatalistic manner the announcement of the relocation. They believed that the decision had been made by higher authorities, and that they had neither the right nor power to question it."[10]

The development model of relocation had its limitations. In particular, its econocentric and "undemocratic" features were criticized. The assumption that relocatees benefit indirectly from relocation was challenged, as was the premise that the system as a whole somehow redistributed fairly the benefits accruing from forcing people to move and facilitating the development of private industry. Some critics argued that if one included social-psychological factors in one's conception of costs, the relocatees could be seen as subsidizing the rest of the system. The criticism had some effect, and the liberal-welfare model became increasingly common.[11] One official explained:

In the fifteen years since [urban renewal's] inception, we have seen a progressive broadening of the concept and a strengthening of tools. We have seen, increasingly, both the need for, and realization of, rapprochement between physical and social planning, between renewal and social action. But the fully effective liaison of the two approaches has almost everywhere been frustrated by the absence of the tools to deal as effectively with the problems of human beings as with the problems of physical decay and blight.[12]

Another writer has observed,

social welfare can no longer be treated as the responsibility of private and more or less bountiful ladies and gentlemen or as the less respected branch of the social welfare community and the city government. Tied as it is to the concerns as dear to the heart of the country as economic prosperity it merits a place in the inner sanctum, particularly of planning commissions.[13]

THE LIBERAL-WELFARE MODEL

The "rediscovery" of poverty,[14] the war on poverty, the increasing pressure "from below" upon the development model, and the broadening definition of urban renewal led to the widespread emergence of the liberal-welfare-oriented approach. The liberal-welfare model, like the development model, emphasized expertise and technical knowledge in its operation and administration, and invariably was initiated by public authority. The principal difference is that the liberal-welfare model purported to benefit the relocatees primarily and directly. Under this model, welfare officials often saw themselves as "caretakers" for the relocatees; one relocation official has said, "the department of relocation is the tenants' advocate."[15] The liberal-welfare model of relocation was characterized by a host of social welfare programs supplemental to housing policies and was regarded as an opportunity for a multifaceted attack on poverty and other problems. It was this liberal-welfare model and its assumptions that shaped the rhetoric underlying the 1963–64 decision to relocate Africville.

Ideologically, the liberal-welfare model was much like the development model in that it tended to operate with a consensus model of society and posited a basic congruency between the interests of relocatees and those of society as a whole, it was "undemocratic" in the same sense as the development model; the low-status relocatees were accorded little attention, either as participants in the implicit political process or as contributions to specific policies or plans of action. There was an effort, however, to persuade rather than to ignore the relocatees. Criticism of the liberal-welfare model of relocation was related primarily to the ideological level. Some writers noted that liberal welfarism had become part of the establishment of contemporary North American society.[16] Its proponents were presumed to be handmaidens of strong vested interests, reconciling the disadvantaged and patching up the symptoms of social malaise. Critics pointed out that the special

programs associated with the liberal-welfare model of relocation tended to be short-term and unsuccessful. The welfare rhetoric often diverted attention from the gains and benefits accruing to the middle-income and elite groups in society. The critics attacked the liberal-welfare model on the premise that the social problems to which it is ostensibly directed could be solved only through profound structural change effecting a redistribution of resources, and by providing relocatees with the consciousness and resources to restructure their own lives.

The liberal-welfare model is best illustrated by the Africville relocation…. The community of Africville was defined as a social problem, and relocation was regarded as an intervention strategy designed to help solve the "social and economic problems of Africville residents." The central actors in the formation and implementation of relocation policy were politicians, bureaucrats, experts, and middle-class caretakers; there was no meaningful *collective* participation by Africville residents. The relocatees were to be major beneficiaries through compensation, welfare payments, and rehabilitative retraining programs. The major problem with the relocation was that, although rooted in liberal-welfare rhetoric, it failed to achieve its manifest goals.

THE POLITICAL MODEL

The liberal-welfare model of relocation was revised and developed both as a response to criticism at the ideological level and in reaction to its lack of operational success. There was a growing interest in citizen participation in all phases of relocation; in the firmer acceptance, structurally and culturally, of the advocacy function of relocation officials; in the coordination of relocation services; and in the provision of resources. It is difficult to assess how far this interest has been translated into fact. There appeared to be a shift in the 1970s, at least conceptually, to the political model of relocation and a frank recognition that relocation usually entailed a conflict of interest, for example, between the relocatees and the city. There was an attempt to structure the conflict by providing relocatees with resources to develop a parallel structure to that of the government. Although society and the relocatee were considered to benefit equally, this political perspective assumed that relocatees benefited both directly and indirectly; directly in terms of, say, housing and other welfare services, and indirectly by participating in the basic decision-making and the determination of their life situation. The political model of relocation was based on the premise that social problems were political problems and emphasized solutions through political action; relocation was approached primarily as a situation in which problems were solved not by the application of expertise but by the resolution of conflicting interests.

Beyond the considerable costs (the dollar cost is less hidden than in the other relocation model) and administrative difficulties entailed, there were other grounds for criticism of the political model. There was a tendency to overemphasize the solidarity and common interests of relocatees, to exaggerate the multiplying effects of political participation in relocation,[17] and to raise serious questions about how far government could proceed or would proceed in fostering extra-parliamentary political action.

Citizen participation, a core element in the political model, was institutionalized in the United States by the community action programs of the 1964 Economic Opportunity Act. Numerous books and articles, far too many to cite, have discussed the reasons, operations, and failures of "maximum feasible participation" of the poor in the war on poverty.[18] Citizen participation was also part of the United States model city programs, which required that local residents be involved in the planning process and implementation of changes in their neighbourhoods. Contrasted with the United States, Canada has relatively few examples of related social-animation projects. The rise of "mili-

tant" citizen groups was a phenomenon which developed later in Canada. The public outcry against the community work of the Company of Young Canadians and the subsequent governmental intervention to close this organization may be an indication of the limits of this perspective. The only Canadian publication illustrating the political model of a relocation is Fraser's study of Toronto's Trefann Court. Trefann Court residents successfully fought off a development-type relocation project; subsequently, the conflict arising from different interests was recognized as an integral part of the city's social organization. Despite internal community conflict between homeowners and tenants, a number of community residents, leaning heavily on outside: "resource people," developed a cohesive organization and set up a working committee (a parallel structure) to establish a conceptual scheme for community change in conjunction with the existing city bureaucracy. The Trefann Court case also pointed to a key problem in the political model, that of assessing the representativeness of any one group of citizens to speak, argue, or vote for an entire community. With the establishment of "parallel structures," many citizens grow frustrated with the tedious detail involved in committee work. In Fraser's words:

The fact that the Working Committee operated under formal rules of order, dominated by minutes, reports, rules of procedure and legislative decorum widened the gap between the committee and the community. As debates became more lengthy, detailed and technical, the meetings became harder to follow for the ordinary Trefann resident who might drop in.[19]

THE TRADITIONAL MODEL

Finally, there is the traditional model of relocation in North American society. This is a limiting type of relocation carried out under governmental auspices, for it is a form of planned social change characterized by self-help and self-direction. It is the neighbourhood or community leaders, often indigenous minority-group leaders working through indigenous social organizations, who plan and carry out the relocation, generally with official support and some resource commitment by government agencies. The traditional model entails a largely laissez-faire strategy whereby the relocatees benefit directly and technical expertise is used to advise rather than to direct. Criticism of this approach contends that, without political action, neither the available resources nor the generation of initiative can be effective in the case of low-status groups.

There are numerous examples of the traditional model of relocation. Group settlement and resettlement in various parts of Canada have been common. The relocation of Beechville, a black community on the outskirts of Halifax, is an example within the Halifax metropolitan area. Community leaders, anticipating a government attempt to relocate the residents, organized themselves into a co-operative housing association, received funds from Central Mortgage and Housing Corporation, and reorganized their community partly on their own terms. The scope available for traditional relocation models lessens as society becomes more technocratic and centralized.

CONCEPTUAL FRAMEWORK

...[O]ur emphasis will be on the liberal-welfare model of planned social change and its implementation during the Africville relocation. During the analysis we focus on questions of power and exchange among the various participants of the relocation. Thus, from the perspective of power and exchange,[20] we can examine the power resources and relationships among the individual persons and groups involved in the relocation, the historical evolution of these social facts, the goals held by the different parties, and the strategies and tactics employed in establishing the terms of the relocation "contract." We can also analyse the role of outsiders, experts, and community "leaders" and focus on questions

such as the mobilization of advocacy, relocation resistances and alternatives, and the relation of rhetoric to action. It is vital in the Africville case to have a larger historical view, observing the historical exchange patterns between the city and the Africville people and tracing the implications of these patterns in making Africville "ripe for relocation" and in influencing the relocation decision-making and mechanics.

An aspect of this perspective concerns the context of negotiations and the bargaining strategies developed by the parties involved. Accordingly, attention was devoted to probing the relocatees' knowledge about the relocation; their strategies (use of lawyers, co-operation with fellow relocatees, and development of special arguments in dealing with city officials), and their perceptions of the city's goals, strategies, and resources. The relocation social worker completed a questionnaire concerning each relocated family which paid considerable attention to his negotiations with relocatees and his perception of their goals, strategies, and resources. This perspective included the concepts of rewards, costs, profits, and distributive justice. It would appear, for instance, that relocatees would have been satisfied with the relocation if rewards exceeded costs and if they thought that the city and other relocatees would not "get a better deal." Information concerning rewards, costs, sense of distributive justice, and satisfaction was obtained through the questionnaires, the interviews, and the case studies.

Despite problems in measuring each relocatee's perception of the relative profit accruing to himself or herself, other relocatees, and the city of Halifax, and problems occasioned by differences between long-term and short-term effects, this power and exchange approach is significant for the relocation literature which often appears to keep aloof from the "blood and guts" of relocation transaction. Equally important, by placing the Africville relocation within a typology of relocation models, it is possible to explore the domain consensus (that is, the basic terms of reference held in common and prerequisite to any exchange) associated with the liberal-welfare approach, and especially how such *domain* consensus (for example, "disadvantaged communities or people have few intrinsically valuable resources and need to be guided by sympathetic experts") develops and how it sets the limits and context of bargaining and reciprocity.

RESEARCH STRATEGIES

The methods employed in this study were varied: questionnaires, in-depth interviews, historical documents, newspapers, case studies, and "bull sessions" with relocatees. A useful baseline source of data was the survey of Halifax blacks, including Africville [residents], conducted in 1959 by the Institute of Public Affairs, Dalhousie University. The original questionnaires were available for re-analysis, an important consideration since many of the data were not published and the published material contained several significant inaccuracies.[21] The 1959 survey questionnaire provided basic demographic data as well as information concerning mobility aspirations, employment, education, and social life.

The collection of data for this study began in 1968. The researchers arranged for two students from the Maritime School of Social Work to prepare twenty case studies.[22] A review of the students' case studies and field notes, guided by the perspective developed by the researchers, aided the drafting of a questionnaire. In 1968 current addresses of the relocatees were also traced and brief acquaintance interviews were conducted.

The most intensive data collection period was June to December 1969. One of the researchers (D.W.M.) conducted in-depth, tape-recorded interviews with individual people associated with the relocation decision-making and implementation: politicians, city officials, middle-class caretakers, the relocation social worker, consultants, and Africville relocatees involved in the decision-making. During these interviews an open-ended interview guide[23] was used to explore knowledge of Africville and awareness of pre-1964 relocation attempts and also the actual relocation decision-

making and mechanics. Each of the approximately two-hour interviews was transcribed and analysed for patterns. Many quotations used in this book are taken from these tape-recorded interviews.

Concurrently, the other researcher (D.H.C.), with two assistants, was meeting informally with the relocatees, individually and in "bull sessions." On the basis of these experiences and the case studies, we all drafted and pre-tested an extensive questionnaire. From September to December, 1969, the questionnaire was employed by interviewers hired and trained by the researchers. The lengthy questionnaire[24] asked about the relocatee's background characteristics: life in Africville, personal knowledge of relocation decision-making processes, relocation strategies, negotiations, costs, rewards, and post-relocation conditions. The questionnaire was given to all household heads and spouses who had lived in Africville and had received a relocation settlement of any kind. Approximately 140 persons were interviewed, several in places as far distant as Winnipeg and Toronto.

In June, 1969, the relocation social worker spent eight days answering a questionnaire[25] on the relocatees' background characteristics, his relocation bargaining with each relocatee, and his perception of the latter's rewards, costs, and strategies. Such data enabled us to analyse more precisely the relationships among parties to the relocation, for similar data from the relocatees and their perception of the relocation social worker were obtained from the relocatee questionnaire.

Two other research tactics were employed at the same time as the interviews were conducted. One of our assistants was conducting in-depth, tape-recorded interviews with black leaders in the Halifax area concerning their assessment of Africville and the implications of relocation. Another assistant was gathering historical data and interviewing selected Africville relocatees concerning the historical development of the community. Important sources of historical data were the minutes of Halifax City Council (read from 1852 to 1969), reports of the Board of

Halifax School Commissioners, the Nova Scotia Public Archives, files in the Registry of Deeds, the Halifax *Mail-Star* library, and the minutes of the Halifax Human Rights Advisory Committee. In all phases of research, the Africville files in the Social Planning Department, City of Halifax were of especial value.

PHASES OF THE AFRICVILLE STUDY

The Africville Relocation Report, in addition to being an examination of relocation and planned social change and a contribution to the sparse literature on blacks in Nova Scotia, represents a fusion of research and action. The researchers did not begin the study until virtually all the Africville people had been relocated, and the research strategy resulted in the study being more than an evaluation.[26] The process of obtaining collective as well as individual responses, and of establishing a meaningful exchange with relocatees, fostered collective action from former Africville residents. Some local government officials objected to what they have referred to as the researchers' "activist" bias. The researchers maintain, however, that exchanges had to be worked out with the subjects of research as well as with the funding agencies. The liberal ethic posits informed voluntary consent as fundamental to adult social interaction; informed voluntary consent requires, in turn, meaningful exchange among the participants.

The study began in October, 1968 with a meeting of relocated Africville people. This was the first time since relocation that former residents of Africville had met collectively. This stormy meeting, called by the researchers, was a public airing of relocatee grievances and led to relocatee support of the proposed study. Subsequent talk of forming committees to press grievances with the city of Halifax was an important result of the meeting. The researchers encouraged this tendency, for the expressed grievances appeared legitimate, and the researchers considered that it would be both possible and important to tap a collective or group dimension in the relocation process as well as to study the usual social-psychological considerations.

Later in the same week, at a meeting that the researchers had arranged with city officials, relocation caretakers, and civic leaders, the researchers related the expressed grievances of the relocatees and urged remedial action. General support for the proposed study was obtained at this second meeting, and the pending reconsideration of relocation by the city's newly created Social Planning Department was crystallized.

During the winter and spring of 1969, as the present study was being planned in detail, the action-stimulus of the researchers' early efforts was bearing fruit. Social Planning Department officials were meeting with the relocatees and, as it were, planning the second phase (not initially called for) of the Africville relocation. With provincial and municipal grants totalling seventy thousand dollars, the Seaview Credit Union was organized to assist relocatees experiencing financial crises; in addition, plans were formulated to meet housing and employment needs, and special consideration was to be given to former Africville residents whose needs could be met within the city's existing welfare system. A relocatee was hired to manage the credit union and to assist with other anticipated programs.

During the main data-gathering period, the summer of 1969, and in line with a decision to obtain collective as well as individual responses, the researchers met with informed groups of Africville relocatees to discuss current and future remedial action, it became apparent that the so-called second phase of the relocation would be inadequate to meet the people's needs. There was little identification with the credit union and it was floundering, for many relocatees who became members were either unable or unwilling to repay loans. Other anticipated programs and action promised by the city were delayed or forgotten due to bureaucratic entanglements and to lack of organization and pressure on the part of the relocatees.

The relocatees still had legitimate grievances related to unkept promises made at the time of relocation and later. With the formation of the Africville Action Committee, a third phase of the relocation began in the fall of 1969 and winter of 1970. The task of this new committee, developed from group discussions held between the researchers and relocatees, was to effect governmental redress through organized pressure. Several position papers were developed by the Africville Action Committee and negotiations were reopened with the city of Halifax. Although numerous meetings of relocatees were held during the first half of 1970, problems within the Africville Action Committee and the absence of resource people until the fall of 1970 hindered progress. With the committee stumbling along, and the credit union and other city-sponsored projects either ineffectual or nonexistent, the relocation process appeared to have petered out. The action committee was reactivated when one of the authors (D.H.C.) returned to Halifax permanently in the fall of 1970 and groups of relocatees were subsequently reinvolved in reading and criticizing a draft of the present study and in evaluating the relocation and the remedial action taken. Since the fall of 1970, the Africville Action Committee was active. Widespread support for its claims was obtained from community organizations, subcommittees were established to deal with questions of employment, housing, and financial compensation; and city council authorized the establishment of a city negotiating team to meet with representatives of the action committee.

In 1974, at the time of publication of the first edition of this book, the Africville Action Committee, to all intents and purposes, had ceased to function. Although it could claim some credit for a special employment training program through which a number of unemployed Africville relocatees had found jobs, the action committee fell far short of its goals.

The city's lack of a positive imaginative response and the internal organizational problems of the action committee hindered other proposals. What remained in 1974 was a reorganized credit union, a modest base for further redress and group action. However, by 1999 the Seaview Credit Union was no longer in existence; it had collapsed over two decades ago. However, the community is not dead.... Africville still thrives in the hearts and minds of many of the relocatees. In addition, Africville still has rich symbolic value for fostering black consciousness in Nova Scotia.

POSTSCRIPT

Throughout the study, we consciously and deliberately attempted to achieve a viable fusion of research and social responsibility. The research focussed on the collective responses of the group as well as on individual responses. At each stage in the study (conception, data gathering, data analysis, and preparation for publication) the collective and individual inputs that gave the study an action potential were obtained from relocatees. Drafts of appropriate chapters were sent for critical comment to officials and others involved in the relocation. The study became a stimulus to action because the normal researcher-subject exchanges could be worked out in concrete, actual terms. This was preferable to the usual research situation where, in effecting exchanges with the people being studied, the researcher typically makes vague references to the possible benefit of the study and does little or nothing to follow up implied promises of action.[27] But of course, our research strategy has its weakness too. It is difficult to feel satisfied that the kind of exchange relations that we established had productive consequences. Despite our involvement (in the early 1970s) with petitions, committee work, and attempts at rational problem solving, little redress of the inadequacies of the relocation program was achieved and the manifest goals of the liberal-welfare rhetoric of the relocation remain, in large measure, unrealized.

NOTES

1. *Social Theory and Social Structure* (Glencoe, Ill.: The Free Press, 1949), p. 80.

2. Gordon Stephenson, *A Redevelopment Study of Halifax, Nova Scotia* (Halifax, N.S.: City of Halifax, 1957).

3. *The Condition of the Negroes of Halifax City, Nova Scotia* (Halifax: Institute of Public Affairs, Dalhousie University, 1962); and G. Brand, *Interdepartmental Committee on Human Rights: Survey Reports* (Halifax, N.S.: Nova Scotia Department of Welfare, Social Development Division, 1963).

4. Minutes of the Halifax City Council, Halifax, N.S., September 14, 1967.

5. The Government of Newfoundland initiated the program in 1953. In 1965 a joint federal-provincial program was initiated under a resettlement act. In 1970 the program was placed under the direction of the Federal Department of Regional Economic Expansion. For an overview of the resettlement program, see Noel Iverson and D. Ralph Matthews, *Communities In Decline: An Examination of Household Resettlement in Newfoundland,* Newfoundland Social and Economic Studies, No. 6, (St. John's, Nfld.: Memorial University of Newfoundland, Institute of Social and Economic Research, 1968). For a critical assessment of studies of the resettlement program, see Jim Lotz, "Resettlement and Social Change in Newfoundland," The *Canadian Review of Sociology and Anthropology 8* (February, 1971): 48–59.

6. See Table 4, "Completed Redevelopment Projects" in *Urban Renewal* (Toronto: Centre for Urban and Community Studies, University of Toronto, 1968). Reprinted from *University of Toronto Law Journal,* 18. No. 3 (1968): 243.

7. David A. Wallace, "The Conceptualizing of Urban Renewal," *Urban Renewal* (Toronto: Centre for Urban and Community Studies, University of Toronto, 1968), 251.

8. An example of such a project is one reported by Thurz in southwest Washington, D.C. Little was done for the relocatees, but the relocation was widely acclaimed for its futuristic redevelopment design. For a critique of this approach, see Daniel Thurz, *Where Are They Now?* Washington, D.C.: Health and Welfare Council of the National Capital Area, 1966). See also, Jane Jacobs, *The Death and Life of Great American Cities* (New York: Random House, 1961).

9. Graham Fraser, *Fighting Back: Urban Renewal in Trefann Court* (Toronto: Hakkert, 1972), p. 55.

10. John Matthiasson, "Forced Relocation: An Evaluative Case Study," paper presented at the annual meeting of the Canadian Sociology and Anthropology Association, Winnipeg, 1970.

11. In recent years some minor progressive modifications have been introduced with reference to the development model; these deal with advance notice and public hearings, relocation compensation, and the availability of housing stock. See, Robert P. Groberg, *Centralized*

Relocation (Washington, D.C.: National Association of Housing and Redevelopment Officials, 1969).

12. William L. Slayton, "Poverty and Urban Renewal," quoted in Hans B. C. Spiegel, "Human Considerations in Urban Renewal," *Urban Renewal,* op. cit., 311.

13. Elizabeth Wood, "Social Welfare Planning," quoted in Spiegel, op. cit., 315.

14. For a discussion of this, see Kenneth Craig, "Sociologists and Motivating Strategies," M.A. thesis, University of Guelph, Department of Sociology, 1971.

15. Groberg, op. cit., p. 172.

16. See Alvin W. Gouldner, *The Coming Crisis of Western Sociology* (New York: Basic Books, 1970), pp. 500–02.

17. Relocation is a short-term consideration, for most services brought to bear on relocatee problems rarely extend beyond rehousing. A more general critique of the multiplying effect of citizens' involvement in relocation is given by S. M. Miller and Frank Riessman, *Social Class and Social Policy* (New York: Basic Books Inc., 1968).

18. The historical antecedents and reasons for the legislation are discussed in Daniel Moynihan, *Maximum Feasible Misunderstanding* (New York: Free Press, 1970). For an alternative interpretation, see Francis Fox Piven and Richard A. Cloward, *Regulating the Poor: The Functions of Public Welfare* (New York: Random Vintage Books, 1972), pp. 248–84. The operation of the program is discussed by Ralph M. Kramer, *Participation of the Poor: Comparative Community Case Studies* in *the War on Poverty* (Englewood Cliffs, N.J.: Prentice Hall, 1969).

19. Fraser, op. cit., p. 262.

20. For a discussion of this theoretical perspective, see Peter M. Blau, *Exchange and Power in Social Life* (New York: Wiley, 1964); and George Caspar Homans, *Social Behavior: Its Elementary Forms* (New York: Harcourt, Brace and World, 1961).

21. *The Condition of the Negroes of Halifax City,* Nova Scotia, op. cit.

22. Sarah M. Beaton, "Effects of Relocation: A Study of Ten Families Relocated from Africville, Halifax, Nova Scotia," Master of Social Work Thesis, Maritime School of Social Work, Halifax, N.S., 1969; and Bernard MacDougall, "Urban Relocation of Africville Residents," Master of Social Work Thesis, Maritime School of Social Work, Halifax, N.S., 1969.

23. The interview guide is published in Donald H. Clairmont and Dennis W. Magill, *Africville Relocation Report* (Halifax, N.S.: Institute of Public Affairs, Dalhousie University, 1971), pp. A131–A135.

24. Ibid., pp. A97–A128.

25. Ibid., pp. A83–A96.

26. Some relocation studies have been carried out as part of the relocation decision-making, see William H. Key, *When People Are Forced to Move* (Topeka, Kansas: Menninger Foundation, 1967), mimeographed, others have been concurrent with the relocating of people, see

Herbert J. Gans, *The Urban Villagers: Group and Class* in *The Life of Italian Americans* (New York: The Free Press, 1962). The present study is unique in that it fostered collective action carried out after the relocation.

27. See Craig, op. cit.

43

Rich Planet, Poor Planet: Global Environment and Poverty in 2001

Christopher Flavin

A visit to Brazil's tropical state of Bahia provides contrasting views of the state of the world at the dawn of the new millennium. Bahia's capital, Salvador, has a population of over 3 million and a thoroughly modern veneer. Its downtown is full of large office buildings and busy construction cranes, and its highways are crammed with sport utility vehicles. The state is also rich in natural resources: the wealth provided by gold and sugarcane made Salvador the obvious location for colonial Brazil's leading port and capital for two centuries.[1]

Once a backwater—slavery was not outlawed until the end of the nineteenth century, one of the last regions to ban this practice—Bahia's economy is now booming. The state has a prospering manufacturing sector and has become popular with many leading multinationals, including automobile companies that have put some of their most advanced factories there. The information economy is in a particularly competitive frenzy. Brazilian Internet service providers are connecting customers for free, and cell phones appear to be almost as common as they are in many European cities.

Scratch the surface, however, and another Bahia is still there. The large favelas that ring Salvador's outskirts are crowded with thousands of poor people who lack more than cell phones and computers: Toilets, running water, and school-books are among the basic services and products that are unavailable to many of Bahia's poor. Similar gaps can be seen in the low hills that run south of Salvador along Bahia's rugged coast: The collapse of many of the country's rich cacao farms due to a devastating pathogen called witches'-broom and a sharp decline in world chocolate prices have left thousands of farm workers jobless and unable to provide for their families.

Source: From Lester R. Brown et al. *State of the World 2001* of the Worldwatch Institute, New York: Norton's 2001.

Bahia's environmental condition is just as uneven. Considered by ecologists to be one of the world's biological "hot spots," the Atlantic Rain Forest covers more than 2,000 kilometers of Brazil's subtropical coast. In 1993, biologists working in an area south of Salvador identified a world record 450 tree species in a single hectare. (A hectare of forest in the northeastern United States typically contains ten species.) In the last decade, Bahia's political and business leaders have come to recognize the extraordinary richness of their biological heritage—wildlands are being protected, ecological research facilities are being set up, and ecotourist resorts are mushrooming. A sign at the airport even warns travelers that removing endemic species from the country is a felony.[2]

And yet, signs of destruction are everywhere: Cattle ranches sprawl where the world's richest forests once stood; 93 percent of the Atlantic forest is already gone, and much of the remainder is fragmented into tiny plots. Pressure on these last bits of forest is enormous—both from powerful landowners and corporations eager to sell forest and agricultural products in the global marketplace, and from poor families desperately seeking a living.[3]

This picture of Bahia in the year 2000 is replicated at scores of locations around the globe. It is the picture of a world undergoing extraordinarily rapid change amid huge and widening disparities. Unprecedented economic prosperity, the emergence of democratic institutions in many countries, and the near instantaneous flow of information and ideas throughout a newly interconnected world allow us to address challenges that have been neglected for decades: meeting the material needs of all 6 billion members of the human race and restoring a sustainable balance between humanity and Earth's ecological systems.

This moment is historic, perhaps even evolutionary, in character. Tragically, it is not being seized. Despite a surge in economic growth in recent years and significant gains in health and education levels in many developing nations, the number of people who survive on less than $1 of income per day—the poverty threshold used by the World Bank—was 1.2 billion in 1998, almost unchanged since 1990. In some parts of the world, including sub-Saharan Africa, South Asia, and the former Soviet Union, the number living in poverty is substantially higher than the figures recorded a decade ago.[4]

The struggle to restore the planet's ecological health presents a similar picture: a number of small battles have been won, but the war itself is still being lost. Double-digit rates of growth in renewable energy markets, plus a two-year decline in global carbon emissions, for example, have failed to slow the rate of global climate change. Indeed, recent evidence, from the rapid melting of glaciers and the declining health of heat-sensitive coral reefs, suggests that climate change is accelerating. The same pattern can be seen in the increased commitment to protection of wild areas and biological diversity: new laws are being passed, consumers are demanding ecofriendly wood products, and ecotourist resorts are sprouting almost as quickly as dotcom companies. But foresters and biologists report that this host of encouraging developments has not reversed the massive loss of forests or the greatest extinction crisis the world has seen in 65 million years.[5]

Long considered distinct issues, consigned to separate government agencies, ecological and social problems are in fact tightly interconnected and mutually reinforcing. The burden of dirty air and water and of decimated natural resources invariably falls on the disadvantaged. And the poor, in turn, are often compelled to tear down the last nearby tree or pollute the local stream in order to survive. Solving one problem without addressing the other is simply not feasible. In fact, poverty and environmental decline are both embedded deeply in today's economic systems. Neither is a peripheral problem that can be considered in isolation. What is needed is what Eduardo Athayde, General Director of Bahia's Atlantic Forest Open University, calls "econology," a synthesis of ecology, sociology, and economics that can be used as the basis for creating an economy that is both socially and ecologically sustainable—the central challenge facing humanity as the new millennium begins.[6]

The challenge is made larger by the fact that it must be met simultaneously at national and global levels, requiring not only cooperation but partnership between North and South. Responsibility for the current health of the planet and its human inhabitants is shared unequally between rich and poor countries, but if these problems are to be resolved, the two groups of nations will need to bring their respective strengths and capabilities to bear. This will require a new form of globalization—one that goes beyond trade links and capital flows to strengthened political and social ties between governments and civil society.

A select group of large industrial and developing countries—a collection that can be called the E-9, given that they are key environmental as well as economic players—could have a central role in closing the North–South gap. Together, this group of countries accounts for 57 percent of the world's population and 80 percent of total economic output. (See Table 43.1.) This [reading] uses data on these nine diverse countries and areas to illuminate key economic, social, and ecological trends. But this grouping has more than just analytical value. As argued at the end of the [reading], E-9 cooperation could be a key to achieving accelerated economic and environmental progress in the new century.[7]

A TALE OF TWO WORLDS

Halfway through the year 2000, two stories from the Philippines made headlines around the world. In June, a computer virus dubbed the "love bug" appeared almost simultaneously on every continent, crashing the computer systems of scores of multinational corporations and government offices, ranging from the U.S. Pentagon to the British Parliament. The estimated total cost of the resulting disruptions: $10 billion. Computer

Table 43.1   The E-9: A Population and Economic Profile

Country Grouping	Population, 2000	Gross National Product, 1998
	(million)	*(billion dollars)*
China	1,265	924
India	1,002	427
European Union[1]	375	8,312
United States	276	7,903
Indonesia	212	131
Brazil	170	768
Russia	145	332
Japan	127	4,089
South Africa	43	137

[1] Data for European Union do not include Luxembourg.

Source: World Bank, *World Development Indicators 2000* (Washington, D.C.: 2000), 10–12; Population Reference Bureau, "2000 World Population Data Sheet," wall chart (Washington, D.C.: June 2000).

security experts and FBI agents quickly traced the diabolical love bug to a small Manila technical college and a 24-year-old student named Onel de Guzman. For computer experts, this may have been an indication of the vulnerability of the global Internet, but in the Philippines it quickly became a source of national pride. People took the love bug debacle as an encouraging sign that their developing nation was leapfrogging into the top ranks of the global economy's hottest sector.[8]

Across town, a Manila neighborhood called the Promised Land was hit by a different kind of news a month later: more than 200 people were killed in a massive landslide and subsequent fire. Although this tragedy was precipitated by Typhoon Kai-Tak, it was anything but a natural disaster. The Promised Land, it turns out, is a combination garbage dump/shantytown that is home to 50,000 people, most of whom make their living by scavenging the food and materials discarded by Manila's growing middle class. When two days of heavy rain loosened the mountain of garbage, it came crashing down on hundreds of homes as well as the dump's electrical lines, starting a massive fire. Scores of

Promised Land residents were buried, others were burned alive, and still more were poisoned by toxic chemicals released by the fire.[9]

Economic successes and social failures are now found side by side, not just in the Philippines, but around the world in this supposed time of plenty. The annual output of the world economy has grown from $31 trillion in 1990 to $42 trillion in 2000; by comparison, the total output of the world economy in 1950 was just $6.3 trillion. And in 2000, the growth of the world economy surged to a 4.7-percent annual rate, the highest in the last decade. This increase in economic activity has allowed billions of people to buy new refrigerators, televisions, and computers, and has created millions of jobs. Global telephone connections grew from 520 million in 1990 to 844 million in 1998 (an increase of 62 percent), and mobile phone subscribers went from 11 million to 319 million in that time (up 2,800 percent). The number of "host" computers, a measure of the Internet's expansion, grew from 376,000 in 1990 to 72,398,000 in 1999—an increase of 19,100 percent.[10]

The economic boom of the last decade has not been confined to the rich countries of the North. Much of the growth is occurring in the developing nations of Asia and Latin America, where economic reforms, lowered trade barriers, and a surge in foreign capital have fueled investment and consumption. Between 1990 and 1998, Brazil's economy grew 30 percent, India's expanded 60 percent, and China's mushroomed by a remarkable 130 percent. China now has the world's third largest economy (second if measured in terms of purchasing power parity), and a booming middle class who work in offices, eat fast food, watch color television, and surf the Internet. China alone now has 420 million radios, 344 million television sets, 24 million mobile phones, and 15 million computers.[11]

Still, the global economy remains tarnished by vast disparities. (See Table 43.2.) Gross national product (GNP) per person ranges from $32,350 in Japan to $4,630 in Brazil, $2,260 in Russia, and just $440 in India. Even when measured in purchasing power terms, GNP per person among

Table 43.2   Economic Trends in E-9 Nations

Country	GNP per Person, 1998	Purchasing Power per Person, 1998	Population Earning Below $2 per Day, 1993–99[1]	Share of Income or Consumption	
				Lowest 20 percent, 1993–98[1]	Highest 10 percent, 1993–98[1]
	(dollars)		(percent)	(percent)	
Japan	32,350	23,592	—	10.6	21.7
United States	29,240	29,240	—	5.2	30.5
Germany[2]	26,570	22,026	—	8.2	23.7
Brazil	4,630	6,460	17.4	2.5	47.6
South Africa	3,310	8,296	35.8	2.9	45.9
Russia	2,260	6,180	25.1	4.4	38.7
China	750	3,051	53.7	5.9	30.4
Indonesia	640	2,407	66.1	8.0	30.3
India	440	2,060	86.2	8.1	33.5

[1] Data are from a single year within the time frame.

[2] Comparable data for European Union not available; Germany is most populous EU member.

Source: World Bank, *World Development Indicators 2000* (Washington, D.C.: 2000), 10–12, 62–64, 66–68.

these countries varies by a factor of 10. Per capita income has increased 3 percent annually in forty countries since 1990, but more than eighty nations have per capita incomes that are lower than they were a decade ago. Within countries, the disparities are even more striking. In the United States, the top 10 percent of the population has six times the income of the lowest 20 percent; in Brazil, the ratio is 19 to 1. More than 10 percent of the people living in "rich" countries are still below the poverty line, and in many, inequality has grown over the last two decades.[12]

The boom in global consumption over the past decade has been accompanied by improvements in living standards in many countries and declines in others. The U.N. Development Programme estimates that the share of the world's population suffering from what it calls "low human development" fell from 20 percent in 1975 to 10 percent in 1997. Still, World Bank figures show that 2.8 billion people, nearly half the world's population, survive on an income of less than $2 per day, while a fifth of humanity, 1.2 billion people, live on less than $1 per day. An estimated 291 million sub-Saharan Africans— 46 percent of the region's population—now live on less than $1 a day, while in South Asia, the figure is 522 million. This is a staggering number of people to enter the new century without the income needed to purchase basic necessities such as food, clean water, and health care.[13]

Worldwide, some 1.1 billion people are currently estimated to be malnourished. Most of these are poor people in rural areas who have insufficient land to grow the food they need and not enough income to buy it from others. Many of these people live in countries with food surpluses, but while well-off farmers sell their products to middle-class consumers in distant nations; the proceeds have no benefit for millions of starving children. In some African countries, such as Kenya, Zambia, and Zimbabwe, as much as 40 percent of the population is malnourished.[14]

Roughly 1.2 billion people do not have access to clean water. In China, the portion that fall in this category is 10 percent (125 million people), in India it is 19 percent, and in South Africa, 30 percent. Toilets are even rarer in many countries: 33 percent of Brazil's population does not have one, nor does 49 percent of Indonesia's or 84 percent of India's.[15]

Polluted water is a major contributor to one of the largest disparities today's world faces: the health gap. Although infant mortality rates have dropped 25 to 50 percent in many countries in the past decade, they still stand at 43 per thousand live births in China and 70 per thousand in India. (See Table 43.3.) Much of the wide difference in this number around the world results from undernutrition and common infectious diseases that remain rampant in many poor countries. More intractable diseases such as cholera and tuberculosis are also becoming epidemic in many areas.

More alarming still is the fact that AIDS, which has been brought under control in some rich countries, is spreading rapidly in many developing nations. The crisis is particularly acute in southern Africa, which a decade ago had relatively low rates of infection. By 2000, HIV infection rates had reached a stunning 20 percent in South Africa, 25 percent in Zimbabwe, and 36 percent in Botswana. Decades of rising life expectancy are being reversed in a matter of years, as hundreds of thousands of young adults and children succumb to the disease. Health care budgets are being overwhelmed, and education undermined by the early deaths of many teachers. It is no accident that the countries most ravaged by AIDS are those with high rates of social disruption and limited government health services. In China, poor people who sell their blood in order to make ends meet are paying a high price in the form of HIV infection from contaminated needles. Ironically, in parts of Africa, it is those who are just emerging from poverty that are being hit the hardest—devastating a generation of educated young workers, a cataclysm that may forestall the growth of an economically secure middle class.[16]

Table 43.3   Health Indicators in E-9 Nations

Country	Health Expenditures per Person, 1990–98[1]	Infant Mortality 1980	Infant Mortality 1998	Tuberculosis Incidence, 1997	HIV Prevalence Among Adults, 1997
	(dollars of purchasing power)	(per thousand live births)		(per 100,000)	(percent)
United States	4,121	8	4	7	0.76
Germany[2]	2,364	12	5	15	0.08
Japan	1,757	13	7	29	0.01
South Africa	571	42	31	394	12.91
Brazil	503	70	33	78	0.63
Russia	404	22	17	106	0.05
China	142	90	43	113	0.06
Indonesia	73	115	70	187	0.82
India	38	67	51	285	0.05

[1] Data are from the most recent year available.

[2] Comparable data for European Union not available; Germany is most populous EU member.

Source: World Bank, *World Development Indicators 2000* (Washington, D.C.: 2000), 90–92, 102–04, 106–08.

One of the key ingredients of economic progress is education, and on this front, the world is doing better than it was two decades ago. (See Table 65.4.) In India, the share of children in secondary school has risen from 41 percent to 60 percent; in China, it has gone from 63 [percent] to 70 percent; and in South Africa, from 62 [percent] to 95 percent. But even with these improvements, many countries are failing to invest adequately in their young people, who are unlikely to be able to participate in or benefit from today's most vibrant economic sectors, which demand not only basic literacy but often specialized training. Girls in particular are receiving inadequate education in many countries. Adult female illiteracy rates remain as high as 25 percent in China and 57 percent in India, levels that virtually guarantee a host of social and economic problems—and that make environmental threats more difficult to address.

TESTING THE LIMITS

When the Russian icebreaker *Yamal* reached the North Pole in July 2000, the scientists abroad were confronted with a strange sight: an expanse of open, calm water in place of the two or three meters of pack ice that is common to the region even at the height of summer. In the 91 years since Robert Peary and Matthew Henson reached the North Pole by dogsled in 1909, nothing like this had been reported. But human memory is the wrong scale on which to measure this development: Scientists estimate that the last time the polar region was completely icefree was 50 million years ago.[17]

The dynamic, shifting character of the Arctic ice pack suggests that the open water over the pole itself was, for now, a fleeting phenomenon. But recent scientific evidence confirms the underlying trend: Earth's frozen top is melting at an extraordinary rate. Submarine sonar measurements indicate a 40-percent decline in the average thickness of summer polar ice since the 1950s, far exceeding the rate of melting previously estimated. Based on these observations, scientists now estimate that by the middle of this century the Arctic could be ice-free in summer.[18]

Among the myriad signs of human-induced global climate change—fossil fuel combustion was recently estimated to have raised atmospheric concentrations of carbon dioxide to their highest

Table 43.4   Education in E-9 Nations

| Country | Adult Illiteracy Rate | | | | Share of Children in Secondary School | |
| | Female | | Male | | | |
	1980	1998	1980	1998	1980	1997
	(percent)				(percent)	
Germany[1]	—	—	—	—	82	95
Japan	—	—	—	—	93	100
United States	—	—	—	—	94	96
Russia	2	1	1	0	98	88
Brazil	27	16	23	16	46	66
South Africa	25	16	22	15	62	95
Indonesia	40	20	21	9	42	56
China	48	25	22	9	63	70
India	74	57	45	33	41	60

[1] Comparable data for European Union not available; Germany is most populous EU member.

Source: World Bank, *World Development Indicators 2000* (Washington, D.C.: 2000), 74–76, 82–84.

levels in 20 million years—this one may be the most dramatic. In late 2000, the Intergovernmental Panel on Climate Change (IPCC), the scientific body that advises government negotiators, produced its latest report. It included the strongest consensus statement yet that societies' release of carbon dioxide and other greenhouse gases "contributed substantially to the observed warming over the last fifty years." By the end of the century, the IPCC concluded, temperatures could be five degrees Celsius higher than in 1990—an increase greater than the change in temperature between the last Ice Age and today.[19]

While the shipping industry is already beginning to view the Arctic meltdown as a potential short-term opportunity—perhaps cutting the transit distance between Europe and the Far East by as much as 5,000 kilometers—the full economic and ecological consequences would be far more extensive and hard to predict. Scientists have recently learned that Arctic ice is a key part of the "engine" that drives the powerful oceanic conveyor belt—the warm Gulf Stream—that provides northern Europe with the relatively temperate and stable climate that allowed European societies to flourish. Shutting it down could change the climate of Europe more than at

any time since the last Ice Age. And because the Gulf Stream is a dominant feature in the oceanic circulation system, any major change in its course would have ripple effects globally. Moreover, with less ice to reflect the sun's rays, the warming of Earth that caused the ice to melt in the first place would accelerate.[20]

Some 10,000 kilometers south of the North Pole lies a very different environment—the world's tropical oceans and their abundant coral reefs, a biologically rich ecosystem that has been described as the rainforest of the ocean (65 percent of fish species are reef dwellers). One of the richest is the Belize Barrier Reef on the Yucatan Peninsula in the Caribbean, the site of a recent diving expedition by marine biologist Jonathan Kelsey and journalist Colin Woodard. What was intended to be an exciting exploration of the region's spectacular, multihued marine life turned out to be a disturbing disappointment: "Bright white boulders dotted the seascape in all directions, a sign of severe coral distress," Woodard reported. "A centuries-old stand of elkhorn coral as big as an elephant was now dead and smothered in a thick two-year growth of brown algae.... Across the plane, the corals appeared to be dying."[21]

Around the world, from the Caribbean to the Indian Ocean and Australia's Great Barrier Reef, similar observations have been reported in the past two years. Coral polyps are temperature-sensitive, and often sicken or die when ocean surface temperatures rise even slightly. The temporary warming of ocean waters that accompanies El Niño anomalies in the Pacific is generally hard on coral reefs, but the 1998 El Niño was something different: Reports of sick coral were soon being filed by marine biologists around the world, who estimated that more than one quarter of the coral reefs were sick or dying. In some areas of the Pacific, the figure is as high as 90 percent. For many small island nations, the loss in income from fishing and tourism, as well as increased storm damage from the loss of coral reefs, may be enough to trigger the collapse of their economies.[22]

Following another serious episode of coral bleaching just a decade earlier, this recent epidemic of coral disease is another strong indication that the world is warming. But it is more than that: Coral reefs are sort of a marine version of the famous canary in a coalmine—vulnerable to many environmental stresses that now run rampant, including urban sewage, agricultural runoff, and the sedimentation that comes from deforestation. The recent decimation of coral reefs and the growing frequency of such events suggest that the world's ecological balance has been profoundly disturbed.

Whether it is Arctic ice, tropical corals, oceanic fisheries, or old-growth forests, the forces driving ecological destruction are varied, complex, and often dangerously synergistic. Population is one factor. The nearly fourfold expansion in human numbers over the past century has drastically increased demands on natural resources. The combination of population growth and deforestation, for example, has cut the number of hectares of forest per person in half since 1960—increasing pressures on remaining forests and encouraging a rapid expansion in plantation forestry. Demand for water, energy, food, and materials have all been driven up by the unprecedented expansion in human numbers. And increasingly, it is in the world's developing countries that natural systems are declining the fastest and people face the most serious environmentally related stresses. (See Table 43.5.)[23]

Table 43.5   Ecological Health of E-9 Nations

Country	Share of Land Area That is Forested, 1995[1]	Change of Average Annual Deforestation, 1990–95	Share of Mammals Threatened, 1996	Share of Flowering Plants Threatened, 1997	Share of Land Area Nationally Protected, 1996
		(percent)			
Russia	22	0	11.5	—	3.1
Brazil	16	0.5	18.0	2.4	4.2
United States	6	−0.3	8.2	4.0	13.4
China	4	0.1	19.0	1.0	6.4
Germany[2]	3	0	10.5	0.5	27.0
Indonesia	3	1	29.4	0.9	10.6
Japan	0.7	0.1	22.0	12.7	6.8
South Africa	0.2	0.2	13.4	9.5	5.4

[1] Data may refer to earlier years.

[2] Comparable data for European Union not available; Germany is most populous EU member.

Source: World Bank, *World Development Indicators 2000* (Washington, D.C.: 2000), 126–28.

Population growth alone could not have tested environmental limits this severely, however. The pressures it imposes have been magnified by rising consumption levels as each individual demands more from nature. Meat-based diets and automobile-centered transportation systems are among the highly consumptive practices first adopted by the billion or so people living in rich countries, and now proliferating quickly in many parts of the developing world. Meanwhile, government regulations and emission control technology have lagged well behind the pace of adoption in richer countries. As a consequence, the most serious air pollution is now found in cities such as Jakarta and São Paulo. (See Table 43.6.)

The combination of population growth and increased consumption is projected to cause the number of people living in water-deficit countries to jump from 505 million to over 2.4 billion in the next twenty-five years. In countries that already face severe water shortages, such as Egypt, India, and Iran, water scarcity is likely to require large-scale food imports. In northern China, the water table under Beijing fell 2.5 meters in 1999, bringing the total decline since 1965 to 59 meters. Similarly, surging demand for oil—particularly in North America and East Asia—contributed in the

year 2000 to the highest sustained oil prices the world has seen since the early 1980s. Beyond the proximate political reasons for higher oil prices, the underlying cause is clear: world oil production is nearing its eventual all-time peak, and producers are struggling to meet the combined demands of first-time car owners in China and those who are buying the large SUVs now found in nearly half of U.S. garages.[24]

While the last decade's growth in affluence contributed to many environmental problems, keeping people poor is not the answer—either morally or practically. In impoverished areas around the world, the rural poor are pushed onto marginal, often hilly lands, from which they must hunt bushmeat, harvest trees, or clear land for pasture or crops in order to survive. A 2000 study on the root causes of biodiversity loss, sponsored by the World Wide Fund for Nature (WWF), concluded that together with other forces, poverty often plays a major role.[25]

In the Philippines, for example, the country's rich array of coral reefs, forests, and mangroves—home to an estimated 40,000 species—are shrinking rapidly in area, while the remaining pockets lose much of their original diversity. According to the WWF study, rural poverty and the unequal distribution of land in the Philippines are among

Table 43.6   Air Pollution in E-9 Nations

Country	Sulfur Dioxide, 1995	Suspended Particulates, 1995	Nitrogen Dioxide, 1995
	(micrograms per cubic meter)		
Germany (Frankfurt)[1]	11	36	45
Japan (Tokyo)	18	49	68
South Africa (Cape Town)	21	—	72
United States (New York)	26	—	79
India (Mumbai)	33	240	39
Brazil (São Paulo)	43	86	83
China (Shanghai)	53	246	73
Russia (Moscow)	109	100	—
Indonesia (Jakarta)	—	271	—

[1] Comparable data for European Union not available; Germany is most populous EU member.

Source: World Bank, *World Development Indicators 2000* (Washington, D.C.: 2000), 162–64.

the major causes of biodiversity loss that must be remedied if the country's natural wealth is to be preserved for future generations. Similarly, a study in the southern Mexican state of Campeche found that much of the pressure on the Calakmul Biosphere Reserve is coming from the efforts of local indigenous people to meet their material needs. Meeting those needs sustainably is a key component of any effective program to reverse environmental decline.[26]

NORTH MEETS SOUTH

Bridging these gaps between North and South will require a combination of innovative market reforms and a common commitment by governments to fill the gaps left by the private sector. Most of the recent emphasis has been on the market, pointing to developments such as the certified forest products market and booming consumer interest in ecotourism. And even government negotiated treaties such as the Kyoto Protocol on climate change now rely on market mechanisms as primary tools for achieving their goals. Greenhouse gas trading schemes are being viewed as a way of not only trimming emissions as efficiently as possible, but also distributing the burden of addressing the problem among various countries.

Market mechanisms are often effective, and private innovation is key to solving many problems, but North–South cooperation will have to be based on something more than commercial relationships if the world's current problems are to be surmounted. Cooperation among NGOs, for example, allows innovative social programs and political techniques to be transferred rapidly from one country to another, dramatically speeding the rate of progress. The recent surge in the number of these groups in the developing world is being spurred by the support of foundations in industrial countries, as well as by the spread of democracy in many poor nations. And the Internet is proving a boon to the spread of civil society in countries where it has been weak in the past. The ability of citizens to communicate easily among themselves—and with people in distant lands with similar concerns—is rapidly transforming the political equation in many countries, and is creating more favorable conditions for addressing social and ecological problems.

Government leadership is also key: Governments need to forge strong partnerships and provide sufficient funding to invest in the public infrastructure needed to support a sustainable economy. The failure of many industrial countries to meet the financial commitments they have agreed to under various international agreements and the failure of some developing countries to carry through on political and economic reforms have left a residue of distrust that must be overcome. Although it is unlikely that foreign aid levels will ever return to the figures that were typical in the 1960s and 1970s, a steady flow of well-targeted grants is essential to sustain progress. And with private capital taking up much of the burden of industrial growth and large-scale infrastructure, government aid can be targeted at pressing needs, with multiplier effects on human progress and environmental protection: areas such as education, health care, the status of women, micro-credit, and broad Internet access. One essential step is reducing the developing-country debt burden, which has reached onerous levels in recent years.

The economic and political weakness of many developing countries has prevented them from taking the more central position on the world stage that is now logically theirs. With 80 percent of the world's population, the bulk of its natural resources, and an opportunity to learn from the historical mistakes of today's industrial countries, it seems clear that the South will increasingly dominate the twenty-first century. Today's industrial powers will likely resist this shift, but they will soon find that they cannot achieve their own goals without the cooperation of the South. The summer of 2000 saw an intriguing sign of the changing balance of power when Mexico elected its first president from outside the traditional ruling party. Vicente Fox, a charismatic modern leader, traveled to Washington and called for allowing workers to travel as freely across the Mexico–U.S. border as capital now does.[27]

The existing structure of international institutions such as the World Bank and the World Trade Organization will have to be reformed to allow developing countries to take the more central role that is now essential to solving the world's most difficult problems. With shared power will come shared responsibility—a role that seems far more achievable today than it did two decades ago, when participatory political systems were still rare in the developing world.

One new organizing principle for countries that is particularly appropriate is the E-9 group described earlier—a coalition of northern and southern countries that between them have far greater impact on global social and ecological trends than do the Group of Eight (G-8) industrial

countries. Between them, the E-9 have 60 percent of the world's population, 73 percent of the carbon emissions, and 66 percent of higher plant species. (See Table 43.7.) They have both the ability and the responsibility to lead the world in addressing the main challenges of the twenty-first century.

NOTES

1. Based on author's visit to Bahia, August 2000.
2. James Brooke, "Brazilian Rain Forest Yields Most Diversity for Species of Trees," *New York Times*, 30 March 1993.
3. "Latin America and the Caribbean: Brazil," *The Nature Conservancy*, **www.tnc.org/brazil/forest.htm**, viewed 12 October 2000.
4. World Bank, *World Development Report 2000/2001* (New York: Oxford University Press, 2000), 21–3.
5. Christopher Flavin, "Wind Power Booms," and idem, "Solar Power Market Jumps," both in Lester R. Brown, Michael Renner, and Brian Halweil, *Vital Signs 2000* (New York: W.W. Norton & Company, 2000), 56–9; Seth Dunn, "Carbon Emissions Fall Again," in ibid., 66–7; Clive Wilkinson, *Status of Coral Reefs of the World, 2000:*

Table 43.7   The E-9: Leaders for the Twenty-first Century

Country	World Population, 1999	PPP Gross Domestic Product, 1998	World Carbon Emissions 1999	World Forest Area, 1995	World Vascular Plant Species, 1997
			(percent)		
China	21.0	10.2	13.5	4	11.9
India	16.5	5.4	4.5	2	5.9
European Union	6.3	20.5	14.5	3	—
United States	4.6	21.3	25.5	6	6
Indonesia	3.5	1.3	.9	3	10.9
Brazil	2.8	2.9	1.5	16	20.8
Russia	2.4	2.4	4.6	22	—
Japan	2.1	8.0	6.0	0.7	2.1
South Africa	0.7	0.9	2.0	0.2	8.7
E-9 Total	**59.9**	**72.9**	**73**	**56.9**	**66.3**

Source: Worldwatch calculations based on Population Reference Bureau, "1999 World Population Data Sheet," wall chart (Washington, D.C.: June 1999); World Bank, *World Development Indicators 2000* (Washington, D.C.: 2000), 10–12; BP Amoco, *BP Amoco: Statistical Review of World Energy* (London: June 2000), 38; U.N. Food and Agriculture Organization, *State of the World's Forests 1999* (New York: 1999), 125–30; World Conservation Union–IUCN, *1997 IUCN Red List of Threatened Plants* (Cambridge, U.K.: 1998), xvii, xxvii–xxxiii.

Executive Summary, 9th International Coral Reef Symposium, 23–4 October 2000, Bali, Indonesia; National Snow and Ice Data Center, "Mountain Glacier Fluctuations: Changes in Terminus Location and Mass Balance," **www.nsidc.colorado.edu/NASA/SOTC/glacier_balance. html**, viewed 2 February 2000; Alexander Wood, "An Emerging Consensus on Biodiversity Loss," in Alex Wood, Pamela Stedman-Edwards, and Johanna Meng, eds., *The Root Causes of Biodiversity Loss* (London: Earthscan, 2000), 2.

6. Eduardo Athayde, Atlantic Forest Open University, Salvador, Bahia, Brazil, discussion with author, 10 August 2000.

7. The E-9 concept was first introduced as the E-8 in *State of the World 1997*. This chapter adds South Africa to the group and substitutes the European Union (EU) for Germany, which substantially extends its breadth of economic and ecological coverage. The sector-specific tables that follow, however, use statistics for Germany (the EU's most populous member), due to the lack of comparable data for the EU as a whole.

8. " 'Love Bug' Suspect Charged," *Associated Press*, 29 June 2000; Mark Landler, "A Filipino Linked to 'Love Bug' Talks About His License to Hack," *New York Times*, 21 October 2000.

9. Casualties from "Payatas Relocation Coordination Ordered," Manila Bulletin, **www.mb.com.ph/umain/ 2000%2D07/mn071805.asp**, viewed 10 September 2000; Typhoon Kai Tak from Roli Ng, "Garbage Slide Kills 46 in Manila's Promised Land," Planet Ark, **www.planetark.org/dailynewsstory.cfm?newsid=7412 &newsdate=11-Jul-2000**, viewed 10 September 2000; number of residents from "Manila Urges Payatas Residents to Get Out of Dumpsite," *China Daily Information*, **www.chinadaily.net/cover/storydb/2000/ 07/15/wnmanila.715.html**, viewed 10 September 2000.

10. Growth of world economy from Angus Maddison, *Monitoring the World Economy 1820–1992* (Paris: Organisation for Economic Cooperation and Development [OECD], 1995), 227, and from Angus Maddison, *Chinese Economic Performance in the Long Run* (Paris: OECD, 1998), 159, using deflators and recent growth rates from International Monetary Fund (IMF), *World Economic Outlook* (Washington, DC: October 1999); growth estimate for 2000 from IMF, *World Economic Outlook* (advance copy) (Washington, DC: September 2000); International Telecommunications Union (ITU), *World Telecommunication Indicators '98*, Socioeconomic Timeseries Access and Retrieval System database, downloaded 24 August 1999, and ITU, *World Telecommunication Development Report 1999* (Geneva: 1999); number of host computers from Internet Software Consortium and Network Wizards, "Internet Domain Surveys," **www.isc.org/ds**, viewed 20 February 2000.

11. Growth of various economies from World Bank, *World Development Indicators 2000* (Washington, DC: 2000), 182–83; China's economy from ibid., 10–12; consumer products in China from ibid., 300, and from Population Reference Bureau, "2000 World Population Data Sheet," wall chart (Washington, DC: June 2000), with computers from Ye Di Sheng, "The Development and Market of China's Information Industry and its Investment Opportunity," **www.caspa.com/event/augdin2.htm**, viewed 10 November 2000.

12. Wealth disparities from World Bank, op. cit. note 4, 282–83; trends in per capita income from U.N. Development Programme (UNDP), *Human Development Report 1999* (New York: Oxford University Press, 1999), 2–3; income disparities from World Bank, op. cit. note 11, 66, 68; 10 percent based on UNDP, op. cit. this note, 149, 197; inequality growth from ibid., 3.

13. UNDP, op. cit. note 12, 25; number of people living on less than $1 per day from World Bank, op. cit. note 4, 3, 23.

14. Number of people malnourished is a World Watch estimate based on U.N. Administrative Committee on Coordination, Sub-Committee on Nutrition in collaboration with International Food Policy Research Institute (IFPRI), *Fourth Report on the World Nutrition Situation* (Geneva: 1999), and on Rafael Flores, research fellow, IFPRI, Washington, D.C., e-mail to Brian Halweil, Worldwatch Institute, 5 November 1999, and discussion with Gary Gardner, Worldwatch Institute, 3 February 2000; selected countries with chronic hunger from Gary Gardner and Brian Halweil, *Underfed and Overfed: The Global Epidemic of Malnutrition*, Worldwatch Paper 150 (Washington DC: Worldwatch Institute, March 2000), 17.

15. Number without access to clean water from Peter H. Gleick, *The World's Water 1998–1999* (Washington, DC: Island Press, 1998), 40; percentages by country from World Bank, op. cit. note 11, 14–6; toilets from World Bank op. cit. note 11, 94–6.

16. Joint United Nations Program on HIV/AIDS, *Report on the Global HIV/AIDS Epidemic—June 2000* (Geneva: June 2000), 124; Elizabeth Rosenthal, "In Rural China, a Steep Price of Poverty: Dying of AIDS," *New York Times*, 28 October 2000.

17. John Noble Wilford, "Ages-Old Polar Icecap Is Melting, Scientists Find," *New York Times*, 19 August 2000.

18. D. A. Rothrock, Y. Yu, and G. A. Maykut, "Thinning of the Arctic Sea-Ice Cover," *Geophysical Research Letters*, 1 December 1999, 3469; Ola M. Johannessen, Elena V. Ahalina, and Martin W. Miles, "Satellite Evidence for an Arctic Sea Ice Cover in Transformation," *Science*, 3 December 1999, 1937; Lars H. Smedsrud and Tore Furevik, "Toward an Ice-Free Arctic?" *Cicerone*, February 2000.

19. Paul N. Pearson and Martin R. Palmer, "Atmospheric Carbon Dioxide Concentrations Over the Past 60 Million Years," *Nature*, 17 August 2000, 695; Andrew C. Revkin, "A Shift in Stance on Global Warming Theory," *New York Times*, 26 October 2000.

20. Carsten Rühlemann et al., "Warming of the Tropical Atlantic Ocean and Slowdown of Thermohaline

Circulation During the Last Glaciation," *Nature*, 2 December 1999, 511.

21. Percentage of fish species as reef dwellers from Norman Myers, "Synergisms: Joint Effects of Climate Change and Other Forms of Habitat Destruction," in Robert L. Peters and Thomas E. Lovejoy, eds., *Global Warming and Biological Diversity* (New Haven, Conn.: Yale University Press, 1992), 347; Colin Woodard, "Fall of the Magic Kingdom: A Reporter Goes Underwater in the Belize Barrier Reef," *Tuftonia*, summer 2000, 20.

22. Daniel Cooney, "Coral Reefs Disappearing," *Associated Press,* 23 October 2000; Wilkinson, op. cit. note 5; Ove HoeghGuldberg et al., *Pacific in Peril,* available at **www.greenpeace.org**.

23. Hectares of forest per person from Robert Engleman et al., *People in the Balance: Population and Natural Resources at the Turn of the Millennium* (Washington, DC: Population Action International, 2000), 12.

24. Number of people living in water-deficit countries from ibid., 9; Beijing water table from James Kynge, "China Approves Controversial Plan to Shift Water to Drought-Hit Beijing," *Financial Times*, 7 January 2000; oil prices from U.S. Department of Energy, *Monthly Energy Review*, September 2000; near peak production of oil from Colin J. Campbell and Jean H. Laherrere, "The End of Cheap Oil," *Scientific American*, March 1998, 78–83.

25. Pamela Stedman-Edwards, "A Framework for Analysing Biodiversity Loss," in Wood, Stedman-Edwards, and Meng, op. cit. note 5, 15–6.

26. Wood, Stedman-Edwards, and Meng, op. cit. note 5, 283, 231–54.

27. Developing-country share of population from United Nations, *World Population Prospects: The 1998 Revision* (New York: December 1998); Fox proposal from Mary Jordan, "Mexican Touts Open Borders: Visiting President-Elect Pushes N. American Convergence," *Washington Post*, 25 August 2000.

Part XXI

Collective Behaviour and Social Movements

44

On the Origins of Social Movements

Jo Freeman

Most movements have inconspicuous beginnings. The significant elements of their origins are usually forgotten or distorted by the time a trained observer seeks to trace them out. Perhaps this is why the theoretical literature on social movements usually concentrates on causes (Gurr, 1970; Davies, 1962; Oberschall, 1973) and motivations (Toch, 1965; Cantril, 1941; Hoffer, 1951; Adorno et al., 1950), while the "spark of life" by which the "mass is to cross the threshold of organizational life" (Lowi, 1971: 41) has received scant attention....

From where do the people come who make up the initial, organizing cadre of a movement? How do they come together, and how do they come to share a similar view of the world in circumstances that compel them to political action? In what ways does the nature of the original center affect the future development of the movement?

Source: From *Social Movements of the Sixties and Seventies,* ed. Jo Freeman, pp. 8–13, 17–30, copyright © 1983 by Jo Freeman. Reprinted by permission.

Before answering these questions, let us first look at data on the origins of [two] social movements prominent in the sixties and seventies: civil rights...and women's liberation. These data identify recurrent elements involved in movement formation. The ways in which these elements interact, given a sufficient level of strain, would support the following propositions:

Proposition 1. The need for a *preexisting communications network* or infrastructure within the social base of a movement is a primary prerequisite for "spontaneous" activity. Masses alone do not form movements, however discontented they may be. Groups of previously unorganized individuals may spontaneously form into small local associations—usually along the lines of informal social networks—in response to a specific strain or crisis. If they are not linked in some manner, however, the protest does not become generalized but remains a local irritant or dissolves completely. If a movement is to spread rapidly, the communications network must already exist. If only the rudiments of a network exist, movement formation requires a high input of "organizing" activity.

Proposition 2. Not just any communications network will do. It must be a network that is *co-optable* to the new ideas of the incipient movement.[1] To be co-optable, it must be composed of like-minded people whose backgrounds, experiences, or location in the social structure make them receptive to the ideas of a specific new movement.

Proposition 3. Given the existence of a co-optable communications network, or at least the rudimentary development of a potential one, and a situation of strain, one or more precipitants are required. Here, two distinct patterns emerge that often overlap. In one, a *crisis* galvanizes the network into spontaneous action in a new direction. In the other, one or more persons begin *organizing* a new organization or disseminating a new idea. For spontaneous action to occur, the communications network must be well formed or the initial protest will not survive the incipient stage. If it is not well formed, organizing efforts must occur; that is, one or more persons must specifically attempt to construct a movement. To be successful, organizers must be skilled and must have a fertile field in which to work. If no communications network already exists, there must at least be emerging spontaneous groups that are acutely attuned to the issue, albeit uncoordinated. To sum up, if a co-optable communications network is already established, a crisis is all that is necessary to galvanize it. If it is rudimentary, an organizing cadre of one or more persons is necessary. Such a cadre is superfluous if the former conditions fully exist, but it is essential if they do not.

THE CIVIL RIGHTS MOVEMENT

The civil rights movement has two origins, although one contributed significantly to the other. The first can be dated from December 7, 1955, when the arrest of Rosa Parks for occupying a "white" seat on a bus stimulated both the Montgomery Bus Boycott and the formation of the Montgomery Improvement Association. The second can be dated either from February 1, 1960, when four freshmen at A & T College in Greensboro, North Carolina, sat in at a white lunch counter, or from April 15–17, when a conference at Shaw University in Raleigh, North Carolina, resulted in the formation of the Student Non-Violent Co-ordinating Committee. To understand why there were two origins one has to understand the social structure of the southern black community, as an incipient generation gap alone is inadequate to explain it.

Within this community the two most important institutions, often the only institutions, were the church and the black college. They provided the primary networks through which most southern blacks interacted and communicated with one another on a regular basis. In turn, the colleges and churches were linked in a regional communications network. These institutions were also the source of black leadership, for being a "preacher or a teacher" were the main status positions in black society. Of the two, the church was by far the more important; it touched on more people's lives and was the largest and oldest institution in the black community. Even during slavery there had been an "invisible church." After emancipation, "organized religious life became the chief means by which a structured or organized social life came into existence among the Negro masses" (Frazier, 1963: 17). Furthermore, preachers were more economically independent of white society than were teachers.

Neither of these institutions represented all the segments of black society, but the segments they did represent eventually formed the main social base for supplying civil rights activists. The church was composed of a male leadership and a largely middle-aged, lower-class female followership. The black colleges were the homes of black intellectuals and middle-class youth, male and female.

Both origins of the civil rights movement resulted in the formation of new organizations, despite the fact that at least three seemingly potential social movement organizations already existed. The wealthiest of these was the Urban League, founded in 1910. It, however, was not only largely restricted to a small portion of the black and white bourgeoisie but, until 1961, felt itself to be "essentially a social service agency" (Clark, 1966: 245).

Founded in 1909, the National Association for the Advancement of Colored People (NAACP) pursued channels of legal change until it finally persuaded the Supreme Court to abolish educational segregation in *Brown* v. *Board of Education*. More than any other single event, this decision created the atmosphere of rising expectations that helped precipitate the movement. The NAACP suffered from its own success, however. Having organized itself primarily to support court cases and utilize other "respectable" means, it "either was not able or did not desire to modify its program in response to new demands. It believed it should continue its important work by using those techniques it had already perfected" (Blumer, 1951: 199).

The Congress of Racial Equality, like the other two organizations, was founded in the North. It began "in 1942 as the Chicago Committee of Racial Equality, which was composed primarily of students at the University of Chicago. An offshoot of the pacifist Fellowship of Reconciliation, its leaders were middle-class intellectual reformers, less prominent and more alienated from the mainstream of American society than the founders of the NAACP. They regarded the NAACP's legalism as too gradualist and ineffective, and aimed to apply Gandhian techniques of non-violent direct action to the problem of race relations in the United States. A year later, the Chicago Committee joined with a half dozen other groups that had emerged across

the country, mostly under the encouragement of the F. O. R. to form a federation known as the Congress of Racial Equality" (Rudwick & Meier, 1970: 10).

CORE's activities anticipated many of the main forms of protest of the civil rights movement, and its attitudes certainly seemed to fit CORE for the role of a major civil rights organization. But though it became quite influential, at the time the movement actually began, CORE had declined almost to the point of extinction. Its failure reflects the historical reality that organizations are less likely to create social movements than be created by them. More important, CORE was poorly situated to lead a movement of southern blacks. Northern-based and composed primarily of pacifist intellectuals, it had no roots in any of the existing structures of the black community, and in the North these structures were themselves weak. CORE could be a source of ideas, but not of coordination.

The coordination of a new movement required the creation of a new organization. But that was not apparent until after the Montgomery bus boycott began. That boycott was organized through institutions already existing in the black community of Montgomery.

Rosa Parks's refusal to give up her seat on the bus to a white man was not the first time such defiance of segregation laws had occurred. There had been talk of a boycott the previous time, but after local black leaders had a congenial meeting with the city commissioners, nothing happened—on either side (King, 1958: 37–41). When Parks, a former secretary of the local NAACP, was arrested, she immediately called E. D. Nixon, at that time the president of the local chapter. He not only bailed her out but informed a few influential women in the city, most of whom were members of the Women's Political Council. After numerous phone calls between their members, it was the WPC that actually suggested the boycott, and E. D. Nixon who initially organized it (ibid.: 44–5).

The Montgomery Improvement Association (MIA) was formed at a meeting of eighteen ministers and civic leaders the Monday after Parks's conviction and a day of successful boycotting, to provide ongoing coordination. No one then suspected that coordination would be necessary for over a year, with car pools organized to provide alternative transportation for seventeen thousand riders a day. During this time the MIA grew slowly to a staff of ten in order to handle the voluminous correspondence, as well as to provide rides and keep the movement's momentum going. The organization, and the car pools, were financed by $250,000 in donations that poured in from all over the world in response to heavy press publicity about the boycott. But the organizational framework for the boycott and the MIA was the church. Most, although not all, of the officers were ministers, and Sunday meetings with congregations continued to be the main means of communicating with members of the black community and encouraging them to continue the protest.

The boycott did not end until the federal courts ruled Alabama's bus segregation laws unconstitutional late in 1956—at the same time that state courts ruled the boycott illegal. In the meantime, black leaders throughout the South had visited Montgomery, and out of the discussions came agreement to continue antisegregation protests regularly and systematically under the aegis of a new organization, the Southern Christian Leadership Conference. The NAACP could not lead the protests because, according to an SCLC pamphlet, "during the late fifties, the NAACP had been driven out of some Southern states. Its branches were outlawed as foreign corporations and its lawyers were charged with barratry, that is, persistently inciting litigation."

On January 10, 1957, over one hundred people gathered in Atlanta at a meeting called by four ministers, including Martin Luther King. Bayard Rustin drew up the "working papers." Initially called the Southern Leadership Conference on Transportation and Nonviolent Integration, the SCLC never developed a mass base even when it changed its name. It estab-

lished numerous "affiliates" but did most of its work through the churches in the communities to which it sent its fieldworkers.

The church was not just the only institution available for a movement to work through; in many ways it was ideal. It performed "the central organizing function in the Negro community" (Holloway, 1969: 22), providing both access to large masses of people on a regular basis and a natural leadership. As Wyatt Tee Walker, former executive director of SCLC, commented, "The Church today is central to the movement. If a Negro's going to have a meeting, where's he going to have it? Mostly he doesn't have a Masonic lodge, and he's not going to get the public schools. And the church is the primary means of communication" (Brink & Harris, 1964: 103). Thus the church eventually came to be the center of the voter registration drives as well as many of the other activities of the civil rights movement.

Even the young men and women of SNCC had to use the church, though they had trouble doing so because, unlike most of the officers of SCLC, they were not themselves ministers and thus did not have a "fraternal" connection. Instead they tended to draw many of their resources and people from outside the particular town in which they were working by utilizing their natural organizational base, the college.

SNCC did not begin the sit-ins, but came out of them. Once begun, the idea of the sit-in spread initially by means of the mass media. But such sit-ins almost always took place in towns where there were Negro colleges, and groups on these campuses essentially organized the sit-in activities of their communities. Nonetheless, "CORE, with its long emphasis of nonviolent direct action, played an important part, once the sit-ins began, as an educational and organizing agent" (Zinn, 1964: 23). CORE had very few staff in the South, but there were enough to at least hold classes and practice sessions in nonviolence.

It was SCLC, however, that was actually responsible for the formation of SNCC; though it might well have organized itself eventually. Ella Baker, then executive secretary of SCLC, thought something should be done to coordinate the rapidly spreading sit-ins in 1960, and many members of SCLC thought it might be appropriate to organize a youth group. With SCLC money, Baker persuaded her alma mater, Shaw University, to provide facilities to contact the groups at centers of sit-in activity. Some two hundred people showed up for the meeting, decided to have no official connection with SCLC beyond a "friendly relationship," and formed the Student Non-Violent Co-ordinating Committee (Zinn, 1964: 32–4). It had no members, and its fieldworkers numbered two hundred at their highest point, but it was from the campuses, especially the southern black colleges, that it drew its sustenance and upon which its organizational base rested.…

THE WOMEN'S LIBERATION MOVEMENT[2]

Women are not well organized. Historically tied to the family and isolated from their own kind, only in the nineteenth century did women in this country have the opportunity to develop independent associations of their own. These associations took years and years of careful organizational work to build. Eventually they formed the basis for the suffrage movement of the early twentieth century. The associations took less time to die. Today the Women's Trade Union League, the General Federation of Women's Clubs, the Women's Christian Temperance Union, not to mention the powerful National Women's Suffrage Association, are all either dead or a pale shadow of their former selves.

As of 1960, not one organization of women had the potential to become a social movement organization, nor was there any form of "neutral" structure of interaction to provide the base for such an organization. The closest exception to the former was the National Women's Party, which has remained dedicated to feminist concerns since its inception in 1916. However, the NWP has been essentially a lobbying group for the Equal Rights

Amendment since 1923. From the beginning, the NWP believed that a small group of women concentrating their efforts in the right places was more effective than a mass appeal, and so was not appalled by the fact that as late as 1969 even the majority of avowed feminists in this country had never heard of the ERA or the NWP.

The one large women's organization that might have provided a base for a social movement was the 180,000-member Federation of Business and Professional Women's Clubs. Yet, while it has steadily lobbied for legislation of importance to women, as late as "1966 BPW rejected a number of suggestions that it redefine…goals and tactics and become a kind of 'NAACP for women'…out of fear of being labeled 'feminist'" (Hole & Levine, 1971: 89).

Before any social movement could develop among women, there had to be created a structure to bring potential feminist sympathizers together. To be sure, groups such as the BPW, and institutions such as the women's colleges, might be a good source of adherents for such a movement. But they were determined not to be the source of leadership.

What happened in the 1960s was the development of two new communications networks in which women played prominent roles that allowed, even forced, an awakened interest in the old feminist ideas. As a result, the movement actually has two origins, from two different strata of society, with two different styles, orientations, values, and forms of organization. The first of these will be referred to as the "older branch" of the movement, partially because it began first and partially because it was on the older side of the "generation gap" that pervaded the sixties. Its most prominent organization is the National Organization for Women (NOW), which was also the first to be formed. The style of its movement organizations tends to be traditional with elected officers, boards of directors, bylaws, and the other trappings of democratic procedure. Conversely, the "younger branch" consisted of innumerable small groups engaged in a variety of activities whose contact with one another was always tenuous (Freeman, 1975: 50).

The forces that led to NOW's formation were set in motion in 1961 when President Kennedy established the President's Commission on the Status of Women at the behest of Esther Petersen, then director of the Women's Bureau. Its 1963 report, *American Women,* and subsequent committee publications documented just how thoroughly women were denied many rights and opportunities. The most significant response to the activity of the President's commission was the establishment of some fifty state commissions to do similar research on a state level. The Presidential and State Commission activity laid the groundwork for the future movement in two significant ways: (1) It unearthed ample evidence of women's unequal status and in the process convinced many previously uninterested women that something should be done; (2) It created a climate of expectations that something would be done. The women of the Presidential and State Commissions who were exposed to these influences exchanged visits, correspondence, and staff, and met with one another at an annual commission convention. They were in a position to share and mutually reinforce their growing awareness and concern over women's issues. These commissions thus provided an embryonic communications network.

During this time, two other events of significance occurred. The first was the publication of Betty Friedan's *The Feminine Mystique* in 1963. A quick best seller, the book stimulated many women to question the *status quo* and some women to suggest to Friedan that an organization be formed to do something about it. The second event was the addition of "sex" to the 1964 Civil Rights Act.

Many thought the "sex" provision was a joke, and the Equal Employment Opportunity Commission treated it as one, refusing to enforce it seriously. But a rapidly growing feminist coterie within the EEOC argued that "sex" would be taken more seriously if there

were "some sort of NAACP for women" to put pressure on the government.

On June 30, 1966, these three strands of incipient feminism came together, and NOW was tied from the knot. At that time, government officials running the Third National Conference of Commissions on the Status of Women, ironically titled "Targets for Action," forbade the presentation of a suggested resolution calling for the EEOC to treat sex discrimination with the same consideration as race discrimination. The officials said one government agency could not be allowed to pressure another, despite the fact that the state commissions were not federal agencies. The small group of women who desired such a resolution had met the night before in Friedan's hotel room to discuss the possibility of a civil rights organization for women. Not convinced of its need, they chose instead to propose the resolution. When conference officials vetoed it, they held a whispered conversation over lunch and agreed to form an action organization "to bring women into full participation in the mainstream of American society now, assuming all the privileges and responsibilities thereof in truly equal partnership with men." The name NOW was coined by Friedan who was at the conference doing research on a book. When word leaked out, twenty-eight women paid five dollars each to join before the day was over (Friedan, 1967: 4).

By the time the organizing conference was held the following October 29 through 30, over three hundred men and women had become charter members. It is impossible to do a breakdown on the composition of the charter membership, but one of the officers and board is possible. Such a breakdown accurately reflected NOW's origins. Friedan was president, two former EEOC commissioners were vice presidents, a representative of the United Auto Workers Women's Committee was secretary-treasurer, and there were seven past and present members of the State Commissions on the Status of Women on the twenty member board. One hundred twenty-six of the charter members were Wisconsin residents—and Wisconsin had the most active state Commission. Occupationally, the board and officers were primarily from the professions, labor, government, and communications fields. Of these, only those from labor had any experience in organizing, and they resigned a year later in a dispute over support of the Equal Rights Amendment. Instead of organizational experience, what the early NOW members had was experience in working with and in the media, and it was here that their early efforts were aimed.

As a result, NOW often gave the impression of being larger than it was. It was highly successful in getting in the press; much less successful in either bringing about concrete changes or forming an organization. Thus it was not until 1970, when the national press simultaneously did major stories on the women's liberation movement, that NOW's membership increased significantly.

In the meantime, unaware of and unknown to NOW, the EEOC, or the State Commissions, younger women began forming their own movement. Here, too, the groundwork had been laid some years before. The different social action projects of the sixties had attracted many women, who were quickly shunted into traditional roles and faced with the self-evident contradiction of working in a "freedom movement" but not being very free. No single "youth movement" activity or organization is responsible for forming the younger branch of the women's liberation movement, but together they created a "radical community" in which like-minded people continually interacted or were made aware of one another. This community provided the necessary network of communication and its radical ideas the framework of analysis that "explained" the dismal situation in which radical women found themselves.

Papers had been circulated on women and individual temporary women's caucuses had been held as early as 1964 (see Hayden & King, 1966). But it was not until 1967 and 1968 that the groups developed a determined, if cautious, continuity and began to consciously expand themselves. At least five groups in five different cities (Chicago, Toronto, Detroit, Seattle, and Gainesville,

Florida) formed spontaneously, independently of one another. They came at an auspicious moment, for 1967 was the year in which the blacks kicked the whites out of the civil rights movement, student power was discredited by SDS, and the New Left was on the wane. Only draft resistance activities were on the increase, and this movement more than any other exemplified the social inequities of the sexes. Men could resist the draft. Women could only counsel resistance.

At this point, there were few opportunities available for political work. Some women fit well into the secondary role of draft counseling. Many didn't. For years their complaints of unfair treatment had been forestalled by movement men with the dictum that those things could wait until after the Revolution. Now these political women found time on their hands, but still the men would not listen.

A typical example was the event that precipitated the formation of the Chicago group, the first independent group in this country. At the August 1967 National Conference for New Politics convention a women's caucus met for days, but was told its resolution wasn't significant enough to merit a floor discussion. By threatening to tie up the convention with procedural motions the women succeeded in having their statement tacked to the end of the agenda. It was never discussed. The chair refused to recognize any of the many women standing by the microphone, their hands straining upwards. When he instead called on someone to speak on "the forgotten American, the American Indian," five women rushed the podium to demand an explanation. But the chairman just patted one of them on the head (literally) and told her, "Cool down, little girl. We have more important things to talk about than women's problems."

The "little girl" was Shulamith Firestone, future author of *The Dialectic of Sex,* and she didn't cool down. Instead she joined with another Chicago woman she met there who had unsuccessfully tried to organize a women's group that summer, to call a meeting of the women who had halfheartedly attended those summer meetings. Telling their stories to those women, they stimulated sufficient rage to carry the group for three months, and by that time it was a permanent institution.

Another somewhat similar event occurred in Seattle the following winter. At the University of Washington an SDS organizer was explaining to a large meeting how white college youth established rapport with the poor whites with whom they were working. "He noted that sometimes after analyzing societal ills, the men shared leisure time by 'balling a chick together.' He pointed out that such activities did much to enhance the political consciousness of the poor white youth. A woman in the audience asked, 'And what did it do for the consciousness of the chick?'" (Hole & Levine, 1971: 120). After the meeting, a handful of enraged women formed Seattle's first group.

Subsequent groups to the initial five were largely organized rather than formed spontaneously out of recent events. In particular, the Chicago group was responsible for the formation of many new groups in Chicago and in other cities. Unlike NOW, the women in the first groups had had years of experience as trained organizers. They knew how to utilize the infrastructure of the radical community, the underground press, and the free universities to disseminate women's liberation ideas. Chicago, as a center of New Left activity, had the largest number of politically conscious organizers. Many traveled widely to leftist conferences and demonstrations, and most used the opportunity to talk with other women about the new movement. In spite of public derision by radical men, or perhaps because of it, young women steadily formed new groups around the country.

ANALYSIS

From these data there appear to be four essential elements involved in movement formation: (1) the growth of a preexisting communications

network that is (2) co-optable to the ideas of the new movement; (3) a series of crises that galvanize into action people involved in a co-optable network, and/or (4) subsequent organizing effort to weld the spontaneous groups together into a movement. Each of these elements needs to be examined in detail.

COMMUNICATIONS NETWORK

...The women's liberation movement...illustrates the importance of a network precisely because the conditions for a movement existed *before* a network came into being, but the movement didn't exist until afterward. Analysts of socioeconomic causes have concluded that the movement could have started anytime within a twenty-year period. Strain for women was as great in 1955 as in 1965 (Ferriss, 1971). What changed was the organizational situation. It was not until new networks emerged among women aware of inequities beyond local boundaries that a movement could grow past the point of occasional, spontaneous uprisings. The fact that two distinct movements, with two separate origins, developed from two networks unaware of each other is further evidence of the key role of preexisting communications networks as the fertile soil in which new movements can sprout.

References to the importance of a preexisting communications network appear frequently in case studies of social movements, though the theoretical writers were much slower to recognize their salience. According to Buck (1920: 43–4), the Grange established a degree of organization among American farmers in the nineteenth century that greatly facilitated the spread of future farmers' protests. Lipset has reported that in Saskatchewan, "the rapid acceptance of new ideas and movements...can be attributed mainly to the high degree of organization.... The role of the social structure of the western wheat belt in facilitating the rise of new movements has never been sufficiently appreciated by historians and sociologists. Repeated challenges and crises forced the western farmers to create many more community institutions (especially cooperatives and economic pressure groups) than are necessary in a more stable area. These groups in turn provided a structural basis for immediate action in critical situations. [Therefore] though it was a new radical party, the C. C. F. did not have to build up an organization from scratch" (1959: 206).

Similarly, Heberle (1951: 232) reports several findings that Nazism was most successful in small, well-integrated communities. As Lipset put it, these findings "sharply challenge the various interpretations of Nazism as the product of the growth of anomie and the general rootlessness of modern urban industrial society" (1959: 146).

Indirect evidence attesting to the essential role of formal and informal communications networks is found in diffusion theory, which emphasizes the importance of personal interaction rather than impersonal media communication in the spread of ideas (Rogers, 1962; Lionberger, 1960). This personal influence occurs through the organizational patterns of a community (Lionberger, 1960: 73). It does not occur through the mass media. The mass media may be a source of information, but they are not a key source of influence.

Their lesser importance in relation to preexisting communications networks was examined in one study on "The Failure of an Incipient Social Movement" (Jackson, Peterson, Bull, Monsen, & Richmond, 1960). In 1957 a potential tax protest movement in Los Angeles generated considerable interest and publicity for a little over a month but was dead within a year. According to the authors, this did not reflect a lack of public notice. They concluded that "mass communication alone is probably insufficient without a network of communication specifically linking those interested in the matter.... If a movement is to grow rapidly, it cannot rely upon its own network of communication, but must capitalize on networks already in existence" (p. 37).

A major reason it took social scientists so long to acknowledge the importance of communica-

tions networks was because the prevailing theories of the post–World War II era emphasized increasing social dislocation and anomie. Mass society theorists, as they were called, hypothesized that significant community institutions that linked individuals to governing elites were breaking down, that society was becoming a mass of isolated individuals. These individuals were seen as increasingly irresponsible and ungovernable, prone to irrational protests because they had no mediating institutions through which to pursue grievances (Kornhauser, 1959).

In emphasizing disintegrating vertical connections, mass society theorists passed lightly over the role of horizontal ones, only occasionally acknowledging that "the combination of internal contact and external isolation facilitates the work of the mass agitator" (Kornhauser, 1959: 218). This focus changed in the early seventies. Pinard's study of the Social Credit Party of Quebec (1971) severely criticized mass society theory, arguing instead that "when strains are severe and widespread a new movement is more likely to meet its early success among the more strongly integrated citizens" (Pinard, 1971: 192).

This insight was expanded by Oberschall (1973), who created a six-cell table to predict both the occurrence and type of protest. As did the mass society theorists, Oberschall said that even when there are grievances, protest will not occur outside institutional channels by those who are connected, through their own leadership or patron/client relationships, with governing elites. Among those who are segmented from such elites, the type of protest will be determined by whether there is communal, associational, or little organization. In the latter case, discontent is expressed through riots or other short-lived violent uprisings. "It is under conditions of strong...ties and segmentation that the possibility of the rapid spread of opposition movements on a continuous basis exists" (p. 123).

The movements we have studied would confirm Oberschall's conclusions, but not as strongly as he makes them. In all these cases a preexisting communications network was a necessary but insufficient condition for movement formation. Yet the newly formed networks among student radicals, welfare recipients, and women can hardly compare with the longstanding ties provided by the southern black churches and colleges. Their ties were tenuous and may not have survived the demise of their movements.

The importance of segmentation, or lack of connection with relevant elites, is less obvious in the sixties' movements. The higher socioeconomic status of incipient feminists and Movement leaders would imply greater access to elites than is true for blacks or welfare recipients. If Oberschall were correct, these closer connections should either have permitted easier and more rapid grievance solutions or more effective social control. They did neither. Indeed, it was the group most closely connected to decision-making elites—women of the Presidential and State Commission—who were among the earliest to see the need of a protest organization. Women of the younger branch of the movement did have their grievances against the men of the New Left effectively suppressed for several years, but even they eventually rejected this kind of elite control, even when it meant rejecting the men.

Conversely, Piven and Cloward show that the establishment of closer ties between leaders of local welfare rights groups and welfare workers through advisory councils and community coordinators led to a curtailment of militance and the institutionalization of grievances (1977: 326–31). They also argue that the development of government-funded community programs effectively co-opted many local black movement leaders in the North and that federal channeling of black protest in the South into voter registration projects focused the movement there into traditional electoral politics (ibid.: 253). In short, the evidence about the role of segmentation in movement formation is ambiguous. The effect may be varied considerably by the nature of the political system.

CO-OPTABILITY

A recurrent theme in our studies is that not just any communications network will do. It must be one that is co-optable to the ideas of the new movement. The Business and Professional Women's (BPW) clubs were a network among women, but having rejected feminism, they could not overcome the ideological barrier to new political action until after feminism became established....

On the other hand, the women on the Presidential and State Commissions and the feminist coterie of the EEOC were co-optable largely because their immersion in the facts of female status and the details of sex discrimination cases made them very conscious of the need for change. Likewise, the young women of the "radical community" lived in an atmosphere of questioning, confrontation, and change. They absorbed an ideology of "freedom" and "liberation" far more potent than any latent "antifeminism" might have been....

Exactly what makes a network co-optable is harder to elucidate. Pinard (1971: 186) noted the necessity for groups to *"possess* or *develop* an ideology or simply subjective interests congruent with that of a new movement" for them to "act as mobilizing rather than restraining agents toward that movement," but did not further explore what affected the "primary group climate." More illumination is provided by the diffusion of innovation studies that point out the necessity for new ideas to fit in with already established norms for changes to happen easily. Furthermore, a social system that has as a value "innovativeness" (as the radical community did) will more rapidly adopt ideas than one that looks upon the habitual performance of traditional practices as the ideal (as most organized women's groups did in the fifties). Usually, as Lionberger (1960: 91) points out, "people act in terms of past experience and knowledge." People who have had similar experiences are likely to share similar perceptions of a situation and to mutually reinforce those perceptions as well as their subsequent interpretation. A co-optable network, then, is one whose members have had common experiences that predispose them to be receptive to the particular new ideas of the incipient movement and who are not faced with structural or ideological barriers to action. If the new movement as an "innovation" can interpret these experiences and perceptions in ways that point out channels for social action, then participation in a social movement becomes the logical thing to do.

THE ROLE OF CRISES

As our examples have illustrated, similar perceptions must be translated into action. This is often done by a crisis. For blacks in Montgomery, this was generated by Rosa Parks's refusal to give up her seat on a bus to a white man. For women who formed the older branch of the women's movement, the impetus to organize was the refusal of the EEOC to enforce the sex provision of Title VII, precipitated by the concomitant refusal of federal officials at the conference to allow a supportive resolution. For younger women there were a series of minor crises.

While not all movements are formed by such precipitating events, they are quite common as they serve to crystallize and focus discontent. From their own experiences, directly and concretely, people feel the need for change in a situation that allows for an exchange of feelings with others, mutual validation, and a subsequent reinforcement of innovative interpretation. Perception of an immediate need for change is a major factor in predisposing people to accept new ideas (Rogers, 1962: 280). Nothing makes desire for change more acute than a crisis. Such a crisis need not be a major one; it need only embody collective discontent.

ORGANIZING EFFORTS

A crisis will only catalyze a well-formed communications network. If such networks are embryon-

ically developed or only partially co-optable, the potentially active individuals in them must be linked together by someone…. As Jackson et al. (1960: 37) stated, "Some protest may persist where the source of trouble is constantly present. But interest ordinarily cannot be maintained unless there is a welding of spontaneous groups into some stable organization." In other words, people must be organized. Social movements do not simply occur.

The role of the organizer in movement formation is another neglected aspect of the theoretical literature. There has been great concern with leadership, but the two roles are distinct and not always performed by the same individual. In the early stages of a movement, it is the organizer much more than any leader who is important, and such an individual or cadre must often operate behind the scenes. The nature and function of these two roles was most clearly evident in the Townsend old-age movement of the thirties. Townsend was the "charismatic" leader, but the movement was organized by his partner, real estate promoter Robert Clements. Townsend himself acknowledges that without Clements's help, the movement would never have gone beyond the idea stage (Holzman, 1963).

The importance of organizers is pervasive in the sixties' movements. Dr. King may have been the public spokesperson of the Montgomery Bus Boycott who caught the eye of the media, but it was E. D. Nixon who organized it. Certainly the "organizing cadre" that young women in the radical community came to be was key to the growth of that branch of the women's liberation movement, despite the fact that no "leaders" were produced (and were actively discouraged). The existence of many leaders but no organizers in the older branch of the women's liberation movement readily explains its subsequent slow development….

The function of the organizer has been explored indirectly by other analysts. Rogers (1962) devotes many pages to the "change agent" who, while he does not necessarily weld a group together or "construct" a movement, does many of the same things for agricultural innovation that an organizer does for political change. Mass society theory makes frequent reference to the "agitator," though not in a truly informative way. Interest groups are often organized by single individuals and some of them evolve into social movements. Salisbury's study of farmers' organizations finds this a recurrent theme. He also discovered that "a considerable number of farm groups were subsidized by other, older, groups.... The Farm Bureau was organized and long sustained by subsidies, some from federal and state governments, and some by local businessmen" (Salisbury, 1959: 13).

These patterns are similar to ones we have found in the formation of social movements. Other organizations, even the government, often serve as training centers for organizers and sources of material support to aid the formation of groups and/or movements. The civil rights movement was the training ground for many an organizer of other movements.... The role of the government in the formation of the National Welfare Rights Organization was so significant that it would lead one to wonder if this association should be considered more of an interest group in the traditional sense than a movement "core" organization.

From all this it would appear that training as an organizer or at least as a proselytizer or entrepreneur of some kind is a necessary background for those individuals who act as movement innovators. Even in something as seemingly spontaneous as a social movement, the professional is more valuable than the amateur.

NOTES

1. The only use of this significant word appears rather incidentally in Turner (1964): 123.
2. Data for this section are based on my observations while a founder and participant in the younger branch of the Chicago women's liberation movement from 1967 through 1969 and editor of the first (at that time, only) national newsletter. I was able, through extensive correspondence and interviews, to keep a record of how each group around the country started, where the organizers got the idea from, who they had talked to, what conferences were held and who attended, the political affiliations (or lack of them) of the first members, and so forth. Although I was a member of Chicago NOW, information on the origins of it and the other older branch organizations comes entirely through ex post facto interviews of the principals and examination of early papers in preparation for my dissertation on the women's liberation movement. Most of my informants requested that their contribution remain confidential.

REFERENCES

Adorno, L. W., et al. 1950. *The authoritarian personality.* New York: Harper & Row.

Blumer, H. 1951. Social movements. In *New outline of the principles of sociology,* ed. A. M. Lee. New York: Barnes and Noble.

Brink, W., and L. Harris. 1964. *The Negro revolution in America.* New York: Simon & Schuster.

Buck, S. J. 1920. *The agrarian crusade.* New Haven, Conn.: Yale University Press.

Cantril, H. 1941. *The psychology of social movements.* New York: Wiley.

Clark, K. B. 1966. The civil rights movement: Momentum and organization. *Daedalus,* Winter.

Davies, J. C. 1962. Toward a theory of revolution. *American Sociological Review,* 27(1): 5–19.

Ferriss, A. L. 1971. *Indicators of trends in the status of American women.* New York: Russell Sage Foundation.

Firestone, S. 1971. *Dialectics of sex.* New York: Morrow.

Frazier, E. F. 1963. *The Negro church in America.* New York: Schocken.

Freeman, J. 1975. *The politics of women's liberation.* New York: Longman.

Friedan, B. 1963. *The feminine mystique.* New York: Dell.

———. 1967. NOW: How it began. *Women Speaking,* April.

Gurr, T. 1970. *Why men rebel.* Princeton, N.J.: Princeton University Press.

Hayden, C., and M. King. 1966. A kind of memo. *Liberation,* April.

Heberle, R. 1951. *Social movements.* New York: Appleton-Century-Crofts.

Hoffer, E. 1951. *The true believer.* New York: Harper & Row.

Hole, J., and E. Levine. 1971. *Rebirth of feminism.* New York: Quadrangle.

Holloway, H. 1969. *The politics of the Southern Negro.* New York: Random House.

Holzman, A. 1963. *The Townsend movement: A political study.* New York: Bookman.

Jackson, M., et al. 1960. The failure of an incipient social movement. *Pacific Sociological Review,* 3(1): 40.

King, M. L., Jr. 1958. *Stride toward freedom.* New York: Harper & Row.

Kornhauser, W. 1959. *The politics of mass society.* Glencoe, Ill.: Free Press.

Lionberger, H. F. 1960. *Adoption of new ideas and practices.* Ames: Iowa State University Press.

Lipset, S. M. 1959. *Agrarian socialism.* Berkeley: University of California Press.

Lowi, T. J. 1971. *The politics of discord.* New York: Basic Books.

Oberschall, A. 1973. *Social conflict and social movements.* Englewood Cliffs, N.J.: Prentice-Hall.

Pinard, M. 1971. *The rise of a third party: A study in crisis politics.* Englewood Cliffs, N.J.: Prentice-Hall.

Piven, F. F., and R. Cloward. 1977. *Poor people's movements: Why they succeed, how they fail.* New York: Pantheon.

Rogers, E. M. 1962. *Diffusion of innovations.* New York: Free Press.

Rudwick, E., and A. Meier. 1970. Organizational structure and goal succession: A comparative analysis of the NAACP and CORE, 1964–1968. *Social Science Quarterly,* 51 (June).

Salisbury, R. H. 1969. An exchange theory of interest groups. *Midwest Journal of Political Science,* 13(1), (February).

Toch, H. 1965. *The social psychology of social movements.* Indianapolis, Ind.: Bobbs-Merrill.

Zinn, H. 1964. *SNCC: The new abolitionists.* Boston: Beacon Press.

Part XXII

Social Change and Modernity

45

The Disenchantment of Modern Life

Max Weber

Scientific progress is a fraction, the most important fraction, of the process of intellectualization which we have been undergoing for thousands of years and which nowadays is usually judged in such an extremely negative way. Let us first clarify what this intellectualist rationalization, created by science and by scientifically oriented technology, means practically.

Does it mean that we, today, for instance, everyone sitting in this hall, have a greater knowledge of the conditions of life under which we exist than has an American Indian or a Hottentot? Hardly. Unless he is a physicist, one who rides on the streetcar has no idea how the car happened to get into motion. And he does not need to know. He is satisfied that he may "count" on the behavior of the streetcar, and he orients his conduct according to this expectation; but he knows nothing about what it takes to produce such a car so that it can move. The savage knows incomparably more about his tools. When we spend money today I bet that even if there are colleagues of political economy here in the hall, almost every one of them will hold a different answer in readiness to the question: How does it happen that one can buy something for money—sometimes more and sometimes less? The savage knows what he does in order to get his daily food and which institutions serve him in this pursuit. The increasing intellectualization and rationalization do *not,* therefore, indicate an increased and general knowledge of the conditions under which one lives.

It means something else, namely, the knowledge or belief that if one but wished one *could* learn it at any time. Hence, it means that principally there are no mysterious incalculable forces that come into play, but rather that one can, in principle, master all things by calculation. This means that the world is disenchanted. One need no longer have recourse to magical means in

Source: Excerpts from *From Max Weber: Essays in Sociology* by Max Weber, edited by H. H. Gerth & C. Wright Mills, translated by H. H. Gerth & C. Wright Mills. Translation copyright © 1946, 1958 by H. H. Gerth and C. Wright Mills. Used by permission of Oxford University Press, Inc.

order to master or implore the spirits, as did the savage, for whom such mysterious powers existed. Technical means and calculations perform the service. This above all is what intellectualization means....

Science today is a "vocation" organized in special disciplines in the service of self-clarification and knowledge of interrelated facts. It is not the gift of grace of seers and prophets dispensing sacred values and revelations, nor does it partake of the contemplation of sages and philosophers about the meaning of the universe. This, to be sure, is the inescapable condition of our historical situation. We cannot evade it so long as we remain true to ourselves. And if Tolstoi's question recurs to you: As science does not, who is to answer the question: "What shall we do, and, how shall we arrange our lives?" or, in the words used here tonight: "Which of the warring gods should we serve? Or should we serve perhaps an entirely different god, and who is he?" then one can say that only a prophet or a savior can give the answers....

To the person who cannot bear the fate of the times like a man, one must say: May he rather return silently, without the usual publicity build-up of renegades, but simply and plainly. The arms of the old churches are opened widely and compassionately for him. After all, they do not make it hard for him. One way or another he has to bring his "intellectual sacrifice"—that is inevitable. If he can really do it, we shall not rebuke him. For such an intellectual sacrifice in favor of an unconditional religious devotion is ethically quite a different matter than the evasion of the plain duty of intellectual integrity, which sets in if one lacks the courage to clarify one's own ultimate standpoint and rather facilitates this duty by feeble relative judgments. In my eyes, such religious return stands higher than the academic prophecy, which does not clearly realize that in the lecture-rooms of the university no other virtue holds but plain intellectual integrity: Integrity, however, compels us to state that for the many who today tarry for new prophets and saviors, the situation is the same as resounds in the beautiful Edomite watchman's song of the period of exile that has been included among Isaiah's oracles:

He calleth to me out of Seir, Watchman, what of the night? The watchman said, The morning cometh, and also the night: if ye will enquire, enquire ye: return, come.

The people to whom this was said has enquired and tarried for more than two millennia, and we are shaken when we realize its fate. From this we want to draw the lesson that nothing is gained by yearning and tarrying alone, and we shall act differently. We shall set to work and meet the "demands of the day," in human relations as well as in our vocation. This, however, is plain and simple, if each finds and obeys the demon who holds the fibers of his very life.

46

The Information Age: Apartheid, Cultural Imperialism, or Global Village?

R. Alan Hedley

INTRODUCTION

The concept of development does not have a long history. It dates back to the industrial revolution, which first produced global differences among the peoples of the world in terms of socioeconomic development. The most profound result of this revolution was the huge gain in human productivity, which in turn significantly raised individual income (Hedley, 1992, pp. 63–97). Between 1801 and 1901, total national income in Britain increased more than 600% (Mitchell, 1962, p. 366). By 1870, workers in industrial nations earned 11 times more than their counter-

parts in nonindustrial countries. Moreover, the advantages of industrialization have been cumulative: Today, as we embark on the so-called information revolution, per capita income is 52 times greater in developed than less developed countries (World Bank, 1995, p. 53), thus magnifying what one author has termed a *Global Rift* (Stavrianos, 1981).

The term *sustainable development* is even more recent. It gained widespread currency as a result of the report produced by the World Commission on Environment and Development (1987). Established in 1983 by the United Nations due to the growing realization that "the development paths of the industrialized nations are clearly unsustainable" (p. xii), the Brundtland Commission defined sustainable development as "development that meets the needs of the present without compromising the ability of future generations to meet their own needs" (p. 43). According to Michael Jacobs (1991, pp. 60–61), the "core meaning" of sustainable development as defined by the Brundtland Commission

Source: Hedley, R. Alan. (1999). The information age: Apartheid, cultural imperialism, or global village? *Social Science Computer Review,* 17(1): 78–87. Reprinted by permission of Sage Publications, Inc.
Author's Note: This article is a revised version of a presentation that was given at the 14th International Conference of the World Association for Case Method Research and Application, Madrid, 1997.

involves three key elements: (a) the necessity of considering the biosphere in making economic policy, (b) commitment to more equitable distribution of economic and natural resources to present as well as future generations, and (c) concern for nonfinancial aspects of human welfare in the determination of development (e.g., health and education).

We are thus learning that to ensure the development of humankind and, indeed, to safeguard our very existence on this planet, we must heed the environmental context in which development occurs, distribute the products of human labor and the Earth's resources more equitably now and in the future, and modify our values to emphasize the quality of human life. In this article, I focus on two of these aspects of sustainable development—the distribution of resources and the quality of life. Specifically, I examine the structure of the emerging information revolution and assess what implications it has for reducing the gap between rich and poor nations, providing greater balance among cultures, and improving the quality of life for all peoples.

THE INFORMATION REVOLUTION

Marc Porat (1977) made one of the first efforts to define and measure the information economy. Using the Standard Industrial Classification Codes, Porat found that information goods and services accounted for approximately half of both gross national product and employment in the United States in 1967. However, Porat's classification grouped both modern and traditional information activities. Most of the industries he identified either predated the original industrial revolution (e.g., real estate, insurance, banking, law, accounting, and architecture) or grew out of the transportation and communication revolution occurring at the turn of the 20th century (e.g., publishing, telephone, radio, and photographic and motion picture industries). Consequently,

Porat simply reconfigured the existing economy to emphasize its information component. Although this is a legitimate endeavor, as it illustrates a general transformation from physical to intellectual activities, it does not reveal the direct impact of the modern information revolution. Porat's analytical strategy, and others like it (Bell, 1976), adopt an inclusive view of an information society.

A more exclusive approach focuses on that part of the economy that emerged directly as a result of the microelectronic revolution of the late 1960s (Gilder, 1989). For the purposes of this article, information technology refers primarily to computer hardware, components, software, services, and also the new telecommunications infrastructure essential to computer networking. The Organisation for Economic Co-operation and Development (OECD, 1996, p. 3) adopts a similar approach in defining the information sector. Although admittedly conservative in its specification of what to include and exclude in the information revolution, this strategy offers two definite advantages: (a) It permits a clear analytical distinction between "old" and "new" information technology, and (b) it provides an explicit empirical base for comparative research.

A major problem in measuring the modern information revolution is that economic and labor force data are classified into traditional industrial categories. Thus, although we can identify the manufacturing component of this technological innovation in terms of computers produced and numbers employed in producing them, it is next to impossible to measure the applications of this innovation within the economy. These data are hidden throughout all the standard industrial and occupational codes. As a result, we are limited to those applications specifically identified as computer services. Commenting on this problem, a *Business Week* article notes that "government statistics track goods and jobs, not flows of information... [which] means... [there is] a large and vibrant 'ghost economy' that traditional economic indicators don't measure" (Mandel, 1994, p. 26). Consequently, the actual impact of computers in the world economy is vastly under-reported. However, until data are organized into categories more indicative of the microelectronic transformation, this is the only reliable way to measure it.

Table 46.1 presents a number of dimensions that reflect what an information revolution entails. For example, there must be a discernible body of information workers who are organized in some fashion to produce innovative goods and services. In turn, this requires infrastructural support. Finally, to the extent that a revolution does take place, its effects should be noticeable in the larger society. Table 46.1 specifies each of these dimensions along with available empirical indicators that can be used to measure them. Employing these multidimensional empirical indicators, a researcher could conceivably collect cross-national data over time to plot both individ-

ual and aggregate change. These data would permit estimates to be made of information and communications technology (ICT) development both within countries over time and compara-tively between nations (or world regions) at particular points in time. This kind of research design would provide the necessary empirical foundation for more careful analyses of the worldwide effects and impact of ICT.

Applying the empirical indicators in Table 46.1, we may conclude that the information revo-lution is still very much in its beginning stages and is limited primarily to the developed coun-tries. Just five G-7 nations (United States, Japan, Germany, France, and United Kingdom) accounted for 80% of the information technology market in 1994, and American and Japanese corporations dominate the industry (OECD, 1996, pp. 7, 37). By July 1996, developed coun-tries had 201 personal computers per 1,000 people compared to only 6.2 per 1,000 in the rest

Table 46.1   Dimensions and Measures of an Information Society

1. Economic activity/labor
   a) Percentage of labor force in computer hardware, software, and services industry
2. Economic output/productivity
   a) Percentage contribution of computer industry to gross domestic product (GDP)
   b) Percentage share of value added in computer manufacturing to GDP
3. Organization/structure
   a) Computer companies as a percentage of total business corporations
   b) Number of employees per company in the computer industry
   c) Use of information technology in business
   d) Computer literacy among employees
4. Technological infrastructure
   a) Computer power (MIPS) per capita
   b) Investment in telecommunications as a percentage of GDP
   c) Internet hosts per 1,000 inhabitants
   d) Digital main lines as a percentage of total main lines
5. Technological innovation
   a) Computing R&D as a percentage of total manufacturing R&D
   b) Computing professional and technical workers as a percentage of all professional and technical workers
   c) Information technology patents granted as a percentage of total patents
6. Technological diffusion
   a) Computers per capita
   b) Percentage of households with personal computers
   c) Information technology spending as a percentage of GDP

Source: Organisation for Economic Co-operation and Development (1996) and *World Competitiveness Report 1995* (1995).

of the world (World Bank, 1997, p. 286). Analysis of the Internet, the worldwide network of personal computers connected to host computers, indicates that it is overwhelmingly American based, English speaking, and Western focused. In January 1997, 63% of the estimated 16.15 million host computers connected to the Internet were in the United States, 74% in English-speaking nations, and fully 90% of the Internet operated out of Western countries (Network Wizards, 1997). To date, despite claims to the contrary, the nascent yet burgeoning information revolution is not a worldwide phenomenon.

These data hold few surprises. Similar to the previous two industrial revolutions, the information revolution has its origins in the West. However, because it is just beginning, it does not necessarily have to follow the same trajectory. Although the information revolution could well exacerbate existing economic and cultural fault lines, thus widening the global rift between North and South, it also offers the possibility of a truly interconnected global village. In the following section, I examine these possibilities, paying particular attention to the concept of sustainable development.

THREE DEVELOPMENT SCENARIOS

1. Apartheid. Left to grow unchecked in the global marketplace, the information revolution will more than likely solidify and reinforce existing cleavages. Indeed, a current world map displaying the location of the four largest computer networks (including the Internet) divides the world along the same North-South axis originally drawn in the 1980 Brandt Report (Matrix Information and Directory Services, 1997). This "do-nothing" approach to development is basically a strategy of exclusion or apartheid; it is also inherently unstable and therefore unsustainable. Given that the income gap between North and South continues to increase

and that the South represents a growing proportion of the world's population, it is only a matter of time before those in the South perceive these disparities as intolerable (Hedley, 1985). In fact, signs of increasing world disorder are already apparent: escalating acts of terrorism and civil disobedience, rising illegal migration and refugee flows, spiraling crime rates, widespread famine and disease (including AIDS), and many local disputes that erupt into international conflicts. Clearly this is not the path to sustainable development. As the United Nations Commission on International Development warned us almost three decades ago, "Before long, in our affluent, industrial, computerized jet society, we shall feel the wrath of the wretched people of the world. There will be no peace" (Pearson Report, 1969).

2. Cultural imperialism. Given the statistics already cited, another likely development outcome could see the world becoming increasingly Westernized. Although the theory of cultural convergence (Kerr, Dunlop, Harbison, & Meyers, 1964) has been heavily criticized, it appears particularly applicable to the emerging information and communications revolution. The central thesis of convergence theory states that upon the introduction of technologically superior techniques, structural adaptations are made that in turn affect other aspects of society until eventually all societies, no matter how dissimilar they were initially, converge in certain patterns of social organization and behavior. Concerning the introduction of computer and telecommunications technology, unlike previous technological revolutions, a significant part of the technical process is itself cultural. Even though computer software commands computers in binary code, the software originates in words, the effective currency of culture. According to Einstein (1941/1954), "The mental development of the individual and his way of forming concepts depend to a high degree upon language. This makes us realize to what extent the same language means the same mentality" (p. 336).

And Gilder (1989) further adds that we are now reaching the stage where "the distinction between hardware and software will all but vanish" (p. 328).

Although earlier technologies incorporated aspects of culture in their designs in the form of standards and regulations, these were more limited in scope. But information technology, by its very nature, is cultural. "The notion that information and communication are, in fact, culturally neutral is the greatest myth of our time" (Mowlana, 1996, p. 179). Consequently, to the extent that only one culture or one linguistic group produces the bulk of software, as is presently the case, and "as hardware designs increasingly embody software concepts" (Gilder, 1989, p. 329), then certainly the possibility exists for cultural imperialism on a massive scale.

Microsoft CEO Bill Gates (1995) speaks directly to the evolution of ICT and the prospect of (American) cultural convergence:

American popular culture is so potent that outside the United States some countries now attempt to ration it. They hope to guarantee the viability of domestic-content by permitting only a certain number of hours of foreign television to be aired each week. In Europe the availability of satellite and cable-delivered programming reduced the potential for government control. The information highway is going to break down barriers and may promote a world culture, or at least a sharing of cultural activities and values. (p. 263)

What will this "world culture" look like? Which "cultural activities and values" will be adopted? According to recent newspaper reports (Weise, 1997), it could be a "Bill Gates" world. In a bid to position himself for the next phase of the information revolution, Gates has formed a new company, Teledesic Corporation, which is investing $9 billion to ring the planet with 840 satellites to provide worldwide Internet access (see **http://www.teledesic .com**/). Although a truly global Internet could bring about a new age in which all human beings have access to the same information (see below), it is also possible that

this heavenly infrastructure could increase Western cultural and economic dominance on a scale never before even imagined. Should this development approach take precedence, it would by definition also be accompanied by strategies of exclusion and therefore be unsustainable for the same reasons advanced earlier.

3. Global village. As already indicated, a third development option exists. Given that the Internet (and its likely successor) is a configuration of two-way, horizontally connected computers accessed mainly by individuals via personal computer, its technology represents a significant break with previous one-way, top-down, mass communication media and, consequently, the potential for mass indoctrination. Although the Internet still permits the exercise of widespread power, as argued in the cultural imperialism scenario, its multiple interactive, real-time capability combined with its potential for universal access are novel features never before experienced on a world scale. According to Brown and Brown (1994), the information revolution "will provide a virtually seamless world communications network capable of reaching every inhabitant on earth" (p. 3). For the first time ever, a true global village in which all people have the opportunity to interact and to voice their individual concerns is possible, if not yet realized. For the hitherto disenfranchised of the world, the information revolution could thus provide the means to organize and to articulate their needs, such that they could eventually participate in a more just and humane and, therefore, sustainable world society.

How likely is this development outcome? Given the first two scenarios, and the fact that entrenched interest groups are committed to maintaining the status quo, it does not seem at all probable. However, to the extent that we can find empirical support for this third option on the Internet, we would at least have some grounds for cautious optimism. Such evidence comes from a content analysis of one Internet discussion group, established prior to a 1997 conference on Knowledge for Development in the Information Age (Global Knowledge 97). Sponsored by the United Nations Development Programme and the World Bank, it was set up "to facilitate broad discussion of the Conference themes at all levels of civil society" (Majordomo, 1997). Participants were informed

that the List offers a major forum for the exchange of ideas as well as an important channel for input into the Conference itself. The UNDP and other Conference sponsors encourage those from around the world, especially those in the South, to use the list to express their own needs, experiences, and suggestions related to Conference themes. (Majordomo, 1997)

Although my analysis is not based on a comprehensive survey of the Internet (if indeed that is possible), it does provide limited information on the extent to which the global village option is available on the Internet and the kinds of access that marginalized groups have to it. Notice of the availability of this particular on-line discussion was published widely on the Internet by the United Nations, the World Bank, and the Canadian government (Global Knowledge 97, 1997).

My period of observation began on March 24, 1997 (the time of the first e-mail posting), and ended 1 month later (April 23). During this time, 98 discussants (65% male) from 23 countries (43% from the North) posted 170 messages on a variety of development issues. (Altogether, there were approximately 700 subscribers to the GKD97 list discussion; J. Brodman, e-mail communication from the master moderator of the GKD97 list, May 7, 1997.) Although more Southern than Northern countries were represented, the vast majority of individual discussants (80%) were from the North. However, it should be noted that some people writing from the South were in fact Northern development workers and that several Northern writers were originally from the South. Because I could determine only where messages originated (and not the national-

ity of the authors), it is impossible to provide a breakdown by nationality. Most of the discussants ($n = 77$) made reference to their work in their messages; they constituted four major occupational groups: government-affiliated professional development workers, 30% (of whom close to half worked for UN agencies); academics, 22%; private development and information technology consultants, 21%; and nongovernmental organization (NGO) representatives, 18%. Graduate students occupied the remaining group (9%). Finally, it is interesting to note the major issues discussed. As requested in the information for participants, they related broadly to the themes of the forthcoming conference: the North-South gap, global information flow, communications infrastructure development, universal (scientific) knowledge versus local indigenous knowledge, development and empowerment initiatives, overseas and distance education programs, brain drain, and implications of the information revolution for global development.

These data are not remarkably different from what could be found in a traditional face-to-face development conference, except for the fact that on-line, many individuals from all over the world can engage in extensive real-time discussion at just a fraction of the cost of physically bringing these people together. Because of this, some on-line discussants were not the traditional development workers and researchers usually found at conferences; they were part of the group targeted for development. Although they made up only a small proportion, these people offered viewpoints not usually voiced at conventional conferences. For example, one stressed the need to wire the rural South with appropriate technology (e.g., conventional and cellular telephones and community radio) "to enable the majority to learn what is going on and air their views too.... [As a result,] the North would be able to receive more accurate information about the situation in the South." Thus, both the Internet in particular and electronic communication in general provide the technological means to broaden the constituency of discussion.

A particularly distinctive feature of on-line discussion is the references made to various sites on the Internet. Table 46.2 provides a listing of the 54 sites directly mentioned by these discussants (although in some cases the actual electronic addresses were not provided). Of these, 50 are located on the central Internet as Web sites, whereas 4 are e-mail addresses. Concerning the Web sites, it is important to note that each one in turn provides direct hyperlinks with other related Web sites. From these 50 Web sites, therefore, it is possible to link up with literally hundreds of other sites (and e-mail addresses) that are in some way involved with development. As a result, Table 46.2 provides the means to tap into conceivably all that exists about development on the Internet. For example, a visit to the Global Knowledge Internet site in 1998 revealed a listing of 192 Web sites pertaining to development, which in turn are linked to hundreds of other electronic addresses.

Table 46.2 reveals a wide variety of development resource centers available on the Internet. Although the list is not representative, given the particular issues addressed and discussants involved, it does reflect great diversity in terms of focus, sponsorship, language, and point of origin. For example, in addition to major development organizations, there are national government agencies, not-for-profit information centers, charitable foundations, educational institutions, research centers, environmental enterprises, private consultancy firms, and large and small NGOs that offer everything from technical advice and information to solidarity, protection, assistance, and "community."

There is also substantial representation from the South in terms of communications infrastructure development (Grameen Communications), electronic networks (Isis, QuipuNet, Red Caldas), and NGOs (ABANTU for Development,

Research Network on Sustainable Structural Adjustment Policies). These organizations were established by people of the South to address particular development concerns as they defined them. They are currently engaged in a wide variety of innovative projects. Furthermore, much of their work is complemented by the more numerous development agencies operating from the North.

The list in Table 46.2 constitutes evidence of at least the nucleus of a global village, especially to the extent that one realizes it is illustrative of a much larger and more diverse development network. For example, the SD Gateway (**http://sdgateway.net**), operated by the UN International Institute of Sustainable Development, contains an archive of 88 electronic mailing lists, including GKD97, covering "topics ranging from ecology to economics to ethics to community initiatives." Consequently, thousands of concerned people (experts and laypersons alike) from both the North and the South are communicating with each other on a wide variety of development issues. Thus, we may conclude that the Internet can provide an interactive forum for many different kinds of groups to disseminate particular points of view and to engage in dialogue with interested others. It also represents a widely varied information resource available to all who have access to it. Although the issue of access remains a serious problem, there are indications even now that strategic access to the Internet is currently being gained by a small core of those traditionally without voice. Moreover, as the electronic communications infrastructure becomes more broadly established, largely as a result of the efforts of organizations such as those listed in Table 46.2, we may expect even greater and more diverse representation on the Internet. And with the establishment of a virtual global village, truly inclusive discussion and debate on development could finally take place—a necessary precondition to achieving sustainable development.

Table 46.2   Internet Development Resource Centers Identified on the GKD97 Internet List Discussion and Global Knowledge Website*

Communications infrastructure development
Association for Progressive Communications (**http://www.apc.org/english/**)
Bellanet International Secretariat (**http://home.bellanet.org**)
Grameen Communications (**http://www.grameen-info.org/gc/**)
Internet Society (ISOC) (**http://www.isoc.org/**)
National Telecommunication Cooperative Association (NTCA) (**http://www.ntca.org**)
Network Startup Resource Center (NSRC) (**http://www.nsrc.org/**)
Partnerships for ICTs in Africa (**http://www.uneca.org/aisi/pict**a)
UNDP Special Unit for Technical Cooperation Among Developing Countries (**http://tcdc.undp.org**)
World Bank InfoDev Program (**http://www.infodev.org**)

Electronic networks/building community
Association for Community Networking (AFCN) (**http://www.afcn.org**)
Centre for Community & Enterprise Networking (**leesing@sparc.uccb.ns.ca**)
Isis—Women's International Cross-Cultural Exchange (**http://www.isis.org**)
Letslink (**http://www.letslinkuk.org**)
QuipuNet (**http://www.quipunet.org**)
Red Caldas (**http://www.colciencias.gov.co/redcaldas/**)
Web Networks (**http://community.web.ca/**)
World Association of Community Radio Broadcasters (**http://www.web.apc.org/amarc/**)

Distance education
COL Knowledge Finder (**http://www.col.org/kf/**)
Global Distance Education Network (GDENet) (**http://www.ouhk.edu.hk/cridal/gdenet**)
Rivers of Life (**http://cgee.hamline.edu/rivers/**)
School Net Africa (**http://www.schoolnetafrica.org.eg**)
Virtual University (**http://www.vu.org/campus.html**)

Development assistance and research Government organizations
Canadian Bureau for International Education (**http://www.cbie.ca/**)
Canadian International Development Agency (**http://www.acdi-cida.ca/**)
Centre for International Research and Advisory Networks (**http://www.nuffic.nl/ciran**)
International Development Research Centre (**http://www.idrc.ca**)
Netherlands Directorate General for International Co-operation (**http://www.os.minbuza.nl/**)
Swedish International Development Agency (SIDA) (**http://www.sida.se/**)
UN Development Programme (**http://www.undp.org/**)
UN Economic Commission for Africa (**http://www.un.org/depts/eca**)
UN Food and Agricultural Organization (**http://www.fao.org/**)
UN International Institute for Sustainable Development (**http://www.iisd.org**)
UNESCO Early Childhood and Family Education Section
    (**http://www.unesco.org/education/educprog/ecf/**)

Nongovernmental organizations
ABANTU for Development (**http://www.abantu.org**)
Alliance for Democracy (**http://www.thealliancefordemocracy.org**)
Environment & Development of the Third World (Enda Third World) (**http://www.enda.sn/indexuk.htm**)
International Co-operative Alliance (ICA) (**http://www.coop.org/**)
Research Network on Sustainable Structural Adjustment Policies (**http://www.jp.or.cr/catedra/**)
Urban Popular Economy Programme (**ecopop@enda.sn**)
World Information Transfer (**http://www.worldinfo.org**)
World University Service of Canada (**http://www.wusc.ca**)

Charitable foundations
Benton Foundation (**http://www.benton.org**)
Rockefeller Foundation (**http://www.rockfound.org/**)
The MacArthur Foundation (**http://www.macfdn.org/**)

Private organizations
African Management Services Company (AMSCO) (**http://www.amsco.org**)
Consultant, Global Information Analysis (**rlabelle@web.net**)
Global Village for Future Leaders of Business and Industry (**http://www.lehigh.edu/~village**)
Management Systems International (**rwebster@msi-inc.com**)

Development Information centers
Development Gateway (**http://www.developmentgateway.org**)
Enterprise Development Website (**http://www.enterweb.org**)
Global Digital Opportunity Initiative (GDOI) (**www.markle.org**)
Global Information Infrastructure Commission (GIIC) (**http://www.giic.org/**)
UN Global Urban Observatory Network (GUONet) (**http://www.unhabitat.org/guonet/**)
Union of International Associations (**http://www.uia.org**)

---

*This table was revised in January 2004 for inclusion in this book. It reflects current names and Web contact information for the organizations concerned.

CONCLUSION

The development scenarios just examined are not mutually exclusive; yet to the extent that apartheid and cultural imperialism, that is, processes of exclusion, continue to gain in ascendancy, there is diminishing likelihood of the inclusive global village option. However, analysis of the Internet reveals that technologically greater opportunity exists now for the previously excluded to participate. Is this sufficient? Some who are deeply committed to the concept of inclusion have grave reservations. Consider the following excerpt from a (Northern) discussant in my case study:

Poverty is a choice the world has made. It is a political choice. The information revolution will be another instrument to implement that choice. Only a governance revolution would represent a real change. And to link the information revolution with democratization is naive in the extreme, parallel to the current leap of faith linking democratization and open markets.

Given the history of humankind since the industrial revolution, it may well be naive to expect that we can tear down the many institutionalized structures of exclusion that are currently in place. However, if we do not try, all of us will eventually lose. At stake is the very survival of our species (Piel, 1992). My case study and other data I presented on development via the Internet indicate that both the technological infrastructure and the will to make a difference are growing. It is possible to reduce the North-South gap, to provide greater cultural balance, and to improve the quality of life for all human beings—but then again, it always has been.

REFERENCES

Bell, D. 1976. *The coming of post-industrial society.* New York: Basic Books.

Brandt Report. 1980. *North-South: A program for survival.* Cambridge, Mass.: MIT Press.

Brown, F. B., and Y. Brown, 1994. *Distance education around the world. In Distance education: Strategies and tools,* ed. B. Willis, 3–39. Englewood Cliffs, N.J.: Educational Technology.

Einstein, A. 1954. The common language of science. In *Ideas and opinions by Albert Einstein,* ed. C. Seelig. New York: Wing Books. Reprinted from Advancement of Science, 2(5), 1941.

Gates, B. 1995. *The road ahead.* New York: Viking.

Gilder, G. 1989. *Microcosm: The quantum revolution in economics and technology.* New York: Simon and Schuster.

GKD97. 1998. The GK virtual conference: Recommendations and cases from the GKD97 list. [Online] Available: **http://www.globalknowledge. org/english/ search/index.html.**

Global Knowledge 97. 1997. International conference on knowledge for development in the information age, Toronto (June 22–25). [Online] Available: **http://www.globalknowledge.org.**

Hedley, R. A. 1985. Narrowing the gap between the rich and the poor nations: A modest proposal, *Transnational Perspectives,* 11(2/3): 23–27.

———. 1992. *Making a living: Technology and change.* New York: HarperCollins.

Jacobs, M. 1991. *The green economy: Environment, sustainable development and the politics of the future.* London: Pluto.

Kerr, C., J. T. Dunlop, F. Harbison, and C. A. Meyers. 1964. *Industrialism and industrial man.* New York: Oxford University Press.

Majordomo. 1997. Welcome to the Global Knowledge for Development Conference Internet list discussion. Information provided for Internet discussion group participants by **Majordomo@tristram .edc.org.**

Mandel, M. J. 1994. The digital juggernaut. Business Week special issue, *The Information Revolution:* 22–29.

Matrix Information and Directory Services. 1997. Current world map of the Matrix and the Internet (March 28). [Online] Available: **http://www.mids .org/.**

Mitchell, B. R. 1962. *Abstract of British historical statistics.* Cambridge, U.K.: Cambridge University Press.

Mowlana, H. 1996. *Global communication in transition: The end of diversity?* Thousand Oaks, Calif.: Sage.

Network Wizards. 1997. Internet domain survey (January). [Online] Available: **http://www.nw.com/.**

Organisation for Economic Co-operation and Development (OECD). 1996. *Information technology outlook* 1995. Paris: Author.

Pearson Report. 1969. *Partners in development: Report of the Commission on International Development.* New York: Praeger.

Piel, G. 1992. *Only one world: Our own to make and keep.* New York: Freeman.

Porat, M. 1977. *The information economy: Definition and measurement* (Special Publication 77-12, U.S. Department of Commerce, Office of Telecommunications). Washington, D.C.: U.S. Government Printing Office.

Stavrianos, L. S. 1981. *Global rift: The Third World comes of age.* New York: William Morrow.

Weise, E. 1997. Plan would launch 840 satellites to deliver Internet. *New York Times* (March 18).

World Bank. 1995. *World development report 1995.* Oxford, U.K.: Oxford University Press.

———. 1997. *1997 world development indicators.* Washington, D.C.: International Bank for Reconstruction and Development.

World Commission on Environment and Development. 1987. *Our common future.* Oxford, U.K.: Oxford University Press.

World competitiveness report 1995. 1995. Lausanne, Switzerland: IMD and World Economic Forum.